Contents

Introduction

This book has been written specifically for the new AQA specification introduced for first teaching in September 2015. The writers are all experienced authors, teachers and subject specialists with examining experience who provide comprehensive and up-to-date information that is both accessible and informative.

As a textbook it has been written to build student understanding through a concept-driven approach to the AQA AS and A-level specifications. Each chapter is self-contained, providing content to generate the knowledge and skills required for successful completion of the AQA specification. It has been written to develop student skills to enable them to evaluate theories and research, as well as build up their knowledge to master sociological topics.

The content of this book covers all topics in the new specification. Each chapter has a range of features designed to give students confidence and to present the content of their course in a clear and accessible way, as well as supporting them in their revision and exam preparation.

Summary of the specification and its coverage in *AQA Sociology for A-level* books 1 and 2

Content	Covered in
AS Compulsory content	
3.1.1 Education	AQA Sociology for A-level 1
3.1.2 Methods in Context	
3.2.1 Research Methods	
AS Optional – one of these topics must be studied	
3.2.2.1 Culture and Identity	AQA Sociology for A-level 1
3.2.2.2 Families and Households	
3.2.2.3 Health	
3.2.2.4 Work, Poverty and Welfare	

A-level Compulsory content	
4.1 Education with Theory and Methods 4.1.1 Education 4.1.2 Methods in Context 4.1.3 Theory and Methods	All covered in AQA Sociology for A-level 1 *except* Theory, which is covered in AQA Sociology for A-level 2
4.3 Crime and Deviance with Theory and Methods 4.3.1 Crime and Deviance 4.3.2 Theory and Methods	All covered in AQA Sociology for A-level 1 *except* Methods, which is covered in AQA Sociology for A-level 2
A-level Optional – one topic from each set of options must be studied	
4.2 Topics in Sociology	
Option 1 4.2.1 Culture and Identity 4.2.2 Families and Households 4.2.3 Health 4.2.4 Work, Poverty and Welfare	AQA Sociology for A-level 1
Option 2 4.2.5 Beliefs in Society 4.2.6 Global Development 4.2.7 The Media 4.2.8 Stratification and Differentiation	AQA Sociology for A-level 2

This title (Book 1) covers the AS or your first year of A-level, including all the options. There is also an introduction to theory section, which will help you to understand all the different sociological concepts. Year 2 of A-level, including all the options as well as a full theory chapter, is covered in Book 2.

The book has been meticulously designed to strengthen learning and revision through each stage of the course with plenty of practice questions and extension exercises. As an innovative textbook it offers the following qualities:

The AQA specification

Each chapter begins with a table illustrating how the content reflects the AQA specification. Every topic in the AS/Year 1 A-level AQA specification has a full chapter in this book. The content of every chapter has been carefully chosen in conjunction with the AQA specification to develop knowledge and understanding of key sociological concepts in a contemporary context.

GETTING YOU STARTED

Each section begins with an opening activity involving text or images with questions designed to develop sociological skills with practical activities. A combination of open and closed questions is used to stimulate thinking about key ideas appropriate to the chapter. The questions may be completed individually or used to stimulate discussion and group work.

Key terms

Key terms are written in **bold type** or *in orange* and defined in a simple way in the glossary towards the end of the book. The terms are mainly sociological, but also cover important terms from other disciplines that are relevant but may need explaining.

IN THE NEWS

This section includes articles adapted from contemporary newspapers, websites and journals; it is used to discuss topic events that you may have seen in the news. It is designed to demonstrate the application of sociological ideas to the social world around us.

STUDY TIPS

These are designed to give pointers towards improving students' knowledge of sociology and skills development. They offer careful and balanced advice on concepts, ideas and theories in ways that will add depth and quality to students' work.

CONTEMPORARY APPLICATION

This section offers a contemporary example of how each section within a chapter can be applied to the social world we live in. The content is designed to provoke thought and possibly offer examples and evidence that can supplement students' written work.

RESEARCH IN FOCUS

These extracts offer an insight into interesting and relevant contemporary research. The questions that follow them are designed to provoke understanding of the findings as well as consideration of methodological approaches and issues.

Check your understanding

This end-of-chapter section offers a set of questions designed to test knowledge and understanding of the chapter's content.

Practice questions

These are designed to offer study practice. A range of questions are asked along with the provision of items as appropriate.

Theory and methods

1

Understanding the specification

AQA specification	How the specification is covered in this chapter
• What is sociology? • Macro- and micro-sociological theory	*Section 1* • Functionalism • Marxism • Interactionism • Feminism • New Right • Postmodernism
• Quantitative and qualitative methods of research; research design • The relationship between positivism, interpretivism and sociological methods; the nature of 'social facts'	*Section 2* • What makes a good research design? • What are quantitative and qualitative methods of research? • What is the relationship between positivism, interpretivism and sociological methods?
• Sources of data, including questionnaires, interviews, participant and non-participant observation, experiments, documents and official statistics	*Section 3* Why do researchers use: • Questionnaires? • Interviews? • Participant and non-participant observation? • Experiments? • Documents? • Official statistics?
• The distinction between primary and secondary data, and between quantitative and qualitative data	*Section 4* • What is the distinction between primary and secondary data? • Why do researchers use different types of sampling and pilot studies?
• The theoretical, practical and ethical considerations influencing choice of topic, choice of method(s) and the conduct of research	*Section 5* • What theoretical considerations influence research? • What are the practical issues associated with research? • What ethical factors must sociologists consider?

Section 1: Sociological theory

This section will explore the following debates:

- Functionalism
- Marxism
- Interactionism
- Feminism
- New Right
- Postmoderism

Sociological theory is not an explicit part of the AS specification, but studying 'sociological theories, perspectives and methods' is one of the two 'integral elements' which are intended to be immersed within the study of individual topics. This section is included here to support students in order that they have some grasp of the main theoretical debates before they start the more detailed examination of, for example, the functionalist or Marxist approaches to the role of education. The brief discussion of theory here is designed to assist students and teachers as an introductory 'What is sociology?' module.

1.1 What is sociology?

Sociology is the systematic and, some would say, scientific study of the social world around us. Sociology emerged as an academic subject in the nineteenth century in the wake of the Industrial Revolution that first took place in Britain (1740–1850) and the democratic revolutions of the USA (1776) and France (1789).

It is often said that sociology evolved as a response to **modernity**. Modernity can best be understood as the modernising process whereby agricultural societies gave way to industrial and urban societies. Modernity can be seen to be centred on three significant changes: the economic evolution of industrial **capitalism**, the political global development of nation states and the cultural shift as rationality and scientific thinking began to replace religion and traditions.

The three 'founders' of sociology responded to modernity differently. Karl Marx (1818–83), as a revolutionary socialist, saw modernisation as an opportunity for creating a progressive society that could reflect the interests of the people. Émile Durkheim (1858–1917) had mixed views on change; he advocated reforms but was concerned that too much rapid social change could undermine the stability of society. Max Weber (1864–1920) was the most negative, fearing that the emerging industrial society was becoming increasingly bureaucratic and stifling. He referred to the growth of bureaucratic structures as like an 'iron cage' around society. What follows is a brief introduction to the central modern sociological perspectives that were, to varying degrees, influenced by these three founders.

What is the functionalist perspective?

As its name implies, this theory is centred on how the component parts that make up society operate in a way that is both functional to its members and the maintenance of society as a whole. The origins of functionalism go back to influential thinkers of the nineteenth century, including Herbert Spencer (1820–1903) and Émile Durkheim.

Spencer, heavily influenced by Charles Darwin, emphasised the evolutionary development of society and its component parts. Through his **organic analogy** he also compared society to the human body. Just as an organism is made of organs that are interrelated and interdependent, society is made up of **social institutions** (such as family, education, work) that are interrelated and interdependent.

Durkheim, a contemporary of Spencer, developed a key understanding of the role that consensus **values** play in reinforcing social order and stability in society. He developed key concepts, such as the **collective conscience** to describe the moral values that were core to any society, serving to bind people together. Such ideas were to prove highly influential to a group of sociologists in the mid-twentieth century in the USA who developed 'structural functionalism'. As a theory, it is heavily influenced by Durkheim's consensus view of society. It also reflects Spencer's ideas, though its focus on integration derived from interrelationships between **institutions** and their members.

One of the leading structural functionalists was Talcott Parsons (1902–79). He stressed the importance of the role of **socialisation** in promoting consensus values, arguing that a commitment to a common morality (**core values**) ensured social order. Parsons developed a sophisticated model of society which he called 'systems theory'. Besides Durkheim, Parsons was also influenced by Weber and his action theory. He attempted to synthesise Durkheim's focus on the structures that make up society with Weber's ideas of what shapes people's actions.

Within the system of society, Parsons argued there were four sub-systems: economic, political, kinship and cultural. Each of these sub-systems functions to meet essential human needs. So important are they that Parsons refers to them as imperatives or prerequisites of society. For society to be healthy and survive, it has to deal with four problems: adaptation, goal attainment, integration and latency (also called pattern maintenance).

Functionalism dominated sociology until the 1960s, when it became increasingly challenged by Marxist and interactionist thinking. Its critics argue that it is a naïve and overly optimistic theory, choosing to over-emphasise consensus while ignoring the widespread conflict that exists in society. As a theory it also struggles to adequately explain social change.

What is the Marxist perspective?

Like functionalism, Marxism is a response to modernism. It evolved out of the writings of Karl Marx who observed, first-hand, the new industrial society of capitalism.

Like functionalism, this theory is structuralist in that it places a lot of emphasis on the structures that make up society. The two theories have also been described as macro-theories, as they are top-down theories that explain the operation of society as a system. However, in contrast to the social system theory of Parsons, Marxism is preoccupied with the economic system of capitalism.

Politically, functionalism and Marxism are poles apart. In contrast to the consensus basis of functionalism, Marxism is based on a conflict analysis of society, especially that centred around class conflict. Marxism is much better equipped to deal with and explain social change, as this is a cornerstone of Marx's theory. Through his theory of historical materialism, Marx portrayed capitalism as merely a stage or 'epoch' in the history of human development. The end of history, he argued, will be a truly equal communist society.

The driver of social change, Marx argued, is class conflict. He shows that all societies are class societies with a dominant and a subordinate class. The interests of these two classes can never coincide, and ultimately the subordinate class will sieze power and overthrow the dominant class. Under capitalism, the dominant class is the **bourgeoisie** and the subordinate class the **proletariat**. However, Marx showed that the subordinate class can be duped and fooled into supporting the society that actually exploits it. He referred to this process as **false consciousness**.

Marx was clearly aware of how ideologies can distort reality and prevent workers seeing their true class position – exploited, alienated beings. Institutions such as the media, religion, education and the family all divert people's attention away from revolutionary thought. Marxism has been criticised for being over-negative and crudely deterministic in that all social problems are inevitably blamed on the capitalist system. Critics argue that people (not the economic system) make their own history and, for that reason, the assumed future of **communism** cannot be predicted. Functionalists argue that Marxism places too much emphasis on conflict at the expense of recognising the fair amount of consensus in society. Feminists argue that focusing solely on class ignores **gender relations**.

What is the interactionist perspective?

Interactionism, also called symbolic interactionism, derives particularly from the work of Max Weber, and was developed by sociologists at the University of Chicago, in particular Herbert Blumer and George Herbert Mead in the mid-twentieth century. As a perspective it is fundamentally different to both functionalism and Marxism. It rejects any attempt to make sense of society as a system, choosing instead to try and understand the meanings behind individual actions. As a consequence it is described as **micro-sociology** because its starting point is how individuals make sense of the world, not how society works. It has three key characteristics:

- It focuses on the interaction between the individuals (which it calls actors) and the world (effectively the 'stage' on which the actors perform a variety of roles).
- It is interested in the actions of individuals (such as why people choose to behave the way they do, 'voluntaristic' behaviour), rather than the structures in which they operate (such as family obligations, compulsory education, speed cameras, etc.).
- It stresses the importance of an actor's ability to interpret the social world, arguing that there is no objective reality; instead the world is real inside the head of each individual.

Much of interactionism centres on the concept of the self, which is at the very hub of this perspective. As individuals we are very conscious of the people around us and how they think about us and our behaviour. As such, the self can be interpreted in three ways:

- how we imagine we appear to others
- how we imagine their judgement of that appearance
- our response to those perceived judgements, such as pride, anger or humiliation.

Erving Goffman (1959) developed the idea of the self. He recognised the discrepancy between our 'all-too-human selves and our socialised selves'. The tension is between what people expect us to do, and what we spontaneously want to do.

The concept of power relations and **labelling** theory were introduced by Howard Becker (1963). He noted how powerful groups can impose labels on the less powerful. Such labels often stick and can become self-fulfilling, so a teacher may negatively label a student as 'stupid' or 'troublesome' which can become a shared meaning and even internalised by the student who may feel an obligation to live up to the label.

To interactionists, there is no such thing as objective reality. Reality is what is inside people's heads – individual's interpretations of the world. This is an idea that would be adopted subsequently by postmodernists. Both functionalists and Marxists criticise interactionism for neglecting social structures, which they argue impact directly on people's lives and shape **life chances** and opportunities. Marxists argue that the structure of **social class** is particularly important, whether or not actors are consciously aware of it or not.

What is the feminist perspective?

Feminism developed as a specific **theoretical perspective** because its supporters claimed that sociology can render women invisible simply by ignoring them and their experiences, or else it marginalised the importance of women's **roles**. Feminists argue that this is largely as a result of the systematic biases and inadequacies of what they refer to as 'malestream' theories. A feminist theory is necessary as a check to the male domination.

Feminism offers an alternative view and constructs reality by drawing on women's own interpretations of their own experiences and interests. Feminist theory can be complex. It is a structural theory in the sense that it is centred on how **patriarchy** shapes the experiences of women (and men) across society. However, it is also interpretive since it seeks to make sense of women's experiences by portraying the meanings of being a woman in patriarchal society. As a perspective it is divided into different types of feminisms, reflecting disagreement on the nature, causes and solutions to patriarchy.

Liberal feminism

This type of feminism views gender inequality as stemming primarily from the ignorance of men that derives primarily from the strength of socialisation and 'sex-role conditioning'. The solution to gender inequality is simply the education and reform of men, although they recognise this sometimes needs the 'stick' of anti-discrimination legislation. This is, therefore, the least radical of all the feminisms and is often criticised by other feminists for glossing over the true oppression and exploitation that women experience. Other feminists also claim that men are not simply ignorant, but have a vested interest in maintaining the patriarchal ways of living and thinking that empower them.

Marxist-feminism

As their name implies these are feminists who adopt the Marxist view that the economic dependence women have on men has been created by capitalism. This serves two functions: firstly, to provide cheap female workers who can be exploited even more than men, and secondly to ensure that household chores are done cheaply. When women do enter the workforce they traditionally work in low-paid, low-status, mainly part-time jobs (although this can now be viewed as somewhat simplistic and changing).

Marxist-feminists argue that the solution to women's oppression is the abolition of capitalism. This would eradicate the double oppression of patriarchy in the home and economic exploitation in the workplace.

Radical feminism

As the name implies, this is the most extreme form of feminism. Radical feminists focus their attention on the power relations between men and women, which is referred to as 'sexual politics'. They argue that all women are oppressed by men, in particular within the home, and need to break this imbalance of power through a collective identification of their interests through a sense of 'sisterhood'. Radical feminists see gender as a shared class identity. They argue that women share the same sex-class position because they are controlled and sometimes abused by the violence of men. Women's liberation can only be achieved by actively challenging and eradicating the prevailing systems of patriarchy.

Black feminism

Black feminism evolved because black women felt that white feminists failed to recognise that some women were oppressed not only by patriarchy but **racism** as well. Black feminists criticised the ethnocentricity of most feminism for being blinkered and focused on just white women's experiences. Therefore, in order to eliminate women's subordination, the system of racism must be challenged alongside patriarchy and capitalism.

Postmodernist feminists

The claim of some that we now live in a postmodern society has led to two polar strands in feminism. Some people, called post-feminists, argue that the shift towards an increasingly gender-equal society has made feminism no longer relevant. The battle has largely been won! Clearly the bulk of feminists would challenge this assertion.

The other strand, postmodernist-feminism, embraces the essential argument of postmodernism, that we are now living in an increasingly fragmented and pluralistic society centred on individuality and multiple identities. While they recognise that gender is clearly a very important determinant of life chances, the experiences of individual women differ. Factors such as social class, age, ethnicity, physical appearance and even locality all shape and individualise women's experiences. Clearly some women are more oppressed by men than others, so a more individualistic approach is necessary, rather than a one-size-fits-all approach.

What is New Right theory?

Strictly speaking the New Right perspective is a neo-liberal political theory rather than sociological. However, its contribution has penetrated so much of sociology, especially topics like the family, education and poverty, work and **wealth**, that it simply cannot be ignored. In addition, as the influence and popularity of functionalism declined after the 1960s, New Right thinkers became the new right-wing voice of sociology.

The New Right shares much in common with functionalism, such as support for a meritocratic society and the traditional family, but is far more focused on and influenced by neo-liberal ideology. This openly advocates minimal government and sees the free market as the most efficient way to allocate resources. As a perspective, the New Right is clearly isolated and commands little support except from its enthusiastic advocates. It is generally criticised for being ideologically blinkered and over-focused on looking for simple scapegoats to blame for society's problems. These include feminists generally and specifically groups such as single-parent mothers and the so-called **underclass**. This is seen as simplistic and short-sighted, ignoring the complexities of modern society and reinforcing a world view that lacks evidence. Instead New Right ideas, like those of one its leading proponents, Charles Murray, are seen as being more reliant on 'innuendos, assertions and anecdotes' (Walker, 1990).

What is postmodernist theory?

As noted above, the period of modernity is associated with industrialisation. Since society today is very different to that of the Industrial Revolution, some argue that we are now living in a postmodern society. It is worth stating here that not everyone supports this view. Marxists, for example, argue that society is fundamentally the same capitalist system, with the same **economic relations** of class exploitation. Those who believe we are still in the modern period sometimes use the term 'late modern' to concede some social and cultural differences to the nineteenth century.

Supporters of postmodernism argue that society is fundamentally different now than it was during the era of industrialisation. They argue that it is now characterised by its preoccupation with consumerism, shopping and style, which is fundamentally different to the old society centred on production and work. Postmodernists argue that society has become considerably fragmented and individualistic – there is so much **diversity**, allowing people to make personal choices in almost every field of life. Like interactionism, postmodernism does not recognise objective reality. Reality is what is inside people's heads. Since there are multiple versions of reality, postmodernism rejects the very idea of **grand theories** like the ones discussed above, although it is ironically a theory (of sorts) itself.

STUDY TIP

In your notebook, or on a sheet of paper, construct a two-column grid with lots of rows. In the first column write the terms 'collective consciousness', 'false consciousness' and 'systems theory'. In the second column write an explanation for each term. Add to your list all unfamiliar terms you encounter relating to theories and methods.

Section 2: Sociological research

This section will explore:

- What makes a good sociological research design?
- What are quantitative and qualitative methods of research?
- What is the relationship between positivism, interpretivism and sociological methods?

Figure 1.1 Doing sociological research

GETTING YOU STARTED

What makes good research?

Figure 1.2 Collecting data in the field

Good sociological research is both valid and reliable. To be valid, it must accurately record or measure what you originally wanted to explore. To be reliable, your research methods need to be applicable to a different example of the same situation and give the similar results.

To achieve validity you need to define your terms. For example, you may want to compare and measure intelligence levels among certain groups. You would need to decide exactly what you meant by the term 'intelligence' as well as the groups you want to look at, to pinpoint what it is you are hoping to record.

It is sometimes easier to ensure validity in qualitative research where all the relevant details of a respondent's situation can be explored. In survey-based quantitative research where you are relying on a small number of short-answer questions, you need to design and test the questions carefully to make sure that the respondents understand them as you intended.

It's important to understand that research can be reliable without being valid and vice versa. For example, a poorly designed questionnaire might yield consistent (reliable) but misleading (therefore not valid) results. Research can also be valid without being reliable. For example, if you achieve a fascinating case study that offers insight into an aspect of society, but it is impossible to repeat the methods used, or to show that the study could not have been interpreted differently, then it can't be said to be reliable.

Adapted from Economic and Social Research Council (2014) Methodologies: What makes good research? (www.esrc.ac.uk/_images/what-makes-good-research_tcm8-32679.pdf).

Questions

1. How does the extract define good sociological research?
2. In what ways does the extract imply the use of the word 'work' is problematic?
3. What is meant by validity?
4. What is meant by the term 'reliable'?
5. Why is it easier to ensure validity in qualitative rather than quantitative research?

2.1 What makes a good sociological research design?

In this section you will learn about the fundamental qualities that make sociological research successful: representativeness, validity, reliability and generalisability.

Common sense versus sociological research

People make judgements about other people's behaviour all the time. However, these tend to be based on 'gut feelings', prejudices, or on the basis of common-sense reasoning. As a result of this, people's judgements may be biased, inaccurate and consequently of no real value. To really make sense of human behaviour and how society is organised, sociologists need a research approach that is both different and better than that used by ordinary people. For sociological research to be able to stand up to close scrutiny, it must be designed in such a way that it avoids the characteristics of common-sense thinking. To ensure this, sociological research must satisfy two conditions: it must be **rigorous** in its execution, and be based on **empirical** evidence. Sociological research therefore needs to adopt a systematic approach.

Representativeness and generalisability

Good sociological research should be representative. This means that the group of people being studied (normally called a **sample**) shares the characteristics of the larger group or **target population**. This means that the findings of the research can be applied to them. By choosing the type and size of the sample carefully, researchers can help ensure that their research is good quality (see page 38).

Good research is also generalisable. Generalisability means that information that is collected about a small group can be applied to larger groups. For example, if a representative group of young people reported that bullying was a common experience, then it could be generalised that bullying probably had a real impact on young people across society. Generalisability derives from research that is valid, reliable and representative.

Validity and reliability

Validity means that the research findings are true to life. Research findings that are high in validity tend to derive from qualitative research (see page 11). In qualitative research, researchers tend to sample small numbers of people and take very detailed accounts of their emotions or behaviour. Researchers have to be careful however, because people will not always tell the truth. For example, asking car drivers if they ever drink alcohol over the legal limit and then drive may get dishonest responses as this is an example of irresponsible behaviour. To gain qualitative data rich in validity, researchers tend to use research methods such as in-depth interviews or participant observation (see pages 20–26). If the researcher suspects someone is not telling the truth, their data gets discarded.

Research findings that are high in reliability tend to derive from quantitative research (see page 10). Reliability means that the data collected would be the same if the researcher or anyone else was to repeat the research. In sociological research this can be difficult because groups can change over time and because people can change their attitudes or behaviour simply because they know they are being studied. To gain data high in reliability, researchers tend to use research methods such as social surveys (questionnaires or structured interviews) and experiments.

Sociological research must apply academic rigour and be systematic in its attempt to understand human behaviour. Sociological research must:

- be based on evidence
- be verifiable (it can be tested) and
- be able to be cross-referenced (checked against other findings).

It is important to recognise that validity, reliability and representativeness are sometimes lacking in research. You should assess research design against these criteria: will it produce valid, reliable, representative data? How might the research design be compromised by using this method?

KEY SOCIOLOGISTS

Alan Bryman wrote the influential, *Social Research Methods* (2004). It outlines and evaluates important research practices with regard to both qualitative and quantitative methods.

STUDY TIP

There is generally an inverse relationship between validity and reliability. If a piece of research can be shown to offer elements of validity and reliability, discuss evidence for this but make sure you don't conflate them – use two separate sentences.

CONTEMPORARY APPLICATION

All sociological research has a duty to uphold the reputation of the subject and its members. Therefore all researchers must adhere to the British Sociological Association's Code of Ethics, and maintain good practices in the course of their research. Otherwise they run the risk of bringing the subject into disrepute.

RESEARCH IN FOCUS

Accessing insular groups

Figure 1.3 Amish communities tend to be very private

Natalie Jolly undertook a study of a very private religious sect, the Amish, who reject most aspects of modern American society. She wanted to gain an understanding of community power within Amish society – who has power, how it is gained, and how it is exercised. She gained access to the Amish community through a 'gatekeeper' – a non-Amish

midwife who permitted Jolly access to this secretive religious society.

She undertook an ethnographic study in the form of a two-year participant observation. Jolly acted as a volunteer health care worker and apprentice to the non-Amish midwife. She gained her primary data from observing 40 Amish homebirths as well as countless prenatal visits and postnatal checkups over a period of 30 months.

Jolly describes the tension she felt between becoming a fully active participant and a completely detached passive spectator. She describes a potential pitfall of subjectivity, or what she calls the 'vulnerable observer'. On the other hand, she felt active participation enhanced the quality of her research in two ways. Firstly, it enhanced the quality of the data obtained during fieldwork. Secondly, it enhanced the quality of the interpretation of the data.

Jolly's primary source of data was the notes on her conversations and observations. Frequent examination of these notes yielded themes of interest, substantiating and elaborating on the patterns that came out of her participant observations. Using this data, Jolly was able to gain an insight into the mechanisms by which power operates and is transacted between individuals and groups within the Amish community.

Adapted from Natalie Jolly (2014) In this world but not of it: Midwives, Amish, and the politics of power. *Sociological Research Online*, *19* (2), 13.

Questions

1. What was the key research method used by Jolly?
2. In the context of research methods, what is meant by the term 'gatekeeper'?
3. What is meant by the term 'active participation'?
4. What do you think Jolly meant by being a 'vulnerable observer'?
5. Why is the research of insular groups like the Amish potentially difficult for sociologists?

2.2 What are the methods of research?

When you are studying quantitative or qualitative methods, both these approaches as well as the research methods that are associated with them and how they are associated with the respective approaches of positivism and interpretivism are important.

The quantitative approach

When sociologists accumulate data for their research they can collect either **quantitative data** or **qualitative data** (or both). Quantitative data refers to data that is essentially factual and generally takes a numerical form. It is the type of data that is traditionally associated with positivist sociologists.

Most sociologists in the nineteenth century adopted the positivist position. Positivists believe that people's behaviour is shaped by factors that are directly observable, so they undertake a scientific method of collecting **social facts**. As a consequence, quantitative data is often numerical in nature and expressed in the form of statistics. Because it is easier to replicate quantitative research, the data is said to be higher in reliability.

Some research methods are more appropriate than others for collecting quantitative data. The most common research method is using a social survey, based on a closed-question questionnaire or **structured interview**. When sociologists collect their own data this is known as **primary data**. However, they can also simply use data that has already been collected by someone else. This is known as **secondary data** and is comprised of findings from existing research and official statistics. Often secondary data will come in the form of quantitative data, such as official crime statistics, marriage rates, or the percentage of pupils who attain five A*–C GCSEs. The quantitative approach is favoured by researchers who are studying trends or statistical truths.

The qualitative approach

In contrast to quantitative data, which is usually numerical, qualitative data is made up of words. Those who gather and use qualitative data are known collectively as interpretivist sociologists, adopting an approach modelled on social action theory, originally devised by Max Weber. Researchers can interpret the motives and meanings behind people's experiences by exploring their behaviour and feelings.

The most common research methods used to collect qualitative data include **unstructured interviews** and participant observation. Whereas collecting quantitative data involves the objective accumulation of factual and measurable data, qualitative data is subjective; essentially it is data about how people feel. Qualitative data consequently tends to be viewed as richer in detail than data obtained by quantitative means. Because it gets to the heart of the matter, qualitative data is generally considered higher in validity.

It is important to recognise that while quantitative data is associated particularly with a positivistic approach, all sociologists will inevitably collect some numerical data in the course of their research.

	Positivist/structural approach		Interpretive/social action approach
Sociology perspective	Functionalism, New Right	Marxism, neo-Marxism, feminism*	Interactionism, labelling theory, feminism, phenomenology
Emphasis on	Consensus	Conflict	Meanings and motives
Views on behaviour	Determinism – behaviour is determined by structures that surround individuals		Voluntarism (agency behaviour) – behaviour reflects free will and derives from within the individual
Characteristics	Scientific, value-free, objective, quantitative data, high in reliability		Non-scientific, value-laden, subjective, qualitative data, high in validity
Giddens' contribution (see page 14)	Structuration theory (structure + agency)		

Table 1.1

* Feminism can be viewed as both structural (focusing on the structure of patriarchy) and interpretive (focusing on the meanings of gender oppression)

KEY SOCIOLOGISTS

Emile Durkheim (1897) sought to collect quantitative data through a positivist approach in his study of suicide. It was a ground-breaking analysis of statistical data from which Durkheim concluded that social factors rather than individual personalities caused suicide. Later, interpretivists argued that Durkheim's positivistic approach overlooked the meanings that lay behind not just suicidal behaviour but also how statistics were interpreted by people such as coroners.

STUDY TIP

As you study this topic make a note of examples of methodological pluralism as you come across them. Being able to cite them will strengthen your work.

RESEARCH IN FOCUS

Gay men and ageing

Figure 1.4 A gay couple

Paul Simpson (2013) undertook an ethnographic study into gay men and ageing. His methodology was to use participant observation in the bars of Manchester's gay village and semi-structured interviews conducted in private places. He used this qualitative approach as he felt it was better suited to accessing the personal stories and practices of his target population.

Simpson was aware of a common problem associated with observation – the observer effect. This is when close contact with the people whose actions are being studied can distort their behaviour in their 'natural' habitats. In addition, there is a danger of the researcher going native. This is when the researcher gets so close to the people they are studying that it makes the findings biased and no longer objective.

There were also ethical issues. Because Simpson could not ask the people he observed for their permission, his research had to be covert. The British Sociological Association's Code of Ethics approves covert research provided there is no other way of obtaining the data and that the possibility of causing harm is minimised as far as possible.

Finally, Simpson chose to sample for difference. This was because Manchester's gay village is a dynamic, multi-sited, cultural space where different behaviours occur. His observations took place in different kinds of bars – 'mixed' or associated with younger or older men, some with huge dance floors, others small and intimate.

Adapted from Paul Simpson, 'Doing Ethnography', Sociology Review, vol. 23, 2, pp.9–11.

Questions

1. What methods did Simpson use in his research of gay men?
2. Why did Simpson adopt a qualitative approach for his study of gay men?
3. Outline and explain the two potential problems associated with observation that Simpson was aware of.
4. What is meant by covert research?
5. Why do you think Simpson 'chose to sample for difference'?

2.3 What are the main sociological perspectives?

If you are studying the relationship between positivism, interpretivism and sociological methods, you will develop an awareness of each of these two approaches and how sociologists typically embrace them both in contemporary research.

The sociological perspectives that tend to adopt the positivist, scientific, macro approach and focus on structure are: consensus-orientated functionalism, New Right, and conflict-orientated Marxism and feminism.

The sociological perspectives that tend to adopt the interpretivist, micro approach and focus on action and agency are: interactionism, labelling theory, phenomenology and feminism.

Positivism

Most early sociologists felt their research should adopt the methodological approach of the natural sciences in order to ensure it was sufficiently rigorous, objective and based on empirical evidence. This scientific approach, which had been advocated by Auguste Comte (1798–1857) somewhat earlier, was known as positivism. It argued that only by adopting a rigorous methodological approach based on the scientific principles of collecting objective evidence in the form of facts, could sociology stand up to academic scrutiny.

Such research was based on evidence, subject to verification (it could be tested) and was considered truly objective. The approach and results were believed to be genuinely value-free and, like scientific research, could be cross-referenced against existing research findings. Positivism researches society by focusing on the macro level; it does this by observing how the social structures of society influence and shape the behaviour of individuals.

Interpretivism

Max Weber (1864–1920) challenged the positivist approach when he pointed out that sociology's subject matter was not the same as that of the natural sciences. Unlike crystals, cells or earthquakes, human beings have consciousness and are normally aware when they are being studied. Therefore they tend to stop behaving naturally, simply because they know they are being observed. To truly understand human behaviour, Weber advocated a totally new approach which he called verstehen, which literally translates as 'understand'. He said we should try to understand human behaviour by putting ourselves in the shoes of those we are studying and by focusing on interpreting the meanings behind people's actions.

Weber's 'action theory' focuses on the micro-level of social life – the way in which individuals behave with one another. Behaviour is seen as agency driven, being shaped by personal choice and hence voluntaristic, as opposed to being constrained by structures. This approach still stresses the importance of adopting a rigorous and systematic approach, stressing that making sense of human behaviour requires a careful interpretation of it – hence this alternative approach is known as interpretivism.

Realism

Sociological researchers rarely fall neatly into the positivist or interpretivist approaches. The reality is that when undertaking research sociologists use a combination of the two approaches. The approach of realism recognises strengths and weaknesses within positivism and interpretivism and seeks to use their respective strengths.

The analogy of an onion is sometimes used to illustrate the strengths of a realist approach over a positivist approach. The positivist approach is centred on the observation of structures. If this approach was applied to an onion, it would conclude that onions are dry and papery. Realists believe that a structured reality exists but, unlike positivists, disagree that this reality is necessarily directly observable. Sometimes you have to probe beneath the surface. If applied to onions, a realist perspective would reveal their moist texture and ring structure.

Realists also identify with the interpretivist view that people operate as conscious actors who behave in meaningful and voluntaristic ways. It is important, therefore, to research the meanings and feelings that shape their behaviour.

Realists collect both quantitative and qualitative data and tend to use each to offset the weaknesses of the other. To do this they embrace **triangulation**, the process of using two or more research methods in a single piece of research to check the reliability and validity of research data. Using triangulation means that researchers are not boxed into theoretical corners and can use one set of data to offset the weaknesses of the other.

Structuration

Structuration was developed by Anthony Giddens (1976) to illustrate the complex interplay that exists between structures and **agency**. He argues that it is impossible to isolate structure and action from each other – as a result of action we create structures. For example, we choose to get engaged and thereby create the structures of the family and **marriage**. On the other hand, structure is what enables us to act at all. For example, if we are in an unhappy marriage we can choose the agency action of divorcing our partner. Giddens makes the useful point that structure and agency therefore cannot be viewed in isolation.

Post-structuralism

Post-structuralism argues that, to get to the truth, researchers need to go beneath the surface of society. The post-structuralist criticism of the structure/agency polarisation is that all perspectives actually include both. They conclude that the sensible conclusion to draw from the structure versus agency debate is that the distinction does not so much present a problem to be solved but rather is a way of describing reality.

KEY SOCIOLOGISTS

Karl Popper (1959) is associated with the deductive approach (see laboratory experiments, page 27) and the idea of **falsification**. Popper advocated that all researchers should constantly attempt to falsify or disprove their theories. By doing so they do not take any hypothesis for granted (no matter how many times it proves true) and demonstrate their duty to be objective.

STUDY TIP

While quantitative data is associated particularly with a positivistic approach and qualitative data with interpretivists, this is a simple analysis of how these methods interact. Be aware of methodological pluralism, the realist approach and Giddens' structuration theory.

Knowing and understanding Figure 1.5 will ensure that you demonstrate a joined-up understanding of the different approaches to sociological research.

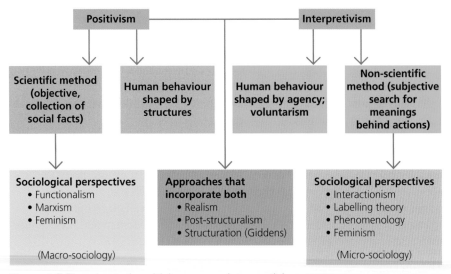

Figure 1.5 Flowchart of positivism versus interpretivism

It would probably be fair to say in the twenty-first century that sociology has risen above the stale and polarised debate of positivism versus interpretivism. Today most sociological research involves elements of both approaches. This is known as a realist approach and involves collecting both quantitative and qualitative data.

Playing it dumb in the field

Figure 1.6 Single-room occupancy hotel

Terressa Benz undertook interpretivist research by living as a resident for 14 months in a seedy single-room occupancy (SRO) hotel in Los Angeles. Such establishments are a common feature of 'skid rows' in the USA, where mainly single, non-white, middle-aged to elderly males live with a degree of permanence. As a female researcher she highlights how doing interpretive studies in the field can be wrought with challenges. These challenges are well covered in sociological literature. However, she argues, neither the emotions involved nor the specific techniques for dealing with this emotional fallout are openly discussed.

In her research Benz explores not only the emotions of fieldwork, specifically as a woman in a male-dominated research setting, but actual tactics for dealing with these feelings – tactics she calls 'flanking gestures'. Flanking gestures are techniques that allow the researcher to blur and stretch their gender, which she suggests provides a certain amount of emotional relief in the field.

As part of her research strategy, Benz chose to play the role of an incompetent observer. 'Playing dumb' has long been a technique used by ethnographers to not only gather information but also to build rapport. She suggests that playing dumb can also serve as a tactic for dealing with the emotional challenges of fieldwork, especially for a female in a male-dominated setting. SRO hotels tend to function according to very traditional gender norms in which women are assumed to be less knowledgeable than men.

Benz reports finding it infuriating when people in her everyday life treat women as less intelligent than men; in research settings she is able to embrace this demeaning gendered assumption in a constructive way. She says: 'Embracing the role of the less-intelligent female in the field means that your research subjects are underestimating you, which is, in my opinion, a very good thing. When research subjects underestimate you they tend to share more information as they expect you are unlikely to fully understand or remember what they have said. They will also try to teach you different things which build their confidence while also developing rapport.'

Adapted from Terressa Benz (2014) Flanking gestures: Gender and emotion in fieldwork. *Sociological Research Online*, *19* (2), 15.

Questions

1. What aspect of research has received little discussion according to Benz?
2. Why does Benz suggest some researchers play the role of the 'incompetent observer'?
3. How does Benz 'embrace this demeaning gendered assumption in a constructive way'?
4. Why might some feminists disapprove of this research strategy?
5. Make a list of the potential problems that an academic female researcher might experience while doing participant observation in a single-room occupancy hotel.

Check your understanding

1. How is sociological knowledge different to common-sense knowledge?
2. What does 'valid' mean?
3. What does 'reliable' mean?
4. What is the difference between structure and agency?
5. What does 'representative' mean?
6. What does 'generalisability' mean?
7. What is the difference between primary and secondary data?
8. What is meant by the term 'positivist approach'?
9. What is meant by the term 'interpretivist approach'?
10. What is meant by triangulation?

Practice questions

1. Outline two characteristics of a positivist approach to sociological research. [4 marks]
2. Evaluate how and why sociological knowledge is different to common-sense knowledge. [16 marks]

Section 3: Sources of data

This section will explore:

- Why do researchers use questionnaires?
- Why do researchers use interviews?
- Why do researchers use participant and non-participant observation?
- Why do researchers use experiments?
- Why do researchers use documents?
- Why do researchers use official statistics?

GETTING YOU STARTED

Attitudes of poor, white working-class boys in a high-achieving school

The participants for the study were in Year 10 (approximately 14–15 years of age) and selected by their free school meals (FSM) status. The students were interviewed in the school. The problem with using FSM status is that it is something of a blunt instrument for social class analysis. The study was designed not to select participants based on poor behaviour or lack of engagement in an effort to learn more about the heterogeneity of white working-class boys' educational experiences.

With parental consent, the first stage in the data-collection process was classroom observation. As attitudes and perceptions are actively constructed in social contexts, it is critical to observe participants among their peers. Since observation is always filtered through the researcher's interpretive frames, the study used these observations to access the boys' perceptions of the lesson, their role in the lesson and their understanding of the expectations in the lesson. The study also used interviews, being mindful of the impact of the interviewer on the interview process.

At no point in the research were the boys made aware that they were selected on their FSM status. However, they were asked their own social class identification. Pseudonyms were used in the presentation of the data.

Adapted from Garth Stahl (2013) Habitus disjunctures, reflexivity and white working-class boys' conceptions of status in learner and social identities. *Sociological Research Online*, 18 (3), 2.

Questions

1. Why do you think the researcher chose to use boys receiving free school meals for his sample?
2. Why did the researcher not select participants based on poor behaviour or lack of engagement?
3. What do you think the researcher meant by the phrase 'observation is always filtered through the researcher's interpretive frames'?
4. Why do you think the researcher was careful to hide from the boys the fact that they were selected on their FSM status?
5. Why were pseudonyms (false names) used in the presentation of the data?

3.1 Why do researchers use questionnaires?

If you are discussing questionnaires, you could start by developing an awareness of their strengths and weaknesses, their favoured use by positivists and their association with quantitative data. It is also important to critically compare the alternative methods, such as interviews or observation.

Self-completion questionnaires are a series of written questions distributed directly, electronically or by post, to a group. The respondents answer in their own words. The questionnaire is most associated with the positivistic approach and is generally used to collect quantitative data in response to **closed questions**.

Open questions can be used to collect some qualitative data, but respondents tend not to write very much in questionnaires, even when invited to do so. This means questionnaires are of limited use in collecting data about people's feelings or experiences.

Because of their association with quantitative data, questionnaires are regarded as a method that generally produces data high in reliability. Because of their problem with collecting qualitative data, they are generally viewed as being low in validity.

Questionnaires are associated with a positivistic approach. As a method they are generally associated with functionalism and Marxism, but all types of sociologists can and do use questionnaires in their research.

Social surveys use either questionnaires or involve structured interviews. Structured interviews are effectively questionnaires, as the interviewer uses a schedule where the questions are read out in the same order and responses written down.

Traditionally, a lot of questionnaires were distributed through the post or were expected to be returned to the researcher by post. It is increasingly common, however, for self-completion questionnaires to be distributed electronically using online tools such as SurveyMonkey.

Self-completion questionnaires have certain benefits:

- Financial – when funds are low and travel costs for the researcher are prohibitive, this method can be attractive.
- Potential **sample size** – electronic or postal questionnaires are really the only practical method to use when samples are very large.
- Privacy – they allow respondents time and privacy to give the questions a considered response, particularly useful when researching a sensitive or delicate subject matter. If respondents are honest and reflective with their answers, this should increase the validity of the research.
- Removing the interviewer – the absence of face-to-face interaction may make people answer more honestly and removes any interviewer effect.

The biggest problem with electronic and postal questionnaires is the poor response rate, which undermines the representativeness of the sample and the ability to make generalisations from the findings.

Advantages of self-completion questionnaires	Disadvantages of self-completion questionnaires
Questionnaires administered at specific locations have the advantage of allowing the researcher to distribute and collect them. This allows the sociologist to explain what they want and clarify any difficulties that may arise.	Response rates can be low when individuals are given the responsibility of returning the completed questionnaire.
It is possible to research very large samples as it is both quick and relatively cheap in comparison to other methods.	Sometimes respondents can be guided in their responses. For example, if a researcher was not present in a school, teachers could possibly influence pupils in how to respond.
In institutions like schools, the nature by which they are organised can provide easy sampling approaches, through providing sampling frames such as the school roll, year groups and classes. This facilitates giving out questionnaires within a school setting.	Questionnaires may be returned incomplete, illegible or incomprehensible.
Questionnaires produce data that is generally high in reliability.	Questionnaires can still be biased and involve researcher imposition factors as a result of the way questions are asked.
Because questions are standardised it is possible to collect quantitative data and identify patterns. Comparisons can be drawn between different groups, such as social class, gender or ethnicity.	Questionnaires and quantitative data are poor at indicating the meanings or experiences that individuals might have wanted to share.
If questionnaires encourage respondents to reflect on their responses then they can still provide valid, in-depth qualitative data.	Questionnaires may not generate data high in validity.
Because questionnaires are completed in private it is a good method to use when researching personal or sensitive issues.	Researchers cannot control for how individuals may interpret questions, making comparisons potentially difficult.
When questions are pre-coded and standardised, analysing the results is a relatively quick process.	If the sample size is very large, analysis might be time consuming, especially if computer technology cannot be used.
Analysis of large sample results is even easier when done by a computer using pre-coded answers and optical character reader (OCR) technology.	It is impossible to check whether individuals have answered honestly in questionnaires.
When researchers have to negotiate 'gatekeepers' (such as head teachers), it may be easier to access their sample through questionnaires than through interviews or observation.	

Table 1.2 Advantages and disadvantages of self-completion questionnaires

Operationalisation means defining an abstract concept in such a way that it can be measured and subsequently studied. Problems can arise when individuals operationalise concepts or define terms in ways that differ to the interpretation of the researcher.

◀ KEY CONCEPT ●

KEY SOCIOLOGISTS

Carolyn Jackson (2006) studied lads and ladettes in Year 9, researching gender and fear of failure. Because her sample was big she used self-completion questionnaires to explore: academic goals and disruptive behaviours, academic performance and aspirations, and views about laddishness and popularity. Pupils responded to statements on a five-point agreement scale with anonymity encouraging honesty. The questionnaire had to assume pupils understood her concept of 'laddishness' and there was the potential problem of pupils exaggerating their laddishness.

CONTEMPORARY APPLICATION

Although there will always be a place for the paper questionnaire, it is likely that the medium for the delivery of questionnaires will increasingly be electronic. This is because software packages not only facilitate the writing of questionnaires but increasingly collate responses, producing graphs, charts and tables that enable swift analysis of results.

RESEARCH IN FOCUS

Does fear of debt put students off going to university?

Figure 1.7 Students graduating

Claire Callender and Jon Jackson (2005) used self-completion questionnaires to measure the fear of debt arising from university study. They researched the attitudes of prospective students in England towards debt and their decisions about whether or not to apply to university. Their research involved the postal distribution of 3,582 questionnaires to 101 school sixth forms and further education (FE) colleges. Responses were received from 1,954 students in 82 schools and colleges; the response rate for the student questionnaires was 55 per cent. The research was quantitative and positivistic in style.

The self-completion questionnaires were handed out to students in classes by teachers. There were three specific questions designed to gather information about student attitudes to debt. To operationalise social class, the researchers had to translate this concept into a way that was measurable. To do this they used a variant of the Office for National Statistics' (ONS) Socio-Economic Classification, but reduced the six levels to three, which were lower income, middle class and upper class.

Callender and Jackson's conclusion was that debt aversion is a class issue. They found that fear of debt was considerably higher among those from the lower-income group than the other two classes. This was still the case when other factors were held constant, such as type of institution they attended (FE college, state or independent school), gender, ethnicity and age. The lower-income group was also more likely to evaluate going to university as having more costs than benefits.

Adapted from Blundell, J. and Griffiths, J. (2008) *Sociology Research Since 2000.* Cooksbridge: Connect Publications.

Questions

1. What was the response rate to Callender and Jackson's postal questionnaire?
2. Do you think the response rate would have been higher or lower if they had posted questionnaires to each student's home? (Explain your reasons.)
3. What does the term 'operationalise' mean when applied to social class?
4. Explain why this research was both quantitative and positivistic in style.

3.2 Why do researchers use interviews?

When thinking about interviews, knowledge of the different types of interview (structured, semi-structured, unstructured, group interview and focus groups) along with their strengths and weaknesses, together with the association with qualitative data and research generally high in validity, is important.

Interviews come in a variety of forms and can be used to collect both quantitative and qualitative data.

Structured interviews are another way of conducting social surveys. In-depth interviews are either unstructured or semi-structured and provide rich qualitative data, generally high in validity. Besides providing spoken narratives about people's experiences and emotions, they can raise new ideas that the researcher had not necessarily thought of. These can then be probed further.

Interviews are associated with the interpretivist approach. As a method they are generally associated with interactionism, labelling theory and phenomenology, but all types of sociologists use interviews in their research.

Structured interviews

A structured interview (sometimes referred to as a formal interview) involves the interviewer asking a series of questions from an interview schedule (effectively a questionnaire). As with questionnaires, all respondents are given the same set of questions in the same order. Transcribing answers is normally straightforward as questions tend to be closed with simple tick boxes or multiple-choice answers. The interviewer normally checks the appropriate boxes on the interview schedule or records word-for-word the answer of respondents. The data collected is therefore usually quantitative.

Open questions can be asked to collect some qualitative data, but there is a danger that interviewers may abbreviate answers and potentially exclude key points. Positivists view structured interviews as scientific because they are standardised, high in reliability and generate quantifiable results.

Semi-structured interviews

Semi-structured interviews involve a set of common questions, but the interviewer can develop and expand on these according to the answers given. So, for example, in response to an interesting reply, the interviewer might invite the interviewee to expand on their answer. Or, if an answer given was vague or unclear, the interviewer could ask them to clarify what they meant.

An advantage of using semi-structured interviews is that it allows researchers to generate both quantitative and qualitative data. As a research method it offers elements of reliability (as common questions can be replicated) and the qualitative data gained from follow-up questions adds to the validity of the findings. The follow-up questions allow for some rapport to be built between the respondents and the researchers.

Unstructured interviews

An unstructured interview (sometimes called an informal interview) are extended sessions of conversation where an interviewer asks open-ended questions about a topic, during which the respondent is able to answer freely and in-depth. Because unstructured interviews can be quite lengthy in time (sometimes repeated over several sessions) trust and rapport can build between

Figure 1.8 An interview

the interviewer and the respondent. This can produce rich qualitative data, high in validity. Because interviewers are not constrained by fixed questions, the conversation can flow freely, adding to the validity of the data produced because respondents feel that their input is valued.

Group interviews/focus groups

Researchers sometimes find that interviewing people collectively can be useful. Group interviews (sometimes called focus groups) provide a quick way of interviewing a larger number of people. Group interviews or focus groups involve intensive discussion and interviewing on a given topic.

This method generates qualitative data by building up a rapport with and between respondents and encouraging them to volunteer data rich in validity. The 'group dynamics' encourage one person's answer to stimulate answers from someone else, adding to the richness of the data recorded. Group interviews are becoming increasingly common in sociological research.

The interviewer effect can derive from the personal bias, values or judgements an interviewer brings to the interview. It can also stem from the social characteristics of the interviewer. For example, teenage girls are unlikely to open up and discuss female issues with a male interviewer. The validity of the qualitative data generated in interviews can be compromised by the interviewee feeling uncomfortable with the characteristics of the interviewer.

 **KEY CONCEPT**

Advantages of interviews	Disadvantages of interviews
Response rates are high as responses are collected directly by the interviewer.	The nature of structured interviews does not encourage elaboration as it invites short answers (often multiple-choice answers).
The interviewer is able to clarify terms and explain questions that individuals may not have understood.	Pupils may respond to interviewers as authority figures and hold back information.
Interviews offer the opportunity for the individuals to clarify their responses if the researcher feels that this is necessary.	There is a danger of the 'interviewer effect' where the very presence of an interviewer can influence the quality of data.
The interviewer can pick up on non-verbal signs, such as facial expressions of respondents, in order to detect lying.	The interviewer's tone of voice, dress, gender, age and ethnicity could influence respondents and their answers.
With structured interviews, individuals are asked the same questions in the same order, which means comparisons can be made.	Interviews are more costly and time consuming than questionnaires.
With semi-structured interviews the researcher can collect both quantitative and qualitative data. This reflects a triangulation or realist approach.	Interviews may be inappropriate for researching sensitive and embarrassing issues. Individuals may be unwilling to verbalise responses that they would write in a questionnaire.
With semi- and unstructured interviews a rapport between interviewer and interviewees can build and contribute to the richness and validity of qualitative data.	Samples tend to be small with non-standardised questions in semi- and unstructured interviews, making generalisations and production of statistics difficult.
The interview can be carried out in a familiar place where individuals feel safe. This can encourage the free response of valid qualitative data.	Some argue that observation is a more appropriate method for the study of areas such as education, allowing the pupils/teachers to be relaxed and therefore behave more naturally.

Table 1.3 Advantages and disadvantages of interviews

KEY SOCIOLOGISTS

Louise Archer (2003) studied Muslim boys and education in the context of race, **masculinity** and schooling. Working with two non-academic Asian British women, Archer held group interviews using a semi-structured interview schedule. Archer discovered that the boys were willing to talk about racism with Asian interviewers but that her whiteness silenced the boys in some of the discussions. This is a classic example of an interviewer effect.

STUDY TIP

It is important to demonstrate knowledge of strengths and weaknesses of the different types of interviews. In addition, you need to be able to compare and contrast interviews with other research methods such as questionnaires and observation. Finally, it is helpful to locate them as a method favoured by interpretivists for the collection of qualitative data, high in validity.

CONTEMPORARY APPLICATION

There is no reason why interviews have to be face-to-face. Researchers may increasingly use electronic software such as Skype or Facetime to conduct interviews. This saves on travelling. In addition, although researchers may still encounter 'gatekeepers', there may be fewer risks and barriers to conducting an interview.

RESEARCH IN FOCUS

Why are African-Caribbean students subject to more exclusions from school?

Cecile Wright *et al* (2005) researched the high level of exclusions of African-Caribbean boys. They noted that official figures show that for both African-Caribbean boys and girls, they are at least four times more likely to be excluded than white boys and girls. The fact that official statistics do not take into account unofficial and unrecorded exclusions means that this figure is probably an underestimate.

They used four data collection processes that involved interviewing. The initial interview of excluded boys was followed by a friendship group interview. They undertook a third interview ten months after the first, although not all of the young people were interviewed three times. Finally, they interviewed family members and carers. All interviews were recorded.

Their findings were that many African Caribbeans felt labelled and discriminated against and that their exclusion had been unjust. They also found it difficult to return to school because they were viewed as troublemakers by both teachers and other students. This led some to develop a sense of resistance against the schooling system. Exclusion understandably often led to poor qualifications and poor employment opportunities, though Wright *et al* found that some students had returned successfully to full-time education.

The strength of this research is that the consequences for both students and families of exclusion are discussed in detail. However, Wright *et al* say little about the causes of the exclusion other than referral to racism by the schools, teachers and other pupils. The full complexity of the exclusions therefore remains unpacked.

Adapted from Cecile Wright, Penny Standen, Gus John, Gerry German and Tina Patel (2005) School exclusion and transition into adulthood in African-Caribbean communities. Joseph Rowntree Foundation (www.jrf.org.uk/publications/school-exclusion-and-transition-adulthood-african-caribbean-communities).

Questions

1. What were the four data collection processes that involved interviewing?
2. Given that many of the researchers are from BME groups, including the African-Caribbean community, could there be any potential methodological pitfalls associated with this research?
3. What is highlighted as a weakness of the research?
4. In what ways is this a qualitative piece of research?

3.3 Why do researchers use participant and non-participant observation?

When studying participant and non-participant observations, you will develop an awareness of the strengths and weaknesses of this method, together with its association with qualitative data and research generally high in validity.

Participant observation involves immersion by the researcher within the group that is being studied. It can be **overt** or **covert**, but when covert it is felt people act most naturally, producing data that is high in validity. Classic examples include John Howard Griffin (1961) who dyed his skin to discover what it was like to be black in 1960s USA, and Erving Goffman (1961) who became a porter and physiotherapist in a psychiatric hospital in order to understand the meanings of being a mental patient. Non-participant observation occurs when researchers observe a group from outside without actively participating within it. This can also be overt or covert.

Observation as a research method is widely used by interpretivist sociologists, especially interactionists. It is therefore most commonly associated with the collection of qualitative data that is rich and meaningful, hence high in validity. The key attraction is that it can be **naturalistic**, that is, people are observed behaving in their natural environment. It provides a perfect opportunity to exercise Weber's concept of *verstehen* whereby the researcher can interpret the behaviour through the eyes of those being observed. It is this interpretation of those being studied that forms the basis of this research method. There are four types of observation:

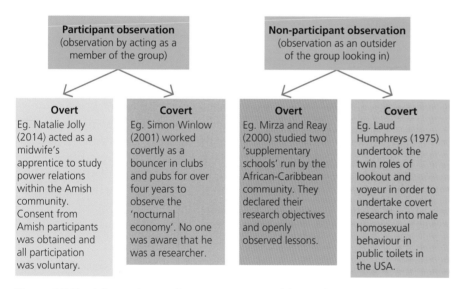

Figure 1.9 Participant observation versus non-participant observation

Overt observation occurs when the researcher joins a group with their full knowledge in order to observe their behaviour. For example, when Paul Willis (1977) was doing classroom observations, the pupils in the class were aware of his presence as a researcher. Covert observation has lots of ethical implications since it involves studying a group without their knowledge and hence informed consent. The BSA Code of Ethics only permits this when there is no other way of obtaining the data and that the possibility of causing harm in minimised. When Willis was pretending to be a snack bar worker in the school his research was covert because none of the pupils knew he was researching their behaviour.

Remember successful observation has much to do with acceptance of the researcher by the group. The social class, gender, ethnicity and age of the researcher can all act as barriers to acceptance. Even the presence of a stranger among the group can influence behaviour and make it less natural.

	Advantages	Disadvantages
Overt research	The researcher is being honest and open about her/his role. No one is being deceived. As the group is aware of the researcher and the research being undertaken, the participants may agree to take part in interviews or self-complete questionnaires as well.	When researching certain deviant behaviour or groups closed to outsiders, only someone on the inside can really gain access to their behaviour and secrets. Even a researcher considered sympathetic by the group may still not be fully trusted by its members.
Covert research	Because groups are unaware they are being researched their behaviour should be natural. There should be no 'observer effect'. Researchers can penetrate deviant groups and other areas considered forbidden. Such research can produce insightful data rich in validity.	It can be hard to gain entry into a remote or insular group and then to achieve acceptance from its members. It is ethically wrong to spy on people behind their backs. In addition, if the group studied breaks the law this puts the researcher in a compromised legal position. Covert research can be dangerous if the cover of the researcher is blown. Several sociologists have had to flee groups they have been studying, fearing for their lives. Making notes in the field is difficult when you are pretending to be an ordinary member of the group.

Table 1.4 Advantages and disadvantages of overt and covert research

Ethnography

Ethnography was a method originally applied to research in anthropology but is often used synonymously in sociology to refer to participant observation. It literally means the study of the culture and structure of a group of people in a society. Ethnographic research involves the production of highly detailed accounts of how people in a particular social setting lead their lives, based on systematic and long-term observation of, and interviews with, informants. Ethnography often uses **gatekeepers** to gain access to groups on the margins of society. It can use different research methods but the most common is participant observation. In-depth interviews and the use of qualitative documents can also be used in ethnographic studies.

The 'observer effect' is a key concept relevant to this debate. This occurs when people are aware that they are being watched and occurs particularly when observation is overt. When this occurs there is a danger that those being studied will not behave normally or naturally, rendering the research worthless. Even when research is covert, the presence of a stranger or extra person can affect the dynamics of a group and change people's behaviour. However, many researchers are surprised at how quickly their presence can be 'forgotten' by those they are overtly observing. When this happens the group's behaviour seems to become quite natural.

Advantages of observation	Disadvantages of observation
It is a naturalistic approach studying individuals in their natural environment.	Covert observation raises ethical concerns: spying on individuals without their knowledge or informed consent has to be justified in terms of the BSA's ethical code.
If observation is undertaken covertly, it is least likely to result in an imposition factor.	When observation is overt there is the danger of an 'observer effect'. The observer's presence may change or influence the behaviour of the group (the **Hawthorne effect**).
Observations offer an opportunity for small-scale, detailed research. The qualitative data obtained tends to be rich and high in validity.	The researcher could become too involved ('going native'), fail to remain objective and can become influenced by the values of those they are observing.
Observation is a highly suitable method for interpretive study of environments, offering the kind of sociological insight generally not found in surveys.	Some small-scale observations are not generalisable, meaning the data has limited value.
Observation offers an opportunity to study the interaction among individuals and between them and outsiders, offering validity to the research.	With observation it can be difficult to gain access to certain groups protected by 'gatekeepers', such as hospital patients.
Providing access can be gained, observation is a good way of penetrating the underworld of **subcultures**, gaining insight into their behaviour, values and language.	Researchers can encounter problems when trying to penetrate certain groups in order to observe them, such as gangs.
By its nature, observation can take the researcher in unexpected directions, possibly generating new research questions.	It can be very time consuming compared to other methods.
Within the certain environments, observation can form a useful preliminary method in order to develop research questions when subsequently carrying out a questionnaire or interviews.	Practically, it is difficult to record information when observing. Relying on memory is problematic, but microphones and video recorders are intrusive or raise ethical issues of not having informed consent if covert.
	Observation as a method is low in reliability. It is very difficult to replicate research.

Table 1.5 Advantages and disadvantages of observation

KEY SOCIOLOGISTS

John Hughes (1976) once described good sociological research as 'getting the seat of your pants dirty', implying researchers should immerse themselves fully into their area of investigation. He also advocated that observation should 'become part of a daily round, learning languages and meanings, rules of impersonal, relations ... and in short, living the life of the people under study'.

STUDY TIP

It is important to demonstrate an ability to compare the strengths and weaknesses of participant and non-participant observation, but be careful to avoid just using narrative lists in extended-answer questions requiring AO2 and AO3 skills. You will need to critically evaluate this method.

CONTEMPORARY APPLICATION

Structured observation was originally a quantitative method of data gathering adopted by positivist anthropologists such as Bronislaw Malinowski and Margaret Mead in the 1920s and 1930s. It is now almost exclusively associated with qualitative research and the interpretivist approach. There may still be a place for mixed-methods research; structured observation could provide valuable pointers for case selection in an otherwise interpretivist research project.

'Ordinary' young people's experiences of the everyday antisocial

This ethnographic project involved 14 months of youth work in a traditional youth club and a street-based project. As well as participant observation, groups of young people were engaged in 'task-based' activities including walkabouts, photo diaries and 'mapping' exercises. Methods were designed to engage young people in discussion about antisocial behaviour while avoiding abstract adult-led concepts. For example, the term 'antisocial behaviour' was avoided during the research. Activities and discussions were instead centred around general topics such as growing up in Robbiestoun, schools and friendships, and the places and spaces important to young people.

This provided a route away from a simplistic categorisation of behaviours or activities as antisocial and also evaded values and labels in favour of a more 'neutral' starting point.

The research focused on the 'middling' young people who were the majority of those involved in the project. These young people identified themselves as neither conformists nor troublemakers. Indeed, their narratives about school, friendships and involvement in crime revealed that their experiences and their identities fell somewhere in-between these two categories. While their lives 'in the middle' lacked the everyday drama, chaos and vulnerability of the minority groups, antisocial behaviour remained a salient and everyday issue.

Adapted from Emma Davidson (2013) Between edges and margins: Exploring 'ordinary' young people's experiences of the everyday antisocial. *Sociological Research Online*, *18* (1), 5.

Figure 1.10 Research is vital for sociologists

Questions

1 What methods were used besides participant observation?
2. Why do you think the term 'antisocial behaviour' was deliberately avoided by Davidson?
3. Why do you think Davidson focused her research on 'middling young people' rather than the minority groups either involved in crime and deviance or victims of antisocial behaviour?
4. What were her findings about this middling group?

3.4 Why do researchers use experiments?

When studying experiments, you will learn to distinguish between laboratory and field experiments, develop an awareness of the strengths and weaknesses of this method, and its association with quantitative data and research.

Though experiments are frequently used in natural sciences and psychology, there are fundamental problems with their use in sociology and they are rarely used.

Positivist sociologists argue that research should be carried out under controlled conditions, but even positivists rarely use experiments. This is because of ethical concerns and the clinical environment of the laboratory. Human behaviour is infinitely complex and humans will not behave in a natural way if they believe they are being experimented on.

Interpretivist sociologists, in particular, argue that because humans are conscious, they know they are being experimented on. Therefore, they argue, it is impossible to observe natural behaviour and gain consistent results from overt experiments. This then brings in the case for carrying out covert experiments on people, which may be unethical as they have not given their informed consent.

Laboratory experiments

Where laboratory experiments are used within sociology they are used in specific circumstances. For example, Karl Popper (1959) advocated a **deductive approach** to research. This approach has many similarities to the scientific approach of positivism, but differs in that researchers start with a theory that is subsequently tested against empirical evidence. (Conventionally sociologists formulate theories out of evidence.)

If a sociologist wanted to test a theory, they may choose to undertake a laboratory experiment where very precise evidence can be consistently collected. This method might be used if the researcher wanted to observe how independent **variables** may be influencing the **dependent variable** they are studying. The **independent variable** in an experiment is the variable that is subject to variation by the researcher, whereas the dependent variable is the response that is being measured. The independent variable is the presumed cause, whereas the dependent variable is the presumed effect. Typically experiments are undertaken when there is a need to demonstrate that when certain variables are controlled the resulting outcome can be measured and studied. When a variable is subject to control in an experiment, it is either held constant or changed in order to measure its impact. In natural sciences a researcher may control the variables of light, moisture or soil fertility on plant growth. However, within sociology it is both unethical and impractical to influence variables such as income, status or popularity, which makes conducting sociological experiments difficult.

A classic example of a psychological laboratory experiment is that of Albert Bandura (1965) who was investigating the effects watching media violence on children. All children were shown a film of a man hitting a Bobo doll (an inflatable doll that always returns to an upright position when knocked over) with a mallet. The children were then divided into separate rooms and exposed to various independent variables: in one room the man was criticised for his violence; in another room the man was praised; in a third room neither criticism nor praise was offered. Subsequently all the children were individually placed in a room with a Bobo doll and secretly observed. It was found that the children in the first room, where the man had been criticised for being violent, displayed least aggression. Although Bandura claimed that his experiment successfully showed media effects, many critics have argued that the unnatural nature of this experiment proves little.

Field experiments

Because it is difficult, some would say impossible, to control for all variables, laboratory experiments are only used occasionally. When sociological experiments are undertaken they tend to be 'in the field'. An experiment in the field involves undertaking research in the social world and isolating certain variables so that a hypothesis can be tested. These are sometimes referred to as 'natural experiments' since the researcher is covert and people are unaware that they are being experimented on. For example, Jonathan Raban (1991) undertook a study of homeless people on the streets of New York. Raban experimented by performing each of the two identities of pedestrian and a 'street person'. As a pedestrian he describes how he focused on an imaginary point in the distance to avoid eye contact; the street people he described as 'bits of stationary furniture, on a level with fire hydrants and the trash cans'. Then Raban sat on a fire hydrant and pretended to be one of the 'street people'. He records his feelings: 'It was interesting to feel oneself being willed into non-existence by total strangers. I'd never felt the force of such frank contempt.' This simple experiment gives an insight into the emotions and feelings of the two groups on the street.

In another field experiment, J.W. Sissons (1970) used the same actor, firstly dressed in a suit and bowler hat and secondly dressed as a labourer. He was asked to stand in Paddington Station, London, and ask strangers for directions to Hyde Park, using exactly the same question and words each time. Sissons was able to observe the different reactions: people responded far more positively and gave more detailed directions when the actor was dressed in a suit. He concluded that the variable of social class was the key factor in explaining people's reaction to being asked to give directions, since all the other variables were held constant.

Comparative research

Comparative research is a sociological interpretation of the experiment. Sociologists as diverse as Émile Durkheim (a positivist) and Max Weber (an interpretivist) have used the comparative method to systematically compare differences in social phenomena between groups within a society. In this way relationships or **correlations** may be observed. Therefore with the comparative method the social world effectively becomes the laboratory. The comparative method is associated with positivists, who use it to test hypotheses or **causal relationships**.

Advantages of using experiments	Disadvantages of using experiments
Experiments reflect the positivist belief that research should be undertaken in controlled conditions. The structured nature of some organisations could help facilitate this.	Attempts to conduct experiments can produce doubtful results if people are aware that they are being studied – the 'experimenter effect'.
Experiments can be repeated time and time again, so they are regarded as being high in reliability.	Any attempt to replicate a laboratory creates an unnatural environment, reducing the chance for natural behaviour.
Field experiments are generally favoured by sociologists over laboratory experiments as they are more natural and have fewer ethical and practical problems.	In most laboratory situations it is impossible to replicate normal life and to control all the variables that influence people's behaviour.
Popper argues that experiments enable researchers to test precise predictions. Theories can be tested by the collection of empirical evidence.	If experiments are done in a covert way, it raises ethical issues as people cannot give their informed consent.
When the interaction between variables can be measured experiments achieve the goal of positivist sociology: evidence of cause-and-effect relationships.	

Table 1.6 Advantages and disadvantages of using experiments

STUDY TIP

Locate the use of experiments primarily with positivism and the collection of quantitative data. Remember not to just list off a range of advantages and disadvantages in extended-answer questions requiring AO2 and AO3 skills.

KEY SOCIOLOGISTS

Elton Mayo (1925) undertook research at the Hawthorne plant of the Western Electric Company designed to increase workers' productivity. The team tried various interventions and saw inexplicably varied results. They found that what changed the workers' work rates was the fact they were being studied rather than any of changes consciously made by the research team. This experimenter effect has since become known as the Hawthorne effect.

3.5 Why do researchers use documents?

If you are discussing documents, you could include the different types of document (personal, public and historical) together with their respective strengths and weaknesses. In addition, you could build on this to discuss their association with both quantitative and qualitative data and, accordingly, qualities of reliability and/or validity.

The word 'document' means any paper-based or electronic resource. Examples of documents include **personal documents** (such as diaries and letters), **public documents** (such as government reports) and **historical documents** (such as parish records, census data and school inspection reports), as well as audio and video recordings, including broadcast programmes. Documents can be an important source of information for researchers. A key part of any research is to undertake a **literature search** in order to establish the nature and extent of existing data. Researchers can use this information to shape the direction of their research or their research questions. Sometimes the existence of high-quality documents makes the planned primary research unnecessary as it would simply replicate the data already in existence. However, as with any secondary data, documents may contain errors or personal biases, so they must be used with caution. There is also the general problem of how secondary data was collected and what methodological errors were committed in its compilation.

Personal documents

The term personal document refers specifically to diaries, memoirs and letters, photographs and, as of recently, emails and personal electronic documents. Personal documents can be historical or contemporary – that is, they might have been created recently or a long time previous.

Personal documents are viewed as reflecting a naturalistic arena where individuals can explore their own thoughts and feelings. Because of the personal nature of these documents, they are often viewed as a source of rich qualitative data, high in validity. Indeed, because most personal documents are not written for public consumption, they may have greater validity. Personal documents have to be used with some care: they can reflect partisan or biased views, or may even be forgeries.

Diaries are a very subjective document since the diarist can be very selective about what they choose to record. Equally they can disregard any experience they wish because the diarist organises their thoughts and feelings in the way they choose. Diaries are, therefore, potentially biased and not necessarily representative. Consequently it may be difficult to generalise from such a personal and individual source of data.

Fulcher and Scott (2011) suggest that the reliability and validity of any historical document can be assessed by asking four key questions:

● How authentic is the document? Is it complete and can it be credited to a particular author?
● What were the motives for writing the document? Is it creditable or exaggerated or biased?
● Is the document representative or typical?
● Are the feeling and emotions expressed in the document clear?

In a sense, personal documents can provide a more ecologically valid method than many other research methods. For example, personal documents can provide a 'window' into participants' thought processes that may not be apparent from other research methods. When writing personal documents people are located in their natural environment and not the slightly contrived setting of a researcher-led interview and/or observation.

Sociologists sometimes ask respondents to keep diaries. Examples include Young and Willmott (1973) in their study of London families, Charles and Kerr (1988) in their study of families and food, and Jacqui Gabb (2008) who, in her study of families, invited them to draw emotion maps. Such diaries may be lower in validity than diaries discovered by chance. Alan Bryman (2012) notes that while email has replaced many letters of the past, it can still offer an alternative document source.

Public documents

Public documents are resources produced for the public domain and refer to records created or received by government departments and their executive agencies, the armed forces, NHS authorities and the courts. There may consequently be an overlap here with official statistics. In the UK public records considered appropriate for preservation are kept in The National Archives or a place of deposit approved by the Lord Chancellor. Public records are not normally retained beyond the 30-year period, unless authorised by the Lord Chancellor. Sociologists do not need consent to access public records and confidentiality is not required in the case of information available within them.

Public documents are normally accurate and reflect facts about society at any one moment in time. They offer mainly quantitative data but, if offering any insight into society, could also be considered qualitative. Many interpretivist and **conflict sociologists** question the usefulness of public documents: like official statistics they believe the only useful thing public documents reveal is something about the people or organisations that produced them.

Advantages of using documents	Disadvantages of using documents
Using data from earlier research in the form of secondary documents can save time.	Since documents offer a very personal account of individuals, they may not be representative or provide generalisable data.
Personal documents, such as diaries, can give genuine insight into behaviour and experiences, offering rich qualitative data.	There is no way of knowing how honest individuals have been and, hence, how valid or biased the data is in personal documents.
Diaries can provide a reliable alternative to the traditional interview method for events that are difficult to recall or are easily forgotten.	The way people operationalise concepts (see page 19) or define terms in personal documents may not be the same as the researcher.
Personal documents, such as diaries, may be used as a useful supplementary method, in addition to questionnaires, interviews or observation.	Researchers rarely investigate 'ordinary people' so if personal documents from their research are used they often reflect interesting but untypical examples: truants, gang members, etc.
The content of personal documents, such as diaries, tends to be very high in validity because they are generally not written for public reading.	With historical documents there is often no way of checking their accuracy, especially if the authors are now dead.
Getting individuals to keep diaries can be very useful if the researcher cannot collect data first hand, say because of financial or distance issues.	It can be difficult to interpret ambiguities in historical documents whose author is uncontactable.
In the wider context of research, historical documents may be the only source of information about certain establishments, policies or groups.	
Where there are sufficient public documents it is possible to create a statistical database of the information.	

Table 1.7 Advantages and disadvantages of using documents

STUDY TIP

It is important to demonstrate that, although underused, secondary sources such as diaries can provide access to rich qualitative data, if used carefully. Remember to not just list arguments for and against documents in extended-answer questions requiring AO2 and AO3 skills.

KEY SOCIOLOGISTS

In a study concerned with how working-class ideas and **identity** shape young people's life choices, such as whether to go to university, Archer *et al* (2007) got eight students to complete photographic diaries. They found that young people who subscribe to working-class youth styles were self-limiting their own access to routes for academic success.

RESEARCH IN FOCUS

Using diaries with learners

Figure 1.11 Diaries are a useful source of information

Krishan and Hoon (2002) studied the way courses are designed in education. They identified three advantages of using diaries in research:

- they provide 'voices' to the respondents (they write in their own words)
- they give an insight into the individual's 'learning agenda'
- they provide a means of 'listening' to the respondents.

However, success in using diaries rests entirely on the quality and frequency of entries. Clearly the usefulness of this method is compromised if entries are short and only done on an infrequent basis.

Krishan and Hoon found that huge gains could be made in course design if teachers were aware of the learners' perception of what content they wanted to learn, as well as the ways to achieve the learning. Too often teachers focus on their own beliefs regarding course content and the nature of the delivery. What is frequently problematic is the level of disjointedness between the teachers' and the learners' learning agendas. Although it is very difficult, if not downright impossible, to completely match these two agendas, arriving at a level of compatibility is essential if meaningful learning and teaching is to proceed.

Therefore by 'listening' to individual 'voices' through the diaries, it is possible for the teacher in the classroom to make certain adjustments to accommodate individual learning needs.

Adapted from Tom Farrelly (2014) *Diaries in Social Research.* Academia.edu (www.academia.edu/4127274/Diaries_in_Social_Research).

3.6 Why do researchers use official statistics?

When studying official statistics, you will develop an awareness of the strengths and weaknesses of this form of data, together with its association with quantitative data and research generally high in reliability.

Official statistics consist of the wide range of data collected by government departments and agencies. Such data tends to be both extensive and up to date. In addition, this volume of data could not be collected by researchers – only governments are able to finance such large-scale data collection. Official statistics can cover the whole of the population, as with the census or statistics about birth, marriage, **divorce**, death, unemployment and crime rates. At other times very large sample sizes can be used. For example, a sample of 50,000 **households** is the source of data for the annual Survey of Crime for England and Wales (formerly the British Crime Survey).

Most official statistics are readily available and free, and are accurate. They cover a wide range of social areas, from calculating the size of population to the distribution of income and wealth. Researchers use official statistics because they can be very useful for demonstrating trends over time. In addition, they can highlight significant and meaningful regularities within society. Researchers

Questions

1. What were the three advantages of using diaries in research according to Krishan and Hoon?
2. What threatens to undermine the use of diaries in research?
3. Do you think that researchers generally, like the teachers in this study, do not 'listen' enough to their respondents?

frequently take advantage of the existence of official statistics to use as a benchmark in order to make comparisons with the data they have collected personally. In addition, official statistics can help identify patterns between different social group using criteria such as social class, gender, ethnicity and age.

There are some doubts about the accuracy of some official statistics, such as the crime rate or suicide statistics. The official crime rate is published annually as police recorded crime (PRC). Positivists tend to take official statistics at face value. Interpretivist sociologists describe the official crime rate as little more than a **social construction**: it is based on the number of crimes reported and recorded by the police, but a lot of crime is never reported and so not recorded. Interpretivists consider that a 'dark side' exists between the real level of crime and the official level.

Many sociologists argue that a lot of official statistics are objective and reflect the social facts of society. They argue that their criticisms have been exaggerated, overdrawn and extended illegitimately beyond the fields such as suicide and crime in which they were originally developed.

● KEY CONCEPT ➤

Non-official statistics are numerical data collected by organisations other than government departments and agencies. These can be private organisations (such as charities, for example the Joseph Rowntree Foundation), pressure groups (such as Greenpeace), interest groups (such as trade unions) and even corporate firms (such as Sky TV).

Advantages of using official statistics	Disadvantages of using official statistics
Positivist sociologists largely accept official statistics as accurate, reflecting objective social facts.	Conflict and interpretivist sociologists question the accuracy of official statistics; they argue that they are inevitably socially constructed. They only offer information about those who produced the data.
Official statistics are accessible and inexpensive.	
Official statistics can be used to check and confirm research findings elsewhere.	Researchers may derive different interpretations from official statistics, making drawing comparisons potentially difficult.
Official statistics, such as educational statistics linked to government educational policies, can support research questions.	As with any secondary source of data the researcher has no control over the processes by which official statistics were gathered.
Governments tend to keep official statistics updated, usually annually but sometimes even monthly, enabling monitoring of trends over time.	Official statistics frequently underestimate real problems, such as truancy and exclusions in education. They therefore do not reflect the 'real' rates and consequently lack validity.
Official statistics are frequently based on very large samples. These would be impractical and costly for a researcher to produce.	Marxists question the ideological role of official statistics. For example, statistics on the success of government policies may be manipulated to put a gloss of them.
Official statistics may form the inspiration for subsequent sociological research. For example, interest in male educational underachievement was sparked off by GCSE examination results.	Feminists have also criticised official statistics, arguing they can be used to promote patriarchal interests. For example, gender exam attainment levels created a 'problem about boys' rather than a 'celebration of female achievement'.
Official statistics may provide useful background material to research, providing further insights.	

Table 1.8 Advantages and disadvantages of using official statistics

KEY SOCIOLOGISTS

Kellett and Dar (2007) undertook research on whether poor childhood literacy was linked to subsequent adult poverty. Their starting point was official statistics which indicated a limited improvement in literacy rates following the government targeting literacy over the ten-year period prior to their research. They found that, despite their high profile, the impact of these policies has in fact been quite limited.

CONTEMPORARY APPLICATION

The official statistics on crime published as police recorded crime have come in for repeated criticism over the years as the police have been accused of not recording all crimes reported to them (a process known as 'cuffing'). In January 2014 the UK Statistics Authority stripped police recorded crime of its gold standard status as official statistics. There is an alternative official statistic on crime, the Crime Survey of England and Wales (CSEW), which is a victim survey and therefore not interested if crimes have been recorded or not.

STUDY TIP

It is useful to recognise that conflict and interpretivist sociologists question the validity and reliability of this data, as every sociologist will use official statistics at some point.

Check your understanding

1. What type of question is generally asked in self-completion questionnaires?
2. What circumstances might make a postal questionnaire (or an equivalent electronic version) an obvious choice of method?
3. What is a key problem with postal (or electronic) questionnaires?
4. Name the four types of interview.
5. What sort of data is collected and what type of questions are asked in unstructured interviews?
6. What does 'going native' mean in the context of observations?
7. Why is covert research generally viewed as unethical?
8. Why is the experiment rarely used in sociological research?
9. Why must sociologists be wary of using personal documents?
10. What are official statistics?

Practice questions

1. Outline two advantages of using questionnaires in sociological research. [4 marks]
2. Evaluate why sociologists use official statistics in their research. [16 marks]

Section 4: Data and sampling

This section will explore:
- What is the distinction between primary and secondary data?
- Why do researchers use different types of samples and pilot studies?

GETTING YOU STARTED

Kyla Ellis-Sloan (2013) undertook primary research to understand experiences of teenage motherhood. She specifically focused on the **stigma** attached to teenage pregnancy and parenting. Her research draws on first-hand accounts of teenage mothers as they discuss their paths to motherhood. Ellis-Sloan utilised the work of Erving Goffman (on stigma (1963), face-work (1967) and impression management (1969)), to demonstrate the strategies deployed by young mothers in the face of a stigmatising identity.

Figure 1.12 Young mother

Her research began with participant observation undertaken at three young parent support groups in the south east of England. Ellis-Sloan attended the group's weekly two-hour sessions for a year. Conversations during periods of observation formed a vital part of data collection. They also offered the possibility for relationships and rapport to be built between the researcher and participants. In addition, they were used to enhance the more formal interviews which followed participant observation. Informal conversations allowed insights into experiences to develop. These were then used to sensitise the researcher to issues and questions that were relevant to individual participants.

The research began with two focus groups. These worked to generate data but additionally functioned as a space to co-construct an interview guide. Group dynamics can impact on the data generated by producing agreement rather than differing views. Further interviews were sought on a one-to-one basis. In addition to the focus groups, the research included 23 semi-structured interviews drawing on narrative and **biographical approaches**. The findings were that being a teenage mother continues to be a stigmatising identity and that young mothers are keenly aware of this.

Adapted from Kyla Ellis-Sloan (2013) Teenage mothers, stigma and their 'presentations of Self'. *Sociological Research Online*, *19* (1), 9.

Questions

1. Why did Ellis-Sloan start with participant observation?
2. How did the informal interviews (conversations) conducted during observation aid the research?
3. Why did Ellis-Sloan use two focus groups?
4. What point does she make about group dynamics within a focus group?
5. What was the primary focus of research by Ellis-Sloan?

4.1 Primary and secondary data

If you are discussing the distinction between primary and secondary data, you could cover the difference between these two types of data.

Theoretical perspectives will inform each sociologists' choice of data source based on their skills and factors like practical and ethical considerations. Those adopting a realist approach (see page 13) will seek, as a matter of good practice, both quantitative and qualitative data, which may require them to use both primary and secondary sources.

Primary data

Primary data is collected first hand by the researcher and is unique. It is collected by the researcher personally, or using a team, through methods such those described in Section 2. For the researcher, the advantage of collecting primary data is that:

- they have control over how the data is collected
- they can adjust their research strategy and research questions to obtain data specific to the aims of their research or hypothesis
- it is up-to-date data that does not currently exist within the public domain.

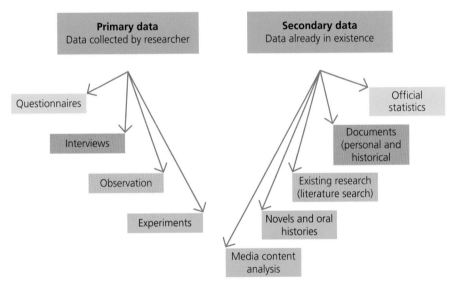

Figure 1.13 Primary versus secondary data

Secondary data

Secondary data is data that has been collected by someone else that is used by a sociologist to ask new questions or to pool with other research. Secondary data can take the form of literature searches of published academic research, historical and personal documents and official statistics. Other examples of secondary data include journals and academic papers, novels, oral histories and media content analysis of newspaper and magazine articles or transcripts of audio/video recordings.

One of the key problems in using secondary data for any researcher is that they have no control over the research procedures and how it was collected. Consequently, researchers need to be alert to the fact that secondary data is highly variable in terms of its quality. If a researcher is confident that the data has been produced by a dependable source, it can offer significant benefits in saving both time and money. There is little point in replicating data that already exists, unless to check the reliability of the data. Secondary data needs to be used carefully, but can be a useful component in the researcher's strategy.

Meta-studies rely heavily on published secondary material on a given subject.

Oral history

Oral history is where the researcher and research participants spend extended time together engaged in a process of storytelling and listening. It is a collaborative process of narrative building rather than an in-depth interview. Getting people to reflect on their life experiences is becoming more popular in certain areas of sociological research. Such individuals are seen as an important asset with important stories to tell about the social world while they are still living. By empowering subjects to see their experiences as important, interviews can yield rich qualitative data, high in validity. However, some feel that there is a danger here of people exaggerating, selectively remembering or possibly putting a subjective slant on their recollections. Any of these factors would serve to undermine the validity of the data and render it biased. Equally, if individuals give a slightly different version of the past each time they are interviewed, the data would be low in reliability. An example of using oral histories is Rachel Slater's (2000) study of how four black South African women experienced urbanisation under apartheid.

Media content analysis

The mass media offers a colossal amount of potential data. The nature of this data can be either quantitative or qualitative. By adopting a systematic approach it is possible to produce high-quality, objective data when analysing media content.

It is important to remember that media content is often biased, especially media that is allowed to openly support political parties. The Glasgow Media Group (GMG) (see 'Key sociologists') has adopted highly sophisticated techniques to ensure that their analyses are scientific and objective. Not all researchers are this thorough in their analysis however, with the risk that a researcher's analysis ends up being little more than a subjective (personally biased) interpretation of the content.

Novels

Novels, by their nature, are fiction, so must be used with extreme care in sociological research. However, many novelists undertake careful and systematic research when writing their novels. The usefulness and validity of novels will depend on the integrity and authenticity of the research they have undertaken. Sometimes sociologists will use respected novels in order to verify information obtained from more traditional sources. A feminist might use the representation of gender in novels to offer an insight into gender relations and how these might be influenced by age, social class, ethnicity and location.

When sociologists use secondary sources they must be aware that the motive behind its construction may reflect bias. Documents may well reflect a desired viewpoint or official statistics may have been constructed to reflect government **policies** more favourably.

KEY SOCIOLOGISTS

The Glasgow Media Group (originally the Glasgow University Media Group) have undertaken many rigorous and systematic analyses of media content, including the portrayal of strikes (1976 and 1990), war and conflict (1995, 2004, 2008, 2011), mental illness (1996, 2010), disability (2011) and refugees (2013). These studies demonstrate the usefulness of media analysis as a data source.

CONTEMPORARY APPLICATION

It is worth noting how both academics and the public are benefiting from the growing accessibility of secondary sources as more become available as they are published, particularly on the internet. In addition, the government is frequently subject to mandatory publication of information following Freedom of Information requests.

STUDY TIP

When discussing secondary methods and data, be sure to include official statistics and documents, discussed in Section 3, as well as novels, oral histories and media content analysis discussed in this section.

Using existing secondary data

Paterson used data from secondary sources to ascertain whether there was a correlation between overall educational attainment and various attributes that are relevant to democracy, such as a tendency to be active, to vote and to hold views on important public issues.

Paterson used the British Social Attitudes Survey (BSAS), the Scottish Social Attitudes Survey (SSAS) and the British and Scottish Election Surveys carried out to coincide with elections to the UK parliament in 1979, 1992 and 1997. The BSAS is an annual cross-section survey with a sample size of around 3,500 that has taken place since 1983. It is reliably able to measure change over time. The SSAS is also an annual cross-section survey, with an annual sample size of around 1,200 conducted annually since 1999.

She also used the National Child Development Study (NCDS) and the 1970 British Cohort Study. The NCDS is a longitudinal survey of everyone born in Britain in a single week in 1958. It has followed the sample for half a century. It measured social attitudes and civic participation in 1991 and 2000, with some measures also from 2004. Adult educational attainment and social class were measured in 1981, 1991 and 2000. The 1970 study is a longitudinal study of the cohort of everyone born in Britain in a single week in 1970.

Paterson also used the British Household Panel Study (BHPS) interviews from 1991 to 2008. The BHPS is a panel study of households selected by clustered and random sampling, first interviewed in 1991.

Paterson concluded from her research that there appear to be no neat conclusions about trends between education and civic values. For some it strengthens, for some it weakens, and for some it broadly remains the same. The rising participation of young people in higher education in the past 30 years has not led to a constantly rising participation in civic life, or to a steady trajectory towards more liberal views.

Adapted from Lindsay Paterson (2013) Education, social attitudes and social participation among adults in Britain. *Sociological Research Online*, *19* (1), 17.

4.2 What are samples and pilot studies?

When you study sampling, you will develop an awareness of the differences between types of sample and why one might be chosen in preference to another.

Before detailing the different sample types, there are some important terms and concepts to explain.

The target population is the whole group that is being studied. This can be very large (in the case of the census it is the population of the UK). Time and financial constraints usually prohibit studying the whole target population. Instead researchers will study a sample population. A sample is a group of individuals with the same social characteristics of the target population selected from a wider population.

A sampling frame lists members of the target population from which the sample is drawn. Research in a school might use the school roll as a sampling frame or may use selected tutor groups as sampling frames. A potential problem is when samples are incomplete; this can happen with deviant or secretive groups when it is not necessarily known if they reflect the target population.

With all samples, researchers must be mindful that if the sample size is too small the data might not be representative of the target population. Samples must be of a sufficient size or researchers should use alternative sampling techniques.

Questions

1. Why do you think Paterson chose to use secondary data rather than collect her own primary data?
2. What is a longitudinal survey?
3. What are the problems in using the same sample in a longitudinal survey?
4. What were Paterson's findings?
5. Why is it good to use data in succession?

Representative samples	Non-representative samples
Random sample	Snowball sample
Stratified random sample	Purposive sample
Systematic sample	
Cluster sample	
Multi-stage sample	
Quota sample	

Table 1.9 Types of samples

Representative samples

Although there are exceptions, the golden rule of research is that samples should be representative – that is, samples should be a smaller group that shares the same social characteristics of the large group being studied.

Random sampling: this is the simplest and most basic type of sample. The advantage of this type of sampling is that everyone in the sampling frame has an equal chance of being chosen. It is fundamentally like drawing names from a hat or raffle tickets from a tombola drum.

Stratified random sampling: this also involves choosing people at random but from predefined categories designed to reflect the characteristics of the target population. Groups are created to reflect social class, gender, ethnicity, age groups and anything else considered relevant. If the target population comprised ten per cent from black and minority ethnic groups (BME) then ten per cent of the sample should be drawn from this group. This will improve representativeness.

Systematic sampling: this chooses people for a sample by drawing the nth person from the sampling frame. For example, every third, fifth or tenth name is chosen. The size of the sampling frame or the desired size of the sample may well affect the size of gap between each name chosen.

Cluster sampling: sometimes an obvious sampling frame is neither apparent nor available. In such circumstances researchers randomly choose individuals or households that are grouped together. If their choice is flawed then the sample may not be representative.

Multi-stage sampling: this involves selecting a sample from another sample. A target population may live in a particular geographical area. The researcher may then choose random or typical roads from within this area and, from these, randomly choose people to research. Providing typical roads are chosen, along with the people, the sample should be representative.

Quota sampling: this features more in market research than sociology. It involves giving each interviewer a quota to interview from predefined groups of people based on social class, gender, ethnicity, age and anything else relevant. One flaw of this technique is that people's characteristics can sometimes cut across several categories, potentially compromising the data.

Non-representative samples

Snowball sampling

Just as a snowball will gather size as it rolls down a hill, this type of sample relies on participants recommending others to take part in the research. Sometimes snowball samples can begin with just one person who then acts as a gatekeeper providing access to everyone else. Traditionally, it was used when gaining access to deviant or secretive groups such as criminal gangs, groups involved with illegal activities such as drug-taking or paedophilia, or reclusive groups such as religious sects. Because the researcher has no control over who is nominated for the research and because samples tend to be small, there is a real risk of the sample not being representative.

Purposive sampling

This type of sample is used when sociologists deliberately want to research untypical groups in order to test a specific hypothesis. For example, Wright *et al* (2006) in their research into street violence drew their sample from six prisons and correctional institutions. They chose purposive sampling to locate only offenders serving sentences for crimes that seemed to involve street violence such as robbery, grievous bodily harm (GBH), actual bodily harm (ABH) and offences involving firearms.

Sometimes sociologists study untypical groups and societies for a specific purpose. For example, feminists may study gender-equal societies to demonstrate there is nothing natural about patriarchal domination.

Pilot studies

After choosing a sampling type, many researchers carry out a **pilot study** prior to carrying out their main research. The purpose of a pilot study is to check the feasibility of the research. For example, it is important to trial questionnaires and interviews to ensure that the questions elicit the quality and quantity of data required. For example, the wording of a question needs changing if people ignore it or misinterpret the nature of response required. Sometimes interviewers will use pilot studies to act as ice-breakers in order to build up a rapport with respondents. It is also a means of establishing whether respondents have been sufficiently briefed. By trialling the research process among a pilot sample, problems can be identified and rectified at a minimal cost. This avoids costly mistakes and can even terminate research projects if problems seem insurmountable.

Pilot studies are normally carried out on people with similar characteristics to the target population but not normally on those who will form the final sample.

CONTEMPORARY APPLICATION

Samples are generally selected using software, which can remove bias in selection. Sampling can only be automated once sampling lists and target populations have been identified, and this can be where the challenges of sampling for research arise, for example, in identifying secretive or deviant groups members.

KEY SOCIOLOGISTS

Sharp and Atherton (2007) researched the experiences of policing in the community from the perspective of young people in black and minority ethnic (BME) groups. They used a snowball sample to get access to their target population. The sample was gained initially by the researchers' contacts with local youth groups and organisations. These initial contacts then suggested further participants. They found snowballing was functional to the research since it involved participants themselves explaining the research and its purpose to others. It would have been very difficult to find enough young people willing to co-operate without this approach.

STUDY TIP

It is important to show awareness of the advantages and disadvantages of each sample type. A key disadvantage of many types is the risk of being unrepresentative. If a sample lacks representativeness then it is not possible to draw generalisations from it to the wider population.

The English Longitudinal Study of Ageing

Figure 1.14 An active older couple

The English Longitudinal Study of Ageing (ELSA) gathers information on the health of people over the age of 50. The study has been developed through collaboration between University College London, the Institute of Fiscal Studies and the National Centre for Social Research.

The research originally took place every two years and followed a nationally representative

random sample of approximately 8,500 people to avoid unintended patterns emerging. A sample of postcodes was selected from the sample frame of Postcode Address File*, using a random sampling technique. Each selected household was sent a letter explaining the purpose of the research and asking if members would agree to be interviewed and complete a self-complete questionnaire.

The sample has since been refreshed, using respondents selected from Health and Safety Executive (HSE) surveys in the years 2001–2004, 2006 and 2009–2011. The researchers now use a stratified random sample. Through a combination of self-complete questionnaires and interviews, the researchers are able to collect both quantitative and qualitative data, which forms an interdisciplinary resource. The data produced shows wide ranging and detailed information on the health, economic position and quality of life of ageing people.

* A database that contains all known postcodes in the UK.

Adapted from Marmot, M. *et al* (2014) *English Longitudinal Study of Ageing: Waves 0-6, 1998-2013* 21st edition. Colchester, Essex: UK Data Archive.

Questions

1. What was the original sampling frame used by ELSA?
2. What does the term 'nationally representative random sample' mean?
3. Explain two reasons why the researchers used a stratified random sample.

Check your understanding

1. What is primary data?
2. Give two advantages of using primary data.
3. What is secondary data?
4. Give two advantages of using secondary data.
5. Give one disadvantage of using secondary data.
6. What is meant by the term 'target population'?
7. What is a sampling frame?
8. Identify four types of representative sample.
9. Identify two types of unrepresentative sample.
10. Why is it normally considered important for samples to be representative?

Practice questions

1. Outline two characteristics of a positivist approach to sociological research. [4 marks]
2. Evaluate why sociological researchers might use a non-representative sample. [16 marks]

Section 5: Influences on research

This section will explore:

- What theoretical considerations influence research?
- What are the practical issues associated with research?
- What ethical factors must sociologists consider?

GETTING YOU STARTED

White working-class views of neighbourhood, cohesion and change

The Joseph Rowntree Foundation (2011) undertook research into white working-class neighbourhoods and community cohesion. The researchers deliberately adopted a qualitative approach to give white working-class members a voice. The research was conducted in three stages – a scoping stage, followed by active and reflective stages.

The scoping stage established links with community organisations and agencies in the three study areas of Aston (Birmingham), Somers Town (London) and Canley (Coventry). This led to interviews with lead officers from the local authorities to explain the project, identify key stakeholders and examine the physical environment.

Figure 1.15 What are your first impressions about this crowd in light of the article you have just read?

The active stage involved qualitative interviews with a sample of residents, followed by community study days to allow reflective discussion and debates, and finally discussions in three focus groups.

The reflection stage was a policy workshop which allowed residents to hear the research findings and debate the results. This shaped the final report.

The study also used secondary data from a literature review, looking at what has been written about white working-class communities and community cohesion previously. This helped to refine the research questions and to give the study a context. The researchers found there was relatively little previous material on white working-class communities, and in much of it members of this group were stereotyped as perpetrators of racial harassment, hostile to immigrants and inflexible in their views.

Adapted from Joan Garrod (2012). The white working class. *Sociology Review, 22* (1).

Questions

1. Why did the researchers adopt a qualitative approach?
2. Outline and briefly explain the three stages of the research.
3. Why was primary research supplemented by secondary data?
4. What is a literature review?

5.1 What are the theoretical considerations?

When thinking about what theoretical considerations influence research, you will need to understand how sociological theories have either a structural or social action approach and how this can shape research techniques, choice of research area and interpretation of results.

While researchers should strive to be objective and neutral in their research, inevitably their prejudices and values may shape what they research, their approach to the research, their method choice and, finally, the interpretation of their findings. For example, Marxists and feminists have an open political agenda: they would both like to change society and make it more equal with regard to class and gender inequalities, respectively; functionalists will use evidence selectively in order to reinforce their consensus view that a common set of values exists in society. It is therefore important to remember that behind a lot of sociological research lies an agenda with an interest in being supported.

Structural approaches

Structural theorists explain the order and predictability of social life by seeing human behaviour as learned behaviour shaped by external forces. They are sometimes referred to as macro-theories which adopt a **top-down** approach because of their large-scale vision of seeing society-wide structures or institutions as the starting point for explaining human behaviour. Examples of such structures would be family, education, religion, work and **the State**. Examples of macro, structural, top-down sociological perspectives would be functionalism/New Right, Marxism/ neo-Marxism and some aspects of feminism. The favoured methodological approach of structural theorists is quantitative methods aimed at generating facts and statistics. There is an overlap between the structuralist approach and positivism.

Social action approaches

The alternative to the macro, structuralist approach are theories based on the social action approach, originally conceived by Max Weber. Action theory sees society not as the starting point but as the outcome of individuals engaging in an infinite number of meaningful encounters. It is precisely because these encounters are meaningful to the people concerned that they create social order with the semblance of an apparently stable society. These theories argue that society is generated by the sum of social actions, in which people actively interpret and give meaning to social encounters.

Because of the focus on the individual (rather than society) as the starting point from which to make sense of human behaviour, social action theories are sometimes described as micro-theories, generating a **bottom-up**, small-scale view. Action theory argues that making sense of society starts with the extraordinary ability of people to interpret what is going on around them. They then embrace agency in order to make choices and act in a particular way in the light of this interpretation. Examples of micro, agency-based, bottom-up sociological perspectives are interactionism, postmodernism, and some elements of feminism. The favoured methodological approach of action theorists is qualitative methods aimed at generating an understanding of meaning behind behaviour. Action theory is therefore closely associated with the interpretivist approach or phenomenology.

Different perspectives

The starting position of any feminist analysis is the inequalities that exist between men and women across the divisions and institutions that make up society. Their focus on the patriarchal relations that exist across society

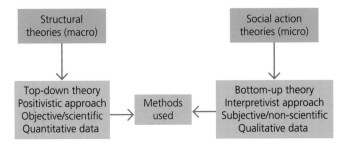

Figure 1.16 Structural theories versus social action theories

will clearly impact on their choice of research areas. Having a clearly stated agenda for change may also influence the way they interpret their results.

RESEARCH IN FOCUS

Researching the 'Moonies'

Eileen Barker (1984) studied the religious sect of the Unification Church, or 'Moonies' as they are more commonly known (after their founder Sun Myung Moon). The research was welcomed by the Moonies themselves who were concerned about the adverse publicity they were receiving, especially from the accusation that they were gaining new members through a process of 'brainwashing'.

Barker adopted a triangulation approach using three methods. Firstly, she sent a 40-page questionnaire to every Moonie couple living in Britain. This was followed by an in-depth interview among a smaller sample that typically lasted between four and eight hours. Finally, Barker undertook a participant observation study, living among a Moonie community for more than two years.

When it came to analysing her data she compared her results with the British population as a whole, and with a sample that had attended a Moonie session but failed to subsequently join up. In this way she was able to find out why people joined the Moonies and their characteristics in terms of age, gender and social class. In a sense she was using a fourth method here, the 'comparative method'.

Barker found no evidence of 'brainwashing'. Instead, she found that certain individuals, who were mainly middle class, were attracted to the sect because it offered structure and meaning in their lives. However, turnover was high, suggesting the needs provided were temporary.

Adapted from Eileen Barker (1984) *The Making of a Moonie: Choice or Brainwashing?* Oxford: Blackwell.

KEY SOCIOLOGISTS

Phil Hadfield (2006) applied a Marxist analysis to the 'nocturnal economy' of pubs and clubs. Hadfield sought evidence to support his view that capitalist enterprises, in following their natural profit-making goal, may end up creating an environment in which certain types of crime flourish. Hadfield demonstrated the irresponsibility of the drinks industry, which ignored the repercussions of their profit-driven behaviour.

CONTEMPORARY APPLICATION

It is rare in contemporary research for researchers to be constrained into either a purely positivistic or interpretivist approach. Significant amounts of research involve a triangulation or realist approach, collecting quantitative and qualitative data.

STUDY TIP

Make sure you are clear on the basic arguments outlined here. Demonstrating a good understanding of the relationship between theoretical approaches and methodological approaches will add depth to any writing on this topic.

Questions

1. Why were the Moonies willing to participate in this research?
2. Why do you think religious sects are normally reluctant to let researchers study them?
3. Outline and briefly describe the three methods she used.
4. Discuss what is particularly interesting about Barker's use of her methods.
5. Would her approach be acceptable and tolerated normally by respondents?
6. What might be described as her fourth method?

5.2 What are the practical issues?

When studying the practical issues associated with research, you will learn how these shape both the nature of research and the subsequent quality of research.

First thoughts might lead to the conclusion that sociologists can research any aspect of social behaviour. However, the reality is rather different. Sociological research is constrained by a range of practical considerations that limit the choices available. The reality is that the nature and type of research undertaken is often determined by very pragmatic factors.

The personal values of the researcher

It is inevitable that individual researchers are drawn to areas of life in which they have a particular personal interest or have chosen to specialise in. In addition, highly principled sociologists, such as Marxists and feminists, will tend to be selective in what they research and hope that it at least raises consciousness and, ultimately, leads to social and political change. Sometimes researchers will engage in research that is currently fashionable or an expanding area of research for the simple reason that it may lead to promotion.

Funding

The influence of funding on research choices cannot be overstated. At its most extreme, a lack of funding will mean research does not go ahead. To a lesser extent, a lack of funding might compel researchers to use cheaper methods. For example, a researcher may be forced to use questionnaires for a large study simply because interviews are more expensive.

Research without funding can rarely be carried out. Many sociologists are compelled to do research for which funding is available rather than what they would personally like to investigate.

Sources of funding: sources of research funding might include government funding, charitable funding or corporate funding. For example, a lot of university-based research is funded by the Social and Economic Research Council (SERC), the Higher Education Funding Council for England and government departments such as the Home Office, the Department of Health or the Department for Education. Businesses may also use sociologists to carry out research, but such funding is usually for a self-interested agenda such as improving their image or selling more products.

Sustainable funding is required for research to be undertaken with confidence – researchers need to know they will be able to see their research through to completion. This is particularly relevant for longitudinal studies, which cannot produce results without long-term funding.

Conflicts of interest: when sociologists rely on an organisation to fund their research, compromises may need to be made on the part of the researcher. For example, big business is unlikely to welcome any pro-Marxist sentiment or anti-capitalist findings, so such findings may be suppressed in corporate-funded research.

Autonomy in funded research: the extent of freedom given to the researcher over the design and nature of research will vary depending on the requirements of the funding organisation and aspects of individual projects.

Accessibility of the target audience

The nature, type and location of the group being studied can influence the research methods chosen. For example, a group that is difficult to access may require a snowball approach (see the example of accessing members of a gang on page 39). Sometimes groups are protected and research methods will have to be agreed with a gatekeeper. Groups with poor literacy skills or language problems will need interviewing rather than questionnaires. Geographically diverse groups may limit method choice to a postal/electronic questionnaire. Deviant, criminal or powerful groups may resist being knowingly studied and may require covert observation.

Size of research team

Where the research team is small, this limits research to relatively small-scale projects. In addition, using the method of questionnaires is a logical choice. Increasing the size of the research team makes interviews a more practical option.

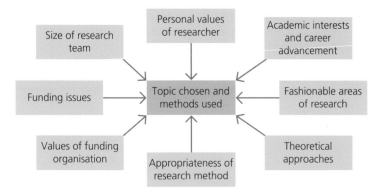

Figure 1.17 Practical issues that influence topic choice and research methods used

Different perspectives

The Marxist perspective stands to be the greatest loser when it comes to receiving funding for research. Because of its ideological and political position it may find it hard to gain funding from government bodies or big business, since they are unlikely to support or agree with the perspective's findings.

KEY SOCIOLOGISTS

Tombs and Whyte (2003) point out that research in Britain is increasingly 'policy driven'. Further, they say policy-related research funders are exclusively looking for positive findings. They note that research criticising the government is increasingly rare; the government frequently makes researchers sign agreements that the government must grant permission for the publication of their research and findings.

CONTEMPORARY APPLICATION

Tombs and Whyte (2003) note that out of 298 articles published by the *British Journal of Criminology* over a ten-year period, only one article was about state crime and only six discussed corporate crime. This suggests that undertaking critical research about the state or big business is either difficult to fund or get published, or both.

STUDY TIP

If you are doing the Extended Project, use your experiences to provide examples to illustrate practical issues in research.

RESEARCH IN FOCUS

Bouncers as 'Badfellas'

Simon Winlow's (2001) in-depth ethnographic research exemplifies how practical issues can affect research.

Winlow's aim was to see how changes in society – such as de-industrialisation and globalisation – had affected masculinity and the role of violence and crime in working-class culture in the north east of England. He used his own physique to pass himself off as a bouncer in order to gain access to the pub and club-going group using covert observational methods to study working-class violence in Sunderland.

Until the recession of the 1980s, many working-class people in Sunderland were employed in heavy industries such as shipbuilding. Because Winlow grew up in Sunderland he was able to use this background to provide an insider's understanding of the social settings he would be experiencing. There were many new clubs opening and Winlow used his local knowledge to gain access to the growing night-time economy and its links with violence and crime.

Winlow was able to observe the links between bouncers, violence and crimes such as cigarette smuggling and protection rackets. In addition he carried out a number of unstructured interviews with young men, especially those who were regularly employed as bouncers, debt collectors, enforcers etc. He shows how, for working-class young men with powerful builds and a willingness to use violence, the development of bouncing provides not only an income but also opportunities to make more money from entrepreneurial crime.

Adapted from Blundell, J. and Griffiths, J. (2008) *Sociology Since 2000.* Cooksbridge: Connect Publications.

Questions

1. How does Winlow's research follow in the tradition of the Chicago School?
2. What does ethnographic mean?
3. How did Winlow use his local knowledge of the area to his advantage in his research?
4. What two research methods did Winlow use?
5. Explain why this is a good example of qualitative research.

5.3 What are the ethical considerations?

All sociological research must conform to professional ethical guidelines, particularly those published by the British Sociological Association (BSA). These guidelines provide a code of conduct and ensure that research is underpinned by moral principles. It therefore means that research should be undertaken in the most appropriate manner. Consequently, this protects everyone involved, including those being researched, as well as the researcher. When planning research, it is important to consider ethical issues before, during and after the research process has taken place.

Informed consent

Unless research is covert, all participants should give a clear agreement of their willingness to take part in the research. They must therefore be made aware of the purpose and nature of the research. At any time participants should have the right to withdraw their consent; subjects should be able to walk away from the research at any time.

The BSA ethical guidelines note that 'covert methods violate the principles of informed consent and may invade the privacy of those being studied'. In such cases the researcher must ensure that participants are protected from the serious ethical issues that could accrue.

Preserve confidentiality

All respondents must be guaranteed anonymity with all data collected treated in strictest confidence. Limiting the context in which a person's statements or actions are described will reduce the chance of anyone being unwittingly identified when the research is published.

Avoid harming people

No one should ever be hurt or disadvantaged by sociological research. Maintaining privacy helps avoid this problem. When sensitive issues (for example, poverty, rape or self-harming) or vulnerable groups (for example, the poor, homeless or elderly) are being researched, great care should be taken to avoid any reinforcement of low self-esteem.

Support should be made available to help research subjects deal with any issues that might arise during the research process. Although participants may be willing to share feelings and experiences, they may be unaware of the subsequent emotions that can arise from sharing these with a researcher.

Competence

Sociologists must constantly strive to uphold the good name of sociology and never bring the subject into disrepute. All findings should be recorded accurately and truthfully. Researchers should abide by all national laws and administrative regulations (for example, the Data Protection Act, the Human Rights Act, copyright and libel laws). Researchers should consider any potential consequences or implications that could result from publication.

Research should not involve an intrusion of privacy

The nature of research (interpretivist in particular) is to get close to the subject matter. However, there is thin line between getting close and intruding on someone's privacy; researchers must be mindful not to cross this line.

Ethical issues with secondary data

Concerns about confidentiality are significant when reusing or sharing secondary data. The protection of both participants and researchers is of paramount importance with secondary data. However, even complex data can be archived and shared, providing informed consent is gained for participation and publication.

Longitudinal data is harder to anonymise, but efforts to maintain confidentiality must be paramount. Visual data can be altered, but at a high cost to integrity and quality.

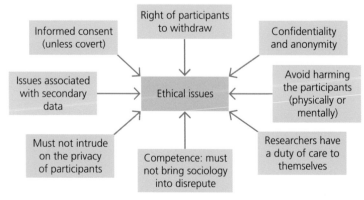

Figure 1.18 Ethical issues in research

Section 5: Influences on research

KEY SOCIOLOGISTS

Laud Humphreys' (1975) covert research into male homosexual activity in public toilets raised many serious ethical issues. Firstly, by pretending to be a lookout/voyeur he was effectively spying on people. Secondly, he misused a police contact to gain addresses of some participants from their car registration numbers. Finally, the publication of his work was used by some people to promote anti-gay propaganda.

CONTEMPORARY APPLICATION

The statement on ethical practice provided by the BSA offers a set of 61 guidelines on a variety of fundamental aspects of professional sociology. Adhering to these guidelines should ensure that sociological research is ethical.

> **STUDY TIP**
>
> Remember that ethical issues underpin all sociological research. Make sure you can demonstrate knowledge of the ethical issues outlined above and summarised in Figure 1.18.

Data can be shared more safely by preventing public access to the data and by requiring users to register and to sign a licence specifying terms of agreement before accessing data.

Different perspectives

Ethical issues apply universally and consistently across all sociological perspectives. If research is more likely to be covert, such as with some interpretivist research, extra care must be taken to protect participants from potential ethical issues.

Check your understanding

1. What is a structural theory?
2. What is meant by the terms 'macro-theory' and 'top-down'?
3. What type of data is assumed to be collected primarily by structural theorists?
4. Why is social action theory described as a micro- and bottom-up theory?
5. Explain why funding issues may result in sociologists not necessarily doing the research of their choice.
6. Why might career advancement influence the choice of research by a sociologist?
7. Why might sociologists from conflict perspectives such as Marxism find it harder to fund research than those from consensus theories?
8. Why do covert methods violate the principles of informed consent?
9. Good interpretivist research involves getting close to those being researched. What are the potential problems with this?
10. What ethical issues can derive from using secondary data?

Practice questions

1. Outline two ethical issues to be considered when undertaking sociological research.   [4 marks]
2. Evaluate the how and why sociological knowledge is different to common sense knowledge.   [16 marks]

Links to other topics

This topic has links to:

● Chapter 3 Methods in context: education.

Education

2

Understanding the specification

AQA specification	How the specification is covered in this chapter
• The role and function of the education system	*Section 1* • What is the role and function of the education system for the individual and society according to conflict and consensus theories? • How are interpretivist and postmodernist theories useful for understanding the role and function of the education system?
• Differential educational achievement of social groups by social class, gender and ethnicity in contemporary society	*Section 2* • How does social class affect educational experience and outcomes, exploring both internal and external factors? • How does gender affect educational experience and outcomes, exploring both internal and external factors? • How does ethnicity affect educational experience and outcomes, exploring both internal and external factors?
• The significance of educational policies, including policies of selection, marketisation and privatisation, and policies to achieve greater equality of opportunity or outcome, for an understanding of the structure, role, impact and experience of and access to education; the impact of globalisation on educational policy.	*Section 3* • What is the impact of education policies developed since 1979, including selection, marketisation and privatisation? • What is the effect of social policies on different groups? Have they led to greater equality of education? • What is the impact of globalisation on access to education and education policy?

Section 1: The role and function of the education system

> **This section will explore the following debates:**
> - What is the role and function of the education system for the individual and society according to **conflict** and **consensus theories**?
> - How are interpretivist and postmodernist theories useful for understanding the role and function of the education system?

There are various views of the role of education, which can broadly be placed into two types: conflict views, which in simple terms argue that the education system reproduces inequalities within society, and consensus theories, which argue that the education system benefits individuals and society.

Questions

Use the images in Figure 2.1 to answer the following questions.
1. How does education prepare children for later life?
2. What kinds of skills and characteristics are seen as important in education?
3. How are students encouraged to do well at school?

GETTING YOU STARTED

Figure 2.1 Educational milestones

When discussing the role or function of education, you could consider what education does both for the individual and for society. You could also explore the functions of the education system on both micro and macro levels. This chapter considers a range of perspectives, including consensus and conflict theories.

1.1 What are consensus theories?

Consensus theories, such as functionalism and the New Right, regard education as having two major functions: **secondary socialisation** and providing the skills needed in preparation for paid employment. The education system therefore maintains society. They also argue that the education system is meritocratic. A **meritocracy** is a fair system that gives everyone an equal chance of success so that, if a student is talented and works hard, they will achieve good results.

Functionalists

The functionalist Émile Durkheim argued that the education system was a key aspect of socialisation which ensures that individuals understand and conform to social values, as well as acting as a form of **social solidarity**, that is, to ensure people are integrated and value society.

Talcott Parsons developed Durkheim's ideas futher. He explains how school acts as a bridge between the home and the wider society. He says that at home children are treated as individuals – he calls these **particularistic standards**. In education, however, children learn to though a meritocratic system, where everyone gets treated the same regardless of who they are – he calls these **universalistic standards**. For example, teachers mark work by the same standards for every student, not differently for each individual.

Functionalists are optimistic about the role of education for society – they believe that education responds to the needs of the **economy** and provides the right amount of workers for the particular skills that the economy demands. The functionalists Davis and Moore claim that education prepares people for their future roles, a process known as **role allocation**. Other perspectives agree that education results in role allocation but view this as a negative (see conflict theories below).

New Right

New Right sociologists and politicians argue that the education system should be run like a business and enable parents to have choice in the school they send their children to. New Right thinkers are optimistic that the education system can offer opportunity for all. They have concerns, however, about the failings of the current education system. Recently, the New Right has aspired to make state education more like private education, viewing the private system as a 'better' model of education.

New Right ideas are seen in Conservative governments and in the Conservative and Liberal Democrat coalition government of 2010–15. The role and function of education for New Right thinkers is to enable individual choice so that individuals can achieve to the best of their abilities. Choice in this context refers to a choice of schools and style of education, including selective and non-selective education. Chubb and Moe (1990) argue that the introduction of market forces into education, known as **marketisation**, is beneficial to the education system as it helps improve standards and efficiency.

Criticisms of consensus theory perspectives

Critics argue that functionalist views ignore the persistent inequalities that occur in education – that particular groups of students (such as some of the working class, boys and some ethnic minorities) achieve much lower results than other groups.

Consensus theories also fail to consider the negative experiences that some students have at school. It assumes that the education system is organised in a beneficial way for all, and this is simply not the case. New Right thinkers have been criticised for failing to acknowledge that when choice is introduced, not all students are able to utilise the choices available. For example, some students may not be able to go to a school a long way away because of transport costs: such choices in fact reproduce inequalities.

1.2 What are conflict theories?

Conflict theorists take a negative view of education – they see it as a way to reinforce inequalities in society. There are two main conflict theories: Marxism and feminism.

Marxism

Marxists argue that the education system acts as a means of socialising children into their respective class position, in a way that makes sure that they are unlikely to challenge the system. Marxists point out that the education system supports **capitalism** by ensuring that working-class students are prepared for mundane repetitive labour while middle-class students are encouraged to aspire to higher levels of education and use school as a way of making connections that will help them later in life. Marxists challenge consensus theorists, arguing that the education system is not meritocratic – they argue that this is a myth to ensure that the system seems fair.

The French Marxist Pierre Bourdieu (1977) developed the idea of education functioning in a way that advantages those with middle-class ideas. He claims that the middle class also possesses **cultural capital**, a set of ideas, tasks, interests and behaviour which result material rewards later in life (see page 159). Cultural capital places them at a distinct advantage (more on this later when we look at the impact of social class). He also argues that the middle class controls the education system and, therefore, working-class students have middle-class knowledge imposed on them, which places them at a disadvantage since this knowledge is not familiar to them. Middle-class students are at an advantage as a result of this.

The Marxist Louis Althusser (1971) argues that capitalist society cannot be maintained by force alone; people might rebel and the system would be challenged. Instead, Althusser argues that a number of institutions, including education, **legitimise** inequalities through subconsciously introducing a particular set of ideas or ideology. Institutions such as education form part of what Althusser calls the **ideological state apparatus**, through which the ruling classes transmit their values. The middle class seeks to persuade all students to accept and adopt capitalist values.

● KEY CONCEPT ➤

According to Marxists Bowles and Gintis (1976), in education there is a **hidden curriculum**; that is, everything that is taught at school is not formally on the curriculum. Functionalists, however, might take a different view of the hidden curriculum and see it as a positive way of students learning the values and norms of society.

Bowles and Gintis developed the **correspondence principle**, which identified the similarities between work and education, and argues that the function of education is to prepare students for work.

Respecting authority	Being polite to teachers and not questioning their decisions or views
Accepting the values of the school	Following the rules of the school, for example in how to treat other students
Being obedient	For example, raising your hand to talk, sitting quietly in class

Table 2.1 Examples of the hidden curriculum

School	Work
School uniform has to be worn	Work uniform has to be worn
Pupils are rewarded for hard work through awards and good grades	Employees are awarded for work through promotions or pay rises
Pupils' time is controlled through a timetable	Employees' time is regulated through contracts and records
Pupils are expected to respect authority, such as the teacher	Employees are expected to respect authority, such as their boss

Table 2.2 Examples of the correspondence principle

KEY SOCIOLOGISTS

Marxists Bowles and Gintis (1976) found that the education system supports the capitalist system in three particular ways: through the **myth of meritocracy**; that education falsely claims to be fair when in fact, they argue, that it reproduces inequalities through the hidden curriculum; and finally the correspondence principle.

Feminism

Although girls now outperform boys at all levels of the education system, feminists still argue that it perpetuates a **patriarchal ideology**, leading to girls moving into lower-paid jobs and weaker economic positions in society.

Until the mid-1990s boys outperformed girls at every level of education. Feminists argued that women were being overlooked in the education system and claimed that girls' relative underachievement was the result of patriarchal society. Since girls began outperforming boys in the mid-1990s, feminists have focused on two key concerns: gendered subject choices, and the subsequent lower-paid and lower-status jobs occupied by women, despite performing well in education.

Gendered subject choices occur when girls, when given a choice of subjects to study, tend to choose subjects that are considered to be traditionally female, and to avoid subjects that are considered to be male. This is the same for both genders. Feminists argue that this is largely due to gendered socialisation at home but is also linked to processes in the school which encourage girls to maintain traditional caring roles.

Criticisms of conflict theory perspectives

Some (such as functionalists and the New Right) disagree with the Marxist perspective of education and argue that education is fair or meritocratic, and it is true that education does offer some students the opportunity to do well and for them to increase their social position, a process known as **social mobility**.

Feminists have been criticised for underestimating the change in girls' position educationally. For the first time in history, young women in their early 20s are now earning more than men, which suggests that women's economic position is changing for the better. Sociologists have also criticised feminists for failing to consider the issue of gender more broadly rather than women only, as there are now many concerns about boys, especially in terms of underperforming working-class boys.

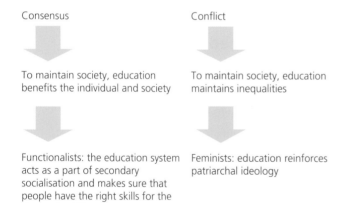

Figure 2.2 Consensus versus conflict theories

	Functionalism and Marxism	Marxism and feminism
Similarities	Both are macro theoretical perspectives that regard education as maintaining society as it is	Both are conflict theories that see society as based on inequality
	Both regard education as playing an important role in shaping the attitudes, norms and values of students	Both regard education as negatively legitimising inequality through a particular set of ideas which prevents people from challenging the system
	Both see education as preparing students for work	Both see education as a way to perpetuate inequalities at work
Differences	Functionalism is positive about the role of education, Marxism is critical	Marxists focus on class inequalities in education while feminists focus on gendered inequalities in education
	Functionalists regard education as meeting the demands of an economy in a way that meets everyone's individual needs as well as the needs of society; Marxists regard education as simply supporting and benefitting capitalism and the ruling classes	Marxists argue that major structural changes are needed within society, whereas liberal feminists argue that greater equality is possible through law changes and a shift in attitudes

Table 2.3 Comparing functionalism and Marxism, and Marxism and feminism

STUDY TIP

You will be expected to understand similarities and differences between the key perspectives on the role of education. These are summarised in Table 2.3.

CONTEMPORARY APPLICATION

The Conservative and Liberal Democrat coalition government, in power between 2010 and 2015, announced that it intended to spend millions of pounds on projects that 'instil character' in students. This would include projects such as ex-army officers working with students to improve their attitude and self-discipline in school. This is a good example of the way in which this coalition government's policies have sought to return to traditional values about discipline.

Questions

1. List the ways that a virtual school is different to a normal school.
2. What are the advantages and disadvantages of virtual schools?

1.3 How are interpretivist and postmodernist theories useful?

If you discuss the function or role of education, it is a good idea to explore interpretivist and postmodernist theories of education as well as functionalism, New Right, Marxism and feminism. These two theories are more contemporary than the classical social theories of education and, as such, may be more relevant to understanding education in a contemporary context.

As we saw in the previous section, there have been a number of theoretical explanations of the role or function of education from functionalists, the New Right, Marxists and feminists. These theories were developed within modern society and, as you are aware, some sociologists claim that there are alternative ways to understand contemporary education.

IN THE NEWS

First 'virtual school' planned

The Department for Education have revealed plans for Britain's first state-funded 'virtual school', which means that hundreds of children might soon be learning from home. One key idea behind the project is to avoid time lost in poor classroom behaviour and travel.

Students will interact with tutors online, taking part in a full curriculum, including GCSEs and A-levels. Their day will follow a similar timetable to school, ending earlier than usual: 1 pm for younger students and 1.45 pm for older students.

Some have criticised the idea, saying that children need face-to-face contact with their peers and teachers.

Adapted from Nicholas Reilly (2014) Britain's first state funded 'virtual school' could open next year. *Metro*, 29 November.

Postmodernism

Postmodernists claim that education reflects the increasing **individualism** in society and that this is reflected within educational policy as well as the experience of education. For example, there are now policies that reflect individual learning programmes. Careful consideration is given to responding to students' individual learning styles (Usher *et al*, 1997). This is partially a reflection of the multicultural society of the UK, which has resulted in a number of different views on the education system emerging.

Postmodernists argue that individual identity is becoming more fluid and that a range of factors shape and influence a person's identity and, therefore, their experience of education. Some postmodernists point out that the increasing emphasis on the individual is positive and leads to a breakdown of one-type-fits-all-style education. This has led to schools becoming customised. **Faith schools**, for example, may reflect the local community in terms of ethnicity. Another example might be **specialist schools** which promote particular subjects, enabling students to make choices on this basis.

Another feature of the postmodern world is globalisation and, as a result, educational specialists and politicians today are learning much more about educational styles around the world and incorporating some of these into UK education. For example, the recent adoption of Swedish-style **Free schools** in the UK. There has also been a massive growth in the use and capabilities of information technology, resulting in greater demand for technologically skilled workers and also changing the way that teaching and learning occurs. From a postmodern perspective, this has led to the development of a greater range of learning and working opportunities. For example, people can work more flexibly, from home for example, or in different locations.

Interpretivists

Interpretivists' views on education emerged in the 1960s and explore education on a micro level, looking at the processes that occur within education and attempting to understand the meanings of behaviour within (and beyond) school. Interpretivists don't regard education as positive or negative. Instead, they have developed ways of understanding, for instance, the way that students are labelled at school and the effect that this might have on their education and later life. Interpretivists believe that teachers (and students) label some students positively and some negatively, resulting in students internalising these labels, creating what is known as a **self-fulfilling prophecy**. The interpretivist view is developed more fully later in this chapter when exploring class, gender and ethnicity (see page 57), looking at the processes that occur in education in relation to interactions between the student and the teacher and students themselves.

RESEARCH IN FOCUS

Paul Willis (1977) is both a Marxist and an interpretivist who carried out research in a comprehensive school in Wolverhampton. Using group interviews and participant observation, he found that the working-class 'lads' that he studied saw education as a waste of time, resulting in them doing minimal amounts of work, which he saw as preparing them for a similar attitude towards their future low-status, low-paid jobs. Willis argues that wider structural inequalities can be explored by taking a micro approach, exploring the meaning given to behaviours. In other words, the behaviour of the working-class lads revealed that school holds very little possibility for social mobility, because this group felt that they were simply 'learning to labour'. Willis' classic study involved a very small sample of 12 people, so the findings cannot be generalised. However, his work does demonstrate the usefulness of group interviews and an interpretivist approach to research.

Willis, P. (1977) *Learning to Labour: How Working Class Kids Get Working Class Jobs*. Saxon House.

Questions

1. Explain how Willis is both a Marxist and an interpretivist.
2. Name some advantages of the research methods that Willis uses.
3. How might a feminist criticise this research?

Questions

1. How is this study interpretivist in its approach?
2. What does this study demonstrate about the influence of teachers?
3. Which students do you think are likely to be labelled positively and which students might be labelled negatively?
4. Name some effects of negative labelling on students.

RESEARCH IN FOCUS

Robert Rosenthal and Lenore Jacobson (1968) used an interpretivist approach to uncover the power of teachers labelling their students. In their study of a single Californian elementary school, all students were given an IQ test. The results were not disclosed to the teachers. Instead the teachers were told that around 20 per cent of their students were 'spurters' who were likely to perform better than their classmates. At the end of the experiment an IQ test was given again and those who had been labelled as 'spurters' had indeed made most progress. Rosenthal and Jacobson concluded that teacher expectation plays a significant role in shaping student performance.

This study could be criticised for ethical reasons as the impact on children involved in this study could be long term. It was also only carried out in one school and so the results cannot necessarily be generalised.

Rosenthal, R. and Jacobson, L. (1968) *Pygmalion in the Classroom*. New York: Holt, Rinehart & Winston.

● **KEY CONCEPT**

Labelling is a process in which meaning is attached to behaviour. This can be positive or negative and, with regard to education, usually refers to the way in which teachers label students. Interpretivists explore the process of labelling and the impact that it has on student achievement.

● **KEY CONCEPT**

Self-fulfilling prophecy is when a person begins to **internalise** the label given to them and begins to act out the label.

Criticisms of interpretivist and postmodern perspectives

Despite taking a more contemporary approach to understanding the role of education, there are problems with postmodern and interpretivist approaches. They do not help to explain why such inequalities continue to persist in education, for example why working-class students continue to underperform. They ignore structural inequalities and both fail to suggest how these might be overcome.

CONTEMPORARY APPLICATION

There have been increasing efforts to develop international educational qualifications, such as international GCSEs and A-levels, which reflects the fact that people are more likely to be studying and working all over the world in a globalised society.

STUDY TIP

Both postmodernism and interpretivism are very different to functionalism, Marxism and feminism. Make sure that you explain how these theories differ in their views on education and talk about how they might be more useful for understanding education in contemporary society.

Check your understanding

1. Explain the difference between universalistic and particularistic standards.
2. How do Marxists argue that education supports capitalism?
3. Explain how the hidden curriculum is seen differently by functionalists and Marxists.
4. Explain how functionalists and New Right thinkers are similar in their views on education.
5. What type of research methods do interpretivists favour when researching education?
6. What are the problems with Paul Willis' research, and how might you overcome these problems?
7. Name one problem with postmodernist views on education and one problem with interpretivist views on education.

Practice questions

1. Outline two ways in which postmodernist ideas are reflected in education. (4 marks)
2. Outline two problems with the interpretivist view of education. (4 marks)

Read Item A below and answer the questions that follow.

Item A

Some sociologists regard the role of the education system positively, claiming that it offers every student an equal chance of success. According to these sociologists, the education system also meets the demands of the economy and ensures that students have the correct skills for the world of work.

However, others disagree and claim that the education system simply reinforces inequalities between different groups in society that already exist and makes sure that those with more power maintain their position. This process, they claim, occurs through hidden messages sent to them throughout their education.

1. Assess the view that the education system provides equal opportunities for all students. (20 marks)
2. Outline three functions of education. (6 marks)

Section 2: Social class, gender and ethnicity in education

This section will explore the following debates:

- How does social class affect educational experience and outcomes, exploring both internal and external factors?
- How does gender affect educational experience and outcomes, exploring both internal and external factors?
- How does ethnicity affect educational experience and outcomes, exploring both internal and external factors?

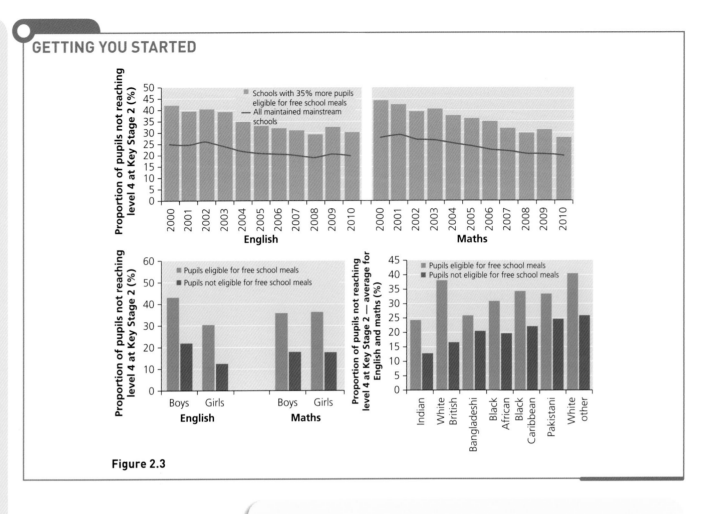

Figure 2.3

Questions

1. What is the relationship between free school meals and educational attainment?
2. Why are free school meals a useful indicator of poverty?
3. Suggest three things that the government could do to improve the results of students from a poor background.

2.1 How does social class affect educational experience?

If you are thinking about education and social class remember it is not just students' results that are important but also the experience of education that might be different for working-class and middle-class students.

Social class remains the strongest predictor of educational achievement in the UK, where the social class gap for educational achievement is one of the most significant in the **developed world** (Perry and Francis, 2010). One common indicator for social class is eligibility for free school meals. Statistics reveal that:

- At Key Stage 2, only 53.5 per cent of students eligible for free school meals reach the expected level. Also, these children are more likely to attend the lowest-performing schools in deprived areas (Kerr and West, 2010).
- Children who are eligible for free school meals are also disproportionately likely to have been in care and/or have special educational needs.

This pattern of inequality between social classes continues into **further education** (16–18 years) and higher education or university-level education. Despite government initiatives, such as Aimhigher, which aim to increase working-class students' aspirations, students with GCSE results above the national average who have been eligible for free school meals are less likely to go on to higher education than more affluent students with the same results (National Equality Panel, 2010).

The number of young people categorised as **NEET** (not in education, employment or training) has also been an issue that reflects continued class inequalities. NEETs are disproportionately working class. These individuals are disproportionately more likely to have truanted or been excluded from school, have few educational qualifications, misuse drugs and alcohol, be a teenage parent, and have mental health issues (Sodha and Margo, 2010). They are also more likely to become involved in crime (Cassen and Kingdon, 2007).

Sociologists have attempted to explain the impact of social class on educational outcome by looking at outside school (external) factors and in-school (internal) factors. **External factors** include material and **cultural deprivation**.

There is some debate about the relative importance of **cultural factors** and **material factors** in leading to underachievement. Some sociologists argue that it is often the low aspirations of the working class which result in a self-imposed barrier to success.

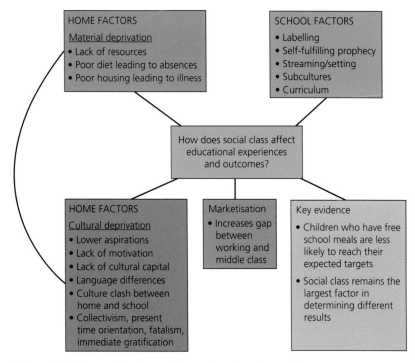

Figure 2.4 How social class affects educational experience

Home factors

Evidence suggests that **material deprivation** is the cause of working-class underachievement. Material deprivation is a lack of things that money can buy that result in educational success. Material deprivation may result in:

- poor-quality housing
- poor diet
- inadequate school uniforms
- poor access to school supplies, including school trips, computers and internet access.

Poor-quality housing and poor diet can to illness and school absences; inadequate uniforms or possessions may lead to bullying and absence, and a lack of school supplies may impact negatively on a student's educational progress.

Material deprivation

Material deprivation may lead to students having to work part time, which can mean that they are too tired to study at home or at school. Interestingly, Leon Feinstein (2003) argues there is evidence that the effects of class difference are apparent even before children reach nursery school. According to the National Equality Panel (2010), by the age of three poor children have been assessed to be one year behind richer ones in terms of communication and, in some disadvantaged areas, up to 50 per cent of children begin primary school without the necessary language and communication skills. Throughout compulsory education the gap between the social classes continues to widen.

Cultural deprivation

Cultural deprivation theorists argue that working-class students lack the appropriate attitudes, norms and values that are necessary to succeed in education. Cultural deprivation theories also link parental attitudes to working-class underachievement stating that parents may be unwilling or unable to support their child in creating a positive attitude towards education – helping them with homework and encouraging a work ethic. Students may experience a **culture clash**. The values of their family clash with the culture of the school, where they are expected to respect learning and their peers and teachers alike.

Generally cultural deprivation leads to students having low confidence and low aspirations, as reflected by low rates of participation in further and higher education. One of the first pieces of research to really highlight the importance of cultural deprivation was a longitudinal study conducted by Douglas (1964, 1970). This research followed the educational careers of 5,362 British children born in the first week of March 1964, through their primary and secondary schools up to the age of 16 in 1962.

Douglas divided the students into groups in terms of their ability, which was measured by a range of tests, such as IQ tests. Douglas also divided the students into four social-class groups, and found significant variations in educational attainment between students of similar ability but from different social classes. Douglas argued that most important factor was the degree of parents' interest in their child's education. He found that, generally, middle-class parents expressed a greater interest in their child's education, for example, visiting the school more frequently to discuss their children's education. They were more likely to want their children to stay at school beyond the minimum leaving age. Douglas found that parental interest and encouragement became ever more important in encouraging children to reach their full potential as they grew older.

Douglas argued that the role of parents in the early years of life of a child is crucial; he suggested that during **primary socialisation** middle-class children receive greater attention and stimulus from their parents. Middle-class parents were more likely to encourage their children to do their best in a wide variety of activities. This leads to higher achievement in the educational system and later in life.

Barry Sugarman (1970) claims that the working class has a particular culture that comprises four characteristics that prevent children from doing well in education. These are:

Collectivism	The idea that the social group is more important than school or school work, and that friendship groups take priority over, for example, getting homework done.
Present time orientation	Focusing in the immediate situation rather than considering the long-term aims; not bothering to put school work first and wanting to have fun without considering the possible long-term consequences.
Fatalism	A belief in the idea that it is not worth working hard in education because you are not likely to do well or get a good job anyway.
Immediate gratification	Wanting to have fun straight away rather than doing school work first.

Table 2.4 A summary of Sugarman's characteristics of working-class culture

Many working-class students, for example, believe that university is 'not for the likes of us' (Archer *et al*, 2007). Such 'low expectations' have been frequently cited by both researchers and policy makers as one of the most significant barriers to working-class educational achievement (Demie and Lewis, 2010). Cultural deprivation includes the view that teachers, typically (though not always) being middle class, even use different language to the working-class students. Also, there are some who argue that working-class students lack the cultural capital to succeed in education (see below).

More recently, studies have explored the culture of the streets where many working-class children spend time. Archer, Hollingsworth and Mendick (2010) describe the way that 'the street' is perceived to be exciting, associated with danger and the complete opposite of school. They found that poorer students often also brought problems from home or their area (or estate) to school. (Their estates were often seen as risky places to be.) Teachers saw the estate as being unstable and difficult, yet they did not have a good understanding of the out-of-school issues faced by working-class pupils. The researchers argue that these problems result in working-class pupils having low self-esteem and feeling looking down on by the rest of society. This leads to them trying to generate self-worth through attachment to objects such as jewellery and trainers.

Cultural deprivation theories have been criticised for two reasons: they tend to assume that being working class may be inferior when it might simply be different. Futher, not all working-class students underachieve, meaning that the theory does not fully explain why some working-class children do manage to succeed despite their cultural deprivation.

Cultural capital

As discussed in the earlier section on Marxist views on education (see page 52), Bourdieu (1977) argues that middle-class students possess cultural capital which gives them a distinct advantage over working-class pupils. Cultural capital refers to the possession of the appropriate tastes, attitudes and values which lead to material rewards later in life. Therefore it is what the middle class has that the working class lacks and therefore finds itself disadvantaged as a result. For more information on Bourdieu see Chapter 4.

Language deprivation

Some cultural deprivation theorists suggest that the working class lacks the appropriate language skills to succeed in education. According to Bernstein (1972) there are two speech codes:

There is **elaborated speech** which is associated with the middle class: it is a type of speech where sentences are more complex, with correct grammar, and

KEY SOCIOLOGISTS

As part of the **cultural deprivation theory**, Basil Bernstein (1972) argues that particular speech patterns develop in working-class and middle-class families which affect educational attainment: restricted and elaborated speech. These speech codes result in greater advantages for middle-class students who are able to learn and use the elaborated speech codes.

meaning is context free, meaning that something is described fully so that you do not actually need to be there to understand. Bernstein argues that the **elaborated language code** provides significant advantages for middle-class children entering education where the elaborated code is used by teachers.

Bernstein argues that a restricted language code is used by the working class: language is simple, with a limited vocabulary and is context bound. This means that you need to be in the particular situation for the sentence to make sense. However, not all children with restricted speech codes necessarily underachieve.

Bourdieu argues that, in effect, the working class is subject to **symbolic violence** in education and beyond. This means that they experience almost unconscious types of cultural and social domination in everyday social habits. Symbolic power becomes part of the discipline used against the working class to confirm an individual's position in the class structure.

In-school factors

There are a number of processes in education which have led to the widening gap between working-class and middle-class achievement.

Sociologists have carried out research that suggests teachers label students according to their social class and have different expectations of different students as a result: working-class students are labelled negatively; middle-class students are labelled positively. Labelling theorists such as Becker argue that these labels become internalised resulting in a self-fulfilling prophecy (see Rosenthal and Jacobsen (1968), page 56).

These judgements about working-class and middle-class students are often reflected in streaming and setting, which reinforces class differences, with middle-class students overwhelmingly occupying the higher-ability streams. Stephen Ball (1981) found that students were put into sets according to their perceived ability, not their actual ability. Furthermore, students themselves form groups that reflect class differences, with the working class forming negative, **anti-school subcultures** while the middle class tend to form subcultures that are positive or at least allow them to succeed.

Colin Lacey (1970) carried out research in which he found that teachers immediately differentiate their students into two groups: the higher-achieving group and the lower-achieving group. Lacey argues that this process results in the polarisation of the two different groups: once labelled, the students are likely to gravitate towards the higher- or lower-achieving end of the spectrum with which they have been associated. This then feeds into the development of pro-school subcultures and anti-school subcultures. A pro-school subculture is a smaller group within the school whose values are positive about education – such views are associated with educational success. The anti-school subculture reflects a smaller group whose values run counter to the school – such views are not associated with educational success.

Figure 2.5 Summary of Lacey's process of differentiation (1970)

Pro-school subculture	Anti-school subculture
Conforming to the school rules, such as attending lessons, wearing the correct uniform	Non-conformity to school rules, such as truancy and disruptive behaviour
Positive attitude towards teachers and learning	Negative attitude towards teachers and learning
Continuing a positive attitude to education outside the school	Negative attitude to education continues outside the school
Higher educational achievement	Lower educational acheivement

Table 2.5 Characteristics of different school subcultures

Labels are often given to students on the basis of their appearance, their language and their attitudes, without teachers really knowing the potential of the student. For example, in his classic research Howard Becker (1971) interviewed 60 Chicago high-school teachers. He found that teachers judged their students on the basis of their appearance and conduct. Becker argued that middle-class students were more likely to be seen as 'ideal students'.

Critics of labelling theories argue that not all students accept their labels – in fact, they may reject them. They say labelling theories also overlook other things which may influence a person's educational success, such as material deprivation.

As well as considering the processes that occur in the school, some sociologists and educational specialists have suggested that the curriculum reflects middle-class values and should be challenged and changed. John White (2005) argues that the curriculum places great emphasis on middle-class knowledge. For example, in history, students study middle- or upper-class figures rather than working-class people. White argues that the curriculum should be reviewed carefully to ensure that what is learnt is relevant to contemporary society and does not contain bias towards the middle class.

Marketisation: widening the gap between middle- and working-class students

The 1988 Education Reform Act introduced market forces in education (see page 80). This meant that schools began to be run like business – giving parents choices about which school to send their child to and encouraging competition between schools. As part of this policy, public information was produced about the performance of each school.

Increased parental choice benefited middle-class students, whose parents were more likely to be able to 'play the system', for example by moving into catchment areas of better-performing schools or paying for their children to attend better schools further away.

Marketisation draws on both internal and external factors as it affects students, parents and the school. The constant focus on driving up standards within education as a result of marketisation policies reinforces processes within the school, which result in widening inequalities (see Gillborn and Youdell, page 75).

Questions

1. Explain what is meant by an 'ethnographic method'.
2. Why did Ingram think that grammar schools are more likely to promote social mobility?
3. Explain what you think is meant by a 'lad friendly' culture.

RESEARCH IN FOCUS

Nicola Ingram (2010) carried out research into 14–16-year-old boys in two secondary schools in the same working-class area of Belfast in Northern Ireland. One school was a grammar school and the other was a comprehensive school. She wanted to explore the impact of school culture on working-class boys by investigating the experiences of boys living in the same neighbourhood attending different schools.

Ingram used an ethnographic approach, including art-based activities, a focus group and one-to-one interviews. The boys were asked to create two models of their identity with plasticine, one model of who they thought they were in school and another model of who they thought they were outside of school. The grammar school was found to promote social mobility and encourage the formation of a middle-class identity, while the comprehensive school supported aspects of working-class culture with its 'lad friendly' culture.

This study shows how important the culture of the school is in shaping or transforming the aspirations of all the students from different social classes.

Adapted from Ingram, N. (2010) School culture and its impact on working-class boys. *Sociology Review*, 20, 2–6.

STUDY TIP

You must acknowledge that both internal and external factors contribute towards class differences in education. It is important to explain how educational success is linked to material and cultural factors.

KEY SOCIOLOGISTS

Diane Reay (2010) claims that there is a damaging 'poverty of aspiration' in Britain that lies not in the working classes but among political leaders. Reay argues that what UK society needs, more than anything else in the contemporary moment, is greater social equality. Reay argues that introducing market forces into education has significantly widened social class inequalities.

CONTEMPORARY APPLICATION

According to one Coalition government adviser, working-class children must be taught to think and act like the middle classes if they are to get into the best universities and top professions. He said that bright working-class children are less likely to apply to top universities because they are worried about not fitting in.

2.2 How does gender affect educational experience?

When studying gender and education, you will address the patterns in relation to both boys and girls. Although the focus in recent years has very much been about concerns for boys' underperformance, it is important not to generalise; not all boys underperform and some girls underachieve. Also consider the impact of social class and ethnicity.

Until the early 1990s boys significantly outperformed girls in all levels of education, although girls had begun to improve their educational achievement in the 1980s. Not only were boys getting better results in many subjects, they were more dominant in the classroom and often expected to do better than girls. Today, the situation has completely reversed, and it is girls who now outperform boys in many areas and levels of education. This section explores the reasons for these huge changes, as well as exploring the implications. It is worth noting that gender differences are not limited to the UK alone: this is a global pattern.

Gender gap widest for ten years

The gap between the number of girls and boys getting A*–C at GCSE is at its highest rate since 2003, with girls achieving higher grades than boys, though boys are achieving a slightly higher number of A* grades.

GCSE results in 2014 reveal the female A*–C rate was 73.1 per cent compared to 64.3 per cent for males, a gap of 8.8 percentage points and a small increase on 2013.

It is quite striking just how wide the gap has remained since GCSEs were introduced in 1989. While the general trend is that both boys' and girls' results have increased, the gap between the two genders has remained the same.

Educational experts argue that the introduction of coursework has contributed to girls' increased educational outcomes, as girls respond well to the demands and skills that are necessary to be successful in this assessment method.

Adapted from Arnett, G. (2014) GCSE results: Biggest gap in 11 years between boys and girls A*–C pass rate. *Guardian*, 21 August 2014.

Questions

1. What is the difference in results between boys and girls according to this article?
2. Suggest three reasons why girls are getting better results than boys apart from coursework.

It is worth pointing out that the differences between girls' and boys' achievement are complex, and girls and boys have changed in different ways, as Arnot, David and Weiner (1996) remind us. They express concern that there are certain 'myths' about the recent gender differences being oversimplified by the media in particular. It is not the case, for example, that boys underachieve across the curriculum – they match girls in achievement in both maths and science. A further myth is that boys and girls have different learning styles, which teaching needs to match. In reality learning styles are controversial. There is no evidence that learning styles can be clearly be separated and neither is there evidence to suggest that these learning styles are gender specific (DCSF, 2009).

Home factors

The role of women within the home and in wider society has undergone much change over the past few decades. For example, feminist campaigns have led to changing attitudes and laws focusing on increasing gender equality in the home, the public sphere and at work. Over the past 40 years there has been a rise in the percentage of women aged 16 to 64 in employment and a fall in the percentage of men. In April to June 2013, around 67 per cent of women aged 16 to 64 were in work, an increase from 53 per cent in 1971 (ONS, 2013). There are now more women at university than men, and women are beginning to occupy more senior positions in society. Despite this, there is still a long way to go before equality between men and women is achieved. Although, interestingly, women in their 20s are now earning slightly more than men, which is a significant turning point. This contributes to the general view that, today, women have increasing numbers of role models to inspire them to have greater aspirations about their education and future prospects.

KEY SOCIOLOGISTS

Stephen Gorard *et al* (1999) challenge some existing beliefs about gender and achievement, arguing that the 'gap' between the achievements of boys and girls is not growing, and may even be shrinking. They claim that the gap, in favour of girls, mainly appears at the higher levels in any assessment. Therefore, they argue that there are other issues which may be of greater importance than gender which need to be measured and researched, such as a lack of interest in education across a range of different groups.

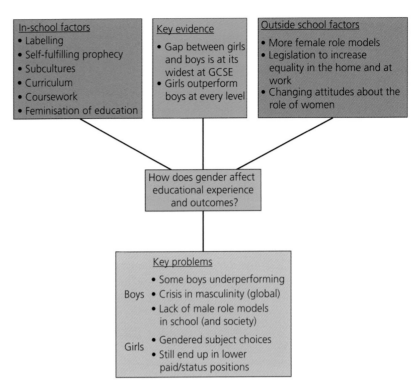

Figure 2.6 The effect of gender on educational experience

Some sociologists claim that the activities they do outside of school actually help girls succeed in education. Interestingly, Kelly (1987) suggests that gender differences in spatial ability (with boys showing greater spatial awareness) may be attributed to the types of toys children play with rather than their genetic make-up. Furthermore, as they grow up, Angela McRobbie (1991) argues that the **bedroom culture** of girls, where girls can create their own subcultures and chat and read, actually contributes towards their communication skills which are now so important and valued within education. Boys, however, tend to carry out activities that are more physical and do not contribute towards their educational development. Boys' subcultures in and outside of school tend to regard hard-working students negatively, placing significant pressure on them to maintain their image of doing the minimum amount of work possible.

● KEY CONCEPT ▶

RESEARCH IN FOCUS

Sue Sharpe (1994) compared the attitudes of working-class girls in London schools in the early 1970s and 1990s. She found that in her later study, in the 1990s, girls were much more confident, assertive, ambitious and committed to greater gender equality. Sharpe asked the girls about their main priorities and found that they were 'love, marriage, husbands and children' for the 1970s girls. By the 1990s these priorities had changed to 'job, career and being able to support themselves' with education being seen as the main route to a good job. In 1994, Sue Sharpe found that girls were increasingly more cautious about marriage. They had seen adult relationships break up around them, and had seen women coping alone in a 'man's world'. Girls' aspirations were more focused on being more independent through becoming highly educated.

Sharpe, S. (1994) *Just Like a Girl: How Girls Learn to be Women – From the Seventies to the Nineties.* Harmondsworth: Penguin.

Questions

1. What is the advantage of repeating research after a period of time?
2. What had happened to the aspirations of girls over the period between the 1970s and the 1990s?
3. Give three reasons why the girls' aspirations had changed so much.

It is becoming clear that girls spend far more of their free time on social media communicating with friends than boys do.

Gendered socialisation often results in boys being socialised into being adventurous and physical, competitive and sporty. These values conflict with the culture of schools, which demand that children listen, conform and often sit still for significant periods of time. There are limited opportunities for boys to learn competitively, leading some to believe that the education system fails boys whose learning styles are not necessarily recognised.

This problem is exacerbated by the fact that, in wider society, the service industry has largely replaced traditional manual jobs, which were almost exclusively carried out by men (for example, mining). The economy today places high value on office-based jobs, presentational skills and interpersonal skills, which are often considered to be more typically female skills. In some cases this has led to boys feeling removed from education and work, sometimes known as the 'crisis in masculinity'. This is demonstrated in boys lacking motivation, having low self-esteem and, as a result, forming anti-school subcultures.

The employment rates for men and women have changed over time:

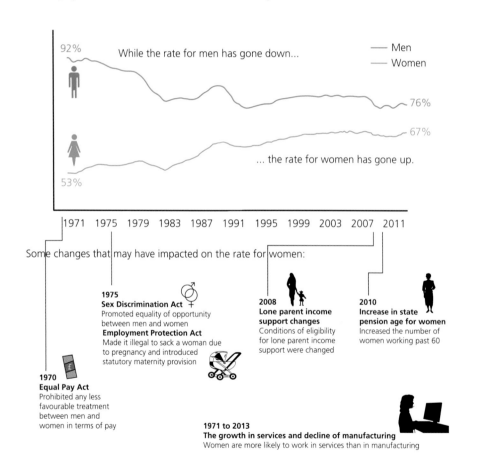

Figure 2.7 Employment rates for men and women over time

Labour Force Survey - Office for National Statistics

School factors

There are a number of processes within schools that have contributed to the current patterns in gender outcomes. Becky Francis (2000a) argues that teachers play a large role in the construction of gender identity in education as well as government policies. Francis is critical of media responses to the recent increase in girls' achievement, which she claims are unhelpful for boys in particular.

Changes in education policies have played a major role in contributing to gender differences, in particular the 1988 Education Reform Act. This act introduced the National Curriculum, which meant that maths and science were compulsory to the age of 16, giving girls no opportunity to opt out of these subjects, which are often perceived to be 'male' subjects. The act also introduced coursework, which girls perform at much better in general than boys.

Evidence-based research carried out into the effects of coursework suggests that it may give girls some advantage. Nonetheless, it cannot account for the gender gap in its entirety. Perceptions of girls' perceived advantage in coursework is high among teachers. Over half (53 per cent) of teachers felt that there was a difference between boys' and girls' ability to do coursework (Bishop *et al*, 1997). At around the same time, the government ran a number of programmes to encourage girls into science and technology.

Girls and boys appear to relate differently to schooling and learning, and girls find it easier to succeed in school settings (Sukhnandan *et al*, 2000). Girls place a high value on the presentation of their work; they spend more time trying to improve what they produce (McDonald *et al*, 1999); they care more about the opinion of their teachers (Bray *et al*, 1997); and they derive more enjoyment from their school life (Arnot *et al*, 1996). Most importantly, girls seem to enjoy reading more than boys.

Machin and McNally (2005) examined the effect of the National Literacy Project (which was designed to drive up standards in literacy in all students) on the attainment of boys and girls. They found that the new teaching methods introduced in 1997 did appear to have an effect on the gender gap by raising the attainment of boys in English, and girls in maths. While both strategies were effective for both boys and girls, the magnitude of the impact was greater for the gender that was generally weaker in a particular subject. For English, the 'literacy hour' had a greater relative impact on boys. However, Machin and McNally argue that one policy alone could not close the gender gap.

Some sociologists have suggested that there has been a process known as the feminisation of education (Sewell, 2010), which means that the school has become a female-dominated environment, which has benefited girls and made boys feel less comfortable with their learning environment. Sewell argues that generally girls are more willing to conform to the rules of the school whereas boys are not, and the disproportionate number of female teachers alienates them further from the school culture.

The feminisation of education refers to the way in which education has become a female-dominated environment.

As girls' educational achievement has improved, teachers have begun to label female students as more likely to succeed, thus creating a self-fulfilling prophecy (see page 55). For boys, on the other hand, teachers are more likely to label them negatively. Research reveals that it is harder for some boys to be seen as hard working as it does not match the 'laddish' subculture that is prevalent in many schools.

This peer pressure, and the need for boys to conform to typically masculine behaviour such as playing sports, breaking rules and doing the minimum amount of work, has of course led to boys creating their own barrier to success. In fact, Epstein (1998) found in her research that working-class boys in particular often experience bullying or being negatively labelled if they are hardworking. Girls on the other hand often have subcultures that focus on working hard and doing well. It is important to remember, however, that subcultures are complex and varied, and not all boys, for example, adopt anti-school values.

RESEARCH IN FOCUS

Forde *et al* (2006) argue that boys are more likely to be influenced by their male peer group, which might devalue schoolwork, and so put them at odds with academic achievement. It is argued that girls do not experience a conflict of loyalties between friends and school to the same extent as boys. Forde *et al* suggest that boys feel it is important to adopt a view of masculinity which sees academic work as feminine and, therefore, being seen to work in school can be seen as a problem. The issue is that this type of masculinity conflicts with the culture of school, where academic achievement is the main way in which students are judged. In order to protect their self-worth and their masculinity, boys will often adopt various strategies: putting off working, withdrawal of effort and rejection of academic work, avoidance of the appearance of work and disruptive behaviour.

Forde, C. Kane, J., Condie, R., McPhee, A. and Head, G. (2006) Strategies to address gender inequalities in Scottish schools: A review of literature

Questions

1. Why do you think boys are more likely to be influenced by their male peer group?
2. Why might school work be seen as feminine by boys?
3. Describe the effects of the strategies that boys often adopt.

Gendered subject choices

One of the clearest examples of gender differences in education is the way in which girls and boys choose different subjects. When presented with a choice, boys opt for traditionally masculine subjects, such as science and maths, while girls tend to opt for traditionally female subjects, such as languages, English and subjects that relate to the caring role. Becky Francis (2000b) claims that despite the fact that girls have recently caught up with boys in the sciences in terms of achievements at GCSE, and continue to outperform boys at languages at this level, there remains a marked difference in subject choice according to gender at A-level and beyond. Francis examined the responses of secondary school students concerning their favourite and least favourite subjects according to gender and claims that there continues to be gender narratives reflected in students' accounts of which they feel able and want to do. Overwhelmingly, gendered subject choices continue.

A number of reasons have been suggested for gendered subject choices, including:

- Gendered primary socialisation (Francis, 2000a): girls are given toys which encourage them to conform to a caregiving role, while boys are given toys which encourage them to be more active.
- The creation of gendered identities at school and outside school through subcultures, the media and other institutions such as the family.
- Peer pressure from both girls and boys, and the 'male gaze' whereby male teachers' and students' behaviour reflects dominant ideas about masculinity, which encourages girls to behave in a stereotypically female way (Skelton, 2002).
- Naima Browne and Carole Ross (1991) describe gender domains, which are imagined areas, tasks and activities that are male and female. These domains encourage girls and boys to choose subjects that tie in with ideas about female or male subjects. Therefore these gendered subjects are relevant to their experiences and existing knowledge.

Questions

1. Using the information here, make a list of all the in-factors which might lead to gendered subject choices.
2. Next consider external factors and make a list of the reasons why there is such gendered subject choices.
3. What might schools and policy makers do to help reduce gendered subject choices?

- These factors contribute to the gendered image that some subjects had which may (or may not) be further reinforced by school brochures, teaching and learning styles. For example, attempting to attract boys to traditionally male subjects by offering activities that are considered traditionally male, such as competitive tasks or tasks which involve physical activity.

Social policy

New Labour introduced a range of policies to tackle boys' underperformance including the Raising Boys' Achievement project, which involved **single-sex** teaching, the Reading Champions Scheme, in which high-profile male public figures supported boys reading, and the Dads and Sons campaign, which included a set of initiatives to encourage fathers and sons to read together. There have also been numerous attempts to attract more men into primary school teaching.

More recently, in the Education Act 2011, the then Education Minister Michael Gove set out his plans for a return to teaching traditional subjects and a reduction of coursework. It is too early to know how these changes will affect gender differences, but the reduction of coursework might favour some boys who tend to do better in exam-based assessment.

Despite the improvements in girls' educational performance, some feminists argue that schools continue to reflect patriarchal ideology. For example, gendered subject choices still remain marked. This means that where students have a choice over which subjects they study, male students tend to choose science- and maths-based subjects while girls tend to gravitate towards traditional female subjects such as languages, English and health and social care. Feminists argue that this reveals how much girls and boys are still encouraged to conform to gendered expectations. For women this often means that they end up in lower-paid, lower-status caring professions.

KEY SOCIOLOGISTS

Máirtín Mac an Ghaill (1996) argues that notions of fixed gender categories are in the process of changing. Further, he says, there is no 'one type' of boy but an array of different constructions of masculinity. He sees the crisis in masculinity experienced by specific sectors of young working-class men, who are low academic achievers and have little prospect of future work.

STUDY TIP

Gender patterns are linked in various complex ways to social class and ethnicity. Make sure that you acknowledge how these factors overlap. Working-class boys have a greater risk of underachievement than middle-class boys. Avoid generalisations about 'all girls' or 'all boys'.

Questions

1. Which two methods are used in this study?
2. What do the researchers find about differences between teachers' and students' interactions with girls and boys?
3. Suggest how these findings help explain differential educational outcomes for boys and girls.
4. Name a limitation of this research.

RESEARCH IN FOCUS

Michael Younger, Molly Warrington and Jacquetta Williams (1999) examined the gender gap at GCSE in eight contrasting English secondary schools. They looked at classroom interactions, focusing on the perspectives of teaching staff and Year 11 students, and observations of teacher–student interactions in the classroom. They explored the extent to which there is less positive teacher support for boys' learning than for girls' learning.

The research suggests that most teachers believe that they give equal treatment to both girls and boys, particularly in support of their learning, but focus group interviews with students and classroom observation suggest that this is rarely achieved; in most schools, boys appear to dominate certain classroom interactions, while girls participate more in teacher–student interactions which support learning.

The researchers argue that if the underachievement of some boys is to be addressed successfully, these patterns of interaction need to be challenged, to enable boys to begin to develop the very learning strategies which many girls employ effectively to enable them to learn.

Younger, M., Warrington, M. and Williams, J. (1999) The gender gap and classroom interactions: reality and rhetoric? *British Journal of Sociology of Education*, 20 (3), 325–341.

2.3 How does ethnicity affect educational experience?

If you are discussing the reasons for differential educational outcomes between ethnic groups, you could try to explain why certain groups achieve well, as well as exploring the reasons why certain ethnic groups underachieve. It is important not to focus on ethnic minorities alone, as the ethnic majority, in particular white working-class boys, is one of the most underachieving groups currently.

Since the 1970s there has been an increase in sociologists exploring the impact of ethnicity on a person's life chances. Nowhere is this more evident than in educational attainment, where there are great disparities between various ethnic groups.

There are clear patterns in relation to those who are likely to achieve in education. In the UK, Chinese and Indian children achieve results significantly above the national average, while Pakistani, Bangladeshi and particularly African-Caribbean boys underachieve. There are a number of reasons for these patterns, some of which are based on factors that lie outside the education system and other factors and processes that occur within schools. Within education:

- While socio-economic factors explain a large part in the inequality of attainment, there are still differences in attainment between ethnic groups among those students who are eligible for free school meals.
- Chinese students remain the highest-attaining ethnic group. Pupils of any black background remain the lowest-attaining ethnic group, although the percentage making expected progress is above the national average.
- Pupils for whom English is an additional language (EAL) perform, on average, less well than students whose first language is English. However, EAL students generally make better progress between Key Stages. Nonetheless, performance of EAL students varies by ethnic group, with Bangladeshi and Pakistani students doing less well than other groups regardless of EAL status.
- Proportionately more black, Pakistani and Bangladeshi students are recorded as having special educational needs compared to white, Chinese and Indian students.
- Black Caribbean students are around three times more likely than white students to be permanently excluded from school. There are proportionately more black students in student referral units compared with the proportion of these groups in mainstream schools.
- Schools that successfully help minority ethnic children have strong leadership and strong systems, a culture of achievement with high expectations and intensive support for students, and close links with parents.
- Black (82 per cent) and Asian (85 per cent) people are more likely to stay on in full-time education at age 16 than young white people (69 per cent). Black Africans of working age are the most likely to be currently studying for a qualification (44 per cent compared to 17 per cent of white people and 24 per cent of Indian people).
- Bangladeshi (44 per cent) and Pakistani (32 per cent) adults are the most likely to have no qualifications.

(Adapted from Bhattacharyya, G. *et al* (2003) and The Department for Education 2012)

The following discussion separates internal and external factors, however it is likely that a combination of the two result in the patterns of educational attainment that occur. Using the 2001 Schools Census and Population Census data Ruth Lupton (2005) explored the level of segregation and isolation experienced by ethnic minorities in nine Local Education Authorities in England. Lupton found high levels of segregation for the different groups, both in school and outside school. She found consistently higher segregation for South Asian students than for black students and concluded that most children from ethnic minorities experience more segregation at school than in their neighbourhood.

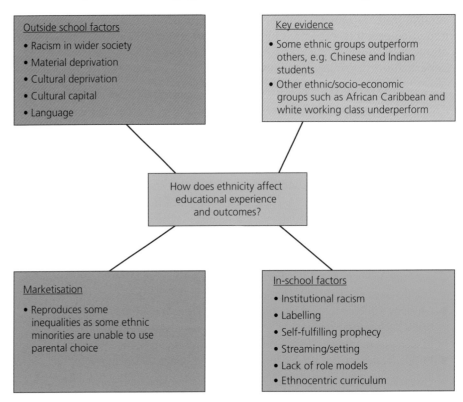

Figure 2.8 How ethnicity affects educational experiences and outcomes

External factors

Racism in wider society has resulted in certain ethnic groups experiencing greater rates of poverty, unemployment, poorer health and over-representation in prisons. Therefore it is no surprise when these groups are also found to be underachieving in education. Therefore the **discrimination** in wider society may be seen as contributing to the lower aspirations of some ethnic groups. For example, this may lead to some feeling there is little point in trying since their chances in life are reduced by either intentional or unintentional racism.

One example of racism in wider society is put forward by Mike Noon (2007) who points to evidence which suggests that, in wider society, managers will overtly discriminate against certain workers based on assumptions about their ethnic group. This pervading racism, either intentionally or unintentionally, informs ethnic minorities of their position, which undoubtedly feeds into attitudes towards school, teachers and society.

Material deprivation

Pakistani, Bangladeshi and African-Caribbean students have a higher than average rate of poverty, meaning that they are less likely to be able to afford important school equipment and uniform. As well as this, diet and housing may not be adequate leading to illness and, subsequently, absences from school.

Cultural deprivation

It is important to remember that some ethnic groups' culture may be seen as different rather than inferior. Some have argued that some ethnic groups regard education as less important, thus leading to a lower value being placed on education and lower outcomes as a result. By contrast, ethnic groups that regard education as important, such as within Indian and Chinese families, have above-average results. Research now reveals that many white working-classes families have lower than average aspirations for their children, which is a significant factor in explaining their relative underperformance. In fact, this has become a key area for policy development.

Family structure

Tony Sewell (2010) argues that one of the reasons for black African-Caribbeans' underperformance is the absence of fathers, which is common in the black community: 59 per cent of black Caribbean children live in lone-parent households, compared with 22 per cent of white children. Sewell claims that the lack of a male **role model** makes it harder for some boys to adapt to the demands of school.

Language

Bereitier and Engelmann (1966) argue that some ethnic minority students lack the language that is used in schools, which places them at an immediate disadvantage. The fact that English is not spoken at home in a high proportion of Bangladeshi families in the UK, for example, has been linked to poorer educational outcomes. However, this is not always the case, and more complex patterns have emerged.

In England, the 2013 School Census showed that one in six primary school students in England – 612,160 – do not have English as their first language. In secondary schools the figure stands at 436,150, just over one in eight. Once special schools and student referral units are taken into account, the total rises to just over a million, at 1,061,010. These figures have more than doubled since 1997. This is a hugely significant increase which reflects the large amount of immigration into the UK.

The census of all children in schools in England (the National Pupil Database) explores the association between the proportion of non-native English speakers in a year group and the educational attainment of native English speakers at the end of primary school. The study finds that an increased presence of children who do not speak English as their first language is not detrimental to the educational attainment of native English speakers.

Research by Geay, McNally and Telhaj (2012), funded by the Nuffield Foundation, found that the number of white non-native English speakers grew dramatically after the EU's eastern enlargement in 2005. Since many of the new immigrants were Polish (and likely to be Catholic), there was a big rise in the demand for Catholic schooling. In general this group of immigrants do not underperform as a result of not having English as their first language. Possible reasons for this include the fact that immigrants from Eastern European countries are often better educated and have substantially higher aspirations than other social groups. The research concludes that children of such immigrants are likely to be a welcome influence in the schools they attend.

Internal factors

A lot of research has been carried out into the processes that occur within the school in relation to the differences between educational performances in ethnic minorities as well as the way ethnic minorities experience school life.

The overwhelming evidence is clear: there are key differences in the ways that certain ethnic groups experience school life. Bernard Coard (1971) in his critique of the British education system claimed that it actually made black children become educationally 'subnormal' by making them feel inferior. Furthermore, Coard stated that West Indian children were told that their way of speaking was unacceptable, implying that they themselves were second-rate as human beings.

There are a number of key processes in the school which contribute to the differences in outcomes of particular ethnic groups. These include labelling, self-fulfilling prophecy, subcultures and the **ethnocentric curriculum** (see page 76).

Labelling

Labelling, attaching meaning to behaviour, is significant in shaping the likely educational outcomes of different ethnic groups. This can result in a self-fulfilling prophecy, where the student internalises a label and it becomes true (see page 55). For example, Fuller (1984) carried out research on black African-Caribbean girls in a London comprehensive and investigated how they responded to negative stereotypes from teachers by forming anti-school subcultures. This means that they did not try to gain approval from their teachers, who they often saw as racist. Rather, they worked hard at their school work while also appearing to reject the school rules. This suggests that students have a variety of responses to labelling and also that negative labelling by teachers does not always lead to failure or underachievement of students. Alternatively, Tony Sewell (1998) found that often teachers regard black students as stereotypically 'macho'. Sewell found that when black boys were labelled negatively or experienced racism, they tended to have a range of different responses.

There have been several policies focusing on raising aspirations and achievement of certain ethnic minority groups. These are known as **compensatory education policies**, for example Sure Start, which also aimed to tackle material and cultural deprivation.

Institutional racism

The intentional or unintentional discrimination that occurs in education may take many forms, for example, not recruiting some ethnic groups to senior management in schools (thus not providing students with positive role models) or only offering certain languages in schools. Mac an Ghaill (1988) describes how black boys and girls might respond differently to **institutional racism**. He claims that black girls will comply with formal rules but will withhold any real engagement with the organisation, while black boys will challenge the school culture more directly and will therefore be more likely to be excluded.

 **KEY CONCEPT**

Institutional racism refers to the intentional or unintentional systematic discrimination that takes place in an organisation such as a school.

The impact of marketisation

As with gender and class, the introduction of market forces within education has contributed to the widening of inequalities in the education system with regards to ethnicity. This is because:

- Some ethnic minority groups are not able to access information about schools that is made available. For example, the school brochures may only be available in English.
- Ethnic groups who experience the lowest educational outcomes are often among the poorest groups in society. As such, they suffer from a lack of cultural capital that disadvantages them in terms of getting into schools through contacts and particular forms of knowledge that make students attractive to some schools.

• Material deprivation in some ethnic groups means that parents are less able to arrange transport for their children to attend out-of-catchment schools. Poorer ethnic minority parents are also less likely to be able to move into more expensive catchment areas for the better performing schools. Also, parents are less able to 'play the system' by using the league tables.

RESEARCH IN FOCUS

David Gillborn and Deborah Youdell (2000) carried out detailed research in two secondary schools showing the real costs of reform in terms of the pressures on teachers and the rationing of educational opportunity. They claim that recent educational reforms have raised standards of achievement but have also resulted in growing inequalities based on ethnicity and social class. League tables have played a central role in the reforms. These have created an A–C economy where schools and teachers are judged on the proportion of students attaining five or more grades at levels A–C. To meet these demands schools are developing new and ever more selective attempts to identify able students. This results in measures of intelligence that label working-class and minority students as likely to fail, which then justifies rationing provision to support those (often white, middle-class boys) already labelled as likely to succeed.

Gillborn, D. and Youdell, D. (2000) *Rationing Education: Policy, Practice, Reform and Equity.* Buckingham: Open University Press.

Questions

1. What is meant by the 'rationing of educational opportunity'?
2. What is the A–C economy?
3. What effects have the A–C economy had on results in terms of social class and ethnicity?
4. Which social group is likely to succeed as a result of the A–C economy?

IN THE NEWS

Chinese and Indian children get better grades than other children

Official figures from the Department for Children, Schools and Families show that Chinese and Indian students gain more top grades than white British children in every school subject. Significant differences in achievement are seen in maths, English, geography, history, chemistry, biology, physics, French and religious education.

The biggest gap in attainment is in GCSE maths. In 2009, 55 per cent of Chinese children and 31 per cent of Indian students achieved an A grade in the subject - whereas for white British students, the figure was 16 per cent, for black African students 14 per cent, for Pakistani students 13 per cent and for black Caribbean students 8 per cent.

Dr Deborah Wilson of Bristol University suggested the attainment differences were due to the contrast in attitudes to education between ethnic minority and white people, including high aspirations among immigrants, who 'almost by definition' are 'keen to get on in life'. She said that, with qualifications linked to social progress, 'it makes sense to focus particular effort at that point'.

Other research shows that Chinese parents are more likely to pay for private tuition to supplement their children's learning at school. According to a study by King's College London, commissioned by the Nuffield Foundation, they are less likely than white British parents to think schools should meet all their children's educational needs.

Adapted from Clark, L. (2010) Chinese and Indian pupils get more top grades at GCSE than British children. *Daily Mail*, 28 March 2010.

Questions

1. Which ethnic minorities achieve higher than average results?
2. In which GCSE subject is the biggest gap in attainment?
3. What percentage of Chinese and Indian students get an A in this subject?
4. What reason does Dr Wilson give for these differences in attainment among ethnic groups?
5. What is the difference between Chinese parents and white British parents?
6. Suggest two other reasons that might explain why some ethnic groups achieve better results than others in education.

The **ethnocentric curriculum** is a curriculum that favours British knowledge and traditions over alternative cultures. While this may not actively result in discrimination, the result is that alternative cultures are not recognised or valued. For example, in a subject such as history, the contribution of various ethnic minority groups or individuals may be overlooked.

Questions

1. What is an ethnographic study?
2. What influences African-Caribbean students' educational performance?
3. Suggest ways in which African-Caribbean boys' performance in particular might be improved?

KEY SOCIOLOGISTS

Tony Sewell (1997) researched how African-Caribbean students were regarded by their teachers, peers and white students at an inner city boys' **comprehensive school**. He found that school expectations and influences such as music and fashion, promoted sexist and racist perceptions of black masculinity. Sewell highlights that concepts of masculinity and ethnicity are complex and shifting requiring more research to be understood.

STUDY TIP

It is very important not to generalise about the outcomes of some ethnic minorities. Also, be careful not to assume that there is no variation in educational performance within ethnic groups. For example, social class differences and gender can result in a wide array of differences within some ethnic groups. Black African-Caribbean girls in particular are to known to be highly successful in education while for black African-Caribbean boys, the story is very different.

CONTEMPORARY APPLICATION

The former Education Minister Michael Gove influenced the decision to allow only British writers to be taught in GCSE English at some schools. This decision was felt by many commentators to be a reflection of a culture which, at worst, discriminates against alternative cultures and, at best, does not value the contribution of key figures who are of ethnic minority descent in the UK and elsewhere.

Questions

Answer these questions using the graph in Figure 2.9.
1. Which group is the highest achieving ethnic group?
2. Which ethnic group is the lowest achieving ethnic group?
3. What has happened in general to results between 2007 and 2011?
4. Suggest three school factors and three home factors which might explain these patterns.

IN THE NEWS

GCSEs and ethnicity

This chart shows the distribution of grades for GCSE and iGCSE, including maths and English, by ethnic group.

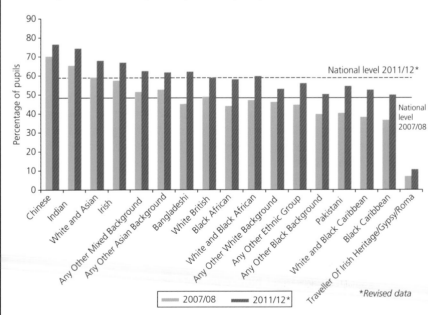

Figure 2.9 Percentage of students achieving five or more GCSEs at grade A* to C or equivalent including English and mathematics GCSEs or iGCSEs by ethnic group, 2007/08 and 2011/12

DfE (2013) *GCSE and Equivalent Attainment by Pupil Characteristics in England: 2011 to 2012.* London: Department for Education.

Check your understanding

1. Identify three characteristics of anti-school subcultures.
2. Name two characteristics of elaborated speech codes and two characteristics of restricted speech codes.
3. Identify two problems with cultural deprivation theories.
4. What is meant by the working class experiencing a 'poverty of aspiration'?
5. Suggest three external factors that have contributed to the gender patterns.
6. Why might boys and men be experiencing a 'crisis in masculinity'?
7. What two problems still exist for girls and women?
8. What impact are the Coalition government policies likely to have had on the gender gap?
9. Which ethnic groups are likely to achieve above average results and which ethnic groups are likely to underperform?
10. Give two examples of an ethnocentric curriculum.
11. Name one weakness of cultural deprivation explanations.
12. What effects does not having English as a first language have on educational outcome?

Practice questions

1. Define the term 'material deprivation'. (2 marks)
2. Using one example, briefly explain how material deprivation may affect educational achievement. (2 marks)
3. Outline **three** ways in which the organisation of schooling may disadvantage boys. (6 marks)
4. Define the term 'institutional racism'. (2 marks)
5. Using **one** example, briefly explain how an ethnocentric curriculum may affect educational achievement. (2 marks)

Read Item A then answer the question that follows.

Item A

There are persistent differences in the achievement of girls and boys in education. In 2014 the performance gap between boys and girls reached its the widest ever – 6.7 percentage points – at the top grades of A* and A. Sociologists argue that a whole range of factors can explain this gap. There has been a huge shift in attitudes towards women in wider society, for example, resulting in women having much higher aspirations educationally. Similarly, over 90 per cent of women now participate in paid employment. However, sociologists also point out that other factors have greater impact on gender patterns, for example, labelling and student subcultures.

Applying material from Item A and your knowledge, evaluate the view that differences in educational achievement between girls and boys are the result of factors and processes within schools. (20 marks)

Section 3: The significance of education policies

This section will explore the following debates:

- What is the impact of education policies developed since 1979, including selection, marketisation and privatisation?
- What is the effect of social policies on different groups? Have they led to greater equality in education?
- What is the impact of globalisation on access to education and education policy?

All three governments since 1979 acknowledge that a major cause of underachievement is poorly achieving schools. Conservative education policies, however, have been heavily criticised for increasing existing inequalities in education rather than reducing them.

New Labour policies reflected their efforts to reduce inequalities in education, although they too used marketisation as a way to try to drive up standards in education. Their policies were widely acknowledged as recognising not just class inequalities but also looking at ethnic and gender-based differences.

The Coalition government of 2010 to 2015 made it clear that they wished to develop marketisation policies and return to a more traditional education system with less coursework and a narrower range of subjects, which many believe will advantage middle-class, male students who tend to do better in these subjects.

This section looks at these policies in more detail.

GETTING YOU STARTED

Immigrants have little effect on school standards

As levels of immigration have risen in recent years, so too has concern about the possible effects of an increase in non-native English speakers into British schools on standards. However, research by the London School of Economics suggests that such worries may be misplaced.

The study, which examined the impact of east European immigrants, concluded there is no reason to be worried about the increase in the number of non-native speakers of English in primary schools.

Although the research found that native English speakers did perform slightly worse at schools that had more immigrant students, the effects were minimal when other factors, such as poverty, were taken into account.

According to the researchers, the proportion of non-native English speakers in primary schools increased by a third from 2003 to 2009, to about 12 per cent.

The main conclusion of the study was that primary-aged students are quick to gain proficient English skills, meaning that they do not negatively affect the progress of those whose first language is English. In fact, maths performance in schools with East European immigrants improved. The families were found to influence other children or the classroom environment in a positive way, possibly because of better behaviour or a stronger work ethos.

Adapted from Cook, C. (2012) Immigrants have little effect on school standards. *Financial Times*, 18 March 2012.

Questions

1. According to this article, what is the effect of increasing numbers of immigrants on school standards?
2. What has happened to the number of non-native English speakers in primary schools over the past ten years?
3. What are the conclusions of the study?
4. What does this article reveal about the impact of broader social policies on education?

3.1 The impact of education policies

There have been many significant changes to education through social policies. This section examines the ways that education has been shaped by successive governments and the ways in which their ideas about the role of education have been communicated through policies. Policies inform students of the prevailing values of society, which they then absorb (Whitty and Young, 1976).

Educational policies before 1979

A working knowledge of some key historical education policies that have shaped ideas about the education system today will greatly improve your understanding of this topic. Some of these are summarised briefly below.

- 1870 Education Act – the first education act making a commitment to provide education nationally
- 1918 Education Act – the age of compulsory education was raised to 14
- 1944 Butler Act – raised the age of compulsory education to 15 and provided free education. This act introduced the tripartite system, or three types of school, which were meant to suit different types of students:
  - grammar schools
  - secondary technical schools
  - secondary modern schools
- 1965 – expansion of comprehensive schools (schools with no entry requirements)

These policies had the intended effect of widening participation in education and encouraging equality between different social groups. However, they had varying degrees of success. For example, despite setting out to provide a range of equally valued schools – a 'parity of esteem' – the Butler Act meant that grammar schools became dominated by middle-class students, which in fact actually reinforced inequalities. Comprehensive schools, which sought to provide all students with an equal chance of opportunity, also led to inequalities in education through processes inside the school such as streaming, where middle-class students overwhelmingly occupied higher sets and achieved more highly.

Educational policies since 1979

In simple terms there are two views of education. These reflect broader left- and right-wing views about society. On the left, the role of education is to reduce social inequality and provide an education system that gives everyone an equal chance of success and social mobility. On the right, the key principle is choice, an education system that offers a range of types of schools, where parental choice is central. These key ideas are summarised in Figure 2.10.

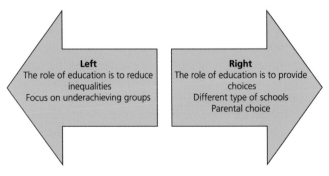

Figure 2.10 Left- and right-wing views of education

In practice, these ideas frequently overlap, and when new political parties form a new government they often continue policies that were begun by the previous government.

Linking social policy and theoretical perspectives

The theoretical perspectives on the role and function of education are also useful for considering **social policy**. The following table illustrates this connection.

Social theory	View on educational policies	Evaluation
Functionalism	Regard educational policies as benefiting the individual and society. They argue that policies are there to create a meritocratic education system, meaning that all students have an equal opportunity to succeed.	There are persistent inequalities in results between different groups, which suggests that educational policies do not result in a meritocratic education system.
New Right	Reflected in many Conservative and Coalition government (2010–2015) policies, the New Right believe in policies which enable marketisation in education, **selective schooling**, increased parental choice and a focus on traditional styles of learning.	Such policies are criticised for creating greater inequalities and benefiting the middle class.
Marxism	Marxists would argue that any of the mainstream political parties support the capitalist economy and ideology. They would argue that the education system and the people creating educational policies are ruling class and therefore policies benefit the ruling class and maintain working-class underachievement.	There are policies specifically targeting the poor and underachieving, such as compensatory education, which challenges Marxist ideas. Also, policies do enable social mobility to occur for some.
Feminism	Liberal feminists argue that policy changes have resulted in the greater educational outcomes for girls at school. However, radical feminists argue that there needs to be a more substantial change in society to really eradicate patriarchy. They would point out that most policy writers in education are men, thus policies reflect patriarchal ideology.	There are still issues for girls despite equal-opportunity legislation and policies. For example, although women are performing better in many areas of education, many still get paid less.
Interpretivism	Interpretivists would be interested in exploring the meaning attached to particular policies, for example the impact of marketisation policies and the effects these might have on processes within the school, such as labelling and the creation of subcultures.	This micro approach may overlook structural causes of inequalities in terms of the types of policy that are created.
Postmodernism	Postmodernists claim that policies reflect the greater choices and individualism in society. They also explore the ways in which learning now takes place as part of a life-long process in a global context.	Postmodernists do not explain the inequalities which persist as a result of educational policy, neither do they offer alternative suggestions.

Table 2.6 A summary of different theoretical perspectives on social policy

Conservative government policies 1979–1997

In 1979 the Conservative party set out an agenda for changing the education system, which continued to 1997. Their most influential policy was the 1988 Education Reform Act. This brought in many significant changes, but the general principle behind the act was the introduction of market forces in education, or marketisation. This means that they applied business ideas to education, creating a marketplace of education. The act included various initiatives designed to help parents and guardians make consumer choices about their children's education:

● League tables, making exam results visible – the idea was to make schools compete to get the best results and drive up standards. In fact another effect of league tables was to make high-performing schools attract middle-class students who are likely to do better at school anyway, reinforcing their

Figure 2.11 Margaret Thatcher visiting a school

success, while schools with poorer results become less successful and less likely to attract students who are likely to do well, widening the gap between successful schools and less successful schools.

- The introduction of Ofsted, a government-funded system of measuring the success of schools and other educational settings – this includes publishing the standard of education achieved by the school.
- Encouraging schools to 'opt out' of local educational authority control – this meant schools could manage their own finances, spending resources where they felt necessary to attract 'customers'.
- The introduction of the national curriculum – a standard curriculum that all students have to follow, decided by central government, standardising what parents were choosing between in terms of areas to be studied.
- Parents no longer had to send their children to their local school but could send them to a school of their choice. Sending a child to a school further away involves paying increased transport costs, which is more likely to be possible for the middle class.

The 1988 Education Reform Act had other effects beyond just greater consumer choice. For example, the national curriculum increased the amount of continuous assesment – assessment at which girls in particular succeed. This, along with other changes in society, led to the closing of the gap in educational attainment and, in many cases, girls' achievements eclipsing boys' in many areas of education.

The national curriculum also made it compulsory for girls and boys to take maths, English and science to 16. This meant that no students were able to 'opt out' of science and maths. This was particularly relevant to girls. Interestingly, this became part of the reason why girls began to perform better than boys. During the 1980s there were a number of policies designed to encourage girls into science and technology, these included GIST (Girls into Science and Technology) and WISE (Women into Science and Engineering).

The effects of marketisation were complex. For example, middle-class parents could 'play the system' by paying to transport their children to better schools outside their area, or move to live in more desirable catchment areas. In fact, some argue that league tables and parental choice led to a polarisation of schools, with the high-performing schools becoming more and more popular while the underperforming schools became 'sink' schools, thus increasing inequalities.

Labour government policies 1997–2010

When New Labour came into power in 1997, Tony Blair famously stated that his priority was 'education, education, education'. Interestingly, New Labour continued many of the Conservatives' marketisation policies, for example through developing a greater range of types of schools and encouraging schools to develop specialisms in particular areas of the curriculum. Other key New Labour policies included:

- The introduction of **academies** – a new type of school partially funded by local businesses to tackle underperforming schools.
- Free childcare for every preschool child – meaning that women could return to work and also helping to ensure that all children start school from a level playing field.
- Sure Start – introduced in 1999 as a means by which preschool children living in the most deprived areas of Britain could receive early intervention and support. It was introduced as a form of compensatory education through

Figure 2.12 Tony Blair visiting a school

clinic and nursery support to improve deprived children's educational prospects while they were still at a preschool age.

- Excellence in Cities – launched in 1999 to replace the prior policy of Education Action Zones (EAZ). It was another form of compensatory education policy targeted at deprived inner-city areas, particularly focusing on raising the aspirations of boys and the working class. Schools received extra resources such as learning support units (LSUs) to tackle truancy and exclusions, while students benefited from low-cost leasing of computers, learning mentors and programmes for gifted students.
- Tuition fees for university – meaning that there was a means-tested fee for university courses. This had the effect that university was only available to those who could afford it.
- Stricter Ofsted guidance on improving 'failing schools'.

Critics such as Whitty (2002) see a conflict between Labour's policies to tackle inequality and the development of marketisation. For example, while compensatory policies such as Education Maintenance Allowances (EMAs) may have encouraged working-class students to stay on until they are 18, tuition fees for higher education may deter them from going to university. Whitty concludes that some of Labour's policies are ineffective and just provide an illusion of equality without actually reducing class inequalities.

Other critics point to the continued existence of both selective **grammar schools** and fee-paying **private schools**. Despite the Labour Party's opposition to private schools, Labour governments have not removed them.

It is difficult to measure the success of Labour's various compensatory policies in reducing inequalities in education. It is clear that while girls continued to achieve highly, many boys continued to underachieve during this period. This period also saw an influx of European immigrants and evidence is only just emerging on their experience of education. Early research suggest that these immigrants actually contribute to the education system and generally achieve above average results.

● **KEY CONCEPT** ➤ Vocational education has been a key area of debate amongst politicians. The Wolf Report (Wolf, 2011) investigated vocational education and was very critical of existing courses, claiming that vocational education often does not lead to jobs and university. In her report, Dr Alison Wolf recommends that all students remain in compulsory education to the age of 16 and longer work-based placements for students aged 16 or older who wish to enter employment.

● **KEY CONCEPT** ➤ Selective education is practised by many private schools and even some comprehensive schools. Where selection takes place, middle-class students are at an advantage as their parents can help prepare them by being more likely to be able to afford private tuition or to have the skills to prepare the child themselves.

● **KEY CONCEPT** ➤ Some sociologists argue that through the increased emphasis on parent choice the education system has become a **parentocracy** – parents are increasingly powerful in shaping the education system. This is very controversial as many sociologists argue that it is only some parents who are able to utilise educational choices. For example, some parents (for example, working-class parents) may not have the skills, time or energy to use the information that is available to make choices for their children.

Coalition government policy 2010–2015

The Coalition government, formed by the Conservative government and the Liberal Democrat party in 2010, introduced a range of controversial changes to the education system. These include:

- Education Maintenance Allowance (EMA) cut – this scheme offered financial help to students with the transport costs, resources and food for example, to encourage poorer students to stay on in education until 18.
- Tuition fees increased – universities in England were able to charge tuition fees of up to £9000 per year from 2012, as the government transfers much of the cost of courses from the state to students.
- Emphasis on old-fashioned discipline – strict uniform codes, and rules such as students standing up when teachers enter the classroom. A pledge to give teachers 'the powers they need' to keep order.
- A 'student premium' for disadvantaged children to resource additional classroom support for students who need it.
- Ofsted inspections to be targeted on failing schools.
- An effort to get more science and maths graduates to be teachers, and state-school students to sit exams such as the iGCSE.
- The introduction of free schools (see page 86).
- Changing the A-level system and reintroducing the two-year A-level.

The policies introduced by the Coalition government have caused considerable controversy. The cuts in certain areas of funding, such as compensatory education, will have undoubtedly led to the increase in inequalities in educational outcome. The effects of returning to a more 'traditional' style of teaching, learning and assessment are yet to be fully understood but it is likely that policies such as reducing coursework are likely to disadvantage girls, who have been so successful in this form of assessment to date. Many coalition policies reflect postmodern ideas about increasing choice in the schools available; however, as previously stated, choice benefits those who are able to utilise it and this normally excludes working-class parents.

The Conservative government elected in 2015 will seek to continue to introduce more Free schools and raise standards through marketisation.

3.2 Social policies in education

When thinking about the effects of social policies on different groups you could consider policies both specific to education but also beyond education, for example changes to immigration.

Figure 2.13 David Cameron visiting a school

STUDY TIP

Make sure that you recognise continuity between all three eras of educational policy. For example, marketisation policies that began in 1979 have been continued by the following governments. Acknowledge that there is some overlap in educational policies.

CONTEMPORARY APPLICATION

There are many changes going on in education today, with a focus recently on using ex-military staff in schools to drive up standards in behaviour. This has received a mixed response as many critics feel that people supervising students should be trained teachers.

IN THE NEWS

Labour vows to overhaul Michael Gove's A-level reforms

Labour accuses Conservatives of 'turning the clock back on social mobility'. The shadow education secretary announced that Labour would put on hold all A-level reforms due to be introduced and scrap the central plan to abolish AS-levels. The Coalition government reforms were designed to toughen up A-levels, moving away from coursework towards end-of-course examinations.

Questions

1. What do Labour mean by saying that Conservatives are 'turning the clock back on social mobility'?
2. Describe the changes to the A-level system planned by the Coalition government in this extract.
3. Why might other groups be critical of the reforms?

But the move has been deeply unpopular with university admissions officers, teachers and students, who complained that their subject choices were restricted. There were also claims that scrapping AS-levels disadvantaged comprehensive-school students in university admissions because they were the most likely to make rapid progress between getting their GCSE and AS results.

According to many Labour politicians, David Cameron's regressive policy to end the current AS-level qualification will close the window of opportunity for many young people wanting to go to university.

Adapted from Adams, R. (2014) Labour vows to overhaul Michael Gove's A-level reforms. *Guardian*, 11 August 2014.

Political era	Impact of policies on social class	Impact of policies on gender	Impact of policies on different ethnic groups
Conservative government 1979–1997	Introduction of marketisation widens inequalities (see page 63). National curriculum means there is less value placed on vocational education with its 'one-size-fits-all' curriculum. The competition between schools means that middle-class parents move into catchment areas with better-performing schools creating a polarisation between high-performing schools and failing 'sink' schools. Better-performing schools get more funding, which means that the gap is widened even further.	The 1988 Education Reform Act had significant effects on gender differences. Girls' results improve partly due to the national curriculum, which means that girls cannot opt out of subjects such as maths and science. Coursework is introduced, which girls perform well at, further improving their results. Specific policies designed to get girls into science and technology (GIST and WISE).	Increasing parental choice disadvantages some ethnic minorities, who are unable to 'play the system'.
New Labour 1997–2010	Continuation of marketisation. Introduction of a greater variety of compensatory educational policies, such as the Education Maintenance Allowance and Sure Start to try to tackle material and cultural deprivation. A focus on raising working-class boys' aspirations.	Continuation of coursework as girls' performance continues to increase. Compensatory policies aimed at encouraging boys to improve their literacy.	Education Action Zones in inner cities with a high proportion of ethnic minorities as well as the introduction of academies to raise standards in failing schools in poorer areas.
Coalition government 2010– Conservative government 2015	A focus on driving up standards and the continuation of marketisation, which results in further inequalities between working-class and middle-class students. Education Maintenance Allowance is cut; student premium replaces other forms of funding for materially and culturally deprived students. University fees are uncapped meaning that universities can charge more, making it too expensive for some students. A focus on a more traditional curriculum with a narrower range of subjects, which benefits the middle class.	A reduction of coursework and more emphasis on written exams, which has been proven to suit boys' style of learning more. Limited policies focusing on compensatory education as funding for compensatory education is cut back significantly.	Greater emphasis placed on marketisation, further disadvantaging some ethnic groups, and less funding for poorer students, which includes some ethnic minorities.

Table 2.7 Educational policies of governments since 1979 and their impact on social class, gender and ethnicity

Ethnicity and education policy

Since the 1960s there has been a growing recognition of the different ethnic groups in UK society, which has led to the development of multicultural education. Multicultural education is a process of reform which challenges and rejects racism and other forms of discrimination in schools and society, and accepts and affirms the pluralism (ethnic, racial, linguistic, religious, economic and gender, among others) that students, their communities and teachers represent. Multicultural education includes the curriculum and strategies used in schools, as well as the interactions among teachers, students and parents.

There has been an increase in recognising the positive contribution of ethnic minorities since the 1960s. However, some have criticised the national curriculum for its focus on white history, culture and general ethnocentrism (see page 76). More recently, the former education minister Michael Gove has been criticised for his claim that the education system needs to prioritise British history and British culture, in the context of a society where there is clear tension between some ethnic groups and a large increase in immigration.

New Right thinkers argue that the education system should focus on ways to drive up educational standards rather than trying to reduce educational inequalities. They also claim that education should focus on traditional subjects such as maths, English, the sciences, history and geography. These are subject areas in which the middle class traditionally perform better. The New Right also believe that education should not widen participation for all students to attend university. This set of ideas mean that workingclass students are unlikely to experience as much social mobility as they might, increasing inequalities within education and society.

What is the impact of marketisation on different social groups?

Marketisation, or running the school like a business, as we have seen, has had a significant impact on the differences between different groups' achievement.

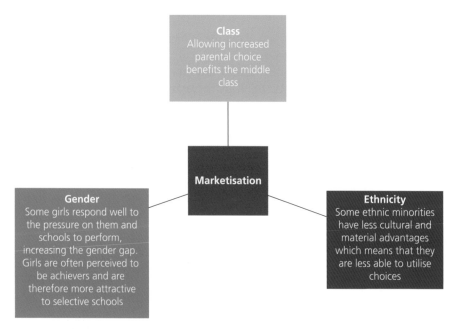

Figure 2.14 Class, gender, ethnicity and marketisation

CONTEMPORARY
APPLICATION

The increased choices in different types of schools and the increase in parental choice reflect greater individualism in education and this links well with postmodern approaches. Today parents are even able to set up their own schools, known as **Free schools**. These were introduced by the Coalition government (2010–2015) as a type of academy, a non-profit-making, independent, state-funded school that is free to attend but which is not controlled by a Local Authority. They can be set up by teachers, charities, education experts and parents. They are set to be expanded under the Conservative government elected into power in 2015.

STUDY TIP

It is also worth considering policies that are not created. For example, there is a lack of policies directly focused on reducing inequalities in terms of girls' lack of participation in traditionally masculine subject areas within the Coalition government.

3.3 How has globalisation affected education?

When studying the impact of globalisation on education you will learn about the way in which the process of globalisation is influencing policy in the UK.

IN THE NEWS

Michael Gove defends Scandinavian-inspired education reforms

The former coalition education minister Michael Gove has defended his Scandinavian-inspired education reforms after Finland and Sweden fell sharply in international school league tables.

At the same time, international evidence suggests that teenagers in Shanghai, Singapore and Korea are improving significantly, surpassing their European counterparts in maths, science and reading.

Mr Gove, whose policy of introducing Free schools was inspired by a similar Scandinavian policy, argued that his controversial changes to the curriculum and teachers' pay were positive, pointing out parallels with successful systems in East Asia.

The UK's performance has remained stable and average in the world's education systems table of performance. Several critics have suggested the UK will have to do more to ensure that students are able to compete successfully with their peers in emerging global economies, arguing that the UK must have higher aspirations as there are fewer jobs for 'poorly educated people'.

Adapted from Warrell, H. (2013) Michael Gove defends Scandinavian-inspired education reforms. *Financial Times*, 3 December.

Questions

1. What does this article suggest about the influence of other countries' education policies on the UK?
2. Where is the UK in relation to global educational performance?
3. What kinds of skills do you think are necessary to allow students to go on to compete with peers in emerging global economies?

Globalisation is the compression of time and distance. In other words, the world is becoming a smaller place and, as a result of the increased movement of people and ideas, education policies have become influenced and affected by other cultures. You can read more about the sociological study of globalisation in Chapter 4 (see page 115).

Globalisation has had two interesting effects on education. Firstly, there is the increased flow of ideas about education as politicians, education specialists and teachers learn about alternative ways of teaching, learning and assessing students. Secondly, globalisation presents a new challenge for education. This challenge involves the changing requirements of the economy as workers are required to be able to use technology and adapt their skills at a much faster rate, possibly also demanding greater geographical mobility and different work practices. This presents a challenge for educators who need to prepare students for this working environment. The other challenge faced by educators is the increasing flow of people into education from other cultures. This, as discussed in this chapter, means that schools must adapt to make sure that immigrants have adequate support and school places. A summary of some of the issues connected to education in a global society are highlighted in Figure 2.15 below.

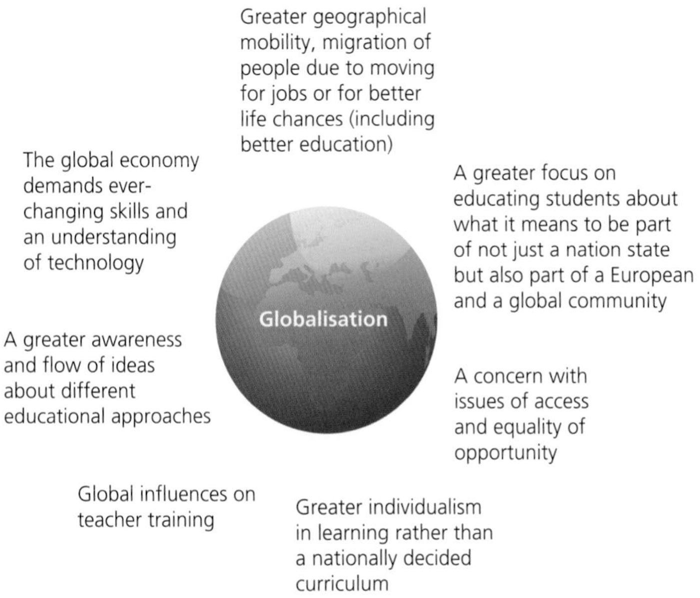

Figure 2.15 Globalisation and education

Policies that reflect the influence of globalisation

An emphasis on lifelong learning

The economy, with its fast-changing technological advances, demands a flexible workforce who can respond to such changes. A culture of learning that recognises that knowledge and skills are not fixed, for example New Labour's programme to get mothers back to work and funding to help with childcare so that women can update their qualifications to return to work. Greater opportunities in adult education, for example access courses and wider participation of mature students at university.

Greater emphasis on individual learning

The greater individualism within society is reflected in education; students are encouraged to think about their own style of learning and to try to develop skills and qualifications that suit them rather than simply conforming to a general education.

Policies which involve greater awareness of a global world view

- The inclusion of global issues within the curriculum, learning about cross-cultural practices, ways of life and the influence of globalisation.
- Policies to enrol more international students, at all levels of education.
- The inclusion of citizenship studies which increase students' awareness of what it means to be a citizen in the UK, as well as to recognise and value the increasingly multicultural nature of the UK and encourage a global view of the world. This involves active citizenship, getting involved with organisations and activities, which leads to increasing understanding of other cultures.
- School policies focusing on equality, diversity and inclusion, to reflect the increasingly diverse cultural backgrounds of students. Ofsted inspections assess schools in terms of their effectiveness in embracing diversity.
- A greater emphasis on supporting students with English as a second language in educational settings.

RESEARCH IN FOCUS

Education for all?

Garrod investigates the participation in education globally. She states that, despite strategies such as the Millennium Development Goals (2000) set out by the United Nations to free people from extreme poverty, great inequalities still exist in education. The targets set by this policy will not be met in relation to primary school children, globally, in terms of having higher participation rates in education.

According to the latest data, in 2012, a fifth of young people aged 15–24 failed to access or to complete primary school and therefore lack the skills for work. However, there has been some improvement in the gender gap, with more and more equality in terms of girls and boys enrolling into schools. One example of success in terms of gender is in relation to Afghanistan, where in 2001 only 5000 girls in the country were enrolled in schools. By 2011, the figure was 2.7 million.

Questions

1. Suggest three reasons why inequalities exist in education today.
2. How has inequality improved in a specific area? Suggest two reasons for this improvement.
3. Why is participation in education particularly important in the context of globalisation?

Check your understanding

1. How are coalition policies similar to Conservative government policies? Give examples.
2. Explain how New Labour policies continued to develop marketisation.
3. What is vocational education?
4. Suggest some possible effects of reducing coursework at GCSE.
5. Which era of policy introduced market forces into education?
6. Explain the positive and negative effects of marketisation
7. Give two effects of globalisation on education.
8. Give two examples of ways in which students are prepared for working in a globalised society

Practice questions

1. Using one example, briefly explain how the introduction of the national curriculum may have affected levels of educational achievement. (2 marks)
2. Outline and explain two educational policies that have contributed to the current patterns of attainment of girls. (4 marks)

Read Item A then answer the question that follows.

Item A

Some social policies seek to reduce inequalities between different social groups through increasing funding for those who experience poverty or those who have low aspirations. These policies focus on making education a level playing field and ensuring that everyone has the opportunity for success in education.

However, other social policies focus on driving up standards in education by introducing market forces into the system. These policies have the effect of widening the gap between high-performing schools and schools that are less effective. This enables some parents to make choices about which school to send their child to while other parents have much more limited choices.

Applying material from Item A and your knowledge, evaluate the view that differences in educational achievement between different groups are the result of social policies. (20 marks)

Links to other topics

This topic has links to:

- Chapter 1 Theory and methods section 1
- Chapter 4 Culture and identity section 4
- Chapter 6 Health, section 2.1 How does social class determine inequalities in health?
- Chapter 7 Work, poverty and welfare, section 1.3 To what extent are poverty and social exclusion linked?

3

Methods in context: education

Understanding the specification	
AQA specification	**How the specification is covered in this chapter**
● Students must be able to apply sociological research methods to the study of education.	● Through the debates, this chapter covers the strengths and limitations of different research methods while investigating issues in education:
	● What is a method in context?
	● What are the key methods that will be examined?
	● How are methods in context questions examined?

Section 1: What is a method in context?

This section will explore:

● What is a method in context?
● What are the key methods, groups and issues which will be examined?
● How are methods in context questions examined?

GETTING YOU STARTED

Figure 3.1 Sociological research in schools

Questions

1. Imagine you are a sociologist with funding to carry out research into education. Come up with four research questions: two about in-school processes and two about issues outside school that impact students' educational outcomes. Once you have your four research questions, decide which method is most appropriate to research each question and write a short statement justifying your decision.
2. What does this activity reveal about the challenges of researching education?
3. What are the positive points about carrying out research on education?

4. Identify some issues with your own personal characteristics that might influence your research.
5. Consider sampling: how would you gather a sample for your research?
6. Are your research questions and methods likely to yield reliable, representative and/or valid data?

This section explores the connection between sociological methods and education. How do sociologists understand or know about what happens in education? See Chapter 1 for more detail on each method as you will need to learn about the methods before you attempt these questions. A range of methods are used by sociologists to understand different processes and different social groups within education.

1.1 Methods

These are the key methods you will need to understand:

- Questionnaires (self-completed, postal – see pages 17–19 in Chapter 1).
- Interviews (structured, unstructured, semi-structured, group – see pages 20–22 in Chapter 1).
- Observation (participant and non-participant – see pages 23–26 in Chapter 1).
- Experiments (see pages 26–28 in Chapter 1).
- Case studies, longitudinal research (see pages 40–47 in Chapter 1 and page 101).
- Secondary research methods (documents, official statistics – see pages 28–33 in Chapter 1).

Factors affecting choice of method

Don't forget that there are a range of factors affecting the choice of a method (see pages 41–48 in Chapter 1). These are summarised below, and usefully remembered as 'PET' – practical, ethical and theoretical issues.

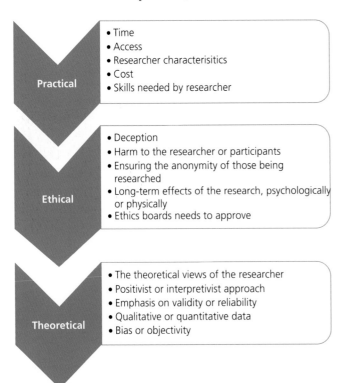

Practical
- Time
- Access
- Researcher characterisitics
- Cost
- Skills needed by researcher

Ethical
- Deception
- Harm to the researcher or participants
- Ensuring the anonymity of those being researched
- Long-term effects of the research, psychologically or physically
- Ethics boards needs to approve

Theoretical
- The theoretical views of the researcher
- Positivist or interpretivist approach
- Emphasis on validity or reliability
- Qualitative or quantitative data
- Bias or objectivity

Figure 3.2 Practical, ethical and theoretical issues in research

A key factor in the type of method used to research education is the theoretical perspective of the researcher. It is important to consider if the method is positivist or interpretivist. For full details of the different research methods associated with different theoretical perspectives, see Chapter 1, pp. 10–14.

Researching students

There are many practical things to consider when studying young people and many of them can be time consuming to negotiate. It is important that you are aware of the many legal and educational rules about involving children in research. For example:

● Before a researcher spends time in a school they must be cleared by the Disclosure and Barring Service, which checks all visitors to the school for criminal records.
● The researcher will need permission from the school and possibly consent from parents and teachers.
● Personal information about students is confidential, as are reports, correspondence and details of any kind on record – researchers cannot rely on accessing these.

Once the researcher has gained access to the school, they need to consider the fact that the students may not be able to read questionnaires and may well need these to be written in the level of language that they would understand, not using complex jargon for example. This is also an issue for interviews, which must be conducted in language appropriate for the age group.

The social characteristics of the researcher may affect the kinds of research that are possible. For example, it might be that the students regard the researcher as an authority figure and may be less willing to open up to them. The social class, gender and ethnicity of the researcher may also affect the research (see Key Sociologist, Louise Archer, page 21).

There is not much free time in the school day when students are able to participate in research. This needs to be considered when selecting a research method – interviews are quite time consuming, for example.

There are also ethical issues in terms of the effects of the research. Ethical guidelines state that research must not affect respondents negatively. Careful consideration therefore needs to be given to any effects that the research might have on students. Anonymity needs to be protected, so that students are not recognisable in the research write-up. This may be a challenge if the research involved detailed observations or unstructured interviews.

Researching student subcultures, inside and outside school

Researching students' subcultures can be a good way of understanding processes such as labelling and self-fulfilling prophecy, ethnicity, racism, gender differences and many other topics. These are hard for a researcher to participate in as the researcher is older and may be different in terms of other social characteristics, such as class, gender and ethnicity.

In school, subcultures may be directly observable, for example in the classroom. Subcultures might also be observable in the playground and other social areas of the school, for example, at lunchtime, in the canteen. Students might also be observed on school trips. It might be even more of a challenge for researchers to research subcultures outside of the school, where gaining access could be difficult. It is also possible to explore student subcultures through interviews.

Researching teachers, head teachers and other school staff

The advantage of researching teachers and head teachers is that they are literate and articulate, and so can express themselves clearly. However, they have very limited time in their working day to take part in research and therefore may be less willing or able.

Head teachers may be unwilling for the research to go ahead if it involves any results that are potentially damaging to the school's reputation.

Teachers may be wary of criticising the school for fear of their jobs and reputation. Teachers are used to being observed in the classroom but still may see this as potentially threatening or be worried about being judged in some way.

Other staff around the school may provide useful insights in to school life. For example, playground attendants and support staff might see school life differently from teaching staff.

Researching parents

Parents influence children's experience of education in many different ways. They influence their children's attitude towards going to school, homework and attendance. Parents also determine the social class of their child, as well as their language skills and values. Therefore parents are very important to investigate.

Researchers might be able to assess the effects marketisation policies and compensatory education policies on parents.

There are significant practical issues connected with investigating parents; for example, gaining access to parents outside the school can be problematic as parents may be busy and simply not have the time. Parents might also be unwilling to open up and discuss their true feelings for fear of being perceived as having inadequate parenting skills. Some parents are more willing and able to articulate their views than others.

1.2 What are the key issues?

There are several key issues that researchers might wish to study such as:

- **Class inequalities** – why working-class students underperform, why middle-class students are likely to perform above average, low aspirations of working-class students, material and cultural deprivation, social capital, culture clash, compensatory education, the effects of social policies such as marketisation, processes in school such as class and labelling, self-fulfilling prophecy, streaming and setting, subcultures in and outside the school, truancy.
- **Gender differences in educational experiences and outcomes** – why some girls outperform some boys, processes in and outside the school which reinforce **gendered identity**, gendered subject choices, the impact of policies on gender differences, gendered subcultures, gendered labelling, interactions between male and female teachers and students.
- **Ethnicity and differences in educational experiences and outcomes** – positive and negative labelling, self-fulfilling prophecy, subcultures in and outside the school, ethnocentric curriculum, institutional racism, racism in wider society, material and cultural deprivation, social capital, marketisation, disciplinary procedures such as permanent exclusion, interactions between students and teachers.

There are also other general issues that might be of interest for sociologists to investigate:

- different levels of attainment across a variety of social groups
- the impact of social policies
- different types of schools
- different documents and events used to encourage parents and students to come to their schools, such as prospectuses, open evenings
- league tables
- government policies on education
- coursework, including attitudes towards it.

Researching education

Table 3.1 summarises some of the practical, ethical and theoretical issues with studying education.

Practical issues	**Time** – teachers/students/parents are busy and may not have time; some methods such as observation and unstructured interviews are time consuming.
	Social characteristics – will it be difficult for social researchers with particular social characteristics to carry out research on a particular social group? For example, having a particular ethnic background when investigating institutional racism could potentially create a barrier between the researcher and the participants.
	Gaining access – schools will require criminal checks (Disclosure and Barring Checks are expected of anyone working in a school). School managers may not want researchers in the school in case they expose any problems within the school. Parents may not be willing to talk to a researcher or may not have time and may not be easy to gain access to. Access to documents about students and teachers may be a challenge due to data protection issues.
	Cost – some methods are more costly than others, such as large-scale postal questionnaires to a large sample of parents/teachers/students or large-scale research involving trained researchers in a number of different schools.
	Researcher skills – some methods, such as unstructured interviews, require considerable skills of the researcher, for example, working with students, parents and head teachers.
	Age – researchers are inevitably older than students and this could be a barrier.
Ethical issues	**Gaining consent** from the school/parents/students can be difficult.
	British Sociological Association ethical code of conduct, informing ethical guidelines.
	Considering the information revealed about teachers, students, parents or other people involved in the research.
	Considering any **short-** or **long-term effects** of the research on the student/teacher's career/school's reputation.
	Anonymity – does this method allow those researched to remain anonymous?
	The findings might be potentially damaging for a student/teacher.
	Informed consent?
Theoretical issues	To what extent does the method allow the researcher to produce **validity/reliability/representativeness**?
	What kind of data does this method produce, qualitative or quantitative?
	How would a **positivist** or **interpretivist** support or criticise the use of this method to study this particular educational issue?
	Is the research testing a hypothesis or exploring and uncovering meanings?

Table 3.1 A summary of practical, ethical and theoretical issues in researching education

1.3 What are the key methods?

Questionnaires

A questionnaire is a survey method where questions are written down with respondents answering either in their own writing or on a computer/phone if the questionnaire is electronic.

Using questionnaires to understand levels of pay following graduation is effective because it is a quantitative method which is appropriate for researching pay. However, questionnaires are not necessarily useful for exploring why it is the case that men get paid more than women in some cases, therefore the findings of questionnaires can lack meaning, depth and validity.

Strengths	Limitations
High in reliability; if the researcher repeats the questionnaire to the same parents/teachers/students they are likely to get similar results.	Low in validity, which means that questionnaire responses are likely to be less truthful. Students might lie, for example, for fear of getting into trouble with their teachers, and give a socially desirable response.
Due to the standardised nature of the questions, it is possible to isolate variables such as the age, gender and social class of each student or teacher to understand how these might affect the findings of the educational issue.	If the research is focused on younger children, they may not be able to read the questions.
Relatively cheap, meaning that the sample of parents/teachers/students may be larger and therefore more representative.	Teachers, parents and students may be too busy to respond to the questionnaire resulting in a low, non-representative sample.
It is possible to identify correlations using questionnaires, for example considering the impact of poverty on educational outcomes.	It is difficult to uncover deep meanings about educational issues using questionnaires, for example, exploring why it is that students reject labels.
	It is possible that the researcher imposes their own views on the questions, meaning that they are biased.
The anonymous nature of the questionnaire means that the respondent is more likely to tell the truth. Students, for example, may be more truthful than with a researcher who they may see as an authority figure.	Having standardised, closed questions means there is a danger that respondents may not be able to tell the researcher about other important issues that the researcher has not considered.
	It may be difficult to get the consent of the school if the questionnaires are to be used on teachers and students. The school may not want research to be carried out into issues that could potentially damage the school.

Table 3.2 Strengths and limitations of questionnaires in education

RESEARCH IN FOCUS

In her research Caroline Benfield (2007) used a large sample of around 25,000 students who were given standardised questionnaires in the three years following their graduation to establish their level of pay. The research established that, despite women often achieving better results in education, they end up being paid less than men who are doing the same jobs. This may reflect the gendered subject choices that affects girls and leads them to choose subjects that lead them to lower-paid, lower-status work.

Benfield, C. (2007) Women graduates paid less. Higher Education Statistics Agency Report

Interviews

A face-to-face research method using open (unstructured) or closed (structured) questions, or a combination of both. These can take place with one respondent or with several. These can be structured, semi-structured and unstructured, as well as carried out in a group setting.

Strengths	Limitations
Very good for uncovering meanings connected to educational issues through building a close rapport with the respondent.	Low in reliability; each interview is very different, which makes it harder to compare responses and come to a specific conclusion about the educational issue.
It is possible for the interviewer to explain questions, which may be particularly beneficial when interviewing younger students.	This method can be very time consuming, and teachers and students have very limited time during the school day. Parents may also be time limited, making this a hard research method to complete. This method is also time consuming to write up.
It is possible for the researcher to observe the body language of the teacher/parent/student, as well as observing group interactions if it is a group interview. This can reveal important insights about the educational issue.	Teachers and students may be suspicious of the researcher, especially if the interviews take place in the school. They may see the researcher as an authority figure, meaning that they may change their responses in order to be socially desirable.
Using interviews can reveal unexpected or unanticipated responses; for example, students may really open up and offer alternative information about an educational issue.	This method requires considerable skill from the interviewer and possibly the ability to interview small children.
	Bias can be a real issue. If the researcher asks leading or subjective questions, the results are likely to be inaccurate or invalid.

Table 3.3 Strengths and limitations of interviews in education

RESEARCH IN FOCUS

George Farkas and Kurt Beron (2001) used structured interviews to investigate the verbal skills of parents and their children. Their vocabulary tests were carried out on children aged 3 to 14. They found that children from disadvantaged backgrounds are more likely to have poorer verbal skills, which leads them to poorer educational outcomes. This study provides further evidence that material and cultural deprivation both contribute to inequalities in education.

Using structured interviews to assess verbal skills is useful as quantitative data about particular language skills can be ascertained, making results comparable and clear. An unstructured method may have provided less-clear results and the answers may have been harder to compare. Furthermore, structured interviews can produce data about correlations between certain variables such as poor verbal skills and social class for example. However structured interviews may be biased as the researcher imposes their ideas about what is important in language skills. The actual abilities of the students may not have been understood for example, using structured interviews.

Farkas, G. and Beron, K. (2001) *Family Linguistic Culture and Social Reproduction: Verbal Skill from Parent to Child in the Preschool and School*. Washington: Population Association of America.

RESEARCH IN FOCUS

Research using unstructured interviews

Ruth Lupton (2004) used unstructured interviews to investigate the relationship between poor neighbourhoods and underachieving schools. Four schools in areas in the top 3 per cent most deprived areas in the country were selected and qualitative interviews were carried out with each head teacher and a sample of teaching staff (six to eight in each school), as well as teaching and support staff with specific roles in relation to attendance, behaviour or learning support. Lupton found a strong correlation between poorer areas and failing schools. However, Lupton also found that compensatory educational policies had had some impact in raising standards for disadvantaged students.

Lupton, R. (2004) Schools in Disadvantaged Areas: Recognising Context and Raising Quality. London: Centre for Analysis of Social Exclusion, London School of Economics.

Unstructured interviews were very useful in this research for the researcher to build a rapport with the respondents, meaning they were more likely to open up about the effect of poor neighbourhoods on schooling. Poverty is a sensitive topic so this rapport may well have produced more valid results. However, it would be hard to carry out many unstructured interviews and so the results of this study will not be generalisable. Also, responses are difficult to compare.

RESEARCH IN FOCUS

Semi-structured interviews

This type of interview is a mixture of structured and unstructured questions, which carries with it all of the advantages and disadvantages of both types of question. The major benefit is of course that both qualitative and quantitative data is created, thus improving the validity and reliability of the results. It may also be that greater rapport can be built through asking more structured questions initially before moving on to unstructured questions.

Cicourel, A. and Kitsuse, J. (1963) Social Problems Vol 11, No.2

RESEARCH IN FOCUS

Research using group interviews

In his research, Paul Willis (1977) carried out a number of group interviews in a school to discover why working-class children get working-class jobs.

Willis studied a group of 12 working-class boys during their last year and a half in school and their first few months at work. He identified two groups of students as the 'lads' and the 'ear 'oles'. Using unstructured group interviews allowed Willis to observe the interactions between the boys and, as a result, Willis found a number of similarities between the attitudes and behaviour developed by the lads in school and those on a shop floor at work. Having a laugh was important in both situations as a means of dealing with boredom, authority and repetitiveness. The lads rejected school and mentally prepared themselves for a place in the workforce invariably at manual level.

This research shows the strengths of group interviews as a way of making respondents act naturally so that the researcher can take into account body language and interactions between participants, which can provide rich data in itself about attitudes to education. However, the study was time consuming and required considerable skill of the researcher. The findings of this research are not representative and generalisable, however.

Willis, P. (1977) Learning to Labour: How Working Class Kids Get Working Class Jobs. Saxon House.

Observation

A method in which the researcher observes participants in a natural setting; this can be overt or covert, participant or non-participant. This method usually produces qualitative data but can also produce quantitative data.

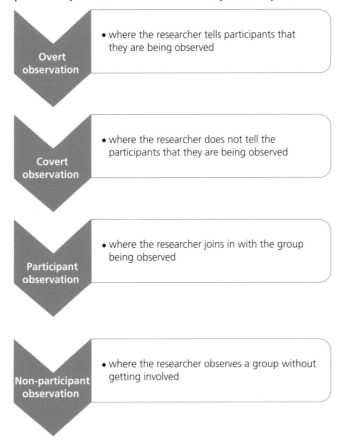

Overt observation
- where the researcher tells participants that they are being observed

Covert observation
- where the researcher does not tell the participants that they are being observed

Participant observation
- where the researcher joins in with the group being observed

Non-participant observation
- where the researcher observes a group without getting involved

Figure 3.3 Observation types

Strengths	Limitations
Preserves natural setting, meaning that participants do not change their behaviour, thus avoiding the Hawthorne effect and producing much more valid results.	It can be difficult gaining consent from a school to carry out observation, especially if the research might reveal damaging information about the school, and covert observation would be very difficult to justify/get approval.
It is possible to observe body language and interactions rather than just verbal responses.	Observation requires considerable skill, especially participant observation, so the researcher might have to learn new skills.
If the research is overt, the researcher can ask teachers/students/parents questions.	Observation of children can be a challenge given that the researcher is older and likely to be perceived as an authority figure.
Observation may uncover new, unexpected information about education.	It can be difficult to record information, and there are many data protection rules concerning children.
There are regular observations in school, such as Ofsted inspectors, so the researcher's presence may not affect teacher or student behaviour very much.	The researcher's social characteristics may make it difficult for them to research issues such as class, gender or ethnicity.
Teachers are articulate and able to express themselves clearly.	The researcher may lose objectivity and give a biased or subjective account of the school.
All aspects of school life can be observed, for example, the playground, classrooms, assembly, meetings, parents' evenings.	Because it is so time consuming, only a small number of participants can be observed, meaning that this method usually has a very small sample; this makes it hard to generalise about other educational settings.

Table 3.4 Strengths and limitations of observation in education

RESEARCH IN FOCUS

Non-participant observation

In their research, Barry Troyna and Richard Hatcher (1992) explored racism in children's lives, carrying out a term of observation in mainly white primary schools in urban areas. They focused on observing the experiences of 10 and 11 year olds and reflected on the behaviour, interactions and responses of the students in their natural setting. They found that where black students are a relative minority racism and harassment are much more likely.

By not participating, it was possible for the researchers to watch the children's body language and behaviour carefully, as well as their behaviour in a natural setting, yielding highly valid results. However, the presence of the researcher could result in the Hawthorne effect, where the children's behaviour changed as a result of their knowledge of being watched.

Troyna, B. and Hatcher, R. (1992) *Racism in Children's Lives: A Study of Mainly White Primary Schools*. London: Routledge.

RESEARCH IN FOCUS

Participant observation

Cecile Wright (1992) also explored racism in her three-year study of four inner-city primary schools in one local education area. She claimed that observation is necessary to understand ethnic minority children's experiences of school, especially in terms of the processes and relationships between teachers and peer groups. Wright carried out classroom observation of 970 students and 57 staff, as well as observation outside the classroom; she also used interviews (see above) with head teachers, teachers and parents. Wright found that the vast majority of teachers seemed genuinely committed to ideals of equality of educational opportunity. However, despite these ideals, there

was considerable discrimination in the classroom. Wright's study concluded that children of different ethnic backgrounds did experience school differently.

By participating in day-to-day school life, Wright would have created a very naturalistic research setting, resulting in more valid results. However, the teachers and students may have changed their behaviour as a result of being watched – the Hawthorne effect may have occurred. Also, teachers may have regarded Wright as an authority figure and social desirability may have occurred, whereby teachers acted in a socially desirable, non-discriminatory way.

Wright, C. (1992) *Race Relations in the Primary School*. London: David Fulton Publishers.

Strengths	Limitations
High in reliability: the same research repeated would produce similar results on an educational topic.	This method has ethical issues as consent is needed from the participants to avoid deception. This would make them aware of the research and possibly change their behaviour as a result, affecting the validity of the research.
The classroom is a relatively controlled environment, which makes it easier for researchers to control all variables.	This method lacks validity or *verstehen*; it is unlikely that the research will provide students/teachers/parents with the opportunity to explain how they feel about a particular topic.
It is possible to isolate variables and understand correlations or cause-and-effect relationships, for example in relation to the effects of student's class, gender and ethnicity, using this method.	The researcher imposes their ideas about what is important about the particular educational issue rather than letting the respondents decide what is important.
This method, using a hypothesis, allows the researcher to produce a definitive answer to a particular educational question.	It can be difficult to control all environments in a school environment as there may be events happening beyond the control of the researcher.

Table 3.5 Strengths and limitations of experiments in education

Experiments

There are three types of experiment but the most commonly found experiment in education is the field experiment. A field experiment is a scientific method of investigation carried out in the real world.

RESEARCH IN FOCUS

Robert Rosenthal and Lenore Jacobsen (1968) carried out a field experiment on a Californian primary school. Rosenthal and Jacobson informed the school that they had a special test that would reveal which children were likely to be 'spurters' or children with particular academic abilities. In reality, this was simply a normal IQ test. Teachers gave the tests to the children and the researchers randomly picked 20 per cent of the sample and reported falsely to the teachers that these students were spurters.

The result was that, a year later, nearly half of those children labelled as 'spurters' had made most gains in terms of their abilities.

This study demonstrates the power of experiments in revealing teacher labelling and how students respond to labelling through their self-fulfilling prophecy. This study has been widely criticised, however, for ethical issues. The researchers ignored the potentially long-term damaging effect on students academically and socially.

Rosenthal, R. and Jacobsen, L. (1968) [2003] *Pygmalion in the Classroom: Teacher Expectation and Pupil's Intellectual Development.* New York: Holt, Rinehart & Winston.

Case studies

A case study is a detailed piece of research that takes place at one particular location, for example a school.

Strengths	Limitations
A lot of detailed, valid information about one educational institution, possibly uncovering unexpected findings.	Non-representative, making it difficult to generalise about all schools, for example, on the basis of researching only one.
Researchers may use a range of methods, known as triangulation, or a combination of positivist and interpretivist methodology, known as methodological pluralism, to build up	Very time consuming and demanding for the researcher to understand all aspects of school life.

Table 3.6 Strengths and limitations of case studies in education

RESEARCH IN FOCUS

Anne Wilkin *et al* (2003) researched the possible effects of extended schools, whereby schools' preschool and after-school activities are established. Telephone interviews were carried out on 50 schools, from which 10 were selected for case studies. The researchers investigated the perceived impact of extended hours of schooling on students, families and the community, as well as on professional roles and teacher workload. The detailed case studies uncovered a number of very positive effects of a range of different styles of extended schooling. Extended school delivery was said to impact positively on student attainment, attendance and

behaviour, offering activities and facilities to increase engagement and motivation. Education and learning was said to be enhanced as the school became regarded as a site of resources and support for the community.

This research shows how useful a case study can be for understanding lots of different aspects of one educational institution. The results are detailed, rich and valid. The disadvantage of a case study is that it is not representative, for example, the school could be very untypical. Therefore the findings from this study cannot be generalised.

Wilkin, A., Kinder, K., White, R., Atkinson, M. and Doherty, P. (2003) *Towards the Development of Extended Schools.* London: National Foundation for Educational Research.

Longitudinal research

A longitudinal study is research that takes place over a significant period of time.

Strengths	Limitations
This is not a snapshot method, meaning that change in relation to educational issues can be understood over time. For example, the impact of educational policies can be observed over a period of time.	Very time consuming and demanding for the researcher; teachers, students and parents can change, which may affect access to the participants.
Researchers may get to know their respondents very well, for example throughout their educational careers, leading to a strong rapport and highly valid data.	Sample attrition can occur, whereby participants drop out of the research for a variety of reasons, such as students/teachers/parents moving away or finding the commitment to the research too high.
The effects of variables on student's lives, such as class, ethnicity and gender, can be understood over a period of time from preschool to school/university and work.	The researcher may lose objectivity and the relationship they have with participants could become subjective.
This method can involve a variety of qualitative and quantitative data, producing rich information on an educational issue.	Issues and concepts in education may change in the way that they are measured over time, making comparisons harder to make; for example, measures of social class.

Table 3.7 Strengths and limitations of longitudinal research in education

---

RESEARCH IN FOCUS

Sue Roulstone *et al* (2011) investigated the role of language in children's early educational outcomes. Specifically, the research looks at the ways young children communicate in their first two years of life, and the role this plays in preparing children for school, using data from a large longitudinal survey of young people. This study examines the environment in which children learn to communicate, such as the activities undertaken with children, the mother's attitude towards her baby, and the wider support available to the family and the extent to which this affects a child's readiness for school entry. This study uses a large, complex dataset from the Avon Longitudinal Study of Parents and Children (ALSPAC), also known as 'Children of the Nineties'.

Data was collected from the children's schools and also supplied by the Department for Education. The researchers found that, despite the strong influence of social class, children's early language made an important contribution to the variation in children's performance when they entered primary school.

Carrying out research over a long period of time illuminates the long-term effects of language use in the first two years of life, rather than simply taking a 'snapshot' view, thus making results more valid. However, this method is time consuming and there is a danger of sample attrition; students can leave the school, move away or simply no longer want to take part in the research.

Roulstone, S., Law, J., Rush, R., Clegg, J. and Peters, T. (2011) *Investigating the Role of Language in Children's Early Educational Outcomes*. London: Department for Education.

Secondary data

There is a huge amount of secondary data available in schools, including qualitative and quantitative data, as well as private and public documents. Beyond the school, policies and national statistics can be used to investigate particular issues within education. This secondary data can reveal particular responses to inequalities within education. Equally, a lack of policies or documentation about an issue can be just as telling. For example, until the 1960s there was very little written about the inequalities that existed between girls and boys in the classroom, which reflects the prevailing attitudes of the time.

It may be that secondary data can reveal historical patterns and provide an indication of shifting attitudes towards issues, such as the incentives to get girls' performance to increase in the 1980s. Marketisation policies such as league tables now mean that there is a lot of information available in public about schools and their students. School data can be interesting in terms of how parents and students perceive the data, and to what extent it informs their views.

Internal school data can yield important information about processes within the school which can be used alongside other primary methods. The use of secondary data is not simple, however, as it needs to be assessed for its credibility, authenticity and reliability.

Secondary data can be either qualitative or quantitative. There is a huge variety of secondary sources of data available on education including those listed in Table 3.8.

Qualitative data	Quantitative data
Ofsted reports	Results information
School brochures, media coverage of issues	League tables
Student reports	Attendance data
Students' work	Exclusion data
Wall displays and posters	Free school meals data
Students' notes to each other/ interactions on social media	Data on the progression of students, targets and test results
Educational policies	National statistics
Educational materials, textbooks and worksheets, curriculum documents, minutes of teachers meetings, websites.	Data produced by non-governmental organisations, already existing sociological research

Table 3.8 Summary of secondary sources of data available in education

Strengths	Limitations
Naturally occurring information which can provide insights into an educational issue.	Data can be difficult to gain access to if it relates to personal data held by schools or parents who may not want to/be able to provide it.
There is a lot of public data available for free, giving researchers a good opportunity to use it in their research on a specific educational issue.	Governments and schools may change the way that data is measured or recorded, making it hard to draw comparisons over time on an educational issue.
Data can reveal information about specific variables such as social class and ethnicity.	Publically available data on education may not provide answers to the research question – that data may simply not be available. For example, data on educational attainment and ethnicity has not always been available.
Data can reveal changes over time with regards to attainment, attitudes towards education or particular groups within education.	It can be difficult getting access and permission to use certain data that concerns students, parents and teachers. Schools may not be willing to share certain information for fear that it might reflect badly on them and damage their reputation.
Qualitative methods can be used to compare results with the quantitative secondary data to get a more valid picture of educational issues.	Secondary data could be biased or have been collected in a subjective way to favour a particular view, for example, recording results differently in order to make them appear better.
Qualitative secondary data on educational issues can reveal deeper meanings about certain educational methods, while quantitative data is high in reliability.	Qualitative secondary data on educational issues is low in reliability, while quantitative secondary data is low in validity.

Table 3.9 Strengths and limitations of secondary data on education

RESEARCH IN FOCUS

Qualitative secondary data

The liberal feminist Lesley Best (1992) carried out content analysis of sex-roles in preschool books and found that school reading schemes portrayed males and females in their 'traditional' stereotypical roles, with women being the caring figure while males are portrayed as being more powerful. Liberal feminists such as Best use these finding to try to raise awareness and reduce sexism and stereotypical views of females in children's books and the mass media.

This method was particularly useful for exploring the meanings attached to gender differences; however, there is a danger of the researcher interpreting the books in a biased way, for example, overstating the sexism in the books as a result of her feminist views.

Best, L. (1992) Analysis of sex-roles in preschool books. *Sociology Review*: Philip Allan.

Quantitative secondary data

This method is very useful for exploring results, however using official statistics and exam results means that the reasons for these patterns are less known. Asthana (2007) speculates about the reasons for girls doing better in single-sex schools, however it is impossible to really know the reasons without deeper investigation, probably using qualitative methodology.

IN THE NEWS

Anushka Asthana (2007) carried out statistical analysis of the results of girls at single-sex independent schools. She found that 68.6 per cent achieved A* and A grades compared with 53.7 per cent in private schools with mixed gender. A similar pattern occurred at A-level. Asthana argues that, according to head teachers, girls at single-sex schools outperform those at mixed ones because teachers tailor their lessons to suit particular girls' skills.

These teaching styles include debate, longer essays and books chosen to interest women.

Asthana, A. (2007) Girls' lessons tailored to suit female brain. *Observer*, 14 October.

Key concept	Definition	How to use this concept for a methods in context question
Positivism	Scientific approach to research favoured by the early classical sociologists. It is centred on the collection of objective social facts.	Is the method favored by positivists? Why?
Interpretivism	Theoretical approach that explains human behaviour through the interpretation of the meanings that lie behind individual actions. It is closely associated with interactionism.	Is the method favored by interpretivists? Why?
Quantitative data/method	Concerned with factual information typically expressed as numerical content.	Does the method produce quantitative data?
Qualitative data/method	Concerned with words that express meaning and emotions (of respondents).	Does the method produce qualitative data?
Standardised	Every participant gets the same questions	Is the method standardised or non-standardised? How easy or difficult does this mean that your data is to compare?
Reliability	The extent to which research, if repeated, would achieve the same results.	Is the method high or low in reliability?
Representativeness	The extent to which a small sample group can be said to reflect the social characteristics of the larger group being studied.	Is the method going to give data that makes it possible to generalise the results?
Validity	The extent to which research is true to life.	How truthful are the results likely to be using this particular method?
Rapport	A trusting relationship between the researcher and the respondent.	Does this method require a rapport between the researcher and respondent, and is this realistic or possible?
Verstehen	The extent to which the researcher sees the world through the eyes of those being researched.	Does this method allow the researcher to see the world through the eyes of those being researched?
Naturalistic	To what extent the research maintains a normal setting.	Is this method set in a naturally occurring situation or is it more likely to be artificial?
Practical issues	Issues with the research which relate to money, cost, time and social characteristics of the researcher.	Does this method have significant practical advantages or disadvantages?
Ethical issues	Potential moral issues which arise as a result of the research.	Does this method have significant ethical advantages or disadvantages?
Theoretical issues	The extent to which the research is based on positivist or interpretivist theoretical ideas.	Does this method have significant theoretical advantages or disadvantages?

Key concept	Definition	How to use this concept for a methods in context question
Social characteristics	The researcher's own individual characteristics which may or may not have an impact on the research.	How will the social characteristics of the researcher impact on the research using this specific method?
Sampling	A small group of people, representative of the larger group, used when the target population is too big to research everyone.	How would you gain access to a sample using this method? Which sampling method might be most appropriate, and why?
Generalisability	When the findings of a study can be applied to describe characteristics of the larger group.	To what extent can the results of the study be applied to the rest of the group?
Macro-level	An approach to understanding society by looking at large-scale institutions and the effects of society on the individual. Associated with positivism.	Methods which involve larger samples and higher reliability, such as questionnaires of large numbers of schools/students.
Micro-level	A small-scale approach associated with the interpretive/interactionist perspective where the focus is on the individual rather than the wider social structures.	Less representative qualitative research methods on small numbers of students/ teachers/parents.
Primary data	Collected first-hand by the researcher.	Is it possible or desirable to collect primary data on the topic?
Secondary data	Collected by people other than the research team so already exists.	What secondary data is available in education? What can it tell the researcher about the topic?
Closed questions	Questions with a determined set of fixed answers, often in the form of multiple choices.	Are these questions appropriate to research this topic?
Open questions	Questions which can be answered freely by the respondent.	What are the advantages of open questions in terms of the topic covered?
Social desirability	Where people respond in a way which makes them appear positive.	Why might teachers/students/parents respond in a socially desirable way?
Operationalise	How sociologist measure sociological concepts.	How can sociological ideas and language be investigated in a way which non-sociologists understand?
Hawthorne effect	Where people behave differently if they know that they are being observed.	How might teachers/students/parents change their behaviour if they know that they are being watched?

Table 3.10 Using key sociological concepts to answer methods in context questions

1.4 How are methods in context questions examined?

Do	Don't
Focus on the specific educational issue	Talk about education generally
Include the method and the issue in every sentence	Focus only on the method
Use concepts specific to the method	Focus only on the issue
Refer to concepts of reliability, representativeness and reliability, making sure that you explain what these mean and how they affect your research	Talk about strengths or limitations only – provide as much of a balanced view as possible
Make sure you consider if your method is favoured by positivists or interpretivists and explain why	Take too long describing one strength or limitation; try to cover several in reasonable depth
Discuss sampling in relation to gaining access; who or what you are studying (parents, students teachers, schools, official statistics)	Provide a list of strengths and a list of weaknesses; make your points feel like a discussion
Talk about the social characteristics of the researcher	Copy from the item; simply say 'as referred to in the item ...'
Bring in an example of a named piece of sociological research	Forget the time you have allocated to plan and answer the question
Have a clear introduction, main section and conclusion	
Use the Item – it will give you clues; for example, it might be describing a concept that you can mention	

Table 3.11 Tips for answering methods in context questions

> **STUDY TIP**
>
> At AS-level the methods in context question is worth a third of the available marks. At A-level this question is worth a quarter of the marks available.
>
> The marks awarded for this question however are the same at AS and A-level:
>
> AO1 8
>
> AO2 8
>
> AO3 4 /20

Example 1

Here is an example of an Item with a question. As you can see, the Item gives you a lot of clues about what you can write.

This means that you need to take at least one idea or a concept from the Item and use it in your answer.

This means that you need to go further than the Item and bring in lots of your own knowledge of methodological studies and concepts.

To 'evaluate' means to consider various views on something. In this case, consider if there are more strengths or weaknesses of interviewing when investigating labelling. In other words, is this a suitable method for this topic?

Question

Applying material from Item C and your knowledge of research methods, evaluate the strengths and limitations of using interviews to investigate labelling. (20 marks)

You need to discuss a range of advantages of interviews and also consider a range of disadvantages with this method in relation to the specific topic. Try to provide a balanced view and give roughly the same amount of strengths as limitations.

This is probably the most important part of the question; it is asking you to apply every single strength and limitation of using interviews to the topic of labelling.

You need to explain that labels vary; in other words, it is not always a negative process. You might like to point out here which students are often likely to be labelled positively, such as middle-class students.

A limitation: if teachers are not always aware of the judgements that they make of students they may not reveal them in an interview.

Make sure that you explain what labelling is, to attach meaning to behaviour.

High in validity: explain that this is a strength of unstructured interviews: they are likely to result in truthful responses.

Define unstructured interviews as a qualitative research method, favoured by interpretivists, in which a series of open-ended questions are asked in a relaxed, conversation-like approach.

Item C

Teachers consciously or subconsciously label students, positively or negatively, and this leads them to raise or lower their expectations of the students. This may result in a number of responses, with some students accepting their labels while others reject them. Negatively labelled students may include working-class students, students from some ethnic groups and boys, who as a result of their labelling may be placed in lower stream sets.

One way of investigating labelling is using unstructured interviews. These are high in validity and have the further advantage of allowing the researcher to build a trusting relationship with the respondent. However, unstructured interviews are generally very time consuming and can be hard to write up without revealing the identity of the person being interviewed.

Fuller (1984) found that not all students accept their labels. In fact the black African-Caribbean girls that Fuller studied actively rejected their negative labels and went on to achieve good results. Where students do accept their label, they may internalise the label and live up to it, a process known as a self-fulfilling prophecy.

Explain that this can lead to a self-fulfilling prophecy.

An ethical issue: unstructured interviews might reveal the identity of the person being researched as they are so detailed.

This is another limitation; unstructured interviews are very time consuming.

A rapport can be built between the researcher and the respondent.

Thinking about Example 1

You could devise a quick comparison of strengths and weaknesses to help you with your planning:

STRENGTHS

- A positive rapport is created between the interviewer and student.

- This method creates valid data.

- Researcher can ask detailed questions about labelling.

- Allows new or unexpected findings to be uncovered.

- Allows the researcher to explore student's feelings in more depth.

- Enables the interviewer to observe body language of respondent.

- Enables the researcher to operationalise complex concepts – e.g. labelling.

- Allows researcher to explain difficult questions.

- Less chance of social desirability from the student if they feel that they can open up and talk about labelling issues.

WEAKNESSES

- Considerable skill is required to conduct an unstructured interview – especially as interviewer is asking personal and challenging questions about negative labelling.

- Hard to conceal identity of student or teacher when writing up the results.

- The research could have negative impact on teacher or student.

- Very time consuming – especially during the busy school day.

- Teacher and students may feel uncomfortable.

- Students may find it difficult to talk to an adult researcher about feeling negatively labelled if they see the researcher as an authority figure.

Decide if on balance the method has more strengths or weaknesses. Perhaps suggest another method that might be better if investigating labelling, such as observation, giving a reason why.

Example 2

Here is another example of a methods in context Item and question with some suggestions of how you might use the Item and break the question down. This time there is a student's response to the question, with a commentary.

Define this concept: a lack of the things that money can buy, which results in poorer educational achievement.

Strength: this means that trends and correlations can be uncovered.

Limitation: this is referring to interpretivists, who say questionnaires on material deprivation would lack validity.

Item C

Investigating the effects of material deprivation on educational achievement.

Some sociologists claim that material deprivation is the main cause of educational underachievement. Some sociologists use questionnaires, given to students, in order to find out the effects of material deprivation, claiming that they enable large-scale research. Questionnaires are also useful because it is possible

to identify the impact of different variables, such as class and ethnicity.

However, questionnaires are criticised by some sociologists who claim that they fail to uncover deeper meanings. For example, they might not explain the causes of material deprivation. Also, students might not be aware of their parents' income, meaning that the results may be inaccurate.

There are also other causes, such as cultural deprivation.

Strength: means greater representativeness.

Limitation: again, low validity.

Bring in a study, concepts and theoretical ideas.

Make sure you define this concept.

Applying material from Item C and your knowledge of research methods, evaluate the strengths and limitations of using questionnaires to investigate the effects of material deprivation. (20 marks)

Student A's answer

School results show that working-class students do not do as well as middle-class students. Sociologists argue that there are many reasons for this, for example, processes in the school such as teachers labelling working-class students negatively, meaning that they are less likely to do well, as well as cultural and material deprivation outside the school. An example of material deprivation is that students cannot afford school uniform and so they might get bullied, leading them to miss school.

The student has correctly identified that there are many causes of class differences in educational achievement. However, it fails to address the question, which is about how to carry out research on the effects of material deprivation. It fails to define material deprivation.

Questionnaires are standardised sets of written questions that are sent by post or carried out electronically. They are usually anonymous and contain closed questions with preset answers for the respondents to choose from. In terms of investigating the effects of material deprivation, questionnaires are useful because the students don't have to write their name on the questionnaire and so they are private. They are also quite quick and easy for the researcher to analyse the results and identify the kinds of effects that material deprivation has. Positivists would favour this method, arguing that it is high in reliability, which means that if the researcher were to repeat the research they would get similar results.

This is a better paragraph because it links the method to the issue, as well as identifying two strengths of questionnaires. The student also links questionnaires to the positivist theoretical perspective.

Questionnaires have the strength of enabling the researcher to break down all of the different parts of the effects of material deprivation, and makes sure that diet, poor housing and educational equipment are investigated. It would be hard to get this sort of detail using another method such as observation.

This is a good paragraph because it compares questionnaires to other methods and also refers to specific types of effects of material deprivation; therefore it is making the issue relevant to the method.

However, there are a number of problems with using questionnaires to study the effects of material deprivation, such as that they lack depth. Questionnaires do not give students the chance to express themselves in more detail about the different effects of material deprivation. Students might lie about the effects of material deprivation because they are embarrassed about them; validity or lack of truthfulness is a problem in questionnaires. There might also be a low response rate, meaning that the findings are not representative.

This is a good paragraph as it connects the issue to the method. However, the student could have suggested a method that would give the students greater opportunities to express themselves, such as unstructured interviews. Some methodological concepts are well used here.

This method has the strength that it avoids the problem of bias found in other methods; for example, in an interview the interviewer might influence the respondent. It also avoids the social characteristics of the researcher affecting the research. For example, a middle-class interviewer might make a working-class student feel intimidated or embarrassed. However, the closed questions in questionnaires do not allow the respondent to develop their answers and ideas, and the questions could be biased or ignore other effects of material deprivation that could be overlooked.

This paragraph is good because it compares questionnaires with interviews, pointing out strengths and limitations of both, which are relevant to studying material deprivation.

Finally questionnaires are anonymous and therefore more ethical than other methods. They are relatively cheap and easy to collect. This means that there can be a larger sample.

This paragraph is referring to the method rather than the method in relation to the specific issue. The student could have gone on here to develop these issues in relation to the specific issue. For example, how might the researcher gain his or her sample, or to point out that younger/less-able students might not be able to read the questionnaire. The student might have referred to a study of education using questionnaires to demonstrate how larger samples can be used, for example Caroline Benfield (2007) used a large sample of around 25,000 when she studied women's pay following graduation.

In conclusion, questionnaires are useful for gaining data on the effects of material deprivation as they are easy to produce, cheap and quick. It is possible to operationalise the concept of material deprivation and, as mentioned in the Item, isolate variables to work out what the possible effects are. However, the results lack meaning and may not provide enough detail about the full effects felt by the respondents.

It is good that the student has referred to the Item here, and they use methods concepts well. They could have used the Item more in their response, however, for example where they discuss theoretical perspectives on questionnaires.

Overall comment

This response is accurate and focused on methods, however it tends to miss opportunities to apply methods knowledge to the issue of material deprivation. However this student does compare the strengths and weaknesses of questionnaires with other methods. This answer lacks the kind of detail needed for higher-level marks.

Example 3

In this example you need to read the Item, the question and Student B's answer. Note carefully where Student B has demonstrated a range of skills. Next, you need to suggest three ways in which you might improve this answer.

Strength: means they are easy to access.

Limitation: this is a practical problem, meaning the results cannot be compared over time.

Interpretivists criticise quantitative methods for lacking validity.

Strength

Item C

Using official statistics to investigate truancy.

Official statistics on education are widely available to the public. However, there have been changes to the ways in which truancy is measured over time. The government is currently focusing on persistent truants, introducing penalties to parents if there is a pattern of missing school without a valid reason. Official statics can show the impact of such policies.

However, some sociologists argue that official statistics are less useful for understanding truancy as they do not explain why students miss school. For example, some students may have genuine health reasons for not being at school while others may be choosing to truant.

Limitation

Explain what truancy means and make sure you say that there are different reasons for students missing school.

Make sure you provide examples of both strengths and weaknesses in balance.

Bring in your own concepts and an example of some research that uses official statistics.

Applying material from Item C and your knowledge of research methods, evaluate the strengths and limitations of using official statistics to investigate truancy.   (20 marks)

Student B's answer

Official statistics are a secondary form of quantitative data which, as the Item suggests, has the advantage of being publically available and free to access, which is a practical advantage. Truancy means where students take time off school. Official statistics include data on truancy from all schools across the UK, so the data is high in representativeness. This makes it possible to generalise about truancy rates, and to find out at which age truancy is more of a problem. Official statistics are favoured by positivists because they are high in reliability.

Researchers and journalists often use official statistics to investigate patterns and trends, such as Anushka Asthana (2007) who carried out statistical analysis of exam results for girls at single-sex independent schools. In terms of truancy, using statistics can provide information on the amount of truancy in different areas of the country, which could provide quantitative information about truancy in different parts of the UK.

However, official statistics have the problem of lacking meaning. This means that although the statistics will give details of the extent of truancy, they do not give the reasons for truancy. An interpretivist would criticise official statistics, saying that they lack meaning and do not provide detail. One advantage however is that official statistics take data on different levels of truancy in different types of schools, so it is possible to identify different levels of truancy in academies or primary schools for example. A disadvantage of this is that official statistics do not include private school truancy figures. Also, there are different reasons for absence and these are not explained in any detail in the statistics. It is also difficult to know which kinds of students are likely to be truants so that possible solutions can be put into place to reduce the problem.

Official statistics may change in the way that they are measured, as referred to in Item C. Until recently, there was little information on truancy rates in different schools. This would make it very hard to be able to make historical comparisons or to see changes over time. Schools might also record information incorrectly and this can lead to further problems of validity with the data.

Official statistics have the advantage of avoiding ethical issues, as they avoid deception or harm, and so they are positive to use because of this. There are no costs to using official statistics. However it would be interesting to follow up the statistics, carrying out research to understand the reasons for truancy on a smaller scale. Interviews, for example, might give more detailed information about why individuals do not attend school.

Example 4

In this final example of a methods in context question, you are expected to plan and write your own answer.

Item C

Using observation to investigate student subcultures.

Student subcultures can tell sociologists a lot about students' attitudes towards education. A subculture is a smaller group with values which are different to the wider group. These can be pro-school or anti-school. Observation can be a very useful way of understanding subcultures, as it means that you can see how these groups operate in a naturalistic setting.

However, participant observation can be problematic as adult researchers are going to have problems gaining access to and participating in student subcultures. This could be due to the differences in age and possibly social class and ethnic group.

Applying material from Item C and your knowledge of research methods, evaluate the strengths and limitations of using observation to investigate student subcultures.　　(20 marks)

Planning checklist

To help you prepare for answering the question, create your own checklist, for example:

- Define 'observation': mention that there are different types.
- Mention that observation can produce both qualitative and quantitative data.
- Present a range of practical, ethical and theoretical strengths and weaknesses in relation to using this method to investigate subcultures.
- Consider how to incorporate key concepts such as the Hawthorne effect, social desirability, *verstehen*, naturalistic setting, social characteristics of the researcher, deception, consent, harm and access.
- Refer to the issues of researching both pro-school and anti-school subcultures.
- Refer to the Item itself.

Issue	Methods
Labelling of some ethnic groups	Questionnaires (postal or self-completion)
Anti-school subcultures	Structured interviews
The effects of marketisation policies	Unstructured interviews
The reasons why boys are underachieving	Participant observation
The reasons why girls may outperform boys	Non-participant observation
The impact of material deprivation on educational achievement	Field experiments
The importance of in-school processes on different gender outcomes	Case studies
Understanding the reasons for truancy	Longitudinal studies
Investigating racism	Using secondary data (documents or official statistics)

Table 3.12

Culture and identity

Understanding the specification

AQA specification	How the specification is covered in this chapter
● Different conceptions of culture, including subculture, mass culture, folk culture, high and low culture, popular culture and global culture.	*Section 1* ● What is culture? ● Can culture be defined? ● What are the different types of culture?
● The socialisation process and the role of the agencies of socialisation.	*Section 2* ● What is socialisation, and what are the roles of the agencies of socialisation?
● The self, identity and difference as both socially caused and socially constructed.	*Section 3* ● Who am I? ● Is identity socially constructed or socially caused?
● The relationship of identity to age, disability, ethnicity, gender, nationality, sexuality and social class in contemporary society.	*Section 4* ● How does age affect our identity? ● What is meant by ethnicity? What does it mean to be British? What are the new ethnic identities in the UK? How has migration produced a diaspora? ● How do people construct their ethnic identities? ● What is disability? What impact might disability have on a person's identity? How might disability be perceived in Western culture? ● What does it mean to be a gendered person? ● What is the process of gender role socialisation? ● How is sexual identity constructed? How is sexuality expressed? ● How does social class affect identity? Is social class important?
● The relationship of identity to production, consumption and globalisation.	*Section 5* ● What are the effects of globalisation on culture and identity? ● How is consumption used to form our identity?

Section 1: Concepts of culture

> **This section will explore the following debates:**
>
> - What is culture?
> - Can culture be defined?
> - What are the different types of culture?

Questions

1. What do these photographs suggest about culture and attitudes towards and food eating?
2. How did they learn to behave in this way?
3. Give reasons for this way of behaving.

GETTING YOU STARTED

Figure 4.1 How do we eat?

1.1 Can culture be defined?

When studying the different definitions of culture, you could consider the similarities and differences between different types of cultures as defined by sociologists.

Culture is one of the most fundamental concepts of sociological analysis. Sociologists seek to study and analyse people's actions, the norms and values that give them a context, and the meanings that they attach to individual and group intentions, behaviours and artefacts. Culture is a key concept in sociology and it allows us to explain how and why members of different societies can behave in similar and familiar, yet also different and unfamiliar, ways. It also allows us to think about what it means to be a human. Culture, as Raymond Williams (1976) has observed, is one of the most complicated words in the English language.

 **KEY CONCEPT**

Issues of **culture and identity** have always been a key theme of sociology. These issues allow sociologists to discuss who we think we are and how we behave as individuals and in groups.

The general definition comes from structuralist theorists (see Section 1.3, page 122) which define culture as 'way of life of society'. This view assumes that there is a shared way of life within society, with shared norms and values, which binds society together. In this definition culture is seen as active and as having a social function. It binds individuals together. It is made up of shared or collective symbols and it patterns our life. It provides the rules by which we live our life. However, we should not assume that all cultures are the same.

The second definition sees culture as a map of meaning. In this view, culture is what we carry around inside our heads, created by our interactions with others. It provides us with symbols and rules, but our role is much more active and creative in producing culture. Culture creates the world we live in. It also allows us to understand and interpret our own actions and the actions of others. Zygmunt Bauman points out that the word culture refers to something that is artificial. Society trains individuals to follow a certain cultural code, which is indicated by signs such as clothes, symbols and words.

Another important aspect of culture is that it is socially constructed, not biologically inevitable. This means that we learn everything about our culture through the process of socialisation. There are three levels of culture that are part of learned behaviour patterns:

- artifacts and behaviours
- espoused values
- assumptions.

The body of cultural traditions that distinguish a specific society

When people speak of English, Croatian, Indian or Chinese culture, they are referring to the shared language, traditions, rituals and beliefs that set each of these peoples apart from others. Horace Miner, in his satirical paper 'Body ritual among the Nacirema' (1956), cleverly demonstrated exactly how cultures can be formed and recognised by these shared aspects (see Research in Focus). In most cases, those who share your culture do so because they were raised by parents and other family members who have it.

RESEARCH IN FOCUS

Body ritual among the Nacirema

'The fundamental belief underlying the whole system appears to be that the human body is ugly and that its natural tendency is to weakness and disease. Encased in such a body, people's only hope is to avoid these characteristics through the use of the powerful influences of ritual and ceremony. Every household has one or more shrines devoted to this purpose. The focal point of the shrine is a box or chest which is built into the wall. In this chest are kept the many charms and magical potions without which no native believes he could live. These preparations are secured from a variety of specialised practitioners. The most powerful of these are the medicine men, whose assistance must be rewarded with substantial gifts...

'The Nacirema have an almost pathological horror of and fascination with the mouth, the condition of which is believed to have a supernatural influence on all social relationships. Were it not for the rituals of the mouth, they believe that their teeth would fall out, their gums bleed, their jaws shrink, their friends desert them, and their lovers reject them. They also believe that a strong relationship exists between oral and moral characteristics. For example, there is a ritual ablution of the mouth for children, which is supposed to improve their moral fibre.

'The daily body ritual performed by everyone includes a mouth ritual. Despite the fact that these people are so careful about care of the mouth, this rite involves a practice which strikes the uninitiated stranger as revolting. It was reported to me that the ritual consists of inserting a small bundle of hog hairs into the mouth, along with certain magical powders, and then moving the bundle in a highly formalised series of gestures.'

Extract from Miner, H. (1956) Body ritual among the Nacirema. *American Anthropologist*, *58* (3), 503–507.

Questions

1. What is your initial reaction to the Nacireman culture (way of life)?
2. Consider any similarities between the Nacireman culture and our own. Make a list of all of them.
3. Find evidence within the article that culture and behaviours are learned rather than biological or innate.
4. Spell Nacirema backwards.

Subcultures

In complex, diverse societies in which people have come from many different parts of the world, people often retain much of their original cultural traditions and form subcultures within a larger culture. For example, in many countries you can find a 'Little India' where there are lots of South Asian residents, restaurants and shops – for instance in Southall, London.

If a particular subculture is characterised by a systematic opposition to the dominant culture, it may be described as a counterculture. Many influential studies of subcultures originate from the Chicago School of Sociology and Birmingham University's Centre for Contemporary Cultural Studies (CCCS). Examples of youth subcultures are: punks, skinheads, emos, goths, skaters, etc.

Hebdige (1995) argued that subcultures bring like-minded individuals who feel neglected by society together and allow them to develop their identity. Functionalists consider that in any given society there is a mainstream or consensus way of life, and those who do not conform to it belong to subcultures – though this does not mean that they are entirely separate from the mainstream culture.

Cultural universals

Cultural universals are learned behaviour patterns that are shared by all of humanity collectively. No matter where people live in the world, they share these universal traits. Examples of such 'human cultural' traits include:

- communication (language)
- classification based on age and gender (woman, man, teenager, elderly person)
- bringing up children in some sort of family setting
- sexual division of labour
- regulating sexual behaviour
- establishing and implementing rules and values
- creating art
- having some kind of leadership role and governing system.

Is culture same as society?

Culture and society are not the same thing. While cultures are complexes of learned behaviour patterns and perceptions of an individual, societies are systems of structural interrelationships (made up of social institutions such as marriage and the family). Societies are groups of people who directly or indirectly interact with each other. People within societies also generally perceive that their society is distinct from other societies in terms of shared traditions and expectations. While societies and cultures are not the same thing, they are closely connected because culture is created and transmitted to others in a society. Cultures are not the product of lone individuals. They are the continuously evolving products of people interacting with each other. Cultural patterns, such as language, politics and economics, make no sense except in terms of the interaction of people.

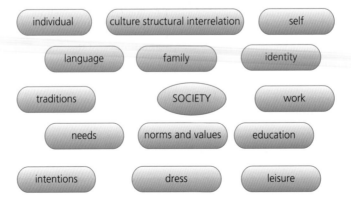

Figure 4.2 The place of culture in society

Culture is located in society as a unique mediating apparatus between the individual on one hand and the system of structural interrelationships (made up of social institutions such as marriage and family) on the other. Any given society is composed of individuals organised into structured social relationships.

1.2 What are the different types of culture?

Do you prefer listening to opera or rap music? Do you like watching horse racing or football? Do you read books of poetry or celebrity magazines?

The term 'culture', as we have seen, refers to the language, norms, values, beliefs, knowledge and customs of a society. However, within this broad definition sociologists refer to folk culture, high culture, low culture, popular culture and mass culture to describe different aspects of culture in society.

Consumer culture can be defined as a culture where social status, values and activities are centred on the consumption – the act of buying goods or services. In other words, in a consumer culture, a large part of what you do, what you value and how you are defined revolves around your consumption of stuff. Keep this in mind when reading through the following sections.

KEY CONCEPT

High culture

High culture, as sociologists define it, is seen to have artistic and/or intellectual value, for example fine art, classical music and literature. An example here might be that classical music is held in higher cultural regard than popular music such as that by Rihanna or One Direction. High cultural products and pursuits are associated with the cultural interests of the rich and powerful. Davis (2000) suggests that high culture is the preserve of very few in society because it involves art, literature, music and intellectual thought, which few can create or even appreciate. Many people today think of high culture in the way that it was thought of in Europe during the eighteenth and early nineteenth centuries – that it reflects inequalities within European societies and their (now former) colonies around the world.

Figure 4.3 High culture

Mass culture

With industrialisation and urbanisation, a new, increasingly commercialised culture has emerged, shaped by media influences and technology. Some sociologists refer to this as mass culture. The idea of mass culture is often based on Marxist theories such as those put forward by sociologists of the Frankfurt School, including Marcuse and Adorno. In their work they argued that, in a capitalist society, mass culture helps to manipulate people into wanting and consuming products they do not really need. Mass culture is essentially a product of the mass media, and examples include popular feature films, television soap operas and recorded pop music. From this viewpoint the audience become passive members of a mass society, unable to think for themselves (Giddens, 2008). Both low culture and popular culture (see below) are forms of mass culture. The main characteristics of mass culture are that it is:

Figure 4.4 Mass culture

- created by commercial organisations
- manufactured
- passive
- inauthentic
- associated with industrial societies
- produced for profit.

Figure 4.5 Low culture

Figure 4.6 Popular culture

Figure 4.7 Folk culture

Figure 4.8 Global culture

Low culture

Low culture is a term for some forms of popular culture and refers to cultural products and pursuits characterised by their production for, and consumption by, 'the masses'. Low cultural products and pursuits are associated with relatively poorer and less-powerful groups of people.

Popular culture

The term popular culture refers to the pattern of cultural experiences and attitudes that exist in mainstream society. Popular culture would include culture which is popular, easy to understand and entertaining to the majority of young people, for example, TV, football, pop music, tabloid newspapers, romantic comedies and soap operas. In modern times, popular culture is often expressed and spread via commercial media such as radio, television, movies, the music industry, publishers and corporate-run websites. Unlike high culture, popular culture is known and accessible to most people. While some do see popular culture as shallow and harmful, others, including some postmodernists, argue that it is just as valid and worthwhile as high culture.

Folk culture

Folk culture consist of local customs and beliefs that directly reflect the lives and experiences of the people, such as folk songs and stories that are handed down from one **generation** to the next.

The main characteristics of folk culture are that it is:

● traditional
● created by ordinary people
● authentic
● associated with active participation
● associated with pre-industrial societies
● rooted in the experiences of ordinary people.

Global culture

Some sociologists today predict that the world is moving closer to a **global culture**. Social forces that are creating it include electronic communications, the mass media, the news media, the internet, international businesses and banks. These forces are leading towards one world culture. The whole world will lose its **cultural diversity** and all people will experience one culture. (See more on globalisation of cultures in Section 5, page 165.)

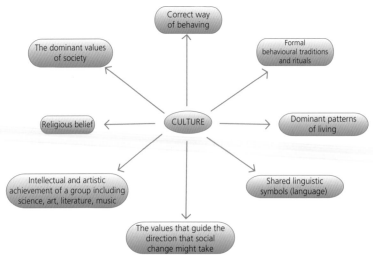

Figure 4.9 What does culture include?

1.3 Different perspectives on culture

As the main theoretical approaches to culture are explored below remember that each one has something to contribute to the following debates: to what extent do social actors (individuals) have the capacity to change social structure or create culture, or is it the case that social structure and culture largely shape our behaviour? In other words does society shape our behaviour? It is important to be able to compare and evaluate different perspectives on culture.

A central theme in the debate about culture and identity is the notion of agency: free will or the freedom to act. Agency is about choice and the ability to exercise choice in the kind of culture that a person has. Central to this notion is reflexivity, the capacity of humans to reflect – to think about themselves and others around them. Humans are the product of their experiences but they also shape and mould these experiences. Culture provides us with possibilities for action, but we take responsibility for what we do through our agency.

Functionalist (consensus theory)

Functionalists are primarily interested in culture in the context of exploring how social order is maintained. They stress the importance of shared common consensus around the main values in regulating social behaviour and ensuring that change occurs in orderly ways. A common consensus or shared culture is placed at the centre of functionalist concerns. According to Émile Durkheim culture bonds the individual to the wider group through the process of socialisation. Culture is necessary for social order to be established and maintained

Critics of the functionalist view of culture suggest that functionalists regard humans as passive or victims of their culture. Interactionist sociologists would criticise the fact that functionalists see individuals as passive, ignoring their potentially active role in creating culture through meaningful interaction.

Marxist: dominant and subordinate cultures (conflict theory)

According to Marx, culture (or ruling-class ideas and values) is produced by the dominant group in order to justify its dominance over others. Culture acts as a constraint on individuals, leading to social order and control. Culture is seen to contain a ruling-class ideology that is socialised into the consciousness of the individuals living in a society. Ideology is created deliberately by the powerful to ensure their continuing domination. Referring to capitalist societies, Marxists use the term 'dominant culture' (capitalism rather than consensus culture as functionalists suggest). Critics of the Marxist view of culture suggest that Marxists see society divided into two groups and do not really consider the role of the individual.

Neo-Marxist

Neo-Marxist theory of culture deviates from classic Marxist theory in at least one important respect – it focuses concern on the super-structure issues of ideology and culture rather than the economic base. The emphasis of neo-Marxist theory is on the culture of the mass media as a powerful influence for preventing fundamental change. Neo-Marxists are concerned in particular with culture and ideology. Antonio Gramsci writes that in capitalist society the ideas and ideology of the capitalist class would secure **hegemony** (leadership or dominance, especially by one state or social group over others), but it was the

Question

1. Give an example for each of the elements of culture in Figure 4.9.

KEY SOCIOLOGISTS

Karl Marx (1818–83) suggested that commodification of culture takes place under capitalism, whereby cultural products are valued for monetary value rather than for the pleasure they can give. He argued that if society becomes too concerned with the purchase of cultural goods, humans fetishise certain goods and 'worship' what they represent (money, wealth and status). This is manipulated by capitalism through advertising and media.

CONTEMPORARY APPLICATION

In the Western world, anyone who cannot understand or does not have access to the internet risks being at a serious cultural disadvantage. Multinational companies are among the most powerful institutions that use media to get their messages across. Many adopt particular brands or signs to achieve instant product recognition, such as the company Nike, which has colonised one of the world's most positive symbols – the tick. Consumer culture spreads in this way.

task of working-class intellectuals and organisations to try to counter these ideas with alternative perspectives. Gramsci suggests that there is continuous struggle through key cultural institutions in which the dominant class seeks to establish its perspectives as common sense while subordinate classes may more or less resist it.

Interactionist (symbolic interactionism)

According to interactionists, culture is maintained through interaction based on communication of signs and signals. Meaning is transmitted symbolically and is generated through the process of interaction. They see identity as the ongoing creation of the interaction of self and culture. George Herbert Mead distinguished between two aspects of the self, namely 'I' and 'me'. Although both developed within society, he considered the 'I' to be the active, decision-making aspect of the self and the 'me' to be the socialised aspect of the self. So, the total reflected the ability to think and act (agency), but was additionally shaped by society (structure). The interpretivist Max Weber also portrays individuals as social actors who typically seek meaning and self-development. Therefore, human beings need not be regarded as mindless products of their culture; instead they have consciousness and can reflect on the cultures they were born into, and they may accept or reject certain aspects of these cultures. Thus, for example, someone born into a Christian environment may decide to become a Muslim.

Feminist

There are several traditions of feminist theory but all of them share the view that culture has played an important part in the subordination of women to the interest of men. Feminists such as Sue Sharpe (1976) maintain that differences in child socialisation serve to generate masculine and feminine cultural identities. Secondary agencies of socialisation, such as the media and peer groups, are said to reinforce gender identities established during primary socialisation within the family. For example, many teenage magazines targeted at female audiences present ideologies of beauty, marriage, domesticity and subordination that serve to strengthen the messages of femininity that families instil into their female members. Gender socialisation of this sort is significant because it helps us to understand why females have traditionally latched on to subjects such as home economics and the arts, which have a femininised image, rather than subjects such as technology and science, which are packaged in a masculine way. Sex role theorists such as Bryne (1978) have argued that the cycle of discrimination against women is therefore created by parents, and teachers reinforce sex stereotypes, which then become the basis for discriminatory practices.

Other sociologists, such as Ann Oakley in *Sex, Gender and Society* (1972), note that from birth, girls are treated differently from boys by the people who care for them. Other studies by Fiona Norman show that girls are expected to play with certain toys, which develop different types of aptitude. These roles may be reflected by the aspirations of the children. (See more on feminist theories and gender later on in this chapter, page 154.)

Postmodernist

Structuralist approaches tend to present identity as single and relatively fixed. The one predominant identity is assumed to dominate; therefore, a person is categorised as working class or middle class and the other aspects of their lives are considered to be set in this identity. However, the postmodernists emphasise that an individual can have multiple identities. A person can be a mother, daughter, student, footballer and cook, and may act and feel differently in each of these roles. Identities are thought of as less fixed or structured and as being quite fluid and open to change. People experience a variety of cultural flows which often cascade to them via the media. Angela McRobbie uses the phrase 'no real me', meaning that individuals have no single essential identity in this postmodern society.

IN THE NEWS

Consumer culture and the 2011 'riots'

Figure 4.10 London riots

David Moxon (2011) suggests that the riots that occurred in England during the early part of August 2011 can only be properly understood if they are located in the situation of a society that is becoming increasingly consumerist in its orientation. The events of August 2011 actually represented conformity to the underlying values of consumer culture. The riots can be read as a demonstration of the current drive of the ideal of the consumer. The initial moment was triggered by the shooting of Mark Duggan by a Metropolitan Police officer. Following this was a greedy moment characterised by looting and a destructive moment characterised by general disorder.

The looting of electrical stores, sports shops, clothing stores and off-licences was perhaps the defining image of the riots. As well as those who stole rather mundane items such as bottled water and doughnuts, and those who merely received stolen goods, there were also those who brazenly posed for photographs with flat-screen TVs and trainers. The suggestion made here is not that the consumer culture of late modern Britain caused the riots in any straightforward manner. Rather, it seems that the acts of those who partook in the riots, both in the greedy and the destructive moments, can only be fully understood if they are analysed in the context of a society that is becoming increasingly consumerist in its orientation. The riots were a manifestation of some of the underlying trends of contemporary society. The riots represented a disruption to social order while simultaneously suggesting the strength and vitality of the consumer culture that is now such a central plank of social life in this country.

Adapted from Moxon, D. (2011) Consumer culture and the 2011 'riots'. *Sociological Research Online, 16* (4), 19.

Questions

1. What is consumer culture?
2. What was the reason for rioting?
3. Why were people protesting with such criminal actions?
4. Are we all just consumers of products?

Check your understanding

1. 'Culture is central to our lives and to who we are.' Briefly explain this sentence as though speaking to a non-sociologist.
2. Identify and explain, with examples, three differences between high culture, mass culture and folk culture.
3. Identify and explain three reasons why the distinction between high culture and low culture is based on class differences.
4. Can you think of any examples today of the social practices still associated with folk culture?
5. What examples of postmodern culture can you identify when looking at buildings, clothes and TV?
6. Do you believe that individuals have free will in determining their own culture or do you believe that people are puppets of society?
7. Explain the difference between low culture and high culture.

Practice questions

1. Define the term 'culture'. (2 marks)
2. Define the term 'mass culture'. (2 marks)
3. Define the term 'folk culture'. (2 marks)
4. Outline three characteristics and/or concepts associated with interactionist views of culture and identity. (6 marks)
5. Outline three characteristics of the postmodernist view of culture. (6 marks)
6. Outline and explain two ways in which sociologists can contribute to our understanding of any two of the following: mass culture, folk culture, global culture, popular culture. (10 marks)
7. Evaluate sociological explanations of the role of culture in society. (20 marks)

Section 2: Socialisation

> **This section will explore the following debates:**
>
> ● What is socialisation, and what are the roles of the agencies of socialisation?

GETTING YOU STARTED

The Dog Girl

From the age of three, Oxana Malaya lived with dogs, eating raw meat and scraps. When she was finally found aged eight, she was walking on all fours, barking and whining to communicate with other members of the pack. Oxana is a **feral child**, one of only about 100 known in the world.

It is understood that Oxana's alcoholic parents left her outside one night, so she crawled into a shelter where they kept dogs. No one came to look for her so she stayed where there was warmth and food, losing what toddler's language she had and learning to survive as a member of the pack.

When years later a neighbour reported that the child was living with animals, Oxana could hardly speak. Though she must have seen humans at a distance, and seems to have occasionally entered the family house like a stray, they were no longer her species: all meaningful life was with the pack.

It has been of huge and continuing interest to sociologists who believe feral children can help resolve the nature–nurture debate. Unfortunately, there is no written documentation about Oxana's physical and psychological state when found, perhaps suggesting that the authorities were not keen to record her case.

Oxana was able to learn to talk again because she had developed some speech before she was abandoned. At an orphanage school, she learned to walk upright, eat with her hands and communicate like a human being. Oxana now lives in a clinic and seems happy to help look after the cows on the clinic farm. However, it is unlikely that she will ever be able to live independently as she lacks the necessary skills to survive on her own.

Adapted from Grice, E. (2006) Cry of an enfant sauvage. *Telegraph*, 17 July.

Figure 4.11 Normal modes of socialisation (clockwise from left): with family, at work, with peers, at school, at prayer

Questions

1. What are 'feral children'?
2. Describe the ways in which Oxana differed from a normal eight-year-old child.
3. Why was she communicating in the same way as dogs?
4. What are the effects of social isolation?
5. Imagine that immediately after your birth you were raised by apes in the forest. If this happened you would lack certain social skills necessary for living in human society, such as the ability to talk a human language and the knowledge of norms such as queuing for buses. But what skills might you have gained?

2.1 Socialisation and its agencies

When thinking about socialisation you could consider how the process of socialisation continues throughout life rather than only in childhood.

Socialisation is the process by which we learn the things that make us 'fit in' with our society, such as language, norms and values, and ways of behaving appropriately in different situations. Socialisation is seen as a lifelong process. It starts at birth and ends when a person dies. Socialisation is also the process by which we acquire the beliefs, habits and skills necessary to play an appropriate role in society. The process of socialisation is learned and controlled through a number of different social institutions. These agencies of socialisation play an important role in the teaching of appropriate norms and values. For example, in the family parents may help to socialise their children into gender roles by buying them gender-specific toys. How individuals are socialised into the social constructs of age, disability, ethnicity, gender, sexuality and social class is explained in detail in Section 4 of this chapter (see page 134)

There are a number of different agencies of socialisation, though these can be broadly divided into primary and secondary agencies.

- **Primary socialisation**, which includes learning the language, gender roles and basic norms and values, largely takes place within the family. These can be formally taught, but they are most likely to be picked up informally by children imitating their parents.
- **Secondary socialisation** is a lifelong process and occurs in a wide variety of organisations, groups and settings such as school, peers, place of work and religion, among others.

4 Culture and identity

KEY SOCIOLOGISTS

Antony Giddens (1989) suggests that socialisation is not a kind of cultural programming in which the child absorbs passively the influences with which he or she comes into contact. Even the most recent newborn infant has needs and demands that affect the behaviour of those responsible for its care. Giddens suggests that the socialisation process is not passive but rather a two-way process in which both parents and children are involved.

CONTEMPORARY APPLICATION

The media's influence as an agent of socialisation is becoming increasingly more powerful than that of the family and the school. Mass media, such as newspapers, magazines, radio, internet, video games, movies, and especially television, is one form of socialisation. Television is an influence on children from a very young age and affects their social development.

KEY CONCEPT

Families socialise young children in different ways.

The family teaches the basic norms and values (see Key Concept below) through process of imitation. Children copy the behaviour of family members and learn the social roles expected of them by looking at role models in their family.

Parents may use sanctions to reinforce approved behaviour and punish behaviour defined as unacceptable. Such processes help children learn how they are expected to behave in a range of social situations. Positive sanctions include praising a child when they behave in a desirable way. When parents want to discourage inappropriate behaviour they can use negative sanctions, such as withholding phone time.

Gender roles within the family are also likely to influence a child's socialisation. If a young boy sees his father going out to work every day and being the main breadwinner than he will want to play the same role in his future.

Figure 4.12 What ideas, attitudes, norms and values do you think you have learnt through these agents of socialisation?

Social policy

Social inclusion is one of the major issues of socialisation. Minority communities and individuals from different ethnic groups and religions may feel excluded and this exclusion leads to a sense of frustration and crime among the youth of the excluded groups. In order to overcome this sense of exclusion, minority groups, and especially the young people of minority groups, have been given special support by government inclusion policies through various social services.

Every society has expectations about how its members should and should not behave. These rules of behaviour are called norms and values.

Wherever you go, expectations are placed on your behaviour. Norms are specific rules that govern human behaviour in particular situations. Examples of norms include appropriate behaviour while eating, rules of mating behaviour, and rules of behaviour in public places, among many others. Norms differ widely among societies and they can even differ from group to group or setting to setting within the same society. For example you would behave differently in church, at home or playing with friends. Norms are place-specific, and what is considered appropriate in one country may be considered inappropriate in another.

Values are beliefs that something is desirable and good, important and worthwhile. Every society has its own value system. Values are the fundamental beliefs that support the community or society and provide the general principles for human behaviour. In most societies, the influence of religion means that many values result from religious teaching. Western societies are likely to reflect values associated with liberalism and capitalism. These would include respect for individual freedom, self-discipline and hard work. Other societies, for example East Asian, may attach greater importance to collectivistic rather than individualistic commitment. Such values stress the importance of remaining loyal to your family, community and sometimes the commercial company that you work for.

Roles and status

Status means the position that someone occupies in society. This position is often a job title but many other types of positions exist: parent, cousin, relative, friend, employee and so forth. Any one individual often occupies several different statuses at the same time: someone can be a teacher, mother and wife simultaneously. Any individual occupies several statuses and thus has several roles.

Sociologists often speak of three kinds of statuses. The first type is ascribed status which is the status that someone is born with and has no control over. There are relatively few ascribed statuses; the most common ones are our biological sex, race, parents' social class and religious affiliation.

The second is achieved status, which, as the name implies, is a status you achieve at some point after birth, sometimes through your own efforts and sometimes through luck (for example, winning the lottery).

The third type is a master status. This is a status that is so important that it overrides other statuses you may hold. A physical disability often becomes a master status because, if you use a wheelchair, to take one type of disability, this confinement becomes more important than the other statuses you have. For similar reasons, gender, race and sexual orientation may also be considered master statuses as these statuses often subject women, ethnicity, and gays and lesbians, respectively, to discrimination and other problems, no matter what other statuses they may have.

Whatever its type, every status is accompanied by a role, which is the behaviour expected of someone – in fact everyone – with a certain status. Because roles are the behaviour expected of people in various statuses, they help us interact because we are familiar with the roles in the first place.

IN THE NEWS

Does letting children watch hours of TV improve academic ability?

A study conducted by researchers at the University of London suggests that the answer may be that it does. The study found that children who watch three or more hours of television a day were ahead of their peers: those who watched less than an hour a day were three months behind them. This contradicts evidence that suggests TV is dumbing down young children.

Dr Alice Sullivan, senior academic at the university's Institute of Education, and the report's lead author, said the educational value of children's television had been under-estimated, and that TV may expose some children to a broader vocabulary than they experience at home.

In tests comparing children of the same social class, regular meal times gave a six-week advantage in terms of reading and writing skills, while set bedtimes put children two months ahead. The report concluded that 'social class and in particular parents' education were the dominant factors' in determining how well children performed academically. The study also found that children whose parents had a steady, above-average income were more than a year ahead of children with unskilled or semiskilled parents.

The study included 11,000 British seven year olds who were tracked since birth in long-term project the Millennium Cohort Study. The study was instigated by politicians' claims that parenting skills were more important in determining how well children excel academically and later on in life, as opposed to the effects of their social backgrounds.

Adapted from Hall, M. (2013) Letting children watch hours of TV improves academic ability, study claims. *Telegraph*, 24 June.

Questions

1. How much can you learn from TV?
2. Is TV more educational than family?
3. What are the things that TV can teach you that your parents can not?

2.2 The role of socialisation

It is important to familiarise yourself with different theoretical perspectives and to develop an argument about the role of socialisation in society.

Functionalist

Functionalists see the socialisation process as beneficial for all of society. From a functionalist perspective, the role of the socialisation process is to integrate individuals into society as a whole. It is important that members of a society see themselves not just as individuals but also as part of a wider group. According to functionalists, socialisation is mainly concerned with transmitting the norms and values of society.

According to Talcot Parsons, socialisation ensures that most people internalise values derived from the cultural system and then operate according to them when performing their roles – mother, employee, son, neighbour etc. – within the social system. The expectations associated with these roles reflect the key values of the cultural system. Parsons believes that behaviour of individuals is powerfully shaped by the impact of the cultural system, particularly through socialisation. The society retains stability because, for a great deal of the time, individuals behave as if programmed to perform to the functional requirements of particular roles. Parsons sees family almost as a 'personality factory', moulding and shaping human identity according to one common cultural pattern. Parsons believes that the process of socialisation involves a series of adjustments in the personality system of a child as it is exposed to increasingly complex social relations (first mother–child relation, then interaction with other members of the family, then with others outside family). Parsons' view simply put is that people as social beings are no more than the values, beliefs and expectations that operate in the social systems of which we are parts. This is a classic structuralist approach which places emphasis on the extent to which social structures or systems shape human behaviour rather than the extent to which human behaviour can change or impact society.

Through socialisation children learn the content of their culture and norms that define their social roles. Individuals learn to conform to role expectations via rewards and punishment, first by family then, later, by other members of society. The individual learns to internalise the norms and values of their society through this process of socialisation. For functionalists, the family is the place that first teaches the child communication skills, appropriate behaviour and general knowledge about the society at large. Religion is a key agent of socialisation that reinforces the collective unity or social solidarity of a group.

Feminist

Feminist perspectives see the socialisation process as a way of reinforcing inequalities between genders. For example, feminists believe that education is an agent of secondary socialisation that helps to impose patriarchy. Feminists view education as a socialisation agent for gender roles, although different aspects are dealt with by different feminists. The education system reinforces the ideology that men are in authority and the 'hidden curriculum' (see page 52) contributes towards it.

Sociologists Tim Heaton and Tony Lawson (1996) argue that the 'hidden curriculum' is a major source of gender socialisation within schools. They believe that schools seem to show or have: textbooks where children are taught from an early age that males are dominant within the family; various subjects aimed at a certain gender group, for example food technology would be aimed at females, leading on to the typical role of females doing housework and cooking; sports that are segregated by gender, with boys playing rugby and cricket while girls play netball and rounders. It could be seen that the majority of teachers are female, but that the senior management positions are mainly male-dominated, although this is not the case in some schools. A number of feminists argue that what is taught in schools still creates gender inequality despite the national curriculum. Students' choice of A-levels still tends towards traditional patterns of gender segregation.

Marxist

Marxists argue that society is characterised by social inequality and class exploitation, and maintained by ruling-class ideology. This is the set of ruling-class ideas and attitudes that is passed on via the socialisation process. Marxists are more likely to emphasise the role of the education system in maintaining **social control**. From a Marxist perspective, the role of the socialisation process is to get people to accept the beliefs and values of the dominant class. All the agencies of socialisation play a part in the promotion of these beliefs and values. For example, according to Marxists religion encourages conformity and an acceptance of hierarchy. This serves the interests of the rich and powerful in society. A Marxist argument, such as that provided by Samuel Bowles and Herbert Gintis (1976), would be that schooling is the site for the instilment of values such as punctuality, discipline, obedience and diligence within the individual, qualities that are regarded by Marxists as those needed within a capitalist workforce. Thus, the 'hidden curriculum' serves to preserve the economic *status quo*.

Social action theory

Social action theory approaches place more emphasis on the way in which individuals create their own identity through interaction with others. This theory sees socialisation as a negotiated process. According to George Herbert Mead the development of self occurs during socialisation through social interaction. For him, play is important to development of self: through play children develop into social beings. Taking the role of others allows children to take into account the reactions of others. Significant others play an important role in enabling children to see how their actions generate specific social reactions.

RESEARCH IN FOCUS

The looking-glass self: how our self-image is shaped by society

Charles Cooley's (1998) theory of the looking-glass self states that a person's self grows out of a person's social interactions with others. The view of ourselves comes from the contemplation of personal qualities and impressions of how others perceive us. Actually, how we see ourselves does not come from who we really are, but rather from how we believe others see us. The looking-glass self theory has three elements. The first element is how we imagine we appear to others. The second element is the judgement we imagine that other people may be making about us, and the third element is our self-image based on the evaluations of others.

How do you know you look good today? Because when you wear your best outfit, you feel confident and happy, and thus, every time you wear your favourite outfit, everyone always tells you how good you look in it. As children we were treated in a variety of ways. If parents, relatives and other important people look at a child as smart, they will tend to raise them with certain expectations. As a consequence the child will eventually believe that they are smart. This is a process that continues when we grow up.

Cooley, C.H. (1998) *On Self and Social Organisation*. University of Chicago Press.

Postmodernist

Postmodern theorists, such as Baudrillard, Lyotard and Jameson, argue that culture and identity are much more important in the twenty-first century. They all agree that in the postmodern era there is a loss of faith in grand belief systems or **meta-narratives**. Postmodernists believe that the norms and values of our society are not transmitted through agents of socialisation in order to benefit rich businessmen. They argue that, in a postmodern society such as ours (which celebrates diversity), we as consumers choose our identity and pick up the norms and customs of our society ourselves. This is done through personal experience. Postmodernist sociologists emphasise both the shifting interpretation of 'self' to an individuals and degree of choice, whereas more traditional views see identity as being shaped in more deterministic manner, for example by class.

Check your understanding

1. How do Marxists say that ruling-class ideas and attitudes are passed on via the socialisation process?
2. Identify different ways in which socialisation reinforces inequalities between genders.
3. Explain how the hidden curriculum plays a role in socialisation.
4. Identify one weakness of the functionalist perspective on socialisation.
5. Explain the meaning of looking-glass self.

Practice questions

1. Define the term 'socialisation'.   (2 marks)
2. Outline and explain two ways in which two of the following agencies may shape the process of socialisation: family, education, mass media, religion.   (10 marks)

Read Item A then answer the question that follows.

Item A

Functionalists argue that society has certain functional prerequisites (basic needs or requirements). One of these is the need to socialise new members into the norms and values of society. Society needs everybody to internalise these norms and values, and the resulting consensus helps to create and maintain social order. For example, from a functionalist point of view, the education system may help to promote social solidarity. The socialisation process helps to guarantee the smooth functioning of society.

Applying material from Item A and your knowledge, evaluate two contrasting sociological approaches to understanding socialisation.   [20 marks]

Read Item B then answer the question that follows.

Item B

Interactionist sociologists emphasise the importance of the self. Individuals develop a self-concept, a picture of themselves, which is an important influence on the way they act. This self-concept is developed through interactions with other people and helps to shape a person's social identity.

Applying material from Item B and your knowledge, evaluate interactionist views of how social identity is shaped by interactions with others.   [20 marks]

Section 3: The self, identity and difference

> **This section will explore the following debates:**
>
> - Who am I?
> - Is identity socially constructed or socially caused?

GETTING YOU STARTED

Have a look at the following list of some of the things that might shape your identity. Pick the ones that are most relevant to your identity and explain why this is the case:

- Age
- Ethnicity
- Religion
- Class
- Gender
- Sexual orientation
- Language
- Nationality
- Location
- Dress sense or code
- A particular team or group you support
- Food or lifestyle choices e.g. veganism

Questions

1. Which of the aspects of identity in the Getting you Started box opposite are given by society (ascribed) and which are chosen (achieved)? Explain why.
2. Which groups do you share a sense of identity with and why?

Identity is a concept used by sociologists to describe the way we see ourselves in relation to other people. Through the process of socialisation we acquire social identity and develop roles for ourselves in our relations with other people. Identity is a social construction. There are different forms of identity, such as social, cultural and individual identities. Sociologists explore to what extent our identity is shaped by society and the interactions with others around us.

3.1 Who am I?

When studying social identity, you can look at any of the following: age, gender, ethnicity, class or disability.

Identity can be defined as the way we think of ourselves, how we think other people see us, and what we think others think of us. Identity means being able to work out who we are as a person. In order to understand ourselves we must also understand others and what they might think about us. Some parts of a person's identity are unique to us and other parts are shared.

Identity is a very widely used and important concept, used in many different fields including psychology, politics, society and culture. Identity is particularly important in a postmodern world that emphasises individuality. In fact, identity has become a key feature of society today, and is at the centre of many contemporary small-scale and global issues, such as wars, issues concerning individual rights, ethnic conflict, gendered identity and much more. Individual choices help to form a person's identity, but that identity is also shaped by society; Sometimes an aspect of a person's identity may be **stigmatised** by society; for example, having a disability may shape an individual's experience in society and, for some people, this disability may take on a master status.

Culture and identity are often linked but they should not be seen as being exactly the same. While our culture often establishes our sense of identity, sociologists usually separate the two concepts. Culture is seen from the macro perspective – the big picture – and identity from the micro meanings we have as individuals. In general, the link between identity and culture is that individuals and groups learn to express their identities through culture. Whatever individuals' biological inheritance may be, they learn to express their identity mainly through the cultural means available to them in the society in which they live.

3.2 Identity: socially constructed or socially caused?

The process of acquiring identity involves the recognition of both similarity and difference. During socialisation we learn to share identities and symbols with people we believe are like us. We subscribe to **collective identity** yet we also distinguish ourselves as different from others. Identity, therefore, involves the consequent defining of some people as outsiders. We may view them as deviant and collectively band against them.

Each person can have several identities: someone can be a British, South Asian, atheist, middle class and a man, all at once. In different situations members of society choose which identity is the most relevant. Of course, social conditions may limit the choices we have in our identities. Being able to rationally choose identities is an indicator of freedom. Identity also involves a certain amount of choice, in that we actively take identities. We choose our political allegiances and our degree of involvement in the community. Interpretivists would argue that the very sense of being an individual, and the way in which we are encouraged to perceive ourselves as individuals, is socially constructed rather than socially caused.

Gordon Marshall (1998) notes that there is no clear definition of identity in modern sociology, although he suggests that the term is mainly used by sociologists to refer loosely to our sense of self and one's feelings and ideas about oneself. Our sense of self is partly structured by how others see and interpret our behaviour. Sociologists note that feeling and ideas about self are partly a product of our adoption of **social identities**, which are formed when we react to **cultural expectations**.

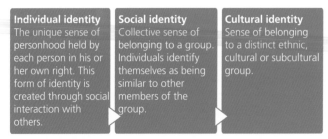

Figure 4.13 Different forms of identity

Identity is a complex, dynamic and changing aspect of an individual and the groups the individual belongs to, and can be understood both at an individual and group level. One interesting aspect of identity for sociologists is the extent to which individuals themselves can shape their own **achieved identity**, that is, the identity that is selected by an individual and the extent to which it is given through society, known as **ascribed identity** (see previous section on status, page 128).

KEY CONCEPT

Stereotype

A stereotype is an exaggerated or distorted generalisation about an entire category of people that does not acknowledge individual variation. For example, we stereotype the young, elderly, heterosexuals, homosexuals, police officers, rich and poor, male and female. People stereotype when they are unable or unwilling to obtain information about the particular individual or the group. Stereotypes form the basis for prejudice and discrimination. They generally involve members of one group that deny access to the opportunities and rewards that are available to that group. Stereotypes are learned at a young age and often remain untested, unchallenged and confused with reality throughout our life. We learn stereotypes from parents, family members, teachers, peers and the media, and they have profound affect on our behaviour and beliefs.

Different perspectives on identity

Many sociologists who adopt an action or micro approach claim that identity is negotiated by individuals. This concept of identity in present sociology allows us to see humans as active and thinking beings, rather than as passive victims or puppets of a culture which controls them.

Interactionist perspectives suggest that identity emerges partly as a result of social interaction. For example, people may deliberately present a version of themselves in public to manipulate how others see them. Some groups may have difficulty presenting a positive view of themselves because they suffer from social **stigma**. For example, people with disabilities may be labelled negatively by other members of society. Interactionist theories emphasise the importance of the self. Individuals develop a self-concept, a picture of themselves, which is an important influence on the way they act. This self-concept is developed through interactions with other people because it is based partly on how others react to the individual. This idea was developed by Cooley, who introduced the term 'looking-glass self' to describe this process (see page 129).

Structural perspectives, such as functionalism, feminism (see page 153) and Marxism, are more likely to focus on the role of social institutions or inequalities of power in shaping identity. According to Marxists and functionalists, in modern society the individual's identity is largely fixed. Marxists see our identity as stemming from our class position, while functionalists see it as a result of being socialised into shared culture.

Postmodernism argues that today's society is too complex to be understood and theorised. In today's society there are so many choices available to us in relation to how we should live our lives. Our identity is continually created and re-created through our consumption of cultural products and symbols. Bauman (1996) argues that identity no longer has a stable basis, identity has now become a matter of choice – individuals can change their identity as and when they want. Postmodernist Hobswarn notes that most identities are like 'shirts' that we choose to wear, rather than the skin we are born with. Instead of one mainstream culture we now have a variety of cultures to choose from. The dominant mainstream culture is being replaced by a wide variety of 'taste groups' and an increasing diversity of lifestyles.

> **KEY SOCIOLOGISTS**
>
> According to Stuart Hall (1992) contemporary societies are increasingly characterised by the existence of fractured identities. People no longer possess a single, unified concept of who they are. The postmodernist view is that individuals build their identity by selecting and focusing on an aspect of themselves, such as gender, ethnicity or religion, and use range of material objects to create, maintain and change their identity.

> **CONTEMPORARY APPLICATION**
>
> Identities are no longer determined or bound by factors such as class, gender or ethnicity, but can be chosen, shaped and changed by individuals through the use of cultural products including clothes, music and lifestyle.

Check your understanding

1. How do we construct our identity?
2. Explain the difference between achieved and ascribed identity.
3. What is a master status?
4. Explain how interactionist perspectives suggest that identity emerges partly as a result of social interaction.
5. Give reasons how contemporary societies are increasingly characterised by the existence of fractured identities.
6. Explain how structural perspectives (such as functionalism and Marxism) are different from interactionists in their view of identity.

Practice questions

1. Define the term 'identity'. (2 marks)
2. Outline two ways of how social identity is shaped by interactions with others. (10 marks)

Section 4: The relationship of identity to other factors

This section will explore the following debates:

- How does age affect our identity?
- How do people construct their ethnic identities?
- What is meant by ethnicity?
- What does it mean to be British?
- What impact might disability have on a person's identity?
- How might disability be perceived in Western culture?
- What does it mean to be a gendered person?
- How is sexual identity constructed?
- How does social class affect identity?

GETTING YOU STARTED

Figure 4.14 Three generations of the same family

Questions

1. Explain the main differences between different age groups.
2. What are the legal rights of each generation?
3. How do roles and statuses change as you enter each new age group?

4.1 How does age affect our identity?

If you are discussing age and identity, you could consider the life cycle and not only focus on one aspect of age, such as old age.

Age usually describes the number of years since a person's birth (although not all societies measure age in this way). In Western culture, a person's age is counted in a chronological, numerical way, beginning from their year of birth to the current point of reference or, in the case of death, until the year in which death occurred. In Western societies age is extremely important. It is used to prohibit, force or permit individuals to participate in certain activities: for example the ages at which you can buy alcohol or tobacco, drive a car, have sex, leave home, marry, join the army, vote, serve as a juror or be expected to retire, are all legally defined. People who reach 100 years of age are specially acknowledged with a message from the Queen. In other cultural traditions, particularly pre-industrial societies, chronological age may not be recognised in the same way as in the West.

Different age groups are assigned both different amounts of social status and different legal rights. However, societies range from those in which age is not particularly important to those in which it is the key structural principle. Societies institutionalise the transition from one age to another through rituals, such as **initiation rites**, which publicly signal the change from one social role to another. In the UK, people ritualise birthdays with presents and parties; 18th and 21st birthdays are significant ages at which to have special social events marking the transition to adult status. Another feature is the extent to which becoming old or being defined as 'old' is associated with a significant loss of status. As the populations of Western societies are all **ageing populations**, with a growing proportion of the population in the higher groups, this situation may change. While those defined as children have traditionally had few legal rights, this situation is being increasingly challenged.

Generation refers to reproduction; each family experiences a sequence of people passing through it. Generations are often used as metaphors for age groups in society, such as 'older generation' referring to retired people, or 'hippy generation' referring to people who were young in the 1960s. They form a **cohort**, an identifiable group whose shaping years have given them common attitudes, values and perceptions. These common experiences may lead to a common sense of identity and interest.

The roles and norms allocated to age groups create both barriers and opportunities. It is important to note that age categories are not fixed by objective criteria: they are social constructions. Society tends to locate individuals together in society on the basis of similar calendar age, so that many sociologists have argued that we need to think about our age in society based on **life course** events. The life course can be described as going through several stages. Life is both a biological and cultural journey that each person goes through at any given time and space. It allows people to see where they are in their lives and to compare where they are in relation to other people of similar and different ages. The life course is seen to be universal, to apply to all humans, and therefore features in all societies.

Childhood (5–16?)

Childhood is a distinct stage. The status differences between children and adults are emphasised and regulated in a number of ways. Children's special status is also marked out through the products and services that are provided for them – clothes, toys and games, reading materials, snack foods and fast food, playgrounds, television channels and programmes. Children are defined primarily in terms of their lack of competency and relative immaturity, compared to adults.

Youth and adulthood (16–64)

Youth is seen as a key stage of transition between the dependent and powerless stage of childhood and the independent and powerful stage of adulthood. Two key components of this transition are the move from education to employment and the move from the parental home to an independent household. During youth individuals become entitled to participate in certain adult activities, such as voting, drinking alcohol, driving, gambling and sex. Once gaining these rights, adults enter a period of full-time employment, adult responsibility and family building.

Old age (65+)

In Britain, the majority of people are no longer in paid employment by the age of 65, and are in receipt of a state pension. Old age is characterised by dependence on others. However, the institution of retirement and provision of a state pension are relatively recent developments and were not available to earlier cohorts of elderly people. Ideas about old age have changed a lot over the past decades, because of the ageing population, as people are living longer and are often healthier and more active for longer.

Different perspectives

Elderly people are now able to choose from a wide diversity of lifestyles. The postmodernist perspective suggests that the life course is becoming destructured: common social patterns determined by chronological age are becoming less critical to people's life experience. Andrew Blaikie (1999) suggests that at the end of the twentieth century we witnessed a shift towards an increasingly individualised, consumer-driven society, in which the avoidance of old age can apparently be accomplished through a range of youth-preserving techniques and lifestyles. Postmodernists argue that in contemporary British society the boundaries between age and the roles specific to age groups and generations have become increasingly blurred. Age-specific experience is declining and age itself is no longer associated with certain events and not others. For example, the elderly are now seen to be able to experience sex and have sexuality – something not generally associated with the elderly 20 years ago. There are a growing number of older couples remarrying in the twenty-first century.

Social policy

The Equality Bill, published in 2009, makes it unlawful to discriminate against someone aged 18 or over because of age when providing services or carrying out public functions. The law was created to stop age discrimination where it has negative or harmful consequences.

The recent Children and Families Act 2014 has the clear aim of protecting children and dealing with their welfare needs. This will mean changes to

---

KEY SOCIOLOGISTS

Chris Phillipson (1982) suggests that living within a capitalist economy creates particular problems for the elderly and, in particular, working-class elderly people. As capitalism is based on the notion that people must be useful to the continuation of the capitalist economy (useful for their labour power), some see the elderly as a drain on the resources of capitalism through their use of welfare provision.

CONTEMPORARY APPLICATION

The ageing of the total population in Britain is driven by two major factors: the decline in **infant mortality rates** and the general decline in **birth rates**. More people have survived into old age, but women have had fewer babies, so the subsequent cohorts are smaller. We are facing the onset of an ageing society: in the near future, dependent, elderly people may outnumber people of an age to work. This is seen to have massive implications for welfare provision and the structure of the economy. It also assumes that elderly people are dependent and offer nothing to society.

the law to give greater protection to vulnerable children, better support for children whose parents are separating, a new system to help children with special educational needs and disabilities, and help for parents to balance work and family life. The act also ensures that vital changes to the adoption system can be put into practice, meaning more children who need loving homes will be placed faster. Reforms for children in care can also be implemented, including giving them the choice to stay with their foster families until their 21st birthday.

IN THE NEWS

The Chisunga initiation ceremony of the Bemeba people of Zambia

According to study by Richards (1982) this ceremony secures the transition from a calm but unproductive girlhood to a potentially dangerous but fertile womanhood. The ceremony takes place after the girl has had her first period and after this event has itself been marked by a separate puberty rite. The puberty rite may involve ceremonial washing of the girl and isolation indoors before her return to the community. The girl then waits until it is convenient for her Chisunga ceremony to begin. The ceremony is composed of mainly individual rituals, including the physical testing of the girl through various ordeals, her social isolation as a form of ritual separation and the singing of ritual songs. The ceremony lasts for over a month and ends with the girl's change of status being marked by her social isolation. The girl is bathed, dressed in new clothes, brought out of the hut and placed on a new mat outside its door. The girl sits in silence in front of the villagers, who throw small presents on the mat. At the end of the ceremony, girls are considered ready for marriage, and a marriage ceremony often follows immediately.

Adapted from *Sociology Review*, September 1995.

Questions

1. Why do they separate girls in the Chisunga initiation ceremony?
2. Why are girls tested during this ceremony?
3. How does life for girls change after the ritual?
4. Is there a similar ceremony for girls in the UK?

Check your understanding

1. What is the life course?
2. List the major changes of the life course.
3. What does it mean when the postmodernist perspective suggests that the life course is becoming destructured?
4. Why are the elderly perceived to be a burden to society?
5. How does age define your identity?

Practice question

1. Outline and explain two ways in which an individual's social experiences may be affected/shaped by their age.

(10 marks)

IN THE NEWS

The Life in the UK Test

Figure 4.15

In November 2005 a 45-minute 'citizenship test' entitled 'Life in the UK' was introduced for those wishing to settle in Britain. The latest changes to the immigration rules came into effect on 14 May 2014. According to the Home Office these reforms make 'fundamental changes' to the system. Specifically they will 'limit the factors which draw illegal migrants to the UK and make it easier to remove those with no right to be here'. The new citizenship test for aspiring Britons is intended to place more emphasis on British history and achievements than previous versions.

Take the sample questions below and see whether you score the 75 per cent (six correct answers) necessary to pass:

1. Which landmark is a prehistoric monument which still stands in the English county of Wiltshire?
2. What flower is traditionally worn by people on Remembrance Day?
3. At her jubilee in 2012, how many years as queen did Queen Elizabeth II celebrate?
4. What is the title given to the person who chairs the debates in the House of Commons?
5. What is the name of the admiral who died in a sea battle in 1805 and has a monument in Trafalgar Square, London?
6. In 1801, a new version of the official flag of the United Kingdom was created. What is it often called?
7. The second largest party in the House of Commons is usually known by what name?
8. From what age can you be asked to serve on a jury?

Adapted from Life in the UK Test (www.gov.uk/life-in-the-uk-test).

Questions

Many citizens who were born and bred in the UK would struggle to know the answer to many of these questions. See answers to the test on page 146.
1. Would you pass the new citizenship test?
2. What were the reasons for the introduction of a citizenship test?
3. What questions should be included in it?
4. Can citizenship be tested by questions in the first place?
5. List the advantages and disadvantages of living in a multi-ethnic society.

What is meant by ethnicity?

Ethnicity is used in sociology to refer to the shared characteristics of social groups, usually based on common cultural factors. It is frequently used to describe smaller groups not originally part of the native population, who are often referred to as 'ethnic minority groups'. Members of ethnic minority groups sometimes experience a variety of social disadvantages. This may be due to prejudice or outright racial discrimination within the society where they live.

One aspect of culture that may be part of someone's identity is a subculture. In complex, diverse societies in which people have come from many different parts of the world, they often retain much of their original cultural traditions. As a result, they are likely to be part of a particular subculture in their new society. The shared cultural traits of subcultures set them apart from the rest of their society. Examples of easily identifiable subcultures in the UK include ethnic groups such as Indian, Polish, Pakistani and Somali. Members of each of these subcultures share a common identity, food tradition, dialect or language, beliefs and other cultural traits that come from their common ancestral background and experience. As the cultural differences between members of a subculture and the dominant national culture blur and eventually disappear, the subculture ceases to exist except as a group of people who claim a common ancestry.

Nationality and identity

Nationality is the legal relationship between a person and a country. It involves having rights and responsibilities attached to being a citizen of a nation state.

The concept of a nation relates, geographically, to the idea of dividing the world into various states. A state is simply an area of land that is administered by some form of national government. Nation states are usually clearly defined in terms of geographic boundaries (England, France, Croatia and so forth). Anderson (1983) introduced the concept of the 'imagined community'; people who are born and live within certain geographic boundaries have a sense of belonging to or being a part of a particular nation – people imagine themselves, for a number of reasons, to have a specific nationality.

The Populus Survey for the Searchlight Educational Trust (2011) suggests an individual's nationality, such as being British, is having a declining influence as an identity source. People no longer identify themselves as British, but are now adopting distinct English, Scottish and Welsh identities. The survey found that 39 per cent of people would rather class themselves as 'English' than 'British'.

The process of globalisation and the rise of a 'global culture' is eroding traditional national values and customs. British society is made up of a wide range of ethnic groups (Welsh, Scottish, Irish, English, Indian, Pakistani, African-Caribbean etc.) so it is difficult to define the term 'British identity'. The rise of multiculturalism in British society, some sociologists argue, created a second generation of ethnic minorities who thought of themselves as mostly but not entirely British. They said this was because they didn't feel fully accepted by the majority of white, British people. They therefore adopted a 'hybrid identity' (see later in this chapter).

In 2004 a British Social Attitudes Survey found that most people defined 'Britishness' as speaking English, holding citizenship and respecting the country's laws and institutions.

One of the major political controversies of the moment is the relationship between Britain and the European Union (EU). The argument revolves around the idea that by joining with countries such as France, Germany, Spain and so forth we are in danger of 'losing our national identity'. That is, we will gradually lose our identity as 'Britons' and, instead, become simply 'Europeans'.

The ideas of nationality (related to concepts of patriotism and national identity) have been – and continue to be – powerfully emotive cultural forms in modern societies.

KEY SOCIOLOGISTS

Hall (1992) suggests that every nation has a collection of stories, images and symbols about its shared experience, which people draw on to construct and express their national identity. National identity is formed through agencies of socialisation through which it is passed on from one generation to the next. Furthermore, national identity is reinforced through rituals and ceremonies.

Palmer (1999) suggests that national identity is promoted and maintained by heritage tourism, using historical symbols of the nation as a means of attracting tourists.

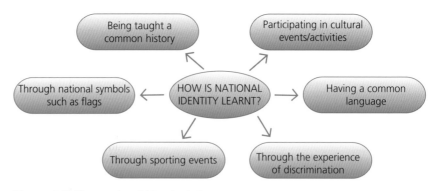

Figure 4.16 How national identity is learnt

IN THE NEWS

Should teachers promote British values?

There has been a great deal of discussion recently by politicians about the concept of 'Britishness'. This debate has taken on greater importance in the wake of certain events that seem to challenge the idea that living in Britain means we all share a common culture and set of values. One of the events that fuelled this debate is what became known as Operation Trojan Horse in Birmingham, where Muslim groups were alleged to have plotted to install governors at a number of schools. This event played out against the backdrop of the increasing diversity of Britain's population; a diversity of ethnic group, culture, faith and country of origin.

From September 2014 every school in England was required to promote British values. This means that every school in England has to tell pupils that British values are as good as or better than other people's values. The Department for Education explained that it wanted to create and enforce a clear and rigorous expectation on all schools to promote the fundamental British values of democracy, rule of law, individual liberty and mutual respect and tolerance of those with different faiths and beliefs.

It means that pupils will learn shared British values and study national identity in the UK. Prime Minister David Cameron said that values including freedom, tolerance of others, accepting personal and social responsibility, and respecting and upholding the rule of law were not optional.

Adapted from Wintour, P. (2014) David Cameron joins calls for promoting 'British values' in schools. *Guardian*, 15 June.

Questions

1. What might be the values and beliefs shared by all British citizens?
2. Can British values be taught and, if so, can they be taught in schools?
3. How would you describe your own national identity?
4. How much choice do you have in choosing your own ethnic identity?
5. Do you think schools should promote a feeling of duty to the state? Why or why not?

What does it mean to be British?

Britain is a multicultural society and is becoming more so by the year. Ethnic identity as a concept is no longer simply a matter of cultural difference. It is developing into a collective urban culture that takes elements of popular culture, such as fashion and music, and merges them with aspects of both minority and majority cultures. This hybrid culture may have positive effects on the relationship between majority and minority cultures in the UK, which has generally been characterised by suspicion, hostility and, in the case of majority culture, racism.

All of this raises a number of important questions. Do we really know what is meant by British values today? To what extent can government policies help to bring about shared values of society?

What are the new ethnic identities in the UK?

Many young British people have complex heritages. How do they construct their identities today, and what role does popular culture play? Sociological research indicates that new ethnic identities are emerging, especially among Britain's younger minority ethnic citizens.

Hybrid identities

Les Back (1996) has observed how new hybrid identities have been emerging among young people in Britain. In his study of two council estates in South London, he found that British white, black and Asian young people were trying out new cultural masks. His research showed that interracial friendships and interaction were common in and around the capital, and that this produces considerable cultural 'borrowing' and experimentation in relation to music, dress and language. This meant that white and Asian youngsters living in these areas were more likely to listen to rap and reggae music than pop and rock.

Johal and Bains (1998) reinforced the idea of hybridity in their research. They developed notion of 'dual identities', best represented by the third-generation British Asians or, as they call them, 'Brasians'. They argue that British Asians use a number of different identities depending on whom they are with and where they are. They claimed that these young people engage in a process of code switching: they may assume a more Western, white identity and behaviour when among white peers and friends in school settings and then revert to a more traditional Asian identity when at home with parents or at their place of worship. However, this behaviour at home may be subjected to social restrictions due to family pressure and cultural expectations. For example, Pakistani girls might have hidden relationships with non-Pakistani boys outside the home and without their parents' knowledge, as this kind of relationship is often regarded as unacceptable.

However, while British Asians may be more likely to construct new identities that are influenced by other cultures; as an ethnic minority in Britain they are still one of the least likely to marry outside their own ethnic group. Style might be one thing but making a life commitment across ethnic boundaries is something different.

Race and ethnic groups

Ethnicity is not the same as 'race'. Sociologists find the term 'ethnic group' more meaningful than 'race'. An ethnic group is based on shared culture rather than physical characteristics. Ethnic groups have a common language, nationality, areas of origin and customs such as food laws and dress. Victorian writers who attempted to classify people according to their size of their skulls and other various physical characteristics used the word 'race'. Their system of categorisation rested on assumption that white people were superior to all. Their supposed greater capacity for civilised behaviour was used as justification for taking control of the countries belonging to other 'races', for example, the colonialisation of Africa by Europeans. Such notions of race are linked with the desire for power over other people. Scientific research suggests that there are few distinctive genetic differences between members of what most people think of

KEY SOCIOLOGISTS

David Mason (2000) defines ethnicity as some kind of cultural distinctiveness, revolving around the belief that descent or origin and traditions are shared. Mason argues that British people see ethnicity as something other groups have. Such categorisation may lead to the construction of statements that make stereotypical and imagined assumptions about other ethnic groups.

Sometimes categorisation is use to justify the cultural superiority of the powerful group. Edward Said (1935–2003) was a Palestinian-American intellectual and literary critic who believed that romanticised representations of the Arab world lead Westerners to form caricatured views of both Islam and Muslims.

STUDY TIPS

Research about new identities highlights the highly fluid nature of ethnic identities in multicultural societies today. Ethnic identities not only change over time but can also change in relation to place and context.

KEY SOCIOLOGISTS

Sanjeev Joha (1998) suggests their ethnic identity is very important for young Muslim women. The domesticity of first-generation Asian women is in stark contrast with the educated and 'Westernised' ambitions of many young, British-Asian females today. Not only do they have to assert their rights to organise their lives, often against male and female opposition in their own communities, but they also have to work at dispelling the myths of the dominant white majority.

STUDY TIPS

You can use Johal's study to show how the experience of women in constructing their ethnic identity is much more complex than for men.

Figure 4.17 Portobello Market, London, where many cultures meet and interact.

as different races, whereas members of the same 'race' often have clear genetic differences such as blood groups and right- or left-handedness.

Different perspectives

Postmodernist perspectives have developed the idea of hybridity to refer to the mixing of two or more cultures in a pick-and-mix approach to identity creation. Taylor (1999) described this process as 'something that resembles a shopping mall where people have much greater choice about how they look, what they consume and what they believe in'. Individuals are subject to range of influences, including media, family, religion and their peers. It is important to note that sociologists face difficulties in determining how far one culture influences or is more important than the other. Ethnic cultures and identities are not fixed or characterised by obvious boundaries. Rather, the opposite is true in this fast-paced postmodern world where cultures and identities are fluid and subject to constant change.

Social policy

Ethnicity is a form of difference that can cause division and conflict in society. A multicultural society has to ensure that it is not so culturally divided. A government might try to integrate different ethnic minorities by adopting housing and education policies that ensure people from various ethnic groups mix with one another. One such example of social policy, seen as the equal rights policy, is the Race Relations Acts of 1965 and 1968, which made racial discrimination in the UK illegal in employment, housing and commercial services. The citizenship test is another example of how government is trying to integrate minority ethnic groups in the UK. Often the policies directed at integration of ethnic minorities have an emphasis on Britishness.

How has migration produced a diaspora?

During the post-Second World War industrial boom, the British government invited a select number of its Commonwealth subjects, particularly those from the Caribbean and the Indian subcontinent, to come and work in the UK. For the African-Caribbean and southern Asian families coming to settle in the UK in the 1950s and 1960s, the experience of migration had a powerful impact on their sense of identity and culture. On arrival many immigrants faced open hostility and experienced discrimination in work, housing and education. The response to racism and harsh economic conditions was a strengthening and reaffirmation of traditional forms of ethnicity and identity. It was sometimes supposed that children of migrant families might face a 'culture clash' being educated in British schools, mixing with white children, learning English and yet experiencing pressure to retain traditional customs within the migrant home and communities.

With the chain of migration, which saw other family members enter this country during the late 1960s, the various south Asian migrant communities had begun to effect a major reconstruction of the British social, cultural and political landscape. The influence of **diaspora** is now highly significant and is reflected, for example, in the popularity of world music or the interest in different styles of cooking. Another example of the impact of migration can be seen in the rising status of black working-class fashion and music within popular culture, which has an enormous influence in many parts of the world. This is partly because black populations have dispersed to so many different societies, and partly as a consequence of the global reach of the mass media, which highlights particular aspects of black style, music and fashion.

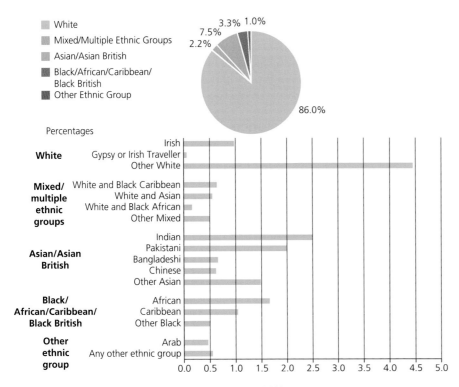

White
Mixed/Multiple Ethnic Groups
Asian/Asian British
Black/African/Caribbean/ Black British
Other Ethnic Group

3.3% 1.0%
7.5%
2.2%
86.0%

Percentages

White
- Irish
- Gypsy or Irish Traveller
- Other White

Mixed/ multiple ethnic groups
- White and Black Caribbean
- White and Asian
- White and Black African
- Other Mixed

Asian/Asian British
- Indian
- Pakistani
- Bangladeshi
- Chinese
- Other Asian

Black/ African/Caribbean/ Black British
- African
- Caribbean
- Other Black

Other ethnic group
- Arab
- Any other ethnic group

0.0 0.5 1.0 1.5 2.0 2.5 3.0 3.5 4.0 4.5 5.0

Figure 4.18 Ethnic groups, England and Wales, 2011

Census – Office for National Statistics

Questions

Use Figure 4.18 to answer these questions.
1. What is the largest ethnic group in the UK?
2. What is the largest non-white group?
3. What do you think this tells us about multi-ethnic society in the UK?
4. How has life in Britain changed as a result of immigration?

Ethnic minority

In Britain ethnicity is mainly associated with minority groups from the former British colonies of the Indian subcontinent, the Caribbean and Africa. It is problematic because it emphasises skin colour rather than common cultural characteristics. It ignores significant white ethnic groups resident in the UK such as Greek Cypriot, Jews, Irish and Polish. It also means that differences between minorities and the majority white population are exaggerated while differences between ethnic minorities are neglected.

How do people construct their ethnic identities?

Ethnic identities are created and reinforced by both primary (family) and secondary socialisation (education, media, peers, religion, etc.). The family is the most important agent of primary socialisation. This is the period of life when an individual first learns about their ethnic heritage. Tariq Modood (2005) describes this process as the first time we become aware of our ethnic culture through food, language, dress, rituals and traditions. Miri Song's (2003) study on British Chinese found that Chinese parents were very influential in reinforcing Chinese values by positively sanctioning children who choose to help out in the family business. These children were seen as more 'Chinese' as they had adopted the Chinese cultural characteristics of family solidarity and collective loyalty. A second way in which the family may shape the formation of ethnic identity is through sharing cultural characteristics such as a shared history, language, politics, religion and geographical origin.

Religion and ethnicity

People use different sources to construct their ethnicity. For example, many British Muslims perceive their religious identity as being as important as their national identity, maybe of even greater importance, although they may well prefer not to have to choose between the two.

Ethnic identities as resistance

There are number of assertive ethnic identity reactions to being denied British identity, which may act as ritual of resistance. For example, Jessica Jacobson (1997) notes that young Pakistanis see Islam as being more important in structuring their identity than cultural or national loyalties. They see Islam as overcoming national differences. Islam has a strong impact on their identity in terms of their diet, worship, dress, behaviour and everyday routines and practices.

The role of the school in the formation of ethnic identities

One way in which the school shapes ethnic identity is through the negative experience of some ethnic minority students. Máirtín Mac an Ghaill (1991) found that some teachers held racist attitudes. He found that in response to such racism pupils develop survival strategies in order to resist negative labelling. This included ethnic minority groups forming close relationships and subcultures. Mary Fuller (1994) has also documented how ethnic identity may be used to resist racial stereotyping in schools. She outlined how young black females resisted discrimination forming a close group and resisting negative non-academic labels.

The role of the media in the formation of ethnic identities

One way in which the media helps to shape ethnic identities is through allowing geographically dispersed communities to keep in touch with cultures that exist in their perceived countries of origin. For example, Marie Gillespie (2010) shows how television and video are used to recreate the culture of south Asians in Britain.

Question

Using two sources from Figure 4.19, outline and explain two ways in which individuals may be socialised into their ethnic identity.

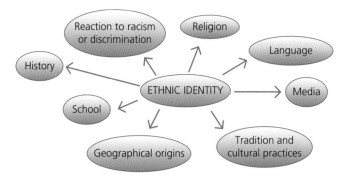

Figure 4.19 Sources from which ethnic groups may construct their identity

In Britain, the ability to make choices about self-identity may be constrained by the categorisation of others with more power and opportunities. People categorise objects in order to understand them; in a very similar way we categorise people (including ourselves) in order to understand the social environment. We use social categories such as black, white, Croatian, Christian, Jewish, student, taxi driver, and so on, because they are useful.

KEY SOCIOLOGISTS

Abercombe and Warde (2000) identify 'project identities', ethnic identities subscribed to many by young African Caribbeans that draw on ethnic history, everyday urban experience and popular culture to subvert and challenge exclusion and racism. They note that music such as gangsta rap and hip-hop is central to this type of identity because it is interpreted as a reaction to white oppression.

CONTEMPORARY APPLICATION

Teacher expectations, an ethnocentric curriculum, negative media representations, policing, the courts, immigration laws, discrimination in jobs and housing allocation, and racial violence, may all serve to negativly categorise minority identities.

Social policy

The UK has a long history of immigration. As a result it has an Immigration Act that regulates and controls immigration into the UK. The purpose of the 2014 Immigration Act is to stop migrants using public services to which they are not entitled, reduce the pull factors that draw illegal immigrants to the UK and make it easier to remove people who should not be here.

IN THE NEWS

My lost Bangladeshi identity

Momtaz Begum-Hossain reflects on her own life and growing up, as well as what ethnic identity means to her and how she learnt to become who she is now.

It's now a year since I was orphaned. [After losing my parents] I felt as though I had lost the last link to my cultural identity.

'As a child, I felt simultaneously English and Bangladeshi. I had a preference for indie music but liked going home to okra curry. At school I excelled in geography and art, and at home I made my parents proud when I recited passages aloud from the Qur'an. There were aspects of both cultures that I liked and loathed.

'At university I immersed myself in a world of miniskirts and clubbing, changing back into a floral tunic and trousers when I went home at the weekends. I closed my ears when my mum showed me yet again how to fold samosas and ignored her offers to show me how to make rice. Then, just before my 21st birthday my mother fell ill and died shortly afterwards. I felt a deep sense of loss, but having my dad around still made me feel complete. It wasn't until I lost him, too, that I realised just how privileged I had been to have two cultures in my life.

'And now they are gone I feel neither English nor Bangladeshi. I've come to realise that my parents played a major role in shaping who I am, what I believe and the decisions I've made in my life. Without their physical presence, I am less cultured.

'My father … was the upholder of religion. In his absence I find it hard to take in any new teachings on Islam: it's as though my own religious education has come to a standstill without him being there to tutor me. Hearing acquaintances talk about religion has no impact on me. We can't teach ourselves culture, no matter how desperately we try. It's something that's passed on from our parents and is far more powerful than anything we read or hear.

'Later this year I am marrying an Englishman. Yet it hasn't given me a stronger connection to the English culture I craved as a child. We are trying to organise a multicultural celebration, but without my parents being present I'm finding it difficult to put my Bangladeshi side across – I feel like a fraud making up traditions as I go along.'

Adapted from Momtaz Begum-Hossain (2010) My lost Bangladeshi identity. *Guardian*, 1 September.

Questions

1. Who taught Momtaz her ethnic identity?
2. Why is she confused about her religious and ethnic identity?
3. How did she construct her own identity?

Check your understanding

1. How important is religion in shaping ethnic identity?
2. Examine some of the ways in which people use different sources to construct their ethnicity.
3. Explain how postmodernist perspectives see hybrid identities as a new form of ethnic identity.
4. What is the role of the media in the creation of ethnic identities?
5. List three ways in which ethnic groups construct their identities.

Practice questions

1. Define the term 'diaspora'. (2 marks)
2. Outline and explain two ways in which an individual's social experiences may be shaped by ethnicity. (10 marks)

[Answers to the Life in the UK Test on page 138: 1. Stonehenge; 2. Poppy; 3. 60; 4. Speaker; 5. Nelson; 6. Union Jack; 7. the Opposition; 8. 18]

4.3 What is disability?

Disability is a concept that has been understood in different ways. Perceptions of disability have evolved significantly in recent decades. To appreciate what disability is, it is important to be aware of the different interpretations proposed by different models (see Different perspectives, page 148). How societies perceive disability has a very strong impact on the type of response that is provided on disability issues, and on the way people with disabilities are viewed.

There are different views of disability within social groups as well as between them. People with physical and psychological impairments have been represented in many ways by Western society over the years – as holy, special and, unfortunately, also in many less-respectful ways. Disabilities can affect people in different ways, even when one person has the same type of disability as another person. Some disabilities may be hidden or not easy to see. Anyone can have a disability and a disability can occur at any point in a person's life.

Disabilities are not hard and fast categories and there are different degrees of disability, as well as ability, which may overlap.

What impact might disability have on a person's identity?

Nancy Scheper-Hughes and Lock (1987) argue that as our society has become increasingly 'healthist' and body conscious, so the politically correct body has become lean, strong and physically fit. **Impairment** and ill health are no longer seen to arise from bad luck or misfortune, but from an individual's failure to live right, eat well, exercise and so on. This individualisation of health can lead to stigmatisation of any who do not conform to the professionally determined norms.

Tom Shakespeare (1994) has argued that disabled bodies are judged negatively in terms of how their bodies are seen as being inferior to those of able-bodied people. For this reason disabled people are negatively judged. The media regularly portray disability as misfortune. The disabled are frequently shown as being deserving of charity. Shakespeare suggests that our culture objectifies the disabled, which leads to the disabled being treated as things or objects, not as people. He explains the cultural values and

Physical disability	Visual disability	Hearing disability	Intellectual disability	Psychological disability	Disabling diseases
Disorders that can cause partial or total impairment of mobility, including the upper and/or lower body (walking difficulties, difficulty in maintaining or changing position, and in manipulating or performing certain actions).	People who are blind but also, in most cases, people with visual impairments. In some professions a colour-blind person can be recognised as disabled.	Total hearing loss is rare. As with visual disabilities most people with a hearing disability have 'residual hearing' for which hearing aids provide a real boost. Depending on circumstances, this disability can lead to a difficulty in expressing things verbally. A number of deaf people use sign language and also lip-reading to communicate.	Intellectual disability represents a difficulty in understanding and a limitation in the speed of mental functions in terms of comprehension, knowledge and perception. Related disabilities occur to different degrees and can be disruptive to the processes of knowledge retention, attention, communication, social and professional autonomy, emotional stability and behaviour.	People with psychological difficulties suffer from an illness that may result, at times, in disturbing behaviours for others that are different from usual habits and conventions.	Respiratory, cardiovascular, digestive and parasitic diseases (for example, diabetes, haemophilia, AIDS, cancer, hyperthyroidism) can lead to deficiencies or constraints in varying degrees. They may be temporary, permanent or progressive. Nearly half of disabling diseases have a respiratory or cardiovascular origin.

Figure 4.20 Categories of disability

cultural representations of the disabled through several key points. We live in a patriarchal masculine society that seeks perfection in the human body and is afraid of death. The disabled person might remind the able-bodied of the impermanence of life and the inevitability of body decay and death. Disability is socially constructed and it is society that disables people. The socially dominant culture shapes the way in which disability and impairment are viewed, and has contributed to the oppression of disabled people. However, what is clear from this one discussion alone is that disabled people do not have single identity.

How might disability be perceived in Western culture?

Cross-cultural examples highlight the culturally constructed nature of disability. For example, Aaron Lippman (1972) observed that in many European countries, such as Denmark and Sweden, citizens with disabilities are more accepted than in the UK. He also found that these countries provided more effective rehabilitation services. The dominant philosophy in Scandinavian countries is an acceptance of social responsibility for all members of the society, without regard for the type or degree of disabling condition. In some communities, such as Benin in Africa, children born with anomalies were seen as protected by supernatural forces. As such they were accepted in the community because they were believed to bring good luck. This shows how disability can be perceived and treated differently in different cultures and at different times.

History shows that ignorance, neglect, superstition and fear are social factors that have made the isolation of persons with disabilities worse. Most of these negative attitudes come from a lack of proper understanding of disabilities and how they affect functioning.

Figure 4.21 Paralympians at the London 2012 Olympics

KEY CONCEPT ➤ **Disablism** is an important concept to this debate. It is discriminatory, oppressive or abusive behaviour arising from the belief that disabled people are inferior to others.

Different perspectives

The social model of disability suggests that disability is caused by the way society is organised rather than by a person's impairment or difference. It looks at ways of removing barriers that restrict life choices for disabled people. Barriers are not just physical. Attitudes found in society are based on prejudice or stereotype, or disablism. When barriers are removed, disabled people can be independent and equal in society, with choice and control over their own lives. Disabled people developed the social model of disability because the traditional medical model did not explain their personal experience of disability or help to develop more inclusive ways of living.

The medical model of disability says that people are disabled by their impairments or differences. Under the medical model, these impairments or differences should be 'fixed' or changed by medical and other treatments, even when the impairment or difference does not cause pain or illness. The medical model looks at what is 'wrong' with the person, not at what the person needs. It creates low expectations and leads to people losing independence, choice and control in their own lives. In the medical model of disability, a person's functional limitations (impairments) are the root cause of any disadvantages experienced and these disadvantages can therefore only be rectified by treatment or cure.

These two models can be seen in the following example: a wheelchair user wants to get into a building with a step at the entrance. Under a social model solution, a ramp would be added to the entrance so that the wheelchair user is free to go into the building immediately. Using the medical model, there are very few solutions to help wheelchair users to climb stairs, which excludes them from many activities.

Figure 4.22 Social model of disability

KEY SOCIOLOGISTS

Kay Tisdall (1997) focuses on the culture and identity of young disabled people. She notes that young disabled people have been marginalised by the social mainstream. Traditionally they are seen as troubled, unformed, dependent, needy and other. These negative attitudes exclude them from many aspects of citizenship, which is reflected in the fact that many young homeless people and young members of the prison population have mental health problems and learning difficulties. Tisdall argues for the creation of participation, which would value the lives of young disabled people, and the creation of positive identities. The cultural diversity of young people needs to be more widely acknowledged.

CONTEMPORARY APPLICATION

Transhumanism is an international intellectual and cultural movement supporting the use of science and technology to improve human intellectual and physical characteristics. Those developing technology have always strived to match the incredible sophistication of the human body. Now electronics and hi-tech materials are replacing whole limbs and organs in a fusion of machine and human. For example, a team of researchers are trying out the first bionic eye implant in the UK, hoping to help a blind patient see for the first time. Technology is also fast becoming a way of recreating the identity of individuals.

STUDY TIPS

When discussing disability and identity, be sure to show your understanding of both models of disability. It is also important to recognise that disability has been and continues to be an oppressive experience for many. This discussion needs to recognise that some people are disabled only temporarily – do not make assumptions about all disabilities being permanent experiences.

Stereotypes attached to people with disabilities include that they:

- are seen as dependent
- cannot contribute to society
- are non-sexual
- are specially gifted
- cannot express their own preferences.

Social policy

People with disabilities have the same human rights as anyone else. The United Nations Convention on the Rights of Persons with Disabilities (CRPD) is a treaty that is binding for state parties and which reaffirms the rights of people with disabilities to fully enjoy their human rights and fundamental freedoms on an equal basis with others.

There have been some key improvements in both the socio-economic experiences of disabled people in the last 20 years, and in related government policies. The British government wants to make sure that disabled people are treated fairly in a whole range of ways. There are already laws to make sure that disabled people are treated fairly at work or in places where they learn. There are also laws to make sure they are treated fairly in other places (like shops, cinemas, theatres and banks). These laws are outlined in the Disability Discrimination Act 2005. These laws and policies may be difficult to put into practice and people with disabilities may be at a disadvantage in reporting discrimination, making them particularly vulnerable.

Bad news for disabled people – report reveals extent of media misrepresentation

A study of how media are reporting disability in the context of government spending cuts reveals a major shift in how disabled people are portrayed and the negative impact this is having on public attitudes and on disabled people themselves.

Inclusion London commissioned the Glasgow Media Group and the Strathclyde Centre for Disability Research to carry out a study to analyse the changes in the way the media is reporting disability and how it has affected public attitudes towards disabled people.

In conducting the study they compared media coverage of disability in five newspapers in 2010 and 2011. A large-scale, detailed content analysis was conducted focusing on *The Sun*, *The Mirror*, *The Express*, *The Mail* and *The Guardian*.

http://www.gla.ac.uk/media/media_214917_en.pdf

The report presents compelling evidence to suggest that there has been a notable change in the way that disability is being reported by much of the UK media. The findings clearly demonstrate that there has been a significant increase in the number of articles that focus on disability, together with a change in tone in how the articles are then being reported.

People with disabilities feel that this negative coverage is causing them to worry about their acceptance by able-bodied people and it reduces their confidence in their personal safety. There was a high level of concern among the participants about the effects of benefit changes on their quality of life and on their ability to participate in society.

The future of robotics: in a transhuman world, the disabled will be the ones without prosthetic limbs

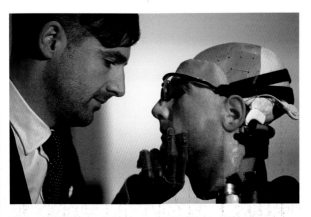

Figure 4.23 Bertolt Meyer, who is fitted with a sophisticated i-limb bionic hand

Bertolt Meyer was born with a stump where his left hand should have been, and spent his childhood wearing a hook connected to an uncomfortable harness. 'To stop it chafing my skin, I had to wear a shirt underneath it at all times. I was always sweating ... You have to understand, this is a stigma.

People think it's weird and that is how you come to perceive it. You walk around with a sense of shame.'

Things are very different now. In 2009 Meyer, a social psychologist at the University of Zurich, was fitted with a state-of-the-art bionic prosthesis. The 'i-limb', developed by Scottish company Touch Bionics, has an aluminium chassis and 24 different grip patterns. Meyer simply taps an app on his iPhone to choose from a whole new suite of movements. 'This is the first prosthesis where the aesthetics match the engineering,' he says. 'It's part of me and I'm proud of it.'

The current bionic hands can grasp and manipulate objects, but cannot feel. And cost is a huge issue: an i-limb costs £30,000, and an artificial heart £70,000. However, some scientists believe that in the future bionic hands could be engineered to improve on human performance. Nick Bostrom, head of the Future Humanity Institute, says that this will happen, but added 'we should not underestimate the technical challenges in getting to that stage.'

Since being fitted with his i-limb, Meyer says that he can now easily perform actions that he never believed would be possible for him, such as wheeling a suitcase through duty free while talking on his mobile phone: a long way on from his childhood feelings of inadequacy.

Adapted from Honigsbaum, M. (2013) The future of robotics: in a transhuman world, the disabled will be the ones without prosthetic limbs. *Observer*, 16 June.

Questions

1. Why was Bertolt ashamed when he had a hook connected to his hand?
2. Why is the i-limb so expensive?
3. What are the ways that your life is enhanced by technology? Give examples.
4. Do you think that technology will surpass our biological nature in the near future?

Check your understanding

1. What is the definition of disability?
2. Explain some of the ways in which disability identity is constructed by society.
3. Identify and briefly explain the two different models of disability.
4. Why is disability seen as oppressive for those who are affected by it?
5. How might disabled people be oppressed in their societies?
6. It is society that disables people. What does this statement mean?

Practice questions

1. Outline and explain two perspectives of disability.   [10 marks]
2. Outline and explain two stereotypes that have been attached to people with disabilities. [10 marks]

4.4 What does it mean to be a gendered person?

When discussing gender and identity, it is important to include analysis of both genders in your study and analysis.

Figure 4.24 What do these photos suggest about identity and gender?

While 'sex' refers to biological difference between males and females, 'gender' is used to describe the range of social and cultural characteristics associated with being masculine or feminine. These characteristics differ from society to society and are mostly learned through the process of socialisation. Feminist sociologists have pointed to the importance of gender as an influence on people's chances, in particular with reference to power. Although there have been many changes in the twenty-first century, such as girls outperforming boys at school, men and women still do not occupy an equal position in society. For example, women still do the majority of housework and childcare, most low-paid workers are women and, on average, women earn much less than men.

Recent studies have usefully pointed out that there is no single way of being male or female in any particular society; however, patriarchy appears to be a common theme universally in relations between men and women. There is some debate over the degree to which individuals have control over their gendered identity; many women in particular experience structural repression. For example, for many women, to resist dominant models of gender can leave an individual vulnerable to persecution or **marginalisation**. However, many individuals today can enjoy a considerable degree of agency, which can be used to create a gendered identity. In terms of how sociologists understand gender, there has also been great progress; increasingly, sociologists study gender rather than just women. Also, recent studies have also looked at the construction of masculinity.

What is the process of gender-role socialisation?

Gender refers to culturally constructed ideas about what it means to be a man or a woman in a specific place or time. There are a number of processes involved in reinforcing ideas about gender identity including socialisation, rituals and rites of passage. One question that interests many sociologists (particularly feminists) is why patriarchy (male-dominated society) appears to be almost universal. Furthermore, to what extent do biological differences between men and women shape the roles they play? The 'normal' way to behave like a man or a woman has nothing to do with reproductive organs but rather with how one is taught to act. We are socialised into learning how to act in feminine or masculine way through the instilment of gender roles. The process of **gender role** socialisation starts early in the family setting and continues through education and into the world of work, reinforced by media representations.

The differences in power between men and women may be expressed in many ways, for example through decision making, political roles, domestic roles, sexual relations and rituals. Also, agreed conventions and expectations about gender roles may not actually be carried out by individuals in practice. Gender is not a fixed marker of identity; ideas about gender are subject to change.

In many societies it is a social norm to take a binary view of gender – that is, to regard male and female as the dominant gender patterns. Feminist sociologists have been influential in showing that gender is an important aspect of identity. Women experience the social world in different ways from men in areas such as education, work and the family. Different gender roles and expectations are a feature of the socialisation process. However, some sociologists emphasise the differences between people of the same gender. There are now a variety of ways to be a woman or a man. For instance, the experience of being female has fragmented, and it varies depending on factors such as age, ethnicity and class. Furthermore, some postmodernist writers argue that people can choose their gender identity from a range of identities that are now on offer in society.

Masculinity and identity

We have to think of the masculine identity as a social construct too. The patriarchal culture also affects males. The expectations of what it means to be a man changes over time and in different societies. According to sociologist Raewyn Connell (2005) masculinity can take a variety of forms. He argues that these forms develop and change – some decline, and some become more prominent. According to him, hegemonic masculinity is the dominant form of masculinity in any society. In contemporary Western societies, white middle-class heterosexual masculinity tends to be the most dominant. It tries to maintain dominance over subordinate groups, for example, gay men. However, it is always subject to challenge, and alternative masculinities may exist alongside it without being fully accepted. In his research Connell found four groups of men in which there was evidence of a crisis in the gender order:

- The first group wish to 'live fast and die young'. These young working-class men engaged in an exaggerated form of masculinity that involved an acceptance of violence. It involved hostility towards homosexuals, but also an element of contempt towards women.
- Another group were involved in the environmental movement, which emphasises equality and co-operation rather than competitiveness. These men were consciously opposed to elements of hegemonic masculinity.
- The 'very straight gays' were homosexual but generally acted in ways that were typical of conventional masculinity. However, they tended towards more **egalitarian relationships** with partners than is typical of heterosexual hegemonic masculinity.

Gender role socialisation is done through the process of **canalisation**. This is the way in which parents channel children's interests into toys and activities that are seen as normal for that sex.

Different perspectives

Simone de Beauvoir (1972) claimed that one is not born, but rather becomes a woman. This means that females become women through a process whereby they acquire feminine characters and learn feminine behaviour. Masculinity and femininity are thought to be products of **nurture**, or how individuals are brought up. They are socially constructed. When they are born, humans are either male or female. Feminists argue that since gender is a product of society then discrimination against women is a cultural creation and can therefore be changed. Feminists believe that women are treated unfairly and they want to change society so that there is equality between women and men.

> **KEY SOCIOLOGISTS**
>
> In 1974 the feminist Sherry Ortner asked the controversial question 'Is female to male as nature is to culture?' Ortner claimed that male dominance was universal, and that because of the association between men and culture, it would be 'natural' for men to control women. Women are universally subordinated by their involvement with non-cultural activities (such as having babies, cooking and so on) which are seen as beneath cultural activities men are involved with, such as socialisation and developing ways of thinking which are seen as 'above' nature. This difference leaves men in a position to control women. However, Ortner later criticised her own theory saying that her claim that male dominance was universal was too strong.

> ◀ **KEY CONCEPT** ◉
>
> **CONTEMPORARY APPLICATION**
>
> The increased participation and success of women in paid work means that traditional notions of female identity are being abandoned. New generations of young females are becoming more assertive about their rights. There has been an increase in divorce initiated by women. More women nowadays are choosing to pursue careers instead of marriage and children. As women participate more extensively in labour markets, they also gain more recognition as significant consumers. The mass media are increasingly targeting single women. This means that women are more likely to see consumption and leisure as key factors in their identity. Being a good mother and housewife, which is the traditional domestic role, is becoming less significant.

STUDY TIPS
Make sure you have a clear understanding of the social construction of gender, and theoretical perspectives such as feminism, and are able to demonstrate this.

Social policy

In 1970 the Equal Pay Act legislated that women should be paid the same as men for doing the same or broadly similar work. In 1984 an amendment stipulated that women should get equal pay for work of equal value.

Check your understanding

1. Explain why men and women still do not occupy equal positions in society.
2. How are different gender roles and expectations taught through the socialisation process?
3. Explain what Sherry Ortner means by 'Is female to male as nature is to culture?'
4. What is canalisation?

Practice questions

1. Define the term 'gender'. (2 marks)
2. Evaluate the view that gender identities are increasingly varied in today's society. (20 marks)

4.5 How is sexual identity constructed?

When thinking about sexuality and identity, try to consider different sociological approaches to sexuality rather than just agreeing that heterosexuality is the norm and other alternative sexual identities are an anomaly.

Questions

Use the images in Figure 4.25 to answer the following questions.
1. What is sexuality?
2. What are the differences between the people in these pictures?
3. Which one is perceived as a norm in our society and why?

Figure 4.25 (L to R) A same sex couple, a transgender couple and a heterosexual couple

Sexual identity refers to a person's choice, desire and participation in the sex act. It describes how important sexual expression is in a person's life; how they choose to express that sexuality, if at all, and any preference they may have towards the type of sexual partner they choose. There is a huge variety of sexual expression (heterosexual, homosexual, bisexual and trans).

According to sociologists sexuality is socially organised and regulated. In many societies, including Britain, individuals are usually categorised as either heterosexual or homosexual on the basis of sexual preferences. However, sexuality is a much more complex concept. In sociology many theories of sexualities can be categorised as either essentialist or social constructionist.

Essentialism is the belief that our sexuality is biologically determined, fixed and beyond individual choice. According to this view, sexuality is an instinctual drive that must find an outlet. Also men's sexuality is regarded as naturally active and women's sexuality as naturally passive and submissive. While some believe that homosexuality is just an example of biological variation, many others believe it to be a pathological deviation from a healthy, heterosexual norm. In this biological perspective sex and sexuality are linked to child-producing ethics. Of course, these kinds of views can and do lead to many prejudices and discriminations.

Social constructionism views the very concept of sexual identity as a social invention. Sexual behaviour has come to represent sexual identity. There are many religious, moral and legal rules and regulations about who it is appropriate to do it with, when and how. This suggests that sexuality is shaped by society. Given that the sex act is regulated so much, and that some means of sexual satisfaction are defined as acceptable and other as deviant, sexuality should be understood as cultural process.

This section shows that sexual identity cannot simply be explained by biological terms. The ways we express our sexuality are influenced by culture and are socially constructed. In order to understand why different people have different sexual preferences we have to consider the socialisation process and the influence of cultural norms. Instead of focusing on biological factors that cause homosexuality, sociologists have explored why sexuality has become an organising principle in society. Sociologists have taken into account social, historical and political factors rather than an idea that sexuality is an individual characteristic.

How is sexuality expressed?

The way in which sexuality is expressed and organised varies widely between human societies and even individuals. **Heterosexuality** is seen as being the norm in many cultures because it is linked to biological reproduction; however, homosexual behaviour is accepted as an alternative to heterosexuality in many others. According to Nanda (1990), in India sexual variants such as Hijras are acknowledged, although they are often marginalised. Hijras are culturally defined as neither man nor woman; born as males, through a ritual surgical transformation they become an alternative third sex/gender category. Their traditional employment is to perform at marriages and after a child has been born. They sing and in return receive traditional payments of money, sweets and cloth. Hijras are seen as different at best, but inferior to homosexual men and women. They have usually been rejected by their families, and usually occupy lower caste positions.

The belief that heterosexuality is superior to other forms of sexuality is called **heteronormativity**. In some countries, known homosexuals are subject to punishment, imprisonment and even death. This view prevents same-sex couples enjoying the benefits granted to heterosexual couples and leads to **homophobia** (fear of homosexuals).

KEY CONCEPT

Kinship and family systems	Economic and social organisation	Social regulation
Rules about marriage and incest. The nature of this rule is culturally specific and defines who we mate with. This is done through incest taboos.	Changes in wider society affect sexual behaviour and attitudes. For example, in the early nineteenth century the industrial revolution disrupted the traditional way of courtship and marriage and caused an increase in births outside of marriages.	Shift from moral and religious regulation to medicine, psychology and welfare. Homosexuality is still subject to more legal constraints than heterosexuality.

Figure 4.26 Regulation of sexuality

Jeffrey Weeks (1986) argues that because sexuality is expressed in so many different ways it must be socially constructed. He rejects the essentialist view that sexuality is reduced to biological drives only because it fails to acknowledge the wide variety of ways in which sexuality can be expressed. According to him sexuality is organised and regulated through the following ways:

KEY SOCIOLOGISTS

Michael Foucault (1979) produced an account of the processes involved in the social invention of sexuality and sexual identities. He dismisses the essentialist view and claims that the very notion of sex as an underlying biological instinct which must be controlled and regulated is an invention. He argues that new ways of classifying sexual behaviour first developed from the eighteenth century as governments sought to regulate sexual behaviour and control population growth. According to Foucault, homosexuality was invented as a deviant label in the 1860s.

CONTEMPORARY APPLICATION

Developments in the scientific investigation of human biology since the nineteenth century have led to increasingly sophisticated searches for a biological basis for homosexuality; however, research has yet to produce conclusive results. Recent interest, for example, has focused on genetics, leading to the idea of a gay gene.

Despite legal changes in some countries (for example, in the UK Civil Partnership Act 2004), across the world heterosexuality retains higher value and status than homosexuality, and in many cases it is given special protection in both legal and cultural practices.

Social policy

The Civil Partnership Act 2004 enables same-sex couples to enter into a status that provides many of the same rights and responsibilities that married couples have in respect to each other and the wider community. From March 2014 same-sex couples could marry in a civil ceremony or religious ceremony where the religious organisation allows it.

Different perspectives

There are many explanations of why people's sexuality differs. Many theories have been put forward citing genetic predetermination, childhood influences and peer-pressure among other reasons. However, neither attempts to find a single cause for an individual's choice of sexual orientation nor attempts to influence or change an individual's sexuality have been successful. Like many of our other characteristics, sexuality seems to be largely a chance product of our individual nature which is then further developed by our early interactions.

STUDY TIP

Remember both the essentialist and social constructionist perspectives of sexual identity. Make sure to show an awareness of the treatment of homosexuals across different societies. Also show an awareness that sexuality and its regulation changes over time and in different places. For example, homosexuality in the UK was classified as type of mental illness until 1971.

Check your understanding

1. What is sexuality?
2. How does the essentialist perspective explain sexuality?
3. What are the ways in which sexuality is socially organised and regulated?
4. What is homophobia?
5. What is heteronormativity?

Practice question

1. Outline and explain two ways in which sociologists can contribute to our understanding of sexual identity.

(10 marks)

4.6 How does social class affect identity?

When studying social class and identity you should try include the Marxist perspective in your discussions.

Figure 4.27 (L to R) A builder, a doctor, and MP Hilary Benn

Questions

1. How do we identify social class? What indicators do we use in order to place people in different classes?
2. Choose one of the people from Figure 4.27 and explain what their lives would be like.

This section examines the way in which class and power relations influence culture and identity. Marxist theories have made a major contribution to concepts such as ideology and hegemony. These concepts point out the way in which those who have power in society play a decisive role in shaping our identities. Not all of the groups in society have an equal influence in defining cultural norms. Difference in power and wealth, in other words class, remain a significant element in the creation of our identities.

Social class refers to a group of people with similar levels of wealth, influence and status. Social class is an economic category and usually refers to the amount of economic power and material wealth an individual has. Class is one way of putting the people of a society into different groups. Class itself is most associated with the writings made by Marxist sociology. Karl Marx believed that in a capitalist society there would be ultimately just two classes: **bourgeoisie** (those who owned **means of production**) and **proletariat** (those who sell their labour to bourgeoisie). However, in our current postmodern society a more complex classification was needed to classify people into more than just two social classes.

How do we measure social classes?

It is hard to classify people into different classes but the following examples show the objective and subjective ways to measure social class.

157

Objective social class is based on the idea that people can be placed in a social class through the use of a scale and measurement device. The government uses the National Statistics Socio-Economic Classification, which creates eight different classes based on type of occupation/income (see Figure 4.28).

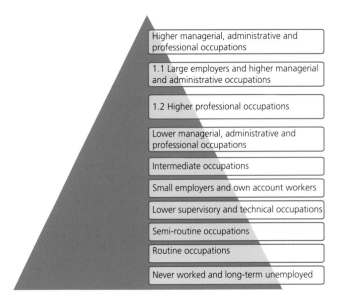

Higher managerial, administrative and professional occupations

1.1 Large employers and higher managerial and administrative occupations

1.2 Higher professional occupations

Lower managerial, administrative and professional occupations

Intermediate occupations

Small employers and own account workers

Lower supervisory and technical occupations

Semi-routine occupations

Routine occupations

Never worked and long-term unemployed

Figure 4.28 Graph of the NE-SEC scale

Adapted from the NE-SEC scale.

The measurement of social class differs in that it is based on what people think they are themselves. This may be based on their occupation but may also be based on a number of other factors, such as housing, health, education, consumption, leisure time and so on.

Mackintosh and Mooney (2000) note that one crucial way in which occupation is linked to identity is through social class. Our judgements about our own and other people's jobs usually involve the classification of ourselves and others into social classes. As Mackintosh and Mooney argue: 'Social class can provide us with a sense of belonging; it can tell us who "we" are and who "they" are and, hence, how to relate to the world around us.' There are other important sources of identity, for example age, gender, ethnicity and so on, but there is evidence that class identity based on occupation is an extremely powerful influence on how we see the world and the social relationships within it.

There is often a very close relationship between social class and life chances. The higher the class position of a child's parents, the more likely the child is to attain high educational qualifications and a well-paid, high-status job. Research conducted by Reay (1998) shows how middle-class mothers are able to influence their children's primary schooling more than working-class mothers. This research shows how demands on working-class mothers affects the time they have to devote to their children. Therefore the children miss out on important socialisation with their mothers.

Social class is an important influence on people's lives. An individual's social class has a major influence on his or her life chances (the chance of obtaining those things defined as desirable and avoiding those things defined as undesirable in any society). There are wide, measurable differences in life chances between social classes.

Is social class important?

Pete Saunders (1990) suggests that old class divisions based on work are becoming less and less relevant. For Saunders, what you do with your money is more significant than how you get it. He believes that society is now characterised by a major consumption cleavage (a split based on what people do with their money). In particular, Saunders argues that home ownership has encouraged more well-off members of the working class to focus their attention on their home and family lives. This has loosened their ties with other members of the working class. The middle class is therefore characterised by more insular values – rather than depending on others in the same economic situation as themselves, they look inwards to their own families for support.

Capital: class as culture

Pierre Bourdieu (1979) attaches as much importance to the cultural aspects of class as he does to the economic aspects. Bourdieu does not see culture and lifestyle simply as products of economic differences. Culture and lifestyle can themselves shape chances of upward social mobility and becoming better off. Bourdieu argues that there are four main sources of capital in society:

1. Economic capital consists of material goods – wealth in such forms as shares, land or property, and income from employment and other sources. Wealth can be passed on quite easily through gifts or inheritance from parents to children.
2. Cultural capital can take a number of forms. First, it includes educational qualifications. Second, it includes a knowledge and understanding of the creative and artistic aspects of culture, such as music, drama, art and cinema. In this artistic sense of culture, Bourdieu distinguishes different levels of cultural capital.
3. Social capital consists of social connections – who you know and who you are friendly with, who you can call on for help or favours.
4. Symbolic capital is similar to the concept of status and refers to 'a reputation for competence and an image of respectability and honourability'.

These different forms of capital relate to one another. For example, it may be difficult to accumulate economic capital without the possession of some cultural, social or symbolic capital. Without educational qualifications, the appropriate taste to enable you to mix in the right circles or to impress at an interview, the 'right' social contacts, or a reputation for competence, it might be difficult or impossible to get a well-paid job.

Classes can be distinguished according to both the type and the amount of capital they possess and their past history. Groups high in cultural capital but low in economic capital (such as teachers) tend to have rather different lifestyles from those with plenty of economic capital but little cultural capital (such as successful small business people).

It is generally agreed that four broad social classes exist in the UK.

The upper class

The upper class is a small class. It refers to those who are the main owners of society's wealth, for example, wealthy industrialists, landowners, traditional aristocracy. Often these people do not work for others as they have such a large amount of assets. For those of the upper class, work is not necessary to survive.

The middle class

This is a very large class. It refers to those in non-manual work. Jobs in this class don't involve heavy physical work and are usually performed in offices and involve paperwork and IT, for example secretary or teacher. However, some argue that lower levels of non-manual work such as supermarket checkout operators should be classed as working class, as their pay and working conditions are more like those of manual workers.

The working class

This is one of the largest social classes. It refers to those working in skilled, semi-skilled and unskilled manual jobs, for example, working in a factory or some form of labouring work. The working class generally enjoys fewer privileges than the middle class and has fewer life chances.

The under class

This is a small class. It refers to a group of people who are right at the bottom of the class structure. This group is allegedly work-shy, happy to live off state benefits, involved in crime and promiscuous. Their 'poverty' usually excludes them from full participation in society.

Max Weber defined **life chances** as your chances of enjoying the good things a society (wealth, good health, a university education) has to offer and of avoiding the bad things (imprisonment, dying young, homelessness) that may happen to you.

Social class influences how people operate within society. Most people are socialised into a certain class from a very early age through primary socialisation. Different ways in which individuals may be socialised into a class identity include:

- the education system
- norms and values taught by family
- class-related leisure pursuits
- the experience of work
- living in a particular community
- influence of peer group.

Different perspectives

One of the most prominent theorists on class is Karl Marx. He saw the cultural aspects as being shaped by the economic infrastructure. In Marx's theories, stratification is a key aspect of the capitalist system. All stratified societies have two major classes: a ruling class and a subject class. The ruling class owns the means of production (land, capital, machinery, etc.) and the subject class does not. The ruling class exploits the subject class. The ruling class uses the superstructure (for example, legal and political systems) to legitimate (justify) its position and prevent protests by the subject class.

In capitalist societies the main classes are the bourgeoisie (the capitalist class that owns the main means of production: capital) and the proletariat (the working class that has to sell its labour to survive). The bourgeoisie exploits the working class through the system of wage labour. Capitalists pay wages to workers, but make a surplus because they pay workers less than the value of what they produce. Marx believed that capitalism was the newest type of class society but that it would also be the last. Eventually it will be replaced by a communist society in which the means of production (land, capital, factories, machinery, etc.) will be communally owned. The transition to communism will not be straightforward because it requires revolutionary action by the proletariat. However, the bourgeoisie uses the superstructure (for example, the media, education system, and political and legal systems) to suppress the proletariat by creating false consciousness (which means that workers do not realise that they are being exploited). Eventually, though, class consciousness will develop – workers will realise that they are being exploited and will rise up to change society.

Functionalists say that the social class system helps society to run smoothly. According to functionalists, society is a meritocracy (that is, the most-able people rise to the top). They have the strong belief that the class system enables each individual to find their right place and role in society (i.e. in the division of labour). The most important positions in society must be filled by the brightest and most-able people. According to functionalism, the people who do well in terms of the common values of society will be at the top of the stratification system. High status, power and high income are rewards for conforming to society's values. Most people don't object to people in powerful positions getting extra status and rewards. According to functionalists, this shows that they support the values that underpin the system.

Postmodernists argue that class is no longer a signifier of identity or culture. Instead it is consumption that dictates lifestyle rather than class. This has been generated by media images of possible lifestyle options (and copying of designer goods by high-street shops). Postmodernist views of society include the idea that people are able to create their own identity around their leisure and consumption choices. In the past, social class was a significant factor in shaping social identity but, according to postmodernists, this is no longer the case. (See more on leisure on page 166.)

KEY SOCIOLOGISTS

Giddens and Diamond (2005) argue that social class is no longer the main source of inequality in the UK. According to them gender, age, ethnicity and disability are much more important sources of inequality. They argue that the working class is no longer important because changes in the economy have led to a dramatic decline in the number of traditional manual workers. Consequently, the working class is now only one group among many that experience economic and social deprivation.

Carter and Coleman (2006) researched planned teenage pregnancies and reported that the risk of becoming a mother was almost ten times higher for a girl from an unskilled background compared to a professional background. In interviews with 41 teenage mums, they found that many spoke of the norm of settling down early: most of their own mums were full-time mothers, many of whom had been teenage mothers themselves. For the girls in the study, family background and, in particular, poverty and disadvantage in childhood, played a major part in their decision to have a baby, which they believed would give them a new identity and purpose. Interestingly, only a minority of interviewees regretted their decision.

Murray (1994) sees the underclass as a 'new rabble' with a totally different culture. They are work-shy, prefer to live off crime and welfare, and they make irresponsible parents. This culture of dependency sees families not fending for themselves but caught in a 'poverty trap' of welfare dependency.

Brah (1999) studied a group of white skinheads in Kempton Dene in the West Midlands. He showed how the working–class identity was crucial for this group of males who worked hard at constructing a culture of whiteness. They followed the norms and values of a key leader called Adam, copying his cultural practices. The creation of a cultural comfort zone (based on social class and a shared culture/identity) is a key factor in the formation of a peer group.

CONTEMPORARY APPLICATION

The idea that identities and lifestyles are now characterised by diversity, choice, globalisation and consumption began to dominate sociological thinking to the extent that some sociologists argued that social class was no longer a subject worthy of sociological analysis.

STUDY TIPS

When discussing social class and identity, remember the difficulties in measuring social class.

Social policy

Government policies aimed at social inclusion have focused on bringing truants back to school, getting single mothers into work, reducing dole queues, and so on.

The **habitus** is 'a structured and structuring structure' consisting of a 'system of schemes generating classifiable practices and works' and 'a system of schemes of perception and appreciation (taste)' (Bourdieu, 1984). In other words, the **habitus** consists of the subjective ways in which different classes understand and perceive the world, and the sorts of tastes and preferences that they have. A habitus tends to produce specific lifestyles. For example, it will influence the sort of leisure pursuits that different classes follow, who they mix with, what sort of television programmes they watch, which newspapers (if any) they read, how highly they value education, what food they eat, and so on. Bourdieu argued that the dominant class has the power to impose its own habitus in the education system, giving those from upper-class and middle-class backgrounds an inbuilt advantage over those from working-class backgrounds.

RESEARCH IN FOCUS

A phenomenology of working-class experience

Simon Charlesworth's (1999) study is based on interviewing people from Rotherham, a town in Yorkshire suffering from the decline of traditional industries and high levels of unemployment. Rotherham has traditionally relied on mining and steel production for employment. However, the nearby pits and steelworks have both closed down, leaving what Charlesworth describes as 'devastation'. At one point Rotherham had 'the largest areas of industrial dereliction in Europe'. It suffered badly during the recessions of the 1980s, losing 8000 jobs (out of a total of 82,000) in 1981 alone. It has not benefited as much as other areas from economic revival, with rates of unemployment, poverty and long-term illness all being much higher than the national average.

Friday and Saturday nights in Rotherham town centre are a key feature of the social life of many of the residents. However, even this is not exactly uplifting. People go out drinking in the pubs and clubs largely to be seen and to pick up, or to be picked up by, others. There is little in the way of meaningful conversation. Having a good body, looking healthy and dressing well enough to appear to have some money are the criteria by which people are valued.

Charlesworth believes that the working class in towns such as Rotherham develops a distinctive habitus because of the conditions under which they live. Most of the residents of Rotherham are working class. Their lifestyle, habits, attitudes, values and physical appearance all stem from the limitations they experience as members of the working class. Charlesworth says, 'the phenomenon of class, inequality, deprivation and powerlessness must be understood through their effect on the manner in which people come to exist in the world' and through the 'states and sensibilities that are social in the sense that they are prior to a particular individual's feeling and govern the range of feelings available'. The class habitus produces 'powerful affinities and aversions to persons, things and spaces' – and this tends to reproduce classes, encouraging them to stick to things which are familiar and appealing to them.

Charlesworth, S. (1999) *A Phenomenology of Working-Class Experience*. Cambridge: Cambridge University Press.

Questions

1. Why has the closing of the mines left Rotherham devastated?
2. What do people in Rotherham do on Friday evenings?
3. What is the working-class habitus?
4. Why does Charlesworth believe that social class is still the main influence on identity in contemporary Britain?

RESEARCH IN FOCUS

Kath Woodward (2000) notes that when we meet someone for the first time we tend to ask them what they do for a living. This interaction is not just about making polite conversation. It is essentially about identity because both our sense of self and how others see us, that is, our social identity, are shaped by the judgements we make about the job we have or don't have in contrast with the jobs others have. If we perceive them to have a better job we may grow quite concerned about how they see us. For example, if we have a manual job and they have a professional job, will they treat us in a condescending manner? Should we show deference? Are we likely to establish a strong friendship or are we unlikely to move in the same social circles ever again? In other words, both our social identity (our public persona) and our self (our subjective awareness) may be strongly bound up with our employment and the income, wealth, status and lifestyle associated with it.

Chapman, S., Toffs and snobs? Upper-class identity in Britain, *Sociology Review* 11.1 (September 2011), p.30

Questions

1. Why is our job important for our identity?
2. Can people from different classes feel equal?

IN THE NEWS

Britain now has seven social classes – and working class is a dwindling breed

A BBC survey of more than 160,000 people has found that Britons can no longer be categorised into the traditional upper, middle and working classes.

The findings, presented at a British Sociological Association convention, show that at the top are a privileged 'elite' of only six per cent of the population, with savings of £140,000 or over, who are described as having 'high levels of economic, cultural and social capital'. Their 'sheer economic advantage' sets them apart from the other classes, according to Professor Mike Savage of the LSE.

At the very bottom are the so-called 'precariat', the most deprived 15 per cent of people in the UK who have only low levels of all three capitals, due to which their everyday lives are precarious.

Professor Fiona Devine of the University of Manchester said the area between the traditional working class and traditional middle class had become blurred. The report sets out the categories in between the top and bottom as:

- Traditional working class: this class scores low on all forms of the three capitals, but they are not the poorest group. The average age of this class is older than the others.
- Emergent service workers: this new class has low economic capital but has high levels of 'emerging' cultural capital and high social capital. This group are young and often found in urban areas.
- Technical middle class: this is a new, small class with high economic capital but seem less culturally engaged. They have relatively few social contacts, so are also less socially engaged.
- New affluent workers: this class has medium levels of economic capital and higher levels of cultural and social capital. They are a young and active group.
- Established middle class: members of this class have high levels of all three capitals although not as high as the elite. They are a gregarious and culturally engaged class.

The results were obtained by analysing people's income, assets, the professions of their peer group and their social activities.

Adapted from O'Brien, L. (2013) Britain now has seven social classes – and working class is a dwindling breed. *Independent*, 3 April.

Questions

1. What factors have sociologists used to identify new classes in the UK?
2. Why is there a much more blurry area between the traditional working class and traditional middle class?
4. Who are the precariats?

Check your understanding

1. Is the upper class in Britain characterised by social closure? (How easy/difficult do you think it would be for a working- or middle-class person to be accepted by the upper classes?)
2. What influence does class have on identity?
3. What is the role of class and class structure in defining cultural tastes?
4. What are the problems of using occupation to define class?
5. Which type of definition, measurement and categorisation of social class do you think is more accurate/valid (i.e. objective, subjective or both)?

Practice questions

1. Define the term 'social class'. (2 marks)
2. Assess the view that social class is no longer a significant factor in shaping social identity. (20 marks)
3. Outline and explain two ways in which individuals may be socialised into a class identity. (10 marks)

Section 5: Globalisation of culture and identity

This section will explore the following debates:

- What are the effects of globalisation on culture and identity?
- How is consumption used to form our identity?

Questions

1. Look at the clothes that you are wearing today. Where were they produced?
2. Take out some items from your bag. Where were the items in your bag produced? Where did you buy them?
3. Who made your mobile phone? Why is it made there?
4. What do you watch on TV or the internet? Where are they made?
5. What is your favourite food? Where does it come from?

GETTING YOU STARTED

Figure 4.29 What is your connection to the rest of the world?

5.1 How has globalisation affected culture and identity?

Globalisation is a very complex and many-sided phenomenon. On the one hand there is the tendency towards **homogenisation** (integration, unity and universalism). On the other hand there is the tendency for **heterogenisation** (localisation, differentiation and diversity). These processes are interconnected and represent – in reality – two faces of the same coin. It is important to understand both sides of the arguments.

This section will discuss how one of the features of the world today is a global culture in which there is increasing interconnectedness between people living in different parts of the world. Technology has allowed people to exchange ideas and information at rapid speed. Sociologists have pointed out that this global culture has both positive and negative impacts on the culture of people in the UK. Cultures and identities are shaped by changes caused by the process of globalisation.

Globalisation is the growing interdependence of societies across the world, with the spread of the same culture, consumer goods and economic interests across the globe. Globalisation is not a new process. Ancient cultures that exchanged goods and travelled in search of new land or riches have always existed, but the speed and awareness of globalisation has intensified in the past 20 years. Today's rapid growth of the transnational flows of capital, people, goods, information and culture has transformed the world. The consequences of these far-reaching economic, political, demographic and cultural changes have affected people's identities all around the world. The globalisation of culture can lead either to a trend towards common codes and practices (homogeneity) or to a situation in which many cultures interact to create a kind of imitation or mixing together, leading to a variety of hybrid identities (**heterogeneity**).

Technology created the possibility a global culture (now a reality, with products such as Disney, Coca Cola and McDonald's found everywhere on the planet). The internet, fax machines, satellites and satellite TV are removing cultural boundaries. Global entertainment companies shape the perceptions of ordinary citizens, wherever they live. Once exposed to globalisation forces, no aspect of social life, customs or economics will remain the same. Everything starts to change. In the twenty-first century, our cultural choices have global consequences. This spread of values, norms and culture tends to promote Western ideals of capitalism. As globalisation makes the world smaller, in terms of time and space, cultures that were once relatively distant and insulated from each other are increasingly coming into contact. The results of these encounters are diverse and often unpredictable.

Resistance to globalisation

Resistance to globalisation takes at least two forms. One is the reassertion of local identities. There has been considerable work on conserving and protecting small-scale cultures from extinction, preserving dying folklore and some of the threatened 1700 threatened languages (of the known 6800) in the world. Reclaiming local culture – music, songs, dance, drama, ceramics, artefacts, traditional textiles and design – is an attempt to preserve it from disintegration. It is significant that cultural disintegration often goes hand in hand with economic integration. This can mean setting up a kind of protection area around declining forms of cultural expression, to try to preserve them in living museums and at craft fairs or cultural festivals.

5.2 How is consumption used to form our identity?

The most common form of cultural conservation in our time is actually **commodification**; that is, packaging and making local cultures sellable abroad.

Thomas Hylland Eriksen (2007) uses an example from his own study in Mauritius. In Mauritius, Creole culture – the culture of the black population – has been elevated to the level of national culture. Most of the popular singers in Mauritius are Creoles. It is seen more or less as a national culture because everything in Mauritius comes from somewhere else – there are Chinese, Indian and European influences, but none of this is seen as truly Mauritian. Creole music and culture is advertised by the national airline: tourists can buy CDs with Séga music at the airport and watch Séga shows and performances at the big tourist hotels. However, Eriksen argues that in reality the Creoles are in a poor social and economic situation. The Creoles have been losing out in virtually every way since the economic transformation started in Mauritius in the mid-1980s, when it was turned into an industrial country almost overnight. Mauritius is such a small place that fairly minor changes can make a great difference, and so it became industrialised very quickly. Most Creoles were hardly affected by this at all. They just remained in the undeveloped villages, often with no tap water or electricity, with no jobs or education.

The other form of resistance is an intense reaction against economic and cultural globalisation, which people all over the world experience as a violation of their identity. The rise of **nationalism** and **fundamentalism** can be thought of as the reaction of people under pressure. We are in an age of destruction of ancient virtues such as self-denial and carefulness, the sparing use of resources, conserving elements that sustain life and reverence for habitats that have nurtured people for millennia. These virtues are replaced by the wasteful habits emerging from the societies of consumption of the West. Identity, especially for young people, seems more strongly attached to lifestyle and consumption issues these days.

An example of this resistance to globalisation can be seen in the movements in the Middle East, such as the Taliban in Afghanistan or the Islamic State in Syria, who reject all symbols of a decadent and immoral West.

Throughout history conflict has occurred around the globe between cultural groupings who seek to preserve or promote their cultural identities, very often by actively suppressing, marginalising and destroying rival cultures. At the moment in Britain there are concerns about culture and identity which lie at the heart of the notion of 'being British'. Through questions about British values or national sovereignty, and the campaign for Scottish independence, 'Britishness' is called into question. The argument that people do not have a fixed identity but a range of cultural identities indicates that cultural identities are socially constructed. This includes national identities.

Leisure opportunities

Leisure is time when one is not working or occupied (free time). The sociology of leisure is the study of how humans organise their free time. Leisure includes a broad range of activities, such as sport, tourism and the playing of games. Many people see leisure time as an opportunity to do as they please. However, it may not be as simple as that. Sociologists suggest that individual differences such as social class, gender, ethnicity and age influence the type of leisure activities we choose.

Age		Class	
Age-related legislation		Time considerations due to nature of work commitments, e.g. unsocial hours	
Different levels of responsibility, e.g. family commitments		Financial resources	
Different levels of income		Cultural expectations about what is appropriate for different social classes, e.g. cultural capital	
Different physical capabilities		The physical demands of work	
Cohort differences, e.g. familiarity with computer technology			
Ethnicity		**Gender**	
Cultural expectations/differences		Women may have less disposable income to spend on leisure activities	
Discrimination, e.g. racism		Women may have less free time because of domestic duties/dual burden	
Time considerations due to long working hours		Social expectations about what sort of leisure activities are appropriate for different genders	
Language difficulties		More funding for male leisure activities	
		Social attitudes make it easier for men to spend more time on leisure activities	
		Women subject to more social control in public spaces	

Table 4.1 Reasons why leisure choices may vary across different groups

Different perspectives

Postmodernists argue that we have freedom of choice over our leisure activities. We are free to choose who we want to be, and our choice of leisure helps to create our identity. Whatever our original class, age, gender or ethnicity, we can become who we want to be through our leisure choices. Postmodernists argue leisure has become privatised and home-centred. Leisure activities that were once available primarily outside the home, e.g. football, music and films, are now available inside the home due to technological advances such as computers and TV. Another such example is tourism. The postmodernist Lyotard (1984) rejects the idea that social characteristics – class, gender, age, ethnicity or, as he terms them, 'metanarratives' – create our identity and therefore influence and determine leisure activities. Postmodernists argue that leisure and consumption choices are now important in determining social identity. People have many more choices and are therefore able to construct any identity they wish. Through consumer and lifestyle choices, people are able to buy the image and status that they wish to present to the rest of society. This enables individuals to create and express their unique identity through their leisure choices.

However, some sociologists suggest that postmodernists exaggerate the changes that have taken place in society. They argue that factors such as social class, gender and ethnicity are still significant in shaping a person's social identity.

For example, feminists point out that social expectations concerning gender roles have an impact on the leisure opportunities and experiences of men and women. Feminists suggest that gender-role socialisation has an impact on women's expectations of leisure and that the lack of affordable childcare stops women from accessing the leisure activities of their choice. Feminists also argue that the leisure opportunities that women have are restricted by men, who expect women to choose home-based activities in their leisure time rather than going out.

From a functionalist perspective, leisure has a number of roles or functions to perform for the wider social system, including helping to bridge the gap between the individual and the wider social system. National sporting events in particular have a role to play in bringing about greater social integration.

KEY SOCIOLOGISTS

Parker (1971) argues an individual's occupation impacts their leisure time. He says there are three patterns: opposition – central life interest and escape from work; neutrality – an escape from work, relaxation; extension – a blurring between leisure and work.

Feminists McIntosh (1988) and Deem (1990) disagree. They argue that women's leisure time is more influenced by the demands of domestic labour and controlled by men than paid employment.

Questions

1. What are the most influential characteristics in the creation of your identity?
2. What are your favourite TV series?
3. How much do you follow fashion?
4. How does the internet spread Western cultural ideas to the rest of the world?
5. Can you create an identity without the influence of global cultures?

KEY SOCIOLOGISTS

The effects of globalisation on culture and identity are far reaching and many different views are expressed by sociologists in relation to these effects. Jeremy Seabrook (2004) suggests that richer Western nations now export the three D's: democracy, development and debt. According to Seabrook there are three responses to globalisation: fatalistic, welcoming and resistant response.

Kenneth Roberts (1999) argues that the functions of leisure are to:

- consolidate the social system
- act as a safety valve for the wider social system by easing stresses and strains
- imprint values such as leadership, teamwork and fair play
- provide people with an opportunity to develop their skills
- help to compensate for the unrewarding and unsatisfying aspects of life.

Pluralist theorists use the capitalist economic framework in their explanation, especially the notion that the consumer is independent and should be free to pursue their own interests. Companies try to make money from leisure, but only if they provide what the public want to buy. Leisure pursuits come and go because of the changing nature of consumer demand.

Figure 4.30 Characteristics of the globalisation of culture

Different perspectives

Postmodernists argue that society is undergoing large social and cultural changes. Important social differences are now the result of different consumption choices and more complex interactions of class, gender and ethnicity. Postmodernists suggest that we can all choose our lifestyle and create our identities. Consumerism is a key aspect of contemporary society and is seen as playing an important role in the formation of self-identity. Robert Bocock (1993) points out that consumption and our ability to buy certain products does affect all members of society. The clothes and food that we buy can be an important indicator of our social position and status. Consumption also can reflect a person's self-image or make a statement about an identity someone aspires to.

Amartya Sen (2002) claims that globalisation is not a Western imposition but rather represents hope for all humanity, and that a universal techno-scientific culture is a universal liberator. Mario Vargas Llosa (2000) argues that because much of the conflict in the world is caused by cultural differences, the sooner cultures unite into a single global culture, the better. Antony Giddens (1999) argues that for those people who follow traditional practices, tradition provides a reliable framework for action that can go largely unquestioned. However, globalisation challenges this sort of traditionalism: local cultures are increasingly exposed to new ideas and traditional ways of living come to be questioned. Day-to-day life became less and less informed by tradition for the sake of tradition.

In a cosmopolitan society individuals have much more freedom to reflect on already existing cultural practices. As a result of this, culture becomes something that is more fluid and more open to debate and adaptation by individuals than ever before in human history. Culture, according to Giddens, becomes more democratic, as more people have a greater say in how it informs their lives.

CONTEMPORARY APPLICATION

Globalisation is now recognised as a key factor influencing the lives of young people. There has been little debate in development education on the relationships between identity and living in a global society. In the UK, like many Western countries, globalisation is having a strong impact at social, economic and cultural levels; economic migration, for example, is increasing rapid social changes. These changes are also often linked to the uncertainty about identity and sense of place in the world. Young people are most directly affected by globalisation and therefore central to current debates on identity. They are experiencing globalisation on an everyday basis through employment patterns, the friendship groups they develop, their usage of the internet and wider cultural influences on their lifestyles.

STUDY TIPS

Globalisation is usually presented as a purely economic process, a vehicle for bringing material improvement to the whole world. However, in reality it can also be very destructive. Globalisation brings its own social and cultural effect. Globalisation is seen as a threat to cultures and identities in societies throughout the **global south** as a crucial to people's reactions, including resistance. In your answers make sure to explore the negative consequences of globalisation in relation to culture and identity.

Social policy

It is argued that the impact of globalisation and global ideologies on social policy can depend on the ways that local cultures reinforce or combat global ideologies and pressures. Debates about identity in response to political devolution, increase in economic migration, global terrorism and the impact of consumer culture have led to UK politicians, for example, promoting the need for a major debate on 'Britishness', which has become linked to citizenship.

Collective identities

Manuel Castells (2004) provides a model for understanding different sorts of collective identities. He refers to legitimate, resistance and project identities:

- Legitimate identities are those introduced and promoted by the dominant institutions of society as legitimate. This means conforming to the socially expected pattern of behaviour. Such identities reproduce the power relations in society. For instance, national citizenship is an identity that confers rights to its holder but also excludes non-citizens, such as immigrants, from such recognition.
- Resistance identity occurs when groups resist the devaluation or stigmatisation of an identity. These identities are those promoted by groups who feel marginalised and devalued by current social conditions. These may be groups that used to enjoy uncontested power but now feel they are losing ground. As a result, they try to resist social change. Examples are the feminist and black liberation movements. Religious fundamentalist groups promote resistance identities.
- Project identity occurs when an alternative identity is constructed, such as one for racial or gender equality. These identities are those promoted by groups trying to build new identities as well as transform the whole social structure. These include the environmentalist and feminist movements.

Figure 4.31 Greenpeace headquarters

A new global identity is the **green identity** where one's whole lifestyle, one's whole being and identity are oriented towards addressing global problems, such as global warming, extinction of species and other environmental issues, at the local and international level, for example through protesting globally and acting locally. An example is Greenpeace, a non-governmental environmental organisation with offices in over 40 countries and with an international co-ordinating body in Amsterdam, the Netherlands. Its purpose is to defend the natural world and promote peace by investigating, exposing and confronting environmental abuse, and championing environmentally responsible solutions.

'Globalisation of fat stigma': Western ideas of beauty and body size catching on in developing nations

Figure 4.32 Crystal Renn became a plus size model following a battle with anorexia. She has since lost weight again through diet and exercise.

In 2011, research from Arizona State University concluded that fat people in developing countries were feeling pressurised to conform to Western ideas of beauty and body size. The team questioned 680 adults in cities in ten countries, asking for yes or no answers to a range of statements such as 'People are overweight because they are lazy', 'Some people are fated to be obese' and 'A big woman is a beautiful woman'.

The report claimed that countries that previously celebrated larger women now have a distorted idea of what is attractive, and concludes that women are now under pressure to be very thin in order to conform to extreme ideals of beauty. In Fiji, for example – a country where a fuller figure is the norm – the influence of Australian and American culture has resulted in an unhealthy image of women's bodies.

Lead researcher Alexandra Brewis said: 'Of all the things we could be exporting to help people around the world, really negative body image and low self-esteem are not what we hope is going out with public health messaging.'

Adapted from Bates, D. (2011) 'Globalisation of fat stigma': Western ideas of beauty and body size catching on in developing nations. *Daily Mail*, 31 March.

Questions

1. What are the problems with this research?
2. Do you think Western ideas of beauty will become the norm around the world?
3. What are different ways that these ideas are spread?
4. Why are people in different cultures accepting these ideas of body images?

Does globalisation lead to homogeneity of cultures?

Figure 4.33 A McDonald's in a shopping mall in Mumbai, India

McDonald's is a very globalised institution, popular in over 100 countries and serving 30 million customers a day. George Ritzer (2007) invented the term McDonaldisation which describes a sociological phenomenon that is happening in our society. He has named a homogenisation theory after this fast-food giant. Ritzer has argued that society is becoming increasingly 'McDonaldised', whereby the principles of a company such as McDonald's are present in various elements of society and life. This is the process of rationalisation, which means the substitution of traditional rules with logically consistent rules. One of the main aspects of McDonaldisation is that any task can be rationalised. McDonaldisation is characterised by efficiency, predictability, calculability and control through non-human technology. McDonald's outlets, as a chain, share a similar look and layout. Customers are served by employees who are scripted in what they say and how they say it. There is an emphasis on numbers and quantity rather than quality – all elements of the food production are timed. Customers are even utilised in the drive for efficiency – they walk up to the counter, walk to their table and clear up after themselves. Ritzer suggests that this conception of rationalisation can be seen in every part of society and is becoming a dominant way of running the rest of the society, such as food, media, education and health care industries. Ritzer believes that McDonaldisation is leading to homogenisation and less diversity. Overall he sees it as a threat to the customs of society as a whole.

Ritzer, G. (2014) *The McDonaldization of Society* (8th edition). Thousand Oaks, California: Sage Publications.

Questions

1. What other institutions have the same process as McDonald's restaurants?
2. Do you think that companies like McDonald's destroy local cultures?
3. What is rationalisation?
4. How does McDonald's exemplify consumer culture?

Check your understanding

1. What is homogeneity?
2. Will consumer values overwhelm people's sense of community and social solidarity?
3. 'Globalisation leaves nothing untouched. It reshapes the elements of life so that they become more matched with the demands of global market.' Identify and explain three examples that would support this statement.
4. Below is a series of statements. For each one, say whether it represents a fatalistic, welcoming or resistant attitude to globalisation:
   a) Globalisation will save humanity.
   b) Globalisation is inevitable and irreversible.
   c) People should conserve local cultures and identities.
   d) Globalisation will help poor people of the world to survive.
   e) People should take action against the disruptions and destructions that are inevitably linked with globalisation.
   f) People are powerless to stop globalisation.
5. Will local cultures inevitably fall victim to this global 'consumer' culture?
6. Is it possible to combine the economic advantages of globalisation while retaining what is of cultural value: linguistic heritage, tradition and customs?
7. How is identity constructed as a result of globalisation?
8. Will English eradicate all other languages? How will this affect local cultures and their languages?

Practice questions

1. Define the term 'global culture'. (2 marks)
2. Outline three characteristics of the globalisation of culture. (6 marks)
3. Outline three characteristics of the postmodernist view of culture and/or identity. (6 marks)
4. Outline and explain two ways in which the culture of the UK is affected by global culture. (10 marks)
5. Outline three reasons why leisure activities may vary across different groups. (6 marks)
6. Assess the view that people today have freedom of choice over their leisure activities. (20 marks)

Links to other topics

This topic has links to:

- Chapter 2 Education, section 2.2 How class, gender and ethnicity affect education
- Chapter 5 Family, section 3 Roles and relationships within the family
- Chapter 6 Health, section 1.7 Social model of health and section 4.1 How is mental health labelled and stigmatised?

Families and households

Understanding the specification

AQA specification	How the specification is covered in this chapter
• The relationship of the family to the social structure and social change, with particular reference to the economy and to state policies	**Section 1** • What is the family? • What is the role of the family for the individual and society? • What is the relationship between the state and the family?
• Changing patterns of marriage, cohabitation, separation, divorce, childbearing and the life course, including the sociology of personal life, and the diversity of contemporary family and household structures	**Section 2** • What is the nature and extent of changes in family structures and households?
• Gender roles, domestic labour and **power relationships** within the family in contemporary society	**Section 3** How have roles and relationships changed in the family? • The sociology of the personal life • How has the domestic division of labour changed? • How have personal relationships changed? • What changes have occurred in parenting and childbearing?
• The nature of childhood, and changes in the status of children in the family and society	**Section 4** • How has childhood changed? • What are the different views on the experience of childhood today?
• Demographic trends in the UK since 1900: birth rates, death rates, family size, life expectancy, ageing population, and migration and globalisation	**Section 5** • What are the key demographic changes in the UK since 1900? • What are the causes and consequences of changing birth, death and fertility rates? • How has migration affected the family?

Section 1: The family in society

This section will explore the following debates:

- What is the family?
- What is the role of the family for the individual and society?
- What is the relationship between the state and the family?

Questions

1. What role might the family play for the individual and for society?
2. What are the positive functions of the family, and what negative consequences might there be for individual members?
3. How might the family be important in preparing children for later life and work?

GETTING YOU STARTED

Figure 5.1 Families

1.1 What is the family?

When studying the family, you will learn to explain what a complex and contested task defining 'a family' is. You will become critical of traditional sociological definitions of the nuclear family as the 'norm' and learn to suggest ways in which the family has changed and how this might affect the kinds of definitions that might be developed today.

This section explores some of the key relationships around which people organise their lives. The family has been and continues to be a very important institution in society for carrying out important functions such as socialising the young. As such, sociologists are interested in understanding the changing role that the family plays for the individual and for society. Some sociologists, such as functionalists, argue that the family is beneficial while others, such as Marxists and feminists claim that the family is negative and damaging, or that it perpetuates inequalities in society.

Defining family and households

Given the complex selection of family structures and relationships that are now possible, defining the family today presents a challenge for sociologists. In the past, functionalist sociologists claimed that the **nuclear family** was the basic and central family structure, that is, two generations living together with biologically related children, headed by a heterosexual couple living under one roof. Today such definitions are clearly challenged by the wide variety of alternative family structures that exist. A household is different from a family as it can include individuals living alone, for example as a result of choice, bereavement or being divorced. Alternatively, a household can refer to group of people living together without necessarily being related, married or committed to each other.

Murdock (1949), a functionalist, claimed that the nuclear family is a universal feature in all societies. His definition was: 'a social group characterised by common residence, economic co-operation and reproduction. It includes adults of both sexes, at least two of whom maintain a socially approved sexual relationship, and one or more children, own or adopted, of the sexually cohabiting couple'.

A broader and more inclusive definition of **the family** might be: a group of people related by kinship ties, relations of blood, marriage, civil partnership or adoption. Note that this definition includes two or more people who are committed to supporting each other in some way, for example through economic, emotional or practical support. Remember that a family can function without necessarily living together under the same roof.

Social policy

Think about the way in which government laws and policies have affected the family. Which kinds of family are seen as desirable and which are not? What role does the state play in policing and regulating family life?

Evaluation

Defining the family is complex and challenging given the rapid changes that have occurred in society and within relationships over the past few decades. These changes reflect broader social changes, in particular the transition from a modern society to a postmodern society. Therefore sociologists need to consider new forms of defining family life as well as recognising that many people today are choosing to live alone. This does not necessarily mean that the family is declining in importance, rather that the family and relationships might be taking different forms that need to be understood using different concepts.

1.2 What is the role of the family?

If you are exploring the role or function of the family, you could include a range of sociological perspectives and consider the way that the family functions for the individual family member as well as the role that the family plays in wider society, for example supporting other institutions.

As mentioned earlier in the chapter, changes in the nature and structure of the family reflect changes in wider society. This is because the family is very much connected with other institutions in society in a whole range of ways. For example, the way that children are brought up affects their experience of education. These changes have been explained by sociologists in a number of different ways, known as theoretical perspectives.

Some of these theories were developed during a period of time known as modernity, and they reflect the ideas and views of that period. Some sociologists claim that this period of time has now ended and that we live in a postmodern era, which means that the family needs to be understood through a postmodern perspective. In brief, the 'modern' family was typically nuclear (two generation, heterosexual married couple with one or more children) in structure, and was stable, with clearly defined gender roles. Typically, women would have cared for the children and stayed at home, taking responsibility for domestic work, while the man would have provided for the family. In postmodern society the family is far less stable and rather than there being one dominant family structure, there are a whole array of different family

STUDY TIPS

Make sure that you know the difference between a household and a family. Understand the definition of a nuclear family and the problems with using this definition to describe different kinds of families in contemporary society. As you work through this section, be aware of the different types of family and households that now exist.

CONTEMPORARY APPLICATION

Defining the family is a huge challenge for sociologists, especially in the context of the increased movement of people or migration that occurs in society today as a result of global processes. Sociologists need to consider the impact of increasing ethnic diversity when defining the family, as well as considering how cross-cultural differences might affect the way that families are regulated by the state.

structures, roles and relationships. This shift from modern to postmodern family life is summarised in Table 5.1 below.

Functionalist theories reflect the attitudes and assumptions of the modern era in which they were developed. Functionalism is a **consensus theory** which regards the family as being positive for both the individual and for wider society. Marxists take a conflict view of the family, arguing that it functions to maintain and reinforce capitalism, while feminists regard the family as a way in which gender inequalities are reproduced, as they reflect patriarchal ideology.

Postmodernists, such as Ulrich Beck (1992), argue that there is no such thing as the family today; instead people can make a range of decisions about the kinds of relationships and family structures that they prefer as individuals. They claim that there is less social pressure on people to conform to expected norms of what is considered appropriate or acceptable. Postmodernists do not regard the family today as positive or negative; rather, they reflect on some of the changes that have occurred. Some postmodernists argue that greater choice and individualism has resulted in greater risk or instability within the family, however.

An alternative way of understanding family life, known as Life Course Analysis, has emerged recently and focuses on the meanings given to particular life choices, events and decisions. Hareven (1978) argues that by understanding what family members see as important, sociologists avoid imposing their own bias on what issues are relevant in studying the family. This approach also has the advantage of not only exploring the family structure but revealing a deeper understanding of gender, roles, relationships and change.

Characteristic	Modern family	Postmodern family
Approximate dates	1900–1970s	1980s to today
Family structure	Nuclear (two-generation family, heterosexual couple, married with one or more children)	Diverse: nuclear, single-parent families, cohabiting couples and families, homosexual families, co-parenting, reconstituted families, beanpole families, lone-person households, LATS, **empty nest** families, class and ethnic diversity, extended families
Roles within the family	Traditional, expressive and instrumental roles, the development of the housewife role	Negotiated, dual-worker families, dual burden, gender scripts, egalitarian
Relationships	Stability: formal, distant, based on women's economic dependence on men, **empty shell** marriage	Instability and choice: closer and deeper, **confluent love** (Giddens), greater individualism
Role of extended family	Less important, nuclear family more geographically and socially mobile, family wage	Grandparents living longer and playing more of a role in their grandchildren's lives as both parents are likely to work
How are children perceived?	Separate, increasingly valued, closer relationships between parents and children	Different views on the experience of childhood, child-centred society/children at greater risk, children and parents share leisure time
Role of the state	Structural differentiation	Increasing involvement of the state, although to different degrees according to the specific political party in power
Role of religion	Religion important in shaping attitudes towards relationships and family life	**Secularisation** means that religion has less influence on family life

Table 5.1 A summary of the characteristics of the modern family and the postmodern family

Functionalism

Durkheim states that the family plays an important role in creating **value consensus**, which refers to the shared ideas about what is considered important. Durkheim argues that the family is central to the process of integrating individuals into society so that society functions positively. Durkheim also argues that the family plays an important role in developing social solidarity (where people feel that they are bound together as part of a group) and a collective conscience (where people have a strong sense of being part of society).

Parsons (1951), another functionalist, claims that over time the family has become more and more specialised, resulting in it carrying out two main roles. The first of these is primary socialisation, where children are encouraged to internalise the norms and values of society; the second role is stabilisation of adult personalities. This means that adults use the family as a source of comfort and support. Functionalists often claim that the different roles within the family are an extension of the biological roles of the man and woman in having children. In other words, they claim that women taking on the expressive role (the caregiving female role) is 'natural' while men taking on the role of provider, working outside the home, is also 'natural'.

Clearly functionalists take a very positive view of family life, which has been criticised for ignoring problems that occur within families, such as domestic violence, abuse and conflict. Many sociologists argue that this theory is no longer applicable to contemporary society due to the changes in family structure, roles and relationships. Feminists are critical of the assumptions that functionalists often make with regards to women being 'naturally' predisposed to taking the caring, housewife role.

The New Right

Sometimes known as political functionalism, the New Right are a group of politicians, sociologists and researchers who argue that the nuclear family and traditional, conservative values are very important. They claim that men and women should take conventional roles in the family, with the woman being responsible for childcare and housework while the man should be the breadwinner. They argue that if the nuclear family breaks down then children will not be adequately socialised. They claim that children need two parents in order to be brought up successfully and warn against **single-parent families** which they believe lack strong male role models for young boys and can lead to delinquency and antisocial behaviour. New Right thinkers stress the importance of individuals taking responsibility for their children. They claim that the state should not be responsible for supporting families with benefits. They have concerns over the growing number of individuals who lack a work ethic and have become reliant on state benefits (welfare dependency), known as the underclass (Murray 1984).

Feminists strongly criticise New Right thinkers, claiming that conservative values in the family are oppressive to women. Others criticise the New Right, claiming that state benefits are important and necessary. Many argue that alternatives to the nuclear family are not only adequate for raising children but also preferable and beneficial.

Marxists claim that the family is simply a way to maintain and reinforce a set of ideas which in turn maintain capitalist society. Marx went as far as suggesting that women in capitalist families are **commodities**, owned by men, like property. Friedrich Engels, another Marxist, argued that the family, in particular marriage and inheritance rules, ensured the ruling class stayed powerful and wealthy as the wealth of capitalism passed through the male line to the son – **primogeniture**. Engels claimed that marriage within a **monogamous nuclear family** was a way to ensure that wealth was kept in certain families, thus

STUDY TIPS

You may be asked to explore the role or function of the family from one particular theoretical perspective or from a range of perspectives. Make sure that you also understand broader arguments which suggest that there has been a shift from modern attitudes to more contemporary postmodern ideas about the family. You may also be expected to identify the difference between ways that the family functions for the individual and also for society.

KEY SOCIOLOGISTS

The poststructuralist Foucault (1975) suggests that to understand the family it is better to explore ways in which the family is observed, checked and regulated by the state (government). He suggested that the family is regularly monitored, for example, by health visitors and teachers. Foucault argued that this knowledge about individuals within families is part of a power relationship between the state and the individual.

KEY SOCIOLOGISTS

The feminist postmodernist Stacey (1997) argues that the increased choice in family life has particularly benefitted women. Stacey challenges the idea that the nuclear family is necessary in order for children to be raised successfully, and she argues that diversity in family structures is going to continue to be the norm.

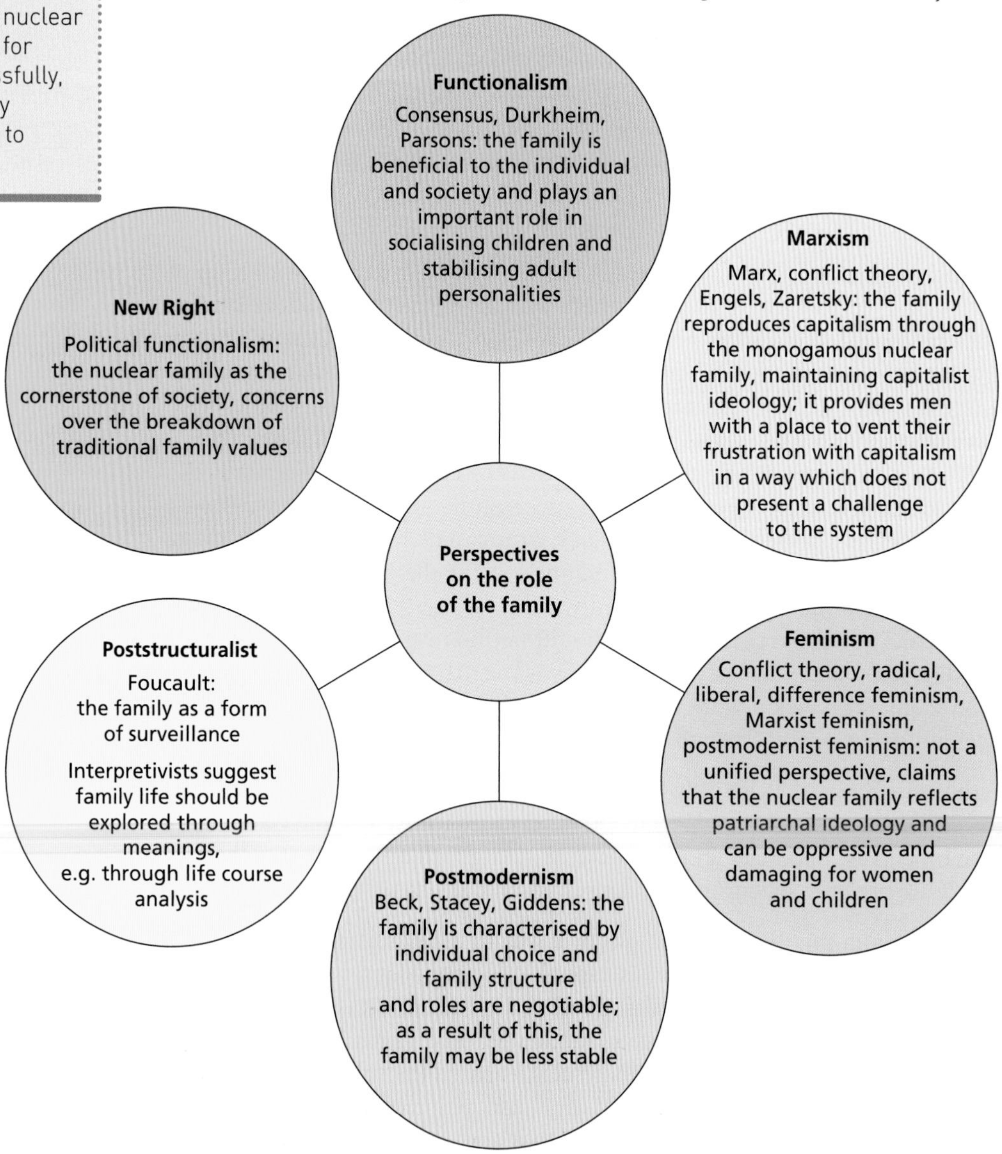

maintaining the power of the wealthy few. The Marxist Zaretsky (1986) argues that the family supports capitalism by providing unpaid labour, reproducing a labour force and being a **unit of consumption**. Zaretsky also claims that the family cushions the pressures of capitalism, allowing individuals to express their frustrations with capitalism in non-threatening ways. He argues that this makes it less likely that the working class would unite and challenge inequalities.

Feminism

Feminism is not a unified perspective and different kinds of feminists take slightly different views on the extent of patriarchy (male dominance) in the family, as well as having different views on solutions to the oppression of women. Figure 5.2 gives more detail on some of the different forms of feminism. Feminists all claim, however, that family life can be and has been far more beneficial to men than women, and that the family is central in the process of gendered socialisation. As well as this, many feminists argue that women take an unfair proportion of the mundane and repetitive housework tasks, as well as taking responsibility for the emotional well-being of family members. They also claim that women have little control or power in relation to decision making, money and other areas of family life. At worst, some feminists argue that it is inevitable that women will experience abuse and exploitation in the family.

Functionalism
Consensus, Durkheim, Parsons: the family is beneficial to the individual and society and plays an important role in socialising children and stabilising adult personalities

Marxism
Marx, conflict theory, Engels, Zaretsky: the family reproduces capitalism through the monogamous nuclear family, maintaining capitalist ideology; it provides men with a place to vent their frustration with capitalism in a way which does not present a challenge to the system

New Right
Political functionalism: the nuclear family as the cornerstone of society, concerns over the breakdown of traditional family values

Perspectives on the role of the family

Poststructuralist
Foucault: the family as a form of surveillance

Interpretivists suggest family life should be explored through meanings, e.g. through life course analysis

Feminism
Conflict theory, radical, liberal, difference feminism, Marxist feminism, postmodernist feminism: not a unified perspective, claims that the nuclear family reflects patriarchal ideology and can be oppressive and damaging for women and children

Postmodernism
Beck, Stacey, Giddens: the family is characterised by individual choice and family structure and roles are negotiable; as a result of this, the family may be less stable

Figure 5.2 A summary of key perspectives on the family

1.3 Feminism: what is the impact of family life on women?

Marxist feminists	Radical feminists	Difference feminism	Liberal feminists
Women are dually oppressed by patriarchy and capitalist ideology. Both systems oppress women for the benefit of men. Families within capitalism require women to be a source of unpaid domestic work to ensure that the man can go to work. Women are also exploited in that they are expected to provide outlets for all the frustration and anger that their husbands experience at work and therefore prevent them from rebelling against their employers. Silvia Federici (2012) argues that many women are now forced into productive and reproductive labour, resulting in a 'double day'.	Radical feminists such as Christine Delphy and Diana Leonard (1992) argued that inequalities in the home are the result of the way that relationships in families allow men to control women. These inequalities in power relations relate to decision making and also control of finances, both of which advantage men. As well as this, radical feminists claim that men benefit from women taking responsibility for the mundane and repetitive tasks such as housework as well as emotional work (where women care for family members and put other people's feelings before their own). This suggests that women experience subordination and oppression while they cater to the needs of their husband – emotionally, sexually, physically – and spend their time raising the children at whatever cost to their own paid work or interests. Radical feminists suggest that major changes are needed in society to improve the position of women.	Offers an interesting, more recent interpretation of the experiences of women in the family. Difference feminists, such as Linda Nicholson (1997) and Cheshire Calhoun (1997), have criticised the other types of feminists for failing to take into consideration the fact that women in different types of households experience family life differently. They claim that it is wrong to claim that all women are exploited in the same way in all types of families. Difference feminists argue that many factors shape the experience that women have of family life. Such factors are social class, race, sexual orientation (lesbian or heterosexual couples) and family structure (nuclear family, extended family, single-parent families and so on).	Liberal feminists such as Ann Oakley are optimistic about greater equality between men and women within the family. They claim that equality between men and women is slowly occurring through a shift in attitudes along with legal changes. Liberal feminists stress the importance of women being socialised and educated so that they have the right and freedom to choose a career, a family role or a combination of the two.

Table 5.2 A summary of feminist theories of the family

STUDY TIP

Students should look up the key terms and key concepts in the glossary at the back of this book for a full definition of the terms which they should be able to understand and explain.

Evaluation

Functionalism	• Ignores negative aspects of the family such as domestic violence. • Many functionalist views of the family may not be relevant to contemporary society.
Feminism	• Highlights the ways in which the family reflects and maintains patriarchal ideology. Research into family life has led to policy and law changes as well as changes in attitudes. • Women in families still experience oppression and a 'dual burden'. Women continue to take responsibility for family life, domestic work as well as paid work. • Women do have greater freedom and choice in family life today according to some; relationships are becoming more equal. Some feminists assume that all women share similar experiences of family life.
Marxism	• The family creates and perpetuates capitalist ideology so that the needs of the economy can be met. This theory highlights the role of the family in relation to other institutions such as education and the economy. • Class may be less relevant in our understanding of the family today while other factors may now be more relevant, for example, ethnicity. • This perspective does not take into account the way that people today may have greater agency in deciding how they themselves choose to construct their family life.
Postmodernism	• It is no longer possible to understand the family though traditional structural theories. Postmodern theorists claim that the family is a product of individual choices and, therefore, family diversity is central. • This perspective highlights the way in which increased choices benefit women and yet, at the same time, result in greater instability in family structures. • This theory does not take into account the influence of structural forces in shaping family life, such as gender and class.
Foucault	• Argues that the family is to be understood as a way in which the state can observe and control individuals through regular surveillance of family life. • The family is not always successfully controlled through the state, for example, there are many examples of the state not intervening in child neglect cases.
Life course analysis	• This approach argues that the family should be understood by understanding the meanings behind practices and decisions. • This theory might be criticised for ignoring the influence of structural forces in shaping people's decision-making process.

Figure 5.3 An evaluation of theoretical perspectives

1.4 What is the relationship between the state and the family?

If you are discussing the relationship between the state and the family then you could explore a range of social policies and their effects on the family. These social policies relate to a range of different areas of family life, for example, marriage, divorce and cohabitation through to parenting, the care of the elderly and much more. It is important to understand that social policies are key to shaping attitudes about what is and what is not acceptable and desirable in family life.

IN THE NEWS

Coalition spending cuts are hitting women 'three times as hard' as men ... and there's worse to come

Consecutive budgets by George Osborne have hit women far harder than men, according to House of Commons library research. Changes to working tax credits have seen some couples lose more than £75 a year.

The shadow home secretary and minister for women and equalities said: 'Since the election they have had many opportunities to change their policies and show that they understand the challenges that women face in their lives. Each time they have failed.'

Female workers in the public sector have been hit the hardest by the austerity measures.

The Child Poverty Action Group said mothers with small children have suffered most from the government cuts, adding that women are more likely to be affected by public sector job losses and more likely to be hit by cuts in welfare benefits. 'It's difficult to see how the government can meet its promise to be the most family-friendly government in history if it carries on being so unfriendly to women.'

Adapted from the *Daily Mail*, 31 March 2012, Paul Milligan.

CONTEMPORARY APPLICATION

A fourth wave of feminism has recently developed consisting of a group of feminists who, using the internet and new forms of social media, voice their concerns about different types of sexism. This has enabled women to have a platform and voice from which they can gain support and hope to encourage change. This has been a particularly useful way to challenge assumptions about the roles within the home as well as elsewhere.

STUDY TIPS

You will need to be able to compare and contrast different perspectives on the family. You will also be expected to offer strengths and weaknesses for each perspective in relation to the family.

Questions

1. Why have these Coalition government policies (see article) hit women harder than men?
2. What message do Coalition policies send to women who work?
3. How might some Coalition policies affect poorer children?

In this section we examine the role that the state or government has in shaping family life. The decisions made by politicians tend to reflect consensus views, in other words, views that are held by many people within society. It is important to remember that the government itself changes according to which political party is in power, as each government has particular views about what is desirable in terms of family structures, roles and relationships. In general, Conservative governments favour traditional views of family life over alternative family structures, while Labour governments tend to be more tolerant and supportive of alternatives to the nuclear family. Some of these differences are highlighted beneath. This section also explores the unintended effects of the policies on the attitudes, roles, relationships and structures in family life.

Which state policies have affected the family?

The government began to develop policies that relate to the family in the late nineteenth and early twentieth century. This coincided with the development of the welfare state. Since then the government has played an important role in shaping ideas about what are considered to be appropriate family arrangements.

Sociological studies play a key role in providing evidence that draws attention to social problems relating to family life. For example, recent research (such as Barter *et al*, 2009) revealed that domestic violence among teenage relationships is a growing concern, which led to policies such as a media campaign to try to inform and support young people. As such there is and has always been a strong relationship between sociology and social policy.

As well examining the policies that have been developed, it is also worth noting where policies are not developed; this can reveal a lot about the way a particular government feels about a particular family issue. For example, not introducing laws that benefit married couples, such as tax breaks for married couples, suggests to everyone that cohabitation is an acceptable alternative to marriage.

What is a social policy?

A social policy is a plan or course of action put into place by a government in an attempt to solve a particular social problem. Social policies are generated in response to social problems, which are identified by sociologists' research, national statistics or data collected by various groups such as governmental departments or non-governmental organisations. Sometimes policies are created by politicians who want to send particular messages about what they see as desirable (or not) in family life. These views vary over time, however; simply put these views fall on the political spectrum outlined in Figure 5.4.

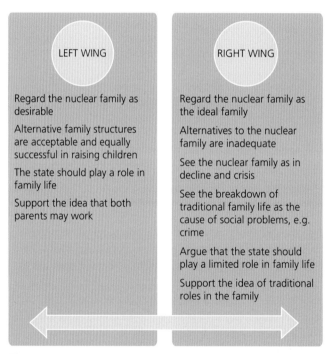

Figure 5.4 Left- and right-wing views on the family

Law or policy	Effect on the family/attitudes towards family life
1942 The Beveridge Report	This report led to the development of the welfare state, a set of policies which included National Insurance – money that is deducted from people's wages that helps pay for people's welfare as well as the National Health Service, which offers free health care to everyone.
	This was a significant report as it was the first to really make family welfare a state issue. It had the effect of reducing poverty and improving the health of some of the poorest and most vulnerable individuals and families in society.
1969 Divorce Reform Act (came into effect January 1971)	This law led to a significant increase to the number of divorces. The divorce rate increased massively from 58,239 in 1970 to 119,025 in 1972. It allowed couples to divorce after they had been separated for two years (or five years if only one of them wanted a divorce). A marriage could be ended if it had irretrievably broken down, and neither partner no longer had to prove 'fault'. This act allowed individuals to leave marriages that were simply unhappy, which provided greater choice for men and women in relationships.
Sex Discrimination Act 1975	This act was developed to make discrimination illegal on the grounds of sex. It also made discrimination on the grounds of marital status illegal. This sent a very clear message about the importance of gender equality in both the public and private spheres.
Equal Pay Act 1970	This act made it illegal to discriminate against men or women on the grounds of their sex in relation to pay. Despite the act coming into force men are still often paid more than women when doing the same job. Despite this, the Equal Pay Act was important in sending a message to women that they were legally entitled to equal pay, even if in reality this was not necessarily practised.
1991 Rape became illegal in marriage	This act was relatively recent, however it attempted to make women especially feel as if the state could intervene in private-sphere issues such as marital rape. In actual fact rape within marriage continues to be very difficult to prove and, as such, very few cases go to court. However, the message to men and women was clear; such behaviour is unacceptable.
Civil Partnership Act (2004) and Gay Marriage Act (2014)	Highly controversial, these acts represented the recognition of homosexual marriage as a positive alternative to heterosexual relationships. This was an important shift from the state labelling homosexuality as a crime (homosexuality was only decriminalised in 1967) to regarding homosexual parents as having the same rights and roles as heterosexual couples. It included recognition of homosexual parents as being suitable for raising children successfully, representing a huge shift in social attitudes.

Table 5.3 Some key social policies that had a significant effect on family life

Political views on the family

There are three key eras of social policy which you will be expected to understand. The first of these is the Conservative government (1979–1997).

Conservative (New Right) government (1979–1997)

The policies developed in this era reflect the general desire of right-wing politicians, sometimes known as New Right politicians, to reinforce the importance of the nuclear family and conservative attitudes towards family life, which they believe were (and are) under threat. This was achieved through a range of policies that were coupled with an attack on alternatives to the nuclear family in the right-wing media. These family policies were coupled with policies in education that gave parents greater choice in an attempt to drive up standards (see more in Chapter 3). At the same time, housing policies underwent significant changes, with the sale of many council homes, meaning many more homes became privately owned. As house prices have risen significantly, this has meant that many poorer people are unable to afford to own their own homes. Here are some key family policies of the Conservative government of 1979–1997:

- Many benefits were cut back in an attempt to encourage individuals, particularly fathers, to become more responsible for their children and families. Single-parent benefits, for example, were cut in an attempt to discourage alternative family structures.
- The Child Support Agency was set up in an attempt to make fathers pay maintenance for their children and discourage people from having children outside marriage. In fact the CSA was very expensive and ineffective.

- The New Right failed to introduce free/reduced-cost childcare to women as well as making assumptions about women staying at home with the children. This reinforced the idea that they favoured traditional roles, with men going to work and women looking after the children.
- Providing people who were married with tax and welfare benefits. This acted as an incentive for people to marry. It also suggested that alternatives to marriage, such as cohabitation, single parents and homosexual couples (who at the time could not get married), were regarded as less desirable.
- Privatising care for the elderly put poorer families in a position of responsibility for elderly relatives, meaning that women were likely to take responsibility for their care, further reinforcing the idea of traditional gender roles.

Evaluation

Many Conservative government policies were criticised by feminists who argued that such policies were counter to improving gender equality. New Right policies were also criticised for 'blaming the victim', in other words, blaming single-parent families for societal problems such as antisocial behaviour. Many single-parent families are, in fact, headed by working parents who do not rely on benefits as the main source of their income. Many sociologists and politicians argue that the family policies developed by the New Right in fact increased inequalities and poverty.

New Labour Policies (1997–2010)

New Labour were the first government to really address the massive changes that were occurring in family structure as well as changes to the contribution that men and women were making to the family in the context of women's increased participation in paid work (Lewis, 2007). New Labour regarded family policy as important, so it is no surprise that they created a new ministerial role, Minister for Children, in 2003.

Furthermore, in 2007 New Labour formed the Department for Children, Schools and Families. They also prioritised education and introduced policies intended to make sure that children from poorer backgrounds were prepared for school, such as Sure Start, as well as specific educational policies designed to assist students from poorer backgrounds. New Labour recognised that in most cases both parents work, and they introduced policies to help women return to work after having children, as well as helping with childcare costs. In terms of housing, New Labour invested funds in improving social housing and set ambitious targets for building affordable housing.

In terms of specific family policies, rather than regarding single parents as a moral problem New Labour introduced policies that supported them, for example helping single parents with childcare so that they could gain qualifications or retrain and return to work. New Labour also introduced:

- More generous maternity leave and pay, and paternity leave. This sent a clear message of support and acceptance that both parents are likely to work, and also recognised the increasing role that many fathers play in their children's life.
- Free childcare for two and a half year olds. Once again this helped parents with the cost of childcare, making it easier for them to return to work. This policy was also developed in an attempt to help children from a range of backgrounds access preschool care so that they were ready for their education, in an attempt to give all children an equal chance of doing well in school.
- Flexible working arrangements for parents.
- The New Deal (1998), which helped **lone parents** enter into paid work after having children by helping with the cost of childcare and training or education.
- Help for the elderly, such as the winter fuel payment, which was intended to help the elderly with their heating costs and, as a result, reduce health issues.

- The Adoption and Children Act (2002), which enables same-sex couples to adopt. This signals very clearly that same-sex couples are acceptable as an alternative to traditional heterosexual couples in raising children. The act also made sure that children's needs should be considered and taken into account.

Evaluation

Many people welcomed New Labour's range of family-friendly policies. Some have suggested that they reflected the large proportion of women in ministerial positions in the government at the time, as well as the fact that Tony Blair, the prime minister, had young children himself when he was in office. However, critics such as the New Right suggested that New Labour intervened too much in family life, arguing that this results in a **nanny state** where individuals rely on what they see as the overly generous benefits the government gives rather than people taking responsibility for themselves and their families.

Coalition government policies (2010–2015)

The Coalition government was formed by the Conservative and Liberal Democrat parties and continued many of the ideas developed by the New Right. The Prime Minister David Cameron highlighted his own concerns about the breakdown of traditional family values leading to 'Broken Britain'. In terms of housing, the government introduced some help for those trying to buy a house for the first time as well as injecting cash into house-building projects. The Coalition government also sought to make significant changes to education, increasing parental choice and cutting back many policies designed to help children from poorer backgrounds as part of their general strategy of reducing state spending.

Interestingly, the Deputy Prime Minister Nick Clegg, leader of the Liberal Democrat Party, was promoting policies such as the increase in paternity benefits, which appears to very much support the idea that gender roles are becoming more equal and shared, acknowledging the increasing role that fathers play in their children's lives. Meanwhile, Cameron continued to promote policies that suggest that he regards the nuclear family, with traditional gender roles, as desirable and ideal. Some of their policies include:

- The reintroduction of the married persons' tax allowance. Cut by New Labour, this policy clearly indicates a preference and adds an incentive for marriage over cohabitation.
- Legal Aid budget cut substantially. Legal Aid enables people on low incomes to access free legal advice. By being cut, it is argued that some vulnerable groups, such as women who have no incomes of their own, will be unable to access legal advice when they most need it, for example if they experience domestic violence.
- Child Benefit became means tested. This significant move meant that what had been a universal benefit for all parents was cut for people earning above a specific threshold. This change suggests that those with higher incomes should take responsibility for the costs of their children themselves, without help from the government.
- Plans to tackle children's exposure to adult content on the internet and other media.
- The scaling back or cutting of benefits, which are replaced by a new benefit called universal credit, designed as a way of making people earn more through working rather than claiming benefits. This was intended to reduce welfare dependency.
- Troubled Families programme (2011), designed to help families who have problems and cause problems to the community around them, putting high costs on the public sector. They claim to do this by working alongside local authorities to get children back into school, reduce youth crime and antisocial behaviour.

KEY SOCIOLOGISTS

Donzelot (1997) argues that family policy reflects the views of the powerful in government who use it as a form of surveillance over individuals and families. Donzelot argues that policies are applied in very different ways according to if someone is middle class or working class, arguing that the policies benefit the middle class. Health visitors, social workers, doctors and other key agents, according to Donzelot, ensure that family life occurs in the ways that the government sees as being appropriate.

KEY SOCIOLOGISTS

Murray (1984) argues that an overgenerous welfare state leads a 'culture of dependency' whereby individuals no longer take responsibility for their own income. His views are very similar to those of the New Right, who argue that the state should reduce benefits and ensure that individuals work and take care of their children themselves, rather than rely on benefits.

Leonard (in Zimmerman, 2001) argues that government policies all reflect a strong preference for the ideology of the nuclear family, with a strong emphasis on the role of women as nurturing and children as subordinated. Leonard argues that family policy encourages individuals to focus on work and consumption, making sure that ideas about traditional gender roles are reinforced.

Evaluation

The Coalition government has come under attack from many who claim that their family policies fail to support alternatives to the nuclear family or, at worst, regard the alternatives to the nuclear family as inferior or inadequate for raising children. Given that such a high proportion of families today are no longer nuclear, these policies are not regarded as reflecting the experiences of family life for many people. Feminists and others have argued that Coalition family policies have hit women hardest, resulting in greater hardship for women and their children in many cases. As the Coalition government attempted to cut back benefits in general, it is the poorest and most vulnerable groups who have been most negatively affected, thus, according to some, widening the gap between the rich and the poor.

CONTEMPORARY APPLICATION

Consider the recent focus of the Coalition government on 'troubled families'. Think about what kinds of family are considered to be troubled and think about why they are being focused on.

STUDY TIPS

Social policy relates to every part of the families topic as policies form and, at the same time, reflect family structures and ideas. Therefore make sure you include relevant policies in family and household essays. Make sure that you also have an awareness of the different ideas about family life that governments have.

Check your understanding

1. Explain the difference between a household and a family.
2. Describe some of the differences between modern and postmodern families.
3. What is meant by 'instrumental' and 'expressive' roles in the family?
4. How, according to Marxists, does the family support the economy?
5. What does 'patriarchal ideology' mean?
6. How is life course analysis a different approach to understanding family life?
7. Which perspectives regard the nuclear family as ideal and which argue that family diversity is positive/desirable?

Practice questions

1. Assess two ways in which social policies have shaped family life. (10 marks)

Read Item A then answer the question that follows.

Item A

Marxists take a conflict view of society and argue that the main role of the family is to reinforce and maintain capitalism. Others, however, disagree and take a more positive view the role of the family, both for the individual and society.

Assess the view that the main role of the family is to reinforce and maintain capitalism. (20 marks)

Item B

Social policies have greatly shaped family life over the past 40 years. For example, there have been policies to increase equality between men and women. Policies have had a number of intended and unintended effects on family structures as well as the roles and relationships in families.

Applying material from Item B analyse two ways in which policies encourage the nuclear family. (10 marks)

Section 2: The changing nature of family structures

When considering family structure or changes in the family you could discuss the nature and extent of family diversity that exists today. This includes exploring the different types of families and households that have emerged or reduced over the past 40 years, offering both causes and consequences as well as describing sociological views on these changes. It is also worth considering the influence of social policies on family diversity.

This section will explore the following debates:

● What is the nature and extent of changes in family structures?

GETTING YOU STARTED

	1961	1971	1981	1991	2001	2011
One person (%)	12	18	22	27	29	29
Two people (%)	30	32	32	34	35	35
Three people (%)	23	19	17	16	16	16
Four people (%)	19	17	18	16	14	13
Five people (%)	9	8	7	5	5	4
Six or more people (%)	7	6	4	2	2	2
Average household size (number of people)	3.1	2.9	2.7	2.5	2.4	2.4

Office for National Statistics

Table 5.4 Households by size in Great Britain

Questions

1. What has happened to the average size of households since 1961?
2. Give three reasons for the trends.
3. How do you think these changes have affected the type of relationships and the roles that people have in the family?
4. What do you think will happen to households size in the future? Why?

188

IN THE NEWS

	Percentages					
	1961	**1971**	**1981**	**1991**	**2001**	**2011**
One-person households	12	18	22	27	29	29
One-family households						
Couple						
No children	26	27	26	28	29	28
1–2 dependent children	30	26	25	20	19	18
3 or more dependent children	8	9	6	5	4	3
Non-dependent children only	10	8	8	8	6	6
Lone parent						
Dependent children	2	3	5	6	7	7
Non-dependent children only	4	4	4	4	3	3
Two or more unrelated adults	5	4	5	3	3	4
Multi-family households	3	1	1	1	1	1
All households						
(=100%) (millions)	16.3	18.6	20.2	22.4	23.9	25.5

Table 5.5 Households by type in Great Britain

Office for National Statistics, Statistical bulletin, 2012

Questions

1. Identify which types of households and families have increased and which have decreased.
2. Suggest reasons for these changes.

2.1 How have family structures changed?

In this section we examine the nature and extent of changes in the size and shape of the family along with a discussion of the causes and consequences.

The symmetrical nuclear family

Sociologists such as Young and Willmott (1973) and Chester (1985) claimed that the most common family structure in modern society was the nuclear family. In their classic study, Willmott and Young argue that the **extended family** is playing much less of a role in day-to-day life. The **symmetrical family**, they claim, arose as a result of society becoming fully industrialised, which also resulted in husbands and wives having a greater amount of leisure time to spend together, which is largely spent around the home. Willmott and Young claim that relationships between husbands and wives have become closer and more equal (more on this view and criticisms of it later) and that there is much more sharing of tasks within the home. Some sociologists, such as Chester, have argued that the nuclear family continues to remain dominant; even if people do not spend all of their lives in a nuclear family, they still aspire to them. However, there is much evidence to suggest that the nuclear family is being replaced with alternative family structures.

Many of the changes in recent years to family structures are a result of the fact that many women now work, meaning that they are often financially independent, giving them greater choices about family life. As we have seen, family structures are also affected by the kinds of policies that the government introduces. There have been a variety of responses to the changes in family structure from sociologists, academics and policy makers, with some, such as feminists, regarding these changes as generally positive while others, such as the New Right, seeing the changes as a sign of **moral decay**. In this section we will explore the key areas of change within family structures.

Probably one of the most significant trends over the past 40 years has been the massive increase in divorce, which has led to a whole range of changes, not only in the structure of the family but also in attitudes towards marriage and relationships. Today, 42 per cent of all marriages end in divorce. Divorce means the legal termination of a marriage and is not the only form of ending a relationship. There is also **separation** of couples who are either married or simply in a relationship and, less frequently, empty shell marriages where couples live separate lives and are married in legal terms only.

Another significant trend in recent years has been the changing number of children that women have. This is more complex than it first appears. Sociologists are interested in which women are having children and when.

One useful way to remember the various forms of family diversity that have emerged is the acronym CLOGS based on the ideas of Rapoport and Rapoport (1982) as shown in Figure 5.5.

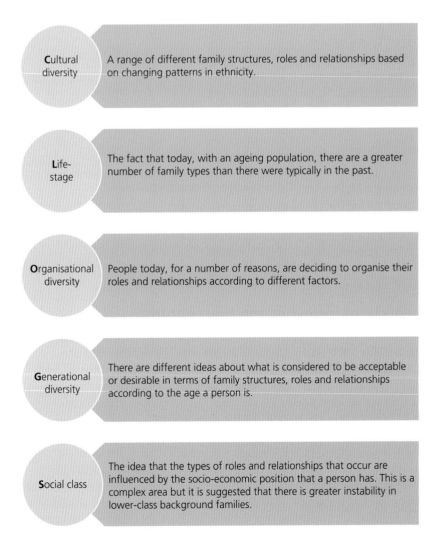

Cultural diversity — A range of different family structures, roles and relationships based on changing patterns in ethnicity.

Life-stage — The fact that today, with an ageing population, there are a greater number of family types than there were typically in the past.

Organisational diversity — People today, for a number of reasons, are deciding to organise their roles and relationships according to different factors.

Generational diversity — There are different ideas about what is considered to be acceptable or desirable in terms of family structures, roles and relationships according to the age a person is.

Social class — The idea that the types of roles and relationships that occur are influenced by the socio-economic position that a person has. This is a complex area but it is suggested that there is greater instability in lower-class background families.

Figure 5.5 Types of family diversity

Type of family	Definition
Household	Either one person living alone or a group of people who live at the same address and share living arrangements – bills, meals, chores, etc.
Family	A group of people related by kinship ties – relations of blood, marriage, civil partnership or adoption.
Nuclear family	A two-generation family with two heterosexual adults and their dependent children – own or adopted. A traditional (or conventional) nuclear family is one in which the parents are married and the gender roles are segregated, e.g. female housewife and male breadwinner.
Extended family	Two or more generations of family members with additions beyond the nuclear family. Horizontal means of the same generation (aunties and uncles/cousins) and vertical means grandparents are included. The classic extended family are kin who live in the same household or close proximity; the modified extended family are kin who are geographically dispersed but maintain regular contact via technology.
Beanpole family	Multi-generational family (three or more generations) but few people in each generation due to increased life expectancy; grandparents play an important role in the care of grandchildren/great-grandchildren.
Matrifocal family	Female-headed families, no adult male. African-Caribbean families have a high proportion of matrifocal families (50 per cent).
Patriarchal family	A male-headed, male-dominated family.
Same-sex family	Families headed by lesbian or gay couples, with or without children.
Single-parent household	Families headed by one adult; over 90 per cent are of these are headed by women.
Living apart together (LAT)	**Living apart together** – families or couples who do not live together, usually for work reasons.
Cohabiting couples	Couples who live together but are not married.
Empty shell relationship	A couple living together but not emotionally committed to one another.
Empty nest family	A family where the children have left home and it is just the parent/s at home.
Single/lone-person household	A person living alone through choice, divorce or bereavement.
Reconstituted families (sometimes known as the blended family)	A family where one or more of the partners brings children from another relationship, commonly referred to as a step-family.
Symmetrical family	A nuclear family with joint conjugal roles; husband/wife or cohabiting couples share domestic labour, childcare and leisure activities; the relationship is egalitarian (more equal).
Neo-conventional family	A contemporary version of the nuclear family where both parents work and share the domestic work. Parents may be cohabiting or married, and the children are their biological or adopted offspring.

Table 5.6 A summary of different types of family

The growth of lone-person households

According to the Office for National Statistics (ONS), there were 26.4 million households in the UK in 2013. Of these, 29 per cent consisted of only one person. There are a number of reasons for living alone including divorce, death of a partner or spouse, choice or separation. Given the wide range of reasons, it is no surprise that lone-person households represent one of the fastest-growing household types in the UK. Living alone is costly, as there is no one to share costs with, so this increase is also a reflection of the increased affluence (or increase in wealth and living standards) in today's society. For example, in the past women were usually financially reliant on their husbands, but today, because most women work, they have much greater financial independence and are able to support themselves. This also means that women are able to choose to live alone. Feminists might argue that living alone through choice offers women a way of escaping or avoiding patriarchal relationships.

Another reason for living alone is divorce, and the steadily increasing divorce rates mean that people often find they are living alone between relationships. As people now live longer, elderly people may outlive their spouses and live alone. This presents some challenges as elderly people may experience poverty and ill health and need support from the state and their families.

The increase of cohabitation

According to the ONS, the number of opposite-sex couples living together with and without children has increased significantly, from 2.2 million in 2003 to 2.9 million in 2013. The number of dependent children living in opposite-sex cohabiting couple families rose from 1.4 million to 1.9 million over the same period. This is a significant development, suggesting that marriage is not necessarily the only family arrangement for long-term stable relationships.

Sociologists have different views on cohabitation. Some regard the increase in cohabitation as a positive sign that couples are choosing their partner carefully and living with them before they marry. Alternatively, some regard **cohabitating couples** as being less constrained by typical male and female roles, suggesting that it might lead to greater negotiation and equality between couples. Others, such as New Right thinkers, argue that cohabitation is less stable and long term than marriage and is therefore contributing to the breakdown of traditional families.

RESEARCH IN FOCUS

Ben Wilson and Rachel Stuchbury (2010) carried out a longitudinal study using a sample of adults who were in a partnership (married or cohabiting) in the 1991 census of England and Wales, and then explored whether these individuals were living with the same partner in 2001. Marital partnerships were found to be more stable. Of adults aged 16 to 54, around four in five adults (82 per cent) that were married in 1991 were living with the same partner in 2001. The equivalent figure for adults cohabiting in 1991 was around three in five (61 per cent), of whom around two-thirds (of those remaining with the same partner) had converted their cohabitation to a marriage by 2001. Long-running partnership stability was also found to vary according to the socio-economic (class) backgrounds of these individuals.

Wilson, B., Stuchbury, R., *Population trends*, 139 Spring 2010

Questions

1. What kind of research method was used in this study?
2. According to the results of this research, are cohabiting couples as stable as marriages?
3. What other factors affect the stability of relationships?

The growth of same-sex families

It is estimated that between 5 and 7 per cent of the population are homosexual. Therefore it is no surprise that attitudes towards same-sex relationships have changed; in general there is much greater tolerance. This shift is remarkable (see below for a brief timeline) and due to great efforts made by organisations such as Stonewall. These changes are reflected in state policies, which now include extending marriage rights to same-sex couples. This trend is of great interest to sociologists who are interested in investigating the types of patterns in roles and relationships that exist between same-sex couples (more on this later). The latest ONS statistics reveal that 7037 civil partnerships were formed in the UK in 2012, an increase of 3.6 per cent since 2011. The Civil Partnership Act 2004 came into force on 5 December 2005 and enabled same-sex couples to obtain legal recognition of their relationship. The Government Equalities Office originally estimated that there would be between 11,000 and 22,000 civil partners in Great Britain by 2010, but there were actually over 79,000 people in civil partnerships at the start of 2010.

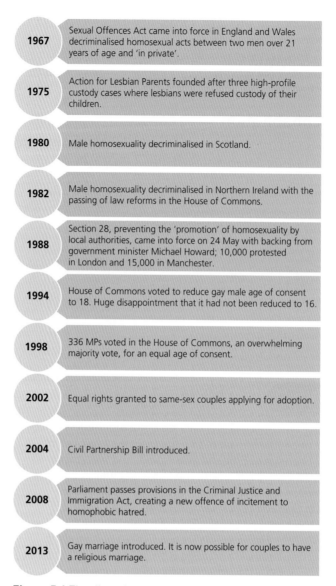

1967	Sexual Offences Act came into force in England and Wales decriminalised homosexual acts between two men over 21 years of age and 'in private'.
1975	Action for Lesbian Parents founded after three high-profile custody cases where lesbians were refused custody of their children.
1980	Male homosexuality decriminalised in Scotland.
1982	Male homosexuality decriminalised in Northern Ireland with the passing of law reforms in the House of Commons.
1988	Section 28, preventing the 'promotion' of homosexuality by local authorities, came into force on 24 May with backing from government minister Michael Howard; 10,000 protested in London and 15,000 in Manchester.
1994	House of Commons voted to reduce gay male age of consent to 18. Huge disappointment that it had not been reduced to 16.
1998	336 MPs voted in the House of Commons, an overwhelming majority vote, for an equal age of consent.
2002	Equal rights granted to same-sex couples applying for adoption.
2004	Civil Partnership Bill introduced.
2008	Parliament passes provisions in the Criminal Justice and Immigration Act, creating a new offence of incitement to homophobic hatred.
2013	Gay marriage introduced. It is now possible for couples to have a religious marriage.

Figure 5.6 Timeline of sexuality regulation

The growth of reconstituted families

This family type is sometimes known as a step-family or **blended family**. According to the ONS the fastest-growing household type was households containing two or more families, increasing by 39 per cent from 206,000 households in 2003 to 286,000 households in 2013. However multi-family households still only represent one per cent of all households. There are various views on **reconstituted families** – some argue that they can be stressful because of the potential conflict between step-siblings and parents.

It has been suggested that there is a greater risk of divorce and separation in marriages where one or both partners have been married before. However, statistics reveal that this is not the case. In 2013, the Marriage Foundation claimed that 45 per cent of first marriages end in divorce but that only 31 per cent of second marriages will end in failure. Functionalists might argue that this is a sign that people today are seeking to improve the quality of their relationships if their relationship breaks down.

The growth in reconstituted families is having interesting effects on parenting practices. For example, **co-parenting**, where separated parents work together as parents, is emerging as an alternative approach to raising children.

Multicultural families

As we are beginning to see, family relationships can be said to be moving away from modern values towards postmodern individualism. In contemporary society there is an increasing amount of migration, resulting in interesting patterns of family structures. Here are two examples of the impact of multiculturalism on family diversity.

African-Caribbean families

Berthoud (2000) carried out research which indicated that only 39 per cent of British-born African-Caribbean adults are married compared to 60 per cent of white adults. It has also been noted that they are more likely to intermarry (marry someone with a different ethnicity or cultural background). Children born into these types of family are more likely to have a dual heritage, adding to the cultural diversity of the UK.

African-Caribbean families are also more likely to be single-parent families, with over 50 per cent containing one adult with dependent children. Berthoud (2003) suggests that the attitude of young Caribbean women is one of 'individualism', which means many choose to live independently from the fathers of their children. Families headed by a woman without the support of a man are known as **matrifocal families**. Grandmothers within the family can also provide a source of unpaid childcare, which allows single mothers to work full time and support the family unit.

Asian families

Berthoud also found that Pakistani and Bangladeshi communities are most likely to live in traditional nuclear families, made up of two adults and their children, however 33 per cent live in extended families, where they have strong connections to their kin and have more than one generation. This extended family often contains grandparents, who can act as a source of support and unpaid childcare for younger family members. Asian communities tend to be more traditional in their views and place high values on marriage, which are often arranged. In Asian families there is little intermarriage and a low divorce rate. Bangladeshi and Pakistani women tend to have more children than Indian and white women – they also tend to have children at a much younger age.

The growth of single-parent families

There were nearly 1.9 million lone parents with dependent children in the UK in 2013, a figure that has grown steadily – but not significantly – from 1.8 million in 2003. In 2011, women accounted for 92 per cent of lone parents with dependent children while men accounted for 8 per cent of lone parents with dependent children. These percentages have changed little since 2001. Women are more likely to take the main caring responsibilities for any children when relationships break down and therefore become lone parents (Office for National Statistics, 2013).

The average age of lone parents with dependent children in the UK in 2011 was 38.1 years, an increase of 2.3 years since 2001. One reason for this increase could be that women have been postponing their childbearing to older ages in recent years. In 2011, 45 per cent of lone parents were aged 40 or over, and only 2 per cent of lone parents were aged under 20, the same percentage as ten years earlier (Office for National Statistics, 2013).

It can be quite challenging to operationalise or measure the numbers of single-parent families since they are difficult to define; for example, there has recently been an increasing tendency for parents to co-parent after divorce. This means that parents still take joint responsibility for their children despite no longer being together as a couple. This is also known as creative singlehood, where a range of options are created and chosen which do not fall neatly into conventional categories of family relationship types. As we have seen, there are a number of concerns over single parents' ability to raise children; New Right thinkers argue that children need a mother *and* a father figure. However, feminists and others disagree and claim that one happy parent is by far more preferable to two parents who are unhappy or dysfunctional. Recent research suggests, however, that it is poverty which has a greater negative effect on children, not the structure of the family (Harkness, 2013).

> ### RESEARCH IN FOCUS
>
> A study by the charity Gingerbread, as part of its Paying the Price project, suggests that 67 per cent of lone-parent families struggle constantly with their finances. Describing its results as 'grim', the group said the push towards flexible working was acting against single parents, with 56 per cent reporting that they cannot get work at all. Others are unable to work the hours they need to meet their living costs.
>
> The survey of 2486 lone mothers and fathers found that 75 per cent had been hit by welfare cuts and 39 per cent were in low-paid jobs, compared with 21 per cent of all workers nationally. Government figures for 2011–2012 showed that the average employment income for single-parent households was £110 a week, compared with £390 for all UK households.
>
> Adapted from Single mothers 'do just as good a job as couples'. *Observer* 19 July 2014.

Questions

1. Why are single-parent families more likely to experience poverty?
2. Why might single parents find it difficult to work?
3. What could the government do to help single parents?

Questions

1. Why are single-parent families more likely to experience poverty?
2. Why might single parents find it difficult to work?
3. What could the government do to help single parents?

The continued importance of the nuclear family

In 2013 there were 18.2 million families in the UK. Of these, 12.3 million consisted of a married couple with or without children. This suggests that, despite the recent changes in family structures, the nuclear family still remains a common family structure. What is interesting to note is that an increasing number of these nuclear families consist of parents whose children have left home or whose children are adults still living with their parents, for example for financial reasons. In 2013, over 3.3 million adults in the UK aged between 20 and 34 were living with a parent or parents. That is 26 per cent of this age group, which is an increase from 1996, when 2.7 million 20 to 34 year olds lived with their parents, 21 per cent of this age group. This means that the number of 20 to 34 year olds living with their parents has increased by 25 per cent since 1996. This may be due to the increased cost of living, meaning that people live with their parents to save money or to save up to buy a home or rent one. It also reflects the fact that the period in which children are dependent on their parents is growing, lengthening the experience of childhood, as well as suggesting that parents and children share increasingly close relationships and leisure time.

Interestingly, it is young men who are more likely to live with their parents than young women. For every 10 women, 17 men aged 20 to 34 lived with their parents in 2013. This is partly due to the fact that women are more likely to form relationships with men older than themselves.

The increase in divorce

The number of divorces generally increased between 1930 and 1990 as a result of changes in behaviour and attitudes. The large increase observed during the 1970s was associated with the Divorce Reform Act 1969, which came into effect in England and Wales in 1971, making it possible for couples to divorce without needing a specific reason. A marriage could be terminated because of 'irretrievable breakdown' in the relationship. Interestingly, the number of divorces fell steadily between 2003

KEY SOCIOLOGISTS

Chester (1985) argues that the nuclear family structure has not disappeared given that, at some point in their lives, most people marry and have children. However, Chester does concede that roles within families are changing, mainly as a result of women entering paid employment. Chester names this type of family a **neo-conventional family**, but he argues that it not a significant departure from the nuclear family.

5 Families and households

and 2009 while, at the same time, there was a significant decline in the number of marriages. This was probably due to the increasing number of couples choosing to cohabit rather than enter into marriage (Beaujouan and Bhrolcháin, 2011).

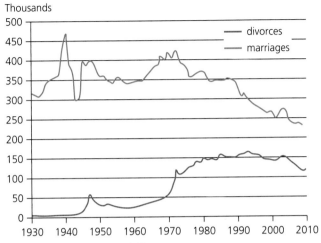

Figure 5.7 Marriage and divorce rates

Key legal changes in divorce

The general pattern is that divorce has become easier with every law change. This marks a real change from when it was very difficult to divorce, especially for women.

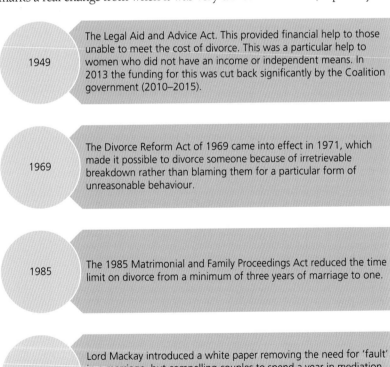

1949 — The Legal Aid and Advice Act. This provided financial help to those unable to meet the cost of divorce. This was a particular help to women who did not have an income or independent means. In 2013 the funding for this was cut back significantly by the Coalition government (2010–2015).

1969 — The Divorce Reform Act of 1969 came into effect in 1971, which made it possible to divorce someone because of irretrievable breakdown rather than blaming them for a particular form of unreasonable behaviour.

1985 — The 1985 Matrimonial and Family Proceedings Act reduced the time limit on divorce from a minimum of three years of marriage to one.

1995 — Lord Mackay introduced a white paper removing the need for 'fault' in a marriage, but compelling couples to spend a year in mediation and encouraging them to negotiate either a reconciliation or a mutually agreeable separation.

1996 — The Family Law Act 1996 allows divorce if the marriage has 'irretrievably broken down' after a period of 'reflection and consideration'. However, since the divorce rate has stayed high, this process has clearly not had the intended effect of making people reconsider divorcing their spouse.

Figure 5.8 Key divorce legislation

Evaluation

Changes in the law are one of many causes for the increase in divorce. So, although some couples are finding the process of divorce easier, it might also be the case that the changes in the law often reflect changes in public opinion, for example, steadily rising levels of divorce in the 1960s prior to the Divorce Reform Act.

IN THE NEWS

Critics warn reforms will make ending a marriage too easy

So-called 'over-the-counter' divorces will make ending a marriage as easy as 'disposing of a carrier bag', a former government minister has warned. Ann Widdecombe said plans under consideration by the most senior family law judge in England and Wales, Sir James Munby, will make obtaining a divorce even easier than it is at present.

Figures from the Office of National Statistics show that between 2011 and 2012 the number of couples divorcing increased by 0.5 per cent. More women than men apply for a divorce – women were granted 65 per cent of all divorces. Interestingly, the incidence of divorce is greatest between the 4th and 8th wedding anniversaries.

Ms Widdecombe told The Times: 'Divorce is already too easy – it makes a nonsense of marriage. I am not saying, go back to the old days when divorce involved tricks and stratagems, but at least it should be something people have to think about and take a great deal of trouble over. It should not be like buying sweets over the counter, or discarding an old carrier bag.'

Adapted from *The Daily Mail*, 23rd June 2014, Darren Boyle

Questions

1. What is meant by an 'over-the-counter divorce'?
2. Why is Ms Widdecombe concerned about the proposed reforms to make divorce easier?
3. Why do you think that women are more likely to apply for a divorce than men?
4. Why do you think that the chance of divorce is greatest between the 4th and 8th wedding anniversaries?
5. How might Marxists, functionalists and feminists explain these proposals?

Changing patterns in childbearing

According to Susanne Whiting, 100 years ago women were having significantly more children. Over the last 70 years, however, the two-child family has consistently been the most common family size and the proportion of mothers with three or more children has remained fairly constant. Interestingly, the total number of births has been increasing since 2000. This may be due to the increase in foreign-born women, who typically have more children. A quarter of all births in 2010 were to mothers born outside the UK, up from 13.2 per cent in 1980.

Women are increasingly delaying childbirth to older ages. In 2010, nearly half of all babies were born to mothers aged 30 and over. Socio-economic class does not seem to impact on family size: the proportion of families with three or more children is fairly evenly distributed across all socio-economic groups. Ethnicity does impact on family size, however, with black and Asian ethnic groups having larger families than white and Chinese ones. Regionally, families with three or more children are most prevalent in Northern Ireland and London.

Social policy

There have been key policy changes that have undoubtedly led to an increase in family diversity, such as the divorce reform legislation, but social policies also reflect and consolidate changing attitudes, such as the legislation legitimising same-sex families. Therefore social policies and family diversity are very much linked.

STUDY TIPS

Avoid making generalisations; while there have been some long-term trends, which are worthy of note, family diversity is complex. For instance, single-parent families vary enormously.

2.2 Different perspectives on family diversity

Functionalism	The recent increase in family diversity means that people have higher expectations about relationships and they are no longer willing to simply conform to what is expected by society. Diversity, therefore, is a positive thing (Riggo and Weiser, 2008).
New Right	The New Right have concerns over the increase in family diversity, which they regard as a symptom of 'broken Britain' where moral decay is occurring. They argue strongly that the state should encourage greater individual responsibility and traditional nuclear family structures, roles and relationships. According to the New Right, traditional family values are essential for the adequate socialisation of children.
Marxism	Marxists tend to assume that the family, particularly the nuclear family, is arranged to support the needs of capitalism. Therefore, it could be argued that the increase in family diversity simply reflects the changes in the economy. For instance, the fact that the majority of parents now both work reflects the increasing cost of living in capitalist society, where the demand for consumer goods has increased phenomenally. Marxists might argue that families today are not more affluent, they are simply being exploited by the ruling classes in more sophisticated ways.
Feminism	Feminists in general regard the increase in family diversity positively as it provides women with greater opportunities to seek alternatives to the nuclear family and the patriarchal ideology that goes with it. Feminists such as Smart and Neale (1999) argue that events in the family, such as divorce, remain gendered, in the sense that men and women still have very different experiences of family life, with women often still experiencing powerlessness.
Life course analysis	This approach focuses on the meanings given to the decisions made by individuals about the kinds of family structures that they find themselves in. Rather than make generalisations about family life, this approach seeks to understand all aspects of family life through small-scale research. This suggests that life course analysis grants individuals a degree of agency or control over their family structures, rather than seeing family structures as being mainly imposed and shaped by social forces.
Postmodernism	Postmodernists comment on the impact of the transition from modern society to postmodern society. This leads to increasing individualism and, at the same time, less pressure on individuals to conform to societal expectations. This results in greater family diversity and also greater instability in family structures. Weeks et al (1999) argue that greater individualism has led to the creation of families of choice, where relationships are created, including same-sex families. Stacey (1996) argues that families within postmodern society can be described as no longer based around one dominant structure. Rather the family structure, roles and relationships are characterised by diversity, choice and fluidity. Stacey bases these claims on her own research carried out into family life in Silicon Valley in California, where women in particular adapt their family life according to the increasing choices that are available to them.

Table 5.7 Sociological perspectives on family diversity

Check your understanding

1. What has happened to the size of the family over the past decades?
2. Give three reasons for the recent decline in the number of divorces.
3. How might divorce law reforms have contributed to an increase in divorce?
4. According to the evidence in this chapter, are cohabiting couples more or less stable than married couples?
5. Give two reasons why there has been a significant increase in lone-person households.
6. Are ethnic minorities experiencing more or less family diversity than the white majority? Explain your answer.
7. What is the average age of single parents?
8. Explain how the state has had a role in shaping attitudes towards same-sex families over the past 50 years.
9. Why do New Right thinkers have concerns about single-parent families?
10. Nuclear families remain the most common form of family, but what has changed about this family structure in recent years?

Practice question

Read Item A then answer the question that follows.

Item A

One reason for the increase in family diversity is that the majority of women now participate in paid employment. Some now claim that the nuclear family is in decline, being replaced by other family structures. For instance, there has been an increase in reconstituted families.

Assess the view that the nuclear family is in decline.   (20 marks)

Section 3: Roles and relationships within the family

When studying this topic it is important that you consider all aspects of roles and relationships, not simply in terms of domestic labour; consider who has power and takes responsibility for which areas of family life.

This section will explore the following debates:

- How has the domestic division of labour changed?
- How have personal relationships changed?
- What are the changes in parenting and childbearing?
- How have roles and relationships changed in the family? The sociology of the personal life.

GETTING YOU STARTED

Forty years of feminism – but women still do most of the housework

Over forty years after the beginnings of feminism, when Western women began questioning the traditional homemaker role, it has been confirmed that married women still do more housework than their husbands.

According to analysis by the Institute for Public Policy Research, eight out of ten married women do more household chores, while just one in ten married men does an equal amount of cleaning and washing as his wife. Just 13 per cent of women say their husbands do more housework than they do. Only three per cent of married women do fewer than three hours a week, with almost half doing 13 hours or more.

Patterns of housework have changed only slightly over the years. More than eight out of ten women born in 1958 said they do more laundry and ironing than their partner, while seven out of ten women born in 1970 agreed with this.

In other words, according to the IPPR research gender imbalance is thriving in the British household, and for truly equal relationships, society needs men to pick up the vacuum cleaner and do their fair share.

Adapted from McVeigh, T. (2012) Forty years of feminism — but women still do most of the housework. *Observer*, 10 March.

Questions

1. What does the article suggest about the nature of relationships today?
2. Why do you think that relationships follow this pattern?
3. Do you think this is likely to change in the future? Give reasons for your answer.

Alongside structural changes in the family there have also been a number of significant changes in relationships and roles. This section explores the causes and consequences of these changes. This is a relatively new area in sociology: until recently sociologists have focused on the more public and measurable aspects of relationships, such as who carries out the domestic work in the home or who is responsible for childcare. Due to the complex nature of

Questions

1. What are gender scripts?
2. Why might lesbian couples lack traditional gender roles?

CONTEMPORARY APPLICATION

Some sociologists have suggested that time spent on housework has been reduced through the introduction of a greater range of domestic appliances. Gershuny and Robinson argue that, between 1965 and 1985, domestic technology has significantly reduced the weekly hours of women's routine housework. Michael Bittman, James Mahmud Rice and Judy Wajcman (2004) challenge this, saying that domestic appliances do not, in fact, reduce the time spent on housework; they may even add time to the task.

STUDY TIPS

It is important to acknowledge that housework is not the only area of responsibility within family life. It is also important to consider the role of men carefully, as they too may experience the dual burden of work and domestic responsibilities. Therefore avoid generalisations and provide a balanced view.

RESEARCH IN FOCUS

Jillian Dunne (1997) investigates same-sex couples to see what the patterns are in relation to who does housework, and if these patterns reflect those of traditional heterosexual relationships. Dunne conducted a survey of 37 cohabiting lesbians with young children, focusing on the negotiation of tasks within the household.

She found that because lesbian couples do not have the traditional gender scripts, that is, traditional ingrained ideas about what roles each partner should take, their relationships were much more egalitarian. On average, the couples in the study relationships had a 40 : 60 split of household chores. Dunne claims that it is no accident that lesbian couples deliberately choose to avoid the traditional male/female imbalance in relation to domestic work.

Dunne, G. (1997) *Lesbian Lifestyles: Women's Work and the Politics of Sexuality.* Macmillan.

Evaluation

This evidence in this section suggests that heterosexual relationships continue to reflect traditional expectations about gender, placing a dual burden on women, the majority of whom are now mainly in paid employment while still taking responsibility for domestic labour. However, it is clear that in some cases men are taking greater responsibility for domestic work and that they too may feel a similar dual burden, which is important not to overlook. Children play a limited role in domestic labour, although this could be due to confusing or inconsistent messages given to them by their parents. Alternatively, lesbian couples are creating new and innovative ways of managing both paid work and domestic work through recreating ideas about gender roles in their own terms, avoiding traditional gender scripts.

STUDY TIP

Consider the methodological challenges in measuring 'responsibility' for domestic work. Some people might exaggerate what they do, therefore careful consideration needs to be given to operationalising concepts such as the dual burden. This discussion also needs to consider the contribution of children to domestic labour (in terms of gender and age) as well as the impact of buying in help with domestic labour such as cleaners.

3.2 How have personal relationships changed?

Following investigations into housework, sociologists have become increasingly interested in the types of relationships that couples have. Specifically, investigating who has control in the relationship and who takes responsibility for the emotional well-being of the family, and what people expect from their intimate relationships. That we are talking about intimate relationships at all suggests that family relationships today are based around a high level of expectation.

Indeed, it is interesting in itself to consider why more people are choosing to live alone and be creatively single; that is to enjoy non-domestic relationships. This does not mean that these personal relationships are any less significant, just different.

In the past, marriage was often based on practical arrangements. Women, for example, would often marry for practical reasons rather than romantic reasons. Today relationships are often based on very different ideas. The postmodernist Beck (1990) argues that **postmodernity** is characterised by increasing emphasis on individual choices or individualisation. This marks a real departure from forming relationships based on social expectations. Smart and Neale (1999) argue that marriage has become more focused on being a relationship in which parenting is shared. They claim that divorce offers women in particular a chance to try to redefine their relationships and find less oppressive relationships. They argue that this has been made more difficult as a result of recent divorce laws, which mean that co-parenting continues beyond divorce. Women are having fewer children and, as a result, families are smaller, which has meant that childbearing practices are changing as well as relationships within families.

What is clear is that relationships are based more on choice and are increasingly negotiated. Carsten (2004) argues that more and more people are favouring chosen family members rather than seeing biological relatedness as primarily significant. Furthermore, Carsten argues that our relationships create the individual and are highly significant. Carsten calls these two processes **relationality**.

Relationality is the twinfold process whereby biology becomes less important in defining family relationships while the importance of relationships and interactions is crucial to defining the individual.

Misztal (2003), in Smart (2013), suggests that sociologists should try to understand family life through exploring people's memories, arguing that people's values shape what is remembered. Misztal says that it is these memories that provide important information about family relationships and that they are used to create and reinforce bonds as well as to change identities. This reveals how important personal life is considered to be in understanding family life today.

Similarly, sociologists such as Rustin (2000), in Smart, argue that to understand family life nowadays, people's biographies should be explored through people presenting their lives through pictures, videos and objects so that their relationships and family life can be better understood.

However, despite the higher expectations of intimacy within relationships, there are still very high levels of conflict and domestic violence within the family. There are also significant imbalances of responsibilities within relationships. For example, according to Duncombe and Marsden (1993) some of the women interviewed in their research felt emotionally deserted, with their husbands leaving them to carry out all of the **emotion work** in the family. Emotion work includes tasks such as offering emotional support, looking after ill children and listening to problems of family members. This leaves many women feeling as if they were carrying out a triple shift, having to take responsibility for not only paid work and housework but also emotion work. So there are many different aspects to intimate relationships, which are complex and can be a challenge for sociologists to investigate.

● **KEY CONCEPT** ►

Emotion work refers to supporting family members' emotional needs; for example, listening to family members' problems, looking after ill children and absorbing other peoples' frustrations.

RESEARCH IN FOCUS

In her study of couples and their money, Jan Pahl (1980) used a combination of secondary quantitative data and qualitative unstructured interviews in which she explored who controls money. Pahl suggests that this offers a lot of information about the nature of relationships within the family. She found that accounting practices were not consistent but, at the same time, they were very meaningful for the couple themselves. The method of money management in couples reflects who earns more. The joint account continues to be a powerful symbol of marital togetherness, but an increasing concern with financial autonomy is showing itself in the growth of 'partial pooling' where couples combine joint and sole accounts. This provides couples with a way of maintaining individual autonomy while also sharing resources.

Pahl, J. (1980) 'Patterns of money management within marriage'. *Journal of Social Policy*, 9 (3), 313–336.

Questions

1. Why is money management a useful aspect of family life to investigate?
2. What is partial pooling and how is it becoming increasingly popular?

CONTEMPORARY APPLICATION

There is a general lack of research into domestic violence between same-sex couples, which partially reflects the fact that until very recently gay couples were not recognised. This could make it harder for homosexual victims to report domestic violence.

KEY SOCIOLOGISTS

Giddens (2004) a postmodernist sociologist, explains how there was little or no intimacy in love relationships before modernity. Public relationships were based on economic factors. In the modern and postmodern era, Giddens argues that it has become possible to create and sustain long-term loving relationships. He claims that modernity led to greater equality and respect, making intimate relationships more possible and desirable; he calls this type of relationship a 'pure relationship'.

RESEARCH IN FOCUS

Arnout van de Rijt and Vincent Buskens (2006) argue that with the increasing availability of effective birth control, casual relationships have become more common. This means that a higher level of trust needs to be created between couples who are looking to commit to each other. In a way the individualisation (the greater focus on individuals needs and desires) that accompanies postmodernity challenges the notion of long-term monogamous (faithful) relationships. Van de Rijt and Buskens argue that Granovetter's (1985) concept of **embeddedness** is useful here.

Embeddedness refers to the specific view of how a particular relationship is seen by the individual and the social networks it may lead to, as well as the way the relationship is perceived publically. They

explore the extent to which relationships become embedded. Using secondary statistical data, they test their hypothesis that embeddedness is an important indicator of trust between a couple who choose not to be married or are considering marriage. They conclude that marriage is confirmation of certain expectations couples have about trusting each other as well as indicating what happens if this trust is broken (for example, childcare payments). They state that their evidence proves that the more the relationship is embedded, the more likely the relationship is to endure. Using the concept of embeddedness to explore relationships is interesting and useful as it helps sociologists to operationalise complex, private aspects of relationships which can be difficult to research.

Van de Rijt, A. and Buskens, V. (2006) 'Dynamics of networks if everyone strives for structural holes'. *American Journal of Sociology*, 114 (2), 371–407.

Questions

1. Why is trust between couples more important today?
2. What is embededness and why might it be a useful concept for understanding relationships today?
3. What is individualisation?
4. Why might relationships be difficult to research?

IN THE NEWS

Figures complied on domestic violence, including findings from the British Crime Survey (BCS) 2001/2, showed that it was much more common than previously thought. The disturbing figures showed that in England and Wales, a quarter of women experienced domestic violence at some point in their lives, and two women per week were killed by their partner. The BCS survey found that there were an estimated 635,000 incidents of domestic violence in England and Wales, of which by far the greater proportion of the victims, were women: only 20 per cent were male.

Domestic violence has a higher rate of repeat victimisation than any other crime, and on average a women will have been assaulted 35 times before she first approaches the police. UK police deal with a domestic assistance call every minute, yet only 35 per cent of domestic violence incidents are reported to the police.

Adapted from http://refuge.org.uk/get-help-now/what-is-domestic-violence/domestic-violence-the-facts/

Questions

1. What do these statistics suggest about power and control in relationships?
2. Suggest two reasons why this data may not be completely valid.

This evidence strongly suggests that for many, relationships are detrimental, particularly to women. However, there has been an increasing awareness of violence by women against men. It must not be forgotten that children and the elderly also suffer domestic violence in the family (more on children later). Also, there is recent evidence that suggests an increase in physical and sexual violence among teenage relationships (Barter *et al*, 2009), an area which until now has been under-researched.

Many feminists argue that relationships are inherently patriarchal and, therefore, domestic violence is inevitable. In fact many feminists argue that society sends messages to both men and women that domestic violence is acceptable and normal, and therefore it is particularly hard to challenge, prevent and control.

Questions

1. Why do you think that younger homosexual people are more likely to report domestic violence?
2. Why was there a tendency for the respondents not to label their experience as domestic violence?

Questions

1. What do you think is meant by 'patriarchal motherhood'?
2. Explain what is meant by qualitative research.
3. How might lesbian couples organise parenting differently to heterosexual couples?
4. Why might women working be more likely to be seen as problematic in heterosexual couples?

RESEARCH IN FOCUS

Using questionnaires, focus groups and interviews, Donovan *et al* (2006) found that domestic violence is a significant problem in same-sex relationships. Domestic abuse is experienced in very similar ways by those in lesbian and gay relationships, although men were more likely to experience sexual abuse. There was a tendency in some cases for the respondents not to define domestic violence as such because it is more likely to be emotional or sexual abuse than physical abuse. As with studies of heterosexual couples, the younger respondents were more likely to report domestic violence. For many, however, many incidents of domestic violence were not reported because they thought they would not receive a sympathetic response and there was a tendency for the respondents to see it as their own fault.

Donovan, C., Hester, M., Holmes, J. and McCarry, M. (2006) *Comparing Domestic Abuse in Same Sex and Heterosexual Relationships.* Swindon: Economic and Social Research Council.

3.3 Changes in parenting and childbearing

One interesting area of recent sociological focus has been to explore the changes in parenting patterns. In the past functionalist sociologists have claimed that due to the fact that women have children, they are somehow inevitably suited to being responsible for looking after them. Things are changing, however, and men are playing an increasing role in their children's lives. Alternative models of parenting, such as same-sex parenting, also show that there are effective ways of parenting beyond the traditional expressive/instrumental roles.

RESEARCH IN FOCUS

Doucet and Dunne (2000) explore how heterosexual and lesbian mothers create new forms of mothering which attempt to challenge and ultimately break down patriarchal motherhood, in which women feel oppressed. They carried out qualitative unstructured interviews with 97 mothers (and 23 fathers) in the UK during the early to mid-1990s. Through their research they hoped to create an alternative, feminist conception of mothering, different from both a 'feminine' conception of mothering and a 'male' model of mothering.

They conclude that the lack of traditional gender scripts (ingrained ideas about the roles of men and women) allowed the lesbians in their study to develop new ways of parenting which are very much linked to being economically independent. Doucet and Dunne argue that rather than seeing women who work as a problem (which they claim is often the case in heterosexual couples) lesbians are resourceful and positive in their solutions to the challenges faced by working mothers.

In other words, the lesbian couples interviewed were able to negotiate the demands of work and parenting positively and productively. They argue that this is more possible among middle-class couples who have the economic and educational advantages to make this happen more easily. This suggests that new forms of parenting may be emerging from same-sex couples.

Doucet, A. and Dunne, G. (2000) Heterosexual and lesbian mothers: challenging 'feminine' and 'male' conceptions of mothering in O'Reilly, A. and Abbey, S. (eds.) *Mothers and Daughters: Connection, Empowerment and Transformation*. Rowman and Littlefield, pp. 103–120.

Social policy

A scheme to let people find out from the police if their partner has a history of domestic violence was brought in across England and Wales in 2014. The Domestic Violence Disclosure Scheme, known as Clare's Law, is intended to provide information that could protect someone from being a victim of attack. The initiative is named after 36-year-old Clare Wood who was murdered by her ex-boyfriend in 2009. The scheme allows the police to disclose information on request about a partner's previous history of domestic violence or violent acts. This suggests that there are ongoing attempts by the government to prevent domestic violence and to send messages to society that it can and will be prosecuted.

Evaluation

Relationships within the family have clearly been challenged and redefined in many cases. Although it appears that women still take responsibility for many areas of domestic life and childcare, there appears to be a shift in attitude towards more negotiated and possibly more egalitarian relationships. It is clear that past patterns of behaviour, often reflecting patriarchal family ideology, are taking time to change fully, and there is a tendency for couples to follow traditionally defined roles. It is clear however that relationships are much more likely to be based on fairly high emotional expectations about love and companionship as opposed to simply practical reasons alone. This evidence suggests that there will be a higher level of negotiation in future relationships, leading to the possibility of greater gender equality. Intimate relationships are a complex area for sociologists to conduct research in as they are often considered to be very private. It is clear that although there has been a significant shift towards a greater expectation for higher quality, fulfilling relationships, there is clear evidence that relationships still reflect patriarchal patterns.

Check your understanding

1. Name two social policies that have shaped roles and relationships.
2. What are time–budget studies?
3. Explain two ways in which personal relationships have changed.
4. How might same-sex couples differ in relationships and parenting?
5. What are pure relationships and why are they more likely to occur today?
6. Why do some feminists suggest that domestic violence is inevitable in heterosexual relationships?
7. What is Clare's Law?
8. Name two ways in which parenting has changed.

Practice questions

1. Explain what is meant by 'lagged adaptation'. (2 marks)
2. Analyse two reasons why women often experience a 'dual burden'. (10 marks)
3. Assess two ways in which power relationships are expressed. (10 marks)
4. Outline and explain two ways in which relationships are becoming more equal. (10 marks)

Read Item A then answer the question that follows.

Item A

According to research carried out by Jonathan Gershuny (2008) relationships are gradually becoming more egalitarian. Gershuny claims that as women are increasingly working full time, men gradually begin to increase their contribution to housework. However, feminists suggest that women today experience a dual burden and continue to take responsibility not simply for housework but for many other areas of family life as well.

Applying material from Item A, assess the ways in which relationships have changed over the past 40 years. (20 marks)

Questions

1. What do these images in Figure 5.9 suggest about the ways in which the experience of childhood has changed?
2. How might changes in the family and society help us to understand the changes in childhood?
3. Suggest some ways in which the experience of being a child varies in different parts of the world.

Section 4: Childhood

There are many key areas to consider for the topic of childhood, including how childhood is socially constructed, the reasons for the changes in the experience of childhood (including if childhood is a positive or negative experience) and, finally, the future of childhood. Remember to consider all children in the UK, as the experience of childhood varies greatly in terms of social class, gender, ethnicity and locality.

This section will explore the following debates:

● How has childhood changed?
● What are the different views on the experience of childhood today?

GETTING YOU STARTED

Figure 5.9 Children's experience of childhood varies greatly

4.1 How has childhood changed?

It may come as a surprise to learn that the period of time in a person's life that is now labelled 'childhood' has not always existed. In the Middle Ages children were simply infants who then transformed into mini adults. As such, there is no inevitable period of time between infancy and adulthood and, therefore, childhood is a social construct; in other words, it is created by society. For further evidence that childhood is a social construct, cross-cultural research reveals that in many parts of the world, children have very different experiences of childhood or, in some cases, no childhood at all, being treated like adults from an early age. Wagg (1992) argues that although all humans experience the same physical stages of development, the experience of childhood is entirely socially constructed.

Childhood emerged largely due to the massive social changes that were associated with the industrial revolution, which took place around 1750 to 1900. Industrialisation refers to the process in which the economy changing from being based on agriculture to being based on machinery. Industrialisation resulted in children moving from being an **economic asset**, where they would have contributed financially to the family, to becoming an **economic burden**, meaning that children are now financially dependent on their families.

There are many reasons for the emergence of childhood as we know it today, and these include the development of the state and social policies. As children and women were prevented from working through laws, the family wage developed, which meant that the father provided the income for the rest of the family. Education also became compulsory, which also meant that children became a concern of the state and, as they were not able to work, children became dependent on adults. This coincided with changing attitudes towards children and childhood, as children became seen as vulnerable and in need of protection. These legal and attitudinal changes were very much linked to the changes in the family. As we have seen, the family became smaller, more geographically mobile and, typically, nuclear in structure. Smaller families meant that parents had the time to establish a closer relationship with their children.

Childhood continues to change and some sociologists have explored the negative and positive aspects of these changes. There is some dispute about children becoming more or less protected, for example. This section explores the future of childhood, with some sociologists suggesting that the boundary between adults and children is in fact becoming more or less distinct.

It is important to note that the experience of childhood depends on the gender, ethnicity and social class of the individual, so it is important to avoid generalisations. These differences are highlighted in Figure 5.10 below.

Gender
The gender of the child is without doubt a factor that shapes the experience of childhood. Socialisation continues to be very much a gendered process, and evidence suggests that girls continue to be far more prepared for school than boys by the time they are four. This is because girls are encouraged to be conformist and develop speaking skills, which prepares them better for school than boys' activities, which tend to be very physical and based on competitiveness. This continues into later childhood and teenage years where girls develop a 'bedroom culture' (McRobbie and Garber, 1975). A bedroom culture is a concept that describe the ways in which girls organise their culture at home in a way that reflects gendered socialisation. According to McRobbie and Garber, girls see their bedrooms as private spaces free from intimidation by males that they feel elsewhere.

THE EXPERIENCE OF CHILDHOOD

Class
The Joseph Rowntree Foundation (2007) states that children from lower income backgrounds are very aware of their disadvantaged position from a very early age. In their research of 220 children aged five to 11 who took part in group interviews in 15 schools, they found that children's experience of school was negatively affected by poverty leading to poorer life chances. Womack (2007) argues that children who are poor often have very negative experiences of childhood. On the other hand, there is some evidence that children who come from more affluent backgrounds may experience 'toxic parenting' where good parenting is being replaced with technology, such as computer games (Pilcher, 2007).

Ethnicity
The experience of childhood is affected by the ethnic background of the child, however the patterns are complex. Certain ethnic groups have higher rates of poverty, for example, among Pakistani and Bangladeshi children. There have been issues raised about the way in which some ethnic groups prepare their children for education, such as African-Caribbean boys (more on this in the chapter on education). However, there is a growing view that it is impossible to generalise about the experiences of particular ethnic groups as experiences vary so enormously.

Figure 5.10 The experience of childhood according to class, gender and ethnicity

Questions

1. What was the research method that Aries used?
2. What problems might there be with Aries' research method?
3. What other contemporary evidence suggests that childhood is a social construct?
4. Why might the rise of childhood as a distinct era be linked to the emergence of the nuclear family?

RESEARCH IN FOCUS

Using portraits of children from the Middle Ages through to the seventeenth century, the academic Philippe Aries (1960) explains how childhood emerged as a social construct from around the seventeenth century. Aries argues that during the Middle Ages, children were simply expected to act in adult ways and were exposed to adult information. The pictures show that children

Figure 5.11 Diego Velasquez, *Las Meninas* (painting)

were given adult responsibilities and clothing. He argues that childhood as we know it in contemporary society is neither inevitable nor natural. He claims that a key factor here was the decline in infant mortality, which meant that parents wished to invest more energy into their children and, as a result, childhood became a more valued experience. Aries argues that at the same time as childhood emerged, the nuclear family took form.

Aries, P. (1960) *Centuries of Childhood: A Social History of Family Life.* London: Vintage.

4.2 Different views on the experience of childhood today

There has been some debate about the nature of the changes to the experience of childhood. There are two main perspectives on this debate.

The conflict view

Conflict theorists, such as Marxists and feminists, argue that the experience of childhood is negative. Feminists claim that children are controlled by adults, which is known as **age patriarchy** (Gittins, 1985). Age patriarchy is a result of children being made to be financially dependent on adults. Alternatively, Marxists argue that children are simply taught to submit to the capitalist system rather than being encouraged to question the system creatively. They also argue that capitalist society results in the exploitation of children. There is some compelling evidence to support this view; for example, 1 in 20 children have been sexually abused and over 90 per cent of children who have experienced sexual abuse were abused by someone they knew. Furthermore, 18,915 sexual crimes against children under 16 were recorded in England and Wales in 2012/13. Sociologists such as Donzelot (1997) argue that new forms of surveillance by the state ensure that parents are being watched and checked, which represents a new way that the state controls adults and children alike.

The march of progress view

March of progress theorists, such as some functionalists, however, argue that childhood is in fact improving as the family becomes more specialised. They claim that changes in attitudes, coupled with greater child centredness in society and social policies, have resulted in happier, safer and more valued children. There is evidence to support this view as well; for example, there has been a 75 per cent reduction in the number of children killed on the roads in England and Wales,

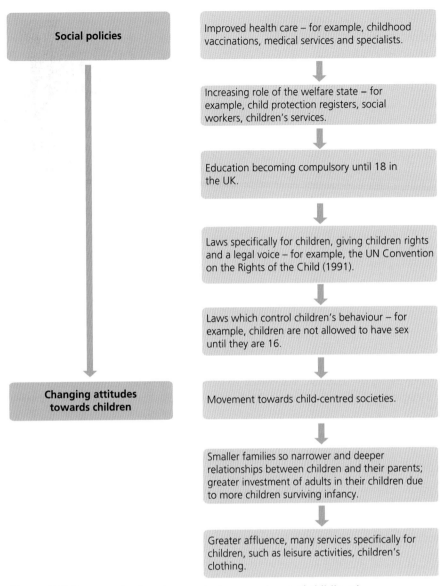

Social policies	Improved health care – for example, childhood vaccinations, medical services and specialists.
	Increasing role of the welfare state – for example, child protection registers, social workers, children's services.
	Education becoming compulsory until 18 in the UK.
	Laws specifically for children, giving children rights and a legal voice – for example, the UN Convention on the Rights of the Child (1991).
	Laws which control children's behaviour – for example, children are not allowed to have sex until they are 16.
Changing attitudes towards children	Movement towards child-centred societies.
	Smaller families so narrower and deeper relationships between children and their parents; greater investment of adults in their children due to more children surviving infancy.
	Greater affluence, many services specifically for children, such as leisure activities, children's clothing.

Figure 5.12 Reasons for the changes in the experience of childhood

either in cars or as pedestrians. Also, the UK tops the European rankings for the use of filters on the internet-enabled devices that children use at home.

Different perspectives

Sociologists have begun to consider the future of childhood in a postmodern society. The postmodernist Neil Postman (1982) argues that the rise and fall of the print media has led to the blurring of the line between children and adults. In other words, in the past children had to read in order to gain access to adult worlds. Today, however, children have much greater access to adult worlds through television, the internet and advertising, for example. Postman claims that this will result in the disappearance of childhood. Others, however, disagree and claim that many children remain separate from adults and protected from the adult world that Postman describes. Postman was also criticised for lacking evidence to support his claims.

The emergence of childhood as we know it is known as the **child-centred society**. It refers to a society in which children's needs are a priority. A collection of legal and attitudinal changes have led to this new status for children.

KEY CONCEPT

Questions

1. Think about the measures of good childhood. Which do you think are most significant to a positive childhood and why?
2. Describe the methodology used in this research.
3. What are the benefits of carrying this research out annually?
4. How might factors such as social class affect childhood?

CONTEMPORARY APPLICATION

There are increasing concerns about the role of technology in encouraging sedentary behaviour in children's lives. The concerns stem from the idea that technology such as computer games is being given to children as a substitute for good parenting. Sue Palmer (2007) calls this **toxic childhood**. Palmer argues that rather than spend quality time with their children, parents are too happy to use television, computer games and fast food to placate them. Palmer suggests that, as a result, children grow up to be easily distractible, self-absorbed and less sociable.

RESEARCH IN FOCUS

The Good Childhood Report 2013 is based on research on the well-being of children, carried out on behalf of the Children's Society. It has been carried out annually since 2005 and includes research on children aged 8–17. The study is based on previously existing research findings, such as the Household Panel Survey, as well as primary research methods such as interviews.

- family
- friends
- health
- appearance
- time use
- future
- home
- money & possessions
- school
- choice

Figure 5.13 The Good Childhood Index

Their latest report reveals that around four-fifths of children are 'flourishing', meaning that they are satisfied with their lives as a whole and find their lives worthwhile. Conversely, about 20 per cent of children aged 8–15 score below the midpoint for one of the two well-being measures used, while 10 per cent, or half a million, are struggling – they score low on both measures.

www.childrenssociety.org.uk/good-childhood-report-2013-online/index.html

Social policy

There is a whole range of policies that relate specifically to children, which have developed as the welfare state expanded. Policies developed for children now tend to focus on a multi-agency approach, whereby different parts of the state work together to protect children.

Here is a brief timeline of some of the most significant policies relating to children. All of these policies reflect the increasing tendency towards a child-centred society.

1946 Universal child benefits introduced (they became means tested in 2013) which is a reflection of how valued children are in society

1991 Child Support Act ensuring the rights of children, making sure that children come first in a divorce, enabling their views to be heard and valued, and making sure that parents provide support for their children

2004 Children Act – 'Every Child Matters' – focusing on the well-being of children from birth to the age of 19

2007 Department for Children established, which focused on improving the quality of life of all children

IN THE NEWS

Why are British children so unhappy?

For several years evidence has been mounting that children in Britain are worse off than those in other developed countries.

In 2007, Unicef published a table of 21 economically advanced countries that compared 40 indicators – including poverty, family relationships, health and safety, education and children's own sense of happiness – that might affect the well-being of children.

The UK came at the bottom of the list, in 21st place (just below the USA). The report concluded that children growing up in the UK were the unhappiest in the industrialised world. Only 40 per cent of UK 11-, 13- and 15-year-olds find their peers 'kind and helpful'. Parents in the UK spent less time 'just talking' to their children than those in more than half the other countries surveyed.

In 2011, a second report from the UN body found that while children said they were happiest spending time with family and friends and 'having plenty to do outdoors', UK parents – particularly in lower-income households – instead felt under 'tremendous pressure' to buy them the latest consumer goods.

In 2012 the Children's Society found that, at any given moment, nearly ten per cent of children in the UK aged between eight and 15 had a low sense of well-being. According to the Office for National Statistics, one in ten UK children aged between five and 16 has a clinically diagnosed mental health disorder.

Adapted from Henley, J. (2012) Why are British children so unhappy? *Guardian*, 27 June.

Questions

1. What position did the UK come in terms of world ranking of childhood?
2. What indicators were used to measure children's happiness?
3. What role might parents take in making sure that children are happy according to this study?
4. How might a conflict theorist and a march of progress theorist explain these findings differently?

Check your understanding

1. Explain some of the reasons for the changes in position of children over the past 100 years.
2. Explain what is meant by child-centred society.
3. What does it mean when someone says childhood is a social construct?
4. How have policies affected the experience of childhood?
5. According to Postman (1982), what is the future of childhood?
6. Give three pieces of evidence that show that childhood is not a protected and privileged time.
7. Explain what is meant by 'toxic childhood' and give an example.

Practice questions

1. Assess two ways in which childhood has changed in the past 50 years.   (10 marks)
2. Outline and explain two ways in which society has become more child centred.   (10 marks)

Read Item A then answer the question that follows.

Item A

According to the conflict view of childhood, children today are likely to be controlled by adults. As well as this, conflict theorists argue that children remain exploited and unhappy. However, march of progress theorists take a different view and argue that today children are more protected and valued, which is linked to their closer relationships with family members.

Applying material from Item A, assess the view that the experience of childhood has improved.   (20 marks)

Section 5: Key demographic changes in the UK

While learning about demographic changes you could examine or analyse changes to the structure or size of the family or focus on a specific change. Remember to discuss these changes specifically in relation to the family and use demographic terms accurately.

> **This section will explore the following debates:**
>
> - What are the causes and consequences of changing birth, death and fertility rates?
> - How has migration affected the family?
> - What are the key demographic changes since 1900?

The UK's ageing population has considerable consequences for public services

The UK is now seeing the rise of the ageing population, a society where there are growing numbers of older people compared to younger people. One important reason for the ageing population is the number of people born during the baby boom of the 1960s. It also stems from increased longevity – a man born in the 1960s lives on average for 84 years. For a boy born today, the figure is 89. The trend for women is similar. A girl born in 1981 might today expect to live to 92. Cohort projections suggest that this will result in demands on public services such as the NHS.

Ten million people in the UK are over 65 years old. The latest projections are for 5.5 million more elderly people in 20 years' time, and the number will have nearly doubled to around 19 million by 2050. Much of today's public spending on benefits is focused on elderly people: 65 per cent of benefit expenditure goes to those over working age.

www.parliament.uk/documents/commons/lib/research/key_issues/Key-Issues-The-ageing-population2007.pdf

Demography refers to the study of the population. Demographic evidence reveals that over the past 100 years there have been significant changes in the population which have had interesting effects on the family and wider society. This section explores key trends in birth, death and fertility rates, exploring the main causes and consequences of these on family life. In simple terms, demographic trends reveal that, in general, women are having fewer children and therefore the family is becoming smaller in size; at the same time there is an increasing number of older people in society.

These population changes over the past century have had two major effects: an ageing population, which is a shift of population age composition towards the older ages, and an increasing **dependency ratio**. The dependency ratio refers to the number of dependents (aged 0–14 and over the age of 65) to the total population (aged 15–64).

There are a number of consequences of an ageing population, both positive and negative, and these include a greater strain on public services such as the health care system and social services, as when people get older they have a higher rate of illness and poverty. Also, increasing costs to the government for public services and pensions may lead to higher taxes for the working population. Due to rising **life expectancy**, there are a greater number of **beanpole families** (Brannen, 2003) in which grandparents may play a more significant role in the lives of their children and grandchildren, helping them financially or with childcare, for example.

There are other effects of an ageing population, such as the fact that as people live longer they are now working for longer, contributing to society for longer (the pension age for women has recently risen to 65). Individuals living longer also have greater opportunity and time to move in and out of various family structures and relationships.

Another area of demography is migration; that is, the number of people moving in and out of a country. This section explores the key trends in migration and suggests reasons for these, as well as discussing the impact of migration rates on family life in the UK.

Questions

1. Explain what is meant by an 'ageing population'.
2. Why do you think people are living longer?
3. Why might people be having fewer children?
4. What impact is the ageing population having on the National Health Service?
5. What kinds of effects might these trends have on the family and households?

5.1 How has the size of the family changed?

Demographic changes have had a number of interesting effects on family structure, roles and relationships. Families tend to be smaller, with extended family members no longer typically living with the family, although extended family may still play an important role in supporting family members, for example, grandparents helping with childcare. Furthermore, extended family members are now able to keep in touch more easily through the internet and by phone. The structure of households is now also far more diverse, as seen earlier in the chapter. The decreasing size of families has led to changes in relationships, with relationships becoming narrower and deeper.

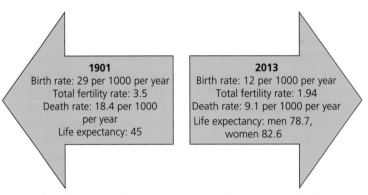

1901
Birth rate: 29 per 1000 per year
Total fertility rate: 3.5
Death rate: 18.4 per 1000 per year
Life expectancy: 45

2013
Birth rate: 12 per 1000 per year
Total fertility rate: 1.94
Death rate: 9.1 per 1000 per year
Life expectancy: men 78.7, women 82.6

Figure 5.14 Summary of key demographic changes since 1900

Birth and fertility rates

Birth rates	Fertility rates
There has been a long term decline in the number of births in the UK. There have been fluctuations in the **birth rate**, which increased with a 'baby boom' after both the First and Second World Wars, but overall the long-term birth rate is in decline.	Fertility has been below the level required to replace the population since 1973 in England and since 1974 in Wales and Scotland. Due to the decline in the birth rate there has been a decline in the **fertility rate** – women are choosing to have fewer children. The fertility rate rose slightly to 1.9 in 2009 due to patterns of immigration (people moving into Britain). Migrant families tend to have slightly larger families than non-migrants. The recent rise is also due to older women having more babies, sometimes with the use of reproductive technologies such as IVF.

Table 5.8 Summary of the key changes in birth and fertility rates

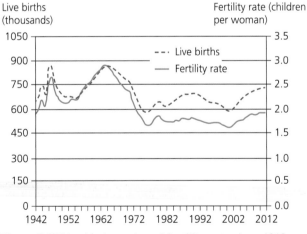

Figure 5.15 Live births and total fertility rate since 1942

 **KEY CONCEPT**

Natural change is an important concept relevant to this debate. **Natural change** is the difference between the numbers of births and deaths, which is a key indicator of population size and growth. If there are more births than deaths a population will experience natural increase.

Cause 1: Change in gender roles

Women's roles have changed a lot over the past 100 years.

Women are delaying having children until later or, in some cases, choosing to remain childless. The average age for women having their first child has increased.

Other reasons for the declining birth rate include: increasingly effective contraception, which has become more widely available; easier access to abortion; the fact that women are less likely to get married.

Many women now work in paid employment – it is difficult to combine a large number of children with working.

Women tend to work in the service sector where there are now more jobs.

Greater legal equality and rights for women, for example the Equal Pay Act.

Increased educational performance for women.

Women leaving having children until later in life may find that they have decreased fertility rates, however fertility rates are rising in older women.

Cause 2: Falling infant mortality

The infant mortality rate (IMR), the number of deaths of infants aged between 0 and 1 in a year per 1000 live births in the same year, has fallen dramatically due to rising living standards, improved hygiene and sanitation, improvements in health care, increased monitoring of child welfare and the developing role of the welfare state.

Cause 3: Children have become an economic burden

In the early nineteenth century, children were often seen as an economic asset because they worked, and contributed to the family income. However, legislation has gradually banned or restricted children working and the length of schooling has been extended. This has made children dependant on their families for longer and means that they are an economic burden rather than asset. People also have higher expectations about living standards and so having fewer children means that this may be more possible.

Figure 5.16 The causes and consequences of the long-term decline in birth and fertility rates

People have become more concerned with their own individual needs. This view is shared by postmodernists such as Beck and Gernsheim (1995) who call this process individualisation. People no longer have to follow traditional norms and values and instead make their own decisions, for example about marriage and having children. This has resulted in fewer people feeling that they should have children.

Consequences of long-term decline in birth and fertility rates

The consequences of the long-term decline in birth and fertility rates include:

- changes in the dependency ratio – that is, the relationship between the economically productive part of the population and non-workers, or dependants such as children and the elderly – falling numbers of children mean there will be less people of a working age, which leads to greater numbers of dependent people
- strain on public services, such as hospitals, while schools may close as a result of the falling numbers of children.
- falling fertility rates can lead to further changes in gender roles, giving women more time for their careers and perhaps leading to relationships between men and women becoming more equal.

Death rates

Since 1901 the number of deaths in the UK has been in steady decline while the population has grown, so the **death rate** has fallen. Falling death rates are reflected in rising life expectancy. Death rates and life expectancy vary between social groups and places. There are a number of causes of the declining death rate:

- decrease in **infectious diseases** such as TB, measles and whooping cough
- **medical advances**, such as vaccines and antibiotics
- improved **maternity care** and the establishment of the NHS have led to a decline in infant mortality rates
- welfare, health and environment – the government has provided better sanitation, sickness benefit and free school meals for those who couldn't afford them. The 1944 Beveridge Report and the development of the National Health Service led to greater government help for the elderly, sick and the young as health care became free to all at the point of delivery. However, there are still significant differences in death rates between various social groups which shows that economic and social factors continue to be important in determining how healthy a person is.

KEY SOCIOLOGISTS

McKeown (1962) argued that the growth in population in the industrialised world during industrialisation to the present was due not to life-saving advancements in the field of medicine or public health, but instead to improvements in overall standards of living, especially diet and nutritional status, resulting from increased affluence.

Questions

1. What are the two main reasons for declining death rates?
2. Why might it be challenging to investigate death rates?

RESEARCH IN FOCUS

Clare Griffiths and Anita Brock (2003) carried out research into declining death rates and explained how infectious diseases have declined to low levels, with the epidemics of the early part of the century no longer occurring. The declining death rates, they claim, are also due to hygiene and improved nutrition, as well as a lack in absolute poverty. This study shows how better nutrition also helped to increase people's resistance to infectious diseases. However, Griffiths and Brock point out how challenging it can be to investigate death rates when definitions of disease and cases of death have changed as well.

ONS (2003) Twentieth century mortality trends in England and Wales. *Health Statistics Quarterly*, 18.

Consequences of declining death rates

The consequences include:

- greater life expectancy
- greater dependency ratio
- more pressure on elderly services/women in families to care for older family members
- cost to the state, for example pensions
- grandparents playing a greater role in their grandchildren's lives
- beanpole families increasing (multi-generational families)
- longer period of life means greater chance of divorce and remarriage
- older people who continue to be well making a greater contribution to society
- increase in the numbers of the 'sandwich generation' (the middle-aged population who feel pressure to care for elderly parents and children/ grandchildren at the same time).

According to Hirsch (2005) by the middle of this century, for the first time ever, there will be no systematic decline in the population in successively higher age groups for the first 80 years of life. Today, there remains significantly fewer 60–80 year olds than people in younger age groups, but by 2041, according to current projections, this will no longer be true. There are numerous effects of an ageing population, both positive and negative. The Griffiths Report (1983) was produced in order to assess the effectiveness of care in the community. The conclusion reached was that government and managers should be involved with increasing the efficiency and the organisation of care in the community. This report coincided with the introduction of the privatisation of some parts of care in the community. The report was partly in recognition of the fact that there were growing numbers of elderly people in society.

Blaikie (1999) describes the effects of an ageing population, which results in a longer retirement period, breaking down the barriers between mid and later life. At the same time, 'positive ageing' also creates new needs and new norms, with new forms of deviance. While baby boomers (people born immediately after the Second World War) may expect a fulfilling retirement, none look forward to the idea of physical decline. Blaikie concludes that living longer is leading to increasing opportunities for older people as well as a shift in popular culture to include 'grey' consumerism and culture. Grandparents are increasingly involved with caring for their grandchildren as well, playing a more significant role in their lives as often both parents now work.

Different perspectives

Feminists would argue that the changing role of women has resulted in greater control over their fertility and less social pressure to conform to traditional gender roles; in other words, women having children. Functionalists might argue that as each institution becomes increasingly specialised, society improves, thus resulting in greater life expectancy and lower death rates.

Social policy

The development of the welfare state and the NHS following the Second World War, when health care became free at the point of service, has had a huge impact on the health of the nation. As a result, death rates have declined as well as infant mortality rates. The state has also developed care of the elderly and thus played a large role in the longer life expectancy.

CONTEMPORARY APPLICATION

The birth rate is linked to the economy. When the economy is strong and growing, the birth rate tends to increase. When the economy is weak or there is a recession, the birth rate generally declines. This partially helps explain the slight growth in the birth rate during the late 1990s when the economy saw a period of growth compared with the decline in the birth rate around 2005–2010 when the economy went into recession. This is not surprising given that, on average, a child costs £186,000 to raise to the age of 18 today. In an economic downturn, people are less likely to be confident in their employment and financial security, and smaller families are more likely.

STUDY TIPS

When discussing demography, be careful not to simply describe trends. Consider the causes, consequences and impact on the family.

5.2 How has migration affected the family?

Migration, the movement of people in or out of a country, has always been a feature of life within the UK. However, there have been significant increases in immigration since the Second World War. Immigration refers to a specific form of migration, where people move into the UK. The first increase was a result of the Second World War, after which immigrants from Asia and Africa came to the UK to work and live. The second wave of migration occurred as a result of the addition of various European countries to the EU, giving people the opportunity to travel, live and work within other EU countries.

Ethnic group	Percentages
White	86.0
Mixed/Multiple ethnic groups	2.2
Asian/Asian British	7.5
Black/African/Caribbean/Black British	3.3
Other ethnic group	1.0

Table 5.9 Composition of the UK population, 2015

www.ons.gov.uk/ons/interactive/index.html

There are a number of reasons why people choose to move into or out of an area, and these are known as **push or pull factors**. Push factors might include war or conflict, lack of jobs, poor education and health system, and political or economic instability. Pull factors might be the reverse: a good education and health care system, political and economic stability, and employment. As well as this, pull factors might include climate and a better standard of living.

IN THE NEWS

A quarter of all babies born in the UK are the children of immigrants

According to a 2012 report by the Office for National Statistics there were 200,000 births to immigrant mothers in Britain in 2011, with forty per cent of these children born in London. The highest numbers of mothers not born in the UK were from Poland, Pakistan, India, Bangladesh and Nigeria.

The report also found that fertility rates for women born abroad were higher than for those born here. The children of women born abroad made up nearly a quarter of all the babies born in Britain. The number of babies born to migrant mothers had more than doubled since the 1990s.

The report indicated the growing impact on the population of historically high levels of immigration in recent years. It said understanding the impact of childbearing among migrants is 'essential for planning services such as maternity provision and schools'.

Adapted from Adams, S. (2012) A quarter of all babies born in the UK are the children of immigrants as mothers from Poland, India and Pakistan give birth in record numbers. *Daily Mail*, 25 October.

Questions

1. How are the fertility patterns of migrants different to non-migrant women?
2. Why is it important to understand the impact of childbearing among migrants?
3. Which countries are foreign-born mothers most likely to come from?

CONTEMPORARY APPLICATION

Increasing migration is a key feature of globalisation. Globalisation, the compression of time and space, has a number of interesting effects on family life. Families have generally become smaller and thus more geographically mobile. This means that they are more able to move for work. Given that many companies are now transnational and often span continents, this provides greater opportunities for people to move. Also, relatives can visit their family members more frequently and communicate with their family members more regularly. Globalisation has led to greater migration and, as a result, increasing numbers of multicultural families have emerged in the UK and elsewhere. This has led to greater diversity in family structures, roles and relationships.

Check your understanding

1. What is demography?
2. Identify three key demographic changes since 1900.
3. What is the life expectancy today?
4. Offer some predictions about what might happen to the population in the future.
5. Why are there more people living alone today?
6. What is the dependency ratio?
7. Why are we likely to see more beanpole families in society?
8. What impact has immigration had on birth rates and why?

Practice questions

1. Outline and explain two factors that might have led to the declining birth rate.　　　　[10 marks]

Read Item A then answer the question that follows.

Item A

The death rate has dropped from 29 per 1000 of the population in 1901, to 12 per 1000 of the population in 2013. The cause of the decline includes better health care, improved sanitation and safer working environments. This has had a number of effects on the family, both in terms of the size of the family and the roles and relationships that exist within the family too.

Applying material from Item A, analyse two effects of the declining death rate on the family.　　　　[10 marks]

Links to other topics

This topic has links to:

- Chapter 1 Theory and methods, section 1
- Chapter 4 Culture and identity, section 2
- Chapter 6 Health, section 2.1 How does social class determine inequalities in health?
- Chapter 7 Work, poverty and welfare, section 1.3 To what extent are poverty and social exclusion linked?

6

Health

Understanding the specification	
AQA specification	**How the specification is covered in this chapter**
● The social construction of health, illness, disability and the body, and models of health and illness.	*Section 1* ● What is health? ● How can sociological perspectives explain health provision? ● To what extent is health and illness a social construct? ● What is meant by the 'sick role'? ● How is disability socially constructed? ● How is the body a social construction? ● What are the models of health?
● The unequal social distribution of health chances in the UK by social class, gender, ethnicity and region.	*Section 2* ● How does social class determine inequalities in health? ● How does gender determine inequalities in health? ● How does ethnicity determine inequalities in health? ● How does region determine inequalities in health?
● Inequalities in the provision of, and access to, health care in contemporary society.	*Section 3* ● How consistent is the NHS as a health care provider? ● How might NHS reforms transform health care provision? ● What is the potential impact of private health provision? ● How might social factors influence the take-up of health care?
● The nature and social distribution of mental illness.	*Section 4* ● How is mental health defined? ● How is mental illness labelled and stigmatised? ● How can social factors influence the demand for mental health services?
● The role of medicine, the health professions and the globalised health industry.	*Section 5* ● What is the current status of the medical profession? ● Are functionalists right to grant medical professionals a high position in the social system? ● Are Marxists right to see the medical profession as an agent of control? ● Are interactionists right to see patient–practitioner consultations as one-sided? ● Are feminists right to still see the medical profession as male dominated? ● Is the postmodernist perspective right to see an increasingly fragmented health service? ● Is there a globalised health industry?

Section 1: Health, illness and disability

This section will explore the following debates:

● What is health?
● How can sociological perspectives explain health provision?
● To what extent is health and illness a social construct?
● What is meant by the 'sick role'?
● How is disability socially constructed?
● How is the body a social construction?
● What are the models of health?

GETTING YOU STARTED

Deprived Glasgow where life expectancy is just 54

Figure 6.1 Calton, Glasgow

There is an inner-city area of Glasgow called Calton where the average life expectancy of a man is just 53.9 years. Although Calton is only a few minutes from Glasgow city centre, its deprivation is so severe that its life expectancy is not only the lowest in Europe but considerably below that of many developing countries. Even in North Korea men have an average life expectancy of 71.3 years.

The explanation for this appalling statistic lies with both structural and lifestyle factors. Deprivation is deep and widespread. For example, 37 per cent live in a workless household, while 44 per cent are on incapacity benefit. In terms of unhealthy behaviour, Calton is characterised by heavy drinking, smoking, drugs and a poor diet. Admissions to hospital for alcohol-related illnesses are above the average for Scotland and smoking rates in Calton are double the Scottish national average. The outcome is levels of cancer, heart attacks, diabetes, drug overdose and suicide that serve to achieve this very low life expectancy.

Adapted from Gillian, A. (2006) In Iraq, life expectancy is 67, minutes from Glasgow city centre, it's 54. *Guardian*, 21 January.

Questions

1. How does life expectancy in Calton, Glasgow, compare to North Korea?
2. Give reasons for the low life expectancy in Calton, Glasgow.
3. List any other factors not mentioned in the article that might be responsible for the low life expectancy in Calton.

223

1.1 What is health?

If you are discussing what health means then you could offer a definition as well as exploring how it is a contested concept because of the different meanings it has for health professionals and lay people.

Mildred Blaxter (2010) argued that we need to distinguish between negative and positive definitions of health. The medical profession tend to define health in a negative manner as 'the absence of disease'. In 1948 the **World Health Organization** (WHO) came up with the following definition:

> (Health is) a state of complete physical, mental and social well-being and not merely the absence of disease or infirmity.

The emphasis on well-being makes this definition essentially positive, rather than negative. There is also an acknowledgement of the importance of individual, social and mental well-being. However, it has been criticised for being rather vague and difficult to measure. Giddens and Sutton (2013) imply it might be 'too utopian to be helpful'. What exactly is meant by physical well-being, mental well-being and, especially, social well-being?

In 1984 the WHO came up with a more complex second definition, intended to address some of the criticisms of the first definition of health:

> '[Health is] the extent to which an individual or group is able, on the one hand, to realise aspirations and satisfy needs; and on the other hand, to change or cope with the environment. Health is, therefore, seen as a resource for everyday life, not the objective for living; it is a positive concept emphasizing social and personal resources, as well as physical capacities.'

This is a stronger, more holistic definition that associates health with individual personal growth and development within the context of meeting basic personal needs. Health has now become a means to an end and not an end in itself or simply the absence of disease. This evolving definition shows that defining health is potentially problematic. Indeed, it becomes even more complex when we look at **lay** definitions.

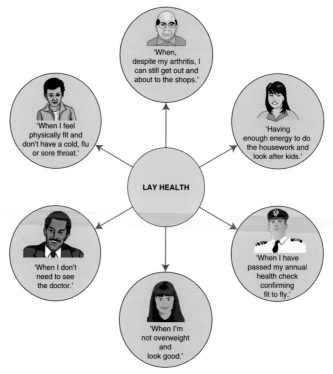

Figure 6.2 Lay health

The interactionist perspective would be interested in how lay definitions of health are subjective in nature, reflecting reality inside people's heads. This shows that lay ideas are shaped by socialisation, culture and identity. Blaxter (2010) also felt that health could be defined as functional and experiential. Functional definitions of health are addressed shortly with Parsons' 'sick role'. The above lay definitions are clearly experiential.

Recognising that definitions of health are shaped by attitudes and interpretation shows the social construction of health. For example, until the 1960s doctors in the UK tried to 'cure' homosexuality with **aversion therapy** in psychiatric hospitals. Being homosexual is no longer a health issue. In terms of social policy, regulating and controlling illness is important to governments as health treatment is expensive and they want to restrict **malingering**. This is dealt with later in the discussion of the sick role.

1.2 How can sociological perspectives explain health provision?

If you study how sociological perspectives explain health care you will develop an understanding of how sociological theories differ.

Health can be defined subjectively, objectively, positively, negatively, functionally and experientially. Interpreting health can also vary with age, gender, ethnicity and social class. We explore some of these interpretations and definitions below.

Marxist perspective

The basis of the Marxist perspective is that the origins of illness are social in nature and derive from the capitalist economic system. Capitalism is seen to cause ill health for two reasons. Firstly, workers can become sick from physical injuries, working with toxic substances or work-related stress. Secondly, many of the products of capitalism can make people ill. Obvious examples are tobacco and alcohol, but as the consumption of convenience and processed food increases, the high levels of fat, sugar, salt and chemical additives all combine to undermine health.

The concept of health as an 'ideological state apparatus' (ISA) is an important concept to this debate. It is associated with the French sociologist Louis Althusser (1969) who argues that ISAs serve to mystify the real exploitative nature of capitalism and therefore act as both a form of social control and a promoter of false consciousness. Health care provision, especially when it is free, acts to make people support capitalism rather than to question its inherent inequalities and unfairness. Vicente Navarro (1979) suggested that doctors serve the interests of capitalism by operating as agents of the state. By supporting the government's emphasis on cultural factors and lifestyle as the key determinant of poor health, this serves to detract from the real cause of ill health: capitalism.

Functionalist perspective

The functionalist perspective of health is heavily dominated by the work of Talcott Parsons and the sick role (covered on page 228). Parsons makes the point that most recognition of illness stems from people's self-diagnosis and reporting to a doctor for confirmation of this. However, people are not consistent in this respect, and reporting to doctors varies with social class, gender, ethnicity and age.

KEY SOCIOLOGISTS

Richard Wilkinson and Kate Pickett (2010) sought to show how health was shaped by social factors such as the degree of inequality in societies, strong communities and friendship networks.

CONTEMPORARY APPLICATION

Since its origins in the 1940s the WHO's definition of health has been widely quoted and is still frequently used. This shows that, while not perfect, it is still useful and has a timeless quality.

STUDY TIP

It is important to be aware not only of the difficulty in defining health but also how the meaning of health will differ between and within health professionals and lay people.

KEY SOCIOLOGISTS

Max Weber (1864–1920) has an important contribution to make to this debate. Weber saw doctors as largely operating out of self-interest. They became powerful through **social closure** to anyone other than the very brightest, who are usually drawn from the upper middle class. Because of their class, status and power over patients, doctors historically and culturally can dominate the consultation process. Note that postmodernists argue that this may be changing.

CONTEMPORARY APPLICATION

Following the Francis Report into the poor-quality treatment and high number of unnecessary deaths at the Mid Staffordshire Trust, the NHS now recognises the importance that good-quality patient–practitioner interaction can have on healing. Simple things like spending time with patients, talking to them, listening to their concerns and addressing issues such as noise, privacy and the quality of food, can make a huge difference. 'People who have a better experience in these terms are happier, healthier and do better' (NHS Confederation).

STUDY TIP

Theoretical perspectives underpin all sociological understanding. Try to include these in your essays where applicable.

Parsons assumes that doctors act out of altruism, and treat all patients equally, but research shows again that the social class, age, gender and ethnicity of patients can have a considerable bearing on the quality and type of treatment provided. Evidence also shows that those higher up the social scale are given both extra time and a more comprehensive explanation of their illness than the lower classes.

Feminists would argue that Parsons was blind to the frequent put-downs female patients receive when their health problems can be reduced to 'feminine neuroses' or 'cured' with problematic drugs such as Valium and Prozac. The elderly are also routinely dismissed with 'what do you expect at your age'.

Interactionist perspective

The interactionist perspective is rooted in the work and ideas of Max Weber, who focused on the dynamics between practitioners and patients. Weber's work has produced the most fruitful findings from the interactionist perspective. For example, interactionists have looked at factors such as length of consultation according to social class, the growing **medicalisation** of society, medicine as a form of 'information control' whereby patients are told only as much as the practitioner feels is necessary, and the labelling and stigmatisation of medical conditions, especially mental illness. Because of these factors, many individuals clearly find the medical profession intimidating. Consequently this may influence the consultation rates of some individuals and groups.

Postmodernist perspective

The scientific, biomedical model and, indeed, the sociological perspectives discussed above, are all rooted in modernity. Postmodernism is characterised by its focus on individualism but also on increased diversity and choice. Postmodernists see the balance of power between practitioners and patients as more equitably distributed than interactionists do. In addition, the postmodernist perspective portrays individuals as acting more like consumers with regard to health care. For example, they shop around more and increasingly embrace **complementary** and **alternative medicine** (CAM) therapies.

The consumerist patient is increasingly educated and challenging, becoming sceptical about intrusive medical methods and the questionable efficacy of biomedical medicine with all its **iatrogenesis**. Postmodernists point out that, in this new climate, the medical profession can no longer bully people into procedures. In addition, it is finding it has to increasingly justify its actions to a questioning public.

1.3 Are health and illness social constructions?

If you discuss the social construction of health and illness, you could bring in the following key ideas.

When sociologists use the term 'social construction', they imply that the things being described are neither natural nor normal. Instead they have been culturally produced to reflect prevailing norms and values about how things should be. When medicine in the Western world is so dominated by the objectivity of science and technology, it might seem odd to even talk about the social construction of health. But consider how the variations in the meaning of health discussed on page 224 and Talcott Parsons' concept of the 'sick role' (see pages 225–226) contribute to how it can be viewed as constructed. While medicine is based on accumulated knowledge, there are still a lot of uncertainties and unknowns. So, for many diseases, doctors do the best they can but there is still a lot they do not understand, and interpretations and treatments will vary across cultures. It is therefore important to bear in mind that the meaning of health and illness can be quite value-laden and lead to stereotyping, labelling and stigmatisation.

With advances in scientific medicine, health practitioners are becoming increasingly successful in understanding how every bodily component is performing (or underperforming), even down to sub-cellular levels. Giddens and Sutton (2013) note that among all the complexity of defining health is that, in Western society, the approach of the biomedical model dominates all the others. It is important to recognise that although it is the dominant means of approaching health and illness, this model is not the only one. There are alternatives to this scientific approach to health, for example Chinese medicine, which adopts a more holistic approach. Within the West some people feel that by focusing too much on detail we run the risk of missing the bigger picture. A scientific approach to understanding medicine would equate with a positivistic approach favoured by functionalists. In contrast, interpretive sociologists would recognise the subjective meaning of health and illness.

CAM and Chinese medicine adopt a holistic approach to health and illness. The holistic approach is relevant to the social construction of health debate because it offers an alternative approach to Western scientific medicine. This shows that the Western scientific medical approach is just one of many ways of understanding health.

CAM practioners believe that the body is made up of interdependent parts. Consequently, focusing on just one part ignores how other parts may be affected. Holistic medicine adopts a method of healing that takes into consideration the whole person: body, mind, spirit and emotions.

In terms of social policy, governments cannot ignore the fact that health inequalities are socially constructed. Their policies on health, however, are increasingly focused on **victim blaming**: the onus is on the individual to take responsibility for their health. Health promotion therefore focuses on encouraging people to exercise, eat healthily, drink moderately and not smoke.

KEY SOCIOLOGISTS

Michel Foucault (1926–84), a post-structuralist, would describe Western medicine as a discourse because it is just one way of looking at health. This shows that while Western scientific medicine is the dominant way of viewing health, especially in the developed world, it is by no means the only way.

CONTEMPORARY APPLICATION

With advances in medical knowledge, scientific medicine has become the dominant means of treating illness not only in the Western developed world but increasingly globally too.

STUDY TIP

It is important to have good understanding of how health is socially constructed and the 'social determinants' perspective, which focuses on the social causes of health inequalities.

RESEARCH IN FOCUS

Social determinants of health

Benoit *et al* (2009) responded to the resurgence of interest in the social causes of health inequities among and between individuals and populations. Although their research is specifically about Canada, it has a universal application to countries in the developed world, such as the UK.

It is worth reminding ourselves about the key message of the social determinants of health, namely that the maintenance and promotion of a population's health is only partly achieved by public investment in health services, such as hospitals, physicians and advanced medical technology.

According to the WHO (2008), we could close the health gap within and across countries in the next decade if, in addition to improving access to primary health care, we take concerted action to reduce the health gap caused by the fundamental factors, including sex and gender, socio-economic status, race, ethnicity, immigrant status, employment and geographical location.

Progressive changes in the Canadian context that are likely to reduce such inequity include an increase in the minimum wage for private as well as public-sector employment; equal pay for work of equal value; policies to raise the value of care work, which is predominantly performed by girls and women; establishment of a national childcare system; public funding for care of the disabled and elderly; improved educational and economic opportunities for Aboriginal peoples, ethnic minorities and new immigrants; and, of course, increased investment in primary health care in an effort to improve health care access and quality of care for its vulnerable populations, including girls and women in rural and remote areas as well as the inner city.

Adapted from Benoit *et al* (2009) Explaining the health gap experienced by girls and women in Canada: A social determinants of health perspective. *Sociological Research Online, 14* (5), 9.

Questions

1. Why is a population's health 'only partly achieved' by public investment in health services, such as hospitals, physicians and advanced medical technology?
2. What is the cause of the health gap 'within and across countries' according to the WHO?
3. List the factors identified by Benoit *et al* which they feel would reduce health inequities in Canada.

1.4 What is the sick role?

The meaning of illness and how it is regulated are important concepts which will form part of your studies.

Illness (like health) is something of a subjective concept. Inevitably, the meanings of illness rest, firstly, on an individual's interpretation and, secondly, on getting someone else (family, employers and, ultimately, doctors) to believe them. Sometimes getting someone to validate sickness is easy, such as when you have a rash, swelling or fever. But what if someone simply does not feel well or has pains or problems with internal organs that are not directly visible? Faking illness can be a good excuse for avoiding activities such as attending school, work, meetings and unpleasant social events. To avoid people abusing illness, Talcott Parsons (1951) developed the concept of the 'sick role'.

This concept is particularly associated with the functionalist perspective as it views being sick as stopping a person from carrying out their normal social functions. People who are genuinely ill should receive sympathy, benefits such as sick pay and be relieved from their work-related duties. However, they have a responsibility to want to get better and follow their doctor's instructions and guidance on how to restore health.

Parsons argued that for society to function properly it must distinguish between those who claim they are ill and those who actually are really ill. Parsons saw doctors as the main group responsible for regulating sickness. The idea of doctors as experts is an important concept for this debate. Because of their long and intensive training, doctors are viewed as experts who use scientific criteria in order to pass judgement on whether someone is healthy or not. This is reflected in patient–practitioner power dynamics as mentioned above. While Parsons, as a functionalist, highlights the role of doctors in 'policing' illness, Marxists have a similar view of doctors being used by the state as agents of social control in order to stop malingering in the workforce. Interactionists point to the unequal power in the doctor–patient relationship which arises from this policing function.

In terms of social policy, regulating the sick role is an important obligation undertaken by doctors on behalf of the government. In 2013 UK workers took an average of 9.1 sick days, nearly double the amount of workers in the USA (4.9 days) and four times more than workers in Asia Pacific (2.2 days). The average for Western Europe is 7.3 days (ONS, 2014a).

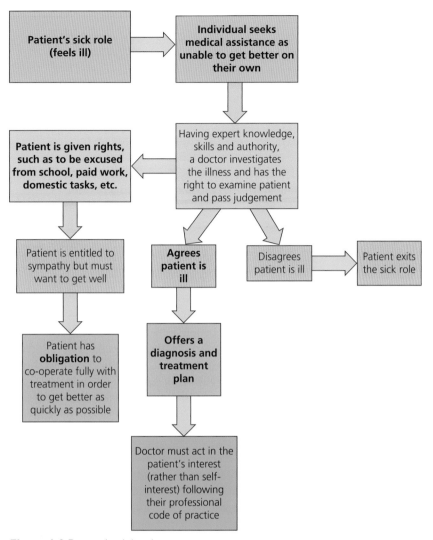

Figure 6.3 Parson's sick role

KEY SOCIOLOGISTS

This concept was developed by the functionalist sociologist Talcott Parsons in his book *The Social System* (1951). He recognised the deviant way that people might use illness as a means of avoiding their responsibilities.

CONTEMPORARY APPLICATION

The concept of the 'sick note' is an important legitimiser of illness. It formalises children's absence from school and worker's time off from their jobs.

STUDY TIP

It is important to be aware of Parsons' 'sick role' and how it can be applied to health situations (mental as well as physical illness).

Questions

1. How are people who enter the sick role, but considered to be 'malingerers', viewed and treated?
2. The legitimacy of both myalgic encephalopathy, or chronic fatigue syndrome (ME/CFS; disparagingly called 'yuppie-flu') and repetitive strain injury (RSI) were challenged by doctors as 'pseudo-illnesses' in the past. Outline their passage through Figure 6.3.
3. What issues might be raised about a person with a mental illness within this sick role model?

1.5 How is disability socially constructed?

When discussing disability it is important to mention its social construction rather than the physical or mental characteristics of a disabled person.

Figure 6.4 How would you cope without a basic sense most take for granted?

KEY SOCIOLOGISTS

Tom Shakespeare, a leading authority on disability, adopts a postmodernist view of disability and describes how people with disabilities have been subject to the process of **othering** throughout history.

CONTEMPORARY APPLICATION

Society is still responsible for the disabling of people with impairments. This is shown by the example of a visually impaired person who becomes disabled because society does not accommodate their needs by providing interventions such as electronic doors, talking lifts in all public buildings or laying tactile pavements.

STUDY TIP

Remember that the term disability is something of a fluid concept. Categories included in this broad term vary across time and between cultures. In the twentieth century there was a huge expansion of people classified as disabled, such as the inclusion of those with specific learning difficulties, for example dyslexia.

When writing about disability, include the factors that serve to socially marginalise and exclude disabled people.

The WHO states that:

> disability is a complex phenomenon, reflecting an interaction between features of a person's body and features of the society in which he or she lives.

While many people's image of disability centres on some form of physical (or mental) impediment, the above quotation challenges this, suggesting that these impediments derive from society's discriminatory treatment.

Roddy Slorach (2012) notes that the WHO's definition still fudges the vital distinction established by the disability movement between impairment (the biological factor) and disability (the treatment) as social discriminations. An inability to walk is impairment; an inability to enter a building because of stairs becomes a disability. Therefore, by not making reasonable adjustments to accommodate the needs of people with impairments, society effectively disables them. The social model of disability thus locates disability as an important dimension of inequality. The cause of such inequality is therefore located in the fabric and structures of society, rather than in individual limitations.

The origins of the sociology of disability are rooted in the work of Talcott Parsons' (1951) sick role model. In the past disability was often equated with illness and disease, and therefore disabled people were relieved of all normal expectations and responsibilities. In terms of contemporary social policy, Roddy Slorach (2012) argues that the Coalition government's 2010 policy of subjecting 2 million people to medical tests as part of the Work Capability Assessment (WCA) shows that the idea of disability equalling a work-shy malingerer still carries weight in the twenty-first century.

Michael Oliver (1986), one of the strongest advocates of the social model of disability, notes how the disabled were encouraged to view their situation as loathsome and undesirable. The term 'stigma' is important here since it is frequently associated with disability. For example, the interactionist Erving Goffman (1963) shows how it is used as a marker for 'moral inferiority'. However, as the social model gained recognition and popularity, Shakespeare and Watson (2002) argued caution, implying that the success of the social model could become its main weakness. He argues that the social model became an ideology that could not easily be challenged – effectively a 'sacred cow'. While society clearly does 'disable' the impaired, impairments cannot simply be ignored as aches, pains and symptoms can be part of everyday life for people with disabilities.

Marxists would see disability as the neglect and marginalisation of a group considered surplus to the requirements of a society based on profit. This shows how capitalism routinely generates impairment then scapegoats and discriminates against those affected.

IN THE NEWS

The disabled and intimate relationships

Having access to intimate sexual relationships is considered a human right and is something most able-bodied people take for granted. However, any attempt to facilitate relationships for disabled people is met with either denial or outright opposition from wider society.

A stranger approached Karen Shook in a supermarket last year. 'He asked if I could still have sex because I was in a wheelchair,' says Shook, laughing as she recalls the incident. 'I told him "Yes, as long as I put the brakes on." Then he told me off for being rude!'

Strangely narrow views exist about disabled people's sexuality, with some assuming that they don't have sex. As with older people and the under-aged, some prefer to believe disabled people are safely tucked up in bed alone.

Characters with a disability appear on TV only rarely, and are often portrayed in the mainstream media as unusually brave, or tragic. 'The mass view seems to be that the only needs of people with disabilities are to be washed and fed.

People with disabilities are cared for as children – you're infantilised – and people don't want to see children as sexual beings.' says Dipa, who has a progressive mobility impairment.

Disabled people are also faced with practical issues. A couple needs to meet first before they can go on to have a relationship. Transport and access issues can deter disabled people from going out to socialise, as can poverty. By denying a sex life, we deny disabled people their full human rights.

Adapted from McNutt, H. (2004) Hidden pleasures. *Guardian*, 13 October.

1.6 How is the body a social construction?

If you are discussing the body then you could focus on its social construction as a source of identity and as a cultural icon.

Just like health and illness, the body, in terms of its shape and size, is also a social construction. For example, the article on page 230 showed how disabled people can be stereotyped and discriminated against simply because their bodies can be different. Further evidence to support the fact that bodies are not just a biological entity but have social meanings is reflected in the global and historical variation in what constitutes the 'ideal', or indeed healthy, body shape. There is no such thing as a natural shape or normal size of either female or male bodies. Instead the body reflects prevailing cultural attitudes, lifestyle decisions and structural factors such as the spread of fast-food culture.

For example, walk into any art gallery and look at paintings of artists such as Rubens and the baroque style. The women portrayed are full-figured and curvy, reflecting the ideal body shape of pre-modern society, when not being skinny demonstrated wealth. This supports the idea that the ideal body shape is shaped by socialisation, culture and identity. Even today, in many parts of the **developing world**, size is still culturally important: when the poor look very thin and malnourished it betrays their socio-economic status. In the past men were probably under less pressure to conform to an ideal body type, but there has always been the ideal of having 'muscle and brawn' (strength). Younger men are increasingly faced with living up to media images of topless men with tight 'six-pack' stomachs. Body size and weight are measured globally with the **body mass index** (BMI). Being overweight (BMI 25–29) or obese (BMI 30+) is linked to numerous health complications, chronic diseases and an increased risk of premature death. In some sections of society, illustrated by magazines which demonise celebrities for 'letting themselves go', there is a perception that being fat indicates a lack of self-control, greediness and laziness. It could be argued that women are fighting a losing battle, with the weight disparity between 'normal' women and models/actresses at 23 per cent. In addition, the gap between what is realistically attainable and the ideal body continues to widen.

The term **clinical gaze** (also associated with Michel Foucault) is important as it shows that the pressure to fit into the prevailing cultural norms about size and shape enhances body dissatisfaction for women far more than for men. Feminists such as Naomi Wolf (1990) have focused on the pressures women are

Questions

1. Why do you think people make narrow assumptions when it comes to disabled people's sexuality?
2. Do you agree that 'by denying a sex life, we deny disabled people their full human rights'?
3. How does the article confirm that disabled people are socially constructed?

6 Health

KEY SOCIOLOGISTS

Sarah Grogan (2007) found that men and children are also beginning to suffer more from perceived body image dissatisfaction (PBID). This shows the power of the media and how it is making us all engage more in critical self-surveillance.

CONTEMPORARY APPLICATION

Giddens and Sutton (2013) note that as Western images that reinforce the ideal of slimness spread around the world via the mass media, there has been a corresponding rise in associated illnesses, such as eating disorders. This also shows the power of the media.

STUDY TIP

When evaluating the factors behind the social construction of the body, remember the difficulty in establishing cause and effect relationships between cultural attitudes and body size.

under to have bodies that are slim, youthful and attractive. This is shown by the estimation that on average women spend 31 years of their lives on a diet. NHS Choices (2015) notes that while women account for the vast majority of eating disorders, it is a growing problem among men too. Ironically, our obsession with body size is occurring when the reality for most societies in the developed world is that bodies are getting bigger.

Perceived body image dissatisfaction (PBID) shows that the body, while a physical phenomenon, has to be viewed just as much in social terms as in biological terms. Julia Twigg (2006) argues that the body cannot be simply reduced to a social construction. This is because bodies have a physical and biological presence that is distinct from the social relationships and cultural forms that shape social life.

Cultural changes to society, such as a shift towards fast food, play a part in changing the body. For example, the journalist Michael Booth (2014) notes that when the USA set up an airbase in Okinawa, Japan, the Okinawans moved from being the healthiest and longest-living people in the world to having the highest rates of obesity in the country.

1.7 What are the models of health?

If you are thinking about models of health it is important to understand the contrasting ways of thinking about how health impacts on the body.

Biomedical model

The scientific medical approach discussed so far is known as the biomedical model. It assumes that illnesses and their causes can be identified, classified and measured using objective scientific methods. Building on this body of knowledge and embracing evermore sophisticated technology, medicine can engage in cure through the use of prescribed drugs or surgery. The biomedical model uses the analogy of the body like a machine and sees the root cause of illness lying within the body and in need of an intervening treatment to cure it. This analogy can be understood when doctors specifically treat the part of the body that isn't working properly. When applied to 'spare-part surgery' (for example, kidney, hip or cornea transplants) it makes even more sense.

The biomedical model has come in for increasing criticism in the past 40 years or so. Social historians have criticised the medical profession's narrow focus on curative and scientific medicine. For example, Thomas McKeown (1976) argues that improvements in public health can be linked to rising living standards, clean water, efficient sewerage removal and improved nutrition rather than the treatment of people with medicines.

Others adopt a more radical view. Ivan Illich (1975) uses the term iatrogenisis, which literally means doctor-generated illness, and refers to sickness produced by medical activity. Illich refers to 'clinical iatrogenesis' as the unwanted side effects of medications or medical malpractice which, together with doctor ignorance, can impair recovery or even kill the patient. Such is the power of the biomedical model and the medical profession that Illich uses the term 'social iatrogenesis' to refer to the way people have become hypochondriacs, resulting in a 'cultural iatrogenesis' whereby people are constantly making appointments to see the doctor and embracing a 'pill for every ill' culture.

Another criticism of the biomedical approach is its view that scientific medicine is superior to all other approaches, for example, complementary and alternative medicine.

Feminists are critical of the biomedical approach as they see conventional medicine as being dominated by men. Women's problems, they argue, become marginalised or masked, such as through the overprescription of tranquillisers or antidepressants.

Critics of biomedical medicine generally suggest that it ignores the opinions and experiences of patients.

Social model of health

Despite the increasing dominance of the biomedical model around the world, observers note that those who become ill are not equally distributed throughout society. Instead, as the item on page 223 about Calton in Glasgow shows, illness and premature death occurs more in deprived backgrounds. The social model of health focuses on diseases of poverty and deprivation, and explains health inequalities in relation to the structural features of society, such as poor housing and deprived environments.

The social model of health also looks at lifestyle and cultural choices. For example, Action on Smoking and Health, a pressure group against smoking, notes that smoking rates are markedly higher among poorer people (ASH, 2014). In 2012, 14 per cent of adults in managerial and professional occupations smoked compared with 33 per cent in routine and manual occupations. In very deprived areas smoking can be as high as 75 per cent, implying a correlation between the stresses of poverty and smoking.

Complementary model

The biggest criticism of the biomedical approach comes from those who adopt a holistic approach. The biomedical model, to its critics, is more concerned with illness than with health. By concentrating on specific parts or symptoms, doctors fail to see the connections between illnesses and the need to restore balance and equilibrium. CAM therapists argue that the biomedical model encourages treatment that suppresses symptoms rather than treating the origins of people's illness. The NHS used to have five dedicated homeopathic hospitals in the UK. However, these have all been closed or have significantly broadened their range of treatments. The social policy within the NHS is clearly based on traditional medicine but some CAM is available on a local and piecemeal basis.

KEY SOCIOLOGISTS

Ivan Illich (1976) offers strong criticism of the biomedical model through his idea of iatrogenesis. This argues that most sickness in society is produced by doctors themselves, either in the form of treatments that don't work or from side effects of prescribed drugs.

CONTEMPORARY APPLICATION

Within the biomedical model there has been a shift towards shared decision making as evidenced by the Expert Patient Programme or the growing interest the King's Fund, an important think tank focusing on medicine.

STUDY TIP

Comparative tables, like Table 6.1, can make very useful revision resources. However, make sure that you avoid listing these points in an essay and present them in a discursive style, as well as linking them to relevant contemporary issues.

Biomedical model	Social model	Complementary model
Separates the mind from body	Examines the impact of social factors on mind and body	Holistic integration of body and mind
Focus on illness and cure	Focus on social factors that impact on health	Focus on restoring equilibrium and balance
Treats the illness or specific body part	Treats the impact of social factors	Treats the whole person
Doctors as 'experts' use intrusive procedures and drugs	Doctors increasingly recognise the impact of social factors	CAM therapists facilitate healing in conjunction with the human body's capacity for self-healing
Overcoming/taming nature	Offsetting the effects of social disadvantages	Harnessing nature's positive forces

Table 6.1 Summary of the different models of health

STUDY TIP

When writing about models of health it is important to recognise the importance of the prevailing biomedical model and the credence it gets from the medical profession. However, it has many criticisms as discussed above. The social model does not exclude biological factors but recognises that social and biological factors interact to produce particular consequences for health linked to class, gender, ethnicity, age and regional differences.

RESEARCH IN FOCUS

Are my bones normal doctor?

Green, Griffiths and Thompson (2006) wanted to research how well the biomedical model was working in practice. Given that contemporary scientific medicine is increasingly saturated with risk and uncertainty, how do health professionals manage patients presenting with specific health problems. They looked specifically at middle-aged women and osteoporosis (the thinning or weakening of bones).

Their overview took in literature on the medicalisation of women's bodies via health interventions such as screening. It examined the role played by medical technologies in defining degrees and forms of risk, which are embedded within and generated by screening processes themselves. They noted how some feminist work has developed frameworks for exploring issues of power and gender within different types of screening programmes. Particularly pertinent are debates about screening as a key process with regard to the medicalisation of women's bodies which become subjected to the 'medical gaze'.

Screening for thinning bones has become increasingly accepted by both women (post and pre-menopausal) and health practitioners as a key route to minimising the risks associated with the onset of osteoporosis. Presented as a 'silent killer', osteoporosis is also widely perceived as a women's disease, with a projected one in three women likely to experience a fracture during their lifetime.

Women perceived as being at high risk of osteoporosis are recommended hormone replacement therapy (HRT) as treatment. Other research highlights growing concerns about the side effects of HRT. Therefore middle-aged women at risk of osteoporosis are faced with a dilemma about what to do next.

The researchers concluded that while the screening results are open to flexible interpretation, they confirm to both patients and practitioners the 'at risk' status of many of the women. Both women and clinicians over-interpret their significance as an indicator of risk.

Adapted from Green, Griffiths and Thompson (2006), 'Are my bones normal doctor?' The role of technology in understanding and communicating health risks for midlife women. *Sociological Research Online*, 11, 4.

Questions

1. What does the phrase 'medicalisation of women's bodies' mean?
2. What is meant by the term 'medical gaze'?
3. Why does this research imply an over-reliance on technology?
4. In what ways does this research support the iatrogenesis argument?

Check your understanding

1. How did the WHO define health in 1948? Offer a critique of this definition?
2. In what ways are health and illness socially constructed?
3. What are the rights and obligations for patients in Parsons' 'sick role'?
4. Briefly outline each of the three models of health: biomedical, complementary and social.
5. What is meant by iatrogenesis? Which model of health is it most critical of?
6. What is the difference between impairment and disability?
7. In what ways are the disabled subject to stigmatisation and othering?
8. What is BMI?
9. Why was a full body shape desirable in pre-modern society?
10. Is the body a biological entity or a social construction?

Practice questions

1. Define the term 'body mass index'.   [2 marks]
2. Using one example, briefly explain what is meant by the 'clinical gaze'.   [2 marks]
3. Outline three characteristics of the social model of health.   [6 marks]
4. Outline and explain two differences between the biomedical and complementary models in their
   understanding of health.   [10 marks]

Read Item A below and answer the question that follows.

Item A

The biological or naturalist approach of 'anatomy is destiny', implying that women and men are inherently different physiologically and therefore have very different roles, is rebuked by feminists. Although women bear the brunt of reproduction, with all that it physically entails, the pressure on women to maintain a slender physique and appear 'sexual' at all times is intense.

Applying material from Item A and your knowledge, evaluate the view that the body is socially constructed. [20 marks]

Section 2: The unequal distribution of health chances

This section will explore the following debates:

- How does social class determine inequalities in health?
- How does gender determine inequalities in health?
- How does ethnicity determine inequalities in health?
- How does region determine inequalities in health?

GETTING YOU STARTED

Health inequalities reflect a north–south divide

Findings from the 2011 census have revealed some interesting facts about the variations in health associated with both region and gender.

Firstly, it was found that people in the north of England are likely to live more years of their lives with a disability than those in the south. Secondly, it was found that, on average, females are expected to live a longer life than males in England but they will spend more of their life with a disability. As females live longer than males, the widening of the gender inequality gap might be partly explained by the prevalence of disabling health problems increasing with age.

Females				Males			
NHS Clinical Commissioning Group (CCG)	Life expectancy (Years)	Disability-free life expectancy (DFLE) (Years)	Years with disability	NHS Clinical Commissioning Group (CCG)	Life expectancy (Years)	Disability-free life expectancy (DFLE) (Years)	Years with disability
Surrey Downs (Highest)	85.1	70.8	14.3	Guildford and Waverley (Highest)	82.2	70.2	12.0
Bradford City (Lowest)	78.6	54.8	23.8	North Manchester (Lowest)	73.5	55.1	18.4
England average	83.3	65.0	18.0	England average	79.2	64.1	15.1

Table 6.2

ONS (2014b) *Census 2011 Analysis, Disability Free Life Expectancy at Birth, at Age 50 and at Age 65: Clinical Commissioning Groups (CCGs) 2010–12* (www.ons.gov.uk/ons/rel/census/2011-census-analysis/disability-free-life-expectancy-at-birth--at-age-50-and-at-age-65--clinical-commissioning-groups--ccgs--2010-12/rpt.html).

Questions

1. What is the average life expectancy for women and men respectively in England?
2. How many years do women and men live with a 'disability' in England?
3. What are the key findings from this table in terms of the healthiest and least healthy areas.
4. What do these figures tell us about people's experience of ageing? What are the implications of this?

2.1 How does social class determine inequalities in health?

If you are discussing social class shaping inequalities in health, you could consider ideas like mortality and morbidity as well as relevant social factors.

RESEARCH IN FOCUS

Does income inequality cause health and social problems?

Karen Rowlingson (2011) undertook a review of secondary data that had been produced about social class inequalities and health. Her report 'Does income inequality cause health and social problems?' examined the following three questions:

1. Whether or not there is a link between income inequality and health and social problems.
2. Who might be most affected by income inequality.
3. Other possible impacts of income inequality, for example, on the economy.

Her findings were that the data agreed the income inequality existed and that health/social problems were correlated. There was less agreement about whether income inequality causes health and social problems independently of other factors, though some rigorous studies found evidence of this. Some research highlights how factors other than income inequality can also contribute to poor health. For example, the role of individual income (poverty/material circumstances), culture/history, ethnicity and welfare state institutions/social policies.

The effect of income inequality may be partly explained by anxiety about status within society. If so, inequality could be said to be harmful because it places people in a competitive hierarchy, causing stress and leading to poor health.

The independent effect of income inequality on health/social problems shown in some studies looked small, but as the studies covered whole populations, they referred to a large number of people. Some of the research suggested that inequality is particularly harmful beyond a certain threshold. Britain rose above this threshold in the mid-1980s, where it has remained.

Adapted from Rowlingson, K. (2011) *Does Income Inequality Cause Health and Social Problems*? Joseph Rowntree Foundation (www.jrf.org.uk/publications/income-inequality-health-social-problems).

Social class inequalities in health have been one of the most enduring areas of research interest. A significant turning point came with the publication of the Black Report (1980). This report, commissioned to find the causes of social class inequalities in health, contained statistical evidence alongside what has proven to be an extremely influential framework for its interpretation. The Acheson Report (1998) was commissioned by the New Labour government to further review the evidence on inequalities in health. It addressed issues which it saw fundamentally as a matter of social justice, namely the widening gap in health between those at the top and bottom of the social scale. It discussed tackling such inequalities through the engagement of the NHS through local partnerships, but primarily addressing inequalities in the settings of schools, the workplace and neighbourhoods. The Marmot Review (2010) offered further evidence-based analysis of the social determinants of health, including the living and working conditions that shape health inequalities. It highlighted the gap in life expectancy between the richest and the rest of society, who not only die prematurely but spend more of their life in ill health.

The Marxist perspective is unsurprised by social class inequalities in health, given how the economic system of capitalism shapes society into a very unequal class structure. The nature of life for the working class (proletariat) is exploitation and alienation in work, or isolation, marginalisation and even greater deprivation for those not working and in receipt of long-term benefits.

Questions

1. What is meant by a review of secondary data?
2. What are the potential problems in using secondary data?
3. What were the key findings of Rowlingson with regard to income inequality and poor health?
4. What useful point is made in the final paragraph?

6 Health

238

KEY SOCIOLOGISTS

Wilkinson and Marmot's (2003) report for the WHO entitled *The Social Determinants of Health: The True Facts* highlighted what they describe as the remarkable sensitivity of health to the social environment. They concluded that good health involves reducing levels of educational failure, reducing insecurity and unemployment, and improving the housing stock. Societies that seek to reduce inequalities will be the healthiest.

CONTEMPORARY APPLICATION

Buck and Frosini (2012) undertook research and found that poorer people engage in 'four key damaging behaviours' (smoking, excessive drinking, poor diet and lack of exercise) which higher social classes increasingly rebuff. The social class health gap (between the richest and poorest) is set to widen not narrow if these differing behaviours continue.

STUDY TIP

You can improve your writing with the inclusion of patterns and statistics. So, in terms of measuring morbidity in the UK, in 2013, 131 million days were lost due to sickness absences (ONS, 2014a), equivalent to 4.4 days per worker.

Questions

1. What two characteristics does social class involve?
2. What are Esping-Anderson's criticisms of using social class categories?
3. What further complications have undermined the usefulness of social class?
4. Why is social class still used prominently when discussing health inequalities?

Other sociologists of health have argued that class analysis is outdated and a Weberian or postmodern approach makes more sense when looking at health inequalities. They argue that as the links between market position and health chances become clearer, social class categories need to be put aside in favour of a focus on market position and non-class based divisions in consumption.

The relationship between social class and ill health is clearly complex. However, there is a correlation showing that, on average, health chances deteriorate the lower down the social scale people are. It is worth remembering that there will also be health inequalities even between households in the same street. In terms of social policy, the state pension age is currently 65 for men and 60 for women. This will to rise to 66 for both genders by 2020, and to 70 for both genders in the next 50 years. This implies that an even greater proportion of working-class people will become sick and die before they retire compared to the current figure of 20 per cent.

Mortality and social class

Mortality means death; the mortality rate or death rate portrays the number of people who die per thousand of a population. Figures from the ONS (2014) show that, remarkably, one in five manual workers (almost 20 per cent) die before reaching the current retirement age of 65. This compares to just 7 per cent for professional and managerial workers. After retirement, working-class men and women enjoy fewer years before they die (14 years compared to 18 years for professions such as lawyers, teachers and doctors).

Morbidity and social class

Morbidity refers to illness. Generally speaking, morbidity increases with age, but some people experience poor health earlier in life; some from birth onwards. In terms of morbidity, research suggests that this stems from multiple factors. Besides structural factors of poverty and material deprivation, the most disadvantaged in society engage in cultural/lifestyle activities that increase their chances of developing a range of serious illnesses. See the Contemporary application box for details of a recent study of this by Buck and Frosini.

RESEARCH IN FOCUS

What is meant by social class?

Williams *et al* (1998) undertook a literature search of existing research and found that a question mark hangs over the meaning of socio-economic status, particularly where social class is referred to.

A concern with social class involves both a 'structural account of relations of power, inequality and exploitation' and, simultaneously, a self-conscious group awareness and identity. Esping-Anderson (1993) argues that class refers to a range of inequalities which distinguish a set of relatively autonomous individuals along a number of axes which are unlikely to align to form a strong collective economic or social identity. Taken a step further, it could be argued that pushing people into constructed 'class groups' creates divisions and hides the heterogeneity of social life. These issues, in turn, have been further complicated by postmodernist debates, such as the transition to a so-called 'risk' society (Beck 1992), and the implication of these changes for health and medicine.

Williams *et al* (1998) The sociology of health and illness at the turn of the century: Back to the future? *Sociological Research Online*, 3, 4.

2.2 Explanations for social class inequalities in health

When explaining social class inequalities in health and illness, you could bring in arguments like the ones below from Shaw *et al*, Graham, Bartley and Blane, and Wilkinson and Marmot.

Shaw *et al* (2008) argue that despite marked and continued overall improvements in life expectancy, health inequalities remain, with income and wealth still retaining a marked influence on life and death. There is an inextricable connection between poverty, inequality, wealth and health which results in the poor suffering higher levels of sickness and premature death. In contrast, the wealthy are more likely to enjoy good health and longevity. They argue that while health inequalities in terms of mortality, morbidity and disability are well documented, explaining their cause is disputed between materialist, lifestyle and psychosocial factors operating over the life course. In addition, inequalities in health widen further when there are inequalities in the provision of health care. Therefore, they argue, policies that reduce poverty and inequality are key to tackling health inequalities. Social security policies have a vital role to play in ensuring adequate income levels.

Hilary Graham (2004) argues that the social factors influencing health and the social processes shaping their unequal social distribution are not necessarily the same. For example, policies could improve specific health statistics without addressing the unequal distribution of the determinants of health between advantaged and disadvantaged groups. Therefore, she argues, if governments are really committed to improving health and reducing health inequalities, they need to address the effects of their policies on the population as a whole. They must recognise the differing consequences of their policies for groups with unequal access to the determinants of good health.

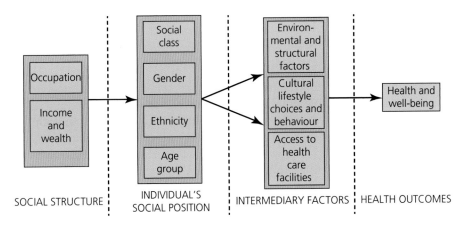

Figure 6.5 Health inequalities

Adapted from Graham and Kelly (2004) Health inequalities, concepts, frameworks and policy. NHS Briefing Paper (www.nice.org.uk/niceMedia/documents/health_inequalities_concepts.pdf).

Bartley and Blane (2008) offer four explanations (or models) to explain social class inequalities in health:

1. **Behavioural model**: this reflects the 'damaging behaviours' identified by Buck and Frosini (see page 238) associated with **cultural factors**

KEY SOCIOLOGISTS

Victoria Cattell (2001) studied 'poor people living in poor places'. Her research shows that deprivation, in itself, is less important than a strong sense of community with regard to health. She found that within stable working-class communities social capital provided good levels of support and emotional well-being. Where the communities were weaker, due to high population turnover, there were fewer social connections resulting in negative health factors: anxiety, depression and fatalism.

CONTEMPORARY APPLICATION

It is estimated that only ten per cent of the causes of health inequalities are under the direct influence of the NHS; the remainder stem from social factors, particularly inequalities in income and education.

STUDY TIP

When explaining the relationship between social class and health inequalities, as well as Bartley and Blane (2008) there is also the artefact explanation. Make reference to this if you can.

and lifestyle. Other behaviours could include the use of immunisation, contraception and antenatal services. However, long-term studies (like Wilkinson and Pickett, see page 225, and the Whitehall II Study, below) have found that differences in health behaviour explain only a minority of social-class differences in morbidity.

2. **Materialist model:** this covers the impact of **structural factors**, such as living in poverty. It considers the consequent exposure to health hazards such as poor-quality housing, run-down housing estates, poor diet, inadequate heating in winter and high stress levels. The now dated but highly influential Black Report (1980) declared that materialist explanations were the most significant factor in accounting for social-class differences in health. However, some critics argue that welfare provision (such as free school meals and housing benefits) tempers some of the problems of poverty and so material factors alone cannot explain all social-class inequalities in health.

Feminists argue that social-class differences and the longer life expectancy of women help to obscure the poorer health of women compared to men. Their poorer health stems from a combination of both biological and social factors. For example, Miller and Glendinning (1989) claimed that women experienced economic hardship more than men.

3. **Psychosocial model:** this argues that social inequality may affect how people feel, which in turn can affect body chemistry. For example, the Whitehall II Study (Ferrie *et al*, 2004) found that an imbalance between effort and reward manifested itself in biological factors. When they tested the blood of low-ranking civil servants, it was poorer in quality compared to higher-ranking civil servants. Low-grade workers had higher fibrinogen levels (making their blood thicker and harder to pump around the body) and a more adverse blood fat profile.

The Whitehall II Study found that smoking, drinking, diet and exercise accounted for less than a third of social-class health inequalities. The remaining two-thirds, they argue, are down to perceived inequalities and status differences within the civil service:

> Inequalities in health cannot be divorced from inequalities in society. The inescapable conclusion is that to address inequalities in health it is necessary both to understand how social organisation affects health and to find ways to improve the conditions in which people work and live.

4. **Life-course model:** disadvantages in childhood tend to have repercussions in adulthood. For example, children brought up in deprived homes tend to be less successful in the education system and hence end up working in low-paid, low-status jobs. This is a relatively recent model that requires the undertaking of longitudinal studies to provide empirical evidence in its support. However, it makes sociological sense in that it is a logical idea that health disadvantages can accumulate over time.

Wilkinson and Marmot (2003) note that however important individual genetic susceptibilities to disease may be, the most common causes of ill health to the wider population are environmental. The conditions under which we live (both structural and cultural) shape health and addressing these explains why health across Europe has generally improved, and why in some countries health has improved while in others it has not. It also explains why health differences between social groups has widened in some countries and narrowed in others.

IN THE NEWS

A 25 year gap between the life expectancy of rich and poor Londoners is a further indictment of our unequal society

In 2014, the London Health Observatory found the gap in life expectancy between those in London's affluent and deprived wards was nearly 25 years. In another study, the Equality Trust discovered that during the last 20 years the gap in life expectancy for those in different UK local authority areas increased by 41 per cent for men and 73 per cent for women.

Income is one of the greatest determinants of a person's health. Differences in average incomes between countries don't seem to have much of an effect, but within societies income inequality matters a great deal: ranking neighbourhoods from the richest to the poorest gives an almost exact match in the order of best to worst health.

However, the issue isn't just related to poverty. Even the neighbourhoods just below the richest ones were found to be slightly less healthy than the richest.

Income inequality, relative poverty, unemployment, under-employment, insecure and volatile incomes and the low-pay economy all have a detrimental effect on health. It's not difficult to see that the daily struggle at the bottom of the heap puts a lot of pressure on people's physical and mental well-being.

Adapted from Kate Pickett and Richard Wilkinson (2014) A 25 year gap between the life expectancy of rich and poor Londoners is a further indictment of our unequal society. *Independent*, 15 January.

Questions

1. What is the current life expectancy gap between the richest and poorest wards of London?
2. How much has the life expectancy gap in local authority areas increased for men and women in the past 20 years, according to the Equality Trust?
3. What other explanations, besides income, do Pickett and Wilkinson offer for this health gradient?

2.3 How does gender determine inequalities in health?

When studying the gender health gap you could cite statistical evidence. It is also important to refer to feminist ideas that the male-dominated medical profession misunderstand and mistreat female health problems.

Mortality and gender

In 1901 life expectancy was just 45 years for men and 49 years for women. By 2014 this had increased to 79.2 years for men and 83.3 years for women. Life expectancy at birth in the UK has reached its highest level on record for both males and females (see the bottom two lines in the graph in Figure 6.6). It is expected that people will continue to live longer. The life expectancy of those born in 2035 is expected to be 94.2 years for men and 97.2 years for women (see top two lines in the graph).

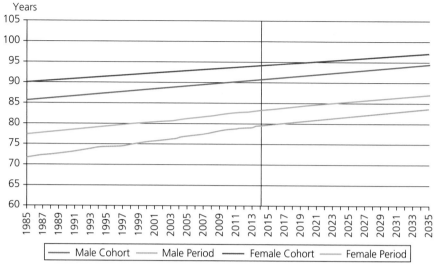

Years

—— Male Cohort	—— Male Period	—— Female Cohort	—— Female Period

Figure 6.6

Adapted from ONS (2011) 2010-based Period and Cohort Life Expectancy Tables (www.ons.gov.uk/ons/rel/lifetables/period-and-cohort-life-expectancy-tables/2010-based/p-and-c-le.html).

Morbidity and gender

Ironically, although women live longer than men on average, they experience more ill health. The two are not unconnected. The Getting you started activity (page 236) shows that, on average, women can expect to spend 18 years and men 15.1 years in less than good health. The article in the activity suggests that this might be due to women's longer lives and the prevalence of health problems increasing with age.

Women also experience poorer health than men before retirement, with men consistently having lower levels of sickness absence from work than women. Women are more likely to work in the public sector, which has higher levels of sickness. Nonetheless, when this and other factors that influence sickness are controlled for, women are 42 per cent more likely to have a spell of sickness than men.

Explanations for this gender health gap range from biological to social factors. The female body, because of its role in reproduction, is considerably more complicated than the male body. Women can suffer from menstrual problems, sickness associated with pregnancy (such as hormone swings and high blood pressure) plus frequent and enduring problems during the menopause.

Feminists question why women appear to consult doctors more. Higher consultation rates are not necessarily because they have more illness but, especially as mothers, they are frequently crossing the surgery threshold anyway. By comparison, men can be notoriously reluctant to consult doctors and often wait until symptoms have become pronounced.

Differential consumption is an important concept illustrated by Hilary Graham (1984) who describes how, when household budgets are tight, women will forego spending on themselves on food and heating in winter if they are at home alone during the day. This means that they will be more prone to illness and supports the French feminist Christine Delphy's notion of self-sacrificing women in order to give their male partners and children more.

KEY SOCIOLOGISTS

Alan Dolan (2011) plays an important role by engaging in research into men's health, a largely neglected area in the past. His study of working-class men shows how male attitudes to health vary, including attitudes to risk-taking behaviour. Dolan found that male risk-taking behaviour varied according to economic circumstances. He therefore challenges the idea of a **homogeneous** culture of masculinity.

CONTEMPORARY APPLICATION

Although men seem to enjoy better health (lower morbidity) than women, they do experience higher rates of injury from accidents. This means that to compare the genders we need to examine the lifestyle choices and risk-taking behaviour of men and women.

STUDY TIP

Remember, if you are comparing women's and men's health, you need to discuss mental illness (see Section 4, page 259) as well as physical illness. In addition, remember that both women's and men's health can also be influenced by social class, age and ethnicity.

6 Health

IN THE NEWS

The wealthiest women get 20 more years of life in good health than the most deprived

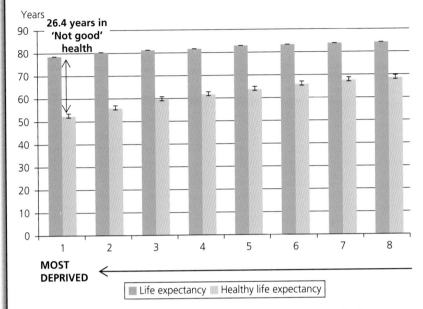

Figure 6.7 Life expectancy for females across the ten income deciles

Research by the Office for National Statistics (ONS) for the years 2009-11 found that women living in the most disadvantaged areas were expected to live 20.1 fewer years in 'good health' than those in the wealthiest. Comparable data for men shows that the gap is slightly less, at 19.3 years.

However, it is worth noting that relative wealth trumps gender as an indicator of life expectancy – a man in a wealthy area will live longer than a woman in a deprived area.

Another factor is the quality of life of those years, and wealthier people obviously get a lot more of those. This means that males in the bottom 10 per cent of the population spend 70.9 per cent of their lives in good health, compared to those in the richest 10 per cent who spend 85.2 per cent of their life in good health.

Adapted from Arnett, G. (2014) The wealthiest get 20 more years of life in good health than the most deprived. *Guardian*, 14 March.

Questions

1. What is the gap between life expectancy and healthy life expectancy for the most deprived women?
2. What does this mean in the real-life experiences of these women?
3. How does this article and graph illustrate the social model of health?

2.4 How does ethnicity determine inequalities in health?

When discussing the ethnic inequalities in health it is important to bring in statistical evidence reflecting genetic but mainly social factors that shape ethnic mortality and morbidity.

Before embarking on this section it is worth remembering that defining ethnicity is problematic in itself. Sociologists use the term in preference to 'race' but its meaning is still complex, embracing aspects of culture, religion and nationality.

It is also useful to note that some people identify themselves with more than one ethnic group. Material factors are important as they are a driver of ethnic health inequalities. This means that because of their location, generally in the lower social classes, black and minority ethnic (BME) groups are more likely to live in poverty with poorer quality housing. The correlation between poverty and poor health is clearly documented (see Section 2.1, page 237).

Mortality and ethnic groups

Statistics show consistently higher premature death rates for non-white men than for white men. Comparative data for women shows a similar picture.

People of Pakistani and Bangladeshi descent, living in England and Wales, have the highest mortality rates from circulatory disease. This increased risk is due in part to an increased prevalence of diabetes. However, the key factor in mortality rates is the social class of most BME groups. Most ethnic groups are concentrated within the working class, so it follows that the factors discussed about class and health are the key determinants of mortality here too.

Morbidity and ethnic groups

BME groups in the UK experience poorer health in general compared to the overall population, although some BME groups fare much worse than others, and patterns vary from one health condition to the next. Ethnic groups reporting the poorest health include Pakistani, Bangladeshi and black Caribbean, with Indian, East African Asian and black African people reporting the same health as white British people. Chinese people report better health than the rest of the population.

As with mortality, evidence suggests that social class is the main factor driving ethnic health. BME groups are frequently located within the working class and therefore occupy a poorer socio-economic position.

A small number of relatively rare genetic diseases appear to specifically affect ethnic minorities. For example, sickle cell anaemia is a serious inherited blood disorder that affects 1 in 300 people of African-Caribbean descent. Thalassaemia is another serious inherited blood disorder that primarily affects people of Mediterranean, Middle Eastern and South Asian descent.

A Weberian sociological approach could offer a useful means of making sense of the general poorer health of BME groups, with its emphasis on class and status differences. The findings of research by Richard Wilkinson and the Whitehall II Study emphasise the importance of status in shaping health chances and could be usefully transferred to BME groups. Frequently located in the lower social classes, and often subject to discrimination, it is no wonder they often have poorer health chances. In terms of social policy the Acheson Report was the first to specifically make recommendations for reducing ethnic health inequalities. These were that:

- policies aimed at reducing socio-economic inequalities should consider the needs of BME groups
- services should be sensitive to the needs of BME groups and promote awareness of their health risks
- the needs of BME groups should be specifically considered in planning and providing health care.

KEY SOCIOLOGISTS

Sproston and Mindell (2006) identified that members of BME groups are more likely to define themselves as suffering from 'poor health' than the majority white population. This means that they either have poorer health as measured objectively or subjectively feel they have poorer health, or both.

CONTEMPORARY APPLICATION

Cultural differences have also been attributed as a factor to explain ethnic inequalities in health. For example, the South Asian community eat a highly saturated form of clarified butter called ghee, which may be a contributing factor to their high levels of heart disease. The Muslim community is also prone to vitamin D deficiency, a factor here being the covering up of skin, especially in women.

STUDY TIP

It is easy to focus on the differences between ethnic groups and forget that the key driver of health chances in society is actually social class. Understanding the connections between social factors such as ethnicity, class and gender is referred to by sociologists as **intersectionality**.

IN THE NEWS

Use of health services by BME groups

Ethnic differences in the receipt of health care and the uptake of services have been reported, although this varies between different parts of the NHS. There are some positive findings. For example, most BME groups access primary care at rates as high as the general population (in relation to need). However, there is also some evidence of lower access to hospital care among BME groups. For example, South Asians have been found to have lower access to care for coronary heart disease.

Looking at prevention, rates of smoking cessation have been lower in BME groups than in white groups. In addition, rates of dissatisfaction with NHS services are higher among some BME groups than their white British counterparts. For instance, South Asians report poorer experiences as hospital inpatients, according to Health care Commission patient surveys.

Adapted from Parliamentary Office of Science and Technology (2007) Ethnicity and Health. *Postnote* 276 (www.parliament.uk/documents/post/postpn276.pdf).

Questions

1. What was an example of a positive finding about BME groups' use of health services?
2. For which illness did South Asians have lower access to care?
3. Why do you think rates of smoking cessation are lower in BME groups?
4. What reasons explain why South Asians might report poorer experiences as hospital inpatients.

2.5 How do regional factors determine inequalities in health?

If you are studying inequality in health, you could cover the correlation between declining health and age, and regional differences which can also apply to health chances, reflecting a combination of social capital and levels of deprivation.

Within the UK, life expectancy varies by country. England has the highest life expectancy at birth – 78.3 years for males and 82.3 years for females – while Scotland has the lowest – 75.4 years for males and 80.1 years for females. Life expectancy at age 65 is also higher for England than for the other countries of the UK. There is also variation according to English region, as shown in Table 6.3.

There can be great variations of health in large cities. For example, in London, men's life expectancy ranges from 71 years in Tottenham Green (Haringey) to 88 years in Queen's Gate (Kensington and Chelsea) – a difference of 17 years. As we saw in Section 1, the poorest parts of Glasgow, like Calton, have a life expectancy as low as 53.9 years.

Social capital is relevant to this conceptual debate. The sociologist Robert Putnam (1995) shows how Émile Durkheim's concepts of social integration and anomie are still relevant in determining health chances across regions. Putman used the term 'social capital' to refer to the social networks and trust that can exist in communities, enabling residents to participate together in the pursuit of a general sense of well-being. Putman's work supports the ideas discussed earlier of Cattell (see page 240), but was criticised by Pevalin and Rose (2006) who argued that the influence of social capital is overshadowed by social deprivation. Wilkinson explains poor health as stemming from an interaction of the two.

KEY SOCIOLOGISTS

Shaw *et al* (1999) looked at mortality rates prior to retirement age across parliamentary constituencies and found that even when they controlled for social class and gender, region still seemed to be a significant factor in the chance of living beyond retirement age. Their explanation was a mixture of spatial, social and economic factors that determine life expectancy within regional areas.

CONTEMPORARY APPLICATION

The Parliamentary Health Committee (2009) casts doubt on the success of recent government policies to reduce regional inequalities in health: 'Despite much hype and considerable expenditure we have not seen the evidence to convince us that any of the specific support given to deprived areas to tackle health inequalities has yielded positive results.'

STUDY TIP

When evaluating the impact of region, remember the very close correlation between deprivation and poor health. Poor health regions tend to be poorer with higher levels of unemployment. This should not be surprising to a sociologist.

Questions

1. Why do you think iconic junk-food brands wish to sign exclusivity agreements with major international sporting events like the Olympics?
2. Why do you think governments 'swallow the big food companies' mantra that healthy eating is all about personal choice?
3. How could WHO's recommendations on food marketing be implemented?

Country / Region	Males		Females	
	At birth	At age 65	At birth	At age 65
United Kingdom	77.9	17.8	82.0	20.4
England	78.3	18.0	82.3	20.6
North East	76.8	17.0	80.9	19.5
North West	76.6	17.0	80.8	19.5
Yorkshire and Humber	77.4	17.5	81.5	20.0
East Midlands	78.1	17.8	82.1	20.4
West Midlands	77.5	17.7	81.9	20.4
East of England	79.3	18.5	83.0	21.0
London	78.6	18.4	83.1	21.2
South East	79.4	18.7	83.3	21.3
South West	79.2	18.6	83.3	21.3
Wales	77.2	17.4	81.6	20.1
Scotland	75.4	16.5	80.1	19.1
Northern Ireland	76.8	17.2	81.4	20.0

Table 6.3 Average life expectancy of UK residents in 2010

ONS (2010)

In terms of social policy, since 2000, the Department of Health has introduced a series of policies aimed at reducing regional inequalities in health. The Cross-Cutting Review (2002) aimed to co-ordinate action across government departments and 'spearhead areas' (the 70 local authority areas with the worst health and deprivation indicators) were given extra resources. Faced by the failure to reduce health inequalities in the spearhead areas, in 2006 the Department of Health created the National Support Team (NST) on health inequalities to work with local authorities and **primary care trusts** (PCTs).

IN THE NEWS

International Olympic Committee fails to support public health policy

Figure 6.8 The Olympic torch relay, London 2012

The Coca-Cola publicity campaign that travelled the UK with the Olympic flame before the games contradicted the ideals of the torch relay. Junk-food companies ignored the reality of the obesity epidemic by targeting children with messages linking their brands to the healthy image generated by high-level sport.

UK governments have ignored their responsibilities for public health, giving in to pressure and swallowing the big food companies' mantra that healthy eating is all about personal choice. There is a huge communication gap between those who want effective action to protect public health and those with a commercial stake who continue to deny the detrimental effects of junk food and poor diet.

The World Health Organization recommends that member states seek to reduce the negative impact of unhealthy food marketing on children. Unfortunately this was not reflected at the London Olympics.

Adapted from Neville Rigby and Amandine Garde (2012) Junk food has no place in the Olympic lineup. *Guardian*, 17 July.

Check your understanding

1. What were the four 'key damaging behaviours' identified by Buck and Frosini (2012)?
2. What is the current average life expectancy for England and Wales for women and men?
3. What is the difference between mortality and morbidity?
4. What are the four models or explanations used by Bartley and Blane (2008) to explain social-class inequalities in health?
5. In what ways does the Whitehall II Study provide evidence to support the biomedical model of health?
6. How do Wilkinson and Pickett (2010) explain health inequalities?
7. Why might health statistics exaggerate the gender health gap between women and men?
8. Which ethnic groups experience the poorest health?
9. Which are the healthiest and least healthiest parts of the UK?
10. What does Putman (1995) mean by the term 'social capital'?

Practice questions

1. Define the term 'life expectancy'.   [2 marks]
2. Using one example, briefly explain what is meant by 'social capital'.   [2 marks]
3. Outline three cultural factors associated with promoting good health.   [6 marks]
4. Outline and explain two material reasons why health among the working class tends to be poorer than among the middle class.   [10 marks]

Read Item A below and answer the question that follows.

Item A

The good news is that gender norms and values are not fixed. They evolve over time, vary substantially from place to place and are subject to change. Thus, the poor health consequences resulting from gender differences and gender inequalities are not static either. They can be changed.

Applying material from Item A and your knowledge, evaluate the view that inequalities in health stem primarily from lifestyle and cultural factors.   [20 marks]

Section 3: Inequalities in health care provision

This section will explore the following debates:

- How consistent is the NHS as a health care provider?
- How might NHS reforms transform health care provision?
- What is the potential impact of private health provision?
- How might social factors influence the take-up of health care?

GETTING YOU STARTED

NHS pushes UK's health care to top of the league table out of 11 Western countries

Cost, efficiency and access to health care in Britain put it at the top of the pile, with Switzerland coming second and Sweden third. The USA comes last.

COUNTRY RANKINGS

	Top 2
	Middle
	Bottom 2

OVERALL RANKING

	AUS	CAN	FRA	GER	NETH	NZ	NOR	SWE	SWIZ	UK	US
OVERALL RANKING (2013)	4	10	9	5	5	7	7	3	2	1	11
Quality Care	2	9	8	7	5	4	11	10	3	1	5
Effective Care	4	7	9	6	5	2	11	10	8	1	3
Safe Care	3	10	2	6	7	9	11	5	4	1	7
Co-ordinated Care	4	8	9	10	5	2	7	11	3	1	6
Patient-Centred Care	5	8	10	7	3	6	11	9	2	1	4
Access	8	9	11	2	4	7	6	4	2	1	9
Cost-Related Problem	9	5	10	4	8	6	3	1	7	1	11
Timeliness of Care	6	11	10	4	2	7	8	9	1	3	5
Efficiency	4	10	8	9	7	3	4	2	6	1	11
Equity	5	9	7	4	8	10	6	1	2	2	11
Healthy Lives	4	8	1	7	5	9	6	2	3	10	11
Health Expenditures/ Capita, 2011	$3800	$4522	$4118	$4495	$5099	$3182	$5669	$3925	$5643	$3405	$8508

Figure 6.9

Culzac, N. (2014) NHS means British health care rated top out of 11 Western countries, with USA coming last. Independent, 17 June.

Questions

1. Which country offers the cheapest health care service in terms of health expenditure per capita?
2. Which country is the most expensive in terms of health expenditure per capita?
3. Why might people in the UK be surprised at the findings of this research?
4. Which country has the least healthy lives?
5. What does Figure 6.9 tell us about the performance of the NHS?

3.1 How consistent is the NHS as a health care provider?

If you are considering the provision of NHS care, then you could bring in ideas of inconsistency according to region and the concept of the 'postcode lottery'.

Credit for the creation of the NHS lies with the 1945 Labour government and its health secretary Aneurin Bevan. As an ex-miner, Bevan had witnessed the impact that accidents and poor health had on ordinary people unable to pay doctor's fees. He was determined that everybody would have access to the health care they needed regardless of income. He believed that the best way to achieve this was to create a centralised, unitary system based on four principles: universalism, equality, **collectivism** and autonomy. Opposition, particularly from the medical profession, forced him to compromise: doctors insisted that private 'pay beds' were retained within the NHS along with their right to work in the private sector alongside their NHS duties. To gain the doctors' reluctant agreement for a state-funded NHS Bevan claimed he had to 'stuff their mouths with gold'.

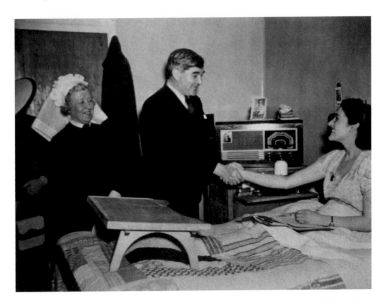

Figure 6.10 Aneurin Bevan opened the first NHS hospital in Manchester, 5 July 1948

Inequalities in provision

Since its creation, the NHS has never truly been a 'national' institution. Although it was available across the nation, regional inequalities quickly became apparent as a built-in feature of the NHS. The quality of hospitals varied, with the prestigious teaching hospitals (especially in London) receiving higher levels of funding and resources than regional hospitals. The Court Report (1973) found that the parts of the country with the greatest need got the lowest provision of services. The report found that in regions with high **birth rates**, a high proportion of children in the population or high infant mortality, the number of GPs and local authority medical staff was low.

Thirty years on, Appleby and Deeming (2001), found the situation has not significantly improved:

> In areas with high needs, such as inner cities and deprived areas, there tend to be fewer doctors working with higher caseloads and sicker patients ... Also, rates of immunisation, and screening for cervical and breast cancer, are significantly lower in people from more deprived areas – areas where cancer mortality rates are highest.

Figure 6.11

Such is the irregular delivery of care within the NHS that some talk of a **postcode lottery** – the way in which the provision of care and treatment within the NHS varies according to the resources available in each **Clinical Commissioning Group (CCG)**.

In 2013 the government commissioned the Keogh Review to investigate the 14 hospital trusts with the worst death rates in England. This followed the exposure of high mortality rates and poor levels of care at the Mid Staffordshire NHS Foundation Trust. Keogh concluded that these 14 hospital trusts were failing in all three dimensions of quality – clinical effectiveness, patient experience and safety – as well as failures in professionalism, leadership and governance. The Keogh team's review methodology has provided a blueprint for the **Care Quality Commission's (CQC)** approach to inspections. The Francis Report (2013) was commissioned to look specifically into the hundreds of premature deaths at the Mid Staffordshire NHS Trust over a three-year period. The report highlighted an appalling failure by medical staff to make the quality of care their primary concern.

Many Marxists would see the NHS as an example of **relative autonomy** – an institution that is not directly controlled by the ruling class but still exists to serve their interests. The public see the NHS as a benevolent gift from the state or capitalist class, but forget that:

- it is funded out of public taxes
- it serves the capitalist class by reinforcing **false consciousness**
- it regulates the public's sickness from work by challenging malingerers.

KEY SOCIOLOGISTS

Julian Tudor-Hart (1971) refers to the discrepancy whereby the better-off have access to superior resources within the NHS as the **inverse care law**. Tudor-Hart suggests that the availability of high-quality medical care varies inversely with need. The poorest communities, who have the greatest health needs, have fewer doctors and inferior resources.

CONTEMPORARY APPLICATION

Because of devolution, patient experience and costs can vary considerably between the four nations that make up the UK. For example, prescriptions are free in Wales, Scotland and Northern Ireland but cost £8.25 (2015) in England per item.

STUDY TIP

Recognising that the NHS was, and remains, a service with regional variations according to how resources are distributed and used is important in understanding differential provision and access.

Survey of NHS treatments reveals wide UK disparities

The largest government analysis of health care in England, the NHS Atlas of Variation, has revealed wide regional disparities in patient treatment that amounts to a postcode lottery.

The NHS Atlas covers 71 key indicators, including hospital admission rates, what treatments health trusts choose to fund, and how children are managed in the NHS.

In 2011 there were variations of more than three-fold in the amount some regions spend on learning disabilities, two-fold in spending on mental health and nearly two-fold on cancer-related spending. The starkest contrast shows in the rate of prescribing anti-dementia drugs, with patients in some areas being prescribed 25 times as many treatments and tablets than others.

Access to care homes for the very frail paid for by the NHS varied considerably. For example, the admission rate for people over 74 was just under three per 100,000 of the population in Devon and Cornwall, but 190 in every 100,000 in Northumberland.

Lifestyle choices may also play a part in the differences. Patients living in the East Midlands were most likely to be granted gastric band operations. This compared to East Anglia where they are least likely.

The health secretary told GPs that 'the degree of variation is considerable and unexplained by simple differences in population'.

The King's Fund said that those commissioning health care should be asked to explain the disparities.

Adapted from Randeep Ramesh (2011) NHS postcode lottery survey reveals wide UK disparities. *Guardian*, 9 December.

3.2 How might NHS reforms transform health care provision?

If you are thinking about the structure of the NHS and reforms, you could discuss how recent reforms are designed to impact on the quality for service users.

In April 2013 the NHS in England began its biggest reorganisation since its creation in 1948. The reforms mean that around £65 billion of the NHS's £100 billion budget (2014 data) will go to the 200 or so CCGs that include all of the GP groups in a geographical area. CCGs purchase health care services (prescription drugs, minor surgery, hospital consultations and operations) on behalf of their patients.

NHS England regulates GP and dentists' contracts and funds directly a few very rare health conditions that affect a relatively small number of people in England. There are around 20 Commissioning Support Units, which provide support to CCGs such as data analysis, contract negotiations and technical advice. Clinical Senates exist to advise GPs (who are not specialists) on complex illnesses. For example, a cardiologist may explain to a GP the treatments needed for someone with a heart condition. In 2015 it was announced that full control of £6 billion a year of NHS health spending was to be handed to Greater Manchester councils as part of a significant extension of devolved powers. It was hoped that this experimental innovation would integrate health and social care services.

Questions

1. What is meant by the term 'postcode lottery'?
2. What is the NHS Atlas of Variation?
3. List three examples of differential access to resources in England.
4. Why do you think there is such a variation in the provision of care and treatment?

Post-2013 NHS provision in England

Following the post-2013 reforms the NHS is now comprised of a variety of trust organisations:

- **Acute trusts**: All NHS hospitals in England are managed by acute trusts, most of which have already gained foundation trust status. Acute trusts employ the bulk of staff within the NHS (such as doctors, nurses, pharmacists, radiographers, midwives and health visitors). The role of acute trusts is to ensure hospitals provide high-quality health care and that they manage their budgets efficiently. They also decide how a hospital will develop.

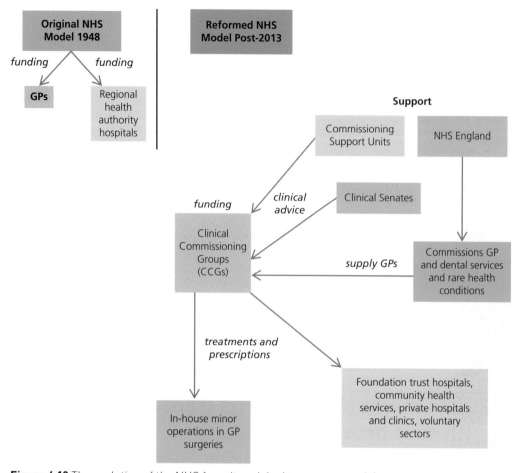

Figure 6.12 The evolution of the NHS from its original to current model

KEY SOCIOLOGISTS

Martin Powell (2008) shows that the change of the public–private mix in the UK has resulted in the decline of direct state provision of health care. He portrays the public health sector as surrendering to 'neo-liberalist' ideas of welfare. Such changes to the public–private mix of welfare provision could be conceptualised as reflecting the wider transformation of the welfare state itself in the twenty-first century.

- **Foundation trusts**: These trusts are similar in status to academy schools in that they are free from government control and operate independently, being responsible to a board of governors (including patients, staff, members of the public and partner organisations). They are free to determine their own future and can raise money from both public and private sectors.
- **Ambulance trusts**: There are currently ten ambulance services (including four foundation trusts) in England, providing emergency access to health care and, in many areas, transport to get many patients to hospital for treatment.
- **Mental health trusts**: There are currently 58 mental health trusts in England, 41 having reached foundation trust status. They provide health and social care services for people with mental health problems. Mental health care can be provided through GPs, such as prescribing antidepressants or providing counselling support. Specialist care for people with severe anxiety problems or psychotic illness is normally provided by mental health trusts in secure psychiatric units.

Private Finance Initiatives (PFIs) have been used to finance the design, construction and operation of hospitals. Their main attraction to government is that they get the facilities now but pay for them over the next 25 years, and it does not count as public borrowing. In theory they are supposed to deliver high-quality, well-maintained assets that represent value for money for the taxpayer. However, so excessive are the guaranteed payments over 25 years that many foundation trusts now find themselves in financial trouble and have to save money by cutting clinical services and making medical staff redundant.

In terms of social policy, the influential King's Fund states that since April 2013, CCGs have replaced primary care trusts as the commissioners of most services funded by the NHS in England. They now control around two-thirds of the NHS budget and have a legal duty to support quality improvement in general practice. Most neo-Marxists are critical of the NHS reforms, claiming that tendering health services to private-sector firms prioritises the making of profit over the clinical interests of patients. However, neo-liberals (who favour capitalism and the free market) respond that tendering drives down costs, therefore market forces result in value for money and bring cost efficiencies.

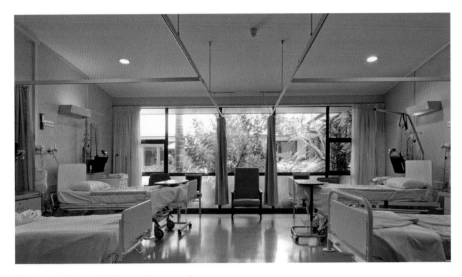

Figure 6.13 An NHS hospital ward

IN THE NEWS

NHS hospitals performing record numbers of private operations

NHS hospitals are doing record numbers of private operations in order to keep their finances afloat. Stark figures show income from private patients rose 12 per cent in 2012 – with further rises predicted.

A Freedom of Information request by Labour MP Gareth Thomas revealed that English NHS hospitals earned £434 million from private patients in 2012–13, up £47 million in a year. Hospitals are forecasting they will earn even more in year (2013–14): about £480 million from private work. Ealing Hospital in London, where the A&E department is under threat, increased the amount it got from private patient income by 250 per cent in the last two years, while the world famous Great Ormond Street hospital saw a 58 per cent rise. Hospitals can now earn up to 50 per cent of their total income from private work.

Concerned doctors fear that the system is creating a situation where those who pay take the lion's share of scarce resources. Mr Thomas said: 'Our hospitals are seeing a huge rise in the amount of money they receive from private patients. With yet more increases to come ... it's clear that under David Cameron a two-tier health service is emerging; pay privately and you'll be seen quickly – don't pay privately and join an increasingly long waiting list.'

Adapted from Jason Beattie (2013) NHS hospitals performing record numbers of private operations in 'two-tier' health service. *Daily Mirror*, 20 September.

CONTEMPORARY APPLICATION

Many people fear the reforms of the NHS in England are an attempt by the Coalition government (2010–2015) to privatise the NHS through the back door. For instance, the Health and Social Care Act 2012 made it compulsory for CCGs to use market mechanisms to commission health services. Many NHS GP surgeries are run by private health care firms such as Virgin Care. Since 2013 NHS hospitals are able to earn up to 50 per cent of their income from private patients.

STUDY TIP

Remember that these health reforms, which became effective in 2013, apply to England only. Although part of the NHS, the organisation of health services in Wales, Scotland and Northern Ireland is different.

Questions

1. What percentage of their income can NHS hospitals earn from private health care work?
2. How much have earnings from private-patient income risen by at Great Ormond Street hospital?
3. What does MP Gareth Thomas mean by a 'two-tier health service'?
4. What are the arguments for and against the NHS increasingly performing private treatment?

3.3 What is the potential impact of private health care provision?

When discussing the impact of private health care provision you could include how it can impact on patient services but also how it can have repercussions on the NHS.

As we have seen, the NHS offers a far from equitable service across nations, regions and individual CCGs. The nature of health care in the UK since the formation of the NHS has always been a two-tier system of state and private health provision. Apart from the very rich, most people cannot afford to purchase private health care. Some, mainly professional and managerial workers, receive access to private health care as a perk associated with their employment. Others can purchase it through an insurance policy. The most obvious benefit of private health care is the bypassing of waiting lists both to see a specialist consultant and to access an operation. Other benefits include private single rooms that are more like hotel bedrooms than hospital wards, improved staff ratios and better-quality food.

Figure 6.14 Most surgeons in England work in both the NHS and the private sector

However, the existence of private health care does more than offer a choice to the privileged minority who can afford it. It contributes to wider health inequalities for the following reasons:

- Consultant surgeons usually work in both the NHS and the private sector. They therefore have a vested interest in having a waiting list for operations. The longer the wait, the more people will be tempted to borrow or draw from savings for a quicker operation.
- When consultants are performing private operations they cannot be performing NHS operations. Private operations make surgeons, anaesthetists and theatres unavailable to public patients.
- Consultant surgeons tend to earn more doing private work, so they may prioritise this side of their work.
- Private patients have access to resources not available to NHS patients. For example, the BUPA website (2014) boasts of prescribing drugs 'not available to NHS patients'.

KEY SOCIOLOGISTS

Hilary Graham (2009) argues that 'all policies likely to have a direct or indirect effect on health should be evaluated in terms of their impact on health inequalities, and should be formulated in such a way that they favour the less well-off'. Graham asserts that private medicine is divisive and serves to widen health inequalities by denying services to those outside the most affluent in society.

In terms of social policy, this two-tier health system becomes increasingly important since, following the NHS reforms, priority of resources may go to those with money who are able to bypass waiting lists to see consultants and have operations. Private health care has always enabled patients to do this, but with NHS trusts allowed to receive up to 50 per cent of their revenue from private patients we may see a two-tier system become more apparent.

The coalition government (2010–15) actively encouraged private firms to run health services within the NHS. For example, in 2013 the health secretary Jeremy Hunt personally stepped in to speed up the private takeover of NHS services by the private health company Virgin Care. Part-owned by Sir Richard Branson's Virgin Group, Virgin Care now runs seven hospitals in his Surrey constituency along with dentistry services, sexual health clinics, breast cancer screening and other community services.

Neo-liberal sociologists would defend the existence of the private sector as being more efficient than state-run services and offering people a choice. They have also welcomed the idea of an 'internal market', first introduced by the Thatcher government in the 1980s, which encouraged hospital trusts to compete with each other. Markets currently function in NHS provision with patients being able to choose their hospital and surgeon for their operation. NHS reforms are clearly going to extend market principles further.

CONTEMPORARY APPLICATION

As living standards improve evidence shows that demand for private health care rises too. Along with other indicators, the UK has seen a phenomenal increase in the private purchase of cosmetic surgery from clinics and hospitals. The value of the UK cosmetic procedures market was worth £2.3 billion in 2010 and it is estimated that it will grow to £3.6 billion by 2015.

STUDY TIP

Note that private treatment outside the NHS can also apply to complementary and alternative medicine (CAM). Although this can still be expensive it does provide a more affordable alternative to the NHS than conventional private health care as well as offering an alternative to the biomedical model approach.

IN THE NEWS

When privatisation of GP practices leaving patients vulnerable

For many patients, doctors, and local politicians, the privatisation of surgeries has been a far from positive experience, and a warning of what can go wrong when parts of the NHS are left to the private sector.

A stable NHS surgery in Camden was abruptly closed by The Practice plc, the UK's largest operator of privatised NHS GP practices, leaving vulnerable patients without a local GP.

Patients in other areas where GP surgeries have been closed have suffered similar difficulties. They have accused the Practice plc of terminating contracts in areas of high deprivation where it finds it cannot make money. However, the Practice plc defended its actions, saying loss-making activities were unsustainable.

An inquiry run by Camden local council was appalled by the lack of accountability. It expressed concern at the manner of the closure, particularly the lack of consultation with other GP practices, which led to unnecessary anxiety for patients and increased pressure on other GPs.

The result has been calls for much more transparency and monitoring of private sector operators in the NHS. Traditionally the NHS has worked outside most formal democratic structures in this country. This mattered less when NHS providers were a public service.

Adapted from Felicity Lawrence (2012) When privatisation of GP practices goes wrong. *Guardian*, 19 December.

Questions

1. Why do you think GP surgeries in deprived areas are more likely to be loss-making for firms offering privatised practices?
2. What implications are there from this article if the trend for privatised GP services continues to grow?
3. How might this example illustrate the idea of an 'inverse care law'?
4. Why does it matter less if public providers work 'outside formal democratic structures' compared to private firms?

3.4 How can social factors influence health care?

When thinking about how any of the social factors influence the take-up of health care, you might discuss this in relation to factors such as social class, gender, ethnicity and age.

In Section 2, page 236, we examined the fundamental inequalities in health associated with social class, gender, ethnicity, age and region. Inequalities can also derive from differential use and take-up of services provided. The **clinical iceberg**, devised by Verbrugge and Ascione (1987) is an important concept in this debate. It uses the analogy of an iceberg to illustrate the considerable amount of unreported illness. The larger submerged part of the iceberg represents the unreported illnesses compared to the visible top, which represents illness that is reported. In terms of social policy, the government sees the Equality Act (2010) as serving to prohibit any discrimination against people when providing a health-related service. It is intended that this will encourage groups previously reluctant to seek medical assistance.

Social class

Christopher Lambkin (in an unpublished PhD thesis) looked into the reasons why so many working-class mothers in Sunderland failed to take up the provision of free health care facilities such as cervical and breast screening, ante- and postnatal clinics, and infant inoculations. Reasons given were partly a resentment and suspicion of middle-class professionals, together with an over-reliance on the wisdom of their own mothers who 'knew best'. Such **fatalistic** attitudes seem to be common among those perhaps living in the most deprived areas with the greatest health risks. However, there are also structural and practical reasons for low consultation rates, such as losing pay from taking time off work and travel costs to visit surgeries and clinics.

Gender

We have seen that, although women live longer than men, they experience more of their lives with disabling ill health (see page 242). As highlighted throughout this section, social class is a major factor in determining health and will clearly differentiate male and female mortality rates. However, across all social classes women consult doctors more than men.

Feminists argue that a lot of the **chronic illness** that women experience is simply tolerated, although breast or cervical cancers receive high-profile campaigns and screening programmes. In contrast, prostate and testicular cancer receives far less attention. Women also appear to be at a greater risk from clinical iatrogenesis, for example, the side effects of oral contraception. As we shall see in a later section, women are more likely to be treated for mental illness. Finally, men have greater economic power to access private health care, but women undertake far more CAM consultations than men.

Ethnicity

We saw in Section 2 how ethnic variations in health are closely associated with social class location. The simple explanation may be socio-economic factors, such as poverty, which many ethnic minority groups experience. Reluctance to lose wages, along with the costs of travel – discussed above in relation to social class – may equally apply here. However, with regard to take-up of services, cultural factors may also explain the lower use of medical resources by people from BME communities. Since communication is an important factor in health consultations, language barriers may be a factor in explaining the differential in take-up of services. Cultural values, such as being uncomfortable with a doctor of the opposite sex, may deter consultations in the first place by some members of BME groups.

Age

The elderly generation may well pre-date the creation of the NHS in 1948. While younger people see access to welfare services as a right as tax payers, older people are often reluctant to 'bother the doctor' about their aches and pains. Health problems are also frequently self-interpreted by the elderly as simply problems with ageing and the body 'wearing out'. One concern of the NHS reforms discussed above is that the elderly may become increasingly rationed out of health care as GPs exercise increasing control over their budgets.

Interactionists theorise about the subjective way that patients experience illness and their consequent actions based on these experiences. They highlight the problems of presuming that people can understand illness through an interpretation of symptoms. Presentation to health professionals will not only depend on the seriousness of symptoms but also on the dynamics of the patient–practitioner relationship and how comfortable people feel about the consultation.

Disability

People of all ages with disabilities are frequently subject to the 'does he take sugar?' syndrome, whereby they are completely ignored while relatives and carers are interrogated for symptoms.

The WHO (2015) report that globally people with disabilities tend to seek more health care than people without disabilities. However, they also tend to have greater unmet needs. For example, they report that 35–50 per cent of people with serious mental disorders in the developed world received no treatment in the year prior to the study. The comparative figure for those in the developing world was between 76 per cent and 85 per cent. The Royal College of Nursing (RCN, 2013) describes how patients with learning difficulties can have undignified experiences when using health services including: discrimination, assumptions being made about individuals with no assessment, lack of communication with the individual and their carers, difficulty in accessing services, staff with a lack of knowledge and skills in learning disabilities, as well as abuse and neglect.

KEY SOCIOLOGISTS

Michael Bury (2005) discusses the patterning of health and illness in contemporary society associated with the social factors of class, gender, ethnicity, age and disability.

CONTEMPORARY APPLICATION

Evidence in the government white paper *Healthy Lives, Healthy People* (2010) found a correlation between mortality for coronary heart disease sufferers and failure to register with a GP. Failure to register with a GP correlates to residence in more deprived areas of society which, ironically, correlates to high rates of heart disease.

STUDY TIP

Remember when discussing any of these social factors to emphasise how they are not homogeneous groups, but will include considerable diversity. Therefore, although the generalisations discussed here will often apply, experiences will also inevitably be individualistic as well.

When discussing any social factor with regard to health, remember the importance of intersectionality (the complexities of overlap between class, gender, ethnicity and age) rather than seeing these as homogeneous groups.

Poor pregnant women missing out on free vitamin D

Figure 6.15

Vitamin D is vital for the growth and maintenance of healthy bones, yet up to 25 per cent of the population (including older people, young children and pregnant women) are at risk of a deficiency.

All pregnant women and those with young children in low-income families are entitled to free vitamin D supplements, but take-up of these vitamins under the NHS's Healthy Start scheme is low. The UK government's senior medical adviser and medical officers say that GPs, midwives and other health workers must ensure that those who are entitled know of their right to the free supplements.

Women qualify for Healthy Start from the 10th week of pregnancy or if they have a child under four years old, or if they or their family receive income support, jobseeker's allowance, employment and support allowance or child tax credit.

Adapted from James Meikle (2012) Poor pregnant women missing out on free vitamin D, health officials claim. *Guardian*, 3 February.

Questions

1. Why do you think the take-up of free vitamin D supplements by pregnant women is greater by higher classes than poorer women?
2. Describe and explain other examples of health-related behaviour associated with pregnancy that can be differentiated by social class.
3. Describe and explain any general health-related behaviour that can be differentiated by social class.

Check your understanding

1. Who created the NHS? When was it founded?
2. Which group within society fiercely opposed the creation of the NHS? Why was this?
3. What is meant by the 'inverse care law'?
4. What does the term 'postcode lottery' imply about access to health resources?
5. Why was the Francis Report commissioned and what were its findings?
6. What is a Clinical Commissioning Group? Why is its role important?
7. How does the existence of private health care contribute to health inequalities?
8. What is meant by the term 'clinical iceberg'?
9. In what ways does health care promote false consciousness according to Marxists?
10. How is the postmodern perspective different in its understanding of health?

Practice questions

1. Define the term 'clinical iceberg'. [2 marks]
2. Using one example, briefly explain what is meant by 'chronic illness'. [2 marks]

▶

3. Outline three ways in which private health care can impact on the NHS. [6 marks]
4. Outline and explain two reasons why gender could influence the take-up of medical care. [10 marks]

Read Item A below and answer the question that follows.

Item A

All sociological perspectives explore aspects of the social model of health. That is, they attempt to understand, sociologically, the concept of health, the role of health professionals and how health institutions work. Where they differ is in their understanding of the nature of engagement people have with health care.

Applying material from Item A and your knowledge, evaluate two contrasting sociological approaches to understanding patterns of usage of health care services. [20 marks]

Section 4: Mental health and illness

This section will explore the following debates:

- How is mental health defined?
- How is mental illness labelled and stigmatised?
- How can social factors influence the demand for mental health services?

GETTING YOU STARTED

Diagnosed depression linked to violent crime, says Oxford University study

Research has shown that people diagnosed with depression are roughly three times more likely than the general population to commit violent crimes, such as robbery, sexual offences and assault. The researchers found that 3.7 per cent of men and 0.5 per cent of women committed a violent crime after being identified as clinically depressed, compared with 1.2 per cent of men and 0.2 per cent of women in the general population.

However, the report emphasised that the overwhelming majority of depressed people are neither violent nor criminal.

The study looked at the medical records and conviction rates of just over 47,000 people diagnosed with depression over a period of about three years, and compared the data with the records of almost 899,000 people with no history of diagnosed depression.

Adapted from: Tran, M. (2015) 'Diagnosed depression linked to violent crime, says Oxford University study'. *Guardian*, 25 February.

Questions

1. To what extent are people diagnosed with depression more likely to commit violent crimes according to the study?
2. Thinking generally about depression, in what ways has it been socially constructed as a feminine illness?
3. What problems do you think men in particular have with dealing with mental illness?

4.1 How is mental illness defined?

If you are considering the issues with defining mental health, you will develop a critical awareness of the realist biomedical definition and the social constructionist definition.

Defining the concept of 'mental illness' is important since, by implication, it has to be defined in behavioural terms. Within the scientific biomedical model of psychiatry, mental illness tends to be viewed as behaviour that is judged as abnormal. Social constructionists respond that this implies that there is a consensus about what constitutes 'normal' behaviour!

Within sociology concepts such as labelling and social construction are used to question the very validity of the term 'mental illness'. Many within the Marxist perspective have criticised the social constructionist approach of Scheff and Szasz (below) for ignoring the wider structures of inequality in society. For Marxists, it is no wonder that the horrors of capitalism – poverty, alienation and unemployment – coincide with the poor mental health of individuals. They argue that Scheff and Szasz never ask why some people appear to cope while others are reduced to 'hysterical' behaviour.

The website Time to Change (www.time-to-change.org.uk) makes the useful point that we all have mental health, just as we all have physical health. Both are subject to fluctuation and change as we progress through life. However, only a quarter of those experiencing mental health problems receive any form of treatment. Mental health is very much the 'Cinderella' of the NHS – unglamorous to work in and chronically underfunded. Yet mental illness is very common, affecting one in four people each year. It is therefore more common than people think.

The realist biomedical approach to mental illness

Psychiatry classifies mental illness into two main groups: the psychoses and the neuroses. Psychoses, or psychotic states, involve a distorted perception of reality. Neuroses, or neurotic states, do not. Within conventional medicine, mental illness is subject to objective classification (diagnosis) in which the cause is linked to factors such as brain chemistry (for example, low levels of serotonin in the brain linked to depression), early childhood experience, and the nature of family relationships. Using accumulated knowledge, psychiatrists claim they can scientifically diagnose and treat mental illness through drug therapy, psychotherapy, electro-convulsive therapy (ECT) and psychosurgery. However, to its critics, psychiatry is a highly imprecise science.

David Rosenhan (1973) conducted a very ethically suspect experiment in which he set out to test the diagnostic skills of psychiatrists. He sent eight **pseudo-patients** to local psychiatric hospitals with instructions that, once admitted, they were to cease simulating any symptoms of abnormality. Rosenhan assumed that anyone behaving normally would quickly get discharged. However, all apart from one of the pseudo-patients were diagnosed as suffering from schizophrenia. When they were all eventually discharged, the psychiatrists maintained their belief that they were correct with their original diagnosis. The medical diagnosis contrasted markedly with the observations of many ward patients, who recognised the pseudo-patients as 'faking it' almost immediately. Although unethical, this experiment is useful in raising questions about who actually is the expert on mental illness in hospitals.

Mental illness as a social construction

In the 1960s some sociologists questioned the very existence of mental illness. Laing and Esterson (1964) controversially argued that the origins of schizophrenia were socially constructed, and lay with tensions within the family. Other social constructionists, such as Thomas Szasz (1961) and Thomas Scheff (1966), argued that mental illness was merely a label applied to any human behaviour that was disturbing or threatening to others. Szasz argues that mental illness becomes a convenient way of resolving social problems while at the same time scapegoating individuals. They argue that psychiatrists, who are typically white, male and middle class, are in a powerful position to label and pass judgement on the abnormality of others. Should we therefore be over-surprised to see a disproportionately high level of mental illness among ethnic minorities, women and the working class?

However, writing in the 1960s Szasz did not have the benefit of the modern diagnostic technology we take for granted in the twenty-first century. Brain scans are now used to identify abnormalities within the human brain that can account for people's dysfunctional behaviour. Walter Gove (1982) challenges the social constructionist view, arguing that most people being treated for mental illness have a serious mental problem.

In terms of social policy, the reforms of the NHS (discussed in Section 3) offer an ideal opportunity to raise the profile of mental health. However, the Economic and Social Research Council (ESRC, 2014) notes that although 'mental illness is now nearly a half of all ill health suffered by people in Britain aged under 65, and accounts for 23 per cent of the total burden of disease … mental health receives only 13 per cent of NHS health expenditure'.

IN THE NEWS

Growth of mental illness among academics

Mental health problems are on the rise among UK academics, with a steady increase in the number seeking help for mental health problems over the past decade. Counsellors and workplace health experts cite the pressures of job insecurity, a constant demand for good results and an increasingly market-driven higher education system as being to blame.

A study published in 2013 by the University and College Union (UCU), which used Health and Safety Executive measures to assess over 14,000 university employees, found high stress levels among academics prompted by a long-hours culture, workloads, and conflicting management demands. Nearly half of academics show symptoms of psychological distress.

A blog in the Guardian Higher Education Network blamed the growth of mental illness in universities as a direct result of a 'culture of acceptance'. Academics and students on the blog gave their personal experiences of mental health problems, including depression, sleep issues, eating disorders, alcoholism, self-harm and even suicide attempts.

Adapted from Claire Shaw and Lucy Ward (2014) Dark thoughts: why mental illness is on the rise in academia. *Guardian*, 6 March.

KEY SOCIOLOGISTS

The French post-structuralist Michel Foucault (1971) located the origins of 'modern' ideas about mental illness in the eighteenth century when the **Enlightenment** was championing rationality, science and technology. He argued that rationality required an opposite – irrationality – and that asylums were used to isolate the 'irrational' from the rational in places where 'rational ideas' of invasive treatment were used to control them.

CONTEMPORARY APPLICATION

In 2011 the Royal College of Psychiatrists called on the media to stop promoting unhealthy body images, claiming it was 'glamorising' eating disorders. It criticises the media for using underweight models and airbrushing pictures to make models appear physically perfect. Increasing globalisation and exposure to Western media have been linked to an increase in the rate of eating disorders in the developing world.

STUDY TIP

A discussion of mental health is relevant to any discussions on health more broadly – mental health *is* health.

Questions

1. What proportion of academics are showing symptoms of psychological distress?
2. What kind of mental health symptoms are being displayed by academics and students?
3. What do you think is meant by a 'culture of acceptance'?
4. What other factors have been highlighted as to why academics are increasingly prone to mental illness?

4.2 How is mental illness labelled and stigmatised?

When studying how mental illness is labelled and stigmatised, you could bring in key interactionist ideas of the process of negative labelling associated with this type of illness.

A major focus for sociological study is the effects of being labelled as mentally ill. The interactionist sociologist Erving Goffman (1968) engaged in a classic participant observation study of an American psychiatric hospital. Goffman used the term **spurious interaction** to describe the treatment of mentally ill patients, because all of their behaviour was evaluated in the context of them being mentally ill (for example, Rosenhan (1973) found that his pseudo-patients reported that what they said was frequently ignored or reconstructed to fit the view of medical staff). Goffman argued that because their voice and behaviour is not taken at face value, mental patients quickly fall into a 'career' in two stages:

- The **mortification of self**, whereby their old identity dies with the construction of a new self.
- The adoption of modes of adjustment that enable the individual to 'get by' on a day-to-day basis and perhaps to salvage some of their sense of individuality.

Interactionists examine how biomedical mental health practices have contributed (however inadvertently) to the negative labelling and stigmatisation of patients. With its emphasis on roles, actions and meanings, the interactionist perspective embraces what Weber advocated through the concept of *verstehen*. Mental illness is perceived from the point of view of the patient, not the medical profession.

Stigma refers to the negative label of shame that marks a person out as different from others in society. Contemporary notions of the stigma associated with mental illness are grounded in Erving Goffman's seminal work *Stigma* (1963). Goffman describes mental illness as one of the most deeply discrediting and socially damaging of all stigmas. Writing in the 1960s, he described people with mental illnesses as starting out with rights and relationships but ending up with little of either.

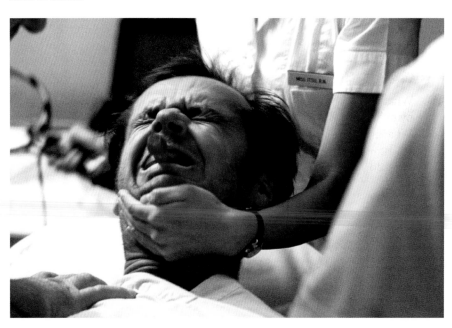

Figure 6.16 Jack Nicholson's character becoming increasingly medicalised as he receives ECT in the film *One Flew Over the Cuckoo's Nest*

Ken Kesey's book *One Flew Over the Cuckoo's Nest* (1962) illustrates the rebellion of McMurphy, originally a perfectly sane recidivist who was placed in a mental hospital for assessment. The storyline highlights the construction of his 'madness' through his increasing medicalisation and personality control. It is said that Kesey's inspiration for the book came from reading Goffman's book *Asylums* (1961).

In terms of social policy, the Equality Act (2010) makes it illegal to discriminate directly or indirectly against people with mental health problems in public services and functions, access to premises, work, education, associations and transport.

IN THE NEWS

Discrimination and stigma against the mentally ill

Research published by the CentreForum Mental Health Commission has urged government ministers to step up the campaign to stamp out discrimination suffered by people with mental health issues.

Despite the Mental Health (Discrimination) Act becoming law in 2011, the research found that:

- 60 per cent of people with mental health problems still feel unfairly treated when looking for a job.
- 75 per cent say they have decided not to apply for some jobs because they were worried about how potential employers might respond to their condition.
- 60 per cent said they had decided not to apply for educational or training courses because of their condition.
- 60 per cent said they were concerned about how workmates might treat them if their condition became known.
- 90 per cent admitted they had concealed their condition from others, and 75 per cent said they avoided having close personal relationships.

Adapted from Kirsty Buchanan (2013) Cruel workplace mental health stigma must end. *Sunday Express*, 29 December.

Questions

1. What evidence is revealed in this research that people feel stigmatised by mental illness?
2. What evidence is revealed in this research that mental illness can lead to discrimination?
3. Why do you think so many people conceal their condition from others?

KEY SOCIOLOGISTS

Erving Goffman wrote *Asylums* in 1961. It was concerned with the process of **institutionalisation** and the ways in which people negotiate new 'mad' identities in situations of powerlessness. It is widely credited with beginning the process of deinstitutionalisation.

CONTEMPORARY APPLICATION

The Mental Health Foundation (2014) says that people with mental health problems report the social stigma attached to it is still significant. Those with mental health problems experience discrimination from society but also from families, friends and employers. Stigma and discrimination can worsen someone's mental health problems and delay or impede their getting help and treatment, as well as their recovery.

STUDY TIP

When discussing labelling theory, remember that it supports the social constructionist definition of mental illness. Labelling theory can be used to criticise the realist approach of the biomedical model.

4.3 How can social factors influence the demand for mental health services?

If you are considering how social factors impact on the demand for mental health services, you could try to show an awareness of how social class, gender, ethnicity and age influence the incidence of mental illness.

Society	Community	Family	Individual
Equality versus discrimination	Personal safety	Family structure	Lifestyle factors (diet, exercise, alcohol intake)
Unemployment levels	House and access to open space	Family dynamics (e.g. high/low expressed emotion)	Attributional style (i.e. how events are understood)
Social coherence	Economic status of the community	Genetic make-up	Debt versus financial security
Health care provision	Neighbourliness	Parenting	Individual relationships and responses to these

Table 6.4 Examples of determinants on mental health

Social class and mental health

There appears to be an inverse correlation between mental health and social class position. Levels of mental illness are between two and two and a half times higher among the most deprived compared to the least deprived. The relationship between deprivation and poor mental health can be seen to be circular, since poor health could lead to social disadvantage and periods of unemployment. Inequities can accumulate over time, making the poor elderly particularly vulnerable to mental health problems.

Gender and mental health

According to the ONS (2014) women in the UK are almost twice as likely to experience anxiety and be treated for a mental health problem than men (29 per cent compared to 17 per cent). Mental illness manifested in eating disorders is also far more common in women.

This discrepancy between the genders may be because women are less reluctant to report symptoms and are more willing to seek medical help: one in four women seek treatment for depression in their life, compared to just one in ten men. Depression, and other mental conditions, may well be underdiagnosed through men not referring themselves to their GPs in the first place. If a man uses words like 'stress' rather than 'depression', doctors may misdiagnose the latter. However, men can manifest mental health issues in other ways, such as addiction. For example, 67 per cent of British people who consume alcohol at 'hazardous' levels, and 80 per cent of those dependent on alcohol, are male; 69 per cent of those dependent on illegal drugs are male.

Feminists, like Phyllis Chesler (2005), have undertaken some interesting analysis into the gendered nature of mental illness. For example, she notes how stereotypes surrounding women expect them to be dependent, emotional and excitable in a crisis. These stereotypical characteristics are also ascribed to the mentally ill. Society's definitions of femininity and madness, it seems, are inextricably linked. This may offer an explanation as to why women are more prone to mental illness labelling, diagnosis and treatment, although such stereotypes are generalised and old fashioned.

Ethnicity and mental health

It is worth stating that different ethnic groups will experience different rates and experiences of mental health. However, the Mental Health Foundation (2013) makes the point that, in general, BME groups living in the UK are more likely to be diagnosed with mental health problems, to be diagnosed and admitted to hospital and to experience a poor outcome from treatment.

A key factor in explaining this is their concentration within deprived groups in the lower social classes. However, as research by Rehman and Owen (2013) found, their experiences are also compounded by discrimination as well. African-Caribbean males are between three and five times more likely to be diagnosed with schizophrenia than white males.

Mallet *et al* (2003) researched the alleged overdiagnosis of African-Caribbeans with schizophrenia. They conducted studies in Trinidad and Barbados and found that the rate of schizophrenia there was significantly lower than among London's African-Caribbean community. Their explanation is that either racial bias and/or a lack of cultural sensitivity is causing psychiatrists to misinterpret psychological distress (a less-serious illness) and overdiagnose schizophrenia. African-Caribbeans are more likely to receive a diagnosis through a referral from the criminal justice system rather than initially through the NHS. This implies that negative labelling may lie behind these statistics. James Nazroo (2001) points out that other BME groups, equally deprived, have much lower levels of mental illness. The higher levels of mental illness among African-Caribbeans cannot, therefore, be entirely explained by racist discrimination and deprivation.

In terms of social policy, the King's Fund (2012) noted that at least £1 in every £8 spent on long-term conditions is linked to poor mental health and well-being – between £8 billion and £13 billion in England each year. It suggests that mental health care could be improved through:

- integrating mental health support with primary care and chronic disease management programmes
- improving the provision of liaison psychiatry services in acute hospitals
- providing health professionals of all kinds with basic mental health knowledge and skills.

CONTEMPORARY APPLICATION

Pickett *et al* (2006), working for the Equality Trust, demonstrated a link between mental illness and income inequality in developed countries. As Figure 6.17 shows, mental illness is more common in countries where income inequality is high. The reason for this may be that inequality has a strong impact on people's emotional well-being.

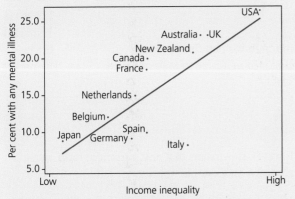

Figure 6.17 Relationship between income inequality and prevalence of mental illness in developed countries

KEY SOCIOLOGISTS

In a study of nearly 600 women living in London George Brown and Tirril Harris (1978) developed the concepts of 'provoking agents' and 'protective factors'. They found that women with children were prone to depression, but that the chances were increased by 'provoking agents' such as overcrowding, poverty, chronic ill health, bereavement and marriage breakdown. They found women could be protected from depression by 'protective factors' such as a a supportive marriage.

STUDY TIP

Cross-referencing is an important skill: the concept of social capital and the work of Robert Putnam (discussed in Section 2) could be a useful concept to use here to explain the differential demand for mental health services associated with class, gender, ethnicity and age.

RESEARCH IN FOCUS

Cognitive therapy rather than pills

Anthony Morrison (2012) undertook research to see if cognitive therapy (CT) could be a successful therapy for people with a schizophrenia spectrum diagnosis who were not taking antipsychotic medication. Although antipsychotic medication is the first line of treatment for schizophrenia, CT had yet to be formally evaluated in its absence. Morrison's study evaluated CT for people with psychotic disorders who have not been taking antipsychotic medication for at least six months.

His methodology was to adopt a longitudinal survey with a sample of 20 participants with schizophrenia spectrum disorder who received CT in an open trial. His means of quantifying the success of CT was to use a Positive and Negative Syndromes Scale (PANSS), which was administered at the start of the research, at nine months (end of treatment) and at 15 months (follow-up). Measurable outcomes were subjective dimensions of hallucinations and delusions, self-rated recovery and social functioning. His finding was that CT is an acceptable and effective treatment for people with psychosis who choose not to take antipsychotic medication.

Adapted from Morrison, A. (2012) *Psychology Medicine, 42* (5), 1049–56.

Questions

1. What is meant by a longitudinal survey?
2. How did Morrison measure the success or failure of their research?
3. What are the potential problems with using subjective judgements as evidence?

Check your understanding

1. How does the biomedical model define mental illness?
2. How do Laing and Esterson explain the origins of schizophrenia?
3. In what ways did Szasz and Scheff argue that mental illness is a social construction?
4. What contemporary criticisms could be made about the social constructionist argument?
5. What message about psychiatry is made by Rosenhan's (1973) experiment?
6. What did Goffman mean by the term 'mortification of self'?
7. What is the correlation between social class and mental health?
8. What did Pickett *et al* (2006) discover about relationship between income inequality and mental illness?
9. Why do higher levels of mental illness among women, such as depression, need to be viewed with some caution?
10. What explanations have been suggested for the high levels schizophrenia among African-Caribbean men in London, compared with Trinidad and Barbados?

Practice questions

1. Define the term 'total institution'. [2 marks]
2. Using one example, briefly explain what is meant by 'stigma'. [2 marks]
3. Outline three reasons why depression appears to be more common in women than in men.
4. Outline and explain two reasons why some feminists see women as more prone to mental illness. [10 marks]

Read Item A below and answer the question that follows.

Item A

One definition of mental illness is deviation from social norms. However, this means that any minority group, outside the consensus, could be defined as extreme, abnormal and, hence, mad – for example, the 'looney left'.

Applying material from Item A and your knowledge, evaluate the reasons why those associated with mental illness are subjected to negative labelling. [20 marks]

Section 5: Health professionals in a globalised industry

This section will explore the following debates:

- What is the current status of the medical profession?
- Are functionalists right to grant medical professionals a high position in the social system?
- Are Marxists right to see the medical profession as an agent of control?
- Are interactionists right to see patient–practitioner consultations as one-sided?
- Are feminists right to still see the medical profession as male dominated?
- Is the postmodernist perspective right to see an increasingly fragmented health service?
- To what extent is there a globalised health industry?

GETTING YOU STARTED

Global skills shortages

In 2011 the government estimated that the NHS would need 108,000 new nurses and 62,000 new doctors by 2020 to cope with an ageing population.

However, a worldwide shortage of medical staff, which is estimated to amount to around half a million vacancies at any one time, means that the UK is facing significant competition from overseas to make up any shortfall.

While the NHS took on 8,500 nurses and midwives from countries such as Pakistan, India and the Philippines in 2010, the number of British staff leaving to work abroad because of pay freezes and low morale hit a ten-year high of 5,500.

The Nursing and Midwifery Council says the number of foreign recruits is higher than the number of newly qualified nurses, despite the immigration cap on workers from outside the EU.

Adapted from Cath Everett (2011) Does the NHS pay staff too much? *Guardian*, 22 June.

Impact of losing nurses from the Philippines

Industrialised countries such as the UK and USA are importing so many experienced and qualified nurses from developing countries that the ability of those countries to adequately address their own health care needs is being compromised.

For example, the Philippines, which supports migration by training a surplus of registered nurses, loses its highly trained and skilled nursing workforce to migration much faster than it can replace them. It is estimated that 85 per cent of nurses trained in the Philippines leave to work overseas, so the Philippines' health service is suffering.

The Philippines has some benefits from this migration: health workers send back substantial sums of money to their families. This boosts the country's GNP as well as enhancing the quality of life of family members.

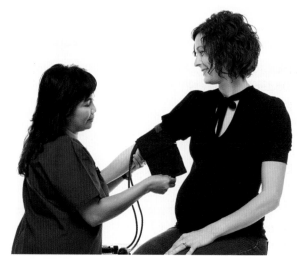

Figure 6.18

Adapted from Littlejohn *et al* (2012) Nursing shortage: A comparative analysis. *International Journal of Nursing, 1* (1), 22–27.

Questions

1. What is the key reason why most developing countries will have to employ more doctors and nurses in the near future?
2. What is the estimated worldwide shortfall in medical staff?
3. Where does the UK import most of its nurses from?
4. Why do nurses want to migrate from the UK?
5. What are the effects of migration by Filipino nurses on the Philippines?

KEY SOCIOLOGISTS

Bloor and Horobin (1975) summed up the inherent conflict surrounding the patient–practitioner consultations which stems from the two assumptions held by doctors about how patients should behave. Patients are expected to use their judgement about when it is appropriate to seek medical advice but, once this advice is sought, they must then totally subsume to the judgement and orders of the doctor.

5.1 What is the current status of the medical profession?

If you are studying the status of the medical profession, you will learn about the power of the medical profession and develop a sociological understanding of how and where that power comes from.

Doctors have traditionally been known as 'pillars of the community', reflecting both their importance to the running of society and the fact that most people look up to them. As we saw in Section 3 this is reflected in the unequal doctor–patient relationship, where patients learn that their expected role is to be passive, co-operative and, above all, obedient. Doctors' status has also been traditionally reflected in their prestige and pay. Doctors, not just in the UK but generally across the world, share an elevated position of high income and power.

However, the image of the general practitioner (GP) in the UK has become slightly tarnished in recent years. According to the Organisation for Economic Co-operation and Development (OECD, 2014), the UK pays its GPs more highly than any other OECD country – and nearly twice as much as France. The British Medical Association (BMA), which represents doctors, point out that the new GP contract pays doctors for raising the quality of the patient care they provide. However, patients complain that it is becoming increasingly difficult to get a GP appointment, that consultations are too short and too often people have to go to A&E when surgeries are closed.

The reputation and status of frontline hospital staff – doctors, nurses and hospital care assistants (HCAs) – has also been tarnished recently by media stories such as 'too posh to wash' (see In the news, page 269) and scandals of poor patient care, such as those at Mid Staffordshire NHS Trust (see page 250). At Mid Staffordshire, the nursing profession and HCAs were singled out by the media for blame with headline stories of 'thirsty patients forced to drink from vases of flowers'. However, frontline staff argue that whistleblowers who tried to raise concerns were punished. Nursing and hospital care assistants argue they were scapegoated and that the true responsibility for poor care lies with senior management for cutting staff levels and costs.

The reputation and status of doctors is constructed differently to that of other health workers. Weber argued that doctors create an aura of professionalism that allows them to achieve high status. He described how doctors create a system of 'social closure' that serves their self-interest rather than the interests of patients or society. Doctors, he argues, are able to create this social closure because of their market position. Doctors are in a particularly strong market position as their supply is restricted: the high educational attainment and extended periods of expensive, unpaid study necessary to become a doctor mean that most doctors come from the higher social classes. The profession is unattainable to all but the very brightest from the working class. Even then, working-class entrants may still experience exclusion from the 'old boy network' of **nepotism** and favours. This limited supply and high demand ensures the high status of doctors.

Postmodernists argue that the power of the medical profession is changing, with power becoming more fluid and less concentrated in one place. Patients increasingly view themselves as empowered consumers of services and are increasingly shopping around, as well as becoming more vocal in their criticism of the services they use.

In terms of social policy, since a new GP contract was introduced by the Labour government in 2004, GPs have experienced a massive jump in earnings while, at the same time, giving up responsibility for out-of-hours care. In 2014 figures from the NHS showed that 16,000 GPs earned over £100,000, including more than 600 on more than £200,000. The Coalition government (2010–2015) announced measures to make GPs provide seven-day consultations, including Sunday appointments.

IN THE NEWS

A Staff Nurse speaks out

Newspapers of the more sentimental type have traditionally been nurses' biggest fans, portraying [us] as angels despite being constantly overworked and underpaid. Now, however, some have taken a U-turn on this view. The Daily Mail has reported that 'student nurses are to be forced to work for a year as health care assistants to improve compassion in the NHS' and that many graduate nurses consider themselves 'too posh to wash'.

The outrageous idea that when a woman is educated she risks losing touch with her compassion has no place in the 21st century. It is implied (not very subtly) that we must choose between one or the other and that we should opt to preserve our feminine 'nurturing instincts'.

However, this is about more than a feminist debate. The demonisation of educated nurses by the media affects their everyday working lives. Nurses still want do their professional best but are finding it hard when some patients and visitors are influenced by what they read and arrive expecting to find snooty, uncaring nurses with academic pretensions. Some even refuse to believe the evidence of their own experience and go home believing that they have been ill-treated by over-qualified but uncaring staff.

Adapted from Stella Backhouse (2013) Learned resentment. *Nursing Standard*, 27 (46), 26–27.

CONTEMPORARY APPLICATION

In response to the scandals about poor care that have recently afflicted the NHS, there has been a concerted shift to get high-quality patient care at the top of the agenda. By applying **person-centred care** frontline health care professionals aim to provide high-quality care by treating patients as individuals, respecting confidentiality, collaborating in making choices, gaining consent and maintaining clear professional boundaries.

STUDY TIP

Remember that health professionals operate in an increasingly global market. The market position of any health professional can be influenced by global forces. The movement of qualified doctors and nurses from the developing world to the developed world is creating market imbalances. Health workers trained in the UK can also seek employment abroad, resulting in potential staff shortages at home.

269

Questions

1. Why are doctors paid more than nurses?
2. What are the positive and negative consequences of making nursing a degree profession?
3. Why do you think parts of the media express resentment towards educated nurses?
4. What does the article imply about people's attitudes to the nursing profession?

5.2 Are functionalists right?

If you are studying the functionalist perspective and the medical profession, it is important to understand how it is viewed and, in particular, the role it plays in the successful functioning of society.

The functionalist perspective's analysis of the role of the medical profession is rooted in the work of Talcott Parsons (1951). In the 1950s and 1960s following the Second World War, the professions experienced considerable expansion as living standards rose. There was increasing demand for services in health, education and legal services. In Section 1 we saw how Parsons viewed the motive to enter the professions as **altruism**. In other words, they wanted to serve and give something back to the community. Parsons felt that this virtuous gesture, on the part of doctors, deserved in return high prestige, status and salaries. For the medical profession their generous rewards were a worthy return for their efficiency and value to society.

Parsons made some fundamental assumptions about patients having a basic understanding of illness and being sensitive to what conditions would require a consultation with a doctor. However, during that consultation the expectation was that they would be docile and compliant. Doctors, in return, were expected to treat everyone equally and professionally. However, the reality was that doctors looked down on their social inferiors, patronised women, frequently discriminated against minorities and were judgemental about homosexuals. A person's gender, ethnicity and social location could have considerable influence on the nature and quality of treatment they received. Therefore, patients from the higher social classes (and therefore considered more equal in social terms) have traditionally been given extended consultations with greater explanation.

Critique of the functionalist perspective on the medical profession

- As a perspective it is viewed as naïve for ignoring differentiation by class, gender, sexuality, ethnicity and age.
- It assumes the population is comprised of over-socialised and conditioned individuals who are passively obedient towards the medical profession.
- Although a popular assumption, especially in TV medical fiction, there is no evidence that the key driver for doctors to join the profession is altruism.
- Parsons viewed the role of doctors uncritically, ignoring their role as gatekeepers and agents of social control when it comes to policing the sick role.
- The idea of 'illness as a job' or occupation is important within the functionalist perspective. Many patients cope with illness by defining it as a 'job', to be successfully managed by hard work, co-operation with others (doctors and kin) and sharing information about their current state of illness. This supports the sick role.

In terms of social policy, the functionalist idea of rewarding professionals for their expertise and knowledge has never been applied to junior doctors. Despite six years of university training, the most junior hospital trainee post (Foundation Year 1) has a basic starting salary of just £22,636 (2015, England). Although a doctor's income tends to rise quickly, this salary is very low considering they are the doctor most often called by nursing staff to see patients on hospital wards, especially on night shifts.

KEY SOCIOLOGISTS

Steve Barber (1963) coherently accounted for what he saw as a functional relationship between professions (like doctors) and society: because we rely on their expert and complex knowledge, it is only fair and just to grant them a high position in the social system in terms of income, status and prestige.

CONTEMPORARY APPLICATION

Otto Pollock (1998), while supporting the 'illness as a job' analogy, argues it is inappropriate to apply it to people suffering from chronic forms of mental illness. This is because the positive notion of coping with their illness is denied to people seen by others as having no control.

STUDY TIP

Ensure that all theories are subject to evaluation. What are their strengths and weaknesses? Functionalism, for example, considers sickness as a form of social deviance but ignores how sick people can be exploited by iatrogenesis, powerful medical professionals, drug companies and health insurance companies.

5.3 Are Marxists right?

If you are discussing the Marxist perspective and the medical profession, it is important to understand the role it plays in helping the capitalist class by acting as agents of control.

Karl Marx, himself, had little to say on the medical profession other than how they were outside the financial reach of the proletariat. For Marxists, medicine is a major social institution in capitalist society. Inevitably they see it as shaped by the interests of the capitalist class (the bourgeoisie). We saw in Section 3 how capitalism is seen to make people ill and how it then uses the medical profession as agents of social control. It does this by obscuring the real cause of people's illness, and by regulating who is sick and who is fit for work. In addition, Marxists are highly critical of the global pharmaceutical industry (known colloquially as **big pharma**) which they say abuses the industry by charging excessive prices for medicines, medicalising non-medical phenomena in order to sell more drugs, and renaming old illnesses to trick people into thinking their conditions are more serious.

The Spanish Marxist Vicente Navarro (2004) argues that, for capitalism to survive, reality has to be obscured so that a situation of false consciousness is constructed. He suggested that doctors act as agents of control, promoting the interests of the capitalist class by explaining health and illness, partly in terms of genetics, but particularly as a result of lifestyle. Focusing on lifestyle personalises illness and removes any connection to structural factors such as deprived neighbourhoods, poor housing, poverty and unhealthy working practices. The social model of health clearly shows that health is influenced by the levels of income, income inequality, people's access to educational opportunities and their recreational opportunities. By failing to recognise and treat these factors, doctors are contributing to the construction and maintenance of false consciousness. Navarro singled out doctors, but other health professionals, such as nurses, also fit into this image of agents of control.

Figure 6.19 The Whitehall II Study showed that capitalism even undermines the health of low-grade white-collar workers

Some Marxists portray the creation of the NHS as a victory for the proletariat by offering free access to professional medical experts, especially consultant specialists. However, Julian Le Grand (1993) challenges this, pointing out that

KEY SOCIOLOGISTS

John McKinley (1985) argues that doctors are themselves just well-paid members of the proletariat, working in a vast, profit-driven health industry. As health care is often delivered by non-profitable organisations, the main profits are made by the pharmaceutical industry. McKinley suggests that the medical profession lacks autonomy, being obliged to prescribe ineffective but profitable treatments.

CONTEMPORARY APPLICATION

The Marxist perspective's concern about the size and power of the pharmaceutical industry is confirmed by data from the WHO (2014). They claim the global pharmaceuticals market is worth in excess of $300 billion a year. By 2017 they expect this figure to rise to $400 billion. The ten largest drugs companies control over a third of the market, several with sales of more than $10 billion a year and profit margins of about 30 per cent.

STUDY TIP

It is good to make critical comparisons between the contrasting views of the medical profession by Marxists and functionalists. Higher-end skills can be demonstrated by not only highlighting the differences but also the fact they share some things in common, such as the role of doctors in regulating sickness and malingering. Make sure you identify your own examples.

Questions

1. What is the implicit purpose of the PIP tests according to the article?
2. How does this article support the Marxist perspective's view of medicine being used as a means of social control?

the poorer members of society have not benefitted as much from the NHS as the middle class. The concept of the 'inverse care law' (discussed in Section 3) appears to support this, with the lower classes arguably receiving poorer quality health care. Many have warned that the 2013 reforms of the NHS will simply perpetuate unequal health care provision among the social classes.

Marxists also note how health and illness are defined in the capitalist system in terms of whether people are able to participate in paid employment. Work is emphasised as the most fundamental of all human activities. Through the sick note system, doctors play an important role in regulating who can legitimately take time off work and who cannot. Their role is therefore to regulate and control the work-shy and malingerers.

The social model of health is a relevant concept to this debate. It would be wrong to see doctors as mere stooges of the system focused solely on the biomedical model. They are increasingly recognising the role of social factors in shaping health chances, for example the impact of poverty or stress in the workplace.

Critique of the Marxist perspective on the medical profession

- While Marxism blames capitalism for poor health and the lack of autonomy of doctors, it cannot explain the diversity of health care provision across capitalist states.
- Functionalists might exaggerate the role of altruism among the medical profession, but Marxists have been accused of understating the role it plays.
- By focusing on social class, it ignores the role that other factors, such as gender, ethnicity and age, can play in shaping people's health experiences.

In terms of social policy, an example of regulating sick and disabled people from malingering is the employment by the Coalition government (2010–2015) of two companies, Capita and Atos, to assess everyone previously on Disability Living Allowance (DLA) for the new Personal Independence Payments (PIP) benefit. Under DLA there were more than 3 million claimants but, by 2018, the UK government believes that under PIP there will be 600,000 fewer claimants.

IN THE NEWS

Assessing the sick and disabled as Fit For Work

Personal Independence Payment (PIP) is a new form of disability benefit which has replaced the previous 20-year-old Disability Living Allowance (DLA). Shortly before it was abolished, the Coalition government cut the DLA by 20 per cent. All new claimants and everyone previously in receipt of DLA have had to have a PIP test to ensure they are incapable of working. Two companies, Atos and Capita, have been appointed by the government to undertake the tests.

The problem has been that the PIP test bears no relation whatsoever to any medical assessment or examination. It is based on a warped interpretation of the biomedical model of disability. Many staff of the French company Atos are not qualified to practise in the UK. You are as likely to be assessed by a midwife for your schizophrenia or a physiotherapist for your cancer as you are by a nurse for complex medical problems. However, the central difficulty is the test itself.

Adapted from Natalie Bloomer (2014) Thousands left in limbo in benefit appeals system grinding to a halt. *Guardian*, 18 June.

5.4 Are interactionists right?

When considering the interactionist perspective and the medical profession, it is important to demonstrate an awareness of their contribution to understanding the dynamics of patient–practitioner relationships.

The interactionist perspective evolved out of the work by Max Weber on the status and market power of professionals. Interactionists have taken this work forward and focused particularly on the power relationship inherent within doctor–patient interactions. The key contribution of this micro-sociological perspective is to recognise the importance of subjective meanings and an awareness that individual experiences may differ. As a perspective, it is therefore very different to the 'one-size-fits-all' approach of the functionalist and Marxist perspectives.

Another driving force for interactionists has been a critique of the functionalist concept of the sick role. Their findings were that sociological research could find no coherent and recognisable fit between the ideal norms of the sick role and the realities of practitioner–patient interactions. This prompted the development of a number of classifications designed to explain variations in practice.

Figure 6.20 Is the consultation an equal interaction?

In a dated, but still relevant, piece of research, Szasz and Hollender (1956) found that the relationship between doctors and patients varies according to where it takes place and with the nature of the medical problem. They identify three types of practitioner–patient interaction:

- Activity/passivity: where the doctor dominates an asymmetrical relationship. Typical of emergency treatment.
- Guidance/co-operation: where the patient gives a co-operative response to treatment. This is closest to the ideal expectations of the sick role.
- Mutual participation: marked by equality between doctor and patient. Found where patients suffer from chronic conditions that involve a great deal of self-care.

Interactionists have also studied what Erving Goffman referred to as 'information control'. Since doctors enjoy what is called **clinical autonomy** they can withhold information from patients as much as the practitioner feels they need to. Because of their years of training, this means that no lay person is in a position to assess the judgement or quality of work of their doctor. Knowing this, doctors (along

KEY SOCIOLOGISTS

Sarah Nettleton (2013) introduced the notion of **e-scaped medicine** to reflect the growing use of ICT in medicine and its effects, for example, how the informatisation of medicine may alter the degree of trust in medical practice and affect relationships between patients and professionals.

CONTEMPORARY APPLICATION

In April 2014 the government announced a £50 million scheme whereby one in ten surgeries are to offer patients the choice of seeing a GP at evenings and weekends, booking appointments online, receiving electronic prescriptions and having check-ups over Skype. The policy highlights the problems patients have in actually arranging a consultation with their GPs. As a consequence, too many people were turning up to A&E, putting pressure on emergency departments.

STUDY TIP

The interactionist perspective and its association with labelling theory and stigmatisation can be particularly relevant when interpreting how illnesses are constructed, particularly negative ones such as HIV Aids or mental illness.

Questions

1. What were the main problems with preparing new GPs in the past?
2. What changes have been introduced to improve GP preparation and training?
3. What do you think are the most common criticisms from patients about GP consultations?

with other professions) will 'close ranks' if a complaint is made against one of their colleagues. In practice, this means that doctors are reluctant to judge the quality of a colleague's work.

The concept of **clinical freedom** reflects the powerful position of the medical profession to take whatever action they consider in their clinical judgement to be best practice. This also manifests itself in a selfish guarding of their privileges and responsibilities as a profession. For example, doctors are very resistant to losing tasks, such as prescribing, to nurses.

Cartwright and O'Brien (1976) found that middle-class patients had six-minute consultations and consequently ended up with more 'patient-centred' treatment than the working classes, who got four-minute consultations and 'doctor-centred' treatment. However, Arber *et al* (2006) videoed consultations in both the UK and the USA and found no evidence that social class, ethnicity or age had any impact on the quality of patient–practitioner interaction or the doctors' behaviour.

Critique of the interactionist perspective on the medical profession

- The strength of the interactionist approach is its focus on power relations and the social construction of the management of health and illness.
- Labelling theory illustrates the imbalance of power in the doctor–patient relationship, and the effects of stigmatisation, such as mental illness.

In terms of social policy, one way of improving the health of the nation, according to the government, is to incentivise doctors (though direct payments) to encourage certain health treatments, such as childhood vaccinations, flu vaccinations for the elderly, or the routine taking of statins for the middle-aged. The government's intention is to roll out personal health budgets, including extending the use of direct payments. This may shape the nature of patient–practitioner consultations, since the doctor has a financial incentive for patients to adopt certain medical procedures.

IN THE NEWS

Preparing new doctors for GP consultations

In the past, newly qualified doctors were expected to refine the skills that they had learned in training, which focused on diagnosis and to develop knowledge and skills with an emphasis on managing patients and their illnesses. However, the usual setting for this was a hospital ward. New doctors had little or no experience of consultations in a general practice, and the skills appropriate for this setting were not taught in medical schools or teaching hospitals.

The development of general practice as a discipline included analysis of the consultation process and the development of a better understanding of it. As time went on, the teaching of the skills required for better consultations and better care of patients improved. They are now taught to undergraduates and it is widely accepted that continuous improvement of these skills benefits both doctors and patients.

www.patient.co.uk/doctor/consultation-analysis

5.5 Are feminists right?

When studying the feminist perspective and the medical profession, it is important to understand their discussion of both the cultural domination of the profession by men and the patriarchy they feel is exerted on female patients.

The feminist perspective is important for highlighting the fact that society is still gendered. The medical profession is still dominated by men and, as a consequence, women feel they are patronised and stereotyped in their consultations with medical professionals. Male domination of the medical profession dates back to the persecution of women healers as 'witches'.

As scientific medicine slowly developed, many countries declared that it was illegal for women to train and practise medicine. Women's role in health care was restricted to providing care in the home and roles subordinate to the expanding male medical profession.

In the UK women were legally excluded from practising medicine until 1885. Anne Witz (1992) discusses how the male medical profession successfully managed to exclude (and later restrict) women's role in medicine in the UK simply by increasing university entry requirements. Those women who gained places to study medicine at university still had to endure men 'who were able to continue to use their powers to exclude women from access to the systematic training and testing necessary to engage in medical practice'.

Feminists argue that the medical profession has continued to exclude women socially through its patriarchal attitudes and sexist barriers to women becoming consultants. The medical profession would argue that such attitudes are now historic, but it remains very masculine, particularly at the top.

Feminists argue that male doctors view female patients the way they do because of the professional socialisation at medical school. New medics are still graduating with preconceived ideas that illnesses such as depression, anxiety, sleeplessness and migraines are predominantly 'feminine' conditions. As we saw in Section 2, most tranquilliser prescriptions are for women, the majority of whom are working-class housewives diagnosed as 'clinically depressed'. Feminists would argue that the lack of satisfaction many women feel about men through being their partners, child-rearers or work colleagues becomes medically transformed into an illness. The real inequalities and conflicts of interest within the family, workplace and society in general become obscured through the 'mists' of Valium or Prozac.

There has been a recent 'genderquake' shift, with 57 per cent of medical entrants now women. Consequently, the medical profession should eventually achieve gender parity, initially with doctors in training and ultimately with consultants. However, feminists point out that women have represented over 50 per cent of medical students since 1991, so the impact should have been greater by now.

Feminists argue that, historically, the control of women and their bodies shifted from the church to the medical profession. They point out that natural female processes, such as menstruation, pregnancy, childbirth and the menopause, have become medicalised. Feminists argue that the motive behind this for the male medical profession was to capture as much of the medical market as it could. As Ann Oakley (1993) notes: 'by the 1950s pregnancy had become a fully medicalised condition'. The ultimate humiliation for women is that the majority of obstetricians and gynaecologists are men, about 85 per cent in the UK.

KEY SOCIOLOGISTS

Arber *et al*'s (2006) research found that the gender of the patient still significantly influenced doctors' diagnostic and management activities. They found that, compared to men, women were asked fewer questions, received fewer examinations and had fewer diagnostic tests ordered for chronic heart disease (CHD). 'Gendered ageism' was suggested, since mid-life women were asked fewest questions and prescribed least medication appropriate for CHD.

CONTEMPORARY APPLICATION

The General Medical Council (April 2014) recorded that 56.1 per cent of all registered doctors are male compared to 43.9 per cent female. Of specialists, 68.1 per cent are male with only 31.9 per cent female. In general practice the gender balance is almost equal with 50.9 per cent male and 49.1 per cent female doctors.

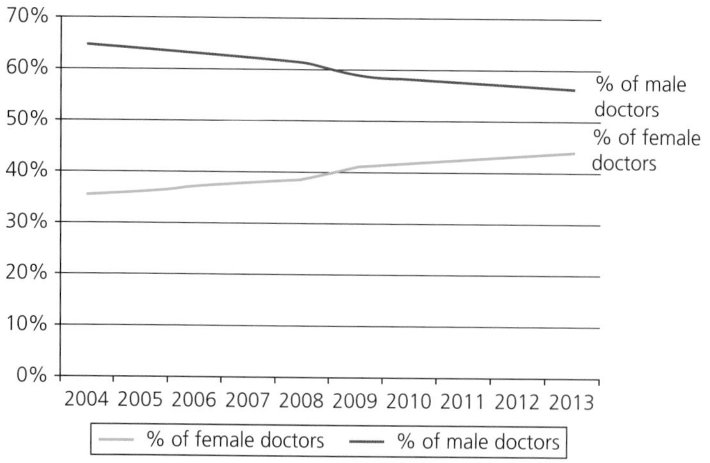

Figure 6.21 Doctors by gender (2004–2013)

General Medical Council (2014) (www.gmc-uk.org/doctors/register/search_stats.asp)

STUDY TIP

Use the feminist perspective to critically evaluate the insufficient focus of other sociological perspectives on gender. While feminists are right to highlight the medicalisation of women's bodies and natural processes like childbirth, it is worth remembering that many women like the security and convenience that medical technology offers. The demand for caesarean births illustrates this perfectly.

Questions

1. What percentage of female consultants are surgeons?
2. Which medical areas have the greatest concentration of female consultants?
3. What factors shape female doctors preferences when it comes to jobs?
4. Why does Black think the medical profession will lose its power and influence?

Critique of the feminist perspective on the medical profession

- Feminism offers a voice to oppressed women who have been subject to patriarchal, patronising and controlling judgements by the male-dominated medical profession.
- As an approach it recognises how women's health, its definition and treatment is related primarily to the 'male-stream' medical profession.
- They have highlighted the growing levels of medicalisation, which obscure genuine grievances in women's lives, such as poverty, poor housing and relationships.
- Some people argue that feminists overstate their case: not all doctors are male, and even those who are can still be sympathetic, caring and non-judgemental to women.

In terms of social policy, the medicalisation of childbirth was highlighted in 2012 when the Southern General Hospital in Glasgow admitted to 'bullying' a mother into taking precautionary antibiotics she didn't want or need. They had threatened that social services would be called to take away her child after the birth. The president of the Royal College of Midwives admitted in the film *Freedom for Birth* (2012): 'we have systems of care that encourage unnecessary interventions or interferences in birth'.

IN THE NEWS

A female-dominated medical profession

The second female president of the Royal College of Physicians since the College was founded in 1518, Dame Carol Black, has warned that the domination of medicine by women will end with the profession losing power and influence.

'We are feminising medicine. It has been a profession dominated by white males. What are we going to have to do to ensure it retains its influence? Years ago, teaching was a male-dominated profession – and look what happened to teaching. I don't think they feel they are a powerful profession any more. Look at nursing, too.'

Many female doctors prefer jobs that involve interaction with patients but also to have more predictable hours that are conducive to family life. Most choose to be GPs, paediatricians, psychiatrists or public health doctors rather than surgeons or cardiologists. Among female consultants, most are paediatricians or work in public health: only 8 per cent are surgeons.

Adapted from Sarah Boseley (2009) The future is female – how women are transforming face of the health service. *Guardian*, 3 June.

5.6 Are postmodernists right?

When discussing the postmodernist perspective and the medical profession, it is important to develop an understanding of their criticism of all other sociological perspectives as 'meta-theories' and how power relations between the practitioner and patient have become fluid.

The postmodernist perspective deconstructs all other sociological perspectives as modernist. The implication here is that they are inadequate theories to explain health in a postmodern society. Postmodernists also challenge the supremacy of the medical profession that is assumed by the other sociological perspectives.

The recent changes to the NHS, including the 'Choose and book' system and the opening up of CAM, has encouraged a fragmented approach to health care. People are encouraged to 'pick and mix' from a range of health care options. Providers argue that this is in keeping with a patient-centred approach to providing care, but postmodernists argue it is merely an extension of a consumerist society and serves to undermine the status and authority of the medical profession.

As a profession, medics have embraced science and denounced CAM medicine. A particular target, despite public endorsement from the royal family and many celebrities including David Beckham, has been homeopathy. CAM, however, continues to receive strong anecdotal support and, as awareness of iatrogenesis filters down to the public, the health profession's position is increasingly questioned.

As noted in Section 2, postmodernists assume that power relations between doctor and patient have become more fluid. Michel Foucault (1963) argues that the origin of power lies in the use of language and its expression through the dominant **discourse**. Traditionally doctors have derived and exerted power over patients through their knowledge of the body. However, patients are empowering and educating themselves through the media and the internet.

Recent work by postmodernists has focused on processes like the growing medicalisation of society, whereby medicine increasingly permeates aspects of daily life. Peter Conrad (2007) notes this has increased particularly in the past 50 years. He argues that there has been a transformation of human events and behaviours previously considered normal into 'medical conditions'. Examples include social anxiety, menopause, 'male menopause', erectile dysfunction and even ageing. Conrad argues that one of the consequences of the expanding medical domain is to disempower the medical profession while empowering the pharmaceutical and biotechnical industries, insurance companies and the patient as consumer.

Michel Foucault (1963) introduced the concept of surveillance as a contemporary feature of postmodern society. This can empower the medical profession, who are increasingly used by employers (annual health checks), insurance companies (evaluating potential risks) and governments (checks in relation to benefits) to monitor the health of the nation. However, at the same time, the medical profession can be bypassed as people engage in **self-surveillance**. Michael Senior (1996) notes how self-surveillance occurs when people use self-diagnosis kits, such as blood pressure or cholesterol testing. In the future people may be encouraged to purchase such kits rather than visit a

KEY SOCIOLOGISTS

David Morris (2000) challenges the practice of the medical profession to separate disease (an objectively verified disorder) from illness (a patient's subjective experience). Postmodern medicine, he argues, can make no such clean distinction; instead, it demands a biocultural model, situating illness at the crossroads of biology and culture. Illnesses such as chronic fatigue syndrome and post-traumatic stress disorder signal our awareness that there are biocultural ways of being sick.

CONTEMPORARY APPLICATION

With society becoming more postmodern, the medical profession remains firmly modernist in its outlook. The difference between these positions is potentially polarising: postmodernists argue that if the medical profession do not respond by changing their reliance on science and technology within a society increasingly distrustful of such a modernist approach, they run the risk of becoming outmoded in the face of the postmodern expectations of its patients.

STUDY TIP

Remember that while the idea of living in a postmodernist society might be convincing to some, not everyone supports this argument. Marxists, for example, argue that however you dress up society, it is still underpinned by the same economic system.

doctor. Technology may introduce widespread self-diagnosis as patients tap in their symptoms to receive a computer-generated diagnosis and a recommended course of treatment.

Critique of the postmodernist perspective on the health profession

- To its credit it recognises the current powerful position of the medical profession and its adherence to the biomedical discourse.
- As a theory it embraces power relations, showing how progressive medicalisation may serve to empower or disempower the medical profession.
- It perceptively sees people operating as consumers of health, choosing from an increasing range and diversity of medical discourses.
- Critics argue that by advocating a DIY approach to diagnosis, it ignores the power of medical profession.

In terms of social policy, the provision of CAM is largely confined to private providers, rendering it out of reach to those on low incomes. NHS provision of CAM is limited, although it is increasingly available as a palliative supplement to patients being treated for cancer. State-funded access to CAM may increase with the introduction of Personal Health Budgets, which people with long-term conditions can spend on their care as they wish.

5.7 To what extent is there a globalised health industry?

When discussing global health inequalities you could include the good health chances of developed countries and compare these to the poorer health chances of the developing world. However, there is considerable variation within countries as well as between them.

Globally there is a huge health divide between richer countries in the developed world and poorer countries in the developing world. In low-income countries, the average life expectancy is 57; in high-income countries, it is 80. However, as the WHO (2011) points out, within both of these global areas there are wide disparities in health status, not only between countries but between different social groups within each country. What is clear is that the lower an individual's socio-economic position within any country, the higher their risk of poor health. For example, we have seen that men in Calton, Glasgow have a lower life expectancy (53.9) than the average for developing countries.

The WHO's (2014) top five facts on global health inequality:

1. Health inequities are unfair and could be reduced by the right mix of government policies.
2. Every day 21,000 children die before their fifth birthday.
3. Developing countries account for 99 per cent of annual maternal deaths in the world.
4. Around 95 per cent of tuberculosis deaths, which is a disease of poverty, are in the developing world.
5. About 80 per cent of chronic diseases are in low- and middle-income countries.

We have come across the term 'big pharma' already in this section. This is a derogatory nickname for the global pharmaceutical industry, which is accused of encouraging a 'pill for every ill' culture. In her book *Big Pharma*, Jacky Law (2006) shows the ways in which major pharmaceutical companies determine which health care problems are publicised and researched. In addition, they are accused of inventing or renaming illnesses in order to sell more drugs. Examples include erectile dysfunction, which some see as naturally occurring process of ageing. The pharmaceutical industry is also accused of malpractice, such as refusing to release the data from negative and inconclusive trials. For example, Ben Goldacre (2012) shows how pharmaceutical companies frequently hide results from bad trials of drugs, exaggerating the benefits. Other questionable practices involve paying doctors to endorse their drugs, ideally in peer-reviewed journals. An example of this was the praise hormone-replacement therapy (HRT) received as a menopausal treatment while downplaying the risk of breast cancer. However, critics of big pharma are often CAM supporters and fail to recognise the contribution that the pharmaceutical industry has made to the advancement of medical knowledge over time. For example, the Ebola crisis in Africa in 2014–15 saw leading pharmaceutical companies rush to create vaccines.

Marxist theory would explain global health inequalities as stemming from global capitalist society, which it sees as serving the interests of making profits at the expense of poorer developing countries. Marxist theory argues that the developing countries have had relatively low levels of development because it has served the interests of rich developed countries to keep them poor, making it easier for them and transnational corporations to exploit their cheap labour and resources. However, as the WHO points out, health is closely linked to living standards. The very poor Caribbean country of Cuba has prioritised health for its people, who enjoy one of the best health services in the world. This, and the example of Bhutan (see Contemporary application), shows that poverty is not necessarily the only factor in driving health. The importance of social capital has been discussed earlier in terms of promoting a sense of well-being and health.

The UN devised the Human Development Index (HDI) in order to measure and compare many factors that contribute towards health, including child mortality rates, life expectancy, access to clean drinking water and sanitation, and access to an affordable diet and shelter. Maternal death is an important concept – the maternal death rate is a key indicator of health inequity because it shows the wide gaps between rich and poor, both between and within countries. An interesting case study is that of Cuba which, despite being a very poor country, has a high HDI. Cuba also gives health care as foreign aid and trains doctors from the developing world for free.

In terms of global social policy, both the World Bank and the International Monetary Fund (IMF) offer loans to developing countries under the banner of Structural Adjustment Programmes (SAPs), whereby countries are usually expected to cut back on welfare expenditure (including on health). Cuts to health spending tend to hit the most vulnerable, such as women and the poor, the hardest. Thus, SAPs are extremely damaging and undermine the health of the least healthy in the first place.

KEY SOCIOLOGISTS

Ben Goldacre (2012) exposes some of the malpractice of the $600 billion global pharmaceutical industry. In addition to hiding unflattering data from their own trials, he describes how the industry is increasingly funding and providing education for medical professionals. He also shows how pharmaceutical products gain government approval through intensive industry lobbying.

CONTEMPORARY APPLICATION

In the South Asian country Bhutan, the key government policy is the pursuit of happiness for its people. Instead of seeking to maximise the size of its economy, its policy is to maximise 'gross national happiness' (GNH). In order to achieve this the government has banned tobacco; traffic lights; various TV channels including MTV; and advertisements for 'false-need products' such as Coca-Cola and Pepsi. Bhutan tops the UN's HDI ranking, demonstrating that its population is not only happy but healthy too.

STUDY TIP

You need to recognise health differences not only between countries but within them too. The poorest parts of developed countries can have health levels equivalent to developing countries.

Questions

1. Which countries had the best and worst health?
2. What does it mean when health shows no correlation with average income?
3. How do Wilkinson and Pickett explain inequalities in health?
4. How does the research of Wilkinson and Pickett support the psychosocial model of Bartley and Blane?

RESEARCH IN FOCUS

The spirit level

In their research of data across many countries, Wilkinson and Pickett (2010) show that health shows no correlation with average income. In other words, a country's health does not improve the richer it becomes. Instead, they argue, there is a strong correlation with income inequality. The wider the income gaps between the rich and poor within a country, the greater the social class health gap. Thus, countries with a narrow income gap, like Japan and the Scandinavian countries, enjoy much better health across the social spectrum than countries like the USA, which has broad income inequality.

Wilkinson and Pickett (2010) *The Spirit Level, Why More Equality is Better for Everyone*. London: Penguin.

Check your understanding

1. What did Max Weber mean when he said doctors created a system of 'social closure'?
2. Why is the status and market position of doctors generally strong in most countries?
3. What is the main motivation to become a doctor according to Talcott Parsons?
4. According to the functionalist Steve Barber, what is the justification for awarding professionals high income, status and prestige?
5. According to Marxists like Navarro, how do doctors obscure the fact that capitalism causes illness?
6. How do Marxists see doctors as agents of control?
7. What is meant by doctors having 'clinical autonomy'?
8. What is happening to the medical profession in terms of gender recruitment?
9. What is meant by the medicalisation of society?
10. What did Foucault mean by 'discourse'?

Practice questions

1. Define the term 'e-scaped medicine'. [2 marks]
2. Using one example, briefly explain what is meant by 'discourse'. [2 marks]
3. Outline three criticisms of the functionalist perspective on health. [6 marks]
4. Outline and explain two ways in which the term 'big pharma' is used to criticise the global pharmaceutical industry. [10 marks]

Read Item A below and answer the question that follows.

Item A

On entering the profession, many physicians did not realise that along with the privileges granted to them came the responsibility to guard and protect those privileges, the most important of which was the responsibility of making sure that things were always done in the best interest of the patient.

Applying material from Item A and your knowledge, evaluate two contrasting sociological approaches to understanding the power of the medical profession. [20 marks]

Links to other topics

This topic has links to:

- Chapter 4 Culture and identity, section 4.3 What is disability?
- Chapter 5 Families and households, section 5.1 Death rates
- Chapter 7 Work, poverty and welfare, section 1.2 To what extent are poverty and social exclusion linked? section 2.2 Why are some groups more likely to be in poverty? section 5.1 What impact does work have on people's lives? section 5.2 What impact does worklessness have on people's lives?
- Global development (Book 2).

7

Work, poverty and welfare

Section 1: Poverty and contemporary society

This section will explore the following debates:

- The definitions of absolute and relative poverty.
- Alternative definitions and measurements of poverty.
- To what extent are poverty and social exclusion linked?
- Theories to explain the existence and persistence of poverty.

GETTING YOU STARTED

Measuring poverty by the Institute of Fiscal Studies

Figure 7.1 The stereotypical image of poverty

The most widely quoted definition of poverty in the UK is the proportion of individuals with household incomes less than 60 per cent of the average.

This measure is used across the EU and was the most high-profile component of New Labour's child poverty targets. It is a measure of 'relative poverty' as the poverty line moves in line with the median from year to year. If median income goes up, then so does the relative poverty line. Essentially, it measures whether poorer households are keeping up with the rest of society. There is a bizarre anomaly of poverty appearing to fall if the poor experience smaller falls in their income compared to average incomes. The reality is that with falling income they are worse off.

Some therefore prefer a measure of absolute poverty, where the poverty line is fixed in real terms, so that poverty goes down when (and only when) the absolute material living standards of poorer households improve. On the other hand, it is difficult to imagine that society's view of minimum acceptable levels of living standards are completely independent of time and place (for example, they are probably higher now than they were in the nineteenth century). The question then becomes how and when the poverty line is changed over time.

Generally speaking, we recommend considering as many measures of poverty as possible in order to gain the richest possible picture – different measures provide different, but incomplete, information, all of which may reasonably be considered relevant. It is also important to consider different poverty thresholds, to ensure that findings are not unique to one specific threshold, and to consider different definitions of income (for example, before and after housing costs).

Adapted from Jonathan Cribb, Robert Joyce and David Phillips (2012) *Living Standards, Poverty and Inequality in the UK: 2012*. London: Institute for Fiscal Studies.

283

Questions

1. What is the measure of poverty used across the EU?
2. Outline and compare the merits of relative and absolute poverty.
3. Why do you think it is important to have many measures of poverty?

1.1 The definitions of absolute and relative poverty

When defining absolute or relative poverty you could critically discuss their competing definitions. Each of these definitions has comparative merits in terms of advantages and disadvantages.

Poverty is an emotive concept and something of an embarrassment to governments, especially the number of children living in poverty. Eradicating childhood poverty is frequently flagged up as a government priority, yet this social problem stubbornly persists across time.

For children, being brought up in poverty significantly increases the likelihood of limited **life chances** and a destiny of adult poverty. Society has a remarkable propensity to reproduce its inequalities, not only at the top, but equally in the deprived sections at the bottom.

Absolute poverty

The concept of **absolute poverty** is rarely applied to contemporary society, with perhaps the exception being those who are truly destitute and living on the streets in rich developed countries, or people living without basic necessities in the developing world. For example, around 2.8 billion people live on less than $2 a day. Roughly 1.2 billion people live on less than $1.25 a day – the UN's consensus definition of 'extreme global poverty'.

In the **developed world** the concept of absolute poverty is normally associated with the past when campaigners such as Seebohm Rowntree and Charles Booth were highlighting the desperate plight of the poor at that time. For example, Rowntree (1901, 1941, 1951) famously conducted three scientific studies of the extent of poverty in York. He used the concept of a **poverty line** to identify who was in or out of poverty. Rowntree calculated the weekly costs of:

- a basic diet
- the 'plainest and most economical' clothes
- rent for basic housing.

These costs then constituted his poverty line. An income less than these basic weekly costs was judged insufficient for effective human life to be maintained. Those whose income was less than these basic costs were below the poverty line.

Application of absolute poverty in contemporary society

Although the concept of absolute poverty is rarely used in rich, developed countries, the concept of what a person or family needs to live on formed the basis of William Beveridge's social insurance, introduced in the 1940s' welfare state. Even contemporary benefit levels, such as income support, are calculated by the government on what they think people need to live on.

The advantages of defining poverty this way are:

- It is a clear and easy way to measure poverty.
- It fits with most people's understanding of poverty as subsistence living.
- It allows easy comparisons of society over time and between countries.

Arguments against defining poverty this way

- It adopts a one-size-fits-all approach. A poverty line ignores individual variations: the cost of living is higher in the south of England than it is the north; heating bills are more expensive in the north of Britain than in the south.
- Basic needs change over time; something considered a luxury in the past may become a necessity, for example, indoor flushing toilets, fridges and mobile phones.
- People living above the poverty line are not immune from deprivation; the closer you are to the line the poorer your quality of life and standard of living.
- The suffering associated with poverty increases over time; people suffer more the longer they are subjected to poverty.

It is worth considering the view that any attempt to construct an absolute measure of poverty could be considered unsociological, since it fails to recognise the important influence of contemporary living standards and lifestyles over individual needs. There is a widespread consensus among sociologists that a relative definition of poverty is the most appropriate; however, the problem of how to measure it objectively remains.

Relative poverty

This definition focuses on the impacts of poverty, especially the way that, over time, poverty leads to **social exclusion**. The most widely accepted definition of **relative poverty** comes from Abel-Smith and Townsend (1966) who claimed to have 'rediscovered' poverty in post-war Britain. Peter Townsend (1979) subsequently defined relative poverty as:

> Individuals, families and groups can be said to be in poverty when … their resources are so seriously below those commanded by the average individual or family that they are, in effect, excluded from ordinary living patterns, customs, and activities.

Relative poverty is inextricably bound up with the idea of inequality. It is set in the context of the average standards experienced by the rest of society. It is, therefore, a dynamic measurement: it changes as society becomes more affluent and varies between societies according to local customs and practices. Townsend used what he called his **deprivation index** criteria as a measurement of relative poverty. Ironically, in the late 1970s he also calculated a poverty line (normally associated with absolute poverty) at approximately 140 per cent of welfare benefit levels; in his deprivation index an ability to access goods and amenities fell much more sharply.

Advantages of defining poverty this way include:

- It demonstrates that poverty is not fixed but becomes a social construction as it will vary across time and possibly between social groups.
- It is a broader definition, linking poverty to lifestyle rather than just necessities.
- It overcomes the bluntness of a poverty line by reflecting degrees of relative poverty.

KEY SOCIOLOGISTS

Peter Townsend (1928–2009) was a British sociologist who pioneered the concept of relative poverty. He identified a close link between poverty and the experiences of the working class, such as poor education, unemployment, low pay associated with unskilled or semi-skilled jobs and long-term reliance on benefits. Townsend's work also established that the working class is more prone to redundancy, accidents and industrial diseases than the middle class.

CONTEMPORARY APPLICATION

Research of people's subjective view of poverty indicates that it is a stigmatised label that many resist. The representation of the poor in British culture is often demeaning. Subjective views on poverty are also gendered: men are more likely than women to deny that they themselves are in poverty, suggesting that men may be more likely to be ashamed with women being more realistic. Poverty rates also differ not only between but within ethnic groups.

STUDY TIP

You need to have a sound knowledge and understanding of these two ways of defining poverty. An ability to evaluate each of these definitions in terms of their strengths and weaknesses is important.

Arguments against using relative poverty

- What constitutes normal or average experiences of the rest of society is a very subjective judgement.
- Measurements of relative poverty cannot be used to compare poverty between societies as it uses the standard of normal experiences within one society.
- Studies of relative poverty tend to concentrate on private life and do not include other deprivations such as public services or the environment.
- There is the absurdity that even rich people can feel relatively poor. Amartya Sen (1983) gives the example of feeling poor in Hollywood if you only owned one Cadillac when the norm was to own two. There is, therefore, a need for some notion of 'basic needs'.

Figure 7.2 The majority of poor people in the UK are in paid work rather than on benefits

Alternative definitions and measurements of poverty

If you are thinking about alternative or contemporary definitions of poverty then it is important to consider and evaluate their relative merits and any disadvantages.

The two definitions of absolute and relative poverty have been compared and debated over the years in terms of their relative merits. New ways of measuring poverty have recently been developed. While these are often variations of the two standard measurements above, they each offer individual characteristics. Some of the key contemporary definitions of poverty are discussed below.

Households Below Average Income (HBAI)

In 1985 the UK government adopted a new way of measuring poverty: Households Below Average Income (HBAI). Poverty throughout the EU and Britain is now officially measured by the number of households receiving three-fifths, or 60 per cent, of the average (median) income. However, a limitation of adopting a relative income poverty line is that it does not take into account other factors, such as how far below the poverty threshold individuals are or the length of time they have been poor. It is important to measure the duration and persistence of poverty as people's suffering of poverty increases the longer they experience it.

The budget standard approach

This is a contemporary attempt to measure poverty in terms of a budget standard that has features similar to absolute poverty. It is associated with Jonathan Bradshaw *et al* (1993) and involves the concept of a 'modest-but-adequate budget' needed to purchase a basket of goods or services assembled by experts. Items were included in the budget if more than half the population had them or regarded them as necessities, such as a television, mobile phones, second-hand car, bicycles, one week's annual holiday and recreational activities. Although this is a form of measurement of absolute poverty, it is very different to Rowntree's **physical efficiency**, which was based solely on the necessities of life.

The consensual approach

Mack and Lansley (1985 and 1990) define poverty as 'an enforced lack of socially perceived necessities'. They developed the 'consensual' approach to poverty from their pioneering Breadline Britain survey (1983). Here the general public (rather than academics) defined what goods and services should be considered as necessities. Their results show that there was a clear consensus on what was deemed to be essential for modern day living in Britain. The Breadline Britain survey defined necessities as items that more than 50 per cent of respondents considered necessities. The approach of Mack and Lansley was well received for using the public rather than relying on expert opinion in defining necessities. However, the researchers still dictated what items would go into their lists in the first place and failed to give the public the opportunity to talk about items not on their list.

Severe material deprivation

Material deprivation figures complement relative poverty rates by providing an estimate of the proportion of people whose living conditions are severely affected by a lack of resources. The severe material deprivation rate measures the proportion of the population that cannot afford at least four of the following items:

● To pay their rent, mortgage, utility bills or loan repayments
● To keep their home adequately warm
● To face unexpected financial expenses
● To eat meat or protein regularly
● To go on holiday for one week once a year
● A television set
● A washing machine
● A car
● A telephone

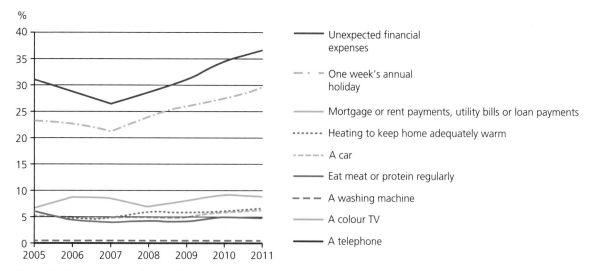

%

Legend:
- Unexpected financial expenses
- One week's annual holiday
- Mortgage or rent payments, utility bills or loan payments
- Heating to keep home adequately warm
- A car
- Eat meat or protein regularly
- A washing machine
- A colour TV
- A telephone

Figure 7.3 Percentage of the UK population unable to afford items, 2005–2011

Figure 7.4 shows data from the Office of National Statistics relating to the percentage of households unable to afford a variety of items in the UK in 2005–2011. In the UK, the overall severe material deprivation rate remained broadly unchanged between 2005 and 2011, with 5.1 per cent of the population being deprived in 2011. Levels of severe material deprivation in the UK are significantly below the EU average of 8.7 per cent.

The concept of **poverty dynamics** plays an important role in this debate. It explores the ways of measuring the total population affected by poverty over a period of time and the extent to which individuals and households move in and out of poverty. To understand poverty and social exclusion, income must be looked at over a sustained period, not just at a point in time. Standards of living will be significantly affected by the duration of any period on low income.

Subjective poverty

The concept of subjective definitions of poverty has been somewhat ignored by sociologists, but it clearly offers an important personal perception of deprivation. People's own definition of poverty inevitably has a degree of relativity to it. Indeed, many people clearly living in poverty are reluctant to define themselves as 'poor'. This is because of the negative connotations of the poverty label. A commonly held subjective view of poverty is that it is a demoralising and challenging situation. Poor people can be subject to stigmatisation by the attitudes of others, so it is often a label that is resisted.

Studies of poor people, such as that by Shildrick and Macdonald (2015), show that many are reluctant to describe themselves as 'poor'. Instead they were more likely to use terms like 'hard up' while at the same time emphasising their ability to 'get by' with their limited budget. They found that 'managing' implied they were 'coping'. It is sometimes felt by people that poverty implies a lack of dignity or cleanliness, and clean homes can be cited as evidence of not being poor. Others will resist what is perceived to be an undesirable classification since representations of the poor in British culture, and particularly in the media, can be demeaning. In terms of gender responses, men appear to deny being poor more than women. This might possibly be because men are more likely to be ashamed while women are more realistic. Cross comparisons across Europe by Franziska Buttler (2013) suggest that ideas of what constitutes subjective poverty vary substantially across countries.

Overall poverty

In 1995 the UN defined overall poverty (to distinguish it from the absolute poverty of lacking the basic necessities of life) as a:

> lack of income and productive resources to ensure sustainable livelihoods; hunger and malnutrition; ill health; limited or lack of access to education and other basic services; increased morbidity and mortality from illness; homelessness and inadequate housing; unsafe environments and social discrimination and exclusion. It is also characterised by lack of participation in decision making and in civil, social and cultural life. It occurs in all countries: as mass poverty in many developing countries, pockets of poverty amid wealth in developed countries, loss of livelihoods as a result of economic recession, sudden poverty as a result of disaster or conflict, the poverty of low-wage workers, and the utter destitution of people who fall outside family support systems, social institutions and safety nets.

UNICEF Report Card on child well-being

This measurement is useful for global comparisons and combines indicators of material well-being, health and safety, educational well-being, family and peer relationships, behaviours and risk, and subjective well-being.

IN THE NEWS

Unattainable UK childhood poverty goals

Evidence that the government will fail to hit its child poverty goals has emerged in a report from the Social Mobility and Child Poverty Commission. The report shows that 3.5 million children are expected to be in absolute poverty in Britain in 2020 – almost five times as many as the target.

The Commission said the absolute child poverty goal was 'simply unattainable' and that this was on course to be the first decade since records began in 1961 not to see a fall in absolute child poverty.

Under the Child Poverty Act 2010, passed by Labour just before it left office, the government is committed to getting relative child poverty (the proportion of children living in households on below 60 per cent median income) below 10 per cent by 2020.

Work and Pensions Secretary Iain Duncan Smith argues that addressing poverty by just increasing benefits is not the answer and that more parents need to be working. The Department for Work and Pensions said it was committed to ending child poverty by 2020 with plans to tackle the root causes of poverty, including worklessness, low earnings and educational failure.

However, the Commission says 'ending poverty mainly through the labour market does not look remotely realistic by 2020', and that increasing the number of working parents would, in many cases, only result in children from low-income workless households to low-income working households. 'The reality is that too many parents get stuck in working poverty, unable to command sufficient earnings to escape low income and cycling in and out of insecure, short-term and low-paid employment with limited prospects.'

Adapted from Andrew Sparrow (2014) UK's child poverty goals unattainable, says report. *Guardian*, 9 June.

KEY SOCIOLOGISTS

David Gordon, director of the Townsend Centre for International Poverty Research at the University of Bristol, states that: 'poverty, inequality and social exclusion remain the most fundamental problems that people face in the twenty-first century'. His involvement with the Millennium Poverty and Social Exclusion Survey provided not only quantitative data on levels of poverty but included information about the goods and services that the British public say are necessary to avoid poverty.

CONTEMPORARY APPLICATION

In terms of social policy the Coalition government (2010–2015) has been criticised for claiming 'we are all in it together' while implementing policies that have hit some of the poorest sectors in society the hardest. At the same time the richest earners have seen the top rate of income tax cut by five per cent. The so-called 'bedroom tax' has cut the benefits of those in social housing with a spare room, often hitting some of the most vulnerable people in society the hardest.

STUDY TIP

The different measurements of poverty in this section offer alternatives to the absolute versus relative poverty debate. It is important to also have knowledge of recent social policy and how this impacts on poverty numbers and the poor themselves.

Questions

1. How many children are expected to be in absolute poverty in 2020?
2. What is the commitment to child poverty made in the Child Poverty Act 2010?
3. What is the key solution to poverty according to the government?
4. Why does the Social Mobility and Child Poverty Commission see this solution as flawed?

1.2 To what extent are poverty and social exclusion linked?

When considering social exclusion it is important that you learn how it differs from poverty in terms of how it is experienced.

Figure 7.4 Young people brought up in poverty can become socially excluded from life chances others take for granted

The meaning of social exclusion

The term social exclusion refers to how the deprived have lower levels of participation across a wide range of areas in society. It was first adopted by the EU in the 1980s, but has only been generally used in Britain since the 1990s. In terms of sociological theory, the interactionist perspective can play a useful role in enhancing our understanding of the meanings of those living in social exclusion. As a term, social exclusion is often used synonymously with poverty, but there are some important distinctions between them. Stephen Sinclair (2003) identifies five key areas of difference:

- Poverty is often concerned with measurement and distribution whereas social exclusion is a relational concept – referring to levels of participation within society.
- Poverty is normally defined in terms of (lack of) income, whereas social exclusion is about experiences: being excluded from social, economic, cultural and even political systems.
- Social exclusion describes a dynamic process rather than a static condition.
- Social exclusion gives consideration to the duration of deprivation.

While Sinclair's points highlight some clear-cut differences between poverty and social exclusion, the reality is that the differences between the two are somewhat fluid. For example, Peter Townsend can take credit for developing both the concepts of relative poverty and social exclusion. He argued that, over time, people evolved from living in poverty to social exclusion when they were increasingly denied the chance to engage in activities that the rest of society takes for granted.

The eradication of social exclusion is a complex and costly task, with governments having to address inequalities in educational opportunity, poor quality housing, health chances, community and environmental inequalities, and being likelihood of being a victim of crime.

Measuring social exclusion

The New Policy Institute (NPI) publishes an annual report on range of areas of need associated with poverty in the UK. The characteristics outlined in Figure 7.5 are not exclusive to the socially excluded but frequently characterise their deprivation and life chances.

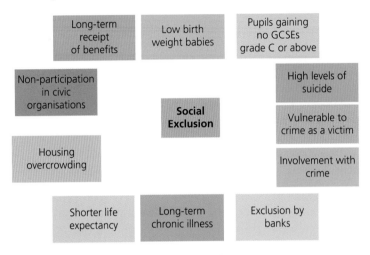

Figure 7.5 Social exclusion and deprivation

The study by Aldridge *et al* (2012) for the New Policy Institute analyses trends that reveal the lifestyle and experiences of those in poverty and social exclusion in the UK today. It says:

- The proportion of pensioners in poverty has halved since the early 1990s, while that of working-age adults without children has risen by a third.
- Over half of children and working-age adults in poverty live in a working household. In-work poverty has been rising steadily for at least a decade.
- Poverty is no longer concentrated in the social rented sector. The numbers of private renters in poverty are now as high, having doubled in the last decade.
- Health inequalities between deprived and non-deprived areas have grown in the last decade. A man in one of the least deprived areas can expect to live longer than a woman in one of the most deprived areas.
- Some 6.4 million people now lack the paid work they want. There are 1.4 million part-time workers wanting full-time work – the highest figure in 20 years.
- The populations of people in poverty and those out of work are not static. While one in six people live in low income at any one time, around one in three has had a spell in low income over a four-year period.
- Similarly, while 1.6 million people are claiming Jobseeker's Allowance (JSA) at any one time, 4.8 million have claimed JSA at least once in the last two years.
- The welfare cuts so far are likely to hit low-income households more than once, through changes to both income-related and housing benefits. Changes to disability benefit could result in low-income disabled people being hit even harder.

Experience of social exclusion

Recent research by the Joseph Rowntree Foundation shows that it is common for parents, especially mothers, to make huge personal sacrifices so that their children can have 'must-have' possessions or take part in extra-curricular

KEY SOCIOLOGISTS

David Byrne (1999) has made a major contribution to our understanding of social exclusion. Borrowing the Marxist term 'reserve army of labour', he defines the excluded as those who move in and out of employment at the bottom end of the labour market. Such movements are clearly influenced by fluctuations in the economy.

CONTEMPORARY APPLICATION

The New Policy Institute (Aldridge *et al*, 2012) concludes that the overall picture is not so much a mixture of success and failure as one of success and neglect. They argue that where governments have intervened and acted to address some of the issues above, change has happened. Where governments have taken no or insufficient action, then the trends outlined have continued.

STUDY TIP

The concept of social exclusion is an important one as it highlights the lived experiences of people living in poverty. It also emphasises the degree of marginalisation from many everyday activities that the poor experience.

activities at school. Children from poor families often report being bullied at school because of their clothes, shoes and gadgets. Many parents reported that they would buy their children what other children saw as normal, even if this meant getting further into debt.

A way of coping with poverty for many people is to spend money on non-essentials, such as alcohol and smoking, as 'stress-reducing' responses to 'make life bearable'. Others buy lottery tickets in a desperate attempt to escape poverty. Social exclusion often means that people frequently go without essential goods, foregoing some meals, having a poor diet, having the heating down or even off in cold weather.

Many poor people were excluded from the normal banking system and often had to resort to disreputable moneylenders. They described themselves as 'drowning in a sea of financial problems' or if lucky 'barely keeping their heads above water'. They were forced to borrow from payday loan shops or 'loan sharks' and to shop at places that allowed weekly payments (which end up being very expensive). Financial problems often manifested into poor emotional support from male partners and sometimes violence. Poverty can drive a wedge between family members. Arguments between parents sometimes drove children away – even to become homeless.

Many feared their electricity or gas would be shut-off creating major health risks in winter. The poor often resort to prepayment meters for gas and electricity, which are the most expensive ways of buying such services, and always with the risk of running out. In homes with water meters there is evidence of health-threatening under-use of water. People who had had their houses repossessed were often rehoused on the worst housing estates with the highest crime levels.

RESEARCH IN FOCUS

Traditional families are the largest UK group in poverty

A 2013 report by the IPPR for Joseph Rowntree found that the largest group experiencing poverty in the UK was the traditional family model, where one parent earns a wage and the other cares for young children.

Where wages are low, the 'traditional' family model does not guarantee that the family will avoid poverty - the report found that a third of these 'working families' are living below the poverty line. This inconvenient truth does not tally with the mantra of many politicians (from all parties) who continually cite work as the best route out of poverty.

Tackling the problem of in-work poverty needs not just a public policy response, it also requires changes within the labour market. The guarantee of a living wage is important, but also necessary are strategies to support progress to better-paid employment, and economic reform to reduce the reliance on low-paid, low-skilled jobs.

People who would like to bring in a second wage to the family face a number of barriers to finding suitable work. Low pay means that much of their earnings are cancelled out by the withdrawal of means-tested benefits, and the cost of childcare can mean that the family budget is in deficit - instead of work paying, they are effectively paying to work.

Policies promoting employment do little for families where one partner actively wants to stay at home to care for children. Tax measures such as raising the tax threshold or a marriage tax allowance would do little to address the issue. There is no advantage for poorer households where earnings are so low that no one is required to pay tax. Similarly, a marriage tax allowance would help only couples who are married or in civil partnerships and earn enough to pay tax.

Adapted from Katie Schmuecker (2013) Traditional breadwinner couples the largest group in poverty in low-pay Britain. Joseph Rowntree Foundation (www.jrf.org.uk/blog/2013/11/breadwinner-couples-largest-group-poverty).

Questions

1. Why is the finding from this research an 'inconvenient truth' for politicians?
2. What solutions to 'in-work poverty' are put forward by politicians?
3. In families with children, what are the potential barriers facing the second earners from entering work?
4. Why might changes to the tax system (e.g. raising tax thresholds or introducing a marriage tax allowance) not necessarily help low-paid families?

1.3 How can we explain poverty?

When discussing the existence and persistence of poverty you will find the sociological theoretical explanations below useful. Ideas about solutions to poverty are studied in greater detail in Section 3.

Feminist perspective on poverty

The explanations for poverty and policy ideas to address it arising from feminist theory are fragmented.

Feminist theorists generally agree that poverty is an issue of gender, and that other sociological theories of poverty tend to ignore gender issues. Feminists argue that such theories are preoccupied with the formal economy and work. As a consequence, feminist theorists argue that they ignore the lived experiences of women and the extent to which women's caring and domestic responsibilities impact on their experiences of poverty.

Women are more prone to poverty than men because the majority of single parents and single pensioners are women. This over-representation of women in the main groups in poverty in the UK gives rise to the phrase the 'feminisation of poverty'.

Kathy Hamilton (2012) notes that women often make personal sacrifices in order that partners and, especially, children are better fed and get expensive branded goods. Such sacrifices, she claims, allows the impression of 'artificial affluence' and are a means of 'stigma management' by low-income mothers. Shildrick and Macdonald (2015) found that there was enormous pressure on mothers to make sacrifices for their children. Failure to make these sacrifices, that is, failure to be seen to be 'maintaining standards', resulted in women being castigated as 'the undeserving poor'. Ironically, the fiercest critics of poor women can be other women, suggesting that it is women's role to protect and project working-class respectability.

Feminists point out that within a household sacrifices and income allocation can be far from equally shared. Jan Pahl (1989) found that men were more likely to have money for personal spending than their partners. Feminists have therefore concluded that women's poverty can only be understood in the context of the gender inequalities that persist throughout life. However, Christopher Pierson (2006) notes that feminists can overstate the gendered nature of poverty. Pierson points out that in some countries like Sweden not only is poverty low but rates are comparable between men and women.

Functionalist perspective on poverty

The functionalist perspective does not really have a coherent view on poverty or its causes, other than to see it as an inevitable outcome for those who do not embrace the opportunities of a meritocratic society.

Functionalist theory includes an element of 'victim blaming' and the 'undeserving poor'. It purports that those who are poor are so because they are lazy or untalented.

The functionalist perspective contributes to our understanding of poverty through the work of Herbert J. Gans. Gans' analysis of the functions of poverty highlights how poverty benefits those fortunate enough to not be living in poverty, and the rich and powerful in particular. Consequently, the bulk of society has a vested interest in maintaining rather than trying to abolish poverty.

Gans identifies three functions of poverty. Firstly, the poor supply workers for the worst jobs in society that no one else wants to do. Secondly, the existence of poverty generates considerable levels of employment for people like social workers, welfare workers and the police. Finally, poverty becomes a reassurance to the rest of society who can use them as a yardstick to measure their success by. In addition, because the poor are relatively powerless they can be scapegoated for a lot of society's problems.

Marxist perspective on poverty

Marxists believe that the cause of poverty lies within the economic system of capitalism, which they argue is incapable of producing social justice. As a consequence they say that it is only possible to eradicate poverty in a socialist society under workers' control, in which human needs, and not profits, determine the allocation of resources.

In capitalism, which is based on the free market system, Marxists argue that the interests of capital and profit are always put before people. This gives rise to low wages, poor protection for workers' contracts, and workers having uncertain hours, such as with zero-hours contracts. Poverty is, therefore, a class rather than an individual or group issue, since all workers – employed or unemployed – are potential victims of the capitalist system.

According to Marxists, poverty also serves to undermine **class consciousness**. Far from giving the poor sympathy, the working class tends to reflect the tabloid media's criticism of them, especially those in receipt of benefits, as 'welfare scroungers'. The Marxist Ralph Miliband (1974) shows how the poor are largely powerless as a group, who not only lack economic resources but political resources as well. He states that 'economic deprivation is a source of political deprivation; and political deprivation in turn helps to maintain and confirm economic deprivation'.

New Right perspective on poverty

The New Right's ideas on poverty became popular in the late 1980s. Right-wing sociologists, such as David Marsland (2003) and Peter Saunders (1990), argued that the generosity of the welfare state encourages fecklessness, which in turn creates a **dependency culture**. Marsland adopts an almost intolerant approach to poverty and the poor, according them no sympathy at all. He accuses organisations like the Joseph Rowntree Foundation of deliberately exaggerating the extent of poverty in order to deceive the public into thinking it is more of a problem than it actually is.

Marsland is very critical of universal benefits and services such as health care, education and child benefits as examples of an overly generous state that simply encourages people to be hopeless and dependent. He describes the welfare state as offering 'sentimentally utopian support for idleness and for reckless lack of foresight, it gradually transforms a free people into a subjugated mass of underclass serfs'. This is a view shared by the American sociologist Charles Murray (1989) who talks of welfare contributing to an underclass 'living outside society' with their own deviant subcultural values.

Such individual and cultural explanations have been criticised, not least because blaming the poor for their poverty is both simplistic and heartless. As a theoretical approach it also ignores obvious structural factors beyond the scope of individuals to control, such as involuntary unemployment, sickness, disability and poverty in old age.

Social democratic perspective on poverty

Social democratic ideology believes that poverty is structural in nature and can be eradicated simply through increased and targeted state spending. In contrast to the New Right, social democratic supporters advocate a strong welfare state with provision to address inequalities, especially intervention to eradicate poverty. Supporters of this ideology give the Scandinavian countries, especially Sweden, as examples of how the state can eradicate inequalities and minimise the hardship of poverty. Sweden has a remarkably egalitarian distribution of income and a low rate of poverty. Accordingly, the poor in Sweden have a standard of living closer to the national average for citizens than in other advanced countries. However, opponents of social democratic ideology point to the very high levels of taxation needed to pay for such a generous welfare state. New Right critics, like David Marsland (2003), would argue that such an approach encourages idleness, an over-reliance on the 'nanny state' and that it strips people of their 'natural capacity for enterprising self-reliance'.

Weberian perspective on poverty

Although the concept of an underclass is most closely associated with the New Right, it is essentially a Weberian concept linked to individual status. Max Weber sought to analyse and explain inequality through the three concepts of social class, status and party. As such, he offers a multi-dimensional approach that essentially explains the existence of poverty as being due to people's inability to secure well-paid employment in the labour market. This can be related to social class but can also explain why groups like women, some ethnic groups and the disabled are more prone to poverty. Therefore, a Weberian analysis of poverty is more sophisticated than that of Marxism since dimensions of status and power are conceptually distinct from economic class or power. Poverty exists simply because there are differences of prestige and authority in society. Groups that lack these inevitably have a poor market position, which in turn generates their material income.

KEY SOCIOLOGISTS

Pete Alcock (2006) helps explain why so many people in poverty are keen to distance themselves from the label 'poor'. It stems from the emphasis within society of a pride in managing in difficult circumstances. He argues: 'to identify oneself as poor is to identify oneself as having a problem and being in need of help'. Poor people are therefore culturally defined as people unable to manage and maintain a degree of respectability, especially around raising a family.

CONTEMPORARY APPLICATION

Shildrick and Macdonald (2015) suggest that it is actually unfashionable to talk about poverty in the contemporary UK. Both politicians and the media have constructed a context of 'political invisibility' with regard to poverty because absolute poverty has been seen to be eradicated (except for the homeless). Therefore, there is an assumption that only a tiny minority of the population can be counted as actually poor, despite measures of relative poverty showing significant numbers of people in marginalised positions of social exclusion.

STUDY TIP

When explaining the existence and persistence of poverty it is useful to show an awareness of the range and diversity of sociological theoretical explanations. While poverty is invariably a class issue, it is important to show that other groups, such as women, many ethnic minority groups, the elderly and people with disabilities, can be more prone to poverty as well.

Check your understanding

1. What is absolute poverty?
2. What is a poverty line?
3. What did Rowntree mean by the term 'physical efficiency'?
4. Give two disadvantages of defining poverty in absolute terms.
5. What is meant by relative poverty?
6. Who is credited with the development of relative poverty?
7. What criticism does Sen make about relative poverty?
8. Give two advantages of defining poverty in relative terms.
9. What is meant by social exclusion?
10. Give four examples of social exclusion.

Practice questions

1. Define the term 'poverty line'. [2 marks]
2. Using **one** example, briefly explain what Rowntree meant by 'physical efficiency'. [2 marks]
3. Suggest **three** ways in which the New Right can explain the cause of poverty. [6 marks]
4. Outline and explain **two** reasons why many people clearly living in objective poverty are reluctant to define themselves as 'poor'. [10 marks]

Read Item A below and answer the question that follows.

Item A

It was estimated by the Office for National Statistics that 14 million people in the UK were at risk of poverty and social exclusion in 2011. In comparisons with other EU countries on a range of poverty indicators, the UK is close to the European average.

Applying material from Item A and your knowledge, evaluate the view that the term social exclusion is a more meaningful way of understanding deprivation than poverty. [20 marks]

Section 2: Poverty, wealth and income

This section will explore the following debates:

● How is poverty distributed in the UK?
● Why are some groups more or less likely to be living in poverty?
● How are wealth and income distributed across society?

Questions

1. Why is the accumulated wealth of £519 billion for the richest 1000 people likely to be an underestimate?
2. Compare and contrast the financial experiences of the richest 1000 with most ordinary workers in the period of austerity (2010–15).
3. What does Rachel Orr of Oxfam say politicians should do?
4. How many billionaires does Britain have?
5. Evaluate the impact of a polarised society as the gap between the richest and poorest widens.

GETTING YOU STARTED

Wealth of Britain's richest 1000 people hits new high of £519 billion

Figure 7.6 The stereotypical image of wealth

The combined fortune of Britain's richest 1000 people has hit a new high, up 15.4 per cent from last year's total of £450 billion. The 26th annual 'Sunday Times Rich List' is based on 'identifiable wealth' – including land, property, other assets such as art and race horses, or significant shares in publicly quoted companies. (It excludes bank accounts, which the Sunday Times has no access to.)

Their wealth has doubled since the financial crisis, the same period in which most workers have seen their incomes frozen and falling, in real terms, as inflation rises between 2 and 3 per cent per annum. In contrast, the richest 1000 have seen their wealth rise from £258 billion in 2009 to £519 billion. Government figures show that in 2014 Britain's richest 1 per cent had accumulated as much wealth as the poorest 55 per cent put together.

Rachael Orr, head of Oxfam's UK poverty programme, said: 'We need our politicians to grasp the nettle and make narrowing the gap between the richest and poorest a top priority. It cannot be right that in Britain today a small elite are getting richer and richer while hundreds of thousands rely on food banks to feed their families.'

Entry to the top 1000 list for 2014 indicated a minimum of £85 million; a top 500 list entry required £190 million, up from £160 million last year. The number of billionaires living in Britain had risen to 104 – more than three times than a decade ago. They share a fortune of more than £301 billion. Britain has more billionaires per capita than any other country. London has 72 billionaires – more than any other city in the world.

Adapted from Julia Kollewe (2014) Wealth of Britain's richest 1,000 people hits new high of £519bn. *Guardian*, 18 May.

2.1 How is poverty distributed in the UK?

When discussing how poverty is distributed you could include which groups are prone to poverty and the reasons behind this.

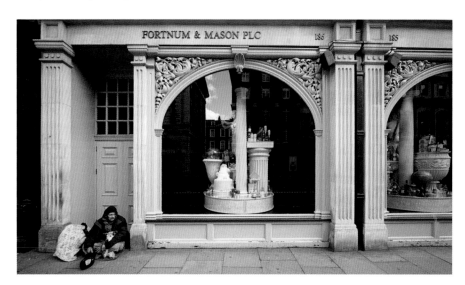

Figure 7.7 An image of contrasting poverty and wealth: a homeless man outside a high-end store in London.

Household composition	Distribution of poverty (percentage)
Single person aged under 65	19.2
Single person aged 65+	24.3
Couple both under 65	7.7
Couple, one or both aged 65+	12.2
Couple with dependent child/ren	15.2
Couple with adult child/ren	3.0
Lone parent with dependent child/ren	10.7
One parent with adult child/ren	2.9
Extended family	1.2
Other	3.6

Table 7.1 Composition of people in poverty in UK, 2013

Household composition, poverty and hardship across Europe, 2013, Eurostat

The elderly

Table 7.2 shows that almost a quarter of people living in poverty in the UK are single persons aged over 65 (24.3 per cent). Couples with one or both people aged over 65 living in poverty represent just 12.2 per cent of people living in poverty. Single elderly are clearly far more prone to poverty than couples. Especially in terms of social class, it is simplistic to consider the elderly as a homogeneous group. Those with good occupational pensions and savings, in addition to the state pension, enjoy a comfortable retirement. Such affluent pensioners are sometimes referred to as grey panthers. Pensioners without savings and dependent solely on the state pension often end their days living in desolate conditions.

Single persons

The next biggest group living in poverty are single persons aged under 65 (19.2 per cent). Couples are generally richer than single people as they can pool their incomes and living costs are not too much higher than for single people.

Households with children

A major social factor associated with vulnerability to poverty is the presence of children in the household. Couples with dependent children are the third highest group (15.2 per cent). Because of the cost of raising children – calculated to be £148,000 from birth until they are 18 (2013) – such households are more likely to live in poverty than childless couples (7.7 per cent).

Lone parents, because they have only one income or are living on benefits, are more likely to be poorer than couples with children or childless single people.

Large families (with three or more children) are more prone to poverty because they are twice as likely to have no parent in employment and, if they do work, are more likely to be earning low incomes. Large families are more likely to have parents with no qualifications. Though having a large family is an additional risk factor, the majority of poor families have only one or two children.

Childless couples

The Joseph Rowntree Trust (Parekh *et al*, 2010) published figures showing that poverty among childless couples has grown to record levels. While New Labour successfully halved the number of pensioners living in poverty and spent billions of pounds on Child Tax Credit, childless couples living in poverty fell to the bottom of the pile. Besides not being targeted by politicians, the main impact on childless adults who receive benefits will be the new way of altering how their benefits are updated annually. This kind of **benefit erosion** can have serious long-term consequences, compounding the real experience of poverty and exclusion for those on the receiving end.

Low-paid people

The annual Monitoring Poverty report (MacInnes *et al*, 2013), produced by the New Policy Institute (NPI), highlights the extent of poverty experienced by people in low-paid employment. They calculated that 4.4 million jobs paid less than £7 per hour. Low-paid work is common among hotels and restaurants, IT, finance and services, and wholesale, retail and transport jobs. Low pay is exacerbated by the insecurities of such work, with people often moving in and out of jobs.

The report found that the number of people experiencing in-work poverty exceeded work-less poverty (6.1 million compared to 5.1 million people, excluding pensioner households). They also found that the number of people working part time but wanting full-time work was 1.4 million, up by 500,000 since 2009. While 18 per cent of people were in low income at any one time, 33 per cent experienced at least one period of low income in a four-year period, and 11 per cent were in low income for more than half of that time The number of working families receiving Working Tax Credit – payments to top up wages – has risen by 50 per cent since 2003, to 3.3 million in 2012.

However, the number of people moving in and out of poverty means that the total number is greater than any snapshot implies. For example, 5 million people have claimed Jobseeker's Allowance (JSA) over a two-year period, around one in six economically active people. The turnover of people moving on and off JSA is substantial: 42 per cent of claims were made within six months of the last claim. Half stop claiming within three months.

Disability and poverty

Around a third of all adults with disabilities aged 25–65 are living in low-income households. This is twice the rate of that for adults without disabilities. The main

KEY SOCIOLOGISTS

Flaherty *et al* (2004) found that people are generally more comfortable applying the term 'deprivation' to nearby estates and areas than themselves. People experiencing poverty frequently tailor their expectations in ways that underplay their own experiences of disadvantage and deprivation as a means of coping with life on a low income, as well as reflecting the social stigma associated with poverty.

CONTEMPORARY APPLICATION

Currently one in five people in the UK are living in poverty. Oxfam (2014a) point out that cuts to social security and public services are combining with falling incomes and rising costs for basics, such as food and fuel bills, to create a deeply damaging situation. Although unemployment numbers are falling, the number of people in insecure jobs is on the rise and many are on wages that don't pay enough to make ends meet.

STUDY TIP

It is useful to be aware of the contemporary predicament of the social groups discussed above. Be aware of trends such as how the elderly have moved from being one of the most vulnerable groups for living in poverty to their present position of nearly a quarter of single people over 65 in poverty. People with disabilities have often been overlooked in sociological discussion but are very vulnerable to welfare cuts.

reason that working-age adults with disabilities are more likely to be in low-income households is because they are less likely to be in work. In terms of the Coalition government's benefit cuts and the shift to universal benefit, the Marxist Roddy Slorach (2012) points out that people with disabilities could be the hardest hit. The introduction of Universal Credit could result in 450,000 people with disabilities and their families losing up to £58 a week.

2.2 Why are some groups more likely to live in poverty?

If you are thinking about the distribution of poverty according to gender or ethnicity, you could include your understanding of intersectionality.

Gender and poverty

As a group, women are marginally more likely to live in low-income households than men (21 per cent compared with 19 per cent in 2014). Specifically, single women are also marginally more likely to live in low-income households than single men (28 per cent compared with 25 per cent in 2014). One reason for this small gender gap is that is that both single female pensioners and female lone parents are more likely to be in low-income households than their male equivalents. One reason why the gap is so small is that there is no such difference for working-age singles without children. A second reason is that most people live in couples.

This gender gap has more than halved over the past decade. One reason for this fall has been the reduction in the numbers of single pensioners and lone parents in poverty – specifically the groups where poor women were traditionally located. By contrast, the two groups where poverty is increasing – working-age singles without children and working-age couples with children – are where women do not predominate.

Ethnic minorities and poverty

Poverty is significantly higher among people from black and minority ethnic (BME) communities, with around 40 per cent of people from BME communities living in low-income households, twice the rate for white people (20 per cent). Specifically, 30 per cent of Indians and Caribbeans, 50 per cent of black Africans, 60 per cent of Pakistanis and 70 per cent of Bangladeshis are living in poverty in the UK. This compares with less than a quarter of the UK population overall.

Within these groups there is significant variation in income and experience. Key factors driving poverty are family size, joblessness and an adherence to the traditional family (hence only one breadwinner). However, none of these factors, together or separately, can fully explain the outcomes.

Discrimination would appear to play a critical role in BME groups' risks of poverty. A Weberian analysis would imply that BME groups lack status compared to other groups and that prejudice and discrimination undermines their market power. Lucinda Platt (2006) undertook research for the Equal Opportunities Commission and found that many men from BME communities experienced unemployment rates up to four times the average for all men. She also found that although Caribbean women are more likely to be economically active than women from any other BME community, including white women, they are still more likely to be in poverty because they are frequently confined to low-paid work.

Barnard and Turner (2011) undertook a review of evidence on the links between poverty and ethnicity. They concluded that an appreciation of **intersectionality** was vital in order to understand the complex ways in which ethnicity overlaps with other factors to affect people's experiences and outcomes. They also concluded that poverty outcomes were shaped by two broad sets of factors: firstly, *informal processes* – the texture of everyday life – and, secondly, the wider *structures* of labour markets, housing options, services, geography and social norms. Finally, they identified four important areas worthy of further investigation:

● How different BME families manage their caring and economic needs.
● How in-work poverty is affected by informal workplace cultures.
● How social networks are changing and enabling BME groups to escape from poverty.
● The influences of the places and communities people live and work in.

Rural areas and poverty

Guy Palmer (2004) challenges the myth that poverty is just confined to urban areas like the inner-city or rundown housing estates. He undertook a study of 400,000 people living in rural areas in the east of England. He found that a sixth of rural households had an income below that used by central government in their definition of poverty. Half of these people were living in households where at least one person was working, highlighting how poverty in rural areas is not just about a lack of paid work; it is also about low pay.

Another key factor contributing to poverty was people with a limiting, longstanding illness; many of these were older people. It illustrates the importance of including older people in any analysis of social exclusion.

Disability and poverty

Because of the low participation rate of people with disabilities in the labour market, they are frequently dependent on welfare benefits. Two changes to the benefit system are seen as making disabled people especially vulnerable to poverty: the move towards universal credit and the introduction of the so-called 'bedroom tax' in 2013. In addition, a planned move to make the application for benefits online will discriminates against people with disabilities: currently, only 58 per cent of people with disabilities have access to the internet compared to the national average of 84 per cent.

All disabled people have been subject to work capacity assessments (WCAs) or 'fit for work' tests since 2008. In 2013 the Disability Living Allowance (DLA) was replaced by the more restrictive Personal Independence Payment (PIP). Roddy Slorach (2012) claims this change was designed to remove benefit from 20 per cent (500,000 people) who previously qualified for DLA. Under PIP there is no equivalent of the mobility component of DLA for those aged 65 or over. The government has also withdrawn the Independent Living Fund, which benefited vast numbers of people with disabilities.

Government figures show that restricting the total amount of benefits to £26,000 will mean that 450,000 disabled people will lose an average of £676 per year. This will clearly impact on both the absolute and relative poverty of this group.

In 2014 the government's welfare reform minister, Lord Freud, famously claimed at a fringe meeting of the Conservative Party annual conference that some disabled people were 'not worth' paying the minimum wage. He also claimed that people with mental disabilities could be paid as little as £2 an hour. Marxists

KEY SOCIOLOGISTS
Helen Barnard (2013) argues that one of the key factors impacting women is the quality of part-time jobs. Many women, she argues, end up working below their skill level in order to get a job that will fit around children. This then impacts on lower-skilled women who are consequently pushed further down the jobs ladder, or out of work altogether.

CONTEMPORARY APPLICATION
Changes, such as the decline of Labour's flagship Sure Start programme and changes to the early years' education curriculum, tend to hit those ethnic groups that are most concentrated in the lower working class. It will take many years for the full effect to impact and be measured in different groups.

STUDY TIP
Make sure you fully understand how and why each of the groups discussed experience poverty. Remember that people in each group are not homogeneous but are differentiated by other social factors, especially social class.

would argue that this reflects how capitalism reduces workers to commodified hands and brains. Workers who do not fit the criterion of profitability are marginalised and seen as disposable.

Questions

1. How many people are living in 'deep poverty'?
2. What factors have led to an increase in poverty?
3. Evaluate the reasons why a rich country like the UK should experience such high levels of poverty.

> **IN THE NEWS**
>
> ### Red Cross to distribute food to Britain's poor and hungry
>
> Families could be forced to turn to the British Red Cross as thousands deal with crippling cuts to their household budgets through benefit cuts or cuts in wages. Rises in basic food prices and soaring utility bills have contributed to more than 5 million people in the UK living in deep poverty.
>
> Records from the Trussel Trust show that in 2012 nearly 500,000 people needed support from food banks. Juliet Mountford, head of UK service development, said the Red Cross agreed to assist FareShare on the basis of 'strong evidence of an increased need for support on food poverty issues ... For the British Red Cross it's a toe in the water. It's the first step in considering whether we ought to be doing more on today's food poverty challenge.'
>
> Adapted from Press Association (2013) Red Cross to distribute food to Britain's poor and hungry. *Guardian*, 11 October.

2.3 How are wealth and income distributed?

When discussing how wealth and income are distributed it is important to develop an understanding of how and why both of these measurements are not evenly distributed across society.

Distribution of wealth

Ruth Lister (2004) points out that **wealth** is considerably less evenly distributed than **income**. Wealth is closely linked to social class; the upper class, as shown below, has the bulk of wealth in the UK. Wealth is a measure of the value of all of the assets of worth owned by a person. It can take the form of money, property, land, stocks and shares, and financial bonds. Wealth is therefore a source of **unearned income**. However, defining and measuring wealth is not clear-cut. For example, some people question whether houses and pensions should not be included because of their use-value. Sociologists often refer to **marketable wealth** when talking of wealth. These are assets a person could reasonably dispose of without interfering too much with everyday life. Housing and pensions are therefore excluded from marketable wealth.

The Office for National Statistic (ONS) produce a Wealth and Assets Survey (WAS) in order to demonstrate how households manage their wealth in the UK. It divides wealth into four categories:

- property wealth (including second homes, property to rent)
- physical wealth (including household contents, cars, paintings, antiques)
- financial wealth (including savings accounts, ISAs, shares)
- private pensions (the accrued value of private and company pensions).

As seen in Figure 7.8, **personal wealth** is very unequally distributed in the UK. For example, the richest family (Gerald Cavendish Grosvenor and family) owns more wealth than the poorest 10 per cent of the population (6.3 million people). According to Oxfam (2014a) the five richest families in the UK are now wealthier than the bottom 20 per cent of the entire population. That means that just five households have more money than 12.6 million people put together – almost the same as the number of people living below the poverty line. It is worth remembering that many people within the working and middle classes can have negative wealth. This stems from the common occurrence of large debts associated with loan arrears, outstanding balances on credit cards or student loan debts.

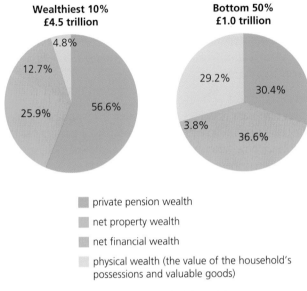

private pension wealth

net property wealth

net financial wealth

physical wealth (the value of the household's possessions and valuable goods)

Figure 7.8 Distribution of household wealth

ONS, 2013

The super-rich in Britain are currently enjoying record amounts of wealth. This highlights the extent of the gulf between the super-rich and the rest of society. To get into the Sunday Times Rich List (2015) of the wealthiest 1000, individuals needed at least £100 million. The combined wealth of the country's top 1000 amounts to £547 billion. In 2015 there were a record number of 117 billionaires (in 2005 there were just 60). Many included in the Rich List have come to live in Britain from overseas, often to avoid paying tax by claiming **non-domicile** ('non-dom') status.

Global wealth inequality

Britain's growth in multimillionaires reflects a wealth explosion occurring globally. Oxfam (2015) reported that, in 2014, the richest 1 per cent of people in the world owned 48 per cent of global wealth, leaving just 52 per cent to be shared between the other 99 per cent of adults on the planet.

Oxfam argues that if the trend of wealth accumulation in the rich continues then the top 1 per cent will have more wealth than the remaining 99 per cent of people by 2016. The collective wealth of this richest one percent is $110 trillion, 65 times the total wealth of the poorest half of the world's population.

Distribution of income

Whereas wealth is an asset, income is a flow concept and refers to the incoming flow of resources over time. It is comprised of four constituent parts:

● earned income from employment (including self-employment)
● income from state support (including benefits, tax credits and state pensions)

- income from private pensions (including occupational and personal pensions)
- other income, such as interest from savings or rent from property.

The distribution of income in the UK is drastically unequal. Oxfam (2014a) describes income inequality as a serious problem facing the UK.

Oxfam points out that between 1993 and 2011 the incomes of the top 0.1 per cent grew by 101 per cent, almost four times faster than the incomes of the bottom 90 per cent of the population, which grew by 27 per cent. What this means in real terms is that the richest 0.1 per cent saw their income grow by more than £461 a week, the equivalent of over £24,000 a year (enough to buy a small yacht or a sports car).

By contrast, the bottom 90 per cent experienced a real terms increase of only £147 a year (insufficient to insure a family car and equating to just to £2.82 a week: as Oxfam puts it, the price of a large cappuccino).

When factors like inflation and the cost of living are taken into account, the income inequality of the past ten years becomes even starker. For example, since 2003 the majority of the British public (99 per cent) have seen a 12 per cent real terms drop in their disposable income (after housing costs), while the richest 5 per cent of the population have seen their disposable income increase.

Income may be supplemented by what is known as the social wage; that is, income in-kind provided in the form of benefits that supplement family income, such as housing benefit, free prescriptions and free school meals. Flaherty *et al* (2004) for instance note that: 'Although the risk of stigma is apparent, many children and parents view free school meal provision as a valuable resource. It enables children to have an adequate main meal when there may be cutbacks at home.'

A call for a 'living wage'

In an attempt to reduce in-work poverty, the national minimum wage (NMW) was introduced in April 1999. In October 2014 it was £6.50 per hour. However, the Living Wage Foundation argues that this is insufficient to live on. This view is supported by poverty pressure groups, who point out that there are currently more working households living in poverty in the UK than non-working ones. The UK living wage for outside of London is currently £7.65 per hour (£8.80 in London). The UK living wage rate is set annually by the Living Wage Foundation and calculated by the Centre for Research in Social Policy at Loughborough University.

Global income inequality

Economic inequality is far from being a UK-only problem – a similar picture of a rapidly increasing gap between the rich and poor can be seen in most countries across the globe. For example, seven out of ten people in the world live in countries where economic inequality has increased in the last 30 years. Oxfam (2014a) points out that one effect of this increasing inequality is that the wealthy are enabled to capture government policymaking through measures such as donating to political parties and funding lobbyists. This means the rules are constantly rewritten in favour of the rich, for example through policies allowing lower taxes for high earners.

KEY SOCIOLOGISTS

Ruth Lister (2004) argues that poverty remains one of the most urgent issues of our time and highlights how it derives from the unequal distribution of both wealth and income. Besides being a class issue, she highlights the plight of other groups such as women and black and minority ethnic groups, who can be prone to poverty as well.

CONTEMPORARY APPLICATION

Oxfam points out that Britain in the twenty-first century is a deeply divided nation. Their research indicates that while the super-rich have never had it so good, millions of families are struggling to make ends meet. Growing numbers of people are turning to charity-run food banks, yet at the same time the highest earners in the UK have had the biggest tax cuts of any country in the world. And while low-paid workers are seeing their wages stagnate, the super-rich are seeing their pay and bonuses spiral up.

STUDY TIP

While it is difficult to remember a lot of statistics, try to become familiar with the key statistics relating to the unequal distribution of poverty, wealth and income in contemporary society.

IN THE NEWS

The American banker JP Morgan believed that the head of a company should not earn more than 20 times those at the bottom. In 1998, chief executives in Britain earned 47 times the average pay in the companies they ran. However, today their earnings rises have accelerated hugely: in 2013 the average pay of a chief executive of a company on the Financial Times Stock Exchange (FTSE) was 143 times the average wage in the company.

In the middle of the twentieth century, when the socialist principles of equality were still taken seriously, the differentials gradually reduced for several decades. But since 1980 that trend has reversed and today seems to be out of control.

Many people understand how serious the problem is, but it seems that no one quite knows how to tackle it. Moves by shareholders to reduce the gap have failed. The government has not intervened. Even the crash of 2008 failed to affect the trend, confirming JK Galbraith's view, still relevant today, that: 'The salary of the chief executive of the large company is not a market reward for achievement. It is frequently in the nature of a warm personal gesture by the individual to himself.'

For many people, especially the young, the outcome is growing feelings of frustration and alienation. As long ago as the 1930s, JM Keynes called income inequality one of 'the outstanding faults of the society in which we live'. That is truer than ever today. Finding an effective way to reduce it is one of the greatest challenges of the age.

Adapted from Editorial (2014) Money madness: Income inequality has reached outrageous levels. *Independent on Sunday*, 17 August.

Questions

1. What was the ratio of earnings JP Morgan regarded as acceptable?
2. What had this ratio risen to in 2013?
3. Why did the ratios become more equal in middle part of the twentieth century?
4. According to the economist JK Galbraith how do chief executives get so rewarded?
5. Do you agree with the editorial's predicted results of this income disparity on young people?

Check your understanding

1. Which group of people represents almost a quarter of people living in poverty?
2. What is meant by the term 'grey panther'?
3. What is the cost of raising a child from birth to the age of 18?
4. Why does the number of people experiencing in-work poverty pose a particular problem for government policy and spin?
5. Why has the gender gap in poverty more than halved recently?
6. Outline the four types of wealth according to the Office for National Statistics.
7. According to Oxfam, the five richest families in the UK are now wealthier than what proportion of UK society?
8. What is the implication of so many rich people in the UK having non-domicile status?
9. How is income different to wealth?
10. What are the criticisms associated with the minimum wage?

Practice questions

1. Define the term 'physical efficiency'. [2 marks]
2. Using **one** example, briefly explain the term 'social wage'. [2 marks]
3. Suggest **three** reasons why those in employment could still be deemed to be living in poverty. [6 marks]
4. Identify two groups in society who are more likely to be living in poverty than others and outline the reasons why this might be. [10 marks]

▶

Read Item A below and answer the question that follows.

Item A

Debates about the distribution of income at some point return to ideas of fairness and opportunity. The idea that society is a meritocracy is used to defend income inequalities, since those who earn the most have earned their rewards through hard work and talent.

Applying material from Item A and your knowledge, evaluate the view that the distribution of wealth and income in society is a fair one.

[20 marks]

Section 3: Responses and solutions to poverty

This section will explore the following debates:

- Can dependency-based explanations help us to understand poverty?
- Different sociological views on the effectiveness of state, private, voluntary and informal providers.
- Can exclusion-based explanations solve the problem of poverty?

GETTING YOU STARTED

The biggest drop in living standards since the war

Figure 7.9 Lines outside job centre

A report by the Institute for Fiscal Studies confirmed that the young have been hurt the most by the era of austerity since the financial crisis of 2007–08.

The employment rate of those in their 20s has fallen, while that of people over 30 has remained fairly stable. As a result, young adults' real incomes have fallen much more than any other age group.

The unemployment rate of 18 per cent of those aged 16–24 contrasted with that of 5 per cent for those aged 25–49, and 4 per cent for those aged 50 and over. Median household income (with housing costs included) for 22–30 year olds in 2013 was 20 per cent less than in 2008. This compares with a fall of 11 per cent for those aged 31 to 59. The fall in income for young adults since 2008 is entirely accounted for by lower employment, as well as sharp falls in real pay for those who are in employment.

The study found that the earnings falls among young workers are partly due to lower hours of work, including more part-time work, as indicators of 'under-employment' have risen. Older workers tend to want fewer hours, while young people want more.

The hourly wages of young workers have fallen particularly sharply. Median hourly wages fell by 11 per cent in real terms for employees aged 22–30 between 2008 and 2013, and by just 3 per cent for those aged 31–59.

Just over a quarter of people aged 22–30 live with their parents. High rents have meant fewer young people can afford to leave home than in the past, while house price increases make buying a first home impossible for many, especially in the South-east and London.

Adapted from David Blanchflower (2014) You won't hear the Chancellor boasting about the biggest drop in living standards since the war. *Independent on Sunday*, 20 July.

3.1 Can dependency help us understand poverty?

When studying dependency-based explanations of poverty it is important to develop knowledge and understanding of the key sociological ideas, such as the stigmatisation of the poor, the culture of poverty, the underclass, administrative costs and the targeting of the poor through means-testing as the key solution to poverty.

Dependency-based explanations

Dependency-based explanations have already been discussed at some length above under the functionalist and New Right perspectives (pages 294–5).

The **culture of poverty** is a concept that is important to this debate. Originating with the work of Oscar Lewis, who studied shanty towns in the developing world in the 1950s and 1960s, it forms the basis of Charles Murray's (1989) work on the underclass. Lewis talked of a culture of poverty whereby individuals felt strong feelings of marginality, helplessness, dependency, present-time orientation, resignation and fatalism.

Lewis argued that the poor themselves prevented any escape from poverty by developing a set of values that stopped them breaking out. Murray's view of **underclass** subculture is very similar. Here was a group of people who possessed deviant 'traits': being welfare dependent, work-shy, promiscuous and criminally violent. The children of the underclass, Murray argued, grow up ill-schooled and ill-behaved, socialised into the 'feckless' attitudes of their parents. Murray therefore talks of the cyclical nature of poverty and particularly associated this with female-headed, lone-parent families. Besides perpetuating a cycle of deprivation, for Murray such families symbolised the fecklessness associated with the absent father-figure, which he saw as particularly damaging for boys.

Questions

1. How does the unemployment rate of those under 25 compare with those over 25?
2. What is the fall in real incomes of those below 30 compared with those over 30?
3. What reasons are given for this disparity in real income?
4. What percentage of young people under the age of 30 still live with their parents?
5. What solutions to poverty would benefit the position of the under 30s?

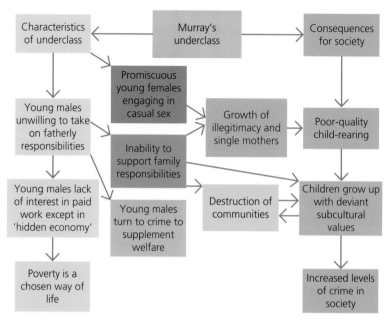

Figure 7.10 Murray's underclass (1989)

New Right solutions to poverty

The New Right favour the use of means-tested welfare benefits to eradicate poverty. This is a welfare approach that targets welfare on the poor. While ideologically opposed to welfare provision, the New Right accept that those most in need of welfare support should be protected by a safety net in order to keep them from absolute poverty.

A means-tested approach is in direct contrast to the principal of universal benefits. A universal benefits approach says that everyone is entitled to receive benefits, regardless of whether they are poor or not. Examples of universal benefits include the state pension and, until 2013, Child Benefit. The New Right believe that universal benefits, because they go to people who do not need them, are not a good use of the state's resources and should be withdrawn. If people who could afford to do so, paid for their own private welfare needs (for example, private pensions, unemployment insurance, private health and private education) it would reduce the tax burden to everyone.

The New Right believes taxation in itself is a bad thing as it acts as a disincentive to work by reducing the rewards. The lower the rate of taxation, they argue, the more incentive people have to work harder and longer, thus creating entrepreneurship, wealth and economic growth. Their argument is that lowering taxation and creating more private wealth ultimately makes everyone better off. This is disputed by social democrats and Marxists.

New Right theorists like David Marsland (2003), Charles Murray (1989) and James Bartholomew (2006) separately argue that one of the dangers of a welfare state, and in particular universal benefits, is that it leads to a dependency culture: the more generous the hand outs, the less incentive people have for taking personal responsibility to support themselves through paid employment. Figure 7.11 above illustrates Murray's argument that this dependency culture leads to crime, female-headed lone parents and participation in the **hidden economy**, rather than the formal economy. The New Right argue that targeting benefits through means-testing is a cheaper, more cost-effective system. However, the exclusion-based explanation of poverty advocates universal benefits because these apply to everyone and promote the concept of citizenship rights and a sense of social solidarity. This argument is outlined below.

Critique of dependency-based explanations

- Victim-blaming explanations for poverty are both simplistic and heartless.
- Holding the poor responsible for their poverty ignores obvious structural factors.
- There is no evidence of the poor having cultural values that are different to the rest of society.
- Means-tested benefits actually leads to more dependency since it creates a 'poverty-trap' whereby people can become worse off in employment.
- A New Right approach results in a residual welfare state with ordinary people having to endure second-class welfare services compared to the rich who can purchase first-class private welfare.

While some people can claim anecdotal knowledge of feckless families, most commentators argue that Murray is wrong and that his analysis is grossly exaggerated. For example, Ken Roberts (2001) does not recognise the homogeneous culture of values that stress dependency, criminality and immorality that underpins Murray's description of an underclass.

Alan and Carol Walker (1987) also reject any clear-cut evidence for the existence of a group of people who form an underclass, and accuse Murray of simply relying on 'innuendos, assertions and anecdotes'.

Steve Craine (1997) makes a useful contribution to the debate through his concept of the **black magic roundabout**. He rejects the idea of an underclass as a group, but agrees that the poor can engage in 'underclass behaviour'. He identifies this as a consequence of their situation of being on a permanent 'carousel' of unemployment, training schemes and low-paid work.

Feminists point out that most single mothers are very successful at child-rearing and the source of their problems is invariably structural, associated with poverty rather than fecklessness.

KEY SOCIOLOGISTS

Shane Blackman (1997) argues the term 'underclass' has been used to heighten fears through the promotion of an idea of an 'other'. Researching the homeless, he found they shared similar aspirations to the rest of society. He found they engaged in 'underclass behaviour', but as a coping mechanism for their situation. While looking 'dangerous, drunken and lazy' and making little effort to improve themselves, this behaviour was a reaction to their situation rather than a way of life.

CONTEMPORARY APPLICATION

As neo-liberal/New Right ideology seems to increasingly influence government policy, there is an increasing demand to remove universal benefits and encourage means-testing. While this appears generally popular with the public, it receives more opposition when applied to making the elderly pay for their care. The issue of the elderly having to sell their home to pay for care or nursing home fees generates criticism and is a problem that governments have struggled to address.

STUDY TIP

When discussing the solution to poverty it is important to unpack theoretical and ideological debates. An awareness of recent social policy is also helpful.

3.2 What are the different sociological views?

If you are discussing the effectiveness of state, private, voluntary or informal providers and their ability to solve the problem of poverty, then you could demonstrate how the latter three have become a major plank of social policy, increasingly supporting state provision.

When Prime Minister Tony Blair famously promised in 1999 to halve childhood poverty by 2010, his strategy to achieve this was through what he termed the **Third Way** – a mixture of both state and private providers to distribute resources. Subsequent governments have followed suit, taking a particular interest in welfare funded privately through charities, voluntary organisations and informal care from family and friends to help address and solve issues associated with poverty.

The reasons for this are partly ideological (the Conservatives, for instance, have never liked the state provision of services) and partly pragmatic (in an era of austerity the government has limited public money at its disposal). David Cameron's idea of the **Big Society** is that the voluntary sector and informal welfare providers should take on welfare responsibilities rather than the state. Therefore his Coalition government (2010–2015) shared the New Right's view that individuals and communities should do more for themselves. This position favours tax cuts and encourages enterprise and entrepreneurship.

The government claims that private, voluntary organisations and informal providers offer more efficient solutions than the state could if it was to intervene directly. In other words, even with grants and subsidies from the government, the private and voluntary sectors and informal providers can achieve the same social and economic outcomes with lower public expenditure.

Criticisms of this neo-liberal approach are that the commitment and funding are insufficient to address the real issues and realities of poverty that people are actually experiencing. In addition, the underfunded informal care that occurs within households is often unpaid and taken for granted. For example, Conor D'Arcy (2013) for the Joseph Rowntree Foundation notes that working-age poverty has risen by 2 per cent, meaning 6.1 million people find themselves in absolute poverty. In addition, the poverty of low-paid workers remains an issue, despite the fact that 'welfare to work' is the government's key solution to poverty. Some sub-groups, such as couples with only one full-time worker, are increasingly likely to be in poverty. At the same time, those in receipt of long-term benefits, such as people with disabilities, are faced with cuts to welfare, deepening their experience of poverty further.

Informal welfare provision is considered by some to be the most important (and underfunded) aspect of care delivery in the UK. It refers to the considerable amount of informal care provision by family and friends to the sick, disabled and, increasingly, the elderly in England and Wales. The Office for National Statistics (2014) estimates that the number of unpaid carers has grown by 600,000 since 2001 to reach approximately 5.8 million. The charity Carers UK estimates the value to the nation of those who look after relatives or friends at around £119 billion a year – almost as much as the entire cost of the NHS.

Informal welfare provision is an important social policy issue because, in addition to providing an important contribution to the supply of care, it also impacts on the employment and leisure opportunities of those providing it. Many informal carers themselves are consequently struggling with little or no help, or are facing cuts in the services and benefits they rely on. Without support, those engaged in the delivery of informal welfare provision may themselves be forced out of work and into poverty, ill health and isolation.

KEY SOCIOLOGIST

Peter Saunders is an Australian-British sociologist who shares many ideas with Charles Murray. He argues that defining poverty at below 60 per cent of the median income confuses inequality (income distribution) with poverty (income adequacy), producing inflated estimates of poverty. This leads to counter-productive policies aimed at income redistribution rather than tackling the deeper causes of the problem. Like Murray he feels an over-generous welfare system simply leads to welfare-dependency.

CONTEMPORARY APPLICATION

The Conservative-led Coalition government (2010–2015) fundamentally supports dependency-based ideas associated with the targeting of welfare. It also favours means-tested rather than universal benefits, as shown by the restriction of child benefit in 2013 to those earning under £50,000. Ideas of the Big Society imply that the voluntary sector rather than the state should take on welfare responsibilities.

Christopher Pierson (2004) suggests that, with the impact of globalisation, the established welfare states of many developed countries, like the UK, will inevitably become smaller and less redistributive. High amounts of state spending on welfare provision will simply become unsustainable. Pierson notes that the most significant change is the growing role for non-state provision, both domestically and internationally.

Faced with increasing international competition for markets and trade deficits, countries like the UK simply cannot afford the kind of state welfare envisaged by Beveridge in the 1940s. Furthermore, there is a growing New Right ideological backlash against such high state welfare as governments distance themselves from the social democratic model. Even the Scandinavian countries have cut back their famously generous welfare states in the twenty-first century.

Opponents to the welfare state, like the New Right Australian James Bartholomew (2006), criticise it on several grounds. Their argument is that any state programme is less efficient than private and voluntary sector provision. Sharing the views of David Marsland in the UK and Charles Murray in the USA, he argues that not only have state welfare programmes performed poorly, but they simply encourage benefit fraud, fecklessness and idleness. Consequently, poverty has not been eliminated or even significantly reduced. However, Baumberg *et al* (2014) debunk the assumption of widespread benefit fraud. They quote the government's own Department for Work and Pensions Report (2013) that estimates that the percentage of claims that are overpaid due to fraud ranges from 2.3 per cent (working-age housing benefit) to 4.2 per cent (lone parents on income support). For all income support and Jobseeker's Allowance claims taken together, the estimate is 3.4 per cent. The public, in contrast, grossly exaggerate the amount of benefit fraud at 25 per cent (British Social Attitudes Survey, 2012). Such ignorance seems inevitable when 30 per cent of all newspaper reporting of social security between 1995 and 2011 made reference to benefit fraud (Baumberg *et al*, 2012).

STUDY TIP

Make sure you can bring current policies and examples into your writing, rather than just a general discussion of the two perspectives of dependency-based versus exclusion-based approaches to poverty.

Questions

1. What is the so-called 'bedroom tax'?
2. How have households been affected by the removal of the 'spare room subsidy' or bedroom tax?
3. What was the intended purpose of removing the spare room subsidy?
4. What have been the consequences of removing the spare room subsidy?

IN THE NEWS

'Bedroom tax' bites as low-income tenants choose between 'heat or eat'

As part of an array of benefit changes introduced on 1 April 2013 under the Welfare Reform Act 2012, the Coalition government added new rules on what it called the 'spare room subsidy'. Under the changes, tenants in social housing have their benefit reduced by 14 per cent if they have a spare bedroom or by 25 per cent if they have two or more. Two children under 16 of same gender are expected to share a bedroom, as are two children under 10 regardless of gender. Tenants affected by the bedroom tax are losing between £14 and £25 a week.

The government said the move was intended to reduce the £23 billion cost of housing benefit and free up housing to help the 300,000 people living in overcrowded conditions. The Department for Work and Pensions (DWP) set a target of 30 per cent of social housing tenants affected by the changes to move home by 2017. Labour said the rule would hit some of the most vulnerable people in society and refer to the rule as the 'bedroom tax'. Disabled people and foster carers are among those worst affected.

In September 2013, the UN special investigator on housing told the government it should scrap the bedroom tax after hearing 'shocking' accounts of how the policy was affecting vulnerable citizens during a visit to the UK.

A study published by the DWP in July 2014 found that 60 per cent of the 523,000 tenants affected were unable to meet the shortfalls in income and claimed that tens of thousands of low-income tenants have been plunged into 'heat or eat' hardship as a result of the bedroom tax. Another survey for the National Housing Federation found that 66 per cent of housing association residents affected by the bedroom tax were in arrears, and more than 15 per cent had received a letter warning them they were at risk of eviction.

Adapted from Haroon Siddique (2014) Bedroom tax: The housing benefit reform explained. *Guardian*, 17 July.

3.3 Can exclusion-based explanations solve poverty?

When studying exclusion-based explanations of poverty it is important to develop knowledge and understanding of how a comprehensive welfare state through universal benefits is viewed as the key solution to poverty.

Exclusion-based (structural) theories of poverty

An alternative to dependency-based explanations of poverty are exclusion-based explanations – that is, an explanation for poverty rooted in structural factors. For example, the 'situational constraints' theory finds the root cause of poverty in the failings of government social policies to successfully allocate resources to ensure everyone's needs can be met. The Marxist view is also structural but sees poverty as an inevitable feature of the capitalist system and contends that, until capitalism is overthrown, poverty will continue to exist.

Unlike dependency-based explanations, exclusion-based explanations see the poor as essentially blameless for their poverty. Instead they focus on the power relations associated with structural factors to explain the causes of poverty. Included in this approach are the reformist ideas of situational constraints along with the more radical ideas of the Marxist perspective.

Situational constraints and exclusion

According to this approach, poverty is caused by structural factors beyond the control of the individual. Key factors include sickness, disability and, especially, not working. When people are unable to access the labour market, either through unemployment, retirement, lone-parenthood or long-term sickness or disability, poverty is often the result. The solution is therefore to compensate those who cannot work and to provide a gateway back into employment for those who can. The favoured ideology here is through **social democratic** ideas of state intervention to eradicate poverty. Any persistence in poverty can be blamed not so much on the individual but on a failure of the state's policies to address the problem. Indeed, individuals are seen as largely powerless and so reliant on the state to provide a solution to their predicament. This typically involves more state spending (either on welfare or to stimulate the economy and hence provide more jobs), the legal setting of a minimum wage at a significantly high level, and a welfare system that ensures that people are not worse off in employment than when in receipt of welfare benefits.

Social democratic solutions to poverty

Social democratic ideology had its golden age in the decades that followed the Second World War (late 1940s to 1970s). It favours an extensive welfare state as envisaged by William Beveridge in which the state should look after everyone from the cradle to the grave. Social democrats favour the use of universal benefits (paid as a right to everyone entitled) as the best solution to poverty, creating a comprehensive welfare state that embraces everyone. They argue that the two-tier approach of means-tested benefits, favoured by the New Right, serves to create a 'residual' welfare state. This means that those who can afford to pay for private welfare (pensions, health care and education) get high-quality services whereas the rest of society get poorer quality services provided by the welfare state.

Universalism is portrayed as the best way of eradicating poverty since benefits are provided for everyone regardless of income. Social democrats see welfare provision as not only helping those in need, but helping to cement society together through reinforcing social solidarity and promoting citizenship rights. The New Right argues that such an approach is wasteful. In addition, they argue that more private welfare (rather than universal benefits) results in lower taxes, which encourages more **entrepreneurial** initiatives and, ultimately, greater wealth and economic growth.

Tony Blair's New Labour introduced a Third Way: it supported the dependency-based idea that people had a personal responsibility to get themselves out of poverty, but would also help them do this through exclusion-based ideas of state support. Underpinning the Third Way was the driving ideology of 'welfare to work'. Getting people into employment not only saves the government (and hence taxpayers) money but equally restores personal dignity and self-respect. Specific policies to help eradicate poverty included:

- making the unemployed proactive in seeking employment by monitoring their activities and providing help with CVs, letters of application, etc.
- the minimum wage to eradicate in-work poverty
- Working Families' Tax Credit, which supplemented low wages with welfare payments to parents with dependent children.

The minimum wage and the Working Families' Tax Credit policies were designed to offset the problem of the 'poverty trap' where people may be materially worse off in employment even if wages are higher than Jobseeker's Allowance or income support payments (due to things like housing benefit and free school meals).

The Third Way was keen to challenge the ideas of social democratic universalism, that the problem of poverty could be solved solely by the state providing universal benefits. It therefore shared some of the ideas of the New Right, with an emphasis on targeting benefits through means-testing and empowering individuals with the personal responsibility to want to get out of poverty.

Marxist explanations of poverty

Marxists are sceptical of social democratic attempts to eradicate poverty. This is because it misses the obvious point that poverty is fundamentally caused by the capitalist system, and capitalism is incapable of producing social justice. Capitalism is based on the free-market system which always puts the interest of capital and profit before people. It is a system that strives to minimise costs, especially wages, and will heartlessly make workers redundant and unemployed whenever demand falls. In a globalised world, workers, are increasingly competing with not only migrant workers, who may undercut their wages at home, but workers across the globe. **Transnational corporations** will often use workers in the developing world to undercut the wages of workers in the developed world. The rise of a transnational labour force means that the nature of work in many places is changing: the UK is now described as a post-industrial society as it manufactures very little now, with most workers employed in the service sector. Jobs that would previously been done in the UK are now being done elsewhere, for example, call centres in India, British Airways ticket offices in India, or the NHS sending patient notes to South Africa to be digitised. Marxists point out that in this cut-throat world, poverty will never be abolished as the capitalist class will always look to produce goods and services in the cheapest way. They would also point to the conditions endured by the workers offshore, which would be unacceptable under UK labour laws. Despite the rights that the UK labour force has won over time, workers can be shed ruthlessly and their jobs replaced either by technology (as in postal sorting offices) or workers abroad.

Figure 7.11 Workers in developing countries can undercut wages in the developed world

This competition between workers and its resulting poverty is actually functional to the capitalist class. The rich have a vested interest in maintaining poverty for the following reasons outlined by Herbert J. Gans (1971):

- Without poverty no one would be prepared to do the dead-end, dirty, dangerous and menial jobs. Such jobs are done by a low-waged pool of workers pressurised into performing these roles that no one else wants to do.
- Secondly, monitoring and supporting the poor creates a number of jobs including workers administering social security systems, social workers, probation officers and the police.
- Thirdly, the poor offer a psychological boost to the rest of society: feeling there is always someone worse off than yourself is something of a consolation and reassurance as people struggle against the forces of capitalism. Poverty thus promotes false consciousness by reassuring the non-poor of their worth.

Marxists argue that there is no incentive for capitalism to eradicate poverty: the only way to eradicate poverty is to get rid of capitalism.

Critique of exclusion-based solutions to poverty

- An extensive welfare state imposes huge administrative costs on society.
- Universal benefits are wasteful and costly, imposing a huge tax burden on society.
- Means-testing ensures welfare is targeted where it is needed most: on the poorest.
- An extensive welfare state encourages a dependency culture.
- There is little appetite among the people for eradicating capitalism soon.

IN THE NEWS

Why can't America be Sweden?

The US does not have a welfare state of the kind that many European countries, including Denmark, Finland, Norway and Sweden, have developed, and despite recent health care reforms many Americans do not have access to the same kind of high-quality health care that their counterparts in these other countries enjoy. They also have much shorter holidays and maternity leave, and do not have access to a variety of other public services more broadly provided in many European countries.

Poverty and inequality in the US have been increasing over the last three decades, and are now higher than in many European countries, In contrast, they have remained broadly the same in Denmark, Finland, Norway and Sweden.

In the US, the richest 1 per cent earn almost 25 per cent of total national income, whereas in Finland and Sweden the top 25 per cent is spread across the richest 5 per cent.

Adapted from Thomas B. Edsall (2013) Why can't America be Sweden? *New York Times*, 29 May.

Questions

1. What are some of the welfare benefits enjoyed by Swedes that Americans lack?
2. What else are much higher and increasing in the US?
3. How does inequality at the top compare between the US and Finland and Sweden?
4. Outline and justify which country has the best system in your opinion.

KEY SOCIOLOGISTS

Steve Craine (1997) developed the 'black magic roundabout' concept. It describes how many young people become trapped in a cycle of unemployment, government schemes and low-paid work in the informal economy. He argues that poverty stemmed from the decline of local manufacturing and neglected local authority housing. Poverty, he argues, is not the result of a pathology of the poor but of exclusion from legitimate opportunities.

CONTEMPORARY APPLICATION

Social democratic ideas are less than fashionable in contemporary society, as neo-liberal, New Right ideas predominate in most government policies. However, the Scandinavian countries have managed to keep extensive welfare states and are perhaps the best contemporary examples of applied social democratic practices.

STUDY TIP

The best applied examples of the exclusion-based approach to the eradication of poverty would be the Scandinavian model of extensive and generous welfare states. However, knowledge of New Right criticisms and how and why their alternative neo-liberal ideology became popular from the 1980s offers an alternative theory to contrast exclusion-based approaches with.

Check your understanding

1. Why are dependency-based explanations of poverty called 'victim-blaming'?
2. Which Victorian sociologist argued that poverty for the weak, incompetent and lazy was 'no more than they deserved'?
3. What does the New Right mean by a 'dependency culture'?
4. Who associated the underclass as having deviant subcultural values?
5. What type of family is viewed as being particularly prone to the reproduction of poverty?
6. What two political ideologies are associated with exclusion-based explanations of poverty?
7. What was meant by New Labour's 'Third Way'?
8. What is the fundamental cause of poverty according to Marxists?
9. In what ways can poverty be viewed as functional?
10. What organisations were relied on by the Coalition government to address poverty?

Practice questions

1. Define the term 'situational constraints'. [2 marks]
2. Using **one** example, briefly explain the term 'informal provision of care'. [2 marks]
3. Suggest **three** forms of behaviour associated with the underclass which Murray argues results in the perpetuation of poverty. [6 marks]
4. Outline and explain **two** ways in which social democratic ideology would address the problem of poverty. [10 marks]

Read Item A below and answer the question that follows.

Item A

Marxists see poverty as an inevitable outcome of the capitalist system and its class structure. The interests of capital will always take preference over those of labour. When workers are no longer needed or their wages are undercut, the necessary outcome is always poverty.

Applying material from Item A and your knowledge, evaluate the Marxist view that poverty is the product of the capitalist system. [20 marks]

Section 4: How is labour organised and controlled?

This section will explore the following debates:

- How is work organised in terms of a division of labour?
- To what extent is the UK a meritocracy?
- To what extent is upskilling occurring in the workplace?
- The significance of technology and the deskilling debate.

GETTING YOU STARTED

Britain: A deeply divided elitist society

The Social Mobility and Child Poverty Commission reported in 2014 that the UK was deeply elitist, with top positions dominated by those born into privileged backgrounds. Its findings were based on a study of over 4000 people in top jobs in business, politics, media and the public sector.

For example, despite the fact that only 7 per cent of the population attends private schools, they account for 71 per cent of senior judges, 62 per cent of senior officers in the armed forces, 55 per cent of senior civil servants and 53 per cent of senior diplomats. Half of the House of Lords was privately educated. Often the top jobs in the UK are dominated not only by private schools, but one school in particular: Eton. For example, the Prime Minister, David Cameron, came in for criticism over the number of his inner cabinet being old Etonians.

Figures for top people who went to Oxford and Cambridge paint a similar picture. Despite the fact that less than 1 per cent of the whole population are Oxbridge graduates, 75 per cent of senior judges, 59 per cent of the cabinet, 57 per cent of senior civil servants, 50 per cent of diplomats, 47 per cent of newspaper columnists and 38 per cent of the House of Lords went to either Oxford or Cambridge University.

According to the former Secretary of State for Education, Michael Gove, in 2010 out of an entry of 4000 only 45 boys and girls eligible for free school meals got into Oxbridge. Because private schools and **Oxbridge** are predominantly filled by people from privileged backgrounds, the report describes these figures as 'elitism so stark that it could be called social engineering'.

Critics of our elitist system argue that talent from poor and even many middle-class homes is simply being locked out. A spokesperson for Oxford University said it was committed to widening its access but added that social mobility is an issue stretching back to birth and that early inequality of attainment is one of the major barriers to progression.

Adapted from Judith Burns (2014) Deeply elitist UK locks out diversity at top. BBC News, 28 August (www.bbc.co.uk/news/education-28953881).

4.1 How is work organised?

When discussing the division of labour you will develop an understanding of the nature of work, and how it is patterned and distributed across society. The growing influence of globalisation is illustrated through the new international division of labour. You could also include how globalisation affects labour markets in your discussion.

What is work?

The term **division of labour** applies to how the variety and range of work tasks within a society are allocated. Conventionally it is most applicable to the workplace, where each person has a specialised role. The meaning of work might seem obvious but a little thought shows that it is rather a complex concept. For example, to most people looking after their own children or elderly or disabled relatives would not be seen as work. However, if you employ a child minder or carer to look after them then it becomes paid employment and this is considered to be taxable work.

Questions

1. What advantages does a private education seem to offer according to the article?
2. Which school in particular seems to offer its ex-pupils the greatest opportunities?
3. Is it fair to describe the private school system and Oxbridge as contributing towards 'social engineering'?
4. What factor does the spokesperson from Oxford University blame for poor social mobility?
5. What solutions could help eradicate elitism in the UK?

Feminists have devoted the past 50 years to trying to raise consciousness about the unfair division of labour in the home with regard to women. The imbalance of this division of labour is probably best summed up by David Morley (1986), who described the home as a place of leisure for men but a place of work for women. So the meaning of work is broad and involves paid employment and household work, as well as a lot of voluntary work. Work is therefore not confined to paid employment. In addition, societies are characterised by a lot of casual work undertaken in what is known as the **informal economy**. Somewhere between the formal and the informal economies lies a grey area of transactions that involve cash but are untaxed, often illegal, and certainly outside the laws that regulate formal economic activity. This would include non-taxed household repairs by craftsmen, car boot sales, prostitution and the sale of illegal drugs. With regard to housework, Marxists point out that this unpaid work of women is functional to capitalism through the social reproduction of labour – daily cleansing, feeding and refreshing the proletariat for another days' work. Feminist sociologists have increasingly questioned why, if housework is so significant, it is differentiated from paid employment? Certainly Ann Oakley (1974) found that housewives often experienced the same alienation as assembly-line workers, and adopted similar coping mechanisms.

The concept of division of labour was originally developed in classical political economics by Adam Smith and David Riccardo. Smith famously showed that by dividing out the 18 separate tasks involved in making pins to ten separate workers, production soared from barely one pin a day to 4800 pins a day per worker. Ricardo's idea of the division of labour focused more on the comparative advantage as the source of specialisation and wealth creation from trade. In sociology, division of labour was developed first by Karl Marx in terms of his two-class analysis, in the sense that the proletariat did all of the work. It was subsequently developed, particularly by Émile Durkheim, who saw the division of labour serving to increase both the reproductive capacity and skills of the workforce. However, he also saw it as having a moral character which was more important because it generates feelings of solidarity across society. The division of labour is therefore both:

- a necessary condition for the intellectual and material development of society
- the means by which social life actually takes place, by virtue of causing individuals to feel a connection to each other and a sense of **social solidarity**.

To Durkheim the division of labour went beyond the workplace: it helped contribute towards the social and moral order within a society.

Mechanical and organic solidarity

Durkheim talked of two kinds of social solidarity: **mechanical solidarity** and **organic solidarity**. Mechanical solidarity refers to the characteristics of pre-industrial society whereby the peasants were strongly connected by sharing a similar status, values and beliefs. Durkheim referred to this bond that bound individuals together in society as the **collective conscience**.

Organic solidarity applies to industrial societies where, although individuals have a distinct job or role, they are actually interdependent on each other. Individuality grows as parts of society grow, with solidarity becoming more organic as society develops a complex division of labour. This division of labour reflects the **moral density** of society and can increase in three ways:

- through an increase of the concentration of people spatially
- through the growth of towns
- through an increase in the number and efficacy of the means of communication.

When one or more of these things happen, labour starts to become divided because society has become more complex and individualistic. Figure 7.14 shows the complex nature of the division of labour and how it has evolved over time.

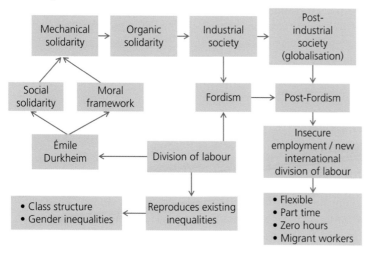

Figure 7.12 Division of labour

KEY SOCIOLOGISTS

Jean Duncombe and Dennis Marsden (1993) undertook an interesting extension of the division of labour concept by claiming that women now perform a 'triple shift' (in comparison to men's one breadwinner shift) since they perform emotional labour as well as employment and domestic chores.

CONTEMPORARY APPLICATION

Women's increased participation in the labour market has not necessarily led to a significant increase in male participation within the home on domestic tasks. Research shows that while there has been a growth in stay-at-home males, in most households domestic work continues to be divided according to gender, with women performing the vast majority of the repetitive indoor housework tasks, while men perform occasional outdoor tasks. Research also shows that women spend more time than men in feeding, supervising and caring for children, although men have increased their time in activities such as physical play. Feminists highlight the huge amount of 'invisible work' women undertake with children, such as remembering when children need to take PE clothes, buying presents and cards for friends' birthdays, providing encouragement, meeting emotional needs and anticipating problems. Finally research shows that if couples share housework before they have children, they often shift to a more conventional gender-based allocation of chores when they become parents.

4.2 To what extent is the UK a meritocracy?

When discussing whether the UK is a meritocratic society, think about unpacking the counter evidence by bringing in examples and sociological theory.

Meritocracy and social mobility

The concept of **social mobility** is important to this debate. It underpins ideas about the fairness of society and the extent to which it is open to movement by individuals up or down the social class structure. If a society is 'closed' to mobility then individuals will occupy the same social position in life as their parents in terms of class, status and occupation. The division of labour in society will therefore be fixed and constant, and the inequalities of society will be reproduced across each generation. As industrial societies developed through the rise of capitalism, so the division of labour became increasingly complex. Within the modern workplace, the division of labour takes on a hierarchal structure with status and material rewards rising through the layers.

The neo-liberal/functionalist justification for this hierarchical division of labour lies with the concept of **meritocracy**. Functionalists and neo-liberals support the idea of a meritocracy as a system that rewards people for talent and effort. Inequality is actually viewed as functional and therefore a positive thing. This is because it acts as a motivator to the poor: if they want to get on then they need to work harder, acquire more qualifications and demonstrate talents previously held hidden.

Marxists and feminists argue that such ideas would be fine if we lived in a truly open society where everyone started from the same position. The reality is, they argue, that the working class and women face oppression and disadvantage from the start. For example, the rich are born into privilege; wealthy backgrounds open all kinds of doors of advantage throughout life.

Postmodernists argue that 'class is dead' and that the distinctions between **blue-collar** and **white-collar** workers has become quite blurred. Many professions, like teaching, have become relatively low paid, with many skilled manual workers, like train drivers, earning at least half as much more than teachers.

KEY SOCIOLOGISTS

Max Weber viewed the skills that individuals brought to the market as the key determinant of the rewards they received for their work. The middle class included professional and managerial workers as well as small businessmen and entrepreneurial self-employed people. Traditionally the working class was made up of manual workers in manufacturing and service industries.

CONTEMPORARY APPLICATION

The social mobility policy entitled: *Opening Doors, Breaking Barriers: A Strategy for Social Mobility* (2011) states that the government's strategy on improving social mobility is based on a life cycle framework. The government's goal is to make life chances more equal at the critical points for social mobility, such as the early years of development, school readiness at age five, GCSE attainment, the choice of options at 16, gaining a place at university or on an apprenticeship and getting into and on in the labour market.

STUDY TIP

An awareness of how private education offers privileges to the upper class and upper middle classes in terms of life chances challenges the meritocratic argument. In addition, it is important to recognise how elements of patriarchy still ensure a **glass ceiling** exists and ethnic minorities are still faced with the 'snowy peaks' of top jobs occupied primarily by white people.

The poor, as discussed earlier, are born with multiple disadvantages such as deprived families, poor housing, poor schooling and a higher risk of poor health. Therefore the reality is that society has a remarkable ability to reproduce its inequalities across the generations. Those born into rich backgrounds grow up to be rich, while those born into poor backgrounds tend to grow up and stay deprived. There are a few 'rags to riches' examples, such as Alan Sugar, David Beckham and Katie Price, but these are very much the exception to the rule. In addition, such people often find that they are not accepted by 'the establishment' and elite because they are 'new money' or the 'vulgar rich'.

A decline of permanent full-time work linked to globalisation?

In the 1980s the concept of a **new international division of labour** was advanced by Frobel *et al* (1981) to reflect a growing trend for global outsourcing and production. Global capitalism encourages the emergence of a world labour market, with transnnational corporations seeking to locate production where labour costs are cheapest. Another response has been from governments, under political pressure from their populations to protect jobs and workers by keeping out migrant workers prepared to undercut prevailing wage rates. Despite these global pressures, employment in 2014 in the UK achieved a new record of 30.6 million people in paid employment. However, a lot of the growth in jobs has been of a temporary and part-time nature, frequently on a **zero-hours contract**. This decline in permanent full-time employment and the growth of part-time, temporary or seasonal employment can be viewed as a feature of falling employment security across Europe and the developed world.

As economies are increasingly subject to world competition, it can be viewed as a feature of globalisation. Global forces have been a factor behind the drive towards **post-Fordist** production techniques, which have resulted in the decline in permanent full-time jobs and the growth of what Michael J. Priore (1995) calls the **secondary labour market**. This is characterised by low wages, low status, low skills and insecure employment relationships with little or no prospect of promotion. Some see this as evidence of Marx's concept of the **reserve army of labour**. The employment figures can disguise the nature and type of work as well as the insecurity and type of contracts people are employed on.

IN THE NEWS

PM warns about immigration while employing a Nepalese nanny

The Prime Minister David Cameron, who talks tough on the number of immigrant workers coming to this country, has defended his decision to employ a nanny of Nepalese origin to look after his children. He recruited the nanny several years ago through a charity that helps immigrants to escape abusive bosses. Despite this he repeatedly makes the point that immigration figures are too high.

His defence of his nanny in 2014 followed the publication of Home Office Minister James Brokenshire's view that immigration and Britain's 'open borders' had benefitted the wealthy most because it allowed them to hire cheap migrant workers as servants.

The coalition government's target was to reduce annual net migration to below 10,000 by 2015. Asked if he would now abandon the target, the Prime Minister stated that immigration has been too high and needed to come down. Since 2010 immigration from outside the EU has fallen by around a third to its lowest level since 1998. The Prime Minister stated we should be training British young people to do more of the jobs that are available. When Ms Lima took a temporary leave of absence in 2012, an Australian nanny filled in to look after the Prime Minister's children.

Adapted from Gander, K. (2014) David Cameron defends hiring Nepalese nanny. *Independent*, 13 March.

Questions

1. Why is it something of an embarrassment for David Cameron to employ a nanny from Nepal?
2. Why does the government want to limit immigration from outside the EU?
3. How does migration to the UK differ between EU and non-EU citizens?
4. Draw up two lists headed 'advantages' and 'disadvantages'. List as many points as you can think of under each heading about the impact of migration both into and out of the UK.

4.3 To what extent is upskilling occurring in the workplace?

When discussing the extent of upskilling, try to understand the term and how it can be applied to contemporary society in a global context.

At the beginning of the 1980s a sociological debate developed over the effects of technology on the demand for skills in the workplace. The debate centred on whether changes in the workplace have led to an expansion (**upskilling**) or decrease (**deskilling**) in skills. The debate has important implications for the workforce. The upskilling supporters believed occupational growth would expand most rapidly in the higher-skilled, technical occupations. In contrast, the deskilling supporters argued that the lowest skilled jobs would vastly outstrip the growth of high technology ones.

The debate also has been applied to the global economy, with the positive upskilling view applied particularly to the developing world. It takes the uneducated and unskilled rural workers in developing countries as its starting point for skill development. It focuses on the growth of literacy and education levels as countries develop and industrialise, so that a growing proportion of the population (including women) become integrated into skilled employment. The more negative deskilling perspective starts with the view that the skilled handicraft work of the early stages of capitalism has been undermined by the growth of technology and global competition. In evaluating the debate, factors such as the growth of the service sector and the impact of women's penetration into the labour force are important.

Upskilling debate

The evidence of the past 30 years has been that high-skilled positions like professional, technical and managerial jobs have expanded while positions like machine operators, labourers and farm labourers have expanded at a considerably lower rate. Even though clerical jobs, which have expanded dramatically, are invariably poorly paid, the upskilling position argues that these are not low-skill jobs. Further evidence of upskilling comes from that fact that skilled workers over the past 30 years have seen their wages rise in real terms over unskilled workers. If demand for more skilled workers increases more rapidly than the supply, the relative wage of skilled workers will rise.

Education is one way of measuring the skills and qualifications in the workforce. Since the 1980s the supply of university graduates has grown substantially. While he was prime minister (1997–2007), Tony Blair set a target of 50 per cent of 18 year olds going into some form of higher education. In 2013 there were 12 million graduates in the UK; such a high number of graduates does imply an upskilled employment market. For example, 30 years ago it was possible to train as a state enrolled nurse (SEN) with three GCSEs; entry to the nursing and midwifery profession is now through university education and graduation. Nurses are increasingly taking on tasks previously restricted to junior doctors, resulting in a blurring of the boundaries between the professions. The advancement in nurses' skills and knowledge means that some of the more fundamental nursing tasks are now delegated to health care assistants.

As manufacturing industries decline and the economy shifts towards an expansion of the tertiary sector, such a post-industrial society needs a workforce with increasing scientific, technological and skilled knowledge. In addition, in an increasingly globalised economy, marketing knowledge becomes increasingly important. In terms of its social policy towards education, the government has put a greater emphasis on teaching and preparing pupils for an increasingly technological workplace that is subject to increasing global competition. From 2014 a new national curriculum was introduced with a greater emphasis on mathematics, science and even simple computer programming for primary schools. Training schemes, like new apprenticeships, have a policy objective of increasing the supply of technically and scientifically trained individuals in employment.

A contemporary example of upskilling is farming, where attendance at agricultural college (now with university status) is considered the norm for anyone expected to be successful in this industry. Farming increasingly relies on skills of soil analysis, crop rotation, the use of very toxic chemicals and financial management. In addition, the technology behind farm machinery, such as combine harvesters, has become increasingly complex, involving new skills to use it effectively.

Countering the upskilling debate is the criticism that expanding the number of individuals graduating from university does not necessarily mean there will be skilled graduate jobs for them to fill. For example, in 2013 the Office for National Statistics (ONS) reported that almost half of 2012 graduates in the UK were in non-graduate jobs. Although the ONS felt the recession since 2007–08 was a contributing factor, the proportion of graduates working in jobs for which a higher educational background is not usually required was 47 per cent. Nonetheless, in 2013 graduates were more likely to be employed than those who left education with qualifications of a lower standard. However, critics argue that the fact that the unemployment rate for recent graduates is much lower than that for non-graduates is due simply to the fact that almost half of those who have recently gained higher education qualifications are entering jobs for which they are overqualified.

The success of women and girls in education over the past decades is well-documented (see Education, page 65). This success in education is not always reflected in the employment market however: a report by the Trades Union Congress (TUC, 2013) blamed this on the collapse of middle-income jobs in manufacturing and administration, referred to below as the 'hollowing out' of the labour market. The report highlights how between 1993 and 2011 the proportion of 16–24 year old females doing low-paid, low-skilled work (such as retailing, waitressing or hotel cleaning) rose from 7 per cent to 21 per cent. In 2011 just one in 100 young women worked in skilled trades compared to one in five young men. In 2011, 14 per cent of young women were economically inactive as a result of looking after family or home compared to just 1 per cent of young men.

Figure 7.15 shows the features and characteristics of the concept of upskilling.

KEY SOCIOLOGISTS

Daniel Bell (1973) is associated with pioneering the upskilling argument. He developed the concept of post-industrial society. He saw the replacement of workers by technology and automation not as a threat but as stimulating a demand for new services and skills. Workers released from manufacturing would be able to take up white-collar jobs in the new service sector. He predicted an upward spiral evolving into what he described as a 'knowledge society'.

CONTEMPORARY APPLICATION

Lord Leitch was asked to undertake a review into the UK's long-term skills needs. His report, *Prosperity for all in the Global Economy: World Class Skills* (2006), presented ambitious goals for 2020 which, if achieved, will make the UK a world leader in skills. The report sets out far-reaching reforms that have implications for the workforce with an agenda of upskilling of workers throughout their working lives.

Figure 7.13 Upskilling of workforce

STUDY TIP

It is important to integrate ideas of upskilling and deskilling to the wider areas of how and why the workplace is organised in terms of a division of labour, and the bigger picture of how this relates to the distribution of poverty, income and wealth.

4.4 How has technology affected labour?

When discussing how technology impacts on workers, try to develop an understanding of how it can impact on identity, roles, surveillance and deskilling.

The impact of technology

Sociologists are divided in their analysis of the impact of technology on both the work process and worker alienation and identity. Michael J. Piore (1995) introduces the concept of the dual labour market, which can be used to explain not only class divides in the workforce but those associated with gender and ethnicity as well. Many female and BME workers are confined to the secondary labour market characterised by low wages, low status, low skills and insecure employment relationships with little or no prospect of promotion. This secondary labour market cuts across manual, white-collar and now, increasingly, into service sector jobs in the modern labour market.

Piore has also studied the impact of technological change and how automation can lead to labour market segmentation. Any threat of being replaced by machines undermines the power of workers and trade union attempts to fight for improvements in pay, conditions and long-term security.

Shoshana Zuboff (1988) draws on the work of Michel Foucault by describing how workers are increasingly subject to forms of surveillance. Subjected increasingly to a 'mechanism of objectification', workers are now constantly under an official gaze: their work performance may be subject to CCTV surveillance but, in addition, their performance is continually evaluated through R&D (review and development) and classified and registered in the official system of files. Such ideas reflect Max Weber's fear of increasingly bureaucratic organisations. However, they have an increased resonance in the information age. Zuboff notes how 'cybernetic identities', which result from the penetrating gaze of the employer, ultimately shape our career and promotion prospects.

When roles involve low skills, employers increasingly look for attributes such as what Ken Roberts (2001) describes as 'aesthetic labour'. Workers are chosen on their ability to 'look right' as attractive individuals to boost the company's image. They are required to come across as human and interested in their commitment

323

to customer satisfaction. George Ritzer (2007) uses the term **McDonaldisation** (a concept first encountered in the Culture and Identity chapter, page 171) to describe an important change to the experiences, identity and satisfaction of workers. Its name belies the fact that this concept extends far beyond the fast-food labour market.

Features of McDonaldisation can be observed across a wide spectrum of occupations, including even professions like nursing and teaching. Across the economy workers are faced with meeting standardised quality measures achieved by breaking down work-based tasks into smaller tasks in order to find the single most efficient method for completing it. The result is efficiency and predictability, and the worker's processes are easily controlled. However, all creativity is stifled and workers are increasingly unfulfilled to the point that they can even be contracted (and therefore threatened with the sack) to smile and be cheerful in front of customers. Decisions about the pace of work have been made elsewhere, often according to some distant managerial protocol developed far from where the tasks are performed.

Alan Bryman (2004) coined the term **Disneyisation**, arguing it complements Ritzer's notion of McDonaldisation in allowing us to understand processes at the heart of workplace practices today. Besides Ritzer's key criteria of efficiency, calculability, predictability and control, Bryman identifies four other trends he associates not only with Disney theme parks but the modern workplace in general: theming, de-differentiation of consumption (multiple consumption opportunities in a particular location), merchandising (selling the brand on as many items as possible) and the development of 'emotional labour' (cheerful workers with fixed smiles). The latter is specifically to control employees, both through scripted interaction with customers but by expecting them to show they are having fun too.

Companies need to define themselves by creating an image, and they look for employees to reflect that image. However, the bottom line for workers is that this type of work is can be stressful and demeaning, often for very low wages. Ken Roberts call this the 'new working class', fragmented, insecure, typically working part time and/or unsocial hours, often on zero-hours contracts. Such workers serve the leisure time of others.

Marxist perspectives on deskilling

The Marxist Harry Braverman (1974) was probably the first sociologist to seriously address the deskilling thesis. Through the adoption of a neo-Marxist approach, he argues that capitalism can only sustain long-term profits by the continued deskilling of the work force. Under such circumstances the wages of workers are constantly under threat, work practices increasingly subject to the control of management, and labour increasingly susceptible to replacement by automated technology. Braverman's ideas were influenced by both the **scientific management** thesis of F.W. Taylor and the practice of **Fordism**. Braverman saw both of these as hallmarks of modern capitalist enterprise. However, critics argue that if skilled manual workers were to suffer such a sustained attack, then the result would be an increasingly homogeneous mass of workers with no real internal differentiation.

While some think Braverman overstates his case, there is a general consensus that the process of deskilling has been a feature of modern industrial society in both blue-collar and white-collar jobs. However, deskilling is seen to be occurring at an uneven pace across occupations: at the same time, some occupations may well have been accompanied by new forms of skilled work.

It is argued that the shift to a post-industrial society, through deindustrialisation and deskilling, weakens the strength of the working class. This can been seen in the decline of union memberships and unions increasingly merging. For example, in 2014 the Trades Union Congress (TUC) was comprised of just 54 unions representing just 5.98 million workers – less than half the membership of the 1980s.

The decline of the industrial work base is associated with an erosion of community life and the cultural reproduction of the working class. In Britain the effect of these two processes has been structural and long-term unemployment, particularly for regions like south Wales, Cornwall, the north west and the north east of England. In these areas substantial sectors of the working class, especially young people, are subject to Steve Craine's (1997) 'black magic roundabout' (see page 315). Another outcome observed by Simon Winlow (2001) in Sunderland is a rise of male violence and crime. Figure 7.16 illustrates some of the key ideas associated with the deskilling debate.

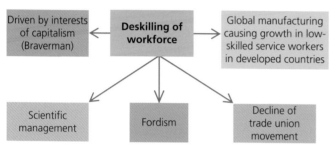

Figure 7.14 Deskilling of workforce

RESEARCH IN FOCUS

Lewis (2011) examined employment trends in a selection of developed economies. What he found was that upskilling the workers did not automatically upskill the work. For example, in the UK he found a significant growth in both low-skilled, low-paid work and high-skilled, high-paid work, despite the fact that educational qualifications across the workforce had been improving. He argues that with the twin impact of new technology and the manufacturing industry's desire to shed labour, all developed economies will have an increasing proportion of low-skilled service workers. Rather pessimistically he adds that 'pursuing the mythical knowledge economy is not a realistic option'.

Adapted from Paul Lewis (2011) Upskilling the workers will not upskill the work. Why the dominant economic framework limits child poverty reduction in the UK. *Journal of Social Policy*, 40, 535–556.

Questions

1. According to Lewis, what is happening to the workforce of the UK economy?
2. Why does Lewis feel there will be an increasing proportion of low-skilled service workers?
3. In what ways does this reflect the work and ideas of: a) Piore, b) Zuboff, c) Ritzer, d) Bryman and e) Roberts?
4. Evaluate the evidence for and against his assertion that 'the mythical knowledge economy is not a realistic option'.

KEY SOCIOLOGISTS

Malcolm Carey (2007) studied social workers and found they continue to extend the process of deskilling and **proletarianisation**. He found that the expansion of the private sector in social care and the continuing reliance on agency workers were two factors in the detrimental change for both social work and service users/carers.

CONTEMPORARY APPLICATION

Adzuna, an organisation that provides labour market data to the government, recently reported that, despite their skills and qualifications, graduates face fierce competition for graduate jobs, resulting in many graduates being forced to take on lower-skilled jobs. They found that in the autumn following graduation there were more than 50 graduates competing for every graduate entry-level job.

STUDY TIP

It is useful to recognise that concepts like upskilling and deskilling have links to the topics of education and global development.

Check your understanding

1. What is meant by the term 'division of labour'?
2. What do sociologists understand by the term 'work'?
3. What is the 'informal economy'?
4. Explain what Durkheim meant by 'mechanical solidarity' and 'organic solidarity'.
5. What is a meritocracy?
6. What is meant by the 'new international division of labour'?
7. What evidence is there to support the idea of upskilling in contemporary society?
8. What was Daniel Bell's vision of a post-industrial society?
9. What two theories influenced Harry Braverman's concept of deskilling?
10. What is meant by 'proletarianisation'?

Practice questions

1. Define the term 'dual labour market'. [2 marks]
2. Using **one** example, briefly explain the term 'division of labour'. [2 marks]
3. Suggest **three** ways in which workers are subject to surveillance. [6 marks]
4. Outline and explain **two** global outcomes that can be attributed to the new international division of labour. [10 marks]

Read Item A below and answer the question that follows.

Item A

The Leitch Review states that 'skills are now increasingly the key lever'. The prize for achieving this ambition is great – a more prosperous and fairer society. The review estimates a possible net benefit of at least £80 billion over 30 years. This would come from a boost in the productivity growth rate of up to 15 per cent and an increase in the employment growth rate by around 10 per cent. Social deprivation, poverty and inequality will diminish.

Applying material from Item A and your knowledge, evaluate the view that the future trend for skills in society is one of upskilling. [20 marks]

Section 5: The impact of work, worklessness and globalisation

> **This section will explore the following debates:**
>
> ● What impact does work have on people's lives?
> ● What impact does worklessness have on people's lives?
> ● What is the impact of globalisation on work?

GETTING YOU STARTED

Globalisation needs a unified plan to work

Following decades of decline in the car industry, Britain is once again at the centre of global car and engine production. In 2013, 1.5 million cars and more than 3 million engines were built in Britain, most of them for export. However, the successful rejuvenation of the car industry has not been accompanied by a significant growth in new jobs: modern production techniques and automation mean that fewer than 150,000 people are directly involved in car or engine manufacture.

An equally successful industry is the fast-food business. In 2012 McDonald's announced that it was creating another 2500 jobs. However, 'McJobs' are low paid, have low status and McDonald's does not earn Britain any export revenue.

Concerns such as these are being raised across the developed world. Will the modern global economy create mass employment at worthwhile wages? Apart from the car industry, Britain has lost most of its manufacturing to factories across the globe in developing countries, especially China. In Britain there is a modest service sector, either integrated with manufacturing or providing self-standing services such as leisure, health, education or fast food. In addition there are many 'cream-skimming' services where 'agentism' dominates, for example financial services and estate agents where a percentage cut is taken on transactions without adding any value.

In economies like Britain where agentism has gone furthest, the manufacturing sector has declined the most, resulting in acute inequalities of income and opportunity. In the UK the agentist service sector has become over-large and over-rewarded.

This has left a pool of workless, unskilled people permanently unemployed or on low wages, a 'squeezed middle' whose wages barely rise and are terrified of losing their jobs, while the rich and privileged enjoy telephone number-sized incomes.

Adapted from Will Hutton (2012) Globalisation can work, but only with a unified international plan. *Observer*, 29 January.

5.1 What impact does work have on people's lives?

When thinking about the impact of work on people's lives you could consider issues like its impact on life chances as well as identity, sense of purpose, fulfilment, alienation and work satisfaction.

Work – from industrial society to consumer society

Although Zygmunt Bauman (1988) talks of society shifting from an 'industrial society' based on production to a 'consumer society', work and employment can still play an important part in shaping our identities. Even if we live in a consumer society, where identity is increasingly shaped by our purchases and how we shop, our ability to do so still depends of disposable income which, for most people, is derived from employment. Our work therefore continues to shape our life chances, what we can afford to consume, and factors like the area where we live and the size and value of the property we live in. The job we do

Questions

1. How many cars and engines were produced in the UK in 2013?
2. Why has the rejuvenation of the car industry not led to a big increase in employment?
3. What is the key problem with 'McJobs'?
4. Explain the meaning of 'cream-skimming' services.
5. Evaluate the argument that 'agentism' has had a negative impact on employment in the UK.

is also still an important marker of identity: when strangers meet one of the first questions is often 'What do you do?'

Karl Marx attempted to show in his writings that work is central to a human being's existence. In short, Marx saw work as separating humans from other animals. According to Marx, work should be a spontaneous, free activity through which humans actively engage in creating an objective world of social institutions. He used the term 'species being' to reflect how people see themselves in the world they have created.

The reality of work however is that few workers own the product of their labour – it belongs to the company. If workers are separated from the value they create in this way, work only serves to alienate most workers because their motive to work is solely financial – to earn a wage to pay the bills. Marx argued that work, for most people, is so unrewarding and such a burden that they no longer know who they really are. The concept of alienation is fundamental to any Marxist analysis of work: it literally means being divorced from one's self. Marx considered four aspects of alienated labour:

1. Alienation from the product – because workers do not own the means of production, they have to sell their labour for a wage. As workers have no control or ownership of the finished product, they gain little or no satisfaction from their productive work.
2. Alienation from productive activity – because workers sell their labour for a wage, their labour is owned by another (the capitalist class).
3. Alienation from species – work should be a creative and rewarding experience, but most workers find it dull, repetitive and unfulfilling. They work solely to get paid.
4. Alienation from fellow humans – work divides individuals from the very essence of humanity, as workers compete in the cut-throat labour market for jobs, bonuses and promotion. Self-preservation becomes the foundation of false class-consciousness.

Robert Blauner (1964) developed Marx's concept of alienation and paints a very bleak picture of working life. He describes how alienation exists in industrial production in four ways:

● Workers have a sense of powerlessness when they do not feel they have control over work processes.
● Workers feel a sense of meaninglessness when the purpose of their work role is not understood.
● Workers feel isolated when they do not see themselves as part of a shared identity or community in the workplace.
● Workers suffer from self-estrangement when their work fails to offer a means for self-expression.

While some employed workers enjoy their role and receive considerable job satisfaction, Blauner's bleak picture of alienation is something that many workers will identify with. Those who are self-employed may escape the levels of alienation experienced by the majority of workers as they have autonomy over when and how hard they work, and reap the rewards of their labour.

Work, satisfaction and 'contradictory class locations'

The American Marxist Erik Olin Wright (1978) identified certain 'contradictory class locations' where workers enjoy a certain amount of autonomy over their work and job satisfaction. These contradictory class locations include managers and supervisors, small business owners, the self-employed and semi-autonomous workers. Wright cited university lecturers as examples of the latter, who are contracted to deliver a certain amount of lectures but have a degree of autonomy over how they spend the rest of their working day. Because workers in contradictory class locations have a degree of control over their work roles (and often power over other workers) Wright regarded them as more likely to be fulfilled with a sense of purpose in their work.

Keith Grint (2008, 2010, 2014) has written a number of books and papers that are particularly critical of the workplace leaders that workers have to endure. He implies that good leadership can alleviate some of the alienation workers inevitably experience as wage slaves, making them feel valued and having some control over the work process. Workers, he argues, are too often let down by poor leadership, which too frequently addresses 'wicked problems' with 'clumsy solutions'. In addition, workers are subject to authoritarian and dominant leadership that imposes from above, rather than listening to their genuine grievances. Grint argues that leaders need to create a culture where workers are empowered and feel they can challenge them freely. In addition, he advocates that employers embrace empathy rather than egotism, whereby effective managers should experience the roles of their workers at a grass-roots level. For example, managers joining the workforce on the production line can gain first-hand experience of the problems that workers have to endure. Figure 7.17 illustrates some of the factors that impact on the meaning of work, including the increasing impact of globalisation.

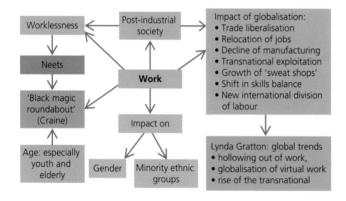

Figure 7.15 Work

5.2 What impact does worklessness have on people's lives?

When discussing the impact of worklessness on people's lives you could consider the meanings of unemployment and underemployment, as well as the impact on those who are retired or unable to work, such as many people with disabilities.

The changing nature of work

More than 50 years ago, Ralph Dahrendorf (1959) predicted that, as a Europe-wide response to globalisation, there would be a decline in permanent full-time employment and the growth of part-time, temporary or seasonal employment. Such workers are not unemployed, as such, but they could be described as underemployed in that they may wish for full-time, permanent employment.

KEY SOCIOLOGISTS

In an attempt to make sense of contemporary society Zygmunt Bauman (2000) uses 'liquid' or 'fluid' as the metaphor of the present-day state of modernity. His point is that fluids cannot hold their shape for long. Liquid makes salient the brittleness, breakability, ad-hoc modality of inter-human bonds. Bauman refers to globalisation as the 'planetarisation' of inter-human dependency and its outcomes.

CONTEMPORARY APPLICATION

The UK government's website GOV.UK has various links to the rules and regulations designed to protect workers in the workplace. These include: flexible working, maximum weekly working hours, night working hours, overtime, rest breaks at work, Sunday working, and workplace bullying and harassment. While the TUC would say governments too often side with employers, these regulations show a commitment to protecting the workforce from higher levels of exploitation.

STUDY TIP

When looking at the impact of work it is important to view this concept in the context of not only social class, gender, ethnicity and age, but also the meanings and opportunities that derive from employment.

Other factors, such as the growth of the 'secondary labour market' (Piore, 1995) and post-Fordist production methods demanding an increasingly flexible workforce, have also accounted for the decline in permanent full-time jobs. Besides part-time workers who would prefer to be full-time, underemployment also includes those workers that are highly skilled but work in low-paying and/or low-skill jobs. In addition, remember the concept of the informal economy (see page 315), which involves work that occurs in the murky and untaxed 'black economy'.

Ethnicity and worklessness

With regard to worklessness and ethnicity, most ethnic minority groups have historically experienced discrimination in the labour market and much higher levels of unemployment. For example, in 2013 unemployment levels in the UK stood at 8 per cent, but for ethnic minority groups it was 14 per cent. Specifically, for black ethnic minorities it was 17 per cent and for Pakistani/Bangladeshi ethnic groups it was 19 per cent. Worklessness impacts particularly on young people from ethnic minority groups, with 16–24 year olds having an unemployment rate of 37 per cent, up from 33 per cent in 2012. For the UK as a whole, unemployment in this age group is 21 per cent.

Education and worklessness

Of particular concern with regard to the workless is the growing number of young people without work across the developed world. It is estimated there are around 14 million young unemployed people in Europe in this category of worklessness (Garrod, 2014a). Fagin and Little (1984) concluded that unemployment and family strain are related, especially for those previously in poorly paid jobs, and for the longer unemployed. Many are university graduates who find themselves overqualified for the jobs that are available. In 2012 graduate unemployment was almost one in ten (nine per cent) six months after graduation. Those who can find employment often do so in non-graduate jobs with low job satisfaction and poor career progression prospects.

The other group that is a cause for concern are the poorly qualified, who typically leave education early. A report by the University and College Union (2013) researched 1000 **neets** (not in employment, education or training) and found a desperately isolated group who felt marginalised and that they lacked control over their lives. A third reported rarely leaving their home and 38 per cent believed they would never gain secure employment. Steve Craine's (1997) 'black magic roundabout' again comes to mind (see Section 3, page 309).

Retirement and worklessness

In 2014 the Department for Work and Pensions announced a desire for the average age of retirement to rise by as much as six months every year. It is currently 64.7 years for men and 63.1 years for women. The state pension age is currently 65 for men and 60 for women. This will to rise to 66 for both genders by 2020 and to 70 for both genders in the next 50 years.

The impact of worklessness on the elderly has been described by Cumming and Henry (1961) who developed disengagement theory, one of the first theories of ageing. It describes how elderly people begin to disengage from their previously social roles as they realise that they will die in the near future.

Hockey and James (1993) challenge the stigmatising role that stereotypes can play in the lives of the elderly. Although most workers look forward to retirement as well-earned leisure in their twilight years, many people continue to seek employment. Reasons include boredom, loneliness and, for many, a necessary income to supplement inadequate pension and savings. Zygmunt Bauman (1988) would describe people whose decision to work after retirement age as an example of the 'repressed' in consumer society.

Those lucky enough to retire with financial comfort are sometimes referred to as 'grey panthers': their high living standard, frequent holidays and indulgence with consumerism would be categorised by Bauman as an example of the 'seduced' in consumer society.

Disability and worklessness

People with disabilities have a level of unemployment, far higher than that of able-bodied people, at around 50 per cent. Their position has been likened to the Marxist concept of a 'reserve army of labour', used when needed but often the first workers to be discarded when no longer required. Even in their leisure time disabled people often have segregated activities, such as day centres and social clubs. Until recently many mainstream forms of leisure, such as cinemas and theatres, excluded wheelchair users on the grounds of health and safety, arguing they were a risk in a fire.

5.3 What impact does globalisation have on work?

When studying the impact of globalisation on work it is important to recognise the growing importance of this concept. Individual economies are increasingly subject to external factors and forces, and these are increasingly outside their control.

Globalisation was defined in the Culture and Identity chapter (page 165) as a key process by which the world is becoming increasingly interconnected due to the significant increase in both international trade and cultural exchanges. Sociologists often use the word 'interpenetration' when referring to the characteristics of globalisation. What they mean by this is that the level of influence on workers is significant to both developed and developing countries.

Over the past 50 years international trade has dramatically increased through **trade liberalisation** (the removal of trading barriers such as tariffs and quotas) and a reduction in transportation costs. The concept of the new international division of labour was introduced in Section 4 (page 320). Since the 1970s this has encouraged a substantial movement of industrial manufacturing to the developing world because labour costs are cheaper.

Globalist theories of poverty

With globalisation the future is seen as somewhat precarious, and living standards previously enjoyed in Western developed countries are seen as potentially under threat. Future unemployment is threatened as transnational corporations (TNCs) increasingly embrace the new international division of labour by switching production to the developing world. This has the effect of weakening the bargaining power of workers globally and leads to increased unemployment in developed countries. As production is increasingly outsourced to the developing world, so the risk of long-term unemployment and dependence on state benefits becomes increasingly common in developed countries. Optimist globalists still see the West the main source of 'high-tech' jobs, but pessimist globalists fear that the future holds little more than non-technical jobs in low-paid sectors such as catering, retail or security. The richer Western European

KEY SOCIOLOGISTS

Joan Garrod (2014a) links the resurgence of right-wing politics in many European countries to the rise in unemployment and a perceived lack of future job prospects among the young. Feelings of hopelessness and despair lead to a sense of alienation, causing people to reject mainstream politics and join more radical political movements.

CONTEMPORARY APPLICATION

A report by the Department for Work and Pensions (Barnes et al, 2011) found that worklessness is particularly concentrated in certain deprived areas in Great Britain. It records that worklessness has actually become entrenched in some areas despite substantial investment in neighbourhood renewal. It concludes that a debate is required at both a national and local level about the causes of worklessness and the nature of regeneration and employment support that is required to get such people back into employment.

STUDY TIP

Remember that the higher level skills of AO2 and AO3 require more than just regurgitating knowledge, which only yields AO1 marks.

countries have seen large numbers of migrant workers from Eastern Europe following the expansion of the EU. Castles and Kosack (1973) see immigrant and migrant workers as a particularly disadvantaged group, arguing that they function as a 'reserve army of labour' that can be drawn on during periods of capitalist expansion and laid off relatively easily during periods of contraction.

To capitalise on TNC investment, many developing nations in the 1970s and 1980s set up export processing zones (EPZs) or free-trade zones (FTZs) in which TNCs were encouraged to build factories producing goods for export to the West. The liberalisation of trade makes economic sense when goods, such as kettles, microwaves and clothes, can simply be made far more cheaply in the developing world then shipped to consumer markets in the developed world. For example, Joan Garrod (2014b) notes that Bangladesh, with its cheap labour, has one of the largest garment industries, second in the world only to China. It employs 4 million workers in 3500 factories with a turnover of £14 billion. However, the workers (invariably female) face very low wages, long working hours and hazardous working conditions, as demonstrated by the collapse of the Rana Plaza factory in Dhaka in 2013, which killed almost 1200 and injured 2500 people.

Figure 7.16 The Rana Plaza factory in Dhaka

The impact of globalisation on work within countries like the UK has been to substantially reduce employment in heavy industries like coal, steel and shipbuilding, as well as the manufacturing of domestic appliances and clothing. Historically Marks & Spencer has been an iconic retailer of 'British quality goods', but it abandoned this policy in the 1980s as clothes made in the UK became increasingly expensive and uncompetitive compared to those made in the developing world. Employment growth in the UK since the 1970s has been in the tertiary (services) sector: education, health care, central and local government services, finance, insurance, retailing, and leisure and tourism.

The impact of trade liberalisation on workers in countries like the UK can vary widely across different groups. For example, Lynda Gratton (2012) identified three trends associated with globalisation: hollowing out of work, globalisation of virtual work and the rise of the transnational. 'Hollowing out' refers to the vulnerability of the middle section of the labour force to the forces of globalisation. Gratton says there will always be a demand for high-skill, high-wage workers – professionals like doctors, lawyers, accountants and highly skilled IT specialists and engineers – and low-skilled workers, like hairdressers, waiters, bank tellers and shop assistants. It is middle-skilled, middle-income jobs – such as

KEY SOCIOLOGISTS

Anthony Giddens (1999) made an important contribution to this debate. He has a pessimistic view of the role that transnational corporations play in global trade. He questions the romantic view of the world as a 'global village'. Instead he describes the oppression and exploitation of the developing world's people and resources as being more like 'global pillage'.

CONTEMPORARY APPLICATION

Marxists see globalisation as serving to worsen the lot of the impoverished in both the developed and developing world. They see global capitalism as creating a world of winners and losers: a few on the fast-track to prosperity, the majority condemned to a life of misery and despair. In the last decade of the twentieth century, the share of the poorest fifth of the world's population in global income had dropped from an already miserable 2.3 per cent to 1.4 per cent.

STUDY TIP

When looking at the impact of globalisation it is important to use examples and evidence from the developed and developing worlds, and to indicate how through trade and transnational corporations they are inextricably connected.

assembly-line workers, managers and secretaries – that are particularly vulnerable as the work can easily be outsourced to a country with lower wages, or they can be replaced by technology.

By the globalisation of virtual education, Gratton means the growth of internet-based distance learning platforms such as Open Yale, iTunesU and Khan Academy, which will enable students across the world to gain very similar learning experiences and work towards similar qualifications. For example, someone in New Guinea can gain the same experience and qualifications as her contemporary in London. These highly-educated people in the developing world, she predicts, will be able to work on online global tasks and projects. This means that employment will be truly global and not determined by the level of economic activity of the country a person lives in, as the virtual market transcends national economies.

Currently platforms like oDesk, eLance and Guru offer employment opportunities to virtual markets for employment to people like software programmers, translators, administrators, web designers and salespeople across the world. Gratton makes the point that good education facilities, such as world-class universities, which currently attract a high number of international students, will lose their significance and importance. In addition, the combination of scaled education and scaled job finding will shift employment of the highly educated and skilled to the most talented and motivated individuals around the globe.

When talking of the 'rise of the transnational' Gratton is not referring to corporations but to individuals who are geographically mobile and willing and able to relocate at any time. This global elite are a truly cosmopolitan group of talented and educated workers, who not only seek out the best global employment opportunities but are highly employable because of their competence, management style, cultural sensitivities and social networks. They are fluent in English, increasingly the global language of business and commerce, as well as other languages, so can facilitate the cross-cultural communication that is so important for global organisations. Whereas in the past transnational workers came from the developed world, talented and motivated individuals are increasingly emerging in developing countries. Gratton predicts a strong cohort from India, followed by China, as these countries' **diaspora** create ever stronger corridors between markets.

Questions

1. What percentage of job losses are caused by international trade and investment?
2. What is the impact on individuals and communities following the relocation of jobs?
3. What other factors, besides globalisation, can lead to job losses?
4. What is the solution offered by Swaim and Torres?

RESEARCH IN FOCUS

Jobs and globalisation

Paul Swaim and Raymond Torres (2005) undertook research for the Organisation for Economic Co-operation and Development (OECD) Directorate for Employment, Labour and Social Affairs in order to assess the impact of globalisation on jobs.

They began with three research questions: Does globalisation really cause job losses? If so, to what extent? And how can we respond?

They found the answer to the first question to be 'yes'.

In terms of the second question, they claimed that data from North America and Europe showed that between 4 and 17 per cent of job losses are caused by international trade and investment. The loss of a job through relocation to another country can be traumatic, causing anxiety and disruption in the lives of individuals, families and communities.

However, global forces were not the only reasons for job losses. Other factors included lack of investment in new technology, capital or skills, or simply poor business management. At the same time, globalisation and world trade can create business opportunities and new jobs.

However, the impact of globalisation on public anxiety was perceived to be large. Whether the reality of relocation of jobs is exaggerated, it is a genuine fear of many workers. Governments should look at various ways of achieving re-employment when relocation does occur. They concluded that 'workers will accept to swim with globalisation, as long as the policies are there to ensure they do not sink because of it'.

Adapted from Paul Swaim and Raymond Torres (2005) Jobs and globalisation: Towards policies that work. *OECD Observer*, 250.

Check your understanding

1. What does globalisation mean?
2. What does trade liberalisation mean?
3. Outline what a transnational corporation is and give three examples.
4. In terms of broad categories of employment, which sector of the economy has grown significantly since the 1970s?
5. What two groups of young people is there most concern about in terms of work and worklessness?
6. How do disabled people fair in terms of gaining work?
7. What is meant by the term 'reserve army of labour'? Give examples of who it can apply to.
8. What did Gratton mean by the 'hollowing out of work'?
9. What did Gratton mean by the 'globalisation of virtual work'?
10. What did Gratton mean by the 'rise of the transnational'?

Practice questions

1. Define the term 'alienation'. [2 marks]
2. Using **one** example, briefly explain the term 'consumer society'. [2 marks]
3. Suggest **three** ways that globalisation can impact on the area of work. [6 marks]
4. Outline and explain **two** groups who are likely to be discriminated against or workless in the labour market. [10 marks]

Read Item A below and answer the question that follows.

Item A

One of the positive impacts of globalisation is that it is helping to generate more wealth in developing countries. However, at the same time, the gap between the richest and poorest people seems to be polarising. A similar phenomenon is occurring in the developed world too.

Applying material from Item A and your knowledge, evaluate reasons for widening gap between the rich and poor in the UK. [20 marks]

Links to other topics

This topic has links to:

- Chapter 2 Education, section 3.1 The impact of educational policies
- Chapter 4 Culture and identity, section 4.6 How does social class affect identity?
- Chapter 6 Health, section 1.7 Social model of health, section 2.1 How does social class determine inequalities in health? section 3.4 How can social factors influence health care?
- Global development (Book 2)
- Crime and deviance (Book 2).

Tackling the AS exam

8

This Chapter will explore:

- The structure of the AS exam
- The skills you will need to demonstrate
- Some advice on tackling short questions
- Tackling paper 1
- Tackling paper 2

The structure of the AS exam

You will take two exams at the end of the year. The first exam paper includes the compulsory topics of Education, Methods in Context and Research Methods. For the second exam, you must answer questions about research methods as well as questions from one of four topic choices:

- culture and identity
- families and households
- health
- work, poverty and welfare.

Paper 1: Education with Methods in Context

You have 90 minutes for this written exam paper, which is worth a total of 60 marks and 50 per cent of your AS level. You should spend approximately 30 minutes answering questions 1 to 4 and 30 minutes each on questions 5 and 6. The questions will look something like this:

1. Define the term … [2 marks]
2. Using one example, briefly explain how … [2 marks]
3. Outline three … [6 marks]
4. Outline and explain two ways in which … [10 marks]
5. Applying material from Item A and your knowledge, evaluate the view that … [20 marks]
6. Applying material from Item B and your knowledge of research methods, evaluate the strengths and limitations of using … to investigate … [20 marks]

Paper 2: Research Methods and Topics in Sociology

You have 90 minutes for this written exam paper, which is worth a total of 60 marks. It counts for 50 per cent of your AS level.

Section A: Research Methods

You should spend approximately 30 minutes answering this section. The questions will look something like this:

1. Outline two problems of using structured interviews in sociological research. [4 marks]
2. Evaluate the problems of using participant observation in sociological research. [16 marks]

Section B: Optional topics

You should spend approximately one hour answering this section. The questions will look something like this:

1. Define the term … [2 marks]
2. Using one example, briefly explain how … [2 marks]
3. Outline three … [6 marks]
4. Outline and explain two ways in which … [10 marks]
5. Applying material from Item A and your knowledge, evaluate … [20 marks]

What skills will I need to demonstrate?

There are three groups of skills that you are required to demonstrate.

A01	Demonstrate knowledge and understanding of sociological theories, concepts and evidence. You can demonstrate A01 skills by writing about the studies and concepts that you have learnt. The way to maximise your marks here is to explain the study accurately, giving the correctly spelled names of sociologists. Concepts must be used correctly and defined thoroughly. You can also show your knowledge and understanding by mentioning an issue that has been in the news or by writing about a relevant policy or law. The important thing is to use relevant information. Another way to show knowledge and understanding is to acknowledge the date of a study and, if appropriate, explain why it may or may not be relevant today.
A02	Apply sociological theories, concepts, evidence and research methods to a range of issues. This can be demonstrated by showing how knowledge or understanding relates to the question. Using phrases such as 'this suggests that …' helps the examiner see that you are not simply writing a list of what you know and hoping that it makes sense. So, if you are talking about a study you might suggest how it supports one side of the argument that you are creating, or the other.
A03	Analyse and evaluate sociological theories, concepts, evidence and research methods in order to: present arguments make judgements and draw conclusions. The hardest set of skills to develop, this will involve you thinking about weighing up arguments, considering which view is the strongest and looking at a debate in a balanced way. Make your work feel discursive, rather than list like.

Table 8.1 A01, A02 and A03 skills

Weighting of assessment objectives for AS Sociology

In the AS course, just under half of the marks available are for AO1, knowledge and understanding, and just over half of the marks are for AO2 and AO3, the higher level skills. It is therefore important that you try to demonstrate both skills in throughout the paper.

Assessment objectives	Component weightings (approx %)		
	Paper 1	Paper 2	Overall weighting
AO1	22	24	46
AO2	18	13	31
AO3	10	13	23
Overall weighting of components	50	50	100

Table 8.2 Weighting of assessment objectives

Some advice on tackling short questions

Do:

- You can be given one out of two for a partially answered question, so make sure that you answer the question as thoroughly as you can.
- If you are being asked for more than one way/example/factor/criticism, make sure that the items you choose are different and do not overlap.
- Be accurate if you are defining a concept.
- Avoid wasting time; for example, you do not need to give any additional information if you will not be given any extra marks for it.

Don't:

- Use one-word answers.
- Overwrite
- Use the word you've been asked to define when defining it; use alternative words.

Tackling Paper 1: Education with Methods in Context

In this section, each question is discussed in detail along with examples of the types of questions that you might get and an explanation of how each question will be marked.

1. Define the term ... [2 marks]

This is a knowledge-based question that requires you to provide an accurate definition of sociological concept related to education.

Example question

1. Define the term material deprivation.   [2 marks]

Answer A

Not having a very good home life.

This answer is very general and does not focus specifically on the concept.

Answer B

A lack of material things which lead to educational success.

This answer uses the word 'material' without explaining what is meant; though it shows understanding that it is a lack of the materials that lead to educational success.

Answer C

Not having the money to buy things that can help a pupil do well in education.

This is a good answer as it shows that the meaning of the concept is understood.

Practice questions

- Define the term labelling.
- Define the term self-fulfilling prophecy.
- Define the term cultural capital.
- Define the term marketisation.
- Define the term correspondence principle.
- Define the term vocational education.
- Define the term privatisation of education.

2. Using one example, briefly explain how ... [2 marks]

This question asks you to explain something by providing a clear example of it. This is likely to be a process that takes place in education or at home.

Example question

2. Using one example, briefly explain how labelling may affect educational achievement   [2 marks]

Here are some sample answers and commentary on question 2.

Answer A

Students from different schools have different experiences.

This response is not relevant to the question.

Answer B

Students who are labelled negatively may join an anti-school subculture.

This response provides a partial answer. It does not go on to describe the effect this might have on their educational outcomes.

Answer C

Students who are labelled as underachievers by teachers may not bother working hard which may lead them to do badly in their exams.

This response has two clear parts; it explains the effect and the consequences of labelling.

Practice questions

● Using one example, briefly explain how material deprivation may affect educational achievement.
● Using one example, briefly explain how the ethnocentric curriculum may affect educational achievement.
● Using one example, briefly explain how ethnic differences may affect educational achievement.
● Using one example, briefly explain how gender may affect educational achievement.

3. Outline three ... [6 marks]

This question awards three marks for AO1 and three marks for AO2 skills, so as well as showing you know and understand something you must also apply your knowledge to this specific issue. It is a good idea to get into the habit of setting out your three points separately.

Example question

3. Outline three ways that gender differences are reinforced in education [6 marks]

Here are some sample answers and commentary on question 3:

Answer A

Gender refers to the socially constructed ideas about what it means to be a girl or a boy. In education this might mean girls are encouraged to take girls' subjects by their teachers. Also boys are encouraged to take boys' subjects. There are lots of things that go on in school which mean that girls do better than boys.

This answer is not set out clearly. It identifies that teachers encourage gendered subject choices, but instead of developing this point it simply repeats the same point for boys.

Answer B

The ways that girls and boys are treated differently by their teachers affects their results. Also, sometimes textbooks contain pictures of girls and boys that portray them in stereotypical ways, for example, with the girls doing dance and the boys doing science, which reinforces the subjects that girls and boys take.

Although the first sentence makes a good point, this point is not developed by saying that by being treated differently, girls might do better than boys. The second sentence is better because it gives a reason (gendered textbooks) and it does explain how this affects the subjects that girls and boys take.

Answer C

Girls are labelled as more hardworking than boys by teachers, meaning that they are likely to feel more encouraged and do better.

Girls and boys are made to do different sports at school, such as boys playing football and girls doing dance. This sends messages to girls and boys about boys being more competitive and sporty while girls are more interested in looking nice.

There are few female headteachers meaning that girls lack powerful role models, which encourages them not to go for powerful positions themselves.

There are three clearly stated responses here which are set out carefully. The three ways do not overlap and each point is developed.

Practice questions

- Outline three ways that school is similar to work.
- Outline three functions of the education system.
- Outline three home factors that affect working-class children's chances of educational success.
- Outline three processes within the school that lead to some ethnic groups having lower educational outcomes.
- Outline three reasons why girls now outperform boys in education.

4. Outline and explain two ways in which ... [10 marks]

This question has five marks for AO1, three marks for AO2 and two marks for AO3. So, there is a focus on knowing studies, concepts, ideas and policies, but equally it is important to apply this knowledge and weigh up different arguments. You are expected to write in prose, so this is a mini essay that needs to be organised into paragraphs.

Example question

4. Outline and explain two ways in which marketisation reinforces inequalities in educational outcomes.   [10 marks]

Sample answer

Marketisation means that a school is run like a business. It was introduced in the 1988 Education Reform Act under the New Right Conservative government. It has been continued ever since then by other governments. It was a policy intended to drive up standards in schools, by making them compete against each other for pupils, who have become like customers.

One effect of marketisation is that it has reinforced class differences. Gilborn and Youdell argue that marketisation made schools focus on their A–C pass rates as this is an important measure of a 'good' school. This means that students who are likely to get A–C grades, such as many middle-class pupils, are likely to get lots of attention because they will make the school look good. However, working-class pupils might get ignored and do much worse.

Another effect of marketisation is that it allows more parental choice, which means that some parents know how to play the system and others do not, giving some pupils an advantage. For example, ethnic minority pupils whose parents do not speak English as their first language might find that their parents are not able to read school brochures or understand league tables, or maybe they cannot afford to move into expensive areas for the top schools. This means that they might end up going to their local school might not be very good, leading to worse results.

Marketisation therefore causes the gap between working-class and middle-class achievement to grow, as well as reinforcing differences between ethnic groups.

This answer clearly shows two ways in which marketisation reinforces inequalities in education. It sets these out clearly and explains them, applying Gilborn and Youdell's study well and applying that knowledge to the question. However, it does not do so well on AO3; for instance it tends to assume that all working-class pupils will underperform. Instead they could have said 'however not all working-class pupils underachieve'. Furthermore it does not evaluate very effectively, and the conclusion tends to repeat the points made earlier rather than offer a criticism or a counter view.

Practice questions

- Outline and explain two ways in which processes in school reinforce class differences in educational outcomes.
- Outline and explain two ways in which Marxists argue that education reinforces capitalist society.
- Outline and explain two ways in which processes outside of school reinforce gender differences in educational outcomes.
- Outline and explain two ways in which educational policies reinforce inequalities in educational outcomes.

Question 6

This question is worth 20 marks, with eight marks for AO1, eight marks for AO2 and four marks for AO3. You are expected to demonstrate your knowledge of sociological methods, concepts and examples of research, as well as knowledge about a particular educational issue. This knowledge of methods is applied to an educational issue; in other words, explaining how methods work in real educational contexts. This question demands a strong understanding of how the method would actually work in a real context.

Due to the fact that this question demands such different skills, there is a whole chapter dedicated to this question (see pages 90–114).

Tackling Paper 2: Research Methods and Topics in Sociology

The second exam paper has some similar questions to the first paper, so this should help you prepare for the exam. The paper is split into two sections, one compulsory section on research methods and a second section that focuses on the topic you have learnt about. Make sure that you only answer questions for the topic you have been taught about.

Section A: Research Methods

1. Outline two problems/strengths/factors [4 marks]

Like question 3 on Paper 1, this question demands that you explain the problem/strengths/factors about a particular research method or research method issue and also that you go on to explain it. Developing your point is therefore important.

Example question

1. Outline two problems with using participant observation in sociological research.

[4 marks]

Here are some sample answers with commentary.

Answer A

Participant observation can be a problem because it is hard for the researcher to record his or her results. Also participant observation can be dangerous for the researcher if they are studying a criminal group. This is because they might break ethical codes that researchers have to work to.

The first sentence is a partial answer because it states a problem without developing it. The second problem in the next sentence is clear and does get developed. This example shows how important it is to state a problem and then go on to consider the impact of this problem on the research.

Answer B

This method is very time consuming, and this can be a problem for a researcher working alone, as they might have to spend considerable amounts of time with the research group, meaning that they might become less objective about the research.

This method can be problematic because the researcher might find it hard to be accepted by the group because he or she has different social characteristics.

This is a slightly unusual answer because the actual problem is stated after the development in both cases. Both parts of the answer are present though.

Practice questions

- Outline two problems with using experiments in sociological research.
- Outline two strengths of using unstructured interviews in sociological research.
- Outline two strengths of using secondary sociological research methods.
- Outline two factors which might affect a researcher's choice of sociological method.
- Outline two ethical issues which may affect a researcher's choice of sociological method.

2. Evaluate the problems of using sociological research [16 marks]

This question requires you to write an essay with a clear structure. There are six marks available for AO1, five marks for AO2 and five marks for AO3. Therefore you must give examples of the problems and strengths of the method as well as deciding if there are more strengths or weaknesses. This question may not be about a method. It might be about general research issues, such as the importance of practical, ethical or theoretical issues, or about qualitative or quantitative research or data.

Example question

2. Evaluate the problem of using postal questionnaires in sociological research.

[16 marks]

Sample answer

Postal questionnaires consist of a set of standardised questions with a set of pre-fixed options for respondents to pick. They are favoured by positivists because they are high in reliability. These questionnaires have the practical advantage of being able to be sent to a wide a range of people as part of a large sample. This means that they can be considered to produce representative results, which can be generalised. Postal questionnaires are also anonymous and so respondents might feel comfortable with answering honestly.

One problem with questionnaires is that people lie and the results might be invalid as a result. There are also problems with questionnaires having a low response rate. The postal questionnaire might be difficult for certain groups in society to answer, for example, illiterate people, children or the elderly or disabled. This means that you are not getting a true picture of all types of views, making the results not representative. Interpretivists might say that this method lacks depth. So, for example, the questionnaire might reveal that there is a social problem, but it may not explain the reasons for this social problem. The responses might not have the answer to a question that a participant wants, causing them to give a wrong answer.

In conclusion, there seem to be more problems with questionnaires than strengths.

This answer is largely accurate and shows some knowledge and understanding. However it lacks depth and the application is limited. It tends to describe or list advantages and disadvantages rather than discuss them. It could have developed each strength or problem further, for example by unpacking and explaining concepts or giving an example. It is generally better to weave strengths and weaknesses of a method together rather than deal with all of the strengths and then all of the weaknesses. This response could have been improved if it had evaluated the method and weighed up the strengths and weaknesses of postal questionnaires.

Practice questions

- Evaluate the problems of using unstructured interviews for sociological research.
- Evaluate the advantages of using official statistics for sociological research.
- Evaluate the strengths of using positivist sociological methods for research.
- Evaluate the problems of using experiments for sociological research.

Section B: Optional topics

In this part of Paper 2, you have a choice of topics. You must only answer questions about one optional topic, so make sure that you are on the correct page before answering the questions.

You can choose one topic from:

- Culture and Identity (Questions 3–7)
- Families and Households (Questions 8–12)
- Health (Questions 13–17)
- Work, Poverty and Welfare (Questions 18–22)

1. Define the term ... [2 marks]

The first question asks you to define a term, which is similar to question 1 in the first paper. It is important that you do this accurately and fully. If you feel that your answer is in any way unclear, add an example.

2. Using one example, briefly explain ... [2 marks]

This question asks you to do two things to explain a process or issue and go on to give an example of it.

3. Outline three ... [6 marks]

Similar to question 3 on Paper 1, this question demands that you explain three factors/ways/reasons and also that you go on to develop these. For an example of how this question is marked, see the families and households example below.

Example question

3. Outline three reasons for increased life expectancy.   [6 marks]

Your checklist for this question could look like this:

- better health care which is free to everyone which means that people stay healthier for longer
- people are better educated about a healthy lifestyle, which means that they are less likely to pick up unhealthy habits such as smoking and so live longer
- people tend to work in safer environments than in the past which means there are fewer deaths at an earlier age and that people live longer
- people are more affluent and so have better diets; this means that people are healthier and live longer.

4. Outline and explain two ways in which ... [10 marks]

Similar to question 4 in paper 1, this question should be written in prose and take the form of a mini essay. This question has five marks for AO1, three marks for AO2 and two marks for AO3. So, there is a focus on knowing studies, concepts, ideas and policies, but equally it is important to apply this knowledge and weigh up different arguments. You are expected to write in prose, so this is a mini essay which needs to be organised into paragraphs.

5. Applying material from Item A and your knowledge, evaluate ... [20 marks]

In this question, there are eight marks for AO1, six marks for AO2 and six marks for AO3, so as well as using relevant studies, concepts, policies and theories, it is important to create a discussion and debate. It is important to read the item as it gives important clues about the views you will be expected to include. The item may also require that you define a concept that is being described. If you are discussing different views in this question, you need to discuss their strengths and weaknesses.

There are examples of this type of question at the end of each section of each topic.

Do	Avoid
Use the item at least once. For example, say 'as referred to in the item'	Copying the item out in your essay; just refer to the ideas in it
Make sure that your essay has a clear structure, a beginning, middle and end	Listing points; work on creating a flowing and discursive debate
Unpack or explain what concepts mean when you use them. Define them accurately and show how they link to the debate	Describing issues; make sure you link them to the question and make them relevant to the topic
Refer to contemporary issues or research	Simply writing what you know about a topic
Come to a clear conclusion, looking at both sides of the argument	Spend too long looking at one view; make sure you give a balanced argument

Table 8.3 General advice on how to approach these questions

Key terms

Absolute poverty: Not having basic necessities of life. It is usually based on a 'poverty line' of a fixed basic minimum income below which effective human life cannot be maintained.

Academies: State-funded schools in England; these are self-governing and most are constituted as registered charities or operated by other educational charities and may receive additional financial support from personal or corporate sponsors. They must meet the same national curriculum core subject requirements as other state schools and are subject to inspection by Ofsted. Introduced in 2000 under New Labour but expanded by Conservative–Liberal Democrat Coalition government (2010–2015).

Access: The process of gaining entry to a group of people to be researched.

Achieved identity: The identity that a person creates through their lifetime.

Age patriarchy: The idea that children are controlled by adults, as a result of their forced dependency on adults.

Ageing population: A process which increases the proportion of old people within the total population. It is one of the main challenges of this century and affects or will affect both developed and developing countries.

Ageing population: the increasing numbers of the population aged 65 or over while there are a decreasing number of children under 16.

Ageism: Prejudice or discrimination against a particular age group, especially the elderly.

Agency: Behaviour that is self-motivated and associated with the concept of voluntarism, whereby actions are derived from choice rather than structures.

Alternative medicine: Similar to complementary medicine, but viewed by its practitioners as a substitute for conventional biomedical medicine.

Altruism: Working to serve the community rather than for self-interest.

Anomie: Concept associated with Durkheim that translates as normlessness, applying when individuals are insufficiently integrated into society's norms and values.

Anti-school subculture: A set of values shared by a group of pupils within a school that run counter to the values of the school.

Ascribed identity: The identity that other people, or society, might impose on individual.

Aversion therapy: Psychological attempt at changing people's behaviour by showing images of what they desire while inducing pain at the same time.

Beanpole families: Multi-generational family with three or more generations (Brannen).

Bedroom culture: The subcultures created by girls which allow them to develop communication skills that are valued within school.

Big pharma: Nickname applied to the powerful global pharmaceutical industry which seems to operate primarily to make profit rather than from a benevolent desire to eradicate disease. Indeed, they seek to medicalise as many activities as possible in order to create a market for their drugs.

Big Society: Term associated with PM David Cameron that advocates the individual responsibility of each citizen to recognise and engage in their civil duties. Cameron naively felt this would bind society together in a classic Durkheimian manner, while permitting further dismantling of the state's provision of services.

Big stories/meta-narratives: What postmodernists call theories like functionalism and Marxism. Such theories attempt to explain how society as a structure works.

Biographical approaches: An approach to research that is focused on the detail of individual lives. Therefore life histories becomes the main focus and source of data for the research.

Biological determinism: A belief that human behaviour is controlled solely by an individual's genes or some component of physiology.

Birth rate: The number of live births per 1000 of the population per year.

Bisexuality: A sexual orientation or sexual attraction towards people of both sexes.

Black magic roundabout: Term coined by Steve Craine to refer to the carousel of unemployment, government training schemes and informal economy that deprived young people are subject to. He notes how many 'fall off' into crime and single parenthood.

Blended family: A step-family where two single-parent families become joined.

Blue collar: A rather outdated and less frequently used term for workers in manual work. The term derives from the blue overalls typically worn in factories in the past to contrast it with the white collars of the shirts worn by those who worked in offices.

Body mass index: A globally used measurement of comparative body weight to height. It is calculated as body mass divided by height squared. BMI is then expressed in numerical units.

Bottom-up theories: These are micro-theories, generally interpretivist, which seek to understand human behaviour by examining how individuals interpret what is going on around them.

Bourgeoisie: The dominant social class in the Marxist dichotomous view. The bourgeoisie own and control the means of production (factories and land).

Camera obscura: A camera obscura projects a 360 degree moving image on to a table, but everything is inverted back-to-front. Marx used the analogy of the camera obscura to show how ideology distorted reality by making circumstances 'appear upside down' and 'inverting' our perception. Ideology therefore promotes false consciousness by altering people's perception of the world – their objective social reality.

Capitalism: A society based on private property, which is divided into social classes. The family structure and roles support this economic arrangement.

Capitalists: The class of owners of the means of production in industrial societies whose primary purpose is to make profits.

Care Quality Commission (CQC): Agency commissioned by the government to inspect hospitals, care homes, GPs, dentists and the care received by people living at home. The CQC's remit is to ensure all care provided in the UK meets national standards.

Causal relationships: When one thing is the direct cause of another.

Child-centred society: A society in which the needs of children are seen as a priority.

Chronic illnesses: Long-term, debilitating illnesses for which there is generally no cure.

Church school: A school which is committed to Christian beliefs.

Class consciousness: An awareness in members of a social class of their real interests.

Clinical autonomy: The practice by doctors of using their professional judgement to withhold information from patients about their medical condition.

Clinical Commissioning Group (CCG): Groups comprised mainly of GPs who receive the bulk of the NHS budget in order to purchase health care treatment for their patients. All GP practices now belong to a CCG, but CCGs include other health professionals, such as practice nurses.

Clinical freedom: The power of the medical profession to take whatever action they consider to be best practice and to protect their own self-interest.

Clinical gaze: Term associated with Michel Foucault to describe the constant judgemental surveillance we are all subject to by others in society that makes us self-conscious about our identity.

Clinical iceberg: Concept associated with Verbrugge and Ascione to describe how most illness is hidden, like the submerged part of an iceberg.

Closed questions: Questions with a determined set of fixed answers, often in the form of multiple choices.

Cohabiting couples: Couples who live together but are not married.

Cohort: A group of people with a shared characteristic.

Collective conscience: Term associated with Émile Durkheim that refers to the shared moral values that serve to enforce social integration and order in society.

Collective identity: Refers to an individual's sense of belonging to a group or collective.

Collectivism: The idea that the social group is more important than school or school work, and that therefore believes that friendship groups are more important than, for example, getting homework done.

Commodification: The transformation of goods and services, as well as ideas or other entities that normally may not be considered goods, into a commodity.

Commodities: Anything which can be bought or sold. In capitalist society, according to Marx, this extends to people and their labour.

Communism: An equal society, without social classes or class conflict, in which the means of production are the common property of all.

Compensatory education policies: Government guidelines, laws or plans which seek to give all children an equal chance of success in education.

Complementary medicine: Similar to alternative medicine but often delivered in parallel with conventional biomedical medicine.

Comprehensive school: A state school that does not select its intake on the basis of academic achievement or aptitude. First began in 1946 but expanded and much more common from 1965.

Conflict sociologists: Supporters of approaches such as Marxism and feminism that focus on divisions and tensions that occur when groups and individuals compete over power or scarce resources.

Conflict theories: Perspectives which focus on the inequalities and conflict between various groups in society.

Confluent love: A relationship in which people hope to have a high degree of emotional intimacy, not neccesarily for life but as long as they are fulfilled and happy.

Consensus theories: Perspectives which regard society as having a beneficial effect on the individual and social groups.

Co-parenting: New style of parenting in which parents who no longer live together share parenting responsibilities.

Core values: The most important and fundamental values of any group of people or society.

Correlations: When a mutual relationship exists between two things.

Correspondence principle: The Marxist idea that school and education are similar and that education is preparation for the world of work.

Cosmopolitanism: Free from local, provincial or national ideas, prejudices or attachments; at home all over the world.

Covert: When research is carried out without the knowledge or informed consent of the group being studied.

Cross-section survey: This is effectively a 'snapshot' survey taken at a moment in time, using a sample that should reflect the characteristics of the target population.

Cultural capital: The Marxist idea that a particular set of tastes, values, interests and knowledge lead to material rewards and success.

Cultural deprivation theory: A theory that suggests that the working class lacks the appropriate norms, values and attitudes that lead to educational success.

Cultural deprivation: The lack of appropriate norms and values which lead to success in education.

Cultural diversity: The existence of a variety of cultural or ethnic groups within a society.

Cultural expectations: Norms and values of that are maintained by a social group.

Cultural factors: Explanations centred on lifestyle and individual choices.

Cultural universals: Elements, patterns, traits or institutions that are common to all human cultures worldwide.

Culture clash: Where working-class pupils feel less comfortable within the middle-class culture of the school, making it harder for them to adapt to the school environment and thus succeed.

Culture of dependency: New Right view that some people have a way of life in which they rely on state benefits rather than aspire to work.

Culture of poverty: A social theory that expands on the cycle of poverty and blames deprivation on the attitudes and values of the poor themselves. It attracted criticism for ignoring structural factors.

Death rate or **mortality rate**: It is normally expressed as the number of deaths per 1000 of the population.

Death rate: The number of deaths per 1000 of the population per year.

Deductive approach: Knowledge is gained by starting with a theory and testing it against evidence.

Dependency culture: A belief that the benefit system actually encourages recipients to live off welfare rather than work. In reality people may be worse off financially working rather than staying on benefits.

Dependency ratio: The percentage of dependent people (not of working age) divided by the number of people of working age (economically active). (The proportion of dependents per 100 working-age population).

Dependency ratio: A measure showing the number of dependents (aged 0-14 and over the age of 65) to the total population (aged 15-64).

Dependent variable: The thing that is being measured/affected in the experiment. It responds to the independent variable.

Deprivation index: Method of measuring poverty used by Peter Townsend. He used ten everyday activities and measured to what extent people participated in each as an indication of relative poverty.

Developed world: High-income countries with mass consumption societies, widespread welfare provision, education and health services for their populations.

Developing world: These are the low- and middle-income countries that do not yet have developed economies and a mass-consumption society for the majority of the population.

Diaspora: The movement or displacement of an ethnic population – which retains cultural and emotional ties – from its original homeland. The term is used to describe the experience of movement and to analyse the social, cultural and political formations that result from it. Diaspora refers to the process of cultural dispersal.

Disability: A physical or mental impairment which has a substantial and long-term adverse effect on a person's ability to carry out normal day-to-day activities. The socio-political definition of disability is: the disadvantage or restriction of activity caused by a contemporary social organisation which takes no or little account of people who have physical impairments and thus excludes them from mainstream social activities.

Discourse: Concept associated with Foucault to describe how language shapes our thinking. At any one moment in time a dominant 'way of seeing' exists, shaping our understanding. However, this could be replaced by another discourse in the future.

Discrimination: The unjust/unfair or prejudicial treatment of different categories of people, especially on the grounds of race, age or sex.

Disneyisation: Term coined by Bryman to reflect how processes originally observed in Disney's theme parks have spread across many other workplaces.

Diversionary institutions: Marxist term for institutions in society that serve to reinforce false consciousness by distracting people's minds from the exploitative and unequal nature of society. Examples would include the family, education, religion and the media.

Diversity: The variety of options and choices available in society.

Divorce: The legal termination of marriage.

Dual burden: When a person has paid work but is also responsible for domestic labour, often resulting in unreasonable pressure being placed on them.

Economic asset: The idea that in the past children were seen to contribute to the household.

Economic burden: The idea that children are financially dependant on their parents.

Economic relations: The way that different groups relate to the economy and work.

Economy, the: An institution which is connected to the regulation of wealth and income, which the family adapts to in various ways.

Egalitarian relationships: Relationships that are considered to be equal.

Elaborated language code: A way of speaking which involves complex sentence structure, a wide vocabulary and is context free; associated with the middle class.

Embeddedness: Refers to the specific view of how a particular relationship is seen by the individual, the social networks it may lead to as well as the way the relationship is perceived publically.

Emigration: The movement of people from an area.

Emotion work: Term originally associated with Duncombe and Marsden who point out the considerable 'work' women in particular engage in within the family supporting partners, maintaining relationships and comforting children.

Empirical: When evidence is subject to test and measurement in an objective manner through supporting data.

Empty nest: A family where the children have left home, just the parent/s at home.

Empty shell: A couple living together but not emotionally committed to one another.

Enlightenment: Period between the first and fourth quarters of the eighteenth century when 'reason replaced faith' and paved the way for the modernisation of society into one increasingly explained in terms of rationality, science and technology.

Entrepreneur: Term for risk-taking business people who are driven by a desire to make money.

e-scaped medicine: Term coined by Sarah Nettleton to reflect the growing use of ICT in medical diagnosis and treatment.

Ethnic identity: The process by which individuals and groups see themselves or are seen by others, in terms of their unique cultural charactersitics.

Ethnicity: The particular cultural beliefs, practices and lifestyles that makes a group unique to the rest of society. Ethnicity should not be confused with race.

Ethnocentric curriculum: A curriculum which regards British culture as superior to other cultures and does not value the contribution of other cultures.

Eugenics: Selective breeding programmes or forced sterilisation of women in order to improve the 'quality' of a population. Examples include Nazi Germany's pursuit of the Aryan race.

Extended family: Two or more generations of family members with additions beyond the nuclear family; horizontal means of the same generation (aunties and uncles/cousins) or vertical meaning grandparents are included. The classic extended family are kin who live in the same household or close proximity; the modified extended family includes kin who are geographically dispersed but maintain regular contact through social networking, for example.

External factors: Experiences and factors that occur outside school that reinforce particular patterns in achievement.

Faith school: A school in the UK that teaches a general curriculum but with a particular religious character or having formal links with a religious organisation. Promoted in 2004 by New Labour but in existence for centuries.

False consciousness: Marxist term that refers to the proletariat's ignorance of their true oppressed class position, a situation that actually causes them to support the economic system of capitalism that is exploiting them.

Falsification: Process advocated by Popper for researchers to constantly try to disprove a hypothesis no matter how many times it proves true. This demonstrates rigour and objectivity being applied to the research process.

Family: A group of people related by kinship ties, relations of blood, marriage, civil partnership or adoption. Note that most families will live in a household but not all households are families.

Fatalistic: The view that we are powerless to do anything other than what we actually do. Taking life as it comes.

Feminine: Possession of the qualities traditionally associated with women.

Feral child (or **wild child**): One who, from a very young age, has lived in isolation from human contact, unaware of human social behaviour and unexposed to language.

Fertility rate: The average number of children a woman would have if she experienced the age-specific fertility rates for a particular year throughout her childbearing life.

Folk culture: Refers to the culture of ordinary people, particularly those living in pre-industrial societies. Examples include traditional folk songs and stories that have been handed down from generation to generation.

Fordism: A term coined by Antonio Gramsci associated closely with the period and process of modernism and the mass production techniques of Henry Ford. It refers to the application of mass production techniques (typically on an assembly line) for the production of standardised commodities for mass consumption.

Free school: A school in England funded by taxpayers that is free to attend but which is not controlled by a local authority.

Fundamentalism: A return to the literal meaning of religious texts and associated behaviour.

Further education: Educational provision for 16–18 year olds.

Gatekeeper: An individual who must be negotiated with in order to gain access to a group to be researched.

Gender: Socially constructed ideas about what it means to be a man or a woman in a specific time and place.

Gender relations: The nature of relationships between men and women in terms of responsibilities, power and decision-making.

Gender role: Socialisation is the process by which boys and girls are socialised into feminine and masculine modes of behaviour.

Gender socialisation: The tendency for boys and girls to be socialised differently.

Gendered identity: The way we see ourselves and are seen by others in relation to culturally constructed ideas of what it means to be a man or woman.

Generalisability: When the findings of a study can be applied to wider society.

Generation: A group of people born and living during the same time.

Glass ceiling: Barrier of prejudice and discrimination that stops women, ethnic minorities and the working classes from accessing top jobs. It is 'glass' because people can see the jobs, but cannot penetrate the barrier.

Global culture: The way cultures in different countries of the world have become more alike, sharing increasingly similar consumer products and ways of life.

Global south: Made up of Africa, Latin America, developing Asia and the Middle East.

Globalisation: Term that refers to the increased global interconnectedness of economic, cultural and political structures due to the exchange of views, products and ideas, and other forms of culture.

Going native: Term which describes the process whereby researchers get too close to their subject matter, a danger especially in covert participant observation. The result is they can become positively biased and over-sympathetic to the group.

Grammar school: A secondary school which requires pupils to pass the 11+ to attend.

Grand theories: The big structural theories of how society works as a system associated with macro-theories like functionalism and Marxism.

Habitus: The cultural framework and set of ideas possessed by each social class into which people are socialised and which influences their tastes in music, newspapers, films and so on.

Hawthorne effect: Term for the so-called observer or experimenter effect discovered by Elton Mayo following his experiments at the Hawthorne plant in the USA. It refers to how groups may respond in unexpected ways simply because they know they are being studied.

Hegemony: Concept associated with Antonio Gramsci to explain how dominant groups maintain power through the subtle use of ideas to win the consent of subordinated groups. Ordinary people are led to believe that the prevailing order is somehow natural and normal and therefore justified.

Heterogeneity: A society or group that includes individuals of differing ethnicities, cultural backgrounds, sexes or ages.

Heterosexuality: A sexual orientation towards people of the opposite sex.

Hidden curriculum: Everything that is taught informally and is not a part of the formal curriculum, for example respecting authority

Hidden economy: Also known as the 'black market' or 'informal economy' because all work sidesteps formal obligations like paying taxes by being paid 'cash in hand'.

High culture: Specialist cultural products seen as having lasting artistic or literary value, which are particularly admired and approved of by intellectual elites and predominantly the upper and middle class.

High modernity: Term favoured by sociologists like Anthony Giddens over postmodernity in order to stress the continuities society still has with modernity.

Historical documents: Term for non-contemporary documents. Usually they are decades or centuries old, such as parish records or census data. However, they can also refer to data from a few years ago, such as school inspection reports.

Homogenisation: The removal of cultural differences, so that all cultures are increasingly similar.

Homogeneous: When a group shares the same characteristics.

Homophobia: An irrational fear of or aversion to homosexuals.

Homosexuality: A sexual orientation towards people of the same sex, with lesbian women attracted to other women, and gay men attracted to other men.

Household: Either one person living alone or a group of people who live at the same address and share living arrangements, for example bills, meals and chores.

Hybrid identity: An identity formed from a 'mix' of two or more other identities.

Iatrogenesis: Term associated with Ivan Illich that refers to any sickness or physical disability caused by the actions of a doctor.

Identity: How individuals see and define themselves and how other people see and define them.

Ideological state apparatus: Term associated with Louis Althusser for socialising agencies that perpetuate ideas that promote false consciousness among the proletariat.

Immediate gratification: The desire to have fun straight away rather than e.g. doing homework first.

Immigration: The movement of people into an area for more than one year.

Impairment: Lacking all or part of a limb, or having a defective limb, organ or mechanism of the body.

Income: The incoming flow of resources over time in terms of money that is either earned from employment or unearned from assets of wealth such as shares, land or financial capital.

In-depth interviews: An intimate form of interview that involves a close exchange of information.

Independent variable: The 'input' which can be modified by the experimenter to determine or affect the dependent variable.

Individualism: Emphasises the importance of the individual, for example the individual's freedom, interests, rights, needs, or beliefs, against the predominance of other institutions in regulating the individual's behavior, such as the state or the church.

Infant mortality rate (IMR): The number of deaths of infants aged between 0 and 1 in a year per 1000 live births in the same year.

Initiation rites: A rite of passage marking entrance or acceptance into a group or society. It could also be a formal admission to adulthood in a community.

Institutional racism: Intentional or unintentional discrimination that occurs at an organisational level.

Institutionalisation: The process by which members of institutions adapt through a combination of social control and socialisation to adhere to its norms, values and, in particular, its rules.

Institutions: Organisations that help society function smoothly.

Internal factors: Experiences and factors that occur in the school which reinforce particular patterns in achievement.

Internalise: To make something internal; to incorporate it in oneself.

Interpretivism: Theoretical approach that explains human behaviour through the interpretation of the meanings that lie behind individual actions. It is closely associated with interactionism.

Intersectionality: A recognition by sociologists that individuals are the result of a complex set of social characteristics such as social class, gender, ethnicity, age and region.

Inverse care law: Term that describes how deprived areas often have the poorest provision of health care services and facilities. Affluent areas often have better resources and doctor–patient ratios.

Labelling: An interpretivist concept which means to attach meaning to behaviour, which can be positive or negative. Highlighted particularly by Howard Becker.

Lagged adaptation: The time delay between women working full-time and men taking more responsibility for domestic work.

Lay: Term that means anything that is applied to ordinary people.

Legitimise: To make something seem fair.

Life chances: The chances of obtaining those things defined as desirable and of avoiding those things defined as undesirable in a society.

Life course: A culturally defined sequence of age categories that people are normally expected to pass through as they progress from birth to death.

Life expectancy: The average number of years a person is expected to live.

Life chances: Weberian concept for opportunities in later life, such as educational success, employment, earnings and health chances.

Literature search: The collation of previous research on a given subject matter that is currently being researched.

Living apart together (LAT): Families or couples who do not live together, usually for work reasons.

Lobby system: Any attempt to influence decisions made by officials in the government. Lobbyists act on behalf of big business, pressure groups and voluntary organisations.

Lone-person household: A person living alone through choice, divorce or bereavement.

Longitudinal survey: This is a survey that is undertaken over time. It therefore allows trends to be identified and comparisons to be made over a period of years.

Macro-sociology: Grand theories such as functionalism or Marxism, where the focus is on how society works as a system made up of interdependent parts. Understanding of human behaviour derives through a comprehension of how this system works and impacts on individuals.

Malingering: When people pretend to be ill when, in fact, they are healthy.

Marginalisation: The process whereby some people are pushed to the margins or edges of society by poverty, lack of education, disability, racism and so on.

Marketable wealth: Assets that belong to individuals that they could dispose of relatively easily without affecting their lifestyle significantly.

Marketisation: Where market forces are introduced into education, which results in running the school like a business.

Marriage: Legally binding contract between two people.

Masculinity: Possession of the qualities/characteristics traditionally associated with men.

Mass culture: Seen as less worthy than high culture or folk culture. It is a product of the mass media and includes popular feature films, TV soap operas and pop music. Critics of mass culture see it as debasing for individuals and destructive for the fabric of society.

Master status: A status which overrides all other features of a person's social standing; a person is judged solely in terms of one defining characteristic.

Material deprivation: The lack of things that money can buy which lead to educational success.

Material factors: Structural factors within society that impact on life chances.

Matrifocal family: Female-headed families, no adult male.

McDonaldisation: Term coined by Ritzer to describe how processes employed by McDonald's fast-food chain have spread across many other workplaces. The key features are efficiency, calculability, predictability and control.

Means of production: The key resources necessary for producing society's goods, such as land, factories and machinery.

Mechanical solidarity: Term associated with Durkheim that refers to pre-industrial societies characterised by tight-knit communities, common roles and a strong sense of shared values.

Median band: This is the income that divides the income distribution into two social groups, half earning income about that level and half earning income below that level.

Medicalisation: The process by which human conditions and problems come to be defined and treated as medical conditions, and thus become the subject of medical study, diagnosis, prevention or treatment.

Meritocracy: Term for a society where rewards are based on merit, talent and effort. Those at the top are seen as justly rewarded in terms of income, wealth and status; the most demanding roles are occupied by the most talented people.

Meta-humiliation: Term that describes the loss of dignity experienced by people living in poverty, exacerbated because their deprivation is experienced amid great and blatant wealth.

Meta-narratives: What theories like functionalism and Marxism are called by postmodernists. Such theories attempt to explain how society as a structure works.

Meta-study: This involves using a significant amount of published secondary material on a given subject.

Micro-level: A small-scale approach associated with the interpretive/interactionist perspective, where the focus is on the individual rather than the wider social structures.

Micro-sociology: Term for sociological perspectives where the starting point to understanding human behaviour lies with an analysis of individual motivations, actions and meanings.

Migration: The movement of people from one area to another.

Modernity: Era of industrialisation and urbanisation that followed the period of the Enlightenment. It is consequently characterised by rational thinking of science and technology. Modernity saw change as progress.

Monogamous nuclear family: The family which perpetuates capitalism, made up of a heterosexual couple and their children who are faithful to each other.

Moral decay: The idea that people are less willing to take responsibility for themselves resulting in a breakdown of traditional attitudes towards family life, leading to family breakdown, the inadequate socialisation of children and antisocial behaviour.

Moral density: Term associated with Durkheim to refer to how progression of the division of labour causes individual parts to extend beyond their limits and act and react on one another.

Mortification of self: Term associated with Erving Goffman meaning how the self or individuality dies as a result of institutionalisation from being treated in a psychiatric hospital.

Myth of meritocracy: A Marxist concept which argues that the idea of fairness and equality of opportunity is a lie, put in place to stop people from challenging the system.

Nanny state: A government which intervenes in many aspect of family life, which results in people being less likely to take responsibility for their own actions.

Nationalism: A sense of pride and commitment to a nation, and a very strong sense of national identity.

Natural change: The difference between the numbers of births and deaths; natural change is a key determinant of population size and growth.

Naturalistic: When behaviour is normal and not subject to the presence or activities of the researcher.

NEETs: Young people who are not in employment, education or training. It is estimated by the World Health Organization (2013) that there are more than 1 million NEETs in the UK.

Neo-conventional family: A contemporary version of the nuclear family where both parents work and share the domestic work. This family may be cohabiting or married. Children are biologically related or adopted (Chester, 1985).

Nepotism: Giving favours, such as providing employment, solely on the basis of family connections.

Net migration: The difference between immigrants and emigrants of an area in a period of time (usually divided by 1000 inhabitants). A positive value would represent more people entering the country/area than leaving it, while a negative value means more are leaving.

New international division of labour: Concept developed by Frobel *et al* to describe the global labour market whereby workers compete globally for jobs through the location of industries. Domestic workers are also increasingly under threat from migrant workers.

Non-domicile: People who live or work temporarily in the UK but are domiciled in another, even though they can spend most of their time in the UK. An example of a 'non-dom' is Lord Rothermere whose family owns the very nationalistic *Daily Mail* through various tax companies in Bermuda. Non-domicile status normally means that people are exempt from paying most taxes in the UK.

Norms: Specific guidelines for action in particular social situations.

Nuclear family: A two-generation family with two adults and their dependent children (biological or adopted). According to Murdock the universal nuclear family is characterised by common residence, economic co-operation, approved (hetero)sexual relationships and reproduction.

Nurture: Generally means upbringing or training. All of the environmental factors, after conception, that shape an individual's expressed characteristics and behaviour.

Objectivism: The assumption that social structures that can be studied independently from individual social actors.

Organic analogy: The comparison of society to a body. The analogy was originally made by Herbert Spencer and developed by Émile Durkheim.

Organic solidarity: Term associated with Durkheim that refers to an individualistic industrial society where people are connected by the wider structure, but isolated in terms of their competition with each other.

Othering: Derogative way of looking down at people who are considered not one of 'us'. Being seen as an 'other' is to be defined negatively and as an outsider.

Overt: When it is clear and obvious that research is being carried out with the knowledge of those being studied.

Oxbridge: Collective term for Oxford and Cambridge universities.

Paradigm: Kuhn uses the term to refer to a viewpoint in science that holds widespread support until a revolution in thinking occurs and it is replaced by another widely supported shared view.

Parentocracy: A system where parents are powerful in shaping education.

Participant observation: Research method that involves observing people by becoming a member of their group and studying them from within. Observation can be overt or covert.

Particularistic standards: The idea that in the family a person may be treated differently from another family member depending on their attributes.

Patriarchal family: Male-headed/dominated family.

Patriarchal ideology: A set of ideas which reflect male dominance.

Patriarchy: Male-dominated society.

Person-centred care: Where frontline health care professionals provide high-quality care by treating patients as individuals, respecting confidentiality, collaborating in making choices, gaining consent and maintaining clear professional boundaries.

Personal documents: Sources of data usually derived from very private documents such as diaries, memoirs and letters. They can be very informative and high in validity, but also subjective and biased.

Personal wealth: Assets that are owned by individuals. Housing and pensions can be included in this definition of wealth.

Phenomenology: Micro-sociological approach developed by Alfred Schütz and Edmund Husserl. It explains human behaviour through the interpretation of the meanings that lie behind individual actions. It is often referred to as interpretivism.

Physical efficiency: Term used by Seebohm Rowntree to refer to a fixed basic minimum income below which effective human life cannot be maintained.

Pilot study: Small-scale study conducted before the main research in order to check whether the research is firstly feasible and secondly to identify any problems that need to be resolved with regard to the research design.

Placebo effect: When healing occurs following dummy treatment or prescribing. It demonstrates the power the mind has to influence the body in order to produce healing.

Policies: A range of actions, plans or laws which attempt to resolve perceived social problems.

Popular culture: Often used in a similar way to the term 'mass culture'. Popular culture includes any cultural products appreciated by large numbers of ordinary people, for example, TV programmes, mass-market films and popular fiction.

Positivism: Scientific approach to collecting data that is centred on the collection of objective facts.

Postcode lottery: Term that refers to the random provision of NHS treatments and care according to where people live.

Post-Fordism: If Fordism is about mass production and consumption, post-Fordism is about tailoring production to individual requirements and niche markets. It involves 'just in time' production or, ideally, production to order, involving the need for a flexible workforce that adapts quickly to demand levels.

Postmodernity: Term used by postmodernists to describe contemporary society. They see society as having distinctly different characteristics to the era of modernity which it replaced, with more diverse and less stable family structures and a greater negotiation of family roles.

Poverty line: Demarcation boundary of a calculated level of income. People with income levels below this are assumed to be unable to purchase basic necessities so are classified as living in poverty.

Power relationships: Understanding the family through exploring who has most control and autonomy in the family.

Pre-modernity: Period of history before the modern era where society was characterised by myths, legends, superstition and traditions.

Present time orientation: Focusing on the immediate situation rather than considering long-term aims. Therefore not bothering to put school work first and wanting to have fun without considering the possible long-term consequences.

Primary care trusts: These no longer exist, having been replaced by Clinical Commissioning Groups (CCGs), but used to commission services on behalf of patients.

Primary data: Collected first-hand by the researcher.

Primary socialisation: The internalisation of norms and values that takes place in the early years of life.

Primogeniture: Inheritance through the male line, common within capitalism until quite recently. Maintains wealth in the ruling classes and therefore the class structure.

Private schools/independent schools/public schools: Fee-paying schools that may or may not follow the national curriculum.

Proletarianisation: Marxist term for a growing identification by the middle class with working class identity, status and values. It reflects a growing class consciousness as proletariat.

Proletariat: The subordinate social class in the Marxist dichotomous classification. The proletariat own nothing except their labour power, which they sell for a wage to the owners of the means of production.

Pseudo-patients: Normal people masquerading as patients when they are in fact healthy.

Public documents: Documents issued for public knowledge or authenticated by a public officer and made available for public reference and use.

Push and pull factors: Reasons which may cause people to move away from an area or attract them to move to a particular area.

Qualitative data: Concerned with words that express meaning and the emotions of respondents.

Quantitative data: Concerned with factual information and typically expressed as numerical content.

Questionnaire: Survey method where questions are written down with respondents answering either in their own writing or on a computer if survey is electronic.

Race: Supposed biological differences between different groups.

Racism: Treating people differently on the basis of their ethnic origin.

Rationalisation: The replacement of traditions, values and emotions as motivators for behaviour in society with rational, calculated ones.

Realism: An approach to research that embraces elements of positivism and interpretivism through the collection of quantitative and qualitative data.

Reconstituted families: A family where one or more of the partners brings children from another relationship.

Relationality: The twinfold process whereby biology becomes less important in defining family relationships while the importance of relationships and interactions is crucial to defining the individual.

Relative autonomy: Neo-Marxist idea that institutions are not under the direct control of the ruling capitalist class. This gives the impression that such institutions are independent, when in reality the economic power of owning capital ensures that the ruling class actually do have control.

Relative poverty: Definition of poverty that is based on living standards judged against normal or average living standards across society.

Relativism: The belief held by postmodernists that there is no such thing as objective reality or truth. The only truth is the pluralistic character of knowledge.

Reliable: The extent to which research, if repeated, would achieve the same results.

Representative: The extent to which a sample can be said to reflect the social characteristics of a larger group (target population) from which it is drawn.

Reserve army of labour: Marxist term that refers to the least secure section of the workforce; employed when the economy is buoyant and dumped when demand for labour is low.

Restricted language code: A way of speaking which involves limited vocabulary, short, broken sentences and is context bound; associated with the working class.

Rigorous: Strict and meticulous approach to doing research.

Role allocation: The idea that education sifts and sorts people into the correct job or role in society.

Role model: Someone who inspires others to try hard to reach a similar status. They display patterns of behaviour which others copy and model their own behaviour on.

Roles: The patterns of behaviour that are expected from individuals in society.

Same-sex families: Families headed by lesbian or gay couples, with or without children.

Sample size: The size of the sample used in research. Clearly the size can play an important part in determining the representativeness of the sample, and hence the researcher's ability to generalise.

Sample: A small group of people, representative of the larger group, used when the target population is too big to research everyone.

Scientific management: A time and motion approach to manufacturing associated with F.W. Taylor (hence sometimes called 'Taylorism') whereby the most efficient production methods are calculated in order to minimise costs and maximise profits.

Secondary data: Collected by people other than the research team, so already exists.

Secondary labour market: Term associated with Anthony Giddens to refer to low status jobs of a flexible, insecure and part-time nature.

Secondary socialisation: The internalisation of norms and values that takes place beyond the family and continues throughout life.

Secularisation: The process whereby religion has less and less influence over people's lives.

Selective education: Any form of criteria that students need to meet in order to go to a particular school. The criteria vary, for example, the 11+ test introduced in the Butler Act involved an IQ test which determined if a student went to a grammar school or not.

Selective school: A school which has some specific form of entry criteria.

Self-fulfilling prophecy: Where a student begins to internalise a label given to them and begins to act out the label.

Self-surveillance: Describes the self-critical inward gaze that acts as a form of self-imposed social control.

Separation: When a couple's relationship somes to an end.

Service industries: Industries that do not manufacture goods but provide intangible services such as retailing, tourism, finance, health, caring, education, etc.

Sex: Refers to the biological features that differentiate men from women.

Sexism: Prejudice or discrimination against people (especially women) because of their sex.

Sexual identity: Self-recognition of one's sexual orientation and sexual behaviours and the meanings one places on them.

Sexual orientation: The type of people that individuals are either physically or romantically attracted to, such as those of the same or opposite sex.

Sexuality: People's sexual characteristics and their sexual behaviour.

Simulacrum: Term associated with the postmodernist Jean Baudrillard that means the blurring of dreams and reality.

Single/lone-parent family: Families headed by one adult; over 90 per cent are of these are headed by women.

Social blurring: The idea that the division between children and adults has become less clear.

Social care services: Support provided by local authorities (LAs) to support patients, and sometimes their families and carers, because of illness, disability, old age or poverty. LAs often subcontract these services to independent care providers.

Social class: A broad group of people who share a similar economic situation, such as occupation, income and ownership of wealth.

Social closure: A system whereby members of a group can act to prevent others from joining the group.

Social construct: Something built or created by society, for example childhood.

Social construction: When something is built up by cultural ideas, rather than being naturally produced.

Social control: Refers to the various methods used to persuade or force individuals to conform to the dominant social norms and values of a society or group.

Social democratic: Political ideology that is centred on the responsibility of the state to help bring about a more equal and fairer society. A key feature of a social democratic society is a well-established and extensive provision of state welfare in the form of health, education and benefits.

Social exclusion: When members of society are denied participation in mainstream activities that other people generally take for granted, such as good housing, transport, health, environment, leisure, etc.

Social facts: External and measurable structural factors that can have a real impact on individuals. Term originally associated with Durkheim to refer to features of objective reality.

Social identities: One's sense of self as a member of a social group (or groups).

Social institutions: The structures that make up society, such as the family, education, religion, work and media.

Social mobility: The ability of individuals, families or households, etc. to change between social strata; a change in social status either upwards or downwards.

Social policy: A plan or course of action put in place by governments which attempts to solve particular social problems.

Social quality: A concept associated with Alan Walker and two Dutch colleagues. Since its creation it has influenced the EU's social policy agenda. Social quality is the extent to which people are able to participate in society under conditions that enhance their individual potential and well-being. It measures the extent to which people are able to thrive.

Social roles: One's position and responsibilities in society, which are largely determined in modern, developed nations by occupation and family position.

Social solidarity: The idea that people feel they belong to society, they feel part of a group.

Social wage: Goods in kind provided as benefits that supplement family income.

Socialisation: The process by which norms and values are transmitted and learned.

Socially constructed: The way something is created through individual, social and cultural interpretations, perceptions and actions of people.

Specialist schools: A government initiative which encouraged secondary schools in England to specialise in certain areas of the curriculum to boost achievement, started in 1994 and continued and expanded under New Labour. When the Coalition government took power in May 2010 the scheme was ended and funding was absorbed into general school budgets.

Spurious interaction: When engagement with people is shaped primarily by the way they have been defined and interpreted.

State, the: A group of institutions which govern and regulate family life to some degree.

Stigma: When people are negatively labelled with a marginalising characteristic which then serves to marks them out as different from others in society.

Stigmatise: A negative marker that is applied to the identity of individuals or groups.

Stigmatised identity: An identity that is in some way undesirable or demeaning and stops an individual or group being fully accepted by society.

Structural factors: External factors which shape individual behaviour in a deterministic way.

Structured interview: Formal interview where pre-written questions are all asked to every respondent in the same order. Data received tends to be quantitative in nature.

Subculture: A smaller culture held by a group of people within the main culture of a society, in some ways different from the main culture but with many aspects in common.

Subjectivism: The view that social structures cannot be studied separately from the study of individual social actors.

Symbolic violence: Where working-class pupils experience almost unconscious types of cultural and social domination in everyday social habits.

Symmetrical family: The widely criticised idea that relationships are becoming more similar and that men and women are beginning to share domestic labour more equally.

Target population: The whole group that is being researched.

Theoretical perspectives: Different views about society that seek to explain change.

Third Way: A middle-way, advocated by New Labour, that embraced elements of both dependency-based ideas, such as the New Right's personal responsibility, and exclusion-based ideas, similar to the social democratic welfare support for the most vulnerable in society.

Top-down theories: These are macro-theories, generally structuralist in nature, that seek to understand human behaviour by examining society as a whole and how individuals fit into its institutions.

Toxic childhood: The idea that technology is being used as a substitute for good parenting.

Trade liberalisation: The encouragement of free trade through the abolition of import tariffs, quotas and export subsidies.

Transsexual: A person who emotionally and psychologically feels that they belong to the opposite sex.

Transnational corporations: Another name for multinational corporations. These traditionally have their head office in the developed world but undertake or outsource their manufacturing to the developing world, where they have been accused of exploiting workers.

Triangulation: Using multiple research methods.

Underclass: Group of very deprived people whose experiences are so distinctly different from the rest of society – including the working class – that they constitute a class in their own right.

Unearned income: Income derived from the ownership of assets rather than from personal toil. This is a key source of income for the rich who use their abundance of assets to contribute significantly to their income.

Unit of consumption: The idea that the family buy things together as a family, for the family, thus providing jobs for people offering family goods and services, and therefore supporting capitalism.

Universalistic standards: The idea that everyone is treated fairly and equally regardless of who they are.

Unstructured interview: An informal interview that takes the form of a conversation. It is designed to build up a close rapport between interviewer and interviewee in order that they open up and provide rich qualitative data.

Valid: The extent to which research is true to life.

Value consensus: Agreement within a society about how society should be ordered.

Values: General beliefs about what is right or wrong or worth striving for.

Variables: Something in research that is subject to change, such as income, status or popularity.

Verstehen: German word that translates as 'understand'. In sociological terms, Weber used it in the context of researchers putting themselves in the shoes of the people they were studying.

Victim blaming: When individuals are blamed for their problems, such blaming the poor for their poverty or the sick for their illness. This approach is favoured by the New Right and right-wing governments.

Vocational education: Education directly linked to a particular occupation or job.

Wealth: A measure of the value of all of the assets of worth owned by a person.

White collar: Simplistic term for office workers. The term derives from the white shirts typically worn in contrast to the blue overalls of factory workers.

World Health Organisation: The public health body of the United Nations.

Zero-hours contract: When individuals are employed but only contracted to work when employers need their services. This results in considerable insecurity of income and the ability to budget.

References

Chapter 1

Althusser, L. (2005) *For Marx*. London: Verso.

Archer, L., Hollingworth, S. and Halsall, A. (2007) 'University's not for me – I'm a Nike person': Urban, working-class young people's negotiations of 'style', identity and educational engagement, *Sociology*, *41* (2), 219–37.

Bandura, A. (1965) Influences of models' reinforcement contingencies on the acquisition of imitative responses. *Journal of Personality and Social Psychology*, *1* (6), 589–95.

Barker, E. (1984) *The Making of a Moonie: Choice or Brainwashing?* Oxford: Blackwell.

Baudrillard, J. (1983) *Simulations*. New York: Semiotext(e).

Benz, T. (2014) Flanking gestures: Gender and emotion in fieldwork. *Sociological Research Online*, *19* (2), 15.

Blundell, J. and Griffiths, J. (2008) *Sociology Since 2000*. Cooksbridge: Connect Publications.

Bruce, S. (1999) *Sociology: A Very Short Introduction*. Oxford: Oxford University Press.

Bryman, A. (2004) *Sociological Research Methods*. Oxford: Oxford University Press.

Callender, C. and Jackson, J. (2005) Does the fear of debt deter students from higher education? *Journal of Social Policy*, *34* (4), 509–540.

Charles, N. and Kerr, M. (1988) *Women, Food and Families*. Manchester: Manchester University Press.

Davidson, E. (2013) Between edges and margins: Exploring 'ordinary' young people's experiences of the everyday antisocial. *Sociological Research Online*, *18* (1), 5.

Economic and Social Research Council (2014) Methodologies: What makes good research? (www.esrc.ac.uk/_images/what-makes-good-research_tcm8-32679.pdf).

Egan, D. (2013) *Poverty and low educational achievement in Wales*. Joseph Rowntree Foundation (www.jrf.org.uk/publications/poverty-education-wales).

Ellis-Sloan, K. (2013) Teenage mothers, stigma and their 'presentations of self'. *Sociological Research Online*, *19* (1), 9.

Farrelly, T. (2014) *Diaries in Social Research*. Academia.edu (www.academia.edu/4127274/Diaries_in_Social_Research).

Fulcher, J. and Scott, J. (2011) *Sociology* (4th edition). Oxford: Oxford University Press.

Gabb, J. (2008) *Researching Intimacy in Families*. Basingstoke: Palgrave Macmillan.

Garrod, J. (2012) The white working class. *Sociology Review*, *22* (1).

Giddens, A. (1976) *New Rules of Sociological Method: A Positive Critique of Interpretative Sociologies*. London: Hutchinson.

Glasgow Media Group (1976) *Bad News*. London: Routledge and Kegan Paul.

Glasgow Media Group (1980) *More Bad News*. London: Routledge and Kegan Paul.

Glasgow Media Group (1982) *Really Bad News*. London: Writers and Readers Co-operative.

Glasgow Media Group (1985) *War & Peace News*. Milton Keynes: Open University Press.

Glasgow Media Group and Eldridge, J. (ed.) (1993) *Getting The Message: News, Truth and Power*. London: Routledge.

Goffman, E. (1961) *Asylums: Essays on the Social Situation of Mental Patients and Other Inmates*. Harmondsworth: Penguin.

Gouldner, A.W. (1962) Anti-minotaur: The myth of a value-free sociology. *Social Problems*, *9* (3), 199–213.

Griffin, J.H. (1961) *Black Like Me*. Boston: Houghton Mifflin.

Humphreys, L. (1975) *Tearoom Trade: Impersonal Sex in Public Places*. New York: Aldine Transaction.

Jolly, N. (2014) In this world but not of it: Midwives, Amish, and the politics of power. *Sociological Research Online*, *19* (2), 13.

Kellett, M. and Dar, A. (2007) *Children researching links between poverty and literacy*. Joseph Rowntree Foundation (www.jrf.org.uk/publications/children-researching-links-between-poverty-and-literacy).

Krishan, L.A. and Hoon, H.L. (2002) Diaries: Listening to 'voices' from the multicultural classroom. *ELT Journal, 56* (3), 227–239.

Locke, R. and Jones, G. (2012) Tackling underage drinking: Reflections on one local authority's response. *Education & Health, 30* (1), 6–10.

Lyotard, J-F. (1984) *The Postmodern Condition: A Report on Knowledge.* Manchester: Manchester University Press.

Marmot, M. *et al* (2014) *English Longitudinal Study of Ageing: Waves 0-6, 1998-2013* (21st edition). Colchester, Essex: UK Data Archive.

McLuhan, M. (1962) *The Gutenberg Galaxy: The Making of Typographic Man.* Toronto: University of Toronto Press.

Mills, C.W. (1956) *The Power Elite.* Oxford: Oxford University Press.

Mirza, H.S. and Reay, D. (2000) Spaces and Places of Black Educational Desire: Rethinking Black Supplementary Schools as a New Social Movement. *Sociology, 34* (3), 521–544.

Paterson, L. (2013) Education, social attitudes and social participation among adults in Britain. *Sociological Research Online, 19* (1), 17.

Philo, G. and Berry, M. (2004) *Bad News From Israel.* London: Pluto Press.

Philo, G. and Berry, M. (2006) *Israel & Palestine: Competing Histories.* London: Pluto Press.

Philo, G. and Berry, M. (2011) *More Bad News from Israel.* London: Pluto Press.

Popper, K. (1959) *The Logic of Scientific Discovery.* London: Hutchinson.

Raban, J. (1991) *Hunting Mister Heartbreak.* London: Pan.

Roberts, K. (2012) Can sociology make a difference? *Sociology Review, 22* (1), 21–24.

Simpson, P. (2013) Doing ethnography: Research an gay men and ageing. *Sociology Review, 23* (2), 9–11.

Slater, R. (2000). Using life histories to explore change: Women's urban struggles in Cape Town, South Africa. *Gender and Development, 8* (2), 38–46.

Sosu, E. and Ellis, S. (2014) *Closing the attainment gap in Scottish education.* Joseph Rowntree Foundation (www.jrf.org.uk/publications/closing-attainment-gap-scottish-education).

Stahl, G. (2013) Habitus disjunctures, reflexivity and white working-class boys' conceptions of status in learner and social identities. *Sociological Research Online, 18* (3), 2.

Sullivan, A., Ketende, S. and Joshi, H. (2013) Social class and inequalities in early cognitive scores. *Sociology, 47* (6), 1187–1206.

Taylor, S. (1982) *Persons Under Trains.* London: Routledge.

Tombs, S. and Whyte, D. (2003) *Unmasking the Crimes of the Powerful: Scrutinizing State and Corporations.* New York: Peter Lang.

Tudor, A. (2008) *Beyond Empiricism: Philosophy of Science in Sociology.* London: Routledge.

Williams, J. (2013) Why is sociology so important? *Sociology Review, 23* (1).

Willis, P. (1977) *Learning to Labour: How Working Class Kids Get Working Class Jobs.* Saxon House.

Winlow, S. (2001) *Badfellas: Crime, Tradition and New Masculinities.* Oxford: Berg.

Wright, C., Standen, P., John, G., German, G. and Patel, T. (2005) *School exclusion and transition into adulthood in African-Caribbean communities.* Joseph Rowntree Foundation (www.jrf.org.uk/publications/school-exclusion-and-transition-adulthood-african-caribbean-communities).

Wright, R., Brookman, F. and Bennett,T. (2006) The foreground dynamics of street robbery in Britain. *British Journal of Criminology, 46* (1), 1–15.

Chapter 2

Adams, R. (2014) Labour vows to overhaul Michael Gove's A-level reforms. *Guardian,* 11 August.

Althusser, L. (1971) *For Marx.* Harmondsworth, Penguin.

Archer, L., Hollingworth, S. and Halsall, A. (2007) 'University's not for me – I'm a Nike person': Urban, working-class young people's negotiations of 'style', identity and educational engagement, *Sociology, 41* (2), 219–237.

Archer, L., Hollingsworth, S. and Mendick, H. (2010), *Urban Youth and Schooling*, Oxford University Press.

Arnett, G. (2014) GCSE results: Biggest gap in 11 years between boys and girls A*–C pass rate. *Guardian*, 21 August.

Arnot, M., David, M. and Weiner, G (l996) *Educational Reforms and Gender Equality in Schools*. Manchester: Equal Opportunities Commission, Research Discussion Series No. 17.

Ball, S. (1981) *Beachside Comprehensive: A Case Study of Secondary Schooling*. Cambridge: Cambridge University Press.

Becker, H. (1963) *The Outsiders: Studies in the Sociology of Deviance*. (revised 1973) New York: The Free Press.

Bereiter, C. and Engelmann, S. (1966) *Teaching Disadvantaged Children in the Preschool*. Englewood Cliffs, NJ: Prentice Hall.

Bernstein, B. (1971) *Class, Code and Control: Volume 1 – Theoretical Studies Towards a Sociology of Language*. London: Routledge.

Bernstein, B. (1973) *Class, Code and Control: Volume 2 – Applied Studies Towards a Sociology of Language*. London: Routledge.

Bhattacharyya, G., Ison, L. and Blair, M. (2003) *Minority Ethnic Attainment and and Participation in Education and Training: The Evidence*. London: Department for Education and Skills.

Bourdieu, P. (1984) *Distinction: A Social Critique of the Judgement of Taste*. London: Routledge,

Bowles, S. and Gintis, H. (1976) *Schooling in Capitalist America: Educational Reforms and the Contradictions of Economic Life*. New York: Basic Books.

Browne, N. and Ross, C. (1991). In Holland, J., Blair, M. and Sheldon, S. (eds) *Pedagogy: A Reader*.

Cassen, R. and Kingdon, G. (2007) *Tackling low educational achievement*. Joseph Rowntree Foundation (www.jrf.org.uk/sites/files/jrf/2063-education-schools-achievement.pdf).

Chubb, J. and Moe, T. (1990) *Politics, Markets, and America's Schools*. Washington: Brookings Institution Press.

Clark, L. (2010) Chinese and Indian pupils get more top grades at GCSE than British children. *Daily Mail*, 28 March 2010 (www.dailymail.co.uk/news/article-1261415/Chinese-Indian-pupils-grades-GCSE-British-children.html).

Cook, C. (2012) Immigrants have little effect on school standards. *Financial Times*, 18 March 2012.

DCSF (2008) *The Extra Mile – How schools succeed in raising aspirations in deprived communities*. London: Department for Children, Schools and Families.

DCSF (2009) *Gender and Education – Mythbusters. Addressing Gender and Achievement: Myths and Realities*. London: Department for Children, Schools and Families (http://webarchive.nationalarchives.gov.uk/20130401151715/http://www.education.gov.uk/publications/eOrderingDownload/00599-2009BKT-EN.pdf).

Demie, F., Mclean, C. and Lewis, K. (2006) *The Achievement of African Heritage Pupils: Good Practice in Schools*. London: Lambeth Research and Statistics Unit.

DfE (2013) *GCSE and Equivalent Attainment by Pupil Characteristics in England: 2011 to 2012*. London: Department for Education (www.gov.uk/government/uploads/system/uploads/attachment_data/file/219337/sfr04-2013.pdf).

Feinstein, L (2003) Very early evidence. *CentrePiece*, 24–30. (http://cep.lse.ac.uk/pubs/download/CP146.pdf)

Francis, B. (2000a) *Boys, Girls, and Achievement: Addressing the Classroom Issues*. London: Routledge/Falmer.

Francis, B. (2000b) The gendered subject: Students' subject preferences and discussions of gender and subject ability. *Oxford Review of Education*, *26* (1), 35–48.

Fuller, M. (1984) Black girls in a London comprehensive school. In Hammersley, M. and Woods, P. (eds) *Life in School: The Sociology of Pupil Culture*. Milton Keynes: Open University Press.

Geay, C., McNally, S. and Telhaj, S. (2012) *Non-Native Speakers of English in the Classroom: What are the Effects on Pupil Performance?* London: Centre for the Economics of Education (http://cee.lse.ac.uk/ceedps/ceedp137.pdf).

Gillborn, D. and Youdell, D. (2000) *Rationing Education: Policy, Practice, Reform and Equity*. Milton Keynes: Open University Press.

Gorard, S., Rees, G., and Salisbury, J. (1999) Reappraising the apparent underachievement of boys at school. *Gender and Education*, *11* (4), 441–454.

Hargreaves, A. (2008) Kentucky Fried Schooling? *TES*, 12 May (www.tes.co.uk/article. aspx?storycode=12019).

Ingram, N. (2010) School culture and its impact on working-class boys. *Sociology Review*, 20, 2–6.

Kelly, A. (ed.) (1987) *Science for Girls*. Milton Keynes: Open University Press.

Kerr, K. and West, M. (eds) (2010). *Insight 2: Social Inequality: Can Schools Narrow the Gap?* Macclesfield: British Educational Research Association.

Lupton, R. (2005) Parallel lives? Ethnic segregation in schools and neighbourhoods. *Urban Studies*, *42* (7), 1027–1056.

Morrow, R. and Torres, C. (1995) *Social Theory and Education: A Critique of Theories of Social and Cultural Reproduction*. New York: SUNY Press.

National Equality Panel (2010) *An Anatomy of Economic Inequality in the UK: Report of the National Equality Panel* (http://eprints.lse.ac.uk/28344/1/CASEreport60.pdf).

Noon, M. (2007) The fatal flaws of diversity and the business case for ethnic minorities. *Work, Employment & Society*, *21* (4), 773–788.

ONS (2013) *Women in the Labour Market*. London: Office for National Statistics (www. ons.gov.uk/ons/dcp171776_328352.pdf).

Perry, E. and Francis, B. (2010) *The Social Class Gap for Educational Achievement: A Review of the Literature*. London: RSA.

Reay, D. (2012) What would a socially just education system look like? Saving the minnows from the pike. *Journal of Education Policy*, *27* (5). 587–599.

Reilly, N. (2014) Britain's first state funded 'virtual school' could open next year. *Metro*, 29 November.

Rosenthal, R. and Jacobson, L. (1968) *Pygmalion in the Classroom: Teacher Expectation and Pupil's Intellectual Development*. New York: Holt, Rinehart & Winston.

Sewell, T. (1997) *Black Masculinities and Schooling: How Black Boys Survive Modern Schooling* Trentham Books.

Sewell, T. (1998) Loose Cannons. In Epstein, D. *et al* (eds) *Failing Boys?* Milton Keynes: Open University Press.

Sharpe, S. (1994) *Just Like a Girl: How Girls Learn to be Women – From the Seventies to the Nineties*. Harmondsworth: Penguin.

Skelton, C. (2002) Constructing dominant masculinity and negotiating the 'male gaze'. *International Journal of Inclusive Education*, *6* (1), 17–31.

Smart, C. (2013) *A Sociology of Personal Life*, Palgrave.

Sodha, S. and Margo, J. (2010) *Ex Curricula: A generation of disengaged children is waiting in the wings...* London: Demos.

Sugarman, B. (1970) Social class values and behaviour in schools. In Craft, M. (ed.) *Family Class and Education*. London: Longman.

Usher, R., Bryant, I. and Johnston, R. (1997) *Adult Education and the Postmodern Challenge. Learning Beyond the Limits*. London: Routledge.

Warrell, H. (2013) Michael Gove defends Scandinavian-inspired education reforms. *Financial Times*, 3 December.

White, J. (2005) *Towards an Aims-led Curriculum*. London: QCA (http://dera.ioe. ac.uk/9704/1/11482_john_white_towards_an_aims_led_curr.pdf).

Whitty, G. and Young, M. (1976) *Explorations in the Politics of School Knowledge*. Driffield: Nafferton Books.

Willis, P. (1977) *Learning to Labour: How Working Class Kids Get Working Class Jobs*. Saxon House.

Wolf, A. (2011) *Review of Vocational Education – The Wolf Report*. London: Department for Education (www.gov.uk/government/uploads/system/uploads/attachment_data/ file/180504/DFE-00031-2011.pdf).

Younger, M., Warrington, M. and Williams, J. (1999) The gender gap and classroom interactions: Reality and rhetoric? *British Journal of Sociology of Education*, *20* (3), 325–341.

Chapter 3

Asthana, A. (2007) Girls' lessons tailored to suit female brain. *Observer*, 14 October.

Best, L. (1992) Analysis of sex-roles in preschool books. *Sociology Review*: Philip Allan.

Farkas, G. and Beron, K. (2001) *Family Linguistic Culture and Social Reproduction: Verbal Skill from Parent to Child in the Preschool and School*. Washington: Population Association of America conference paper.

Lupton, R. (2004) *Schools in Disadvantaged Areas: Recognising Context and Raising Quality*. London: Centre for Analysis of Social Exclusion, London School of Economics.

Rosenthal, R. and Jacobson, L. (1968) *Pygmalion in the Classroom: Teacher Expectation and Pupil's Intellectual Development*. New York: Holt, Rinehart & Winston.

Roulstone, S., Law, J., Rush, R. Clegg, J. and Peters, T. (2011) *Investigating the Role of Language in Children's Early Educational Outcomes*. London: Department for Education.

Troyna, B. and Hatcher, R. (1992) *Racism in Children's Lives: A Study of Mainly White Primary Schools*. London: Routledge.

Wilkin, A., Kinder, K., White, R., Atkinson, M. and Doherty, P. (2003) *Towards the Development of Extended Schools*. London: National Foundation for Educational Research.

Willis, P. (1977) *Learning to Labour: How Working Class Kids Get Working Class Jobs*. Saxon House.

Wright, C. (1992) *Race Relations in the Primary School*. London: David Fulton Publishers.

Chapter 4

Abercombie, N. and Warde, A. (2000) *Contemporary British Society* (3rd edition). Cambridge: Polity Press.

Abercombie, N. *et al* (1994) *Contemporary British Society*. Cambridge: Polity Press.

Albert, B. (2004) The social model of disability, human rights and development. Disability KaR Research Project: Enabling disabled people to reduce poverty.

Back, L. (1997) *Sociology Review*.

Bates, D. (2011) 'Globalisation of fat stigma': Western ideas of beauty and body size catching on in developing nations. *Daily Mail*, 31 March.

Bauman, Z. and May, T. (2002) *Thinking Sociologically*. Oxford: Blackwell.

Begum-Hossain, M. (2010) My lost Bangladeshi identity. *Guardian*, 1 September.

Blaikie, A. (1999) *Ageing and Popular Culture*. Cambridge: Cambridge University Press.

Bocock, R. (1993) *Consumption*. London: Routledge.

Booher-Jennings, J. (2008). Learning to label: Socialisation, gender, and the hidden curriculum of high-stakes testing. *British Journal of Sociology of Education*, *29*, 149–160.

Bourdieu, P. (1984) *Distinction: A Social Critique of the Judgement of Taste*. London: Routledge,

Bowles, S. and Gintis, H. (1976) *Schooling in Capitalist America: Educational Reforms and the Contradictions of Economic Life*. New York: Basic Books.

Butler, T. and Watt, P.B. (eds) (2007) *Understanding Social Inequality*, London: Sage Publications.

Castells, M. (2004), *The Power of Identity* (2nd edition). Malden, MA: Blackwell Publishing.

Chapman, S. (2010) Nobody loves the middle class. *Sociology Review*.

Charlesworth, S. (1999) *A Phenomenology of Working Class Experience*. Cambridge: Cambridge University Press,

Connell, R.W. (2005) *Masculinities* (revised 2nd edition) Cambridge: Polity Press.

Cooley, C.H. (1998) *On Self and Social Organisation*. Chicago: University of Chicago Press.

Cronin, A. (2007) Sociology and sexuality. *Sociology Review*.

de Beauvoir, S. (1972) *The Second Sex* (translated by H.M. Parshley). New York: Penguin.

Focault, M. (1979) *The History of Sexuality: An Introduction*. Harmondsworth: Penguin.

Giddens, A. (1999) *Runaway World: How Globalisation is Reshaping Our Lives*. London: Profile.

Giddens, A. and Diamond, P. (2005) *The New Egalitarianism*. Cambridge: Polity Press.

Gill, B. (2009) New ethnic identities. *Sociology Review*.

Grice, E. (2006) Cry of an enfant sauvage. *Telegraph*, 17 July.

Hall, M. (2013) Letting children watch hours of TV improves academic ability, study claims. *Telegraph*, 24 June.

Hall, S. (2013). *Representation: Cultural Representations and Signifying Practices* (2nd edition). London: Sage Publications.

Honigsbaun, M. (2013) The future of robotics: in a transhumant world, the disabled will be the ones without prosthetic limbs. *Observer*, 13 June.

Johal, S. (1999) Brimful of Brasia.

Kidd, W. (2002) *Culture and Identity*. Basingstoke: Palgrave Macmillian.

Klein, N. (2000) *No Logo*. London: Flamingo.

Lang, R. (2007) *The Development and Critique of the Social Model of Disability*. London: Leonard Cheshire Disability and Inclusive Development Centre.

Lyotard, J-F. (1984) *The Postmodern Condition: A Report on Knowledge*. Manchester: Manchester University Press.

Mason, D. (2000) *Race and Ethnicity in Modern Britain* (2nd edition. Oxford: Oxford University Press.

Mikkola, M. (2012) Feminist perspectives on sex and gender. In Zalta E.N. (ed.) *The Stanford Encyclopedia of Philosophy* (http://plato.stanford.edu/archives/fall2012/entries/feminism-gender).

Miner, H. (1956) Body ritual among the Nacirema. *American Anthropologist*, *58* (3), 503–507.

Mount, F. (2004) *Mind the Gap: Class in Britain Now*. London: Short Books.

Moxon, D. (2011) Consumer culture and the 2011 'riots'. *Sociological Research Online*, *16* (4), 19.

Nanda, S. (2000) *Gender Diversity: Cross-cultural Variations*. Illinois: Waveland Press.

O'Brien, L. (2013) Britain now has 7 social classes – and working class is a dwindling breed. *Independent*, 3 April.

O'Donnel, M. and Chetty, D. (2008) Culture and identity in sociology. *Sociology Review*.

Oakley, A. (1972) *Sex, Gender and Society*. Aldershot: Arena.

Pilcher, J. (1995) *Age and Generation in Modern Britain*. Oxford: Oxford University Press.

Populus (2011) *Fear and HOPE: A Searchlight Educational Trust Project* (www.fearandhope.org.uk).

Riddell, S. and Watson, N. (2003) *Disability, Culture and Identity*. London: Pearson Education.

Ritzer, G. (2007) *The McDonaldization of Society* (2nd edition). Thousand Oaks, California: Sage Publications.

Savage, M. (2000) *Class Analysis and Social Transformation*. Milton Keynes: Open University Press.

Seabrook, J. (2004) *Consuming Cultures: Globalisation and Local Lives*. UK: New International Publications.

Sen, A. (2002) Does globalisation equal Westernisation? *The Globalist*, 25 March.

Shakespeare, T. (1996) Disability, identity and difference. In Barnes, C. and Mercer, G. (eds) *Exploring the Divide: Illness and Disability*. Leeds: The Disability Press.

Shakespeare, T. (2000) *The Disability Reader: Social Science Perspectives*. London: Continnuum-3PL.

Shakespeare, T. (2006) *Disability Rights and Wrongs*. London: Routledge.

Song, M. (2003) *Choosing Ethnic Identity*. Cambridge: Polity Press.

Taylor, P. (2000) *Investigating Culture and Identity*. London: Collins Educational.

Vincent, J. (2000) Age and old age. In Payne, G. (ed.) *Social Divisions*. London: Macmillan Press.

Williams, R. (1976) *Keywords: A Vocabulary of Culture and Society*. Oxford: Oxford University Press.

Willson, G. (2000) *Understanding Old Age: Critical and Global Perspectives*. London: Sage Publications.

Wintour, P. (2014) David Cameron joins calls for promoting 'British values' in schools. *Guardian*, 15 June.

Wolfe, N. (1991). *The Beauty Myth*. New York: William Morrow.

Wood, J.T. (2009). *Gendered Lives: Communication, Gender, and Culture*. Belmont, CA: Wadsworth.

Chapter 5

Adams, S. (2012) A quarter of all babies born in the UK are the children of immigrants as mothers from Poland, India and Pakistan give birth in record numbers. *Daily Mail*, 25 October.

Allen, D. (2001) Is childhood disappearing? *Studies in Social and Political Thought*, *6* (1).

Aries, P. (1960) *Centuries of Childhood: A Social History of Family Life*. London: Vintage

Barter, C., McCarry, M., Berridge, D. and Evans, K. (2009) *Partner Exploitation and Violence in Teenage Intimate Relationships*. NSPCC/University of Bristol.

Beck, U. (1992) *Risk Society: Towards a New Modernity*. London: Sage Publications.

Bittman, M. Mahmud Rice, J. and Wajcman, J. (2004) Appliances and their impact: the ownership of domestic technology and time spent on household work. *British Journal of Sociology*, *55* (3), 401–423.

Blaikie, A. (1999) *Ageing and Popular Culture*. Cambridge: Cambridge University Press.

Brannen, J. (2003) Towards a typology of intergenerational relations: Continuities and change in families. *Sociological Research Online*, *8*, 2, (www.socresonline.org.uk/8/2/brannen.html).

Chester, R. (1985) The rise of the neo-conventional family. *New Society*, 9 May, 185–188.

Donovan, C., Hester, M. Holmes, J. and McCarry, M. (2006) *Comparing Domestic Abuse in Same Sex and Heterosexual Relationships*. Swindon: Economic and Social Research Council.

Donzelot, J. (1997) *The Policing of Families*. New York: Pantheon Books.

Doucet, A. and Dunne, G. (2000) Heterosexual and lesbian mothers: challenging 'feminine' and 'male' conceptions of mothering in O'Reilly, A. and Abbey , S. (eds) (2000) *Mothers and Daughters: Connection, Empowerment and Transformation*. Rowman and Littlefields.

Duncombe, J. and Marsden, D. (1993) Love and intimacy: The gender division of emotion and 'emotion work'. *Sociology*, *27* (2), 221–241.

ESRC (2013) *A woman's work is never done?* Swindon: Economic and Social Research Council (www.esrc.ac.uk/news-and-events/press-releases/27163/a-womans-work-is-never-done.aspx).

Frederici, S. (2012) *Revolution at Point Zero: Housework, Reproduction, and Feminist Struggle*. Oakland: PM Press.

Gershuny, J. (2008). *Time-use Studies: Daily Life and Social Change*. Full Research Report ESRC End of Award Report, RES-000-23-0704-A. Swindon: Economic and Social Research Council.

Griffiths, R. (1983) *NHS Management Enquiry*. London: HMSO.

Hareven, T. (1978) *Transitions: The Family and the Life Course in Historical Perspective*. New York: Academic Press.

Harkness, S. (2013) Women's employment and household income inequality. In Gornick, J. and Jantii, M. (eds) *Income Inequality: Economic Disparities and the Middle Class in Affluent Countries*. Stanford, CA: Stanford University Press.

Henley, J. (2012) Why are British children so unhappy? *Guardian*, 27 June.

Hirsch, D. (2005) Paying for ourselves as we get older: Rethinking resource allocation. Institute of Actuaries/Oxford Institute of Ageing conference 'Ageing population', 8 September.

http://populationmatters.org/documents/family_sizes.pdf

Kegan Paul/

LSE News Update: Internet safety improving for children in the UK finds new report (www.lse.ac.uk/newsandmedia/news/archives/2012/10/internet.aspx).

McKeown, T. (1962) Reasons for the decline of mortality in England and Wales during the nineteenth century. *Population Studies*, 16, 94–122.

McRobbie, A. and Garber, J. (1975) Girls and subcultures. In Hall, S. and Jefferson, T. (eds) *Resistance Through Rituals: Youth Subcultures in Postwar Britain*. London: Hutchinson.

McVeigh, T. (2012) Forty years of feminism – but women still do most of the housework. *Observer*, 10 March.

Murdock, G.P. (1949) *Social Structure*. New York: Macmillan.

Murray, C. (1984) *Losing Ground: American Social Policy, 1950–1980*. New York: Basic Books

NSPCC (2013) How Safe Are Children 2013 (www.nspcc.org.uk/Inform/research/findings/howsafe/how-safe-2013-report_wdf95435.pdf).

Observer (2014) Single mothers 'do just as good a job as couples'. *Observer*, 19 July (www.theguardian.com/lifeandstyle/2014/jul/19/children-little-affected-by-lone-parenthood).

ONS (2003) Twentieth century mortality trends in England and Wales. *Health Statistics Quarterly*, 18.

ONS (2013) *Families and Households, 2013*. London: Office for National Statistics (www.ons.gov.uk/ons/dcp171778_332633.pdf).

ONS (2013) *Women in the Labour Market*. London: Office for National Statistics (www.ons.gov.uk/ons/dcp171776_328352.pdf).

Pahl, J. (1980) Patterns of money management within marriage. *Journal of Social Policy*, 9 (3), 313–336.

Pahl, J. (2000) Couples and their money: Patterns of accounting and accountability in the domestic economy. *Accounting, Auditing & Accountability Journal*, 13 (4), 502–517.

Palmer, S (2007) *Toxic Childhood: How The Modern World Is Damaging Our Children And What We Can Do About It*. London: Orion.

Parsons, T. (1951) *The Social System*. Glencoe, IL: The Free Press.

R.N., Rapoport, M.P. and Fogarty, R. (eds) *Families in Britain*. London: Routledge & Rapoport, R. and Rapoport, R.N. (1982) British Families in Transition. In Rapoport, Scott, J.L. and Plagnol, A.C. (2007) Work–family conflict and well-being in Northern Europe. In Scott, J.L., Dex, S. and Plagnol, A.C. (eds) *Gendered Lives: Gender Inequalities in Production and Reproduction*. Cheltenham: Edward Elgar Publishing.

Smart, C. and Neal, B. (1999) *Family Fragments?* Cambridge: Polity Press.

Stacey, J. (1997) *In the Name of the Family: Rethinking Family Values in the Postmodern Age*. Boston: Beacon Press.

Strinati, D. and Wagg, S. (1992) *Come on Down? Popular Media Culture in Post War Britain*. London: Routledge.

UNICEF Summary of Children's Human Rights (www.unicef.org.uk/Documents/Publication-pdfs/UNCRC_summary.pdf)

van de Rijt, A. and Buskens, V. (2006) Dynamics of networks if everyone strives for structural holes. *American Journal of Sociology*, 114 (2), 371–407.

van de Rijt, A. and Buskens, V. (2006) Trust in intimate relationships: The increased importance of embeddedness for marriage in the United States. *Rationality and Society*, 18 (2), 123–156.

Wagg, S. and Pilcher, J. (eds) (2014) *Thatcher's Grandchildren? Politics and Childhood in the Twenty-First Century*. Basingstoke: Palgrave.

Weeks, J., Donovan, C. and Heaphey, B. (1999) Everyday experiments: Narratives of non-heterosexual relationships. In Silva, E.B. and Smart, C. (eds) *The New Family?* London: Sage Publications.

Wilson, G. (2001) *Globalisation and Support in Old Age*. London: LSE Research Online (http://eprints.lse.ac.uk/archive/00001032).

Womack, S. (2007) Drop age of consent to 14, says academic. *Telegraph*, 16 February (www.telegraph.co.uk/news/uknews/1542843/Drop-age-of-consent-to-14-says-academic.html).

Zaretsky, E. (1986) *Capitalism, the Family and Personal Life*. New York: HarperCollins.

Zimmerman, S. (2001) *Family Policy: Constructed Solutions to Family Problems*. London: Sage Publications.

Chapter 6

Althusser, L. (1971) *For Marx*. Harmondsworth: Penguin.

Appleby, J. and Deeming, C. (2001) Inverse care law. *Health Service Journal*, 111 (5760), 37.

Arber, S., McKinlay, J., Adams, A., Marceau, L., Link, C. and O'Donnell, A. (2006) Patient Characteristics and Inequalities in Doctors' Diagnostic and management Strategies relating to CHD: A video-simulation experiment. *Social Science and Medicine*, 62 (1), 103–115.

Arnett, G. (2014) The wealthiest women get 20 more years of life in good health than the most deprived. *Guardian*, 14 March.

ASH (2014) *Smoking Statistics* (www.ash.org.uk/files/documents/ASH_93.pdf).

Bartley, M. and Blane, D. (2008). Inequality and social class. In Scambler, G. (ed.) *Sociology as Applied to Medicine*. London: Elsevier.

Barton, L. (1996) *Disability and Society: Emerging Issues and Insights*, London: Longman.

Beattie, J. (2013) NHS hospitals performing record number of private operations in 'two-tier' health service. *Daily Mail*, 20 September.

Becker, H. (1963) *The Outsiders, Studies in the Sociology of Deviance*. New York: The Free Press.

Benoit, C., Shumka, L., Vallance, K., Hallgrímsdóttir, H. ,Phillips, R., Kobayashi, K., Hankivsky, O., Reid, C. and Brief, E. (2009) Explaining the health gap experienced by girls and women in Canada: A social determinants of health perspective. *Sociological Research Online*, 14 (5), 9.

Black, D., Morris, J., Smith, C. and Townsend, P. (1980) *Inequalities in Health: Report of a Research Working Group*. London: Department of Health and Social Security.

Blackhouse, S. (2013) Learned resentment. *Nursing Standard*, 27 (46) 26–27.

Blaxter, M. (2010) *Health* (2nd edition). Cambridge: Polity Press.

Bloomer, N. (2014) Thousands left in limbo in benefit appeals system grinding to a halt. *Guardian*, 18 June.

Booth, M. (2014) *The Almost Nearly Perfect People*. London: Jonathan Cape.

Boseley, S. (2009) The future is female – how women are transforming face of the health service. *Guardian*, 3 June.

Brown, G.W. and Harris, T.O. (1978) *Social Origins of Depression: A Study of Psychiatric Disorder in Women*. London: Tavistock.

Buchanan, K. (2013) Cruel workplace mental health stigma must end. *Sunday Express*, 29 December.

Buck, D, and Frosini, F. (2012) *Clustering of Unhealthy Behaviours Over Time*. London: King's Fund.

Cant, S. and Sharma, U. (1998) Reflexivity, ethnography and the professions (complementary medicine). Watching you, watching me, watching you (and writing about both of us). *Sociological Review*, 46 (2), 244–263.

Cant, S., Watts, P. and Ruston, A. (2012) The rise and fall of complementary medicine in National Health Service hospitals in England. *Complementary Therapies in Clinical Practice*, 18 (3), 135–139.

Cattell, V.R. (2001) Poor people, poor places, and poor health: the mediating role of social networks and social capital. *Social Science & Medicine*, 52 (10), 1501–1516.

Chang, H., Wallis, M. and Tiralongo, E. (2012) Predictors of complementary and alternative medicine use by people with type 2 diabetes. *Journal of Advanced Nursing*, 68 (6), 1256–1266.

Chesler, P. (2005) *Women and Madness*. New York: Palgrave Macmillan.

Culzac, N. (2014) NHS means British health care rated top out of 11 Western countries with US coming last. Independent, 17 June.

ESRC (2014) *Cutting NHS Costs with Mental Health Investments*. Swindon: Economic and Social Research Council (www.esrc.ac.uk/_images/ESRC_Evidence_Briefing_Mental_health_NHS_tcm8-26241.pdf).

Everett, C. (2011) Does the NHS pay staff too much? *Guardian*, 22 June.

Ferrie et al (2004) *Work Stress and Health: the Whitehall II Study*. London: CCSU/Cabinet Office.

Foucault, M. (1963) *The Birth of the Clinic: An Archaeology of Perception*. New York: Pantheon.

Foucault, M. (1971) *Madness and Civilisation*. London: Tavistock.

Gillian, A. (2006) In Iraq, life expectancy is 67, minutes form Glasgow city centre, it's 54. *Guardian*, 21 January.

GMC (2014) *List of Registered Medical Practitioners – Statistics* (www.gmc-uk.org/doctors/register/search_stats.asp).

Goffman, E. (1961) *Asylums: Essays on the Social Situation of Mental Patients and Other Inmates*. New York: Doubleday Anchor.

Goffman, E. (1963) *Stigma: Notes on the Management of Spoiled Identity*. Englewood Cliffs: Prentice Hall.

Goffman, E. (1963) *Stigma: Some Notes on the Management of Spoiled Identity*. Englewood Cliffs NJ: Prentice Hall.

Goldacre, B. (2012) *Bad Pharma: How Drug Companies Mislead Doctors and Harm Patients*. London: Fourth Estate.

Green, E., Griffiths, F. and Thompson, D. (2006) 'Are my bones normal doctor?' The role of technology in understanding and communicating health risks for midlife women. *Sociological Research Online*, 11, 4.

Health and Social Care Information Centre (2014) *Statistics on Obesity, Physical Activity and Diet – England, 2014* (www.hscic.gov.uk/catalogue/PUB13648).

Laing, R.D. and Esterson, A. (1964) *Sanity, Madness and the Family*. Harmondsworth: Penguin.

Law, J. (2006) *Big Pharma: How the World's Biggest Drugs Companies Control Illnesses*. London: Constable

Lawrence, F. (2012) When privatisation of GP practices goes wrong. *Guardian*, 19 December.

Littlejohn, L., Campbell, J. Collins-McNeil, J. and Khayile, T. (2012) Nursing shortage: A comparative analysis. *International Journal of Nursing*, 1 (1), 22–27.

Mallett, R., Leff, J., Bhugra, D., Pang, D. and Zhao, J.H. (2002) Social environment, ethnicity and schizophrenia: A case-control study. *Social Psychiatry and Psychiatric Epidemiology*, 37, 329–335.

McKeown, T. (1976) *The Role of Medicine: Dream, Mirage, or Nemesis?* London: Nuffield Provincial Hospitals Trust.

McKinley, J.R. (1985) Towards the proletarianisation of physicians. *International Journal of Health Services*, 5, 161–195.

McNutt, H. (2004) Hidden pleasures. *Guardian*, 13 October.

Meilke, J. (2012) Poor pregnant women missing out on free vitamin D, health official claim. *Guardian*, 3 February.

Mental Health Foundation (2013) *Crossing Boundaries: Improving Integrated Care for People with Mental Health Problems* (www.mentalhealth.org.uk/content/assets/PDF/publications/crossing-boundaries.pdf?view=Standard).

Mental Health Foundation (2014) *Stigma and Discrimination*. (www.mentalhealth.org.uk/help-information/mental-health-a-z/S/stigma-discrimination).

Morris, D.B. (2000) *Illness and Culture in the Postmodern Age*. Santiago: University of California Press.

Morrison, A. (2012) *Psychology Medicine*, 42 (5), 1049–1056.

Navarro, V. (2004) *The Political and Social Contexts of Health*. New York: Baywood.

Nazroo, J.Y. (2003) Patterns of and explanations for ethnic inequalities in health. In Mason, D. (ed.) *Explaining Ethnic Differences: Changing Patterns of Disadvantage in Britain*. Bristol: Policy Press.

Nettleton, S. (2013) *The Sociology of Health and Illness* (3rd edition). Cambridge: Polity Press.

Oliver, M. (1983) *Social Work and Disabled People*. Basingstoke: Macmillan.

Oliver, M. (1990) *The Politics of Disablement*. London: Macmillan.

ONS (2003) *Better or Worse: A Longitudinal Study of the Mental Health of Adults in Great Britain*. London: Office for National Statistics.

ONS (2011) *2010-based Period and Cohort Life Expectancy Tables*. London: Office for National Statistics (www.ons.gov.uk/ons/rel/lifetables/period-and-cohort-life-expectancy-tables/2010-based/p-and-c-le.html).

ONS (2014a) *Sickness Absence in the Labour Market*, 2014. London: Office for National Statistics (www.ons.gov.uk/ons/dcp171776_353899.pdf).

ONS (2014b) *Census 2011 Analysis, Disability Free Life Expectancy at Birth, at Age 50 and at Age 65: Clinical Commissioning Groups (CCGs) 2010–12*. London: Office for National Statistics (www.ons.gov.uk/ons/rel/census/2011-census-analysis/disability-free-life-expectancy-at-birth--at-age-50-and-at-age-65--clinical-commissioning-groups--ccgs--2010-12/rpt.html).

Parliamentary Office of Science and Technology (2007) Ethnicity and Health. *Postnote*, 276 (www.parliament.uk/documents/post/postpn276.pdf).

Parsons, T. (1951) *The Social System*. Glencoe, IL: The Free Press.

Pickett, K. and Wilkinson, R. (2014) A 25 year gap between the life expectancy of rich and poor Londoners is a further indictment of our unequal society. *Independent*, 15 January.

Pickett, K., Oliver, J. and Wilkinson, R. (2006) Income inequality and the prevalence of mental health. *Journal of Epidemiology & Community Health*, 60, 646–647.

Ramesh, R. (2011) NHS postcode lottery survey reveals wide UK disparities. *Guardian*, 9 December.

RCN (2013) *Dignity in Health Care for People with Learning Disabilities*. London: RCN (www.rcn.org.uk/__data/assets/pdf_file/0010/296209/004439.pdf).

Rehman, H. and Owen, D. (2013) *Mental Health Survey of Ethnic Minorities*. London: Ethnos. (www.time-to-change.org.uk/sites/default/files/TTC_Final%20 Report_ETHNOS_summary_1.pdf).

Rigby, N. and Garde, A. (2012) Junk food has no place in the Olympic lineup. *Guardian*, 17 July.

Rosenhan, D.L. (1973) On being sane in insane places. *Science*, *179*, 250–258.

Rowlingson, K. (2011) *Does Income Inequality Cause Health and Social Problems?* Joseph Rowntree Foundation (www. jrf.org.uk/publications/income-inequality-health-social-problems).

Senior, M. and Viveash, B. (1998) *Health & Illness*. London: Macmillan.

Shakespeare, T. and Watson, N. (2002) The social model of disability: An outdated ideology? *Research in Social Science and Disability*, *2*, 9–28.

Shaw, C. and Ward, L. (2014) Dark thoughts: Why mental illness is on the rise in academia. *Guardian*, 6 March.

Shaw, M. *et al* (2008) Health and Disability. In Ridge, T. and Wright, S. (eds) *Understanding Poverty, Wealth and Inequality: Policies and Prospects*. Bristol: Policy Press.

Slorach, R. (2012) *Disability Austerity and Resistance*. London: Socialist Workers Party.

Szasz, T. (1961) *The Myth of Mental Illness: Foundations of a Theory of Personal Conduct*. New York: Harper & Row.

Szasz, T.S. and Hollender, M.H. (1956) A contribution to the philosophy of medicine; the basic models of the doctor-patient relationship. *AMA Archive of Internal Medicine*, *97* (5), 585–592.

Townsend, P. and Davidson, N. (1982) *Inequalities in Health: The Black Report*. Harmondsworth: Penguin.

Tudor-Hart, J. (1971) The Inverse Care Law. *Lancet*, *1*, 405–412.

Twigg, J. (2006). *The Body in Health and Social Care*. Houndmills: Palgrave Macmillan.

Verbrugge, L.M. and Ascione, F.J. (1987) Exploring the iceberg: Common symptoms and how people care for them. *Medical Care*, *25* (6), 539–569.

WHO (2014) *Facts on Health Inequities and Their Causes* (www.who.int/features/factfiles/health_inequities/en/).

WHO (2015) *Disability and Health*. Fact Sheet No. 352 (www.who.int/mediacentre/factsheets/fs352/en/).

Wilkinson, R. and Pickett, K. (2010) *The Spirit Level: Why More Equality is Better for Everyone*. London: Penguin.

Williams, S., Annandale, E. and Tritter, J. (1998) The sociology of health and illness at the turn of the century: Back to the future? *Sociological Research Online*, *3*, 4.

Witz, A. (1992) *Professions and Patriarchy*. London: Routledge.

Wolf, N. (1990). *The Beauty Myth*. London: Vintage.

Young, J. (2007) *The Vertigo of Late Modernity*. London: Sage Publications.

Chapter 7

Aldridge, H., Kenway, P., MacInnes, T. and Parekh, A. (2012) *Monitoring Poverty and Social Exclusion 2012*. London: New Policy Institute.

Barnard, H. (2013) Talk of 'men deserts' doesn't help families or break down gender stereotyping at work. Joseph Rowntree Foundation (www.jrf.org.uk/blog/2013/06/%E2%80%98men-deserts%E2%80%99-families-gender-stereotyping).

Barnard, H. and Turner, C. (2011) *Poverty and Ethnicity: A Review of Evidence*. Joseph Rowntree Foundation (www.jrf.org.uk/sites/files/jrf/poverty-ethnicity-evidence-summary.pdf).

Bartholomew, J. (2006) *The Welfare State We're In*. London: Politico's Publishing.

Bauman, Z. (2000) *Liquid Modernity*. London: Routledge.

Bauman, Z. (2007) *Consuming Life*. Cambridge: Polity Press.

Baumberg, B., Bell, K. and Gaffney, D. (2012) Scroungers, fraudsters and parasites: How media coverage affects our view of benefit claimants. *New Statesman*, 20 November.

Baumberg, B., Bell, K. and Gaffney, D., with Deacon, R., Hood, C. and Sage, D. (2014) *Benefits Stigma in Britain*. Canterbury: Elizabeth Finn Care/University of Kent.

Bell, D. (1973) *The Coming of a Post-Industrial Society*. London: Heinemann.

Blanchflower, D. (2014) You won't hear the Chancellor boasting about the biggest drop in living standards since the war. *Independent on Sunday*, 20 July.

Blauner, R. (1964) *Alienation and Freedom: The Factory Worker and His Industry*. Chicago: Chicago University Press.

Bradshaw, J. (ed.) (1993) *Budget Standards for the United Kingdom*. Aldershot: Avebury.

Braverman, H. (1974) *Labour and Monopoly Capital*. New York: Free Press.

Brinkley, I., Jones, K. and Lee, N. (2013) *The Gender Jobs Split*. London: Touchstone Extras.

Bryman, A. (2004) *The Disneyisation of Society* (2nd edition). London: Sage.

Burns, J. (2014) Deeply elitist UK locks out diversity at top. BBC News, 28 August (www.bbc.co.uk/news/education-28953881).

Buttler, F. (2013) *What determines subjective poverty? An evaluation of the link between relative income poverty measures and subjective economic stress within the EU*. Oldenburg: *Horizontal Europeanisation* (www.horizontal-europeanization.eu/downloads/pre-prints/PP_HoEu_2013-01_buttler_subjective_poverty_0.pdf).

Byrne, D. (1999) *Social Exclusion*. Buckingham: Open University Press.

Carey, M. (2007) White-collar proletariat? Braverman, the deskilling/upskilling of social work and the paradoxical life of the agency care manager. *Journal of Social Work*, 7 (1), 93–114.

Castles, F., Nauman, I. and Pierson, C. (eds) (2012) *The Welfare State Reader* (3rd edition). Cambridge: Polity Press.

Craine, S. (1997) The black magic roundabout: Cyclical transitions, social exclusions and alternative careers. In MacDonald, R. (ed.) *Youth, the 'Underclass' and Social Exclusion*. London: Routledge.

Cribb, J., Joyce, R. and Phillips, D. (2012) *Living Standards, Poverty and Inequality in the UK: 2012*. London: Institute for Fiscal Studies.

Cumming, E. and Henry, W.E. (1961) *Growing Old: The Process of Disengagement*. New York: Basic Books.

D'Arcy, C. (2013) *300,000 More Children in Absolute Poverty Than Last Year – and It's Likely to Get Worse*. Joseph Rowntree Foundation (www.jrf.org.uk/blog/2013/06/more-children-in-absolute-poverty).

Dahrendorf, R. (1959) *Class and Class Conflict in an Industrial Society*. London: Routledge and Kegan Paul.

Duncombe, J. and Marsden, D. (1993) Love and intimacy: The gender division of emotion and 'emotion work'. *Sociology*, 27 (2), 221–241.

DWP (2013) *Fraud and Error in the Benefit System*. London, Department for Work and Pensions.

Editorial (2014) Money madness: Income inequality has reached outrageous levels. *Independent on Sunday*, 17 August.

Edsall, T.B. (2013) Why can't America be Sweden? *New York Times*, 29 May.

Fagin, L. and Little, M. (1984) *The Forsaken Families*. London: Penguin.

Flaherty, J., Veit-Wilson, J. and Dornan, P. (2004) *Poverty: The Facts* (5th edition). London: Child Poverty Action Group.

Frobel, J., Heinrichs, J. and Kreye, O. (1981) *The New International Division of Labour*. Cambridge: Cambridge University Press.

Gander, K. (2014) David Cameron defined hiring Nepalese nanny. *Independent*, 13 March.

Gans, H.J. (1971) The uses of poverty: The poor pay all. *Social Policy*, July/August, 20–24.

Garrod, J. (2014a) Europe's 'lost generation'. *Sociology Review*, 23, 4.

Garrod, J. (2014b) What cost our desire for cheap clothes? *Sociology Review*, 23, 3.

Giddens, A. (1999) *Runaway World: How Globalisation is Reshaping Our Lives*. London: Profile.

Gratton, L. (2011) *The Shift: The Future of Work is Already Here*. London: Collins.

Gratton, L. (2012) The globalisation of work – and people. *BBC News*, 7 September (www.bbc.co.uk/news/business-19476254).

Grint, K. (2008) *Leadership, Management and Command: Rethinking D-Day*. Basingstoke: Palgrave.

Grint, K. (2010) *Leadership: A Very Short Introduction*. Oxford: Oxford University Press.

Grint, K. (2014) The hedgehog and the fox: Leadership lessons from D-Day. *Leadership*, 10, 240–260.

Hamilton, K. (2012) Low income families and coping through brands. *Sociology*, 46 (1), 74–90.

Hockey, J. and James, A. (1993) *Growing Up and Growing Old: Ageing and Dependency in the Life Course*. London: Sage.

Hutton, W. (2012) Globalisation can work, but only with a unified international plan. *Observer*, 29 January.

Kempson, E. (1996) *Life on Low Income*. Joseph Rowntree Foundation (www.jrf.org.uk/publications/life-low-income)

Kollewe, J. (2014) Wealth of Britain's richest 1,000 people hits new high of £519bn. *Guardian*, 18 May.

Lewis, O., Lewis, R. and Mead, M. (1959) *Five Families: Mexican Case Studies in the Culture of Poverty*. New York: Basic Books.

Lewis, P. (2011) Upskilling the workers will not upskill the work. Why the dominant economic framework limits child poverty reduction in the UK. *Journal of Social Policy*, 40, 535–556.

MacInnes, T., Aldridge, H., Bushe, S., Kenway, P. and Tinson, A. (2013) *Monitoring Poverty and Social Exclusion*. London: New Policy Institute and Joseph Rowntree Foundation.

Mack, J. and Lansley, S. (1985, 1990) *Poor Britain*. London: George Allen & Unwin.

Marsland, D. (1996) *Welfare or Welfare State*. Basingstoke: Macmillan.

Marsland, D. (2003) *Real Welfare: Self-Reliance or State Dependency? Economic Notes No. 96*. London: Libertarian Alliance.

Martin, D. (2013) The £148,000 cost of raising a child until they are 18: Figure rises by 4% in a year. *Daily Mail*, 19 August.

Miliband, R. (1974) Politics and poverty. In Wedderburn, D. (ed.) *Poverty, Inequality and Class Structure*. Cambridge: Cambridge University Press.

Morley, D. (1986) *Family Television, Cultural Power and Domestic Leisure*. London: Comedia.

Murray, C. (1989) *In Pursuit: Of Happiness and Good Government*. London: Simon & Schuster.

ONS, (2013) *Graduates in the UK Labour Market 2013*. London: Office for National Statistics (www.ons.gov.uk/ons/rel/lmac/graduates-in-the-labour-market/2013/rpt---graduates-in-the-uk-labour-market-2013.html).

Oxfam (2014a) *A Tale of Two Britains: Inequality in the UK*. Oxfam Media Briefing (http://policy-practice.oxfam.org.uk/publications/a-tale-of-two-britains-inequality-in-the-uk-314152).

Oxfam (2014b) *Working for the Few*. Oxfam Media Briefing (http://policy-practice. oxfam.org.uk/publications/working-for-the-few-political-capture-and-economic- inequality-311312).

Oxfam (2015) *Wealth: Having it All and Wanting More*. Oxford: Oxfam.

Palmer, G. (2004) *Poverty in the Rural East of England*. London: New Policy Institute.

Parekh, A., MacInnes, T. and Kenway, P. (2010) *Monitoring Poverty and Social Exclusion*. Joseph Rowntree Foundation (www.jrf.org.uk/publications/monitoring-poverty-2010).

Pierson, C. (2004) *Late Industrializers and the Development of the Welfare State*. Social Policy and Development Programme Paper Number 16. New York: United Nations Research Institute for Social Development.

Pierson, C. (2006) *Beyond the Welfare State: The New Political Economy of Welfare*. Cambridge: Polity Press.

Piore, M.J. (1995) *Beyond Individualism*. Cambridge, MA: Harvard University Press.

Platt, L. (2006) *Pay Gaps: The Position of Ethnic Minority Women and Men Moving On Up? Ethnic Minority Women and Work*. Manchester: Equal Opportunities Commission.

Press Association (2013) Red Cross to distribute food to Britain's poor and hungry. *Guardian*, 11 October.

Reiner, R. (2007) *Law and Order: An Honest Citizen's Guide to Crime and Control*. Cambridge: Polity Press.

Ritzer, G. (2007) *The McDonaldization of Society* (2nd edition). Thousand Oaks, California: Sage Publications.

Saunders, P. (1981) *Social Theory and the Urban Question*. London: Hutchinson.

Schmuecker, K. (2013) *Traditional Breadwinner Couples the Largest Group in Poverty in Low-pay Britain*. Joseph Rowntree Foundation (www.jrf.org.uk/blog/2013/11/ breadwinner-couples-largest-group-poverty).

Shildrick, T. and Macdonald, R. (2015) Talking about poverty. *Sociology Review*, 24 (3).

Siddique, H. (2014) Bedroom tax: The housing benefit reform explained. *Guardian*, 17 July.

Slorach, R. (2012) *Disability Austerity and Resistance*. London: Socialist Workers Party.

Sparrow, A. (2014) UK's child poverty goals unattainable, says report. *Guardian*, 9 June.

Swaim, P. and Torres, R. (2005) Jobs and globalisation: Towards policies that work. *OECD Observer*, 250 (www.oecdobserver.org/news/archivestory.php/aid/1943/Jobs_ and_globalisation:_Towards_policies_that_work.html).

UCU (2013) Unemployed youngsters want to work, but survey shows a third fear they never will. *UCU News* (www.ucu.org.uk/6729).

Walker, A. and Walker, C. (eds) (1987) *The Growing Divide*. London: CPAG.

Winlow, S. (2001) *Badfellas: Crime, Tradition and New Masculinities*. Oxford: Berg.

Wiseman, J. (1998)

Young, J. (2007) *The Vertigo of Late Modernity*. London: Sage.

Zuboff, S. (1988) *In the Age of the Smart Machine: The Future of Work and Power*. New York: Basic Books.

Index

Brock, Anita   218
Brown, George   265
Browne, Naima   69
Bryman, Alan   9, 324
Bryne   122
BSA *see* British Sociological Association
BSAS *see* British Social Attitudes Survey
Buck, D.   238, 239–40
budget standard approach   287
bullying   68–8
Bury, Michael   257
Buskens, Vincent   205
Butler Act 1944   79
Buttler, Franziska   288
Byrne, David   292

C

Calhoun, Cheshire   179
Callender, Claire   19
Calton, Glasgow   223, 233, 278
CAM *see* complementary and alternative
        medicine
Cameron, David   140, 185, 253, 310, 317,
        320–1
canalisation   153
Capita   272
capital   159–61, 163
    cultural   52, 61, 159
    economic   159
    social   159, 245, 279
    symbolic   159
capitalism   2
    and children   210
    and the commodification of
            culture   121
    and deskilling   324–5
    and disability   230
    and education   52
    and the elderly   136
    and the family   176, 177–8, 179, 198
    global   320, 332
    and health   225, 237, 250, 271–2
    Marxist critique of   3–4, 160–1
    Marxist-feminist critique of   5
    and mass culture   119
    and poverty   294, 313–14
    and socialisation   129
car industry   327
care in the community, privatisation   219
care homes   251
Care Quality Commission (CQC)   250
carers, unpaid   310
Carers UK   310
Carey, Malcolm   325
Carsten   203
Carter   161
Cartwright   274
case studies   100
Castells, Manuel   169
Castles   332
categorisation of others   144
Catholic schooling   73

Cattell, Victoria   240, 245
causal relationships   28, 99
CCGs *see* Clinical Commissioning Groups
CGP *see* Clinical Commissioning Group
change, natural   216
Charlesworth, Simon   162
Chesler, Phyllis   264
Chester, R.   188, 194
Child Benefit   185, 212, 308, 310
Child Poverty Act 2010   289
Child Support Act 1991   212
Child Support Agency (CSA)   183
child-centred society   211
childbearing patterns   189, 193, 196,
        203, 216–18, 220
childbirth, medicalisation   275, 276
childcare   81, 184, 200, 320–1
childhood   136, 208–14
    children as economic assets   208, 217
    children as economic burdens
            208, 217
    exploitation of children   210
    social construction of   208, 210
    toxic   209, 212
    unhappy   213
childhood sexual abuse   210
childless couples   299
Children Act 2004   212
Children and Families Act 2014   136–7
Children's Society   212
Chinese medicine   227
Chinese students   71, 75
Chisunga initiation ceremony   137
Chubb, J.   51
Cicourel, Aaron   97
citizenship tests   138, 142
Civil Partnership Act 2004   156, 183,
        191, 192
class   5
    bourgeoisie   4, 157, 160–1
    and childhood   209
    conflict   3–4
    definition   238
    dominant   4, 121–2
    and education   51–2, 55, 57–64, 66,
            68–70, 73, 81–2, 84–6, 93, 110
    and employment   97, 158, 163
    and families   189
    and health   225–6, 237–41, 256, 271–2,
            274
    and identity   157–64
    importance   159
    and leisure opportunities   166–7
    measurement   157–8, 163
    and mental health   264
    and mortality   238
    researching class inequalities   93
    subordinate   4, 121–2
    theoretical perspectives in   160–1
    upper   159, 163
    see also elite; middle class; ruling
            class; working class

class consciousness   294
Clegg, Nick   185
clinical autonomy   273–4
Clinical Commissioning Groups (CCGs)
        250, 251, 253, 254
clinical gaze   231–2
clinical iceberg   256
CLOGS   189
co-parenting   192
Coalition government (2010-2015)
    and education   78, 83, 84
    and families   185–6, 200
    and health   253, 255, 269, 272
    and poverty   289, 310, 311
Coard, Bernard   74
cognitive therapy   266
cohabitation   190, 191
cohesion   41
cohorts   37, 135
Coleman   161
collective conscience   3, 177, 318
collective identity   132, 169
    legitimate identities   169
    project identities   169
    resistance identities   169
collectivism   61
commodification   121, 166, 177
common sense   8
communism   3, 160
comparative research   28
compensatory education policies   74
competence   47
complementary and alternative medicine
        (CAM)   226–7, 233, 255–6, 277–8
Comte, Auguste   13
confidentiality   47, 92
conflict
    class   3–4
    domestic   204
conflict sociologists   30
conflict theory   50, 51–4, 210
    see also feminism; Marxism
conflicts of interest   44
Connell, Raewyn   153
Conrad, Peter   277
consensus theories   50–1, 53–4, 176, 287
    see also functionalist perspective
consent, informed   26, 28, 46, 94
Conservative party   78, 80–1, 83–4, 181,
        183–4
consultant surgeons   254–5
consumer culture   119, 121, 123
consumer society   327–8, 331
consumerism   7, 168
consumption   166–9, 178
contradictory class location   328–9
Cooley, Charles   129, 133
correlations   28, 95, 99
correspondence principle   52
cosmetic surgery   255
coursework   65, 68, 70
Court Report 1973   249

definition 331
and education 55, 86–8
and employment 320
of fat stigma 170
and the health industry 267–81
and identity 164–5, 168–9
and migration 220
resistance to 165, 166
GMG *see* Glasgow Media Group
GNH *see* gross national happiness
Goffman, Erving 4, 23, 230, 262,
263, 273
'going native' 12, 25
Goldacre, Ben 279
Good Childhood Report 2013 212
Gorard, Stephen 65
Gordon, David 289
Gove, Michael 70, 76, 83–4, 85, 86, 317
Gove, Walter 261
government expenditure 181
government policy 36
see also social policy
GPs *see* General Practitioners
graduates 329, 330
Graham, Hilary 238, 242, 254
grammar schools 79, 82
Gramsci, Antonio 121–2
grand theories 7, 130
gratification, immediate 61
Gratton, Lynda 332–3
Green, E. 234
green identity 169
Greenpeace 169
'grey panthers' 298, 331
Griffin, John Howard 23
Griffiths, Clare 218
Griffiths, F. 234
Griffiths Report 219
Grint, Keith 329
Grogan, Sarah 232
gross national happiness (GNH) 279

H

habitus 162
Hadfield, Phil 43
Hall 139
Hall, Stuart 133
Hamilton, Kathy 293
Hareven, T. 176
harm, avoidance of 47
Harris, Tirril 265
Hatcher, Richard 99
Hawthorne effect 25, 28, 98, 99,
104, 114
HBAI *see* Households Below Average
Income
HCAs *see* hospital care assistants
HDI *see* Human Development Index
health 222–81
biocultural model 278
biomedical model 227, 232–3, 234
complementary model 233

definition 224–5
and disability 229–31
health professionals 267–81
holistic approaches to 226, 227
as ideological state apparatus 225
lay health 224–5
models of 232–4
and the 'sick role' 225, 227,
228–9, 273
as social construction 226–8
social determinants of 227
social model of 233, 234, 272
sociological perspectives on 225–6
see also mental health
health chances, unequal distribution of
236–47
health gap 227–8, 237, 238, 241, 242,
280
health inequalities 227–8
behavioural model of 239–40
and deprivation 291
and ethnicity 243–5
and gender 240, 241–3
global 278–9
materialist model of 240
north-south divide 236
and private health care 254–5
psychosocial model of 240
and regional factors 245–6
and social class 237–41
unequal distribution of 236–47
health care
inequalities in the provision of 247–59
marketisation 255
private 249, 253, 254–5
public-private mix 252, 253
and social factors 256–9
see also National Health Service
healthist consciousness 146
heart disease 257
Heaton, Tim 128–9
hegemonic masculinity 153
Henry, W. E. 330
heterogenisation 165
heteronormativity 155
heterosexuality 154–7
'hidden' curriculum 52, 128–9
'hidden' economy 308
high culture 119
Hijras 155
Hirsch, D. 219
historical materialism 3
Hobswarn 133
Hockey, J. 330
Hollender, M.H. 273
home ownership 159, 183
homelessness 27, 292, 309
homogenisation 165, 171
homophobia 155
homosexuality 154–7
and adoption 185
'cure' 225

and same-sex families 190–2, 202–4,
206
see also gay men; lesbians
Hoon, H.L. 31
hormone replacement therapy (HRT)
234, 279
Horobin 268
hospital care assistants (HCAs) 268–9
Household Panel Survey 212
household surveys 31
households 173–221
by type 188
with children 299
definition 174–5
and poverty 298, 299
Households Below Average Income
(HBAI) 287
HRT *see* hormone replacement therapy
Hughes, John 25
Human Development Index (HDI) 279
human rights 149
Humphreys, Laud 47
Hunt, Jeremy 255
hypotheses 99

I

iatrogenesis (doctor-generated illness)
226, 232, 233, 256
identity 131–4
achieved 133
and age 135–7
ascribed 133
and class 30, 157–64
collective 132, 169
and consumption 166–9, 327
cybernetic 323
and disability 146–7
and ethnicity 138–46
fractured 133
and globalisation 164–5
hybrid 139–42
individual 132
local 165
and masculinity 122, 152
multiple identities 122–3, 132, 133
and nationality 139–40
sexual 154–7
social 132
as social construction 131, 132–3, 135
stigmatisation 132, 133
theoretical perspectives on 133–4
who am I? 131–2
and work 327–8
working-class 30
see also gender identity
ideological state apparatus (ISA) 52, 225
ideology
patriarchal 53, 70
ruling class 121–2, 129
Illich, Ivan 232, 233
illness
chronic illness 256, 270

M

Mac an Ghaill, Máirtín 70, 74, 144
Macdonald, R. 288, 293, 295
Machin 68
Mack 287
Mackay, Lord 195
Mackintosh 158
macro theories 42, 103
Malaya, Oxana 124–5
male dominance 5, 153
male gaze 69
malestream theories 5, 276
malingering 225, 228
Mallet 265
manufacturing 327
march of progress 210
Marcuse 119
marketisation, and education 51, 63,
        74–5, 78, 80–6, 340–1
Marmot 238, 240
Marmot Review 2010 237
marriage 184
    empty shell 176, 190
    same-sex 156
Marsden, Dennis 204, 319
Marshall, Gordon 132
Marsland, David 294–5, 308, 311
Marx, Karl 2, 3–4, 121, 157, 160, 177,
        271, 318, 320, 328
Marxist perspective 3–4
    and childhood 210
    and deskilling 324–5
    and disability 230
    and education 51–5, 80
    and families 176, 177–8, 180
    and functionalism 121
    and globalisation 332
    and health 225, 237, 250, 271–2, 279
    and identity 133, 157, 160–1
    and mental health 260
    and meritocracy 319
    nocturnal economy 43
    and poverty 294, 312, 313–15
    and research funding 45
    and socialisation 129
    and work 318, 328
    see also neo-Marxism
Marxist-feminism 5
masculine cultural identity 122
masculinity
    black 76
    constructions of 67, 69, 70, 76
    crisis in 67, 70
    hegemonic 153
    homogenous culture of 242
    and identity 152
Mason, David 141
mass culture 119
mass media 119, 126
material deprivation 59–60, 72, 75,
        109–11, 287–8, 337 –8

maternal death rate 279
maternity care 218
maternity leave 184
Matrimonial and Family Proceedings Act
        1985 195
Mauritius 166
Mayo, Elton 28
McDonaldisation 171, 324
McDonald's 171, 327
McIntosh 168
McKeown, Thomas 232
Mckinley, John 272
McNally, S. 68, 73
McRobbie, Angela 66, 123
Mead, George Herbert 4, 122, 129
means of production 157
mechanical solidarity 318–19
media
    content 36
    and disability 150
    and eating disorders 261
    effects 27
    and ethnic identity 144
    and gender identity 122
    mass 119, 126
    and nurses 269
    and socialisation 126
media content analysis 36
medical gaze 234
medical model 148
    see also biomedical model
medical profession
    current status 268–9
    globalised 267–81
    see also doctors; General
        Practitioners; nurses
medical technology 218, 277–8
medicalisation of society 226
medicine, feminisation 276
memory 203
mental health 259–66, 270
    defining mental illness 259–60
    discrimination and 263
    labelling of mental illness 262–3
    realist biomedical model 260
    social construction of mental illness
        260–1
    social factors and services 264–6
    stigmatisation of mental illness
        262–3
Mental Health (Discrimination) Act 2011
        263
Mental Health Foundation 263, 265
mental health trusts 252
meritocracy 161
    and education 50, 51, 52, 53
    myth of 52
    in the UK 319–21
metanarratives 130, 167
Meyer, Bertolt 150–1
micro-sociology 4, 13, 42, 103, 133
middle class 159, 163

definition 160
and education 52, 58–64, 81, 82, 158
established 163
and health 274
skills of 320
technical 163
migration 215
    and diaspora 142–3
    and the family 220–1
    and globalisation 220
    and health care staff 267–8
    and labour 267–8, 332
    push/pull factors 220
Miliband, Ralph 294
Millennium Cohort Study 127
Miller 240
Mindell 244
Miner, Horace 117
minimum wage 304, 313
Misztal 203
modernism 3
modernity 2, 7
    end of 175, 277
    and the family 175, 176
    liquid/fluid 329
    and the medical profession 277, 278
Modood, Tariq 143
Moe, T. 51
moneylending 292
Mooney 158
Moonies (Unification Church) 43
Moore 51
moral decay 189
moral density 318
moral inferiority 230
moral order 318
moral values 3
morbidity
    and class 238, 239, 240
    and ethnicity 244
    and gender 242, 243
Morgan, JP 305
Morley, David 317
Morris, David 278
Morrison, Anthony 266
Morrow, Raymond 88
mortality
    common 3
    and ethnicity 244
    and gender 241–2
    and GP registration failure 257
    infant 136, 217, 249, 278
    and regional factors 245
    and social class 238
    see also death rate
motherhood
    feminist conception of 206
    teenage 34, 161
Moxon, David 123
multiculturalism 139, 140–2
Munby, Sir James 196
murder 205